65

D0025353

ML 82 .M8 1983 v.2

The Musical woman : an international perspective.

DATE

ISSUED TO

ML 82 .M8 1983 v.2

The Musical woman : an international perspective.

The Musical Woman

The Musical Woman
An International Perspective

Volume II
1984–1985

JUDITH LANG ZAIMONT,
EDITOR-IN-CHIEF

CATHERINE OVERHAUSER
AND JANE GOTTLIEB,
ASSOCIATE EDITORS

GREENWOOD PRESS
New York • Westport, Connecticut • London

ML
82
.M8
1983
v.2

The Library of Congress has cataloged this serial publication as follows:

Library of Congress Cataloging in Publication Data

The Musical woman.—1983- —Westport, Conn.:
Greenwood Press, 1984-

v.: ill. ; 25 cm.

Annual.
ISSN 0737-0032 = The Musical Woman.

1. Women musicians.
ML82.M8 780'.88042—dc19 84-649117
AACR 2 MARC-S

Library of Congress [8510] MN

Copyright © 1987 by Judith Lang Zaimont,
Catherine Overhauser, and Jane Gottlieb

All rights reserved. No portion of this book may be
reproduced, by any process or technique, without the
express written consent of the publisher.

Library of Congress Catalog Card Number: 84-649117
ISBN: 0-313-23588-0
ISSN: 0737-0032

First published in 1987

Greenwood Press, Inc.
88 Post Road West, Westport, Connecticut 06881

Printed in the United States of America

The paper used in this book complies with the
Permanent Paper Standard issued by the National
Information Standards Organization (Z39.48-1984).

10 9 8 7 6 5 4 3 2 1

Contents

Music Education

Special Topics

Illustrations and Tables

ILLUSTRATIONS

TABLES

Acknowledgments

The editors gratefully acknowledge special support for THE MUSICAL WOMAN Vol. II in the form of generous grants from the Morton and Sophia Macht Foundation, Inc. (Baltimore, Maryland), and the Educational Foundation of the American Association of University Women (AAUW).

Five of the individual chapters in the essay section are outgrowths of papers and panels originally presented at the First National Congress on Women in Music (New York University, March 1981). These chapters—updated, reworked and considerably expanded from the original—are: Joanne Riley's study of the life and work of Tarquinia Molza; Elizabeth Wood's chapter on Ethel Smyth's operas; Barbara Petersen's appreciation of Miriam Gideon's vocal chamber music; Carol Neuls-Bates's portrait of Elizabeth Sprague Coolidge; and Judith Rosen's amended transcript of a panel discussion on electronic music. The editors extend their appreciation to the Editorial Committee of the First Congress for permission to develop the original presentations for publication here.

Introduction

SEPARATE FOCUS ON WOMEN—THE NEED STILL EXISTS

As editors of *The Musical Woman*, we are firmly committed to shedding the spotlight on women's contributions to the world of music in a host of professional capacities. Therefore we have been disturbed to note, in the wake of public and private comment generated by the first volume, a troubling undertone that frequently accompanies discussion of women's achievements in all the arts when these achievements are grouped by gender. Certain "reactive" questions and comments recur, often surreptitiously offered, which reveal fundamental misgivings. Let us bring these questions into the open, so that they can be met head on:

> "According to the most rigorous scholarly standards, aren't conferences/festivals/publications which concentrate on the *woman* aspect of women in music intrinsically suspect, by virtue of the hidden implication that the music itself is not strong enough to take its place in the musical mainstream on its own?"
> "Doesn't the focus on *women* in music inject an unwelcome, perhaps irrelevant, sociological note into what is, or should be, a purely artistic discipline?"
>
> "Are women professionals really viewed differently by the music establishment at large? or is this just a 'sour grapes' myth used to explain the lack of career success for some women composers and conductors?"
>
> "Enough already! I can name three women conductors and five women composers—with this much visibility within the profession, why press for more?"

Why indeed press for more? True, there is no question that women have made significant gains in every segment of the music world in the last several decades. Many have achieved recognition, and some have attained positions of substantial power and authority.

Women have perhaps made the greatest headway in areas where arts administration skills come to the fore. For instance, as of February 1986 in the United States women serve as:

general director/artistic director of several major opera companies (e.g., Sarah Caldwell: Opera Company of Boston, Beverly Sills: New York City Opera, M. Jane Weaver: Texas Opera Theater);

heads of the serious music/concert music divisions of *both* ASCAP and BMI (Fran Richard and Barbara Petersen, respectively);

artist representatives and managers in healthy numbers

orchestra managers—in the second or third echelons, albeit not the top position—for 16 out of the 30 major American orchestras.

Clearly, women *are* finding opportunities for employment in significant numbers in the organizational side of the art, where jobs to be filled coincide well with the traditional feminine strengths: organizational skills, attention to detail, and good interpersonal skills.

It is more difficult to evaluate career progress on the artistic side (e.g., conducting and composing), where career progress follows no set pattern. Even so, several women have recently attained unquestionable prominence. Ellen Taaffe Zwilich was the recipient of the 1983 Pulitzer Prize in composition; the Exxon Corporation/Meet the Composer orchestral residency program has two women in place (Joan Tower and Libby Larsen); and the present roster of composer members of the National Institute of Arts and Letters includes Louise Talma, Miriam Gideon, Betsy Jolas and Vivian Fine. On the podium, too, the last few years have seen increasing attention paid to the activities of relative newcomers (e.g., JoAnn Falletta, Tania Leon), while the careers of more established conductors—such as Eve Queler, Judith Somogi, Catherine Comet, Sarah Caldwell—broaden and deepen. The 1985-86 season saw the inauguration of the Maryland Women's Symphony (Baltimore) and also marked the fifth anniversary of the Bay Area Women's Philharmonic (San Francisco).

So, again, why press for more? Because—particularly on the artistic side—the women cited above represent shining exceptions. These "paragons" (to use John Russell's term from a New York *Times* article on women in the visual arts)—so few, so easy to pinpoint—help us to realize how unequally still women are represented in the music world, particularly in terms of creative impact. Where are the women composers and conductors of middle stature? Does "equal access" to performance opportunities and public notice apply to all women, the best to the worst, as it does for their male colleagues of comparable ability and experience? The uncomfortable conclusion is that at this time, it does not. We seem to be struggling with an unarticulated but entrenched quota system for musically talented women: as long as the public is able to supply a few names in every category of endeavor, there is no sustained impetus to open the gates of opportunity any wider.

An additional burden may be the unsettling suspicion shared by many women that women judge other women more harshly than they do men. (Two of the band directors in Chapter 15 of this volume mention this outright). This relates directly to the question of separatist programming. Critic Karen Monson (Chapter 1) finds any sort of segregated programming a form of distortion and beside the point (all-woman, all-anything). She prefers to use her critical acumen to assess individual pieces solely on their own merits. Similarly, composers Miriam Gideon and Toshiko Akiyoshi explicitly avoid the term "woman" composer as irrelevant to their personal experience.

A final obstacle, particularly for composers, is mentioned by noted patron Paul Fromm in a recent address:

"[There is] a strong tendency for the sword of music criticism against music by women to be double-edged. One edge of the sword is music criticism that patronizes and insults women composers by not taking their work seriously and by substituting gallantry for real evaluation. The other edge of the sword is music criticism that judges music by women more harshly than music by men. A poor or mediocre score by a man is just that; it is not viewed as evidence that all men should immediately cease composing. But a poor or mediocre score by a woman has been and still is often offered as proof that women should not even attempt to compose."*

Such close scrutiny can easily blunt the cutting edge of creativity: in order to grow, all artists need both the space and opportunity to try, and possibly fail.

The first flush of novelty attendant on researching women's contributions is now behind us. A burgeoning round of conferences, festivals, and concerts has sprung up around this special interest, and sustaining these activities takes some doing. Some critics seem impatient to wind down separatist venues: ". . . my own feeling is that a segregated museum [or concert or conference] is no more of a compliment to women artists [or musicians] than a segregated bus was a compliment to blacks."** It's almost as if research on women in music has come to the end of the critical leash—at least in the minds of a few crucial critics.

Should we heed these objections—is it time to cease activities which focus on the contributions of women? We think not—not yet, anyway. Despite the bustle of activity by researchers and significant creative advances by some, women's contribution to music is generally understood to stand apart from the mainstream. "Separate but equal" is a myth, and as Paul Fromm noted, ". . . the point is not [basically] that women artists need their own tradition, but that the arts themselves need both men and women practitioners to be fully expressive of human thought and feeling."***

What is needed now is a concerted effort to ensure that all women music professionals are enabled to take their proper place beside their male col-

*From "Creative Women in Music—A Historical Perspective," an address given by Paul Fromm on February 3, 1986 at the opening session of a contemporary music festival in New Orleans, Louisiana, sponsored by Tulane University and the New Orleans Symphony.

**"One of the Paragons Among Women Artists," John Russell, the New York *Times* August 18, 1985.

***Paul Fromm address, New Orleans, Feb. 3, 1986.

leagues at every echelon; that music by women is enabled to gain its rightful place in the core repertoire; in short, every effort must be made to erase any distinction between all music and "women's music." Constituting 50% of the human race, women should have the right to move forward without hindrance toward their full partnership in the creative quest.

Readers of the first volume of *The Musical Woman* will notice two new elements introduced in the present book. First person interviews proved to be appropriate alternative formats for chapters focusing on individuals, lending additional immediacy to career narratives which include statements of personal perspective seasoned by long experience in the field. (See Joan Briccetti, orchestra manager exemplar [Chapter 2]; Jesse Rosen's discussion of women's participation in this country's only conductor residency program [Chapter 3]; and commentary by ten composers working in the electronic medium [Chapter 10].) A similar immediacy and candor characterize Karen Monson's no-holds-barred look at a critic's high-stress life (Chapter 1); the story of innovative artist manager Susan Wadsworth (Chapter 4); and the frank comments by the women band directors who participated in Carol Feather's survey (Chapter 15).

Continuing the accent on the colloquial we introduce the *Gallery* section devoted to material with a strong visual interest, in this case excerpts from the *Woman Composer* coloring book published by Bellerophon Press. It is refreshing and encouraging to discover that the idea of women writing serious music has penetrated public consciousness sufficiently to spur the publication of such a book.

VOLUME II: THE ISSUES

All of *The Musical Woman's* contributors take their responsibility seriously for setting the record straight, documenting and assessing women's recent and historical contributions to the field, often providing a balanced rewriting of history in the light of new findings. Chief among such reassessments in the present volume are: Joanne Riley's reinterpretation of Tarquinia Molza as the influential creative force in the development of the luxuriant madrigal in late Renaissance Italy (Chapter 18; termed a "revolutionary and important study" by the jury for the 1986 Pauline Alderman Prize); Elizabeth Wood's description of Ethel Smyth as a composer of "more flair and originality than most of her British contemporaries," whose music "compares favorably with that of better-known composers of the period" (Chapter 19); and Laura Mitgang's studied conclusion after extensive critical evaluation of Tailleferre's output that Germaine Tailleferre, while "not an undiscovered master of legendary proportions," or "an influential innovator," did produce a body of music that is "thoughtfully structured and . . . moving" (Chapter 7). Limelight is also shed on nineteenth-century music publisher Arthur P. Schmidt, who emerges as a champion of women composers in conjunction with his interest in American composers (Fried Block, Chapter 6); and due appreciation is given to the considerable contributions of composers Miriam Gideon and Toshiko Akiyoshi, in the areas of vocal chamber music and jazz, respectively (Petersen, Chapter 8; Koplewitz, Chapter 9).

Looking at this second volume as a whole reveals fascinating hard data in the form of significant statistics uncovered in the various essays. Apparently, given any sort of relatively "open" climate within a particular music specialty area, women may expect to achieve a group presence of between 12 and 20 percent; we find this not just in the present time period but in other eras as well. Adrienne Fried Block notes that women composers constituted 12 percent of the total number of composers published in Schmidt's catalogue (1876-1958); particularly in the company's first 45 years, these were the chief American composers of the time. Jesse Rosen provides comprehensive figures to document that women apply to the Exxon/Arts Endowment Conductors Residency program in numbers between 10 and 15 percent of total applicants, and during the program's first decade of operation (1973-1983), 17 percent of the conductors actually appointed to residencies were women. (Interestingly, this corresponds well with Tailleferre's one-sixth "share" of *Les Six*, roughly equalling 17 percent; it also matches the two women resident composers out of 11 residents total in the Meet the Composer orchestra residency program (1985-86), equalling 18 percent.) But when the climate is less "open"—as is the case for women band directors at the college level (Chapter 15)—statistics reveal only token presence: As of June 1980 women held a mere 1¼ percent of band positions in higher education in the United States.

Which music specialty areas are "open" in the sense of being less biased from the gender standpoint? One answer might be the new musical areas that have sprung up or expanded significantly since World War II, such as the entire spectrum of specialties involving electronic technologies (i.e., music publishing via computer, electronic instrument design, recording technician, and composer).

Women also find a more open climate in areas where women are already established as mentors and role models. In an article on American women music critics in *The Musical Woman* Volume I, Barbara Jepson speculated that the notably higher percentage of women critics at *High Fidelity/Musical America* (17 percent in 1981) might be due to the fact that the magazine's editor is a woman. In this volume, Karen Monson notes no barrier to her becoming music critic for the Chicago *Daily News* in the 1970s, implicitly acknowledging that Claudia Cassidy's earlier appointment as music critic for the *Tribune* (1947-1965) may have eased the way for another woman critic in the same city. So, too, St. Louis Symphony Orchestra Manager Joan Briccetti describes her early experiences in orchestra management in which she learned from Sue Staton (now the assistant general manager for the Indianapolis Symphony Orchestra). And Susan Wadsworth (founder and director of Young Concert Artists) speaks of double female models: book editor Lillian McClintock, with whom Wadsworth worked for two ''invaluable'' years while honing administrative skills, and successful real estate broker Anne Popkin, Wadsworth's mother.

The teacher-student relation also forms a natural situation for effective modelling. Among several such instances mentioned in Volumes I and II may be noted pianist Rosalyn Tureck studying with Olga Samaroff (Chapter 16), and Louise Talma's composition study with Nadia Boulanger, where the teacher exerted a ''profound influence'' on the pupil's religious as well as musical life. (Volume I: pp. 130-131).

Where role models are conspicuously absent are in *print*, in the books that comprise traditional tools for learning: texts for courses in music appreciation and music history and especially texts geared for post-secondary-school levels. In a key chapter, Diane Jezic and Daniel Binder survey college-level music texts to report on the mentions of women composers (including printed and/or recorded excerpts from their works) in materials currently in use, among them recent editions of acknowledged standard texts (Chapter 17). Their findings confirm what many have independently lamented: (1) the virtual absence of women composers from these pages; (2) when present, the women are most frequently ''ghettoized''—grouped in a single chapter under the designation ''women composers'' rather than included in an appropriate historical context in the body of the text; and (3) specialized scholarship on women in music has had negligible impact on the more general, as opposed to single-period, texts. For example, in the music appreciation texts surveyed where a woman composer is mentioned, 25 percent of the time she will be a contemporary pop singer-songwriter rather than a composer of serious music; and in three books published in 1985 there are no women composers mentioned at all!

It is frightening to find traditions of bias and ignorance still in place and being perpetuated in the mid 1980s. It is materials in print to which experts refer; it is via materials in print that teachers teach and new generations of musicians learn. Composer and concert producer Katherine Hoover comments, ''Most [critics' prejudices against music by women] are, I think, the result of a conviction that if any of this material were worthy they, as experts, would know of it after so many years in the field'' (Chapter 13). How can we correct a tradition which continues to propagate in print the same misinformation—or lack of information? Jezic and Binder have several pointed suggestions in their chapter.

VOLUME II: COMMON THREADS

While each essay focuses on an individual topic, the editors have noted common themes which surface repeatedly throughout the book, forming a counterpoint of cross-references that connect and illuminate the separate entries.

For instance, geography plays an unexpectedly prominent role. Certain metropolises, at different times, seem to have provided environments in which women were able to flourish in musical life. For example, post-Civil-War Boston, a leader in nineteenth-century American cultural life, saw a positive flowering of women performers and composers (Chapter 6). Baltimore in the 1980s is also home to many prominent musical women: The Dean of the Peabody Conservatory of Music, two composers on its faculty, and the founder-director of its electronic music studio are all women; so are the conductors and founders of three Baltimore community/chamber orchestras (all begun in the 1980s), as well as the director of the city's only new-music performing series. In 1984 Karen Monson became music critic for the Baltimore *Sun*, and Catherine Comet was appointed Associate Conductor of the Baltimore Symphony Orchestra. (As of summer 1986 both Monson and Comet have made subsequent career moves away from Baltimore.) In the last 15 years, St. Louis has welcomed the participation of women in its musical life, centering on the St. Louis Symphony: 33 percent of the orchestra musicians are women; Joan Briccetti has been the Symphony's orchestra manager since 1980; during 1982-84 both the Associate and Assistant Conductors were women (Comet and Antonia Wilson, respectively); and in 1985 Joan Tower succeeded Joseph Schwantner as the Symphony's composer in residence.

The *era* in which a person lives—the political, intellectual, cultural and social climate of the time—similarly plays an important role in the shaping of life and career. Dame Ethel Smyth (1858-1944), composer and iconoclast, was a crusader on many fronts in a crusading age. And Smyth's almost exact contemporary Amy Beach (1867-1944) pursued an independent career as pianist and composer with considerable freedom, also partially a result of the climate of the time.

Of course, for any sort of sustained comparison between figures who are contemporaries it is personal and family situations, financial circumstances, and specific personality traits that seem to make the difference between a successful career and a near miss, or between a career behind the scenes rather than on center stage. For example, there are many similarities in the lives of composer Amy Beach and her exact contemporary, patron Elizabeth Sprague Coolidge (1864-1953): both were born into comfortable circumstances. Both studied piano intensively from childhood, and performed with major orchestras (Beach was a prodigy); both married doctors who encouraged their musical involvements (Coolidge actually began to compose after her marriage); both outlived their husbands by many decades, maintaining lives as independent figures. Yet Amy Beach forged a major career for herself as composer and pianist, whereas Coolidge appears to have regarded her personal musical creative involvements as "a private hobby;" her life suggests she completely internalized the restraining influence of "traditional views about the proper sphere of [artistic activity for] married, wealthy women" (Chapter 5).

An even more revealing contrast—centering on personality, rather than outer circumstances—occurs when one compares the lives of composers Germaine Tailleferre and Toshiko Akiyoshi, born a generation apart, who both struggled against the constraints of poverty. Attempting to make a career in a new country, Akiyoshi went door-to-door to sell tickets for her first Town Hall concert; Tailleferre accepted every commission that came to her, making no bones about composing to earn money. Both composers married more than once, and both had a child. Akiyoshi was fortunate in finding her second husband, saxophonist Lew Tabackin, completely encouraging and supportive. Tailleferre unfortunately had poor luck with men. "Both her first and second husbands, rather than supporting her in her work, considered themselves and their careers to be primary" (Chapter 7). Her first husband's wedding gift to her was a player piano, so Tailleferre would no longer need to spend long hours "bothering" with a real piano. Yet, despite daunting life circumstances, Akiyoshi has succeeded in her career, supporting her demonstrated musical gifts with strong belief in herself, buttressed by continuing collaboration with Lew Tabackin. Tailleferre, however, may not have realized her full potential because of certain innate personality traits, as well as the social constraints of the time. According to Laura Mitgang, Tailleferre suffered from lifelong self-doubts about her gift, reinforced by "being told by her father and both husbands that her talent should not be exploited. . . . She preferred . . . to remain silent and avoid conflicts," shying away from self-promotion and confrontation. The modesty, self-deprecation and conciliation that characterized her personally were no match for the tough challenges inherent in building a high-profile career.

Both Karen Monson and Joan Briccetti are forthright about the quotient of toughness it takes to succeed as a music critic, orchestra manager, or indeed in any professional capacity in a competitive field. Briccetti and Monson echo one another in emphasizing that their spheres of activity are far from glamorous, with jobs demanding long grueling hours of complete attention, with much of the work taking place at night. Each also independently concludes that a husband and children cannot presently be part of her life: their all-consuming jobs conflict directly in total time requirements with family responsibilities and needs. (Tailleferre too realized quite late in life that marriage and a composing career were not compatible. Carol Feather also notes that two-thirds of the women band directors in her study were single.)

By contrast, artist manager Wadsworth and composer Akiyoshi are married mothers with stable, long-term partners. Perhaps the clue here is that their husbands—Charles Wadsworth (director of the Chamber Music Society of Lincoln Center), and saxophonist Lew Tabackin, respectively—are fellow artists who understand and support their wives' career goals.

This leads us to a final commonality touched on by many of the authors. Do the essential attributes of a *woman's nature* outfit her well or ill for a professional career? If we first take the dark side, we can discover in Germaine Tailleferre's personality some traditional feminine traits that conflicted directly with smooth negotiation of the path to success.

The *positive* attributes of a woman's nature appear to be several. We alluded earlier to the traditional feminine strengths: organizational skills, attention to detail, and good social skills. These are not just back-up skills but core necessities for certain jobs: ''I think women make excellent managers, for several reasons: The 'detail' nature of the job and its whole ego orientation—the need to deal with many potentially conflicting demands—suits a female perspective well'' (Joan Briccetti). In addition to these ''innate'' traits, other feminine qualities are cited as significant plusses reflecting individual personality and style: ''A woman's ability to beguile can be as effective as the ability to be forceful and persuasive, and women can express appreciation more freely than men can . . .'' (Susan Wadsworth). Thus, a career strategy for some women could incorporate capitalizing on these inherent, positive feminine traits.

Women's presence in music is beginning to be appreciably felt in every specialty area. To increase women's visibility and clout, it is vital that we applaud every individual accomplishment, continue intensive efforts to research and present a more balanced account of music history, and, above all, press the battle against prejudice on every front. After all, every musician knows that advancement in technique and career really represents the culmination of many small breakthroughs, and that it is *practice* that makes *progress.**

Judith Lang Zaimont
Catherine Overhauser
July 1986

*''Practice makes progress'' is a favorite maxim of noted New York piano teacher Bertha F. Lang, mother of *The Musical Woman*'s editor-in-chief.

Part I

GAZETTE

This second issue of the Gazette continues the task of documentation of activities of women musicians internationally. The original five chapters found in Volume 1 have been expanded into nine chapters: "Performances," "Festivals," "Prizes and Awards/Commissions," "Publications," "Discography," "Films and Videos," "New Books," "Conductors," and "Recent Deaths."

Events are documented for the 1982-1983 season through the 1984-1985 season with forecasts for 1985-1986. The format has been varied in the "Performances" section, with the listings appearing in a single alphabetical sequence rather than broken up by seasons, as in Volume 1. This was done in order to provide easier access to an individual composer's performances. Once again, premieres are indicated by an *, and commissions or awards related to a particular performance are indicated by an †. Those honors not related to a specific performance are listed in the "Prizes and Awards/Commissions" chapter.

Listings in the "Performances" and "Prizes and Awards/Commissions" chapters document the activities of living composers and the deceased, if they were alive at the time of the performance (see Lutyens and Saint-Marcoux). Listings in the "Publications" and "Discography" chapters document historical women composers as well.

The "Conductors" chapter lists the principal affiliations of women conductors during the 1982-1985 seasons. Information was gathered from the American Symphony Orchestra League directories and *Musical America International Directory* issue. It is hoped that there will be additional listings for foreign women conductors in Volume 3.

Information for the Gazette as a whole was once again taken from numerous source materials: newsletters of composer organizations (American Music Center, American Women Composers, International League of Women Composers, etc.), foreign Music Information Centers, publishers' announcements, concert programs, newspapers and other music periodicals, and of course, the composers themselves. Voluminous correspondence was received from both U.S. and foreign composers. This became the primary source material from which the Gazette was created.

Even with all of these resources and the improved documentation of contemporary music in general, it is always impossible to be totally comprehensive. The Gazettes provide a sampling of the varied activities of women composers and conductors worldwide. Critical value judgments are not a factor for inclusion. Activities of more renowned composers are listed alongside those of less well-known composers. The only listings which were eliminated were those in which there was simply too little information.

Once again, we look forward to increased reader participation in the preparation of the next volume's Gazette, and welcome all correspondence.

Performances

(* indicates premiere; † indicates commission or award related to a particular work. Country names in parentheses indicate country of origin or citizenship for composers other than U.S. composers.)

*Ahrens, Margaret. *Agnus Dei.* New York, NY: Merkin Concert Hall, 5/12/83.

*†Alberga, Eleanor (U.K.). *Mobile.* Midlands Dance Co., Jayne Lee, choreographer. London: Stantonbury Theatre, 4/29/83. Commissioned by Midlands Dance Co.

Allen, Judith Shatin. *Aura,* for orchestra. Richmond, VA: 2/16,18/85.

**Glyph,* for viola and piano. Rosemary Glide, viola; Norman Carey, piano. New York, NY: Merkin Concert Hall, 11/13/84.

**Werther.* Da Capo Chamber Players. New York, NY: Carnegie Recital Hall, 5/1/84.

Alotin, Yardena (Israel). *Piano Trio.* Vidom Trio. Cologne: 9/83.

*†*Shir-Hag* . . . Philharmonic Choir. Tel-Aviv: Tel-Aviv Museum, 3/31/84. Commissioned by the Tel-Aviv Foundation for Arts and Literature.

Sonata, for violin and piano. Eric Rosenblith, violin; Michael Freyhan, piano. Paris: 4/83.

*Anderson, Avril (U.K.). *The Grass Harp.* Lontano Ensemble. London: St. John's, Smith Square, 2/29/84.

**Private Energy.* Lorraine Anderson, soprano. London: Purcell Room, 4/26/83.

*Anderson, Beth. *Elizabeth Rex; or, The Well-Bred Mother Goes to Camp*: a a musical. New York, NY: Open Gate Theatre, 12/8-31/83.

Net Work, for SATB saxophones with two keyboards; *Time Stands Still,* and other songs; *Shakuhachi Run,* for shakuhachi; *Preparation for the Dominant,* for ocarina. New York, NY: Third Street Music School Settlement, 12/4/83.

*†*Quilt Music.* Beth Anderson, piano. New York, NY: Riverside Church, 3/2/83. Commissioned by Daniel McCuster Dance Co.

**Revel,* for chamber orchestra. Richmond Symphonia, Jacques Houtman, conductor. Richmond, VA: Virginia Center for the Performing Arts, 1/26/85.

**Riot Rot*: a text-sound opera. Above Midtown Downtown's Dominoes Series. New York, NY: 12/4/83.

*†*Taking Sides Part One*. Beth Anderson, piano. New York, NY: 1/26/84. Commissioned by Daniel McCuster Dance Co.

Torero Piece (1973). Arina Isaacson, Rhiannon, voices, Bay Area Women's Philharmonic Concert. Berkeley, CA: University of California at Berkeley, 5/13/83.

*Archer, Violet (Canada). *Celebration*. Alberta College Brass Quintet. Edmonton: 11/15/83.

**Green Jade*: song cycle for flute, baritone voice, and piano. Jonathan Bayley, Harold Wiens, Albert Krywolt. Edmonton: 3/28/83.

Improvisation, for solo 'cello. Shauna Rolston, 'cello. New York, NY: Town Hall, 10/18/83 (U.S. premiere).

**Reflections*. Madrigal Choir of Cork, Donal O'Callaghan, conductor. Cork, Ireland: 4/3/84.

Soliloquies, for B-flat clarinet and piano. Baton Rouge, LA: Louisiana State University, 2/24/83.

**Songs of Summer and Fall*. University of Alberta Concert Choir, Leonard Ratzlaff, conductor. Edmonton: 3/30/84.

String Quartet no. 3. University of Alberta Quartet. London: Wigmore Hall, 10/6/82 (British premiere).

Arrieu, Claude, pseud. (France). *Woodwind Quintet in C*. Performers of the Bay Area Women's Philharmonic. San Francisco, CA: First Unitarian Church, 1/27/84.

Barnekow, Deborah. *Always to Remember*, for oboe and viola; *The Kraken* (the dragon), for solo trombone; *Whalespeake*, for soprano saxophone, marimba, and tape; *Wildebeests 3*, for three percussionists and several drums. New York, NY: Church of the Good Shepherd, 4/10/83.

*Barnett, Carol. *Four Chorale Meditations*, for solo violin. Jean Marker DeVere, violin. Minneapolis, MN: Walker Art Center, 10/31/82.

**Nocturne*. St. Paul Chamber Orchestra. Minneapolis, MN: Walker Art Center, 9/15/83.

*†*Voices*. Nancy Cox, soprano; Tim Burris, guitar. LaCrosse, WI: Viterbo College, 10/83; St. Paul, MN: Macalester College, 11/5/83. Commissioned by the performers through the Minnesota Composers Forum Commissioning Program, funded by the Jerome Foundation.

*Barrell, Joyce (U.K.). *Sextet*. Hall Family Ensemble. Suffolk: Woolpit Festival, 6/4/83.

*Bingham, Judith (U.K.) *Clouded Windows*. Christine Batty, mezzo-soprano; David Mason, piano. London: Wigmore Hall, 4/19/83.

*†Blaustein, Susan. *Concerto for 'Cello and Chamber Orchestra*. Joel Krosnick, 'cello, Juilliard Ensemble, Paul Zukofsky, conductor. Washington, DC: Library of Congress, 11/7/84. Commissioned by Joel Krosnick and the Fromm Music Foundation.

†*Ricercate*, for string quartet. Arditti String Quartet. Montreal: Université du Québec à Montréal, 10/1/84 (World Music Days). Commissioned by the Group for Contemporary Music. Winner, League-ISCM National Composers Competition.

**Romansa: La Esposa de Don Garcia* (1982). Edward Peterson, baritone;

Martin Goldray, piano. New York, NY: St. Stephen's Church, 12/2/82.

*†*Sextet* (1983). New York New Music Ensemble, Robert Black, conductor. New York, NY: Carnegie Recital Hall, 11/17/83. Commissioned by the New York New Music Ensemble.

*†*Song of Songs*. Barbara Martin, mezzo-soprano; Paul Sperry, tenor; American Composers Orchestra, Bernard Rands, conductor. New York, NY: Symphony Space, 3/19/85. Commissioned by the American Composers Orchestra.

Bliss, Marilyn. *Encounter* (1975). Marilyn Bliss, flute. New York, NY: St. Stephen's Church, 12/2/82.

**Three Farewells*, for soprano, flute, viola, and harp. New York, NY: St. Stephen's Church, 10/16/84.

*Blood, Esta. *Facets*, for flute and piano. Cherry Hill, NJ: Unitarian Church, 11/13/84.

**Fanfare*, for orchestra. Schenectady Symphony Orchestra, Charles Schneider, conductor. Schenectady, NY: Proctor's Theatre, 4/6/84.

*†Bloom, Jane Ira. New work. University of Northern Iowa Jazz Band. Cedar Falls, IA: University of Northern Iowa, 3/3/85. Commissioned by the University of Northern Iowa School of Music.

*Bolz, Harriett. *Poem Cantare*, for flute, 'cello, and piano. Susan Cowden, flute; Jerrie Cribb, 'cello; Harriett Bolz, piano. Columbus, OH: Columbus Cultural Arts Center, 12/10/83.

**Stately March*, for harp. Jeanne Norton, harp. Columbus, OH: Columbus Cultural Arts Center, 3/19/84.

*Bond, Victoria. *Margaret*, for soprano, flute, violin, 'cello, and piano. Judith Otten, soprano; Barbara Boutsikaris, flute; Ruth Herring, violin; Benjamin Whitenburg, 'cello; Max Lifchitz, piano; Victoria Bond, conductor. New York, NY: St. Stephen's Church, 10/18/84.

Bouchard, Linda. *Chaudière à Traction*, for flute and piano (1979). John Ranck, flute; David Carleton, piano. New York, NY: Lincoln Center Library, 5/13/83.

Circus Faces. Beth Anderson, flute; Tina Pelikan, viola; Andrew Luchansky, 'cello. New York, NY: St. Stephen's Church, 5/24/84.

*†*Icy Cruise*, for piccolo, trumpet, viola, 'cello, bass, and harp. Musicians Accord Ensemble, Linda Bouchard, conductor. New York, NY: Carnegie Recital Hall, 5/84. Commissioned by Musicians Accord.

**Pourtinade*. Tina Pelikan, violin. New York, NY: Manhattan School of Music, 4/29/83.

*†*Quartet for Tafelmusik*. Tafelmusik Ensemble. New York, NY: St. Joseph Church, 4/24/84. Commissioned by Tafelmusik.

*†*Revelling of Men*, for trombone sextet and string quintet spatially separated. San Francisco Contemporary Music Players, Linda Bouchard, conductor. San Francisco, CA: San Francisco Museum of Art, 3/84. Commissioned by Quatuor Tromboni de Marin.

Tossing Diamonds. Saturday Brass Quintet. New York, NY: 1/14/84.

*Bouchard, Suzanne (Canada). *Suite pour piano*. Marc-André Demers, piano. Quebec City: 10/29/83.

Boyd, Anne (Australia). *Anglung*, for piano (1974). Selma Epstein, piano. New York, NY: Merkin Concert Hall, 5/12/85 (N.Y. premiere).

Brandman, Margaret (Australia). *Sonorities*, for piano. Selma Epstein, piano.

Hong Kong: Hong Kong Baptist College, 9/26/83; New York, NY: Alice Tully Hall, 10/9/83.

Britain, Radie. *Suite for Strings*. Westwood-Brentwood Symphony Orchestra, Alvin Mills, conductor. Santa Monica, CA: 3/6/83.

*Brockman, Jane. *Character Sketches*, for piano. New York, NY: Carnegie Recital Hall, 5/3/85.

Music for Clarinet and Piano. Bowery Ensemble performers. New York, NY: Symphony Space, 5/22/83.

**Shadows*, for flute and clarinet. David Harman, clarinet; Nancy Harman, flute. New York, NY: Lincoln Center Library, 2/12/84.

*†Brush, Ruth. *The Golden Years*, for SSA chorus. Bartlesville, OK: 1/24/84. Commissioned for the 75th anniversary of the Musical Research Society of Bartlesville.

**River* Moons: Orchestral tone Poem. Bartlesville Symphony Orchestra, L. Green, Conductor. Bartlesville, OK: 11/20/83.

*Callaway, Ann. *Alleluia, Vidimus Stellam*. Gregg Smith Singers. New York, NY: St. Peter's Church, 12/10/83.

**Collections—Recollections*. Rie Schmidt, flute; Marc Shuman; 'cello, Eliza Garth, piano. New York, NY: Columbia University, 12/16/83.

Five Songs for Soprano and Percussion (1984). Manhattan Contemporary Ensemble. New York, NY: Manhattan School of Music, 12/12/84.

*Capers, Valerie. *Sojourner*: opera in one act. Opera Ebony. New York, NY: 2/24/84.

*Carnabucci, Laura. *Suite for Flute and Strings*. Laura Carnabucci, flute; Bay Area Women's Philharmonic. Berkeley, CA: First Congregational Church, 5/17/85.

*Cecconi-Bates, Augusta. *Cabra*, for flute and 'cello. Andrew Bolotowsky, flute; Carol Redfield, 'cello. New York, NY: 10/17/82.

**Praeludium and Allegro*. Ann Eisch, violin; Racine Municipal Band, Delbert Eisch, conductor. Racine, WI: 11/7/82.

**A Touch of Christmas*: children's oratorio. Syracuse University Children's Choir, Barbara Marble Tagg, conductor. Syracuse, NY: 12/5/82.

*Chance, Nancy Laird. *Domine Dominus*: motet for double chorus a cappella. Florilegium Choir. New York, NY: Gustavus Adolphus Church, 6/2/85.

Duos III. Da Capo Chamber Players. New York, NY: Symphony Space, 10/16/84.

**Liturgy*, for orchestra. Columbus Symphony Orchestra, Christian Badea, conductor. Columbus, OH: 4/9/84.

**Rhapsodia*, for marimba quartet. Manhattan Marimba Quartet. New York, NY: Carnegie Recital Hall, 6/4/85.

**Solemnities*, for two brass quartets and three percussion players. Jupiter Symphony Players, Jens Nygaard, conductor. New York, NY: Alice Tully Hall, 5/10/84.

*†*Woodwind Quintet*. Quintet of the Americas. New York, NY: Carnegie Recital Hall, 5/2/83. Commissioned by Quintet of the Americas.

**Woodwind Quintet*: revised version. Vox Nova Quintet. Charleston, SC: Piccolo Spoleto Festival, 6/1/85.

Chaves, Mary. *Pomes*; *Trio no. 3*; *Trio in Two Movements*; *Women's Breath*. Framingham, MA: Framingham State College, 4/1/84.

*†Childs, Mary Ellen. *Chorines*. Choreography by Gina Buntz. American Dance Festival performers, David Stock, conductor. Durham, NC: Duke University, 7/18/83. Commissioned by the American Dance Festival.

*†Clayton, Laura. *Panel*. Choreography by Claire Porter. American Dance Festival performers, David Stock, conductor. Durham, NC: Duke University, 7/18/83. Commissioned by the American Dance Festival.

Clement, Sheree. *Variations/Obsessions*. New York, NY: Merkin Concert Hall, 3/21/85.

Collins, Paula. *Five Pieces for Woodwind Quintet* (1982). Baton Rouge, LA: Louisiana State University, 2/28/83.

*Cory, Eleanor. *Apertures*, for piano. Max Lifchitz, piano. New York, NY: St. Stephen's Church, 10/18/84.

Coulthard, Jeanne (Canada). *Variations on BACH*, for piano. Selma Epstein, piano. New York, NY: Merkin Concert Hall, 5/12/85.

Cowles, Darleen. *Transluscent Unreality Plus I*, for flute. Mary Stolpher, flute. New York, NY: Carnegie Recital Hall, 11/82.

*Cozette, Cynthia. *Adea*: opera excerpts. Thomas Carson, bass-baritone; Cassandra Hayes, soprano; Cynthia Cozette, piano. Philadelphia, PA: 1/9/83.

**Nigerian Treasures*: suite for unaccompanied flute. Cynthia Cozette, flute. Camden, NJ: 3/26/83.

*Crawford, Dorothy. *Portrait of Anne Bradstreet*, for soprano, recorder, violin, and harpsichord. Los Angeles, CA: Westlake School, 2/9/84.

*Danforth, Frances. *Into the Vortex*: dialogue for timpani and tape. John Boudler, timpani. Chicago, IL: American Conservatory of Music, 10/5/83.

Rain Forest, for solo marimba with three multiple percussionists and a timpani. University of Buffalo Percussion Ensemble. Buffalo, NY: SUNY at Buffalo, 9/14/83.

*Dare, Marie (U.K.). *Rhapsody*. Brian Craib, double bass; Kircaldy Orchestra Society, Graeme Wilson, conductor. Kircaldy: Belwearie High School, 3/6/83.

Decker, Pamela. *Passacaglia*, for organ (1980). Pamela Decker, organ. Berkeley, CA: University of California at Berkeley, 6/28/84.

*Dembo, Royce. *Five Brief Pieces*, for two flutes. Bernice and Diane Kliebard, flutes. Madison, WI: Bethel Center, 4/23/83.

**Four Songs*. Lois Dick, soprano, Bernice Kliebard, flute, Mary Ann Harr, harp. Madison, WI: University of Wisconsin, 11/8/82.

**Variations on Transformations*. Warren Downs, 'cello, Ed Walters, piano. Madison, WI: 5/8/83.

De Montigny, Suzanne. *Direct Current*, for piano. New York, NY: La Mama, 3/3/83.

Deschênes, Marcelle (Canada). *Jour J*: electronic. Toronto: Ontario Science Center, 9/22/84.

*Di Bucci, Michelle. *Voice and/or Volumes*. Brooklyn Philharmonia Meet the Moderns Series. Brooklyn, NY: Brooklyn Academy of Music, 11/10/83; New York, NY: Cooper Union, 11/11/83.

*Diemer, Emma Lou. *Bellsong*, for carillon. Margo Halstead, carillon. Ann Arbor, MI: University of Michigan, 5/83.

**Concert Piece*, for organ and orchestra. Emma Lou Diemer, organ; University of Oregon Symphony Orchestra, Karen Keltner, conductor. Eugene, OR:

University of Oregon, 2/25/85 (West Coast Women Conductor/Composer Symposium).

Elegy, for organ, two players. Marilyn Mason, Michele Johns, organ. Ann Arbor, MI: University of Michigan, 5/83.

Fragments from the Mass. Pro Arte Chorale. Media, PA: Delaware County Community College, 3/8/86.

Six Pieces for String Quartet. New Repertory Ensemble. Queens, NY: Queens College, 10/18/83.

**Suite of Homages* (1985). Bay Area Women's Philharmonic. San Francisco, CA; 11/22/85. Commissioned for the fifth anniversary of the Bay Area Women's Philharmonic.

Dinescu, Violeta (Rumania). *Dialogo.* Heidelberg: 3/18/84.

Drei Miniaturen, for saxophone quartet. Rascher Saxophone Quartet. Mannheim: 11/9/83.

*Dlugoszewski, Lucia. *Duende Amor.* Music Theatre Group of the Lenox Arts Center. Stockbridge, MA: 8/83.

Duende Newfallen. New Music Consort. New York, NY: Carnegie Recital Hall, 10/13/83 (New York premiere).

Fire, Fragile, Flight (1976). Manhattan Contemporary Ensemble. New York, NY: Manhattan School of Music, 12/12/84.

*Dusman, Linda. *Nightwatch.* Elizabeth Kirkpatrick, soprano; Carol Yampolsky, piano. Washington, DC: Corcoran Gallery, 5/22/83.

Dvorkin, Judith. *Blue Star*: chamber opera. After Dinner Opera Co., Conrad Strasser, conductor. New York, NY: Lincoln Center Library, 12/5/83.

**Six Zoological Considerations,* for voice and piano. Julia Lovett, soprano. Richmond, VA: Virginia Commonwealth University, 4/29/83.

*Ekizian, Michelle. *Midnight Voices,* for oboe and five players. Henry Schuman, oboe; Laura Conwesser, flute; Anand Devendra, clarinet; Bonnie Hartman, 'cello; Daniel Druckman, percussion; George Fisher, piano; Paul Dunkel, conductor. New York, NY: McMillan Theater, 12/11/84.

†Escot, Pozzi. *Concerto for Piano and Chamber Orchestra.* Yvonne Dupont, piano; New Works Orchestra, Harry Chalmiers, conductor. Boston, MA: New England Conservatory, 6/5/83. Commissioned by Groton Center for the Arts.

†Even-Or, Mary (Israel). *Musikinesis,* for orchestra. Haifa: 6/84. Received ACUM Ltd. first prize.

*†Fine, Vivian. *Drama,* for orchestra. San Francisco Symphony Orchestra, Edo de Waart, conductor. San Francisco, CA: 1/5/83. Commissioned by Dr. and Mrs. Ralph I. Dorfman for the orchestra's 1982-83 season.

*†*Poetic Fires (From the Greeks)*: piano concerto. Vivian Fine, piano; American Composers Orchestra, Gunther Schuller, conductor. New York, NY: Alice Tully Hall, 2/21/85. Commissioned by the Koussevitsky Foundation.

Firsova, Yelena (U.S.S.R.). *Sacrament,* for organ and percussion. Moscow: Moscow Autumn Festival, 10/84.

Fontyn, Jacqueline (Belgium). *Intermezzo,* for solo harp. Sylvia Kowalczuk, harp. New York, NY: New York University, 6/29/83.

Nonetto (1969). Bay Area Women's Philharmonic performers. San Francisco, CA: First Unitarian Church, 1/27/84 (U.S. premiere).

Or Je Vous Dis Bonne Nouvelle. The Occasional Singers, Gil Robbins, director. New York, NY: New York University, 3/14/83.

**Rhumbs*, for brass quintet. New Albion Brass Quintet. San Francisco, CA: San Francisco State University, 3/16/85 (Conference on Women in Music).

*Fowler, Jennifer (U.K.). *Letter from Haworth*, for mezzo-soprano, clarinet, 'cello, and piano (1984). London: 12/5/84.

Piece for an Opera House. Penelope Thwaites, John Lavender, pianists. London: Wigmore Hall, 12/6/82.

Tell Out My Soul, for soprano, 'cello, and piano (revised version, 1984). Great Britain: Harrogate International Festival, 7/84.

†*When David Heard*, for choir and piano (1982). Melbourne, Australia: 12/84. Commissioned by the Collegium Musicum, Austria.

*Fox, Erika (U.K.). *Quasi una Cadenza*. Lontano Ensemble. London: St. John's Smith Square, 2/29/84.

*Frasier, Jane. *Pacific Fantasy*, for soprano and wind ensemble. Estes Park, CO: Alpen Musikfest, 7/84.

*French, Tania G. *Oread*, for chorus, soloists, chamber orchestra, and guitar. Amherst College Friends of Music. Amherst, MA: Amherst College, 10/20/84.

Trio, for oboe, clarinet and bassoon. Adrie Kusserow, oboe; Sue Metzger, clarinet; Elizabeth Midgley, bassoon.

**Variations* for violin and piano. Jonathan Hirsch, violin; Clifton J. Noble, piano. Amherst, MA: Amherst College, 2/24/85.

Frykberg, Susan (Canada). *OM 152—Getting There*: electronic. Toronto: Ontario Science Center, 9/21/84.

Galas, Diamanda. Untitled. Brooklyn Philharmonic, Lukas Foss, conductor. Brooklyn, NY: Brooklyn Academy of Music, 1/28/83 (U.S. premiere).

Gardner, Kay. *A Rainbow Path*: piano version. Kay Gardner, piano. Cambridge, MA: Harvard University, 6/21/84.

Prayer to Aphrodite, for alto flute and strings. Arcady Chamber Orchestra. Blue Hill, ME: 8/28/84.

Rain Forest. Maryland Women's Symphony. Baltimore, MD: 4/20/86.

**Travelin'*. April Kassiver, guitar; Carol Rowe, viola; Nuru Dafina, percussion; Ann Demska, tambura; Kay Gardner, alto flute. Narrowsburg, NY: 9/2/84.

†Garwood, Margaret. *Rappaccini's Daughter*: opera. Pennsylvania Opera Theatre, Barbara Silverstein, conductor. Philadelphia, PA: Trocadero Theatre, 5/16/83.

Gideon, Miriam. *Questions on Nature*. Group for Contemporary Music. New York, NY: 92nd Street YMHA, 4/19/83.

The Resounding Lyre. Constantine Cassolas, tenor; Speculum Musicae, Robert Black, conductor. New York, NY: Alice Tully Hall, 12/1/82.

Rhymes from the Hill. Musicians Accord Ensemble. New York, NY: St. Michael's Church, 12/7/84.

Sonnets from Shakespeare. William Sharp, baritone; Prison Chamber Orchestra, Robert Black, conductor. New York, NY: Symphony Space, 4/3/85.

*Gilbert, Patricia. *A Question of Love*: operatic comedy. London: Conway Hall, 11/7/84.

*Gipps, Ruth (U.K.) *Symphony no. 5*. London Repertoire Orchestra, Ruth Gipps, conductor. London: Guildhall School of Music and Drama, 3/6/83.

Giteck, Janice. *Callin' Home Coyote*; *Thunder Like a White Bear Dancin'*; *Breathing Songs from a Turning Sky*. Seattle, WA: Cornish Institute, 11/83.

Matinee d'Ivresse; *L'Ange Heurtebise*. Thomasa Eckert, soprano; Roger Nelson, piano. Seattle, WA: Seattle Central Community College, 4/17/83.

Glanville-Hicks, Peggy. *Three Gymnopedies*. Bay Area Women's Philharmonic, J. Karla Lemon, conductor. San Francisco, CA: Herbst Theatre, 11/14/82.

Glaser, Victoria. *Plucker's Harvest*, for two 'cellos. Mark Churchill, Martha Kiefer, 'cellos. Boston, MA: New England Conservatory, 6/12/83.

*Glickman, Sylvia. *The Hollow Men*, for SATB, soprano solo, and piano. Pro Arte Chorale, Margery Stanke, director. Media, PA: Delaware County Community College, 11/23/85.

Psalm 96 from *Prayer Service*. Choir of Gladwyne Episcopal Church, Kathleen Holler, director. Wynnewood, PA: 10/84.

*Goolkasian-Rahbee, Dianne. *Pages from My Diary*. Newton String Quartet. Medford, MA: Tufts University, 6/24/84 (American Women Composers Conference).

Phantasie Variations, op. 12 (1980). Sylvia Chambless, piano. Boston, MA: New England Conservatory, 6/12/83.

Gould, Elizabeth. *Andante for Trumpet and String Orchestra*. Janet Entwisle Griffith, trumpet; Keweenaw Symphony Orchestra, Michael T. Griffith, conductor. Houghton, MI: 3/24/83.

*Graham, Janet (U.K.). *Evening Flights*. Marianne Ehrhardt, flute. London: Purcell Room, 10/31/82.

*†Greene, Diana. *Rigorisms II* (1983). Pittsburgh New Music Ensemble, David Stock, conductor. Pittsburgh, PA: Chatham College Chapel, 12/4/83. Commissioned by the Pittsburgh New Music Ensemble.

Gubaidulina, Sofia (U.S.S.R.). *Offertorium*, for violin and orchestra. Gidon Kremer, violin, New York Philharmonic, Zubin Mehta, conductor. New York, NY: Avery Fisher Hall, 1/3/85 (U.S. premiere).

Guraieb, Rosa (Mexico). *Pieza Ciclica*, para piano. Alicia Uretta, piano. Mexico City: Pinacoteca Virreinal, 4/21/83.

*Haas, Jill (U.K.). *Sumai No Ha*. Japan Music Pool. London: Purcell Room, 12/6/82.

Hankinson, Ann. *Variations for Orchestra*. University of Oregon Symphony, Madeline Schatz, conductor. Eugene, OR: University of Oregon, 2/25/85 (West Coast Women Conductor/Composer Symposium).

*Hays, Doris. *Celebration of No*, for tape with alternate versions including film and/or prepared piano, violin, 'cello, chanters. Monika Holszky-Wiedemann, violin; four chanters with tape. New York, NY: Experimental Intermedia Foundation, 3/4/83.

**Harmony*. Maryland Women's Symphony. Baltimore, MD: 4/20/86.

**M.O.M. 'n P.O.P. (Music Only Music, Piano Only Piano)*, for tape, film, slides, and mime. Utrecht, Holland: Academy of Film and Science, 3/28/83.

Sunday Nights (1977). Kathleen Supové, piano. New York, NY: Lincoln Center Library, 12/10/82.

Tunings, for viola. John Graham, viola. New York, NY: Mannes College of Music, 12/17/82 (NY premiere).

Hebert, Melissa A. *The Clowns*, for piano. Paula Collins, piano. Baton Rouge, LA: Louisiana State University, 2/28/83.

*Heilbron, Valerie. *American Suite: Thoughts from a Young Man's Collection*: song cycle for four vocalists and chamber orchestra. Berkeley, CA: Trinity Chamber Concerts, 9/18/83.

*Heinrich, Adel. *Mrs. Forrester, a Lost Lady*: chamber dance-drama. Waterville, ME: Colby College, 2/16/84.

*Hemenway, Edith. *The Twilight of Magic*: children's opera. Downtown Opera Players, Mimi Stern-Wolfe, director. New York, NY: 2/12/84.

Holland, Dulci (Australia). *Scattering of the Leaves* (1965). Selma Epstein, piano. Mexico City: 3/23/84 (Third International Congress on Women in Music).

Toccatina, for piano (1981). Selma Epstein, piano. Ann Arbor, MI: University of Michigan, 5/7/83 (Op. 2: Women in Music Conference).

*Holmes, Shirlee McGee. *Morning Song*; *Song of Spring*; *Acceptance*. Ann Lemon, voice; Suzie Andrew, piano; Iris Reynolds, bass flute; Shirlee Holmes, accordion. Seattle, WA: Seattle Central Community College, 5/15/83.

*†Hoover, Katherine. *From the Testament of François Villon*, for bass-baritone, bassoon, and string quartet. John Cheek, bass-baritone; Leonard Hindell, bassoon. New York, NY: Merkin Concert Hall, 1/9/85. Commissioned by Leonard Hindell.

Images. Verdehr Trio. New York, NY: Merkin Concert Hall, 10/5/83 (NY premiere).

Lyric Trio, for flute, 'cello, and piano (1983). Huntington Trio. Lewisburg, PA: Bucknell University, 3/4/84.

**Songs of Celebration*: Christmas pieces arranged for chorus and brass. Haddonfield, NJ: 12/1/84.

**Suite*, for two flutes. New York, NY: Columbia University, 11/19/84.

*†Hovda, Eleanor. *Ariadnemusic*. Boston Musica Viva and Concert Dance Co. of Boston. Boston, MA: New England Conservatory, 2/10/84. Commissioned by the ensembles.

**Breathing*, for multiple flutes. Lee Humphries, conductor.

Cymbalmusic/Centerflow II. Eleanor Hovda, double bowed cymbals, audience.

Trials III/Crossings. Sharon Friedler, dance and percussion; Louis Friedler, clarinet; Eleanor Hovda, contrabass, percussion, and Audubon birdcall chorus. St. Paul, MN: Walker Art Center, 3/31/83.

Hsu, Wen-Ying. Sky *Maiden's Dance Suite, II*. Women's Music Club Symphony of Columbus, Ohio, Cynthia Capper, conductor. Columbus, OH: Ohio State University, 6/29/83.

*†Ivey, Jean Eichelberger. *Notes Toward Time*. Jubal Trio. Baltimore, MD: Baltimore Museum of Art, 3/11/83. Commissioned by the Chamber Music Society of Baltimore.

Skaniadaryo, for piano and tape. Enid Katahn, piano. New York, NY: Merkin Concert Hall, 3/17/83.

Solstice. Chamber Players of the League-ISCM. New York, NY: Carnegie Recital Hall, 12/8/83 (New York premiere).

**Triton's Horn*. James Cunningham, tenor saxophone; Lily Chang, piano. New York, NY: Carnegie Recital Hall, 3/29/83.

*†Jankowski, Loretta. *Paterson Songs*, for tenor, flute, clarinet, violin, 'cello and piano. George Shirley, tenor; New Jersey Chamber Music Society. Montclair, NJ: 4/13/84. Commissioned by the New Jersey Chamber Music Society in honor of their tenth anniversary.

Jazwinski, Barbara. *String Trio*. New York, NY: La Mama, 3/3/83.

Jolas, Betsy (France). *États*, for violin and six percussionists (1969). Eugène Husaruk, violin, Atelier Percussion de l'Université du Montréal. Montreal:

Université du Québec à Montréal, 10/1/84 (World Music Days).

Kabat, Julie. *The Night Fisherman*. Newband Ensemble. New York, NY: Roulette, 3/6/83.

Kadima, Hagar (Israel). *Sounds*: vocal work. San Diego, CA: University of California, 4/84.

*Kaminsky, Laura. *Enkomios III: A Dream Revisited*. Musicians Accord Ensemble. New York, NY: St. Michael's Church, 12/7/84.

**Twilight Settings*, for soprano, strings, and percussion. Christine Schadelberg, soprano; Hampshire String Quartet, William Trigg, percussion. New York, NY: Symphony Space, 5/28/85.

Kanach, Sharon. *Offrande* (1975). Diamanda Galas, soprano, Brooklyn Philharmonic, Lukas Foss, conductor. Brooklyn, NY: Brooklyn Academy of Music, 4/26/84; New York, NY: Cooper Union, 4/27/84.

Kasilag, Lucretia (Philippines). *Variations on Waylay Angay*, for piano. Selma Epstein, piano. New York, NY: 10/84 (New York premiere).

*Keal, Minna (U.K.). *Symphony*. National Centre for Orchestral Studies Orchestra, Adrian Leaper, conductor. London: St. John's Smith Square, 2/13/84.

Kessler, Minuetta. *Sonata Concertante*, for violin and piano. Marylou Speaker Churchill, violin; Minuetta Kessler, piano. Boston, MA: New England Conservatory, 6/12/83.

Kojiba, Tomiko (Japan). *Hiroshima*: requiem (1979). Boston Symphony Orchestra Strings, Seiji Ozawa, conductor. New York, NY: Carnegie Hall, 12/5/85.

*Kolb, Barbara. *Cantico*: film. James Herbert, filmmaker and painter, Barbara Kolb, producer and composer. New York, NY: Third Street Music School Settlement, 12/5/82.

Chromatic Fantasy. Tony Randall, narrator, New York Philharmonic. New York, NY: Avery Fisher Hall, 5/4/83.

Grisaille. American Composers Orchestra, Thomas Nee, conductor. New York, NY: Alice Tully Hall, 2/27/84 (New York premiere).

Homage to Keith Jarrett and Gary Burton. Richard Craig, percussion. Tampa, FL: University of South Florida, 2/5/84.

**Mille Foglie*. Ensemble InterContemporain, Peter Eötvös, conductor. Paris: 2/27/85.

**The Point That Divides the Line*, for organ and percussion (1982). Leonard Raver, organ; Barbara Kolb, conductor. New York, NY: Church of the Ascension, 3/7/83.

Soundings; Appello; Cavatina. Rochester, NY: Eastman School of Music, 3/4/85.

Koplewitz, Laura. Piece for solo flute. Patricia Spencer, flute. Annandale-on-Hudson, NY: Bard College, 7/84.

*Kosse, Roberta. *And Death Shall Have No Dominion*, for mixed chorus, piano, and percussion. Stonewall Chorale. New York, NY: St. John's Church in the Village, 6/22/85.

*La Barbara, Joan. *Berliner Traume*, for amplified voice and tape. Joan La Barbara, voice. New York, NY: Symphony Space, 3/12/85.

Chandre. Houston Symphony Orchestra, C. William Howard, conductor. Houston, TX: 3/12/83 (U.S. premiere).

October Music: Star Showers and Extraterrestrials. Joan La Barbara, soprano and tape. New York, NY: Symphony Space, 11/5/83.

The Solar Wind III, for voice and chamber orchestra (1984); *Shadow Song*, for amplified voice and tape (1979); *Vlissingen Harbor* (1982). Joan La Barbara, voice; Bay Area Women's Philharmonic, Jeannine Wagar, conductor. San Francisco, CA: Scottish Rites Hall, 5/12/84.

*Laden, Bernice F. *Three Songs*, for voice and flute. Roberta Johnson, soprano; Laura Hamm, flute.

Prelude and Fugue. David Barnes, oboe; David Leistikow, clarinet; Elenore Froelich, bassoon. Seattle, WA: Seattle Central Community College, 4/17/83.

Larsen, Libby. *Bronze Veils*. Bowery Ensemble. New York, NY: Symphony Space, 11/5/83.

Clair de Lune: opera in two acts. Arkansas Opera Theatre, Benson Hess, conductor. Little rock, AR: Arkansas Arts Center, 2/22,24/85.

*†*Fanfare—Introduction*, for orchestra. Minnesota Orchestra. Minneapolis, MN: 9/19/84. Composed as part of the Meet-the-Composer/Orchestra Residencies Program.

Love and hisses, for double woodwind quintet. Bay Area Women's Philharmonic performers. San Francisco, CA: 5/10/86.

*†*Overture—Parachute Dancing*. American Composers Orchestra, Thomas Nee, conductor. New York, NY: Alice Tully Hall, 2/27/84. Commissioned by the American Composers Orchestra.

Sonata in One Movement on "Kalenda Maya", for organ. Philip Brunelle, organ. Minneapolis, MN: 2/5/84 (U.S. premiere).

Travelling in Every Season. Catherine Ciesinski, mezzo-soprano. St. Paul, MN: St. Anthony Arts Forum, 5/5/83.

*†*Water Music*. Minnesota Orchestra. Minneapolis, MN: 1/30/85. Composed as part of the Meet-the-Composer/Orchestra Residencies Program.

*†Lauber, Anne (Canada). *Beyond the Sound Barrier*: symphonic tale for orchestra and two narrators. Toronto Symphony, Mario Duschenes, conductor. Toronto: 11/5/83. Commissioned jointly by the Toronto Symphony and Orchestre Symphonique de Quebec. Denver Philharmonic. Denver, CO: 2/19/84.

Colin-Maillard. Sherbrooke and Ville d'Anjou Orchestras. Canada: 3/83.

*Laufer, Beatrice. *And Thomas Jefferson Said* . . . United States Air Force Chamber Players and the Singing Sargeants. Washington, DC: Anderson House, 2/27/85.

Leach, Mary Jane. *Pieces for Slides, Voices, and Flute*. New York, NY: Experimental Intermedia Foundation, 6/22/84.

Trio for Duo. Mary Jane Leach, voice; Stefani Starin, alto flute; tape. New York, NY: Theater of the Open Eye, 3/9/85.

Leandre, Joelle (U.K.). *Taxi*; *Vidé Obass*; *Cri*. Joelle Leandre, doublebass. London: 8/24/82.

*†LeBaron, Anne. *Lamentation/Invocation*, for bass, clarinet, 'cello, and harp. Christopher Trakas, bass; Charles Neidich, clarinet; Madeline Shapiro, 'cello; Nina Kellman, harp. New York, NY: Carnegie Recital Hall, 11/7/84. Winner of the New Music Consort's Composer Competition.

Planxty Bowerbird, for harp and tape. Sara Cutler, harp. New York, NY: Cooper Union, 1/9/85.

*LeFanu, Nicola (U.K.). *SPNM Birthday Fanfare*. London Sinfonietta Brass, Oliver

Knussen, conductor. London: 5/23/83.

Trio II: Song for Peter. Margaret Field, soprano; Ian Mitchell, clarinet; Helen Verney, 'cello. London: St. John's Smith Square, 3/3/83.

* *Variations for Piano and Orchestra.* Jonathan Dunsby, piano; National Scout and Guide Orchestra, George Odam, conductor. London: Royal College of Music, 12/31/82.

Leon, Tania. *A la Par.* Ursula Oppens, piano, Erik Charleston, percussion.

Momentum, for piano. New Music Consort. New York, NY: Manhattan School of Music, 1/31/85 (NY premiere).

Two Pieces for 'Cello. Michael Rudiakov, 'cello. New York, NY: Whitney Museum of American Art, 3/25/86.

*†Lesiege, Annette. *Star Gazers and Other Pilgrims.* Winston-Salem Symphony, Peter Peret, conductor. Winston-Salem, NC: 3/1/83. Commissioned by the Winston-Salem Symphony.

Levine, Amy Miller. *Joel's Suite,* for oboe and piano. Brenda Schuman-Post, oboe; Suzanne Garramine, piano. San Francisco, CA: San Francisco State University, 3/16/85 (Conference on Women in Music).

Lomon, Ruth. *Dialogue,* for harpsichord and vibraphone. Carol Pharo, harpsichord; Jeffrey Fischer, vibraphone. Boston, MA: New England Conservatory, 6/12/83.

*†*Iatiku . . . Bringing to Life,* for bass clarinet, harp, vibes, marimba, harpsichord, and piano. Boston, MA: 11/12/83. Commissioned by the Eastern Division of the Music Teacher's National Association; received award from National League of American Pen Women.

Loudova, Ivana (Czech.). *Cuarteto No 2, Dedicado a Biedrich Smetana.* Cuarteto Latinamericano. Mexico City: Casa de la Paz, 4/27/83 (Mexican premiere).

Louie, Alexina (Canada). *Pearls.* Magnetic Band, Owen Underhill, conductor. Montreal: Université du Québec à Montréal, 9/29/84 (World Music Days).

Piano Concerto. Robert Silverman, piano, Manitoba Chamber Orchestra, Simon Streatfield, conductor. Winnipeg: 2/12/85.

Songs of Paradise. Toronto Symphony, Andrew Davis, conductor. Toronto: 10/10-11/84.

*Luff, Enid (U.K.). *Mathematical Dream.* Endymion Ensemble. London: 3/14/83.

*Lutyens, Elisabeth (1906-1983) (U.K.). *Encore—Maybe.* Thalia Myers, piano. London: Wigmore Hall, 3/7/83.

String Quartet 1982. Edinburgh Quartet. London: Purcell Room, 3/18/83.

MacGregor, Laurie. *Intrusion of the Hunter.* University of South Florida Percussion Ensemble, Robert M. McCormick, conductor. Tampa, FL: University of South Florida, 3/11/84.

*McIntosh, Diana (Canada). *Double Talk,* for voice, amplified sounds, and tape. London: 11/1/83.

Graditum Ad Summum. Schnabel Piano Duo. New York, NY: 92nd Street YMHA, 2/28/84.

McLean, Priscilla. *Elan! A Dance to All Rising Things From the Earth,* for five instruments. Tempe, AZ: Arizona State University, 3/28/85.

*Maconchy, Elizabeth (U.K.). *L'Horlage.* Sylvia Eaves, soprano; Thea King, clarinet; Courtney Kenny, piano. London: Rosslyn Hill Chapel, 5/21/83.

**Music for Strings*. BBC Prom Orchestra, Edward Downes, conductor. London: BBC Proms, 7/26/83.

**Pied Beauty; Heaven Haven*. BBC Singers, Philip Jones Brass Ensemble, John Poole, conductor. Brompton: Holy Trinity Church, 8/8/82.

Serenata Concertante, for violin and orchestra. Susan Wang, violin, Bay Area Women's Philharmonic. Berkeley, CA: First Congregational Church, 5/17/85 (U.S. premiere).

**Tribute*. Nicolas Ward, violin; Iris Lemare, conductor. Darlington: Civic Theatre, 4/10/83.

**Wind Quintet*. Albion Wind Quintet. London: 9/29/82.

*McTee, Cindy. *Psalm 100*. Pacific Lutheran University Choir of the West, Maurice Skones, conductor. Nashville, TN: 3/12/83.

**Songs of Spring and the Moon*, for soprano and eight instrumentalists. Pacific Lutheran University Contemporary Directions Ensemble, David Robbins, conductor. Tacoma, WA: 4/12/83.

Mageau, Mary (Australia). *Concert Pieces*, for violin, 'cello and piano. Artemon Trio. London: Purcell Room, 1/21/85.

Concerto Grosso. Tasmanian Symphony Orchestra, Keith Humble, conductor. Tasmania: 10/19/83.

**Nach Bach*. Mary Mageau, harpsichord. Queensland, Australia: Kelvin Grove College, 3/20/83.

*†*Pacific Portfolio*. College of St. Margaret Orchestra, Margaret Kendall Smith, conductor. Brisbane: 10/11/83. Commissioned by the College of St. Margaret.

**Soliloquy*, for piano. Choreography by Maggi Sietsma. Brisbane: Woodward Theatre, 11/20/84.

Mamlok, Ursula. *Concerto for Oboe and Orchestra*. Ernest Harrison, oboe, James Yestadt, conductor. Baton Rouge, LA: Louisiana State University, 2/27/83.

Daybreak. Mira Spektor, mezzo-soprano; Dorothy Indenbaum, piano.

From My Garden, for solo violin. Asya Meshberg, violin. New York, NY: West Side YMCA, 3/10/85.

**From My Garden*, for oboe, horn, piano, and crotales. San Francisco, CA: 11/8/83.

**From My Garden III*, for solo viola. David Sills, viola. New York, NY: Lincoln Center Library, 9/7/84.

Haiku Settings. New Music Consort, Judith Bettina, soprano. Queens, NY: York College, 2/27/83.

*Marcus, Adabelle Gross. *Four Piano Compositions*. Ann Arbor, MI: University of Michigan, 5/6/83.

**Song Cycle*. Baton Rouge, LA: Louisiana State University, 2/25/83.

**Textures*, for piano, flute, and strings. Adabelle Gross Marcus, piano; Chicago Chamber Orchestra, Dieter Kober, conductor. Chicago, IL: Chicago Public Library, 2/20/83.

Marez-Oyens, Tera de (Netherlands). *Charon's Gift*, for piano and tape; *Ballerina on a Cliff*, for piano; *Vagaries*, for piano and tape; Untitled new work, for voice and piano. Paris: Centre Pompidou, 10/25/84.

*†*Het Lied de Duizend Angstem*, for two soloists, two choirs, and symphonic orchestra. Holland: 5/4/84. Commissioned by the Fund for the Creation of

Music for National Dutch Remembrance Day.

**Octopus*, for bass clarinet and percussion. Amsterdam: 5/2/83.

Vrede, for soloists, choir, and orchestra. Utrecht: 5/4-5/84.

*†Martin, Judith. *The Moon Dreams Her*, for orchestra. New York, NY: Guggenheim Museum, 10/23/84. Commissioned by Joel Thome's Orchestra of Our Time with funds from the Jerome Foundation of Minnesota.

*†Martin, Ravonna. *Christmas Liturgy*. Jo Ann Pickens, soprano; Fairbanks Children's Choir, Choral Society and Chamber Players, Suzanne Summerville, director. Fairbanks, AK: Ft. Wainwright Chapel, 12/11/83. Commissioned by Festival Fairbanks '84.

Meachem, Margaret. *In Icy Moonlight*. Bowery Ensemble. New York, NY: Symphony Space, 5/22/83.

Miranda, Sharon Moe. *American Fanfare*. American Symphony Orchestra, Jose Serebrier, conductor. New York, NY: Carnegie Hall, 10/14/84.

Monk, Meredith. *Dolmen Music*: Excerpts. New York, NY: Merkin Concert Hall, 12/12/83.

*†*The Games: Days of Wrath*, collaborative work with Ping Chong, for 16 voices, synthesizer, keyboards, bagpipes, and Chinese horn. West Berlin: 11/28/83. Brooklyn, NY: Brooklyn Academy of Music, 10/9/84 (U.S. premiere). Commissioned by the Peter Stein Theater Company of West Berlin.

Quarry: an opera. New York, NY: La Mama, 5/7-11, 14-20, 22-28/85.

Solo; *Turtle Dreams*; *Dolmen Music*; *Quarry*; *Ellis Island*. Vocal and instrumental ensemble, Meredith Monk, conductor. London: Almeida Theatre, 10/5-6/82.

Turtle Dreams: multimedia composition. New York, NY: 4/19/83.

*Moore, Dorothy Rudd. *Frederick Douglass*: opera. Opera Ebony. New York, NY: 6/85.

Moore, Undine Smith. *Before I'd be a Slave*, for piano (1953). Selma Epstein, piano. New York, NY: Merkin Concert Hall, 2/17/85.

Musgrave, Thea (U.K.). *Chamber Concerto No. 2*. Da Capo Chamber Players. New York, NY: Symphony Space, 10/16/84 (N.Y. premiere).

†*Choral Anthem: The Lord's Prayer*. San Francisco, CA: St. Mary's Cathedral, 6/25/84. Commissioned by the San Francisco Chapter of the American Guild of Organists for their 1984 convention.

*†*Harriett, the Woman Called Moses*: opera. Virginia Opera Co. Norfolk, VA: 3/1/85. Commissioned by the Virginia Opera Co. and Royal Opera of England.

Night Music. Alicia Telford, Laura Beatie, French horns, Bay Area Women's Philharmonic, Jeannine Wagar, conductor. Berkeley, CA: First Congregational Church, 3/9/84.

Orfeo I, for flute and prerecorded tape (1975). Patricia Spencer, flute. New York, NY: Cami Hall, 11/25/84.

Mygatt, Louise. *Duets for Violin and Viola*. Guild of Composers Concert. New York, NY: St. Stephen's Church, 2/24/83.

O'Leary, Jane. *Piano Piece II*. Berlin: British Center, 4/25/84.

**Trio*, for flute, clarinet, and piano. Concorde Ensemble. Dublin, Ireland: 1/7/84.

Olivero, Betty (Israel). *Cantigas Sepharadies*, for soprano and orchestra. Amsterdam: International Gaudeamus Music Week, 9/83.

*Oliveros, Pauline. *Rattlesnake Mountain*, for solo accordion. New York, NY: Whitney Museum of American Art, 3/25/86.

Wheel of Time. Kronos Quartet. CA: 2/83.

*Ore, Cecilie (Norway). *Carnatus*, for choir and soprano solo. Elmer Iseler Singers, Elmer Iseler, conductor. Toronto: Roy Thomson Hall, 9/23/84 (World Music Days).

*Panneton, Isabelle (Canada). *Voilage*, for 11 instruments. Instrumental ensemble, Isabelle Panneton, conductor. Montreal: Conservatoire de Musique de Montreal, 4/13/84.

*Parker, Alice. *Elinor Wylie: Incantations*. Hartford, CT: 4/28-29/84.

**Heart and Soul, Awaken*. Appleton, WI: Appleton High School East, 10/25/83.

*†*Invocation: Peace*. Appleton Boychoir. Appleton, WI: 2/2-24/85. Commissioned by the Appleton Boychoir.

Love Songs. The Occasional Singers. New York, NY: St. Joseph's Church, 3/12/84.

**The Ponder Heart*: opera (1982). Alice Parker, conductor. Jackson, MS: New Stage Theatre, 9/10-19/82.

**Revolutionary Overture*. Setauket, NY: Ward Melville High School, 2/15-16/84.

*†*Sacred Symphonies*, for mixed chorus, flute, violin, 'cello, and organ (1983). Harrisonburg, VA: 2/6/83. Commissioned by Eastern Mennonite College.

*†*Songs From the Dragon Quilt*. Juneau Oratorio Choir. Juneau, AK: 11/26-12/3/84. Commissioned by the Juneau Oratorio Choir.

*†*Songstream*, for mixed chorus with piano four-hands. Northampton, MA: 5/1/83. Commissioned by the Hampshire Choral Society.

*Pentland, Barbara (Canada). *Quintet for Piano and Strings*. Robert Rogers, piano; Purcell String Quartet. Vancouver: 1/13/84.

Tellus (1981-82). Magnetic Band, Owen Underhill, conductor. Montréal: Université du Québec à Montréal, 9/29/84 (World Music Days).

**Tides*. Vancouver New Music Society. Vancouver: 12/2/84.

*Perry, Anita (Canada). *Peter Pan*: ballet for children. Anita Perry, flute and clarinet; ensemble. Portland, OR: Eastside Performing Arts Center, 6/29.84.

*Phillips, Bryony (New Zealand). *The Divine Meditations of John Donne*, for tenor and piano (1979). Richard Phillips, tenor; Elisabeth Boulton, piano. Mt. Eden, New Zealand: 1/21/83.

**Ears in the Turrets Hear*, for unaccompanied tenor (1983). Richard Phillips, tenor. Takapuna, New Zealand: 3/1/83.

**The Marriage of True Minds*, for soprano and violin (1982). Lyndsay Freer, soprano; Michael McLennan, violin. Manurewa, New Zealand: 8/11/83.

**Virgin Birth: Christmas Cantata* (1983). Opera Studio with Val Hungerford, piano, Bryony Phillips, oboe. Howick, New Zealand: 12/11/83.

Pierce, Alexandra. *Spectres* (1975). Selma Epstein, piano. Mexico City: Third International Congress on Women in Music, 3/23/84.

Pizer, Elizabeth. *Expressions Intime*, for piano. New York, NY: Cami Hall, 12/16/84.

Kyrie Eleison. Minneapolis, MN: Walker Art Center, 9/13/84.

Lyric Fantasies. Max Lifchitz, piano. Charleston, SC: Piccolo Spoleto Festival, 5/25/83.

*Planick, Annette Meyers. *Seascapes*, for harp and piano. Sydney Wilson, harp, Annette Meyers Planick, piano. Fort Worth, TX: Fort Worth Women's Club, 3/24/83.

*Plonsey, Jennifer. *Alto Flute Concerto*. Kathie Sumrow, alto flute; Sacred Heart University Chamber Orchestra, Leland Roberts, conductor. Bridgeport, CT: Sacred Heart University, 5/1/83.

**Floating Sequence Circle*. Ted Kuhn, violin; Jennifer Plonsey, keyboard; Evan Ziporyn, bass clarinet.

**Three Bypaths*, for woodwind quintet. Gazza Ladra Woodwind Quintet. Stamford, CT: 4/15/83.

*†Polin, Claire. *Kuequenaku-Camiriola,* for piano and percussion. Victor Friedman, piano; Jerry Tanenbaum, percussion. Bryn Mawr, PA: Bryn Mawr College, 4/23/83. Commissioned by William Penn Foundation.

**Mythos*: concerto for harp and strings. Jude Mollenhauer, harp; Hoboken Chamber Orchestra, Gary M. Schneider, conductor. Hoboken, NJ: St. Paul's Episcopal Church, 5/19/83.

*Poston, Elizabeth (U.K.). *Charm Against the Bumble Bee*. Helen Watkins, mezzo-soprano; David Watkins, harp. London: Wigmore Hall, 10/18/82.

*Pradell, Leila. *Psalm 23*, for bass-baritone and piano. Boston, MA: John F. Kennedy Library, 12/84.

Song Cycle of Women Poets, for soprano (1983). Mary Sindoni, soprano; Leila Pradell, piano. Boston, MA: New England Conservatory, 6/12/83.

Preobrajenska, Vera N. *Blue Symphony*. Music Club Symphony of Columbus, Ohio, Cynthia Capper, conductor. Columbus, OH: Ohio State University, 9/29/83.

**Clara Militch*: ballet for pianoforte. Vera Preobrajenska, piano. Santa Cruz, CA: 12/1/84.

**Sonatine*, for piano. Vera Preobrajenska, piano. Santa Cruz, CA: Moraga Concert Hall, 3/4/84.

**Trio Variations*, for oboe, 'cello, and bassoon. Carol Panofsky, oboe; Peter Elsea, bassoon; Joel Schaefer, 'cello. Santa Cruz, CA: 9/30/84.

Presslaff, Hilary Tann. *As Ferns* (1977). LSU Symphony, James Yestadt, condutor. Baton Rouge, LA: Louisiana State University, 2/27/83.

**Doppelgänger*, for solo piano. Chicago, IL: University of Illinois, 4/10/84.

*Ptaszynska, Marta (Poland). *Concerto for Marimba and Orchestra*. Washington, DC: Percussive Arts Society International Convention, 1986.

La Novella d'Inverno. Polish Chamber Orchestra. New York, NY: Carnegie Hall, 4/85; Lisbon, Portugal: 5/85.

Space Model. Cynthia Symanski, percussion. Potsdam, NY: Crane School of Music, 3/17/84.

*Radford, Laurie (Canada). *Masks of Becoming*. Jill Rothberg, flute; Uriel Rosen, trumpet; Louis Dallaire, 'cello; Suzanne Berthiaume, harp. Montreal: McGill University, 4/2/84.

Ran, Shulamit. *Apprehensions*. Da Capo Chamber Players. New York, NY: Symphony Space, 10/16/84.

A Prayer. New York, NY: Sotheby's, 3/4/83.

Verticals. Alan Feinberg, piano. New York, NY: Merkin Concert Hall, 3/2/83.

*Raum, Elizabeth (Canada). *The Garden of Alice*: an opera. Regina, Saskatchewan: Globe Theatre, 1/19/85.

Reed, Marlyce. *Chromasia and Three Short Dialogues*. Green Bay, WI: University of Wisconsin, 5/10/84.

*†Reese, Mona Lyn. *Blessed Is She*. Choir of St. John's Linden Hills. Minneapolis, MN: St. John's Episcopal Church, 7/24/84. Commissioned by the women of St. John's Episcopal Church in honor of the tenth anniversary of the ordination of women.

Diner Romantique, for violin and piano. Jim Ricardo, violin; Celeste O'Brien, piano. St. Paul, MN: Macalester College, 1/23/85; Norfolk, VA: Virginia Wesleyan College, 1/30/85.

†*Nocturne: Black and White Line Drawing of Dreams*, for viola (1982). Minneapolis, MN: Augsburg College, 4/1/84. Commissioned by Larry Peterson.

†*Rhapsody on a Rainy Day*, for two harpsichords (1983). Layton James, Mary Nelson, harpsichords. Mankato, MN: West High Auditorium, 3/11/84. Commissioned by the performers.

The Trim Man, for string trio and mime. Michael Hennessy, mime, Ensemble Capriccio Trio. Minneapolis, MN: Walker Art Center, 4/28/85.

*†*Winter Melodies*, for string quartet (1983). Groveland String Quartet. Minneapolis, MN: The Bakken Library, 4/15/84. Commissioned by the Groveland String Quartet.

Reich, Amy. *Nursery Rhyme*, for multiple guitars. New York, NY: La Mama, 3/3/83.

Remer, Jan. *Union*, for flute and harp. Mary Stolpher, flute; Jan Remer, harp. New York, NY: Carnegie Recital Hall, 11/82.

Richinse, Cecile J. *Miniatures*, for violin, piano, and dance (1982). Dinos Constantinides, violin; Paula I. Collins, piano; Baton Rouge Ballet Theatre Dancers. Baton Rouge, LA: Louisiana State University, 2/24/83.

*Richter, Marga. *Darkening of the Light*, for solo 'cello. Suzanne Valerio, 'cello. Garden City, NY: Adelphi University, 12/8/82.

Lament for Art O'Leary. New York, NY: Alice Tully Hall, 4/23/84.

Requiem, for piano. Selma Epstein, piano. New York, NY: Merkin Concert Hall, 10/21/84.

Songs of Death and Madness. The Occasional Singers. New York, NY: St. Joseph's Church, 3/12/84.

*Rickard, Sylvia (Canada). *Char Hawai*. Norma McCurdy, soprano; Larry de la Haye, clarinet; Kathryn Ely, harp. Victoria, BC: 11/17/83.

*Roe, Betty (U.K.). *Song Cycle: Cat and Mouse*. Sarah Poole, soprano; David Heyes, double bass. London: Dancaster Museum, 10/13/82.

Rogers, Patsy. *A Woman Alive*: vocal drama. Shelagh Vincent, soprano; instrumental ensemble, Patsy Rogers, conductor. Estes Park, CO: Alpen Musikfest, 7/84.

Rubin, Anna. *Laughing the Crying and Golden*: electronic. Amsterdam: 4/84; Brussels: 5/84.

Reflections in a Sound Mirror: video collaboration. Amsterdam: 7/18-21/84.

*Rudow, Vivian Adelberg. *Americana Visited: Crossover Variations*, for viola and piano; *Devy's Song*, for viola and piano; *No Rest for Devy's Spirit*, for solo viola. Richard Field, viola; Jeffrey Chappell, piano. Baltimore, MD: Baltimore Museum of Art, 2/10/85.

**Journey of Waters*. Pamela Jordan, soprano; members of the Baltimore Symphony, Vivian Rudow, conductor. Baltimore, MD: Baltimore Museum of Art, 12/2/84.

*Rusche, Marjorie. *Dance of Death*: opera in two acts. Skylight Comic Opera. Milwaukee, WI: 2/2-3/85.

*St. John, Kathleen. *L'Etoile*. Bay Area Women's Philharmonic. Berkeley, CA: First Congregational Church, 5/17/85.

**Trio*, for piccolo, E-flat clarinet, and oboe. Barrett Cobb, piccolo; Joseph Stone, clarinet; Matthew Sullivan, oboe. New York, NY: Center for Inter-American Relations, 3/14/83.

†St.-Marcoux, Micheline Coulombe (1938-1985) (Canada) *Transit*: music-theatre piece. Montreal: Theatre de l'Eskabel, 10/3/84 (World Music Days). Commissioned by the Canadian Music Council for the 1984 World Music Days.

Samter, Alice (West Germany). *Aspekte*, for flute and piano. West Berlin: 8/3/84.

Duo Ritmico, for piano four-hands. Paris: Fourth International Congress on Women in Music, 10/84.

*Ureufführung von *"Zueignung,"* for flute, trombone, and piano. West Germany: 8/10/84.

Variaten, for piano. West Berlin: British Centre, 3/23/83.

*†Sandresky, Margaret. *A New Song*: solo cantata for soprano, flute, percussion, and piano. Winston-Salem, NC: Wake Forest University, 9/2/82. Commissioned by the Arts Council of Winston-Salem.

Scaletti, Carla. *Lysogeny*, for harp and tape. Alyssa Hess, harp. New York, NY: Columbia University, 10/25/83.

*Scherchen-Hsiao, Tona (France). *Radar*. Anthony de Mare, piano. New York, NY: Symphony Space, 11/5/83.

Schlonsky, Verdina (Israel). *Euphony*, for chamber orchestra. Israeli Chamber Orchestra, Uri Segal, conductor. Tel-Aviv; Jerusalem; Haifa: 11-12/82.

*Schonthal, Ruth. *Aranjuez*. Connecticut Chamber Orchestra, Sayard Stone, conductor. New York, NY: Town Hall, 1/9/83.

Semegen, Daria. *Electronic Study*. New Music Consort. New York, NY: Carnegie Recital Hall, 3/29/84.

*Sheppard, Suzanne. *Fleetings*, for solo flute. Jennifer Keeney, flute. Ann Arbor, MI: University of Michigan, 10/24/83.

**Suite* for solo marimba. Alison Shaw, marimba. Ann Arbor, MI: University of Michigan, 2/4/85.

Shields, Alice. *Coyote*: a scene for electronic tape from the opera *Shaman* (1978). Seattle, WA: 3/25/83.

*†Shore, Clare. *Nightwatch*. Dakota Wind Quintet. Sioux Falls, SD: Augustana College, 1/24/84. Commissioned by the Dakota Wind Quintet.

*†Shrude, Marilyn. *Psalms for David*. Toledo Symphony, Yuval Zaliouk, conductor. Toledo, OH: 3/18/83. Commissioned by the Toledo Symphony.

Sikora, Elzbieta (Poland). Selected works. New York, NY: Kosciuszko Foundation House, 9/26/84.

*Silsbee, Ann. *An Acre for a Bird.* New York Motet Choir, Stephen Sturk, conductor. New York, NY: Merkin Concert Hall, 6/21/83.

*. . . *And Who So Witnessed.* Boston Musica Viva. Cambridge, MA: Longy School of Music, 10/15/84. Commissioned by Boston Musica Viva.

**In and Out the Window*, for piano solo. David Burge, piano. Rochester, NY: Eastman School of Music, 3/13/84; New York, NY: Alice Tully Hall, 3/18/84.

**Journey*, for flute and percussion. Ithaca, NY: Cornell University, 3/17/84.

**The Juggler.* Barbara Nosca, mezzo-soprano; Relache ensemble. Chester Springs, PA: Yellow Springs Institute, 7/84.

**The Nightingale's Apprentice*: a story-opera. Troika Association of Ithaca. Ithaca, NY: 4/13-15/84.

*Silver, Sheila. *Ek Ong Kar.* Gregg Smith Singers. New York, NY: St. Peter's Church, 2/83.

†*String Quartet.* Atlantic Quartet. New York, NY: Carnegie Recital Hall, 11/10/83. Winner of League-ISCM National Composers Competition.

Silverman, Faye-Ellen. *Layered Lament*, for English horn and tape. Bourges, France: 6/9/83.

Oboe-sthenics. Tokyo: Tokyo Gakugei University, 6/27/84.

**Quantum Quintet*, for brass quintet. Mount Vernon Brass Players. Baltimore, MD: 4/17/83.

Speaking Together, for violin and piano. North-South Consonance Ensemble. New York, NY: St. Stephen's Church, 10/18/84.

Winds and Sines. Baltimore Symphony, Sergiu Comissiona, conductor. Baltimore, MD: 2/16-17/84. (Baltimore premiere).

*Simmonds, Rae N. *Bitter Sweet*: a jazz suite. Portland, ME: Westbrook College, 4/18/84.

*†Simons, Netty. *Cityscape #2.* Bowery Ensemble. Buffalo, NY: S.U.N.Y. at Buffalo, 4/11/84. Commissioned by Nils Vigeland, director, Bowery Ensemble.

Illuminations, for two pianos. Tokyo: 3/84.

**Silver Thaw.* University of Redlands New Music Ensemble. Redlands, CA: University of Redlands, 12/9/83.

*Singer, Jeanne. *Trio*, for oboe, viola, and piano. Garden City, NY: Ethical Humanist Society, 1/27/85.

*Smiley, Pril. *Forty-three*: electronic. Speculum Musicae. New York, NY: Columbia University, 2/23/84.

Smith, Julia. *Daisy*: opera in two acts. Rochester Opera Theatre and Philharmonic Orchestra, Sydney Hodkinson, conductor. Rochester, NY: Eastman Theatre, 11/27-28/82.

*Solomon, Elide M. *Piano Concerto.* Purchase Music Ensemble. Purchase, NY: 12/17/83.

Southam, Ann (Canada). *Rivers*, for piano (1982). Christina Petrowska, piano. Toronto: Premiere Dance Theatre, 9/24/84 (World Music Days).

Spektor, Mira J. *Four Songs on Poems by Ruth Whitman.* Bronxville, NY: Sarah Lawrence College, 1/3/84.

Lady of the Castle: one act chamber opera. West Berlin: Judishes Gemeindenhaus, 6/2/85; Acco, Israel: 10/85.

Spiegel, Laurie. *Appalachian Grove #1*, for electronic tape (1974). Bay Area

Women's Philharmonic concert. Berkeley, CA: University of California, 5/13/83.

Immersion, for electronic tape. Downtown Chamber Players. New York, NY: 12/3/84.

**A Stream*, for mandolin. Joanne Faletta, mandolin. New York, NY: St. Stephen's Church, 10/25/84.

*Steinbock, Evalyn. *The Proposal*: opera. New York, NY: St. Peter's Church, 5/10/83.

Sugai, Esther. *Calling*, for three didjeridu and tape (1982). Jon Lellelid, Sean Williams, Greg Powers, didjeridu. *Fantasy*, for soprano saxophone and tape (1978). David Gottlieb, soprano saxophone. Seattle, WA: 3/25/83.

**Five Poems by Andre Breton*, for singer, instruments, and tape (1983). Seattle, WA: Nippon Kan Theatre, 11/18/83.

**Three Movements*, for soprano saxophone and alto flute. Robert Antolin, soprano saxophone; Trudy Sussman, alto flute. Seattle, WA: Greenwood Gallery, 11/17/83.

*Swados, Elizabeth. *Jerusalem*, for 22 singers and five instrumentalists. New York, NY: La Mama, 5/84.

*Swisher, Gloria Wilson. *Joel Variations*. Joel Salsman, piano.

**Sonnets*. Susan Dolachi, mezzo-soprano; Joel Salsman, piano. Seattle, WA: Seattle Central Community College, 5/15/83.

Szonyi, Erzsebet (Hungary). *Toccatina*, for piano (1967). Selma Epstein, piano. Ann Arbor, MI: University of Michigan, 5/7/83 (Op. 2: Women in Music Conference).

Talma, Louise. The Music of Louise Talma: *Sonata for Violin and Piano* (1962); *Soundshots*: 20 short pieces for piano (1974); *Alleluia in Form of Toccata*, for piano (1945); *Lament* for 'cello and piano (1980); *Studies in Spacing*, for clarinet and piano (1982); *Variations on 13 Ways of Looking at a Blackbird*, for voice, oboe, and piano (1979); *Psalm 84*, for mixed voices a cappella (1978); *Let's Touch the Sky*, for mixed chorus, flute, oboe, and bassoon. New York, NY: Hunter College Playhouse, 5/31/83.

**The Ambient Air*. Da Capo Chamber Players. New York, NY: Symphony Space, 10/16/84.

**La Corona*. Gregg Smith Singers, Florilegium Chamber Choir. New York, NY: St. Peter's Church, 1/12/85.

Have You Heard? Do You Know? After Dinner Opera Co. New York, NY: Lincoln Center Library, 10/3/83.

Thirteen Ways of Looking at a Blackbird. Musicians Accord Ensemble. New York, NY: Good Shepherd-Faith Church, 10/16/83.

Terzian, Alicia (Argentina). *Shantiniketan*. London: St. John's Smith Square, 11/25/82. Grupo Encuentros de Musica Contemporanea de Buenos Aires, Alicia Terzian, director. Montreal: Université du Québec à Montréal, 9/3/84 (World Music Days).

*†Themmen, Ivana. *Cupid and Psyche*. Queens Symphony Orchestra, David Katz, conductor. Queens, NY: 1/22/83. Commissioned by the Queens Symphony Orchestra. NACUSA concert. New York, NY: Carnegie Recital Hall, 1/7/85.

*Thomas, Karen P. *Metamorphoses on a Machaut Kyrie*. Contemporary Group String Quartet. Seattle, WA: University of Washington, 5/25/83.

Thome, Diane. *Two Psalms*, for mixed chorus and instrumental ensemble (1980).

LSU Choir, Victor Klimash, conductor. Baton Rouge, LA: Louisiana State University, 2/27/83.

Winter Infinities; *Anais*; *January Variations*; *Silver Deer*. Paris: Ecole Nationale Claude Debussy, 3/83.

Thorington, Helen. *Music for Oil Pump, Violin and Three Others*: processed environmental and instrumental sounds. New York, NY: Experimental Intermedia Foundation, 5/19/83.

Tower, Joan. *Amazon*. Da Capo Chamber Players. New York, NY: Symphony Space, 10/16/84.

Amazon III, for chamber orchestra. Bay Area Women's Philharmonic. San Francisco, CA: 11/22/85.

Black Topaz. Music Today Ensemble, Gerard Schwarz, conductor. New York, NY: Merkin Concert Hall, 3/14/84.

Breakfast Rhythms. New Music Ensemble. New York, NY: Carnegie Recital Hall, 2/15/83.

Breakfast Rhythms I and II (1974-75). Chamber players of the League-ISCM. Toronto: Premiere Dance Theatre, 9/26/84 (World Music Days).

**Cello Concerto*. Andre Emelianoff, 'cello; Y Chamber Symphony, Gerard Schwarz, conductor. New York, NY: 92nd Street YMHA, 9/29/84.

†*Music for 'Cello and Orchestra*. Yehuda Hanani, 'cello; Aspen Festival Orchestra. Aspen, CO: Aspen Festival, 8/85. Commissioned by the Fromm Music Foundation.

Noon Dance. Da Capo Chamber Players. New York, NY: Carnegie Recital Hall, 4/28/83.

Petroushkates; *Wings*. Da Capo Chamber Players. New York, NY: Carnegie Recital Hall, 10/25/83.

Platinum Spirals. Maryvonne Le Dizes-Richard, violin. New York, NY: Carnegie Recital Hall, 3/26/85.

*†*Snow Drops*, for flute and guitar. Carol Wincenc, flute; Sharon Isbin, guitar. St. Paul, MN: Schubert Club of St. Paul, 4/18/83. Commissioned by the Schubert Club of St. Paul. Patricia Spencer, flute, John Lehmann-Haupt, guitar. New York, NY: Cami Hall, 11/25/84.

Wings, for solo clarinet (1981). Robert Yamins, clarinet. New York, NY: Merkin Concert Hall, 3/20/83.

*Ulehla, Ludmilla. *The China Closet*, for percussion. Manhattan Marimba Quartet. New York, NY: Manhattan School of Music, 12/10/84.

Urreta, Alicia (Mexico). *Esferas Noéticas*. Orquesta Sinfonica Nacional, Francisco Savin, conductor. Mexico City: Teatro de Belles Artes, 4/22/83.

*†Van Appledorn, Mary Jeanne. *A Celestial Clockwork*, for carillon. Dr. Judson Maynard, carillon. Corpus Christi, TX: 6/23/83. Commissioned by the American Guild of Carilloneurs. Oklahoma City, OK: 5/19/84.

Concerto for Trumpet and Band. Robert Birch, trumpet; Texas Tech University Band, James Sudduth, conductor. Lubbock, TX: Texas Tech University, 12/4/84.

Legend of Sankta Lucia. Rochester, NY: Eastman School of Music, 5/3/85.

Passacaglia and Chorale, for orchestra. Texas Tech University Symphony Orchestra. Lubbock, TX: Texas Tech University, 10/2/84.

Set of Five, for piano. Virginia Eskin, piano. New London, CT: Billings American Music Festival, 8/4/83.

Van de Vate, Nancy. *Adagio*, for orchestra. Jakarta Symphony Orchestra, Adidharma, conductor. Jakarta, Indonesia: 6/21/84 (Asian premiere).

Concertpiece, for 'cello and small orchestra. Duck Hee Lee, 'cello; LSU Philharmonia, James Yestadt, conductor. Baton Rouge, LA: Louisiana State University, 2/27/83.

**Contrasts*, for two pianos, six hands. Trisutji Kamal, Marusia Nainggolau, Nancy Van de Vate, pianists. Jakarta, Indonesia: 5/23/84.

**Dark Nebulae*. Women's Club Symphony of Columbus, Ohio, Cynthia Capper, conductor. Columbus, OH: Ohio State University, 6/29/83.

**Fantasy*, for harpsichord. Michelle Graveline, harpsichord. Ann Arbor, MI: 5/6/83.

**Gema Jawa*, for string orchestra. New Music Orchestra, John Webber, conductor. Washington, DC: 11/20/84. Jakarta Symphony String Ensemble, Adidharma, conductor. Jakarta, Indonesia: 1/13/85 (Asian premiere).

**Journeys*, for large orchestra; *Concertpiece*, for 'cello and small orchestra. Susan Spengler, 'cello (2d work); University of Oregon Symphony, Marsha Mabrey, conductor. Eugene, OR: 2/25/85 (West Coast Women Conductor/Composer Symposium).

A Night in the Royal Ontario Museum, for soprano and tape. Members of MW2 of Krakow. Katowice, Poland: 5/28/84 (European premiere).

Psalm 121 (SATB); *How Fares the Night?* (SSA); *Make a Joyful Noise to the Lord* (SSATB). Bi-National Choir of the Indonesian-American Friendship Association, Dr. Richard Haskin, conductor. Jakarta, Indonesia: 6/5/83.

**Sonata*, for harpsichord. Susan Erickson, harpsichord. Davis, CA: University of California, 11/12/83.

**Songs for the Four Parts of the Night*, for voice and piano. Lucille Field Goodman, soprano; Deon Nielson Price, piano. Paris: Centre Pompidou, 10.25.84 (Fourth International Congress on Women in Music).

Trio, for violin, 'cello, and piano. Tempe, AZ: Arizona State University, 3/28/85.

*†Vandervelde, Janika. *Ch'i*. Students playing 20 grand pianos, Phillip Brunelle, conductor. Minneapolis, MN: 6/84. Commissioned by the Minnesota Music Teacher's Association.

The Farthest Shore. Elgin Symphony, Robert Hansen, conductor. Elgin, IL: 11/83. Eugene Symphony, William McGlaughlin, conductor. Eugene, OR: 5/84.

**Genesis + II*. Richard Killmer, oboe; Thelma Hunter, piano.

*†*Henry's Fate (Genesis III)*. Vern Sutton, tenor; Joseph Longo, clarinet; Mina Fischer, 'cello; Thelma Hunter, piano; David John Olsen, percussion; Janika Vandervelde, conductor. St. Paul, MN: St. Anthony Park Music Series, 1/84. Commissioned by the Schubert Club of St. Paul in celebration of their 100th anniversary.

*†*Jack and the Beanstalk*. Members of the Minnesota Orchestra, Janika Vandervelde, conductor. Minneapolis, MN: Minnesota Orchestra "Kinder Konzerts," 9-12/84. Commissioned by the Women's Association of the Minnesota Orchestra.

Vasquez, Alida. *Dances of Life and Death*. North-South Consonance. New York, NY: Arcana Studio, 12/7/84 (NY premiere).

*Vehar, Persis. *Faith, Hope, Love,* for SSA, two horns, and string orchestra. Ithaca, NY: Ithaca College, 4/7/84.

Sounds of the Outdoors, for unaccompanied saxophone. Potsdam, NY: S.U.C. at Potsdam, 9/22/84.

**What the Lark Said*, for three-part voices, two flutes, and piano. Clarence, NY: Clarence High School, 5/23/84.

*Vercoe, Elizabeth. *Irreveries from Sappho*: choral version. Mt. Holyoke College Chorus; Allen Boude, piano; Catherine Melhorn, conductor. South Hadley, MA: Mt. Holyoke College, 2/20/83.

**Parodia Sopra "Lasciate Mi Morire."* Susan Allen, harp. Ann Arbor, MI: University of Michigan, 5/7/83 (Op. 2: Women in Music Festival).

Sonaria, for solo 'cello (1980); *Fantavia*, for flute and percussion (1982); *Persona*, for piano (1980); *Irreveries from Sappho* (1981). Paris: Cite Internationale des Artes, 3/13/84.

*Wagner, Melinda. *Circles, Stone and Passage*. Neva Pilgrim, soprano, Society for New Music, Calvin Custer, conductor. Syracuse, NY: 11/1/82.

*Walker, Gwyneth. *Fanfare, Interlude and Finale*. Twin Cities Symphony, Robert Vodnoy, conductor. St. Joseph, MI: 2/13/83.

Wallach, Joelle. *Glimpses*, for orchestra. Haddonfield Symphony Orchestra. Haddonfield, NJ: 12/10/82.

The Kiss of Anima Mundi, for percussion. Paul Price Percussion Ensemble. Bergen County, NJ: Bergen Community College, 10/14/84.

Of Honey and Vinegar; *Organal Voices*; *Plaint for a Prince and King*; *The Kiss of Anima Mundi*; *Mourning Madrigals*. New York, NY: Manhattan School of Music, 2/9/84.

**Orison of St. Theresa*, for chorus and string orchestra. Manhattan Vocal Ensemble, Nelly Vuksic, director, Hoboken Chamber Orchestra, Gary Schneider, conductor. Hoboken, NJ: 5/12/85.

*†*Turbulence, Stillness and Saltation*, for chamber orchestra. Little Orchestra of Princeton. Princeton, NJ: Princeton High School, 2/5/84. Winner of the Little Orchestra of Princeton Composition Competition.

*Wang, An-Ming. *The Christmas Gift*. Hwa Sheng Chorus, Sharon Pan, conductor. Silver Spring, MD: 12/12/84.

**East Wind*. Janese Sampson, flute; Carol Yampolsky, piano. Washington, DC: Corcoran Gallery, 5/22/83.

**Mary's Lullaby*. Welcome to Washington Women's Chorus, Ethel Bornstein, conductor. Washington, DC: British Embassy, 12/11/84.

Warren, Elinor Remick. *Singing Earth*, for soprano and orchestra. Claremont Symphony Orchestra. Claremont, CA: 5/84.

Suite for Orchestra. Maryland Women's Symphony. Baltimore, MD: 4/20/86.

*Watson, Gwendolyn. *Living Piece 1983*: improvisation in six movements. June Watanabe, dancer; Bay Area Women's Philharmonic, J. Karla Lemon, conductor. Berkeley, CA: University of California, 5/13/84.

*Weir, Judith (U.K.). *The Art of Touching the Keyboard*. William Howard, piano. London: Wigmore Hall, 5/13/83.

**Ascending Into Heaven*. Cathedral Choir, Stephen Darlington, conductor. London: St. Alban's Abbey, 7/5/83.

**The Consolations of Scholarship (A Night at the 14th Century Chinese Opera)*. Linda Hirst, soprano, Lontano Ensemble, Odaline de la Martinez, conductor. Durham: Trevelyan College, 5/5/85.

King Harald's Saga. Jane Manning, soprano. New York, NY: Symphony Space, 11/6/83 (N.Y. premiere).

†*Several Concertos*, for flute, 'cello, and piano. Lontano Ensemble. London: St. John's Smith Square, 2/29/84 (London premiere). Commissioned by Lontano with funds from the Arts Council of Great Britain.

**Wild, Mossy Mountains*. David Glyn-Jones, organ. Edinburgh: St. Stephen's Church, 9/10/82.

*Wiener, Eva. *Dream*, for amplified piano. Eva Wiener, piano. Medford, MA: Tufts University, 6/23/84.

Wilkins, Margaret Lucy (U.K.). *Struwwelpeter*, for soprano, three clarinets, percussion, and photographic slides. Great Britain: Huddersfield Contemporary Music Festival, 11/11/84.

*Wilson, Anne. *Magnificat and Nunc Dimittis*, for choir. Girls Choir of the Cathedral of the Incarnation. Garden City, NY: Cathedral of the Incarnation, 12/4/83.

*Wimhurst, Karen (U.K.). *Profit and Loss*. Singcircle; Gregory Ross, conductor; tape. Great Britain: Huddersfield Contemporary Music Festival, 11/28/82.

*Wylie, Ruth Shaw. *Mandala*, for piano. Boulder, CO: Boulder Public Library, 11/17/82.

Music for Three Sisters, for clarinet, flute, and piano (1981). Walter Barzenick, clarinet; Jean Rickman, flute; David Evenson, piano. Baton Rouge, LA: Louisiana State University, 2/24/83.

*†Zaimont, Judith Lang. *Dance/Inner Dance*, for flute, oboe, and 'cello. Huntington Trio. Philadelphia, PA: 7/7/85. Washington, DC: National Gallery, 4/13/86. Commissioned by the Huntington Trio.

Deep Down: a spiritual. David Arnold, baritone. Atlanta, GA: Spellman College, 1/22/84.

From the Great Land: Women's Songs. North Star Consort. New York, NY: Carnegie Recital Hall, 1/14/83 (N.Y. premiere). Morgantown, WV: University of West Virginia, 11/9/84.

**Goldilocks and the Three Bears*: chamber opera for young audiences. Chatauqua, NY: Connecticut Opera Express, 1/5/86. Commissioned by Connecticut Opera.

In the Theatre of Night: six dream songs on poems of Karl Shapiro, for high voice and piano. Conway, AR: University of Central Arkansas, 5/83.

In the Theatre of Night: excerpts. Elizabeth Kirkpatrick, soprano; Carol Yampolsky, piano. Vienna, VA: Wolf Trap Farm, 4/29/84. Pamela Jordan, soprano; Judith Zaimont, piano. New York, NY: 6/10/84.

*†*Lamentation*, for double chorus, piano, and percussion. Gregg Smith Singers. Saranac Lake, NY: 7/8/84. Dale Warland Singers. St. Paul, MN: 5/85. Gregg Smith Singers, Florilegium Chamber Choir. New York, NY: St. Peter's Church, 1/12/85. Commissioned by four professional choruses through the NEA Consortium Commissioning Program.

The Magic World, for baritone, piano, and percussion. James Harp, baritone; Barbra Dahlman, piano; Randy Isles, percussion. Washington, DC: Corcoran Gallery, 11/19/84.

**Music for Two*, for bass trombone and tuba. Baltimore, MD: Peabody Conservatory, 2/22/85.

**Nattens Monolog—Night Soliloquy* (1984). Arleen Augér, soprano, Dalton Baldwin, piano. New York, NY: Alice Tully Hall, 3/13/85. Commissioned by the performers. JoAnn Rice, soprano, Wesley McAfee, piano. New York, NY: 10/24/85.

Nocturne: La Fin de Siecle. (1978); Nancy Roldan, piano. *In the Theatre of Night: excerpts*; Pamela Jordan, soprano, Judith Zaimont, piano. *From the Great Land* (1982); Jean Crichton, mezzo-soprano; Loren Kitt, clarinet; Clinton Adams, piano. *Serenade: To Music* (1981); Florilegium Chamber Choir, JoAnn Rice, conductor. **Stone* (1981); Clinton Adams, piano. *Sunny Airs and Sober* (1975); Florilegium Chamber Choir, JoAnn Rice, conductor. Baltimore, MD: Peabody Conservatory, 11/7/84.

Psalm 23 (1979), for mezzo-soprano, flute, violin, 'cello and piano. Aviva Players. New York, NY: Marymount College, 11/4/85.

Sacred Service: three choral excerpts, for solo baritone, chorus and piano. Amor Artis Chorale, Johannes Somary, conductor. New York, NY: Symphony Space, 2/7/86.

**Serenade: To Music*; *Sunny Airs and Sober.* Florilegium Chamber Choir, JoAnn Rice, conductor. New York, NY: Merkin Concert Hall, 6/11/84.

**Sky Curtains*, for flute, clarinet, bassoon, viola, and 'cello (1984). Barbara Boutsikaris, flute; Raymond Wheeler, clarinet; Carolyn Beck, bassoon; Denise Cridge, viola; Ted Mook, 'cello. New York, NY: St. Stephen's Church, 11/11/84.

*†*Winter Music*: Chantey. University of Kansas Faculty Brass Quintet. Lawrence, KS: University of Kansas, 3/28/85. Commissioned by the University of Kansas Faculty Brass Quintet.

*Ziffrin, Marilyn. *Orchestra Piece.* National Gallery Symphony Orchestra. Washington, DC: 4/1/84.

*†Zwilich, Ellen Taaffe. *Celebration*, for orchestra. Indianapolis Symphony Orchestra. Indianapolis, IN: 10/12/84. Commissioned by the Indianapolis Symphony Orchestra.

Chamber Symphony (1979). Bay Area Women's Philharmonic, Jeannine Wagar, conductor. San Francisco, CA: Scottish Rites Hall, 5/12/84. Bronx Arts Ensemble. Bronx, NY: Wave Hall, 11/6/83.

*†*Double Quartet for Strings.* Emerson String Quartet, Ani Kavafian, James Buswell, violins; Walter Trampler, viola; Fred Sherry, 'cello. New York, NY: Alice Tully Hall, 10/21/84. Commissioned by the Chamber Music Society of Lincoln Center.

Intrada. Da Capo Chamber Players. New York, NY: Carnegie Recital Hall, 5/1/84 (NY premiere).

*†*Prologue and Variations*, for string orchestra. Chattanooga Symphony. Chattanooga, TN: 4/9/84. Commissioned by the Chattanooga Symphony. Caramoor Festival Orchestra, John Nelson, director. Caramoor, NY: 6/30/84.

†*Symphony No. 1.* Indianapolis Symphony Orchestra, John Nelson, conductor. Indianapolis, IN: Indiana State University, 9/84. Pittsburgh Symphony, Andre Previn, conductor. Pittsburgh, PA: 10/19-24/84. University of Oregon Symphony, Frances Steiner, conductor. Eugene, OR: University of Oregon, 2/25/85 (West Coast Women Conductor/Composer Symposium). Winner, 1983 Pulitzer Prize in Music.

Festivals

1985–86

American Women Conductor/Composer Symposium. Sponsored by the University of Oregon School of Music and the Center for the Study of Women in Society. Eugene, OR: University of Oregon, 2/21-23/86.

Atlanta Congress: International Congress on Women in Music. Ruth McDonald, coordinator. Atlanta, GA: Georgia State University, 3/20-23/86.

1986 Bay Area Conference on Women in Music. Sponsored by San Francisco State University Music Department. San Francisco, CA: San Francisco State University, 2/8/86.

International Women's Music Festival. Sponsored by Beer-Sheva municipality, Ben Gurion University of the Negev, and the Israeli Government. Dedicated to 'cellist Jacqueline de Pré. Beer-Sheva, Israel: 6/23-28/86.

National Women's Music Festival. Bloomington, IN: University of Indiana, 6/6-8/86.

Women's Music Festival '85. Sponsored by the Massachusetts chapter of American Women Composers and Boston University School for the Arts. Marjorie Merryman, Elizabeth Vercoe, coordinators. Boston, MA: Boston University School for the Arts, 10/3-6/85.

Works by Women Composers: a festival of music from around the world. Sponsored by the Southern California Chapter of the International Congress on Women in Music. Beverly Grigsby, coordinator. Northridge, CA: California State University, 1/24-26/86.

1984–85

Conference on Women in Music: a regional conference of the International Congress on Women in Music. Dr. Carolynn Lindeman, coordinator. San Francisco, CA: San Francisco State University, 3/16/85.

Op. 3 Women in Music. Lawrence, KS: University of Kansas, 3/28-31/85.

Second National Conference on Women and the Arts. Madison, WI: University of Wisconsin, 6/3-6/85.

Southern California Conference on Women in Music. Northridge, CA: California State University, 3/7-9/85.

Symposium on Women in Music. Sponsored by the Milwaukee Alumnae Chapter of Sigma Alpha Iota. Milwaukee, WI: Mount Mary College, 10/13/84.

West Coast Women Conductor/Composer Symposium. Sponsored by the University of Oregon School of Music and the Center for the Study of Women in Society. Marsha Mabrey, director. Eugene, OR: University of Oregon, 2/23-25/85.

Women Composers Project. Cedar Falls, IA: University of Northern Iowa, 3/1-3/85.

1983–84

Alpen Musikfest 1984: 1st annual festival for women musicians. Jane Frasier, coordinator. Estes Park, CO: 7/22-28/84.

Conference on Women in Music. Cosponsored by the Massachusetts Chapter of American Women Composers and Tufts University. Ruth Lomon and Vivian Taylor, directors. Boston, MA: Tufts University, 6/22-24/84.

Festival of Women in American Folk Music. Woodstock, VT: 8/6-13/83.

Fourth International Congress on Women in Music. Paris: 10/25-28/84.

See Volume 1 for listings of annual events.

Prizes and Awards

Allen, Judith Shatin. 1985 NEA Music Fellowship.

Archer, Violet (Canada). Received Canadian Music Council "Composer of the Year" Award, 1984.

Appointed to the Order of Canada, 1984.

Bay Area Women's Philharmonic, Nan Washburn, artistic director. Received ASCAP Orchestral Award for programming of contemporary music, 1982-83, 1984-85.

Biedrzycki, Sherry. One of the winners of the Fourth International Aaron Copland Competition for Young Composers Ages 5-12, 1984.

Bolz, Harriett. *Sonata for Piano Quartet* received first prize at the National League of American Pen Women Congress, April 1983.

Bouchard, Linda. Received first prize in the chamber/solo composition category of the Sixth Annual Young Composers Competition sponsored by the Performing Rights Organization of Canada, Ltd., 1984.

Icy Cruise, for piccolo, trumpet, harp, viola, 'cello, and double bass received Honorable Mention in the ILWC Sixth Annual Search for New Music, 1984.

Triskelion: a concert-drama received prize from the Performing Rights Organization of Canada, Ltd, 1983.

Brush, Ruth. *Our Heritage, Oklahoma* received first prize in the Oklahoma Heritage Song Contest.

Cant, Stephanie (U.K.). Recieved Arts Council bursary for advanced training.

Chambers, Wendy. 1985 NEA Music Fellowship.

Chance, Nancy Laird. *Odysseus*: song cycle for solo voice, percussion, and orchestra received first prize in the 1984 ASCAP Rudolph Nissim Competition.

NEA Composer Fellowship, 1983.

Chen, Justine. One of the winners of the Fourth International Aaron Copland Competition for Young Composers Ages 5-12, 1984.

Chen, Wendy F. 1984 BMI Award to Student Composers.

Christensen, Suann. 1984 ASCAP Foundation Grant to Young Composers.

Clayton, Laura. 1985 NEA Music Fellowship.

1984-85 John Simon Guggenheim Memorial Fellowship in Music.

Clement, Sheree. Received Goddard Lieberson Fellowship from the American Academy and Institute of Arts and Letters, 1985.

1983 John Simon Guggenheim Memorial Fellowship in Music.

Conant, Deborah. Received Massachusetts Artist Fellowship from the Artists Foundation of Boston, 1984.

Condoret, Brigitte. *Substance of Grace*: electronic, received Honorable Mention in the ILWC 7th Annual Search for New Music, 1985.

Davidson, Tina. *Unicorn Tapestry*, for soprano, 'cello, and tape received first prize in the 1983-84 NACUSA Young Composers Competition.

Dinescu, Violeta (Rumania). *Bewitch Me into a Silver Bird*, for orchestra received Honorable Mention in the ILWC Sixth Annual Search for New Music, 1984.

Received first prize in the Salt Lake City, Utah, Composers Guild Competition, 1983.

Ekizian, Michelle. 1984 ASCAP Foundation Grant to Young Composers.

Fontyn, Jacqueline (Belgium). *Alba: 3 Poesie di Vincenzo Cardelli* was selected for the ISCM 1983 World Music Days.

Fox, Erika (U.K.). Finzi Award, 1983.

Gideon, Miriam. Received Doctor of Humane Letters, Honoris Causa from Brooklyn College.

Gunn, Nancy. 1984 ASCAP Foundation Grant to Young Composers.

Hershey, Sharon L. 1984 ASCAP Foundation Grant to Young Composers.

1983 BMI Award to Student Composers.

Hovda, Eleanor. 1984 McKnight Fellowship.

Hsu, Wen-Ying. *'Cello Concerto* received first prize at the National League of American Pen Women Congress, April 1984.

Praise the Lord, for mixed chorus received Honorable Mention.

Janik, Ada Marie. 1983 Creative Artists Program Service (CAPS) grant for music composition.

Kabat, Julie. 1983 Creative Artists Program Service (CAPS) grant for music composition.

Karpman, Laura. Received 1984 Charles Ives Award from the American Academy and Institute of Arts and Letters.

Kessler, Minuetta. Received Citation for Distinguished Service at the National League of American Pen Women Congress 1984.

Sonata for Clarinet and Piano received award in the Second Annual Chamber Music Composition Competition, 1984.

Kolb, Barbara. 1985 NEA Music Fellowship.

Kuzmych, Christina. *Microtrio*, for violin, viola and 'cello received Honorable Mention in the ILWC 7th Annual Search for New Music, 1985.

Shapes and Sounds IV, for soprano and saxophone received first prize in the ILWC Sixth Annual Search for New Music, 1984.

Larsen, Libby. Meet-the-Composer residency with the Minnesota Orchestra, 1983-85.

LeBaron, Anne. One of the recipients of the Presser Foundation 100th Anniversary Grants for the Publication of American Concert Music to finance publication of a work, 1984-85.

1983 Creative Artists Program Service (CAPS) grant for music composition.

LeFanu, Nicola (U.K.). 1982-83 Arts Council Composers Award.

Lovell, Brenda. One of the winners in the 1984 Utah Composers Guild Composition Contest.

Mamlok, Ursula. *When Summer Sang* was selected to represent the United States at the 1983 International Rostrum of Composers.

Marcus, Adabelle Gross. 1984 Award of Merit from the Parade of American Music, sponsored by the National Federation of Music Clubs.

Merryman, Marjorie. One of the winners of the 1984 New England Composers Competition sponsored by the Boston section of the League-ISCM.

Meyer, Ruth. *Sandsong*, for double bass, violin, viola and 'cello received first prize in the ILWC 7th Annual Search for New Music, 1985.

1984 BMI Award to Student Composers.

Monk, Meredith. *Turtle Dreams* received Villager Outstanding Composer Award, 1983.

Oliveros, Pauline. 1985 NEA Music Fellowship.

Ondishko, Denise M. *Without and Within* received first prize in the World as Mirror Competition, 1983-84.

Pizer, Elizabeth. Received first prize in the choral music category and third prize in the vocal music category of the National League of American Pen Women Biennial Composition Contest, 1984.

NACUSA Certificate of Merit for "outstanding service to the organization," 1983.

Preobrajenska, Vera N. *Third Symphony* received Honorable Mention in the orchestral division category of the National League of American Pen Women Biennial Composition Contest, 1984.

Received Certificate of Merit for distinguished service in music at Nor-Cal's Awards Day, Chico, CA, 1983.

St. John, Kathleen. *Sakura No Hana* received 1985 ASCAP Rudolf Nissim Award.

Shrude, Marilyn. *Psalms of David* received third prize in the 1984 John F. Kennedy Center Friedheim Awards Competition.

Sikora, Elzbieta (Poland). 1984 Kosciuszko Foundation Scholar.

Silas, Renee. *Four Pictures for Woodwind Trio* received second prize in the ILWC 7th Annual Search for New Music, 1985.

Singer, Jeanne. Awarded Honorary Doctorate in Music from World University.

Smiley, Pril. *Forty-three* was selected for the 1985 ISCM World Music Days in the Electroacoustic Works category.

Stone, Dorothea Ferrari. *Wizard Ball*, for flute with ghost electronics received second prize in the ILWC Sixth Annual Search for New Music, 1984.

Sugai, Esther. 1983 ASCAP Foundation Grant to Young Composers.

Tower, Joan. Meet-the-Composer residency with the St. Louis Symphony, 1985.

American Academy and Institute of Arts and Letters Award 1983.

Van Appledorn, Mary Jeanne. Received Outstanding Service to Music Award Medallion from Tau Beta Sigma, national band service sorority, 1984-85.

Van de Vate, Nancy. One of the winners of the 1984 Utah Composers Guild Composition Contest.

Second Sonata for Piano received first prize, piano music category; *Death is the Chilly Night* received first prize, vocal music category; *Dark Nebulae* received third prize, orchestral music category, National League of American Pen Women Biennial Composition Contest, 1984.

The Pond, for SATB a cappella received first prize in the 1983 Composers Guild Competition.

Vandervelde, Janika. 1984 McKnight Fellowship.

Vercoe, Elizabeth. Received Artists Foundation Project Completion Award, 1983.

Wagner, Melinda J. 1984 ASCAP Foundation Grant to Young Composers.

Wallach, Joelle. 1984-85 New Jersey State Council on the Arts Fellowship.
Received Honorable Mention in the Ninth Annual New Music for Young Ensembles Composer Competition, 1984.
Five American Echoes received first prize in the Baroque Choral Guild Annual Competition, 1984.
Forewords, for trumpet and French horn received first prize in the Delta-Omicron Composition Competition 1983.

White, Elizabeth. Received Special Mention in the Third International Aaron Copland Competition for Young Composers Ages 5-12, 1983.

Zaimont, Judith Lang. Received major award in the Georgia State University Bicentennial Composition Competition, 1984.
In the Theatre of Night received Presser Foundation 100th Anniversary Grant for the Publication of American Concert Music to finance publication by Galaxy Music.
1983-84 John Simon Guggenheim Memorial Fellowship in Music.

Zwilich, Ellen Taaffe. 1984 Academy-Institute Award form the American Academy and Institute of Arts and Letters.

Commissions

(See also PERFORMANCES for commissions relating to a specific performance.)

Anderson, Beth. Commissioned by Montclair State College Improvisational Dance Ensemble for a solo piano work, 1984.

Commissioned by the University of Redlands New Music Ensemble, 1984.

Blaustein, Susan. Commissioned by the Jubal Trio through the Nonesuch Commission Awards, 1984.

Bouchard, Linda. Commissioned by Sage City Symphony for a trumpet concerto, to be performed in 1986.

Childs, Mary Ellen. Recipient of Minnesota Composers Forum Commissioning Program Award, 1983.

Coates, Gloria. Commissioned by Musica Viva of Munich for a chamber orchestra work, 1985.

French, Tania. Commissioned by Smith College Glee Club for a setting of *Psalm 100* for women's chorus and organ with optional trumpet and timpani, 1985.

Gideon, Miriam. Commissioned by the 92nd Street YMHA Chorale for a work for chorus and chamber orchestra, 1984.

Commissioned by Sigma Alpha Iota for a chamber work, 1984.

Gilbert, Janet. Recipient of Minnesota Composers Forum Commissioning Program Award, 1983.

Goolkasian-Rahbee, Dianne. Commissioned by Dubrovka Moshfegh for *Discourse* for viola and piano, 1984.

Hurley, Susan. Commissioned by the Sage City Symphony for an orchestral work to be premiered in 1985.

La Barbara, Joan. *Time(d) Trials and Unscheduled Events*, for the medium of radio, was commissioned for the Olympic Arts Festival, 1984.

Larsen, Libby. *Holy Ghosts*: opera was commissioned by the Memphis Opera Co. under the NEA New American Works and Producers Grants Program; projected for premiere during the 1985-86 season.

Symphony No. 1 was commissioned by the Minnesota Orchestra as part of the Meet-the-Composer/Orchestra Residencies Program, 1985. The work will also be recorded by Nonesuch Record Co.

Lauber, Anne (Canada). Commissioned by the Orchestre Suisse Romande for a work for string quartet and orchestra, 1983-84.

LeBaron, Anne. Commissioned by Ensemble Köln for a work for woodwind quintet and trombone, 1984.

Mageau, Mary (Australia). Commissioned by the Queensland Department of Education for four experimental piano pieces to be included in the textbook *In Tune With Music*, Vol. II (McGraw Hill, 1985).

Mamlok, Ursula. Commissioned by the Jubal Trio, 1984.

Oliveros, Pauline. *Shopper's Opera* was composed with support from the NEA for Haleakala/The Kitchen, 1985.

Parker, Alice. *Alleluia* was commissioned by Mari Taniguchi of Appleton, WI, 1984.

Ran, Shulamit. Commissioned by the Mendelssohn String Quartet through Chamber Music America's Commissioning Program, 1983.

Rosewoman, Michele. Commissioned in the Jazz Category of the ASCAP/Meet-the-Composer Commissioning Project for a work written in honor of Aaron Copland, to be premiered by the Brooklyn Philharmonic, 1985.

Rusche, Marjorie. Recipient of Minnesota Composers Forum Commissioning Program Award, 1983.

Tower, Joan. Recipient of Serge Koussevitzsky Music Foundation Commission Grant, 1982.

Van de Vate, Nancy. Commissioned by the University of Redlands New Music Ensemble for a work for trumpet and organ, 1983-84.

Commissioned by MW2 of Krakow for a work for piano, soprano, flute, and 'cello, 1983.

Witkin, Beatrice. Recipient of first Evelyn and William B. Mehlman Commissioning Award from the Hebrew Arts School.

Zaimont, Judith Lang. Commissioned by Florilegium Chamber Choir for a cantata, to be premiered June 1986.

Commissioned by the Huntington Trio for a new work, 1987. *Tarantelle for Orchestra* was commissioned by the Hopkins Symphony Orchestra through a grant from the Maryland State Arts Council.

Zwilich, Ellen Taaffe. Commissioned jointly by Carnegie Hall, the Detroit Symphony Orchestra, and the American Symphony Orchestra League for a piano concerto. The concerto will be performed by the winner of the International American Music Competition as soloist with the Detroit Symphony, Gunther Herbig, conductor, at the 1986 ASOL Conference in Detroit, MI.

Fantasy, for harpsichord commissioned by Concert Artists Guild, 1984.

Commissioned by the Da Capo Chamber Players through Chamber Music America's Commissioning Program, 1983.

Publications

COLLECTIONS AND SERIES

American Artsong Anthology, Vol. I: Contemporary American Songs for high voice and piano, edited by John Belisle. Includes songs by Miriam Gideon, Jean Eichelberger Ivey and Judith Lang Zaimont. Galaxy Music Corp., 1982.

ClarNan Editions: Music by historical women composers. Publication of works by Isabella Leonarda and Camilla de Rossi. ClarNan Editions, 1985 (Address: 235 Baxter Lane Fayetteville, AR 72701).

Da Capo Press Women Composer Series. Complete Contents:

- Beach, Amy Cheney. (1867-1944). *Quintet for Piano and Strings* in F-sharp minor, op. 67.
- Chaminade, Cecile. (1857-1944). *Three Piano Works.*
- Farrenc, Louise. (1804-1875). *Trio in E Minor,* for piano, flute, and 'cello, op. 45.
- Schumann, Clara. (1819-1896). *Selected Piano Music.*
- Clarke, Rebecca. (1886-1979). *Trio* for piano, violin, and 'cello.
- Hensel, Fanny Mendelssohn. (1805-1847). *Trio* for piano, violin, and 'cello in D minor, op. 11.
- Reichardt, Louise. (1779-1826). *Songs.*
- Smyth, Dame Ethel. (1858-1944). *Mass in D.*
- Backer-Grondahl, Agatha. (1847-1907). *Piano Music.*
- Beach, Amy Cheney. (1867-1944). *Piano Music.*
- Lang, Josephine. (1815-1880). *Songs.*
- Moore, Mary Carr. (1873-1957). *David Rizzio.*
- Holmes, Augusta. (1847-1903). *Selected Songs.*
- Malibran, Maria. (1808-1836). *Album Lyrique and Dernieres Pensees.*
- Carreno, Teresa. (1853-1917). *Piano Music.*
- Boulanger, Nadia (1887-1979). *Songs.*
- Chaminade, Cecile (1857-1944). *Album of Songs,* Vol. I.
- Bauer, Marion (1897-1955). *Sonata* for viola (or clarinet) and piano.
- Beach, Amy Cheney (1867-1944). *Violin Sonata,* op. 34.
- Clarke, Rebecca (1886-1979). *Sonata,* for viola or violoncello.

Female Composers: 22 Piano Pieces. Edited by Eva Rieger and Kaete Walter. Includes works by Fanny Mendelssohn Hensel, Cecile Chaminade, Lili Boulanger, Elisabeth Lutyens, and others. Schott, 1985.

Great Women of Rock: Songs written and recorded by women. Warner Bros., 1984.

Historical Anthology of Music by Women. Edited by James R. Briscoe. Includes works by 45 women composers. Indiana University Press, 1986.

Women Composers of Ragtime. Compiled by Carolynn A. Lindeman. Rags by Adaline Shepherd, Julia Lee Niebergall, Irene M. Giblin, and May F. Aufderheide. Theodore Presser Co., 1985.

INDIVIDUAL COMPOSERS

Allen, Judith Shatin. *Gazebo Music*, for flute and piano. Arsis Press, 1983.

Widdershins, for piano. Arsis Press, 1984.

Alotin, Yardena. *Piano Trio*. G. Schirmer, 1983.

Anderson, Beth. *Preparation for the Dominant*, for treble instrument in C; *The Preying Mantis and The Bluebird*, for flute or violin and piano or harp; *The Eighth Ancestor*, for flute or violin, clarinet or oboe, piano and 'cello; *Lullaby of the Eighth Ancestor*, for flute or violin and piano; *Skaters' Suite*, for flute or violin, clarinet or oboe, piano and 'cello; Songs: *Time Stands Still*; *Beauty Runs Faster*; *Womanrite*; *Twinkle Tonight*. Joshua Music Corp.

Armer, Elinor. *Lockerbones/Airbones*, for mezzo-soprano, flute, violin, piano, and percussion. Fallen Leaf Press, 1985.

†Barkin, Elaine. *Plein Chant*, for flute. In: *Six Compositions for Flute Solo.* Mobart. The collection received the National Flute Association's Award for newly published flute music.

Bastet, Patrice. *Deux Pieces Pour Guitare*. Lemoine, 1983.

Bastien, Jane Smisor. *First Pops for Piano*. Kjos, 1984.

Three Miniatures, for piano. Kjos, 1984.

Bate, Jennifer. *Introduction and Variations on an Old French Carol*. Novello, 1983.

Beach, Amy Cheney (1867-1944). *Around the Manger*, for SATB unaccompanied. Salisbury Press, 1985.

Beard, Katherine K. *Look What's Growing in My Garden*: 29 pieces for beginning pianists. Boston Music Co., 1982.

Tomorrow Will Be Better, for piano. Theodore Presser.

†Bishop, Dorothy. *Toward the Horizon*, for piano. Carl Fischer, 1983. Commissioned by *Clavier Magazine*.

Bocquillon, Patrice. *Territoires*, pour three ensembles de flûtes ne jouant qu'avec l'embrouchure. Salabert, 1983.

Bolz, Harriett. *Sonic Essay and Fugue*, for organ. Arsis Press, 1984.

Bond, Victoria. *Margaret,* for alto voice, flute, violin, 'cello, and piano. Seesaw Music Corp., 1984.

Quintet for Woodwinds. Seesaw Music Corp., 1984.

Brenet, Therese. *Suite Fantastique*, pour harpe celtique (1983). Billaudot, 1983.

Brockman, Jane. *Tell-tale Fantasy*, for piano. Arsis Press, 1982.

Brush, Ruth. *Romance Sans Paroles*, for violin and piano; *Sing a New Song to the Lord*; *Song Cycle*, part I; *Songs of Oklahoma*. Bartlesville Publishing Co.

Burnam, Edna Mae. *My Pet Goat*: four piano solos. Willis Music Co.

Clayton, Laura. *Cree Songs to the Newborn*, for soprano and chamber ensemble (1978). Peters, 1983.

Coates, Gloria. *The Beautitudes*. G. Schirmer.

May the Morning Star Rise, for organ. Sonotone.

Tones in Overtones, for piano. Sonotone.

Cooper, Rose Marie. *The Search for God,* for SAB Chorus. Carl Fischer.
Crawford-Seeger, Ruth (1901-1953). *Sonata for Violin and Piano.* Merion, 1984.
Davis, Sharon. *Ballade,* for soprano, saxophone and piano. Western International Music, 1984.
Though Men Call Us Free, for soprano, clarinet, and piano. Western International Music, 198-.
Three Poems of William Blake, for soprano and low clarinet. Western International Music, 198-.
Desportes, Yvonne. *Ceux de Village*: ten quatuors pour clarinette si bémol. Billaudot, 1981.
Hommage à Maurice Emmanuel. Billaudot, 1984.
Imageries d'Antan, pour quintette de cuivres. Billaudot, 1982.
Six Danses Pour Syrinx, pour flûte et guitare. Billaudot, 1982.
Diemer, Emma Lou. *Clap Your Hands,* for SATB chorus and piano or organ. Carl Fischer, 1984.
Encore, for piano. Sisra Press, 1984.
Homage to Cowell, Cage, Crumb and Czerny, for two pianos. Plymouth, 1983.
Summer of '82, for 'cello and piano. Seesaw Music Corp., 1984.
Donahue, Bertha Terry. *The Castle Yonder*: a cycle of songs for soprano with piano accompaniment. Arsis Press, 1982.
Dondeyne, Désiré. *Tubissimo,* pour tuba basse ou saxhorn basse sib et piano. Billaudot, 1983.
Dring, Madeleine (1923-1977). *Three Pieces,* for flute and piano. Cambria, 1983.
Elkoshi, Rivka. *Frames*: six aleatoric pieces for piano. Israel Music Publications, 198-.
Intervals and Intrigues: opera for children's voices, improvised percussion and piano four hands. Israel Music Publications, 198-.
Six Postcard Pictures, for flute and piano. Israel Music Publications, 198-.
Even-Or, Mary. *Esspresioni Musicali,* for children's choir. Israel Music Publications.
Music for Strings. Israel Music Publications.
Fine, Vivian. *The Flicker,* for solo flute and piano right hand; *Four Pieces for Two Flutes*; *Quartet for Brass*; *Romantic Ode,* for string orchestra; *Trio,* for violin, 'cello and piano. Margun Music.
Finzi, Graciane. *Interference,* pour violon et piano ou 2ᵉ violon. Billaudot, 1983.
Rhymes et Sons, for harp. Transatlantiques, 1985.
Fontyn, Jacqueline. *Analecta,* pour 2 violons. Salabert, 1982.
Danceries, for violin and piano. G. Schirmer, 1983.
Mime I, pour flute et harpe. Salabert, 1982.
Mime III, pour saxophone et piano. Salabert, 1984.
Funk, Susan. *Psalm 22,* for mixed chorus with solo baritone. Arsis Press, 1983.
Gaigerova, Varvara Adrionovna (1903-1944). *Vocal Works.* Sovetsky Kompozitor Publishers.
Garwood, Margaret. *A Joyous Lament for a Gilly Flower,* for clarinet and piano. Southern Music Co., 1983.
Gideon, Miriam. *The Resounding Lyre.* C. F. Peters.
Sacred Service for Saturday Morning. Transcontinental.
Glanville-Hicks, Peggy. *Etruscan Concerto,* for piano and chamber orchestra (1954). C. F. Peters, 1985.
Goldston, Margaret. *Adventures of an African Boy,* for elementary piano. Galaxy Music Corp.

The Magic Typewriter, for elementary piano. Galaxy Music Corp.
Windows: intermediate piano pictures. Galaxy Music Corp., 1984.
Gomez, Alice. *Etude in D minor*, for solo marimba. Southern Music Co.
Gotkovsky, Ida. *Baladine*, pour tuba ut et piano. Martin, 1983.
Eolienne, pour saxophone et harpe. Billaudot, 1983.
Invocation Lyrique, pour alto et piano. Billaudot, 1983.
Lied, pour trombone-basse et piano. Martin, 1983.
Romance, pour trombone et piano. Martin, 1983.
Greibling, Mary Ann. *Hornswoggles*, for two horns. Hornist's Nest, 1984.
Hannikainen, Ann-Else. *Pensamientos 1974*, for piano. Fazer, 1982.
Toccata-Fantasia, for piano. Fazer, 1982.
Harcourt, Marguerite Beclard d' (1884-1964). *Chants Peruviens*, for flute and harp or piano. Billaudot.
Hays, Doris. *Southern Voices,* for tape.
Southern Voices, for tape. C. F. Peters, 1982.
Heinkel, Valerie. *Chregalis*, for saxophone quartet. Dorn Publications, 1984.
Hensel, Fanny Mendelssohn (1805-1847). *Trio*, for violin, 'cello, and piano, op. 11. Wollenweber, 1984.
Hester, Gwen. *The Albatross*, for flute and piano. Shawnee Press, 1985.
Holst, Imogen (1907-1984). *String Quintet* (1982). Faber Music, 1984.
Hoover, Katherine. *Suite*, for two flutes. Boelke-Bomart, 1984.
Hyson, Winnifred. *Songs of Job's Daughter*, for soprano with piano accompaniment. Sisra Press, 1983.
Inwood, Mary. *Suite*, for clarinet and bassoon. Seesaw Music Corp., 1985.
Jankowski, Loretta. *Paterson Songs*. ABI Alexander Broude.
Reverie (1982). Continuo Music Press.
Die Sehnsuchten (1982). Continuo Music Press.
Sonata, for B-flat trumpet and piano (1982). Dorn Publications.
Jolas, Betsy. *Caprice a Deux Voix*, pour mezzo-soprano et haute-contre ou contralto. Heugel, 1982.
Episode Troisieme, pour trompette en ut seule. Heugel, 1982.
Stances, pour piano et orchestre. Heugel, 1981.
Jordan, Alice. *Exhortation*, for SATB and organ. McAfee-Belwin Mills.
How Softly Love Was Born, for SATB and organ. McAfee-Belwin Mills.
Name of Wondrous Love, for SATB and organ. H. W. Gray Co.
A Season and a Time, for SATB and organ. McAfee-Belwin Mills.
Take Joy Home, for solo voice and piano. Lorenz Corp.
Kadima, Hagar. *Trio for Flute, 'Cello and Piano*. Israel Music Publications.
Keech, Diana. *Scherzo Rondoso*, for oboe and piano. Cramer, 1982.
Kessler, Minuetta. *Come to the Circus*: easy piano pieces, book 3. Boston Music Co., 1984.
Nocturne in Blue, op. 50, no. 2. Willis Music Co.
Kolb, Barbara. *Chromatic Fantasy*, for narrator and six instruments. Boosey & Hawkes, 1983.
Grisaille, for orchestra. Boosey & Hawkes, 1984.
Larsen, Libby . . . . *And Sparrows Everywhere*: three songs for unaccompanied mixed voices. E. C. Schirmer, 1985.
Double Joy, for six-part chorus, handbells, and organ. E. C. Schirmer, 1982.
Larson, Anna. *The Listeners*, for medium low voice and piano. Arsis Press, 1984.

Last, Joan. *Down to the Sea*: five pieces for piano. Oxford University Press.

On the Move, for piano. Boosey & Hawkes.

Petites Images, for piano. Boosey & Hawkes.

†*Rondo Giocoso*, for piano. Bosworth & Co., Lts., 1985. Commissioned by *Clavier Magazine*.

Three Seascapes, for piano. Oxford University Press.

Time for Leisure: six holiday sketches, for piano. Novello.

Lauber, Anne. *Mouvement*, for flute and piano. Doberman, 1983.

Lejet, Edith. *Metamorphoses*, pour harpe. Transatlantiques, 1982.

Lesiege, Annette. *Star Gazers and Other Pilgrims*, for orchestra. Seesaw Music Corp., 1985.

Lomon, Ruth. *Seven Portals of Vision*, for organ. Arsis Press, 1984.

Loos, Anita. *Sonata no. 2*, for violin and piano. Association for the Promotion of New Music, 1984.

Lovell, Katherine. *Three Summer Sketches*, for 'cello or bassoon and piano. Braydeston Press, 1984.

McGinty, Anne. *Music for a Celebration*, for band. Boosey & Hawkes, 1984.

McLean, Priscilla. *Elan! A Dance to all Rising Things From the Earth*, for flute, violin, 'cello, piano, and percussion; *Fantasies for Adults and Other Children*, for soprano and amplified piano (1981); *The Inner Universe*, for piano, tape, and electron-microscope slides; *A Magic Dwells*, for orchestra and tape. MLC, 1984.

McTee, Cindy. *Psalm 100*. Concordia Publishing House.

Mageau, Mary. *Pacific Ports*, for piano four hands. AMUSE Publications, 1983.

Ragtime I: Elite Syncopations. In: *Contemporary Australian Piano Music*. LaTrobe University Press, 1984.

Mahler, Alma (1879-1964). *Collected Songs*, for medium voice and piano. Universal Edition.

Mamlok, Ursula. *Sextet*, for flute (piccolo), B-flat clarinet (E-flat clarinet), bass clarinet, violin, contrabass, and piano (1977). C. F. Peters, 1983.

When Summer Sang. C. F. Peters.

Marez-Oyens, Tera de. *Het Lied Van de Duizend Angsten* (1984), for choir and orchestra. Donemus.

Möbius by Ear, for viola and piano (1983). Donemus.

Octopus, for bass clarinet and percussion (1982). Donemus.

Masson, Carol Foster. *Carolina Suite*, for flute and piano. Southern Music Co., 1985.

Mekeel, Joyce. *The Shape of Silence*, for solo flute. C. F. Peters, 1983.

Mestral, Patrice. *Intentions III*, pour flute solo et 8 ou 16 flutes. Salabert, 1983.

Mimet, Anne-Marie. *Y Galon Drom (Le Coeur Lourd), Air Populaire Gallois*, pour saxophone alto et piano ou harpe. Billaudot, 1983.

Moore, Sheila Smart. *Prelude and Invention*, for euphonium and tuba. Dorn Publications, 1985.

Musgrave, Thea. *Four Portraits*, for baritone, clarinet, and piano. Theodore Presser Co., 1983.

†*The Lord's Prayer*, for organ. Novello, 1984. Commissioned by the San Francisco Chapter of the American Guild of Organists for the 1984 National Convention.

Peripeteia, for orchestra. Novello, 1983.

Soliloquy I, for guitar and tape. Chester, 1983.

Sonata, for flute, violin and guitar.

Variations for Brass Band. Chester. 1984.

Nelson, Sheila M. *Technitunes*, for violin; *Technitunes*, for 'cello. Boosey & Hawkes, 1982.

Tunes For My String Quartet. Boosey & Hawkes, 1983.

Niamath, Linda. *A Zoo For You*: 10 animal pieces. Frederick Harris Music.

O'Hearn, Arletta. *Jazz Together*, for piano four hands. Kjos, 1983.

Three Piano Preludes in Jazz Stylings. Kjos, 1984.

Owen, Blythe. *Fairest Lord Jesus*. Augsberg Publishing House.

A Little Ballad. Willis Music Co.

A Sunny Day. Willis Music Co.

Parker, Alice. *Holy Michael*, for two part chorus and guitar or harp. Hinshaw Music.

In Praise of Singing, for mixed chorus and orchestra. Hinshaw Music.

It Is Good To Give Thanks, for mixed chorus and keyboard (1983). Hinshaw Music.

Mountain Hymns: song cycle (1982). Hinshaw Music.

The Ponder Heart (1982). Belwin-Mills.

Sacred Symphonies (1983). Augsberg Publishing House.

Philiba, Nicole. *Omaggio a Venezia*: 10 pièces pour piano à 4 mains. Billaudot, 1981.

Venise: 5 pièces faciles pour basson et piano. Billaudot, 1982.

Plé, Simone. *6 Danses*, pour piano, 4 mains. Lemoine, 1983.

Pressman, Lisa Gaye. *Sonata*, for alto saxophone piano. Dorn Publications, 1985.

Ptaszynska, Marta. *Four Preludes*, for vibraphone and piano. Marks Music, 1983.

Scherzo, for xylophone and piano. Marks Music, 1983.

Variations, for solo flute. Marks Music, 1983.

Ran, Shulamit. *Private Game*, for B-flat clarinet and violoncello. Theodore Presser, 1983.

Richter, Ada. *Supersolos*, for piano. Theodore Presser Co.

Richter, Marga. *Duesseldorf Concerto*. G. Schirmer.

Robert, Lucie. *Dialogues Avec Soi-Même*, pour clarinette seule. Billaudot, 1981.

Flash, pour orgue. Billaudot, 1982.

Variations, pour saxophone alto et piano. Billaudot, 1982.

Rocherelle, Eugenie R. *Bayou Reflections, Pages From a Scrapbook*, for piano; *Tierra Del Sol*: characteristic easy duets, for one piano, four hands. General Words, 1984.

Roesgen-Champion, Marguerite. *Suite Francaise*, pour flûte et harpe. Billaudot, 1983.

Roger, Denise. *Pieces en Trio*, for oboe, clarinet, and bassoon. Dorn Publications, 1984.

Sonatine, for flute and piano. Southern Music Co., 1985.

Schaefer, Ruth M. *The Cobblestone Road*, for flute and piano. Shawnee Press, 1983.

Vonni's Guide, for flute and piano. Shawnee Press, 1985.

Watercolors, for flute (violin) and piano. Shawnee Press, 1983.

Schonthal, Ruth. *Miniatures*: study and recital pieces for the early grades. Galaxy Music Corp.

Scott, Katherine. *Andante and Allegro*, for tuba and piano. Queen City Brass, 1984.

Semegen, Daria. *Jeux des Quatres*. In: *ASUC Journal of Music Scores, Vol. 12*, 1983.

Music for Violin Alone. Columbia University Press Music Publications.

Shore, Clare. *Four Dickinson Songs*, for soprano and harpsichord. Arsis Press, 1984.

Simms, Linda Hoffer. *I Am the Vine*, for SATB chorus. Randall Egan and Associates, 1984.

Simons, Netty. *This Slowly Drifting Cloud*, for band or variable ensemble. Merion Music, 1984.

Singer, Jeanne. *Selected Songs Set to Texts by American Poets*. Dragon's Teeth Press, 1982.

Smith, Julia. *Prairie Kaleidoscope*, for voice and piano. Theodore Presser Co.

A Song of Texas, for voice and piano. Mowbray, 1985.

Stirling, Elizabeth (1819-1895). *Six Pedal Fugues*, for organ. McAfee, 1984.

Sung, Stella. *Meditation*, for flute solo and five flute choir. Southern Music Co., 1984.

Talma, Louise. *Thirteen Ways of Looking at a Blackbird*, for voice, oboe (flute or violin) and piano. Carl Fischer, 1984.

Tate, Phyllis. *Prelude-Aria-Interlude-Finale*, for clarinet in B-flat and piano. Oxford University Press, 1983.

Scarecrow, for junior singers, actors, and dancers with instrumental ensemble and piano or percussion. Oxford University Press, 1982.

Tower, Joan. *Wings*. Associated Music Publishers.

Tran, Fanny. *Warszawian Echoes*, for unaccompanied saxophone. Dorn Publications, 1985.

Van Appledorn, Mary Jeanne. *Cacophony*. Carl Fischer.

Elegy for Pepe (1982). Galaxy Music Corp.

Liquid Gold, for alto saxophone and piano (1982). Dorn Publications, 1984.

Lux: Legend of Sankta Lucia. Carl Fischer.

Trumpet Concerto. Carl Fischer.

Vercoe, Elizabeth. *Irreveries from Sappho*, for soprano with piano accompaniment. Arsis Press, 1983.

Sonaria, for 'cello. Arsis Press, 1985.

Wallach, Joelle. *Glimpses*, for orchestra. Carl Fischer, 1982.

Wang, An-Ming. *The Song of Endless Sorrow*. Dale Music.

Warren, Elinor Remick. *Selected Songs*. Carl Fischer, 1983.

Weir, Judith. *Isti Mirant Stella*, for orchestra. Novello, 1984.

King Harald's Saga: grand opera in three acts for unaccompanied solo soprano singing eight roles. Novello, 1982.

Music for 247 Strings, for violin and piano. Novello, 1983.

Wilson, Anne. *Song of the Redeemed*, for two-part chorus with organ accompaniment. Salisbury Press, 1985.

Wylie, Ruth Shaw. *The White Raven*, op. 37/2, for piano, Henmar, 1983.

Ydette, Arline. *Christopher Columbus*: a mini-musical. Shawnee Press, 1982.

Zaidel-Rudolph, Jeanne. *4-Minim*, for 'cello and piano. Seesaw Music Corp., 1985.

Zaimont, Judith Lang. *The Chase* (1972): cantata for SATB and piano. Galaxy Music Corp., 1985.

Nocturne: La Fin de Siecle. Galaxy Music Corp., 1984.

A Woman of Valor (1978), for mezzo-soprano and string quartet. Transcontinental Music Corp., 1986.

Zechlin, Ruth. *Metamorphosen*, für Orchester. C. F. Peters (Leipzig), 1982.

Zwilich, Ellen Taaffe. *Clarino Quartet*, for four trumpets or four clarinets. Margun Music, 1982.

Divertimento, for flute, clarinet, violin and 'cello. Mobart, 1984.
Einsame Nacht, for baritone and piano. Merion Music, 1984.
Fantasy, for harpsichord (1983). Mobart, 1984.
Prologue and Variations, for string orchestra. Merion Music, 1985.
†*String Trio*. Merion Music, 1984. Commissioned by the Lydian Trio.
Symphony no. 1. Margun Music.

Discography

COLLECTIONS

Musica Femina: music by women composers. Includes works by Yvonne Desportes, Anna Amalia, Ivana Loudova, Maria Theresia von Paradis, Gwyneth Walker, Kristen Aspen, and Janna MacAuslan. Musica Femina c-1 (cassette).
Piano Rags by Women. Northeastern (projected release).

INDIVIDUAL COMPOSERS

Allen, Judith Shatin. *Wind Songs*, for wind quintet. Opus One #87.

Anderson, Beth. *Sugar, Alcohol and Meat; I Can't Stand It.* Dial-A-Poem Poets LP.
Yes Sir Ree (If I Were a Poet); I Can't Stand It; The People Rumble Louder Than the Poet Speaks; Preparation for the Dominant; Shakuhachi Run; Ode: An American Song. Widemouth 8619.

Anderson, Laurie. *Big Science.* WB 3676.
Mister Heartbreak. WB 25077-1.

Barkin, Elaine. *Plein Chant,* for flute. CRI SD 513.

Bauer, Marion (1897-1955). *Sonata,* for viola and piano, op. 22. Northeastern NR 222.

Beach, Amy Cheney (1867-1944). *Balkan Variations; French Suite,* for piano. Northeastern NR 223.
Invocation, op. 55. Northeastern NR 222.
Songs and Violin Pieces. Northeastern NR 202.

Beath, Betty. *Piccolo Victory: Images of Colonial Australia,* for piccolo, flute, 'cello and harpsichord (1982). Grevillea GRV-1082.

Berl, Christine. *Three Pieces*, for chamber ensemble. ASUC Record no. 7.

Boulanger, Lili (1893-1918). *Works of Lili Boulanger.* Everest 3059.
D'un Matin de Printemps; *D'un Soir Triste*; *Harmonies du Soir*; *Nocturne*; *Cortège, D'un Vieux Jardin; D'un Jardin Clair.* Unikorn-Kanchana DKP 9021.
Nocturne; *Cortège.* Northeastern NR 222.
Three Songs: *Attente*; *Reflets*; *Le Retour*, for mezzo-soprano and piano. (In: *Music by Women Composers,* Vol. III). Coronet 3127.

Songs. Bridge Records (projected release).

Burgess, Brio. *Auricle in G.* V.E.C. Audio Exchange. *Girl on a Ball.* Audio Child Cassette Edition.

Chaminade, Cecile (1857-1944). *Pierette*; *Serenade Espagnole*; *Romanza Appassionata*. Northeastern NR 222.

Chance, Nancy Laird. *Exultation and Lament*. Opus One #79.

Ciani, Suzanne. *Seven Waves*. Finnadar 90175-1.

Clarke, Rebecca (1886-1979). Choral works. Leonarda (projected release).

Sonata, for viola and piano; *Two Pieces*, for viola and 'cello; *Duo*, for viola and clarinet; *Passacaglia,* for viola and piano. Northeastern NR 212.

Clayton, Laura. *Cree Songs to the Newborn*, for soprano and chamber ensemble (1978). CRI SD 498.

Simichai-ya, for saxophone and electronic tape. CRI (projected release).

Clement, Sheree. *Chamber Concerto*. CRI (projected release).

Cory, Eleanor. *Profiles*; *Apertures*. CRI (projected release).

Cowles, Darleen. *Transluscent Unreality #1.* (In: *Works by Women Composers,* Vol. I.). Capriccio CR 1001.

Crawford-Seeger, Ruth (1901-1953). *Preludes*, for piano; *Piano Study in Mixed Accents* (1930). (In: *Music by Women Composers*, Vol. III). Coronet 3127.

Sonata, for violin and piano. CRI SD 508.

Suite No. 2, for piano and strings (1929). New World NW 319.

Three Songs, for soprano, oboe, and piano. CRI SD 501.

Davis, Sharon. *Cocktail Etudes*, for piano. WIM 16.

6 Songs on Poems of William Pillin, for soprano and piano; *Though Men Call Us Free*, for soprano, clarinet, and piano; *3 Moods of Emily Dickinson*, for soprano, violin, 'cello, and piano; *3 Poems of William Blake*, for soprano and low clarinet. WIM 23.

Diemer, Emma Lou. *Declarations*, for organ; *Sonata for flute and piano*. Golden Crest 7074.

Toccata and Fugue, for organ. (In: *Works by Women Composers*, Vol. I). Capriccio 1001.

Dring, Madeleine (1923-1977). *Dring Dances!* Cambria C-1015.

The Far Away Princess: Songs. Meridian E 77050.

Piano music. Selections. Cambria C-1014.

Shades of Dring: chamber jazz arrangements by Lennie Niehaus on music of Madeleine Dring. Cambria C-1016.

Songs. Selections. Cambria C-1020.

Escot, Pozzi. *Neyrac Lux*, for guitar (1976). Spectrum 128.

Fine, Vivian. Choral Works. Sage City Symphony Rec.

Gideon, Miriam. *The Resounding Lyre*, for tenor and instrumental ensemble (1979); *Spirit Above the Dust*, for mezzo-soprano and ensemble (1981). CRI SD 493.

Sonata for Piano (1977). CRI SD 481.

Sonnets from Shakespeare. CRI 527.

Voices from Elysium, for tenor and instrumental ensemble (1979). New World NW 317.

Goolkasian-Rahbee, Dianne. *Phantasy Variations*, for piano. Educo 3130.

Hays, Doris. *Celebration of No* (tape version); *Southern Voices*, for tape; *Exploitation*, for tape with chant; *Blues Fragments*, for soprano and piano. Folkways FTS 37476.

Hensel, Fanny Mendelssohn (1805-1847). *Gartenlieder*, op. 3; *Songs Without Words*, op. 2 and 8; *Songs* from op. 7, op. 9 and op. 10; *Prelude in F major*, for organ. Northeastern NR 213.

Romances Without Words, for piano; *Songs*; *Piano Trio* in D minor, op. 11. 2-Calliope CAL 1213/14.

Hildegarde, Saint (Hildegarde von Bingen, 1098-1179). *A Feather on the Breath of God*: Sequences and hymns. Hyperion A 66039.

Hoover, Katherine. *The Medieval Suite*, (In: *Music by Women Composers*, Vol. III). solo flute (1982). Leonarda LPI 121.

Howe, Mary (1882-1964). *Goethe Songs* (In: *Music by Women Composers*, Vol. III). Coronet 3127.

Johnson, Laurie. Selections from: *First Men in the Moon*; *Hedda*; *Captain Kronos* and *Dr. Strangelove*, Unicorn-Kanchana DKP 9001.

Selections from: *The Avengers*; *The New Avengers*; *The Professionals*. Unicorn-Kanchana KPM 7009.

Kabat, Julie. *Five Poems by H.D.*; *Invocation in Centrifugal Form*; *On Edge*; *A Mi Hija*; *Kalimba Alight*, for voice and various instruments. Leonards LPI 119.

Karpman, Laura. *Capriccio*, for solo saxophone. CRI (projected release).

Kessler, Minuetta. *Songs*. Afka S-4663.

Kolb, Barbara. *Apello*, for solo piano; *Toccata*, for harpsichord and electronic tape; *Soundings*. CRI (projected release).

Homage to Keith Jarrett and Gary Burton, for flute and vibraphone. Leonarda LPI 121; Contemporary Recording Studios CRS 8425.

Songs Before an Adieu, for soprano, flute, alto flute, and guitar. Bridge Records BDG 2004.

Three Lullabies, for guitar. Bridge Records BDG 2001.

Kroesen, Jill. *Stop Vicious Cycles*. Lovely Music VR 1501.

La Barbara, Joan. *as lightning comes, in flashes*. Wizard 2283.

The Solar Wind (1983); *October Music: Star Showers and Extraterrestrials* 1980); *Vlissingen Harbor* (1982). Nonesuch 78029.

Larsen, Libby. *Aubade* (1982); *Ulloa's Ring* (1980), for flute and piano. Pro Arte 1086.

Symphony No. 1. Nonesuch (projected release).

LeBaron, Anne. *Butterfly Collection*; *Siesta*; *Jewels*; *Transparent Zebra*; *Rare Seal Wolves*; *Ukranian Ice Eggs*; *Drunk Underwater Koto*; *Sudden Noticing of Trees*. Trans Museq Record Co.

Concerto for Active Frogs. Say Day-Bew Record Co.

Dog-gone Cat Act, for harp. Opus One #58.

Leon, Tania. *Haiku*. Opus One #101.

Lomon, Ruth. *Dust Devils*, for harp (1975). 1750 Arch Records 1787.

Five Ceremonial Masks, for piano (1980). (In: *Music by Women Composers*, Vol. II). Coronet 3121.

Soundings, for piano four hands; *Triptych*, for two pianos. (In: *Works by Women Composers*, Vol. II). Capriccio 1002.

Lutyens, Elisabeth (1906-1983). *The Ring of Bone*. ECR 001.

McLean, Priscilla & Barton. *Electro-Surrealistic Landscapes*. Opus One #96

McMillan, Ann. *A Little Cosmic Dust*, for piano and tape. Opus One #79.

Mamlok, Ursula. *Panta Rhei*, for piano, violin, and 'cello. CRI SD 518.
Sextet, for flute, clarinet, bass clarinet, violin, double bass, and piano (1977); *When Summer Sang*, for flute, clarinet, violin, 'cello, and piano (1980). CRI SD 480.

Marez-Oyens, Tera de. *From Death to Birth*, for choir; *Ballerina on a Cliff*, for piano; *Charon's Gift*, for piano and tape; *Ambiversion*, for bass clarinet and tape. BV Haast 054.

Mekeel, Joyce. *Alarums and Excursions* (1978); *Rune* (1977). Northeastern NR 203.

Monk, Meredith. *Turtle Dreams*. ECM Records.

Musgrave, Thea. *Four Madrigals*. Arika AR-002. Choral Works. *Leonarda* (projected release).

Okolo-Kulaks, Alexandre. *String Quartets Nos. 1 & 2*; *Reflections of My Soul: Stormy Road*; *Divertimento: Five Ballet Scenes*. AM-LAT-REC.

Oliveros, Pauline. *Horse Sings from Cloud*; *Rattlesnake Mountain*, for accordion and voice. Lovely Music VR 1901.
Horse Sings from Cloud: quartet version, for harmonium, accordion, concertina, and bandoneon (1975); *The Wanderer*, for solo accordion and accordion orchestra. Lovely Music VR 1902.

Ozaiia, Maria Luisa. *Urte Berri y Ametsa'n Dantza*. ASCE 171538/7.

Pierce, Alexandra. *Variations 7*, for prepared piano. (In: Works by Women Composers, Vol. II). Capriccio 1002.

Procaccini, Teresa. *Quartetto* per archi, op. 42; *Sonatina no. 2*, op. 43, per pianoforte; *Andante e Rondo*, op. 50; *Introduzione e Allegro*, op. 39; *Nove Preludi*, op. 29, per pianoforte. EDI-PAN PRC S20-11.

Radigue, Elaine. *Songs of Milarepa*. Lovely Music VR 2001.

Ran, Shulamit. *Apprehensions*, for soprano, clarinet and piano. CRI SD 509.

Richter, Marga. *Landscapes of the Mind II*, for violin and piano; *Sonora*, for two clarinets and piano. Leonarda LPI 122.

Samter, Alice. Works. Selections. Mars 308328, EMI-ASD.

Samuel, Rhian. *Songs of Earth and Air* (1983). (In: *Music by Women Composers*, Vol. III). Coronet 3127.

Schieve, Catherine. *Labyrinth*. ASUC Record No. 7.

Schonthal, Ruth. *Four Epiphanies*, for unaccompanied viola (1976); *Sonata Concertante*, for 'cello and piano. Orion 83444.
Loveletters, for clarinet and 'cello. (In: *Works by Women Composers, Vol. I)*. Capriccio 1001.

Schumann, Clara (1819-1896). Piano Music; *3 Romances*, for violin and piano, op. 22; *Trio* in G minor, for violin, 'cello, and piano, op. 17. 2-Calliope 1211/12. Songs. EDI PAN NRC 5016.

Shields, Alice. *Coyote*, for electronic sounds. CRI SD 495.
El's Aria. Opus One #90.
Rhapsody, for piano and tape delays: "Homage to Brahms." Opus One #94.
Six Songs from Poems of Pablo Neruda. Opus One #83.

Silsbee, Ann. *Spirals*, for string quartet and piano. Northeastern NR 221.

Silver, Sheila. *String Quartet*. CRI SD 520.

Spencer, Williametta. Choral Music. Golden Crest 5076.

Spiegel, Laurie. *Drums*; *Voices Within*. (In: *Works by Women Composers*, Vol. II). Capriccio 1002.

Strozzi, Barbara (1619-1664). *Che se Può Fare?*; *Non Pavento io non di te*; *Tradimento!* Leonarda LPI 123.

Sutherland, Margaret. *Sonatina*, for piano (1956). Discourses ABM-30.

Szymanowska, Maria (1789-1831). Songs. EDI PAN NRC 5016.

Tailleferre, Germaine (1892-1983). *Sonata No. 1*. Northeastern NR 222.

Piano Music. Selections. Cambria C-1014.

Talma, Louise. *Diadem*: song cycle for tenor and instrumental ensemble. New World NW 317.

Thome, Diane. *The Yew Tree*, for soprano and chamber orchestra (1979). Crystal 257.

Tower, Joan. *Noon Dance*; *Platinum Spirals*; *Amazon*; *Wings*. CRI SD 517.

Petroushkates, for flute, violin, clarinet, 'cello and piano. CRI SD 441.

Sequoia. Nonesuch (projected release).

Snow Drops, for flute and guitar. Pro Arte (projected release).

Van Appledorn, Mary Jeanne. *Concerto for Trumpet and Concert Band*; *Passacaglia and Chorale*. Opus One #110.

†Vercoe, Elizabeth. *Herstory II*: 13 Japanese lyrics for soprano, piano and percussion (1979). Northeastern NR 221. Received grant from the Artists Foundation of Massachusetts for this recording.

Irreveries from Sappho (1981). (In: *Music by Women Composers*, Vol. III). Coronet 3127.

Williams, Grace (1906-1977). *Ave Maris Stella* (1973); *6 Poems by Gerard Manley Hopkins* (1958); *Choral Suite: The Dancers* (1951); *2 Choruses: Harp Songs of the Dane Women; Mariners' Song* (1975). Chandos 1116.

Zaimont, Judith Lang. *Serenade: To Music*, for chamber chorus. Leonarda (projected release).

Zwilich, Ellen Taaffe. *Passages*, for soprano and instrumental ensemble (1981); *String Trio* (1982). Northeastern NR 218.

Prologue and Variations, for string orchestra;

Symphony No. 1; *Celebration*. New World NW 336 (projected release).

Films and Videos

American Composers and Conductors Symposium on Women in Music. VCR tape prepared at the West Coast Women Conductor/Composer Symposium, University of Oregon School of Music, Eugene, OR, 1985.

Brico, Antonia. *Antonia: A Portrait of the Woman.* Directed by Judy Collins and Jill Godmilow. Produced by Judy Collins for Mountain Productions, 1974. 58 minutes.

Hays, Doris. *Southern Voices: A Music Video.* Directed by George C. Stoney. Distributed by Filmmakers' Library and Electronic Arts Intermix. 58 minutes.

Ivey, Jean Eichelberger. *A Woman is . . . a Composer.* Distributed by Louise Tiranoff Productions, New York City. 30 minutes.

Somogi, Judith. *On Stage with Judith Somogi.* Documentary, financed by Phillips Petroleum. 28 minutes.

Themmen, Ivana. Featured composer in *Soundings* series, produced by WGBH-TV of Boston, 1982.

Tower, Joan. Featured composer in *Soundings* series, produced by WGBH-TV of Boston, 1982.

The Music of Joan Tower: interview and performances of her works by the Da Capo Chamber Players. Broadcast on Channel 13 (New York), 7/22/84.

Van de Vate, Nancy. *Panel Discussion with Composer Nancy Van de Vate.* VCR tape, available from producer, c/o North Adams State College, Williamsburg, MA.

New Books

Bowers, Jane M., and Judith Tick, eds. *Women Making Music*. Champaign, Ill.: University of Illinois Press, 1986.

Chissell, Joan. *Clara Schumann, A Dedicated Spirit: A Study of Her Life and Work*. New York: Taplinger, 1983.

Claghorn, Charles Eugene. *Women Composers and Hymnists: A Concise Biographical Dictionary*. Metuchen, N.J.: Scarecrow Press, 1984.

Cohen, Aaron I. *International Discography of Women Composers*. Westport, Conn.: Greenwood Press, 1984.

Cook, Susan, and Thomasin LaMay: *Virtuose in Italy, 1600-1640*. New York: Garland Press, 1984.

Eastman, Sheila Jane, and Timothy J. McGee. *Barbara Pentland*. Toronto: University of Toronto Press, 1983.

Frasier, Jane. *Women Composers: A Discography*. Detroit, Mich.: Information Coordinators, 1984.

Green, Mildred Denby. *Black Women Composers: A Genesis*. Boston: Twayne, 1983.

Handy, D. Antoinette. *The International Sweethearts of Rhythm*. Metuchen, N.J.: Scarecrow Press, 1983.

Hixon, Donald L. *Thea Musgrave: A Bio-Bibliography*. Westport, Conn.: Greenwood Press, 1984.

Leder, Jan. *Women in Jazz: A Discography of Instrumental Music, 1913-1968*. Westport, Conn.: Greenwood Press, 1985.

Le Page, Jane Weiner. *Women Composers, Conductors and Musicians of the Twentieth Century, vol. II*. Metuchen, N.J.: Scarecrow Press, 1983.

MacAuslan, Janna. *A Catalog of Compositions for Guitar by Women Composers*. Portland, Or.: DearHorse Publications, 1984.

Reich, Nancy B. *Clara Schumann: The Artist and the Woman*. Ithaca, N.Y.: Cornell University Press, 1985.

Rosen, Judith. *Grazyna Bacewicz: Her Life and Works*. Los Angeles: University of Southern California School of Music, 1984 (Polish Music History Series, no. 2).

Thomas, Adrian. *Grazyna Bacewicz: Chamber and Orchestral Music*. Los Angeles:

University of Southern California School of Music, 1985 (Polish Music History Series, no. 3).

Tick, Judith. *American Women Composers Before 1879*. Ann Arbor, Mich.: UMI Research Press, 1983.

Von Gunden, Heidi. *The Music of Pauline Oliveros*. Metuchen, N.J.: Scarecrow Press, 1983.

Wood, Elizabeth. *Banners and Music: The Life of Ethyl Smyth*. London: Jonathan Cape, 1986.

Conductors

Primary affiliations of conductors are listed, followed by the year of the source consulted for the information. A - after the year indicates that the appointment was still in effect during the 1985-86 season.

Alsop, Marin. Conductor, Concordia Chamber Orchestra, New York, NY. 1984- .

Atlas, Dalia (Israel). Conductor, Israel Pro-Musica Orchestra/Haifa Chamber Orchestra, Haifa. 1984. Conductor, Technion Symphony Orchestra, Haifa. 1984.

Ben-Dor, Gisele Buka. Conductor, Norwalk Symphony Orchestra, Norwalk, CT. 1984- .

Berger, Jane. Conductor, Siouxland Youth Symphony Orchestra, Sioux City, IA. 1984- .

Bond, Victoria. Conductor, Empire State Youth Orchestra, Albany, NY. 1983- . Music Director, Bel Canto Opera, New York, NY. 1983/84. Music Director, Roanoke Symphony Orchestra, Roanoke, VA. 1986- .

Brooks, Tamara. Conductor, New School of Music Orchestra, Philadelphia, PA. 1983- .

Brown, Beatrice. Conductor, Ridgefield Orchestra, Ridgefield, CT. 1983, 1984.

Comet, Catherine. Associate conductor, Baltimore Symphony Orchestra. 1984- . Music Director, Grand Rapids Symphony, Grand Rapids, MI. 1986- .

Daly, Margaret W. Conductor, McPherson Symphony Orchestra, McPherson, KS. 1984- .

Deutsch, Margery. Acting Music Director, Shreveport Symphony Orchestra, Shreveport, LA. 1983.

Dressler, Janet. Co-conductor, Jackson Symphony Youth Orchestra, Jackson, MS. 1985- .

Falletta, JoAnn. Conductor, Denver Chamber Orchestra, Denver, CO. 1983. Winner, first prize, 1985 Leopold Stokowski Conducting Competition. Received 1985 Toscanini Conductors Award. Associate conductor, Milwaukee Symphony, 1985- . Music Director, Bay Area Women's Philharmonic, San Francisco, CA. 1986- .

Forrest, Harriett. Co-conductor, Northern Ohio Youth Orchestra, Oberlin, OH. 1983.

Fox, Laurine. Conductor, Suburban Symphony Orchestra of New Jersey, Cranford, NJ. 1984.

Freedman, Deborah. Assistant conductor, Annapolis Symphony Orchestra. 1983- . Music Director, Maryland Women's Symphony. 1985- .

Gabbi, Marianna. Conductor, Las Cruces Symphony Orchestra, Las Cruces, NM/ 1983- .

Gipps, Ruth (U.K.). Conductor, London Chanticleer Orchestra, E. Sussex. 1984. Conductor, London Repertoire Orchestra and Chamber Orchestra, E. Sussex. 1984.

Glover, Jane (U.K.). Conductor, London Mozart Players, London. 1984.

Hahn, Marjorie J. Conductor, South Florida Youth Symphony, Miami, FL. 1984.

Hall, Carol A. Co-conductor, North Shore Youth Symphony, Winnetka, IL. 1983, 1984.

Hamilton, Joyce Johnson. Conductor, Napa Valley Symphony Orchestra, Napa, CA. 1983- .

Hampton, Claudette. Co-conductor, Jackson Symphony Youth Orchestra, Jackson, MS. 1983- .

Harrigan, Ann. Conductor, Baltimore Chamber Orchestra, Baltimore, MD. 1984- .

Harrison, Beverly. Conductor, Tyler Youth Symphony Orchestra, Tyler, TX. 1983.

Henke, Margery. Conductor, Akron Youth Symphony, Akron, OH. 1983. Conductor, Tuscarawas Philharmonic, New Philadelphia, OH. 1983- .

Hill, Carolyn. Conductor, Livingston Community Symphony, Livingston, NJ. 1983.

Hillard, Claire Fox. Conductor, Saint Joseph Symphony Orchestra, Saint Joseph, MO. 1984- .

Hillis, Margaret. Co-conductor, Elgin Symphony Orchestra, Elgin, IL. 1983, 1984.

Howard, Priscilla M. Conductor, York Junior Symphony Orchestra, York, PA. 1983, 1984.

Hudson, Nan. Conductor, Denton Community Orchestra, Denton, TX. 1983, 1984.

Kaufman, Roberta. Conductor, Camerata Youth Symphony, Kew Gardens, NY. 1983- .

Keraus, Ruth. Conductor, Southeast Iowa Symphony Orchestra, Mount Pleasant, IA. 1983- .

Kosloff, Doris. Music Director, Connecticut Opera, 1983- .

Lemon, J. Karla. Conductor, Berkeley Youth Orchestra, Oakland, CA. 1983- .

Mabrey, Marsha. Conductor, University of Oregon Symphony Orchestra, Eugene, OR. 1984- .

Martin Carolann. Conductor, Southeast Kansas Symphony, Pittsburg, KS. 1983- .

Min, Elizabeth. Conductor, Bay Area Women's Philharmonic, San Francisco, CA. 1983-1985.

Moore, June. Conductor, Lincoln Youth Symphony Orchestra, Lincoln, NE. 1983, 1984.

Nanna, Marylouise. Conductor, Cheektowaga Community Symphony, Cheektowaga, NY. 1983.

O'Brien, Janina Martin. Conductor, Prince George's County Senior Youth Orchestra, Upper Marlboro, MD. 1984.

Overhauser, Catherine. Music Director, Hopkins Symphony Orchestra, Baltimore, MD. 1983- . Music Director, York Youth Symphony, York, PA. 1983- . Assistant conductor, Prince George's Philharmonic, Silver Spring, MD. 1985- .

Pickar, Catherine J. Conductor, George Washington University Orchestra, Washington, DC. 1984.

Pope, Dianne. Conductor, Greater Des Moines Youth Symphony, Des Moines, IA. 1983- . Conductor, Mankato Symphony Orchestra, Mankato, MN. 1983, 1984.

Queler, Eve. Conductor, Opera Orchestra of New York, New York, NY. 1983- .

Rice, JoAnn. Conductor, Florilegium Choir and Orchestra. 1983- .

Roberts, Kay George. Conductor, New Hampshire Philharmonic Orchestra, Concord, NH. 1983, 84.

Robinson, Kathleen S. Co-conductor, Jackson Symphony Youth Orchestra, Jackson, MS. 1983, 1984.

Schatz, Madeline F. Conductor, Humboldt Symphony Orchestra, Arcata, CA. 1983, 1984.

Schubert, Barbara. Conductor, University of Chicago Symphony Orchestra, Chicago, IL. 1984.

Smith, Carol. Conductor, Sam Houston State Symphony Orchestra, Huntsville, TX. 1983- .

Socolofsky, Byrnina Brooks. Conductor, Youth Orchestra at Glassboro State College, Glassboro, NJ. 1984- .

Somogi, Judith. Conductor, Frankfurt Opera. 1984.

Sonnenfeld, Portia. Music Director, Little Orchestra of Princeton, Princeton, NJ. 1983, 1984.

Stenberg, Patricia. Conductor, Sarasota Community Orchestra, Sarasota, FL. 1983- .

Tamarkin, Kate. Music Director, Fox Valley Symphony, Menasha, WI. 1983- .

Tilloston, Virginia. Conductor, Brevard Chamber Orchestra, Brevard, NC. 1983- .

Tunicka, Maria. Conductor, Brevard Symphony Orchestra, Melbourne, FL. 1983- .

Wade, Janice. Conductor, Des Moines Community Orchestra, Des Moines, IA. 1983- .

Walton, Frances. Conductor, Olympic Youth Symphonies, Seattle, WA. 1983, 1984. Conductor, Thalia Symphony and Chamber Symphony, Seattle, WA. 1984.

Wilson, Antonia Joy. Conductor, Johnson City Symphony, Johnson City, TN. 1984- .

Worby, Rachael. Conductor, Youth Concerts of the Los Angeles Philharmonic, Los Angeles, CA. 1985. Conductor, Wheeling, WV. 1986- .

Recent Deaths

Alderman, Pauline. (1893-1983). U.S. composer, educator, and author, died 11/11/83.

Berberian, Cathy (1925-1983). U.S. singer and composer, died 3/6/83 in Rome.

Dale, Kathleen (1896-1984). British composer, pianist, and musicologist, died 3/3/84 in Woking, England.

Eager, Mary Ann. U.S. popular music composer, died 1/18/84 at the age of 78.

Hanks, Nancy. U.S. arts administrator, died 1/7/83 in New York.

Holst, Imogen Clare (1907-1984). British composer, conductor, pianist, and author, died 3/9/84 in Aldeburgh, England.

Lutyens, Elisabeth (1906-1983). British composer, died 4/14/83.

Petrides, Frederique. Dutch/American conductor, died 1/12/83 in New York.

Saint-Marcoux, Micheline Coulombe (1938-1985). Canadian composer, died 2/2/85 in Montreal.

Tailleferre, Germaine (1892-1983). French composer, died 11/7/83 in Paris.

Part II

ESSAYS

1

Byline Monson: Music Critic

KAREN MONSON

The path to music criticism is ill-lit and sometimes thorny. There are music critics who claim that extensive musical training and experience are not necessary for success and survival, and history has shown that they can be right. I disagree. It is good if a would-be critic is a talented writer, and it can be advantageous for him or her to know something about the journalistic process. But *music* is the important thing. One cannot think of being a music critic before knowing a lot—a whole lot—about music. That knowledge can take any number of different forms, but the more practical the experience, the better. When I recall a Harvard professor's dismissing all of the work of Anton Bruckner with one dull sequence played (correctly but inappropriately) on the piano, I wonder how anyone can approach criticism with training that is solely theoretical or academic.

Even if I had considered becoming a music critic before reaching the pivotal age of 21, I would not have had the vaguest idea of how to go about it. I was a performer, a flutist who had taken courses in music history and theory in high school, at the National Music Camp at Interlochen—wherever I could find them. But all I wanted to do was play. I was aware, during my Radcliffe College years in the mid-1960s, of only two practicing music critics: Michael Steinberg, then of the *Boston Globe*, and Harold Schonberg, then head critic of the *New York Times*. They didn't seem particularly formidable, and I never thought of them as "the others," the enemies of performers. Frankly, I didn't think of them much at all. There are people, including Schonberg, who claim that they intended to be music critics from the time they were children. I'm sure they are telling the truth, but I find it difficult to imagine such determination. How can a ten-year-old have any concept of what is required in this strange and, in some ways, wonderful career pattern?

With my Bachelor of Arts diploma hung on the wall in my parents' house in upstate New York, I departed on a Fulbright Fellowship in performance and music history to West Berlin, where everything—the school, my teacher, my room, the streets, the weather, the food—seemed dismal. I began to think that I didn't want to play the flute anymore. Looking back, I probably just needed a vacation from the instrument that had been my constant companion for 15 of my 21 years. But at the time, I decided to stop performing; I packed my suitcases and went home with no idea of what I would do.

Once back in Boston, I was told by the Radcliffe Employment Service that I was "unemployable"—my Harvard diploma, and other college awards did not matter. I found freelance work (I did not know what the word *freelance* meant at the time) translating from German into English and played a few concerts for friends who were composers; even then I found new music more intellectually interesting than old. Michael Steinberg happened to be at one of the concerts, and I begged his advice. Fortuitously, he was in need of a "stringer," a freelancer, to review a concert for the *Globe* on the coming Sunday afternoon. I recall that the concert took place at MIT, and I remember my companion, but I cannot remember which string quartet was my first victim or what was on the program. It's just as well: the review was dreadful. Not only did I have no idea what I was doing, I could not write and was terrified by the *Globe*'s deadline. Instead of running out the next morning to see my first "byline," I avoided newsstands for days.

For some reason, Steinberg stuck with me. Gradually, I found the courage to see my name in the paper as "contributing critic" two or three times a week for the next few months and began to realize the possibilities inherent in doing something that, at this point, translated into a little money plus a lot of fun. It occurred to me that music criticism might be a way in which I could view the art on a broader spectrum than had been possible when I was playing the flute. When, in 1967, the Rockefeller Foundation offered me a spot in its Project for the Training of Music Critics, I accepted at once. The offer included a stipend of $10,000 over two years, an excuse to move to Los Angeles and the University of Southern California, and the raison d'être that I was sorely lacking.[1]

I still didn't have a clear idea of what music criticism was about, but I would devote myself to it, at least for a while. The Rockefeller Foundation imported professionals to lecture to our class of four men and one woman. We met Virgil Thomson, Paul Hume (then of the *Washington Post*), Alan Rich, Thomas Willis (then of the *Chicago Tribune*), and the famous Harold Schonberg, during whose lectures we perversely counted the number of occasions upon which he mentioned the *New York Times*. I did not even think about the fact that the teachers were all men. The important hours were spent in the office of Martin Bernheimer who, by virtue of his position as music editor of the *Los Angeles Times*, was "resident faculty." Bernheimer's highly subjective teaching style did not work for everyone, but it worked for me. In the second year of the Rockefeller grant, I stayed in Los Angeles as his apprentice critic, working in music and also, as an utter fledgling, in dance.[2]

Rule: It is possible to teach a person of reasonable intelligence and determination to write, given a few years and a great deal of patience. It is not possible to teach a person everything he or she needs to know about music in order to become a critic unless the process starts early, say at about the age of two. Those who would teach criticism have to be able to presume a firm knowledge of music.

The truth is that when I went to California, I knew nothing about opera. I had never heard *La Bohème*. It was my good fortune that Bernheimer was and is the best opera critic in the country. As my mentor (and, of course, in protection of his own reputation and his newspaper's), he saw to it that I attended every local opera performance and spent the rest of my time listening to records. This is the immersion method of instruction, and it worked. When I moved downtown to be the number one (and only) music and dance critic of the *Los Angeles Herald-Examiner* in 1969, I knew enough to admit to what I didn't know. Yes, I was still flying by the seat of my jeans, reviewing operas that I was witnessing for the first time; but I now knew what to watch and listen for and which questions to ask. Reviewing works that are new to him or her is, alas, part of the critic's fate. There is no way that everyone can know everything, and I am aware of situations in which people much older and more experienced than I have found themselves "winging it."

(This works conversely, too: I am probably the only flutist in history to have played Verdi's *Four Sacred Pieces* four times before the age of 21, and Richard Strauss's *Four Last Songs* twice in the same time. There are certain works that you keep encountering, and others you simply miss.)

The prerequisites for becoming a music critic, then, are musical training, a grasp of (and love for) the language, personal sensitivity, curiosity, stamina, an ego that's on the large side, and guts. Especially the last.

In August of 1973, having accomplished nothing particularly noteworthy in the field, I was lucky enough to become the head (again, the only) music critic for the *Chicago Daily News*, succeeding Bernard Jacobson, who had been preceded by Donal Henahan, then of the *New York Times*. Farewell Terpsichore! By then I knew that it was difficult, if not impossible, to give attention to more than one art form. Even those who have accomplished this with some success have been known as "the music critic who also does dance," or "the theater person who also writes about music." Music of the classical or concert variety is a jealous lover; it wants exclusivity.

In return, the muse bestows some blessings. Newspapers are usually dens of generalists, so the specialist music critic tends to be looked upon as the resident effete snob, a little crazy, not to be charged or trusted with many of the responsibilities that would otherwise be considered a normal part of the job. This insults people who know the details of journalism, and it can lead to a limited social life around the office. It does, however, ease the burden.

Chicago is a great city. The *Chicago Daily News* was a great newspaper: brave, literate, venturesome, and full of bright people. Writing mattered there, and so did the arts. The paper met its demise on March 4, 1978, and I left town eighteen months later. I miss the city, the people, and the cultural life. And now, finally, I can say that I also miss the paper. But when it was announced that the *Daily News* would fold, I could not cry. After ten straight years of being a critic, I'd had enough.

Though I have friends who still think that being a critic was and is a glamorous life, I don't remember ever thinking it was glamorous. While it is true that there are free tickets to virtually every concert—sometimes two or three events per night—it does not take long for the critic to realize that, optimistically, only one out of every five concerts is of any real interest. After five or seven years on the job, chances are good that the critic would choose to attend only about one out of every 20 event about which he or she reports. Years passed after the end of the *Daily News* before I was ready to venture out of my house and be in a seat to be entertained promptly at 8:00 or 8:30 P.M.

In addition to the tickets, free records arrive for review, and, on most newspapers and magazines, books, too. These the critic must take home, since there is neither equipment, space, nor time enough to deal with them in the office. Much as one may love records and books, they have a habit of overtaking one's private universe. Fortunately, the critic's day is likely to be flexible. There is no reason to keep to a regular 9-to-5 schedule at the office, since that is neither the time nor the place where the serious work of the job is done. There are matters to tend to during business hours—phone calls to be made, mail to be opened, meetings to be set, and so on. But usually, the critic can arrange his or her day as needed, taking the morning or the afternoon off. This sounds great until you realize that you are free in the daytime and your friends are not. They all work normal hours, with evenings and weekends in which to play, while these same evenings and weekends are the critic's busiest times.

Claudia Cassidy, the distinguished critic emeritus of the *Chicago Tribune*, is credited with having defined her colleagues as "people who eat dinner too early." It's true. Some critics—those who don't have to go directly from the concert hall's keyboard to the one at the computer—have the luxury of dining after the event they have covered. Most of us, though, have to get used to eating at 6 or 6:30 P.M. and then running to get to the concert on time, filled with enough energy and adrenalin to keep going until the review is finished and submitted (which can be at 1 or 2 A.M.).

I was envious of the members of the Chicago Symphony Orchestra when the *Daily News* sent me to cover their European tour in 1974. I do not complain about being sent to Munich, Venice, and Vienna—but I didn't see Munich, Venice, or Vienna. I lived by the musicians' grueling schedule in order to get "color stories," anecdotes that the paper and I wanted and needed. When, after each night's concert, the players went back to their hotels for a drink and a good night's sleep, I went to work. I found a Telex or a cooperative telephone operator, wrote my story, sent it in, and then worried about creature comforts.

At home, during my more masochistic times (my bosses never required it), I set a personal record of covering nine events in one week—seven nights plus weekend matinees. That was stupid, almost as stupid as the seven-day period during which I scheduled myself to review four string quartets, all playing very traditional, even dull, programs. As might have been anticipated, the reviews were clones of one another. One learns to look for variety, just as one learns to avoid what is likely not to be an outstanding performance of the *Eroica* Symphony. Let's face it, there is not much left to be said about the *Eroica*, and you, the critic, are not going to be the one who comes up with an original insight as you sit, late at night, contemplating a mediocre performance. (With your luck, the conductor took all of the repeats.)

The picture is not all gloomy. Had I not been a critic, I might have missed some of the great experiences of a lifetime: Georg Solti conducting Birgit Nilsson and the Chicago Symphony in Strauss's *Salome*; the Paris Opera's controversial production in 1976 of Gounod's *Faust*; Colin Davis conducting the Boston Symphony in Michael Tippett's Third Symphony; soprano Galina Vishnevskaya accompanied in recital by her husband, Mstislav Rostropovich; Elena Obratsova as Marina in the Bolshoi Opera's *Boris Godunov*. I wouldn't have met many of the people whom I can now count as friends. And, in the early 1970s, I did have some fun with the "image" of the critic. I found it amusing to be at the musical "in" spots, where people noticed me and knew my name, often because I was the youngest person in the crowd. I spent a short while dating a young man who drove us to concerts on a large motorcycle. I fear that some impresarios in Los Angeles still remember the motorcycle, not what I had to say about their offerings.

Most of the time, however, I was alone. The chair next to me, my second ticket, belonged to my coat. The best companions were my colleagues; during the first weeks and months in Chicago, they were the only people I knew. The town had four daily papers then, four music critics—three men who were veterans and not exactly fond of each other. My arrival in their ranks civilized our circle a bit; it seemed silly not to speak to the several people whose paths crossed mine four or five times each week. Besides, I liked them all and could prevail upon them for rides in case my car broke down. Sometimes I felt a bit like the mascot of the fraternity, but always in a funny, friendly, whimsical way.

I have never felt that I was condescended to by close male colleagues. I have been put down by a number of men, some of them critics, but I have never sensed professional or sexual discrimination in their verbal abuses. Though I believe that some organizations and institutions continue to avoid critics who happen to be women, I have never been aware of being the object of such bigotry. The fact that I am a woman helped me get my job on the *Daily News*, and it took only a few months' worth of my reviews in Chicago before people stopped referring to me as the new Claudia Cassidy. If this is an example of so-called reverse discrimination, I find no reason to complain.

I also don't complain when men open doors or carry suitcases for me. If this is a sign of my lack of enlightenment, then I probably should add that I despise concerts, exhibitions, anything that is all woman, all black, all Episcopalian, all Opus 1, all anything. I see no reason for such separations, which range from being cute to being downright offensive. But, on the same emotional level, I like to think that chivalry is not dead.

Most of the young people (usually graduate students in music) who came to me to apply to be freelance stringers in Chicago were women. They might have felt comfortable phoning or visiting me because I was female and not much older than they, but I do not think that this was especially relevant. They knew I was the "new kid on the block," and I needed help covering the Chicago beat. They were willing to work hard for very little money, and a couple of them went on to good positions in other cities.

With the exception of the few publications where a woman's work is still thought of as "woman's work," my experience indicates that opportunities for women in criticism are quite as good as they are for men—which is to say that they are not, objectively, good at all. There are very few jobs, and for every full-time position that becomes available on a respectable journal in a city with a full and viable musical life, there are hundreds of moderately well-qualified young people who are willing to try their hands at the assignment for a minimum wage and all the paper clips they can steal. Back in the 1960s, the Rockefeller Foundation's Project for the Training of Music Critics trained critics in numbers greater than existing jobs. And there were appreciably more jobs during those years than there are today.

Though there is some indication in the early 1980s of increased concern for the standards of criticism, and though there is reason to hope for a renaissance in the media as a result of the recovering economy and efficient new gadgetry, it does not seem likely that one axiom of the business will change: the critic's turf is far down on his editor's list of priorities. Music (and dance, theater, and visual arts) does not sell newspapers. Music criticism, in fact, is a lot closer to what used to appear on the society pages of the 1890s than it is to most of what appears on the more widely concerned pages of the 1980s. Writing that Zubin Mehta conducted a Mendelssohn symphony too slowly—or even saying that he conducted it as it has never been conducted before—is about as involving to the average reader as saying that Mrs. Gotrocks entertained her niece Sylvia at tea. (I am speaking here only of the print media, because music criticism has not really entered radio or television except for pop phenomena. Though crossovers from medium to medium might be possible, even successful, this kind of reportage wants the leisure of words on paper and would be difficult to accommodate to the visual and temporal demands of other media.)

Nevertheless, both critics and their editors need to take heed. On the one side, there are still critics who write on and on about a pianist's having missed the B-flat in measure 34. The point would better be: how did he or she play the *music*? The substance is too often ignored for the sake of the notes and technicalities, showing no more than that the writer happened to know what was printed on the page. There are also, regrettably, professional critics who have not recognized that it is a lot easier to write a stingingly negative review than it is to write one that is convincingly positive. This is a serious problem for beginning critics; everything they hear in those first months is the worst they have ever heard. I suppose it is necessary to rid the body and mind of this venom and perhaps enlightened readers understand. Ultimately, however, the reader should not have to care whether the critic liked or hated a work or its performance. The writer must tell his or her audience enough about the music and its delivery to inspire independent thought, let the reader remember the delights (or the dismalness) of the event, and arouse curiosity.

Editors, for their part, must take a broader view. The best and most responsible music critics in this country contribute a great deal more copy, with more variety and substance, than their colleagues on other desks, who must write about labor relations, mayoral races, even sports. Reviews of concerts are but a small part of the job, though they may eat up four nights each week. In addition, there are the book reviews, record reviews, longer pieces that view seasons past and future, "think" pieces on the state of the art, interviews with musical luminaries, updates on financial reports and contract negotiations, analyses of new and different works, short announcements and items about what is happening, and (the worst), calendar listings. In his or her spare time, the critic prepares obituaries. With any luck, these tributes are ready to appear in print when the subject passes on; but, of course, Fate is not considerate of anyone's personal calendar.

The variety and possibilities of the "music beat" are both a liability and an asset. Despite the flexibility and versatility he or she must bring to the job, the critic is often considered to be one of the least essential people on the staff. And, to be sure, some of us are just that. But many—if not most—of today's American music critics are more than earning their salaries.

What happens, though, is that the work wears thin. "Burnout" was not a fashionable disease when I began to experience the symptoms in 1977, but after nine years in the field, that was what I felt. Months before the demise of the *Daily News*, I approached my editor about taking a leave of absence, for which, alas, there were no provisions in the contract. Remembering those times, I still think that I would have quit the paper had it not quit me first.

My primary concerns were practical and, yes, selfish. I was eating too early, alone. I was tired of revving up at 7 P.M. to go to work, then getting home at 2 A.M., when all of my friends were asleep. I had no free weekends. I kept remembering scenes in the little press room at the Ravinia Festival, the North Shore summer home of the Chicago Symphony. The first summer I was there, after my colleagues had sent in their reviews and gone home, I found myself alone with only my typewriter and a visiting raccoon, who looked quite as desolate as I felt. The third summer, I got locked into the park—I was the last to leave, and I am not a slow writer—and had to summon the police to rescue me over the chain fences. Both of these mishaps were funny at the time. By the summer of 1977 they did not seem at all amusing, and I confess that I played a game, trying to write my reviews as quickly as possible. My record was 16 minutes from byline to the end of the text. Pretty good for a computer. Not smart for a critic.

I also noticed that, within my realm of experience, the only critics who were regularly accompanied on evening assignments were the men whose wives did not work. I did know male critics with working wives who went along to occasional special events, as well as male critics whose wives did not work and also did not go to concerts. There were female critics whose husbands sometimes joined them on an evening's assignment—but there were not many females, and not many such evenings. I kept thinking that those concerts and events were special occasions for most people; not for me.

I have been quoted as saying that a woman cannot have a family and be a music critic at the same time. I probably said it, but I was not quite correct. It would be possible, but it would be hard; at least it would be hard for me. Some women have done it, and more will do it in the future. Having never tried the combination, I can only say that I cannot imagine getting home at 2:00 A.M. to a sleeping husband and a fussy child, trying to unwind from the evening's work, and being able to nap only until the baby awakened or the copy desk phoned to check some fact or misspelling (or, worse, to announce a death and order an obituary). I can say, firsthand, that it is the very rare man who will put up with his date's working nights and weekends (even if it is she who has the free tickets) and being in the office until the wee hours of the morning. Perhaps people younger than I will find a compromise; in the meantime, to be honest, I really did not want some bored, sleepy person sitting around the office waiting for me to finish my work. My father did that one night and, even then, I felt guilty.

I had another, more intellectual reservation about the work I was doing. I wondered what good it did, what difference it made. (I can now view that concern as another symptom of the dread "burnout.") I have come to realize that criticism may make no ultimate difference, but that it can do some good. After all, someone must shout loudly and constantly if organizations are ignoring the music of their own era (which is the most important thing). If the emperor is wearing no clothes, someone has to say so, and that person is probably not going to be the one who paid $50 for a ticket. If a young artist or composer offers something outstanding to an audience of six people (and that does happen), someone has to make it known.

Basically, the critic's influence has dwindled over the last thirty or forty years, so that the New York debut review is no longer the die upon which a whole career is cast, and a sharp tongue or swift pen cannot chase a performer out of town. There was a time in the 1970s when I firmly believed that editors were more interested in what toothpaste Herbert von Karajan uses than in what he might think about Beethoven. Fortunately, we seem to have entered a time when some publications care about the toothpaste, but others care about the Beethoven. At least the lines of demarcation are clearer.

As I write this, I can say that I am glad to see these positive developments, but I am not sure that it has made or will make much difference for me. Daily newspaper criticism no longer lures me, though I can thank my years as a critic for much happiness and many unforgettable experiences. Having written two books in the five years after the *Daily News*'s demise, I know that producing a thick volume can be more rewarding than writing a 400-word review. It is difficult to get used to the changed time frame, however; books take years, and reviews take minutes—journalism is, for the most part, a field of instant gratification. I tried my luck as an arts administrator and found that my value systems were very different from those of some other people in that area. I don't rule out the possibility of returning to full-time criticism, but the time and the position must be right.[3]

There are things that I miss very much. I loved teaching criticism, first in Los Angeles for the Rockefeller Project, then for the Music Critics Association Institutes and through some continuing education programs. Wherever I went, the same questions and comments arose; some examples follow.

Rule: You can never please all of the people all the time. Those people who say that they always agree with your assessments either don't read what you write, or are lying.

For whom is the critic writing? For the *interested* reader, but not for musicians and not only for the people who happened to be in the same audience. Just as nothing is going to get me to read a story about wrestling,

I am not going to recruit fight fans to read about a Mozart symphony. Amen.

Rule: Never be wrong. Ninety percent of the time, the critic's assessment, the final vote of yes or no, is subjective and utterly incidental. But on the way to reaching that conclusion, the writer may not err in matters of fact, especially not in print. The critic owes it to the reader to be absolutely correct on every issue except that subjective bottom line.

I know no one in the field who has not pulled the proverbial boner at one time or another. I think I never reviewed a work that was not actually performed, but I did once expound about Verdi's opera *Tosca* (which would have amused Puccini), and I told Californians how proud they should be to have Arthur Rubinstein as a neighbor decades after he had settled in France. I will not rehash friends' mistakes, but when the phone rings very early in the morning and I hear a familiar groan, I know that a critic has put his or her foot in mouth, twisted, and heard about it. The laws of human nature ensure that the critic will be told about every mistake, again and again.

But isn't criticism all subjective? No. That is the reason it does not matter whether the critic approves of a performance or not; there are other, more important things to be said. The byline on a review is one life preserver; the facts are other, better ones. I need to know, for example, whether *Messiah* was offered by forces of 30 or 300. And it does not do to say, "From where I was sitting, the oboe was out of tune." Either it was, or it wasn't.

Should critics take scores to performances? If they do, they should turn the pages quietly. I used to take scores only when I was so tired that I knew I would nap unless I had something tangible to keep me awake. I slept through a world premiere before I learned that strong cough drops can also be great revivers.

Should critics use technical words? Not unless there is a very good reason, one not attached to the ego. *Allegro* and *adagio* are part of the language, but in the event that it is necessary to use a term more obscure, get away from it quickly and pull your untrained reader back into an entertaining and educational prose.

Since we are all in this together, why aren't most critics friendly with musicians, impresarios, managers, and other music professionals? No two critics agree on this issue. It is generally considered awkward and tasteless to write a review of a performance by one's husband or sister, but it has been done. There are critics who have good friends among people whom they review, but there are those who refuse to dine at the same table as a performer or composer. Secure, experienced critics will know that friendship cannot affect a review. The best and most intelligent performers know enough not to worry. I have seen critic/performer relationships sour, but friendships have a way of doing that sometimes. I have also seen critic/performer friendships that seemed unwise, but that was not my business. In the end, the best performer or composer knows better than the critic what was right and what was wrong. Rarely, if ever, will even the most thoughtful of critics be able to tell his or her victim something that he or she did not already know.

Why don't critics stay in the hall after a performance to join in the applause? The answer is not, I think, because they don't want people to see whether or not they approved of the offering. Rather, the critic has only begun his or her work, and the typewriter keyboard must yet be faced. To that end, it is crucial to find a taxi or ransom the car before the rush sets in. This is another of those practical matters, but one that means a lot when everyone else is going either to dinner or to bed and you are off to work.

There is always much to think about on the way from that aisle seat to the typewriter. Fairness does not come as a matter of course, and there were many occasions during a decade of full-time criticism when I had to admit that I resented the waste of my time. Righteous indignation is not to be ruled out entirely, but it must be thoroughly explained before it sees print. The common remark over many breakfast tables is, "Oh, the critic hated the concert again—he/she must have had a bad dinner (or a fight with his/her wife/husband)." Such comments will continue to be made as long as there is criticism, but they *must not* be accurate.

I have two favorite quotations that have satisfied me in some difficult times of questioning. Justice Oliver Wendell Holmes once wrote, "I do expect a rough equation between *isness* and *oughtness*." The critic has to enter the auditorium with a sense of the *ought*; the *is* or the *was* is the performer's problem. And George Bernard Shaw, one of the great music critics, said (albeit on another topic), "If you don't go get what you like, you'll have to like what you get." I like to think that he meant that the critic was responsible for setting the standards—or taking the consequences of reticence. There *is* a moral purpose in music criticism, though it may be hard to find, and should not be taken too awfully seriously.

NOTES

1. The Project for the Training of Music Critics was run through the University of Southern California by the late Raymond Kendall. The first year was spent on campus, where students were invited to attend a variety of classes and sent to numerous concerts, which we were expected to review. During the second year of the Project, we were apprentices on various newspapers around the country, learning the ins and outs of daily journalism. The theory was that with two years of training, it would be possible for the fellows to find jobs. This turned out not to be the case. The Project was abandoned about 1970, when the market was glutted with would-be critics, and remarkably few of the Project's alumni or alumnae are still in the field. At the time of writing, new training projects have been started at several universities. Necessary as it is to improve the general quality of criticism, I hope that young people are not being led along a path that, in the end, can offer no satisfaction.

2. I cannot talk of being a dance critic. I know nothing about dance. But during those years, there was not enough dance in Los Angeles for papers to justify having a separate critic for that very special and specialized art, and it is still common in small markets for the person who is hired to review music also to cover the handful of dance events.

3. *Editor's Note:* Since this essay was written, in 1983-1984, Karen Monson returned to journalism. In the fall of 1984 she was appointed music critic for the *Baltimore Sun* and *Sunday Sun*, covering musical events of note all along the coastal corridor, from Virginia to New York, plus blanket coverage of the home city. After one-and-a-half years at the *Sun*, she left the paper in May 1986 to return to the private sector.

2

Orchestra Manager on the Go: An Interview with Joan Briccetti

On 29 March 1984, *The Musical Woman*'s editor-in-chief, Judith Zaimont, and Associate Editor Catherine Overhauser met with Joan Briccetti, general manager of the Saint Louis Symphony Orchestra. Classified by the American Symphony Orchestra League as a Major orchestra, the Saint Louis Symphony has a 1984-85 operating budget of 11.7 million dollars;[1] its administrative staff of 50 is led by Executive Director David Hyslop. The 101 orchestra members are conducted by Music Director Leonard Slatkin. In 1984-85 the orchestra won two Grammy Awards and undertook its first European tour. We spoke with Briccetti about the Saint Louis Symphony, where she has worked since 1980; her background; and the role of women in today's world of orchestra management.

THE SAINT LOUIS SYMPHONY—UNIQUE ENVIRONMENT FOR AN ORCHESTRA MANAGER

The Musical Woman: You have indicated that your position with the Saint Louis Symphony is multi-faceted. What are some of your principal areas of responsibility?

Joan Briccetti: Our orchestra, like many, is divided into various departments, and the department headed up by the general manager is called simply "Operations." The "operations," most easily summed up, are everything involved in "getting the show on the road." That involves the schedule, the setting up of concerts, arranging of the soloists, and facilitating the repertoire decisions. I am also involved in personnel activities with the orchestra; working with various committees, negotiating individual contracts, and so forth. Also electronic media projects such as recordings and television, touring, and planning future seasons.

TMW: Is there one major tour a year each year?

JB: We come to New York annually, and whatever is built around that we call the East Coast tour. Then we tour every year in the Midwest, which is very important to us for many reasons. We are also in the final stages of planning a European tour, which will be the [Saint Louis Symphony's] first full-fledged tour of Western Europe.

TMW: Are there any specific demands involved in your job because of the character of the Orchestra, or are there other factors associated with the Saint Louis Symphony being located in a city in the center of the United States?

JB: I think the Orchestra is special in many ways and on different levels. I'll give you the most general example. We were described about three years ago as a "sleeper orchestra" by a critic from Milwaukee who was making a comparative critique of various orchestras. In a way that is true. The good news is, in a nutshell, that what this orchestra *does* have is terrific artistic integrity and quality, from every musician right through the music director; there is a good rapport with staff and musicians; and we have an outstanding hall. What we do *not* have at this time, but we're working on every day, is long-term financial security.

TMW: The general pride in the Orchestra's achievement and artistic excellence—that must radiate to everyone on the administrative staff.

JB: It does, and we are less of a "sleeper" all the time. Our recordings constantly receive acclaim, and I think the Orchestra has an emerging recognition level. And although they're improving, at this point our finances need to be significantly strengthened.

TMW: That would probably be echoed by every orchestra in this country.

JB: We have a particularly critical situation right now. There are weak spots in the overall income structure that we are shoring up, and that's what our executive director spends most of his time on—fund-raising, marketing, and that overall, long-range financial picture. But if I had to choose between being financially completely endowed and not having as much of that artistic achievement, I know I'd prefer the way we are: having a very strong quality product, belief in ourselves, and a terrific rapport with the music director. These are essential if you're going to make it in the long haul as one of the top musical ensembles.

We have gotten involved in various artistic activities because of our regional commitment and our American music director, especially Affiliate Artist's Exxon/Arts Endowment Conductors Program and the American Symphony Orchestra League's Orchestra Management Fellowship Program.[2] There are many other orchestras involved in both, but we've really put a lot of energy into sharing as much as possible with the people who visit our organization. And we've also been very, very involved in American music, as you know.

One of my favorite projects is a seven-concert chamber music series that showcases members of the Orchestra in which an American work is featured on every concert. It's interesting that this year 68 members of the orchestra are participating. Now if you know anything about orchestras, that's pretty incredible. It happens because people really like to play.

We are also one of eight orchestras involved in the "Meet the Composer" resident composer program. We adore Joe Schwantner, who is our composer-in-residence. He's been with us for an unprecedented three years [since 1982], and we're looking for ways to hold him hostage permanently in Saint Louis![3]

TMW: That does sound like a special frame of mind, reinforced by what you said about everybody pulling together and being part of the general artistic integrity. It sounds as if there are not separate little empires carved out in the working of your orchestra, but people feel that they are encouraged to participate and make suggestions and work for a common goal.

JB: I think that's really true, and that has so much to do with the attitude that emanates from the top. There is open communication—as much with our executive director, David Hyslop, as with Leonard Slatkin, our music director. All organizations with multiple layers have their problems, too. But I think we have an extremely healthy working situation. And then that travels right through to the orchestra.

TMW: In all this there is a word that I haven't heard mentioned yet, which is *union.* So many orchestras have had union problems in the last few years. Does the good feeling percolate down to the nuts and bolts of contracts and salaries and all?

JB: Well, that's been an objective of this management and music director—a regime which is about five years old altogether. The Orchestra has always been very active in the labor relations arena. I joined the Saint Louis Symphony in the spring of 1980. The 1979-80 season was the Orchestra's centennial year, and it began with a seven-week strike. A West Coast tour was wiped out, recordings were wiped out, the huge centennial gala was obliterated. The volunteers were *not* pleased. It was the fourth strike in seven negotiations, resulting in a real adversarial relationship between management and musicians. David Hyslop had just joined the administration, and one of the things that he set about to do was to improve this relationship; this was something he mentioned to me when he interviewed me. He and I see eye-to-eye on this. We both feel that if you expend your energies battling within, you're going to lose the big battle—making the symphony orchestra flourish in a city like Saint Louis and in this country. We've worked long and hard on this.

So that was 1979-80. But out of the ashes a labor-management committee was formed with assistance from a federal mediator. The committee meets regularly during the nonnegotiating periods, just to keep communication open. These meetings began with lots of musicians and Board members, and we got off to a slow start. The size was cumbersome, so we tried different formats. We all worked at it, and each subsequent orchestra committee that's been elected and has worked with us has demonstrated more receptivity in just understanding how the whole operation works and has generated excellent ideas. We have musicians on the long-range planning committee, and on the investment and endowment committees. So now musicians don't encounter a sudden big surprise or some incomprehensible problem. Over the course of time it has made a huge difference. And the mutual trust and credibility is very good.

FROM ENTHUSIASTIC LISTENER TO ORCHESTRA MANAGER

TMW: Listening to your description of the total relationship between the Orchestra and management makes it clear that there are many very special people involved and that the Saint Louis Symphony is fortunate in having a very special general manager. Can you tell us something about your own background, and how it has shaped your own ideas as far as your working relationship with the Orchestra is concerned?

JB: Well, first of all, I don't want to paint a fairy-tale picture, but I am proud of the organization I work for. And I think that's always half the battle.

In terms of my own musical background, I've always been a jack-of-all-trades. My brother [conductor Thomas Briccetti] began as a concert pianist, evolved into composition, and then into conducting, and he was obviously an influence on me. I come from a large family that has a lot of artistic, creative juices flowing—I have a cousin who is a sculptor—but my brother is the most obvious artistic influence because he is a performer. I grew up outside of New York City in the little teeny town of Somers, New York. It was really the best of two worlds: I grew up in the country, but it was only an hour from midtown Manhattan. My parents both loved music very much, and I spent most of my childhood hearing the piano practiced eight hours a day.

TMW: Did you study music yourself?

JB: Oh yes, I studied. Wonderful memories. I started out with the local piano teacher. My brother was my teacher for a while, and then a very fine pianist who was a friend of his. I played in the band and fooled around with several instruments in college and directed home-grown musicals. But early on I realized that I was an audience person—that "all I knew is I knew nothing." I knew the extent of my talents, and the extent of my limited dedication to perfecting them. And though I didn't train consciously, I've been a good listener since I was a little kid. And I was exposed to new music back then. That's important.

TMW: You mentioned being reluctant to perfect your musical talents. But essentially the role of a manager or producer is to be the supreme detail person involved.

JB: Exactly. That's the way I started to classify my feelings about orchestra management. In the 1960s my brother was music director of the orchestra in Saint Petersburg, Florida, so we'd go down and visit. And there were two realizations I had then. One was just how wonderful rehearsals are. I love performances, but rehearsals are the best. You're sitting there all by yourself, and you feel the performance is all yours. You can hear how the piece comes together as line or color emerges through balancing; intonation is cleaned up; a phrase is defined. You hear it take form, and it's wonderful. Second, I wondered why the people responsible for making the music, including my brother and the musicians, had to worry about all the other details, like, are the lights working, or are there enough music stands. And then my brother, Tom, seeing this interest in me, started plotting and strategizing to interest me in orchestra management! Just before I graduated from college, as a Christmas gift, he set me up in the American Symphony Orchestra League's week-long Orchestra Management Seminar.

I went to that seminar when I was a senior in college, and it "clicked." I hear a lot of the [ASOL Orchestra Management] Fellowship candidates talk about that now. You know—"I love music, but I'm not going to be a performer, and when I read this brochure something clicked." Well, that's exactly what happened to me. It really is an interesting profession, but at that time it was virtually unknown. Now arts administration has emerged as a bona fide career.

I think part of my feeling also comes from my family background; my father was the proprietor of an appliance store, and the old work ethic was potent. In addition to sales, he ran a service department, and he really believed in good service. He had a great reputation of being the best and the most honest, and I think that had a major effect on me.

TMW: For the record, what did you major in at college?

JB: American history, and that's because I decided not to go into chemistry! In my senior year of high school I was ready to go to college and major in science or mathematics.

TMW: You didn't study business adminstration or anything similar?

JB: No, I went to a liberal arts school—Bryn Mawr College. And I liked that place because it is small and it teaches you how to think. I enjoyed my college education and feel strongly about it to this day—about women's schools, about rigorous academic undertakings. There I learned why I want to manage a *symphony orchestra* as opposed to something else.

TMW: Where did you actually earn your spurs as an orchestra manager?

JB: At the end of my senior year in college I started looking for a job and wasn't successful. My brother Tom called one day—at the time he was the associate conductor of the Indianapolis Symphony and the music director of the Fort Wayne Philharmonic. He said, "I don't know how you'll feel about this, but I'm looking at my schedule for next year. I have 130 concerts to conduct, and I really could use somebody to just help me take care of business." I said, "You're on!" And so I did that for two years. It was like fielding batting practice—he'd hit out there and I'd catch it. And what was great was that I worked with two orchestras. I worked for my brother, but also dealt with the big orchestra, where he was part of the overall machinery, and the small orchestra, where he was the music director.

TMW: What kinds of things were you doing?

JB: The wonderful thing was, I really was dealing with the musical production side. I did a lot of library work. He and I still share jokes about certain pieces where I would rant and rave about putting in bowings. But as a result of this "hands-on" experience I became very compulsive about production details. Tom directed all the children's concerts and also created a special series—at that time orchestras were experimenting with movies and lights and this and that. So I became very involved in concert production in Indianapolis and worked a lot with the stage crew and the music library.

Tom is very involved in contemporary music; he is a composer as well as a conductor. I catalogued all of his recordings and his scores—a huge job. But that alone gave me a solid sense of repertoire. Because I did not study music history per se, I would say that the cataloguing, more than anything, gave me a real feeling for the scope of the repertoire. Also, the [Indianapolis] Symphony was in transition at that time; the orchestra was going through some growing pains and I had a wonderful kind of bird's-eye view. It's hard to explain on a résumé, but those two years backstage were probably the most valuable apprenticeship I could have had.

TMW: Hands-on, with the artistic side emphasized. Is this typical of the way careers grow for your colleagues?

JB: I think what was typical until the last couple of years is that each person had his own individual experience. You know, now we have [internship] programs, and there are Master's degree programs in arts administration—the career path is better defined. But in the "old days"—it's only fourteen years ago or so!—each person found his or her own way.

TMW: And that kind of on-the-job training lets you touch bases with many areas that people who go through more formal programs nowadays won't touch if the area is already restricted and specialized. How many people training for orchestra management would do a stint as a music librarian, for example?

JB: I don't know; many, I hope. I think it's important. I have my opinions about the academic approach to orchestra management. Schools offer marketing and all sorts of courses. It may be effective for arts council work or other areas of arts administration, but I really think you also have to be there to learn orchestra management. Learning to work with people is essential.

TMW: Would you know the names of any schools in this country that would grant a degree in orchestra management?

JB: No, not per se. The best place to really focus in on that is through the opportunities the ASOL makes available. They have various [orchestra management] seminars and workshops, in addition to their year-long fellowship program. For arts administration degrees, however, there are several good programs—Wisconsin, Yale, University of Cincinnati, and Duke, just to name a few.

TMW: Would you say that the timing of the way your life plan unfolded was essentially typical of your colleagues in orchestra management? Even if the career path was not exactly the same, you were able almost directly to begin on the job.

JB: Well, to some extent. What happened next was really a fluke, and I think it gave me a leg up early on. After the two years in Indianapolis I wanted to work directly for an orchestra. I went to an [ASOL] National Conference to look for a job, discovered three or four opportunities, and decided to accept a position described as "Assistant to the Manager"—whatever that is—in Richmond, Virginia, because that was "East."—Or so I thought; perspective is a wonderful thing! But I went to Richmond and I stayed there for eight years, and I love Richmond very much.

I was the "new girl in the office" for two months, but that wasn't why I moved there, so we chatted about what my responsibilities would be. It was a small orchestra; at that time it had about a $450,000 budget. There was no one on the staff doing publicity, so I offered to do publicity and public relations. (I had had some really good learning experience with excellent PR people in Indianapolis, including working with Sue Staton, a woman who is now the Indianapolis Symphony Orchestra assistant general manager and for whom I have a great deal of respect.) Because there never had been a PR position in Richmond, I was able to learn on the job and get by alright. I worked very hard to organize a staff position for public relations and publicity, and I wrote program notes, too.

At the end of that season there was some staff turnover. In fact, *I* was getting ready to leave, having accepted a job on the public relations staff of the Cincinnati Symphony. But right at that point the manager's job opened up in Richmond and the Board offered me the opportunity to interview.

Let's face it: This was the South. I was 24. I was a woman. I was a Yankee. I talked real fast and gestured a lot, because I'm from an Italian background. I hadn't managed an orchestra, and that one was facing some big problems right at that moment. But the gentleman who was the president of the Board at the time decided to take a chance with me. I figured he and the Board couldn't be so bad if they'd take that kind of risk, and so I stayed.

It was a tremendous experience. I had to learn a lot and quickly, but I learned to put some faith in my common sense and instincts—and had a good seven subsequent years as manager, and the orchestra grew well.

I developed strong feelings about how you treat the musicians—collectively, and individually, and all year round—not just at contract time. There are so many war stories in our profession, and I'm not really sure why that is—whether they simply rise to the surface, or whether in the past there really was some major problem in perceiving the musicians from the management standpoint. My best theory is that people don't use enough decent common sense and they don't treat others the way they either espouse or would want to be treated. It takes a lot of work to keep a hundred people well organized and apprised of what's going on. There are simple rules like, if it's in the contract, you follow it. If you don't like it, change it the next time around, but in the meantime live with it—*no* exceptions. Don't cut corners or play dumb. That's common sense; obviously, it's your own integrity on the line.

You know, contracts are like the iconography of a painting; you can read a contract and see where all the great hassles have occurred. Some contracts have bizarre things—pages devoted to one particular process or detail, because there was a giant problem or impasse in that area some years before. There's a school of labor relations that says that negotiating a contract takes place every day that you're *not* negotiating: every day you're living that contract. I think that's true. And it sets a whole attitude when you get down to the table. It doesn't mean that things are sweetness and light, but it does at least help people deal with each other more rationally because there is greater credibility and trust built up. I personally prefer thinking in the long term, although what we do is a million nuts and bolts.

Some things I had learned in Indianapolis. I can remember my brother being so frustrated when he would be told by the management, "Now, when it comes to these kiddie concerts you can't use harp and you can't use piano, because we have to pay them extra." Tom would want to do *Petrouchka*, he'd want to do some Copland; you know—the things that are going to turn the kids on. And so I decided back then that was stupid—that *that's* the time when you should invest a little bit. You're not going to short-change there.

TMW: Artistically, you mean.

JB: Yes. Of course you're not going to do the *Alpine Symphony* for the kids! But you've got to weigh all the factors; ultimately I try to go by my basic feelings on what's important. You know, managers have style and technique just like musicians.

TMW: Talking about your style. Several times you've emphasized the pragmatic nature of your job, and your approach to it seems to be to try to be fair with everyone, to try to look at the situation clearly and treat things as a series of nuts and bolts—items that can be dealt with by rational human beings. That's a very fair approach. There doesn't seem to be any sort of personal aura or starving ego or power muscles that you're exercising or anything like that, that one might find in some people who hold the title "manager."

JB: Indeed, one does find that. It's special that David [Hyslop] and I share these same feelings. But sometimes that has its shortcomings. Neither of us loves to go out after every single concert and have a big dinner or spend lots of time socializing, which one really must do. But you're right; I see power as something that is responsibility. You're responsible for your musicians. It's crucial to realize that when a distinguished soloist comes into town, he or she gives a great performance, gets on the plane the next day and goes away, but the orchestra is coming in the next morning maybe for children's concerts or their next rehearsal, and the next rehearsal, and the next—day in and day out. So where do your responsibilities really lie? In the long term they lie first and foremost with your own people.

WOMEN IN ORCHESTRA MANAGEMENT

TMW: It appears again that your personal style and just the way you go about your ordinary business mesh well with what this huge undefined job of being manager of an orchestra seems to require. You are on call all day and all night. How does this very full job commitment square away with the private person, with the demands of home life? Have you at any point had to make sacrifices in either domain to satisfy a requirement within the other—personal or professional?

JB: That's a good question. Yes. . . . How can I put this? Leading a social life is not easy. It starts from the very first moment of somebody being a bit inhibited by a woman who comes along as "the manager of the Symphony." And truthfully it's a high-intensity job. I try to be less so; but one is oneself, and you never realize how strong that might be to other people.

There are so many factors that affect personal life. Part of it is working until 10:00 P.M. most nights. There's no such thing really as having a regular day off—or dare we even suggest two days off! And days when I *can* take personal time I have to go to the hardware store!

Never really being able to wind down can also make personal time difficult. Very honestly, when you do get together with somebody, you're "on"—still in fifth gear, and that can put a strain on personal relationships. Most of my friends and the people that I really get on best with are people in the music world. When you're so involved in your work, it happens that way.

TMW: Do you foresee at any point being able to amalgamate a fuller home life, possibly including children?

JB: I just don't know. I love children, but I already feel negligent about my two wonderful, self-sufficient Siamese cats!

TMW: More generally, do you know of any of your female colleagues who are orchestra managers who have families?

JB: I know of some. Actually, I've never thought about that, because there are more women managers than people realize.

TMW: About how many is this? Are you talking about 15 orchestras, 20 orchestras?

JB: From the big regionals on up—about 40 orchestras—there are quite a few women managers, and I can think of only a few who are married. As for children, I don't know. I know there are women in public relations or other areas of the operation with children. They talk about "super-women." And that is a fair term. People ask me, "Oh, how do you do what you do?"—but I don't think it's *anything* when I think of other women who add the dimension of being responsible to a family—a spouse and children.

TMW: Let's focus for a moment on other people's perception of you in your professional capacity. After being hired as manager of the Richmond Symphony, did being a woman orchestra manager pose any special difficulties in your relations with the Board members, orchestra musicians, or other professionals you were dealing with on a day-to-day basis? Or was it all so new that you weren't aware of "special" problems?

JB: I never felt that I had problems there because I was a *woman* manager, and it could have been for the reason you suggest. When the appointment occurred, my first thought was, "This Board of Directors can't be that conservative if they're hiring me!" There were some women on the Board, and I know in retrospect that some of them supported me. Also, at that time there had been such turnover that the Board was happy to have someone with even one year there for continuity. And I'm sure they were taking a risk and appropriately so. Not necessarily because I was a woman. But I was willing to take on the job at a very modest salary. I had no experience, you know.

TMW: How did that salary compare with the salary of the person who had just left? Was it on the par?

JB: Oh no. Mine was much lower. And when I left after eight years it was still below the par. But during those years things had gone well and I really felt blessed with that experience. We never had any really bad catastrophes; I didn't make too many mistakes. And I left with a lot of love and affection for Richmond and the people, and there was a good feeling in return. When I left they took a long time finding a new manager, and I know the Board paid a substantially higher salary than I had had, i.e., the "going rate."

TMW: Was your successor a male or female?

JB: Male. You could say, "Well, there you see, a man comes in and demands a higher salary because he has a wife and children." But there are two other things that are facts of life. When somebody is in a job for eight years, and starts very low, no matter how determined or well-intentioned an employer is to raise that salary, it's still hard for that employer—the Board or CEO—to swallow it when you say, "Look, I want $3,000 more or $5,000 more this year to adjust my salary." I know; *I've* had subordinates ask for that. I've made a conscious effort to make appropriate adjustments [with employees in Saint Louis], but it's still hard—particularly in our unchanging context of nonprofit. It's in the process of moving from job to job that you really jack up your salary to the competitive level. The career [of orchestra management] was evolving when I was in Richmond. I saw the salaries of other managers go from being maybe a little bit more than mine to a lot more than mine just because there was a lot of movement, and I hadn't moved. That was *definitely* a part of it. I could have demanded more, I suppose, and probably should have. But I was young and it was all new to me.

TMW: Is seven years considered a long tenure as an orchestra manager?

JB: It was fairly healthy.

TMW: Do you think it's harder for women to move around, compared with men? Do families make it more difficult, or is that even an issue?

JB: That's up to the women, isn't it? I mean, if they're not attached, no, but if they are attached it may be harder, depending on that attachment. The problem with orchestra management, like orchestra playing and conducting, is that there's usually only one job in every town. And if you want to change jobs you have to go from town to town—it's like journalism or sports. Relocation then becomes an issue. If a woman has a husband, who's going to move for whom? It just so happens that in this profession, you can't go across town and get a job with the competition. I've seen all the variations—husbands moving or staying put for wives and, of course, vice versa.

TMW: I know that we have a pretty good network for *composers* in this country through various organizations; composers at various career stages can always network and pool their thinking so as to know how to make the best next step. Is there any kind of network for orchestra managers in this country?

JB: Yes. There are orchestra managers' associations organized according to the ASOL's budget classifications: the Metropolitan Orchestra Manager's Association, the Regional Manager's Association, the Major Orchestra Manager's Association, etc. Then within that, you find people networking—for example, executive directors and other peer groups involved with orchestras that have 52-week seasons and that make recordings. And this group of ten or twelve gets together on its own and shares common concerns. In the last couple of years, very informally, five or six of my counterparts that I know best—the "number twos" in certain orchestras—have gotten together for an annual dinner at the ASOL National Conference. And there's more of that encouraged in the senior staff levels, too. It's really important, because in fact you can't go down and pick the brains of the guy at the Jaycee meeting; there just aren't many local colleagues to relate to.

TMW: In the course of your background as you sketched it out there was no real figure of mentor: another working, practicing orchestra manager on whom you modeled yourself. Would you say that your brother was your mentor, perhaps, or was there anyone on the staff of the Indianapolis Symphony with whom you worked particularly closely?

JB: Well, I think in many ways my brother was a mentor because he encouraged me in this field. To me a mentor in many ways sets little guideposts—you know, "Turn left here," so you go off in that direction. And my brother made me aware of certain things that set values for me in the business of dealing with the musicians and the artistic product, which I think is really important. The woman I mentioned before, Sue Staton, who at the time was director of public relations with the Indianapolis Symphony, was—and is—a real professional. Very fastidious. Very detail oriented. Very precise. I learned a great deal from her. There was another public relations person in Indianapolis at the time who freelanced—she didn't work with the Symphony, but handled a lot of special promotional events. And I learned a lot from her, particularly about timing and communication.

Frankly, at the time there were general managers in both Fort Wayne and in Indianapolis who were *reverse* mentors. I learned a lot about what *not* to do from observing work styles that struck me as being very wrong, seeing things that just didn't make sense.

TMW: How about yourself as an example, either during your time in Richmond or now in Saint Louis. Do young people come to you to ask for career guidelines or suggestions?

JB: Yes, it happens a lot. But I don't think it's unique to me, certainly. It happens to the more visible people—people who are in number one or number two positions with the high profile orchestras, and even the smaller ones. If there are young people in any particular town and if they have initiative, they will go and talk to that town's orchestra manager. They need to know that it's not all glamour, not at all. It's a lot of hard work and it's a lot of long hours.

When people come and ask about the profession, I try to give them a broad and realistic view and try to compensate for star dust in the eyes, or try to enlighten the kind of person who thinks that they're going to make a big financial killing. Also, you've *got* to understand the *other* point of view to be an effective orchestra manager. So one better adjust one's frame of reference and recenter the zero point, because otherwise you go crazy real fast. And I don't mean just a superficial adjustment. Otherwise you'll be outraged by the fact that, for example, an orchestra can only travel four hours a day. But have you ever driven on a bus four hours a day and then tried to generate the kind of energy that's required to make an outstanding performance? Then who's accused in the next morning's newspaper of sounding a little road-weary—the management or the orchestra?

You know, there's a lot of validity to almost everything behind a classic orchestra problem. Our personnel manager [in Saint Louis] once said, "In an orchestra like ours there are 101 musicians. That's larger than a lot of small towns, and you're going to get a lot of different people with a lot of different problems and points of view." They come from many different places, they have different values, different personalities. And you just have to be ready to deal with them in as objective a way as possible, without having negative feelings.

TMW: When young people come to you who think they might enter the field of orchestra management and you remove the veil from their eyes about the essence of the profession, is there anything in particular that you tell the young *women* who come to you that is extra or differentiated from what you tell the men?

JB: Not automatically, unless they ask. If I'm asked about being a woman in the profession and should a woman enter into it, I say "yes," because I think women make excellent managers, for several reasons: The "detail" nature of the job and its whole ego orientation—the need to deal with many potentially conflicting demands—suits a female perspective well. I think it's a profession that very much needs good people. It's sort of like musicians in orchestras. You know, auditions are held behind screens now, which is important. But still, the musicians in the orchestra and the conductors really want and need the best person to fill that position, and by God, women are filling the orchestras. It's wonderful.

TMW: What percentage of Saint Louis's complement of orchestra members are women?

JB: A third. We have the only [female] principal trumpet in a Major orchestra. Our principal second violin and principal harp are women. And we have many women as associate and assistant principal strings, assistant principal oboe, assistant principal flute, second flute, and second clarinet; right now on this [East Coast] tour, our assistant principal horn is a woman. And having these women in the orchestra makes a difference. We try to be innovative. Last year we had three pregnant women in the orchestra.

Let's talk about infants in the orchestra families. We had three bouncing babies last year, and all three women wanted to nurse their babies, a perfectly legitimate desire. Our personnel manager is very sensitive, and he tries hard to be fair to the women. Well, we ended up taking a little bitty dressing room and turning it into a nursery. One of the women in the orchestra had a relative who came down and took care of all the babies during the rehearsals. And the funniest thing happened—I have to tell this story. One day our development director, who doesn't hang around the dressing rooms that much, was giving some visitors a tour of our hall, Powell Hall, showing the conductor's room, the concertmaster's dressing room, the women's dressing rooms. He opened a door and there was a crib and Pampers all over and it was decked out with toys, and he had no idea what was going on. He had stumbled into the nursery!

But there were also some problems, because the women's dressing rooms are in one contained area. And other women, who certainly love babies, didn't necessarily want to hear one crying when they wanted to warm up for a concert. They are professionals, too; it was a very delicate problem. Right now we have two pregnancies; we're about to have a baby in May, and we're going to have another one in October, and I suspect that there may be others on the way. So we're going to have to deal with this again, and it will be a trickier problem.

TMW: But it maintains the morale of the group. Do you know if the arrangements that were made to accommodate the newborns in your orchestra are common to the other large orchestras in this country?

JB: Our particular approach? I don't know. I think it was an innovation.

TMW: It shows an extreme willingness on the part of the management to accommodate the players' needs instead of just drawing a hard line and saying, "no children in the building."

JB: Well, I'll tell you something, though. I try to be consistent, and sometimes that means not *looking* consistent. In our discussion about terms for our European tour, some people brought up the desire to take the babies. The staff involved was not thrilled with this, and I was among the most adamant, because it's going to be a rigorous experience. We're going for the first time, and I don't think it's a place for babies. I know what's involved on tour and am sure that, in some way, we would have to expend some of our energy dealing with the babies. Certainly the parents would, but they are professionals too and have to play five or six concerts a week. And that comes first on tour. That's the other side of being a woman; you've got to be professional. Well, we made a reasonable compromise—no children under twelve.

TMW: But the fact is that the matter was considered and hashed out thoroughly, just as the matter of having newborns within the building during rehearsals was accommodated. Do you think that had to do with your being a woman orchestra manager? Do you think that similar concern would have been exhibited by a male orchestra manager?

JB: That's hard to say. How much consideration somebody gives, how thoughtful a person is about a problem—is that sex linked? I hope not!

TMW: How about with other orchestras? For example, in some European countries there is a very definite bias against hiring women in orchestras just because of pregnancy and children as "complicating" factors.

JB: I am sure. Certainly some people have had problems with that—even some women [managers]. . . . The perception of the women in our orchestra [of their long-term treatment], particularly those who have been here more than eight or so years, is not good in terms of previous management. I wasn't there, so I don't know; but there was a feeling expressed. And when I looked at the salaries of the overscale people—the titled players and so forth—and when David [Hyslop] got there and he looked at them, we could see disparities.

This gets back to the question of "What's the job?" When I was forming my ideas about this work, my feeling in a nutshell was that our job is to provide the best working conditions to make the music. That doesn't include just the right temperature and the right lights and the right music and the right chairs (if you can find them). It means having a full house. It means staying solvent, developing income. It means having community support. These are all working conditions that help the artist function as well as he can, unencumbered from all those day-to-day things. On tour, it means having the hotels ready, and talking to mother nature and arranging good weather. . . . It means all these things. . . . In an orchestra there are 101 people, 101 opinions, and somebody's got to decide at some point what's best for everybody, or what's optimum.

That's where a good working relationship with an orchestra committee is essential. When they get involved they start beginning to make discretionary decisions on their own and dissuading somebody from their complaint as opposed to automatically presenting it.

TMW: Do you think that there is a relationship between you and the presence of women in other key positions within an orchestra organization? For instance, the Saint Louis Symphony has had conductors Catherine Comet and Antonia Joy Wilson.

JB: As Exxon/Arts Endowment Conductor and Affiliate Artist Conducting Assistant, respectively. I think some of the women in the Orchestra feel good about that. I know that when I first arrived in Saint Louis, some of the women in the Orchestra expressed to me a personal pleasure to see a woman as a manager. They weren't aware that it was a possibility.

I remember the conducting auditions we had to appoint someone as our Exxon/Arts Endowment conductor. In the preliminary round there were seven candidates, and *four* of them were women. First of all, in just the audition everyone said, "Gee, seven people, and four women." The cut to the finals were three women, and that *really* blew people's minds. I can remember the musicians coming off the stage, and a lot of the women in the orchestra were gloating. I mean, how could you not? It was great. It was also great, though, that the orchestra—which contained 65 men—had chosen these three women. They chose the people they thought had the best talent. And I say *they* chose them, because we do work very much by consensus, especially in the area of auditioning talent—conducting or instrumental. Leonard [Statkin] would not want to choose a conductor that he didn't think the orchestra would be happy with, because he knows they're the people who are going to work under this person.

It was terrific having Catherine [Comet] on the Saint Louis conducting staff. She has a very strong presence on the podium. But some presenters in small Missouri towns were put off by a woman conductor. And what was my reaction to their attitude? I was mad but had to take it; it was a reality. I don't agree with it, of course. But then again, is it her own particular technique? Is it that combined with being a woman? And other presenters were thrilled with her. She's now having a huge success as associate conductor of the Baltimore Symphony Orchestra and making quite a name as a guest conductor, too.

TMW: You mentioned that when you were hired for the position in Saint Louis, several women in the orchestra approached you to say how glad they were that you were hired, specifically being a woman, and that they didn't know that was possible. Has this changed? Can you say something about women's visibility in your profession?

JB: Well, that was only four years ago [1980]. First, a clarification. Usually, most musicians play things close to the chest, especially with management. They are sizing you up, and so forth. They don't come up and say, "How happy I am. . . . " When I started work here I set up a meeting with each orchestra member. It took months to meet them and say, "Hello, this is me; who and how are you?" but I did it just to have a sense of who they were as individuals and make sure I knew names and faces. I didn't realize it, but it meant a lot more. It came across as being very unusual and very progressive.

Now, getting back to your other question. There have been many women in the ASOL Orchestra Management Fellowship Program in the last four years, and there are quite a few orchestras involved. Each Fellow visits several orchestras. And the people in each orchestra more or less have a perception that this person is around—that they're a Fellow, they're being trained for management; and if the orchestra participates in the program year after year, slowly the message gets through.

TWM: But haven't there also been a lot of women involved at the professional level, in addition to the internship program?

JB: Why, sure. But the musicians don't necessarily know that. A musician in an orchestra knows his part. His seat. His stand partner. His section. His repertoire. His conductor. He doesn't spend time thinking on a cosmic level at all. Their whole professional lives are focused on a very small piece of space, and rightly so. They will ask, "What time is the concert tonight? What is the repertoire tonight?" It doesn't mean they're irresponsible. It's just the way that they function—one step at a time.

TMW: So unless they come in personal contact with women either as interns or as manager, they really are not aware of women in orchestra management?

JB: Or unless they have travelled from orchestra to orchestra. But in an orchestra like ours, you don't have people going in and out of the Orchestra every year. You have a small amount of turnover. The average tenure in our orchestra is somewhere around 15 or 18 years. The average age is 42. The point is, a hell of a lot of them have been there since they were whippersnappers, and that's what they know—the Saint Louis Symphony.

TMW: You mentioned before that orchestra management is a profession that seems eminently suited to women. And you've mentioned the strong presence of women both as managers and players in American orchestras. When are we going to see a woman orchestra manager in one of the "big five" orchestras?[4]

JB: You're talking about the "number one" person? The so-called Chief Executive Officer?

TMW: That's right.

JB: I don't know. I wonder myself. First of all, the Chief Executive Officer in a "big five" orchestra is the person responsible for an organization whose annual budget is upwards of ten or twelve million dollars. It's the person who's *not* doing all the nuts and bolts, but is the person responsible for the orchestra's long-range planning, financing, and big-level wheeling and dealing in the big cities. That is the person who's dealing with the Board of Directors more than with the orchestra players. So it becomes a question of guiding, facilitating, and working well with the people who in many cases are, in one way or another, the entrenched leaders of the community. Infrequently they are Young Turks—usually they are members of the old guard. You're talking about the serious establishment. It's one thing to talk about women being hired by executive directors such as David [Hyslop] to be the number two person, as opposed to women being hired by the influential leaders of the community, who are still more conservative and traditional. They also don't relate to women as peers. Symphony leaders epitomize the profile of a symphony subscriber. They are people who are 45 and over, at a high socioeconomic level, and very well educated. If they are men, they are the heads of large corporations, and so forth. So it becomes the same problem as all of those good women bank vice presidents have—when are they going to be presidents of banks? Or take any other profession that you want—a terrific woman surgeon, is she going to be the chief of the hospital? It's that question.

TMW: But we've seen this problem dealt with from two different directions in the world of opera. We have Beverly Sills, who rose through the ranks as performer-turned-executive-director of New York City Opera. We have Sarah Caldwell, who has built an opera company in her own image in Boston and who makes the executive decisions and the artistic decisions and is very active still on the podium.

JB: Well, in both of those cases I would say that their celebrity level—their visibility level—has a great deal to do with it. Beverly Sills is one of the most famous divas/celebrities, and men and women react in a certain way to celebrities. Sarah Caldwell, you're right, is a major presence and force and she built that. Just like women's banks; people went out and said, "I'm tired of not getting a business loan. I'm going to start my own bank." But what you're talking about, is about doing it in an established way. More appropriate to your point is the Chicago Lyric Opera, where you have people like Carol Fox, who rose through the ranks administratively *in management*. Your question really should be, "When is a normal Board of Directors going to consider and *hire* a woman in management?" The answer should be, "When the woman is the best candidate for that position." Now the question is, are they there, and are they being overlooked? I don't know. I do know that there are social considerations that Boards of Directors will have. Just think about what I call the on-duty social aspects of the job. I'll ask you a question. Are single women in chic restaurants yet treated exactly the same way as the couples or the men? It's better than it used to be, but is it exactly the same?

TMW: You're talking about stepping out. It's a double concern. One is, do the women put themselves forth to be in such circumstances, and number two, what is their reception when they do? Do you think that if a woman was nominated to such a position—manager of one of the "big five" orchestras—being the first woman, would she receive as fair a shake as all the male candidates?

JB: I really don't know. I wonder. I can't say, "Yes, sure." And it would be wrong to make the assumption "No." I guess I have a healthy, cautious feeling about it right now.

TMW: The final question. About how much more experience or how many more years would you need under your belt before you yourself might start thinking to look toward the very top positions in orchestra management?

JB: That's a question that I am wrestling with right now. It's certainly not because I'm unhappy; it's because I *am* happy. I'll explain. First of all, I feel a bit spoiled in terms of the things that really count: the quality of the orchestra; rapport with the orchestra, the music director, and executive director—I should almost put them at the top; and my broad range of authority. We work really well together. I doubt if I could work better with anyone else. Remember, the buck stopped with me for seven years [in Richmond]. And a lot of people said, "Are you going to be able to handle being 'number two'?" Well, yes, I am able to handle it. My question is, how badly do I want to be a "number one?" It means going back to an orchestra that plays less well than Saint Louis in order to prove that I can handle it. The logical path for me right now would be either to make some spectacular jump to the "number two" spot in a much bigger orchestra, or else to go on to a slightly smaller orchestra as the "number one" person.

One of the things that has crossed my mind in the past is that some woman needs to be the first. But I have decided that that is a *terrible* reason to do it. There are fatal flaws built in, playing right into certain other traps that women have about being double-and triple-achievers. When you add in "What are you gratified by? What do you want from your life?" and so on, you see that just being a "first" would really be a stupid reason for doing something. It's probable that present conditions make it less likely that the "Cosmos Philharmonia" will call and ask me to head it up. But all I can say, we'll see. And when I decide that's the thing that I want to do, I'll give it my best shot.

NOTES

1. The American Symphony Orchestra League is the national service association for North America's symphony orchestras. It classifies orchestras according to their function and the size of their annual operating income: Youth, College, Community, Urban, Metropolitan, Regional, and Major orchestras.

2. Affiliated Artists, a national nonprofit arts organization, is the largest producer of performing artists residencies in the United States. For further information about its Conductors Program, see Chapter 3. Since 1980 the American Symphony Orchestra League has administered the Orchestra Management Fellowship Program, which seeks to identify and train aspiring orchestra managers. As of January 1985, 20 of the League's 38 Orchestra Management Fellows have been women.

3. Joseph Schwantner served as composer-in-residence with the Saint Louis Symphony Orchestra for a full 3-year term from 1 September 1982 through 31 August 1985 under the auspices of the Meet the Composer program. On 1 September 1985, Joan Tower began her term as composer-in-residence of the Saint Louis Symphony Orchestra under the same program. Meet the Composer is funded by Exxon Corporation, The Rockefeller Foundation, and the National Endowment for the Arts.

4. The New York Philharmonic, Philadelphia Orchestra, Boston Symphony Orchestra, Cleveland Orchestra, and the Chicago Symphony Orchestra are traditionally referred to as the "big five" orchestras of the United States.

Editor's Note: Since the date of this interview, the Saint Louis Symphony Orchestra has added to its major achievements the successful completion of its first European tour; a successful series of recordings for Angel records; 2 Grammy awards, and, together with the Houston Symphony Orchestra, has received a major grant from the National Endowment for the Arts and Southwestern Bell Foundation to participate in a pilot touring program involving 5 midwestern states in a unique funding partnership between the federal government and a private corporation. In November 1986, the Orchestra will embark on its first Far East tour, with performances in Japan and Hong Kong.

3

Equal Opportunity—Assessing Women's Presence in the Exxon/Arts Endowment Conductors Program: An Interview with Jesse Rosen

Affiliate Artists Inc. is a national, nonprofit organization dedicated to the career development of American professional solo performers of all disciplines and to expansion of audiences and sources of support for the arts. It is the leading producer of residencies for performing artists in the United States.

The Exxon/Arts Endowment Conductors Program, developed and administered by Affiliate Artists Inc., is a long-range effort designed to address the problems of career development faced by conductors in the early stages of their professional careers. It is a unique cooperative effort on the part of Exxon Corporation, the National Endowment for the Arts, and leading orchestras and opera companies throughout the country to develop music directors for American symphony orchestras.

The program is designed to bridge the gap between formal training and full-time professional employment by offering up-and-coming conductors on-the-job training with leading musical organizations. Participating conductors are given the opportunity to perform on a full-season basis for up to three years with a major symphony orchestra under the guidance and supervision of both the artistic and administrative staffs of their host orchestra. This varied type of experience, musical and administrative, provides the background that must be acquired by potential music directors.

Each Exxon/Arts Endowment position is created especially to advance and develop the career of the participating conductor. The music directors of the participating orchestras meet regularly with their Exxon conductors to discuss repertoire, program planning, and career counseling; they also observe the Exxon conductors in rehearsal and performance. (Each season the Exxon conductors will conduct approximately 80-100 services with their orchestras, in addition to exchange concerts with other orchestras participating in the program.) And, through their involvement in various nonmusical activities (artistic planning, fund-raising, board relations, etc.), Exxon appointees gain an overview and understanding of the complete operations of their host orchestras.

Each year Affiliate Artists receives grants from Exxon Corporation and the National Endowment for the Arts to cover the costs of operating the program and to pay a portion of each conductor's salary. In addition, participating orchestras contribute funds toward the conductor's salary, which is stipulated to total $20,000 the first year and increases to $22,000 and $24,000 in years two and three.

In 1980 Affiliate Artists instituted a second tier of the program, referred to as Conducting Assistantships, for fledgling conductors who have had little, if any, professional experience. Designed to help the conductor who has just completed formal training, the conducting Assistantships concentrate on devising residencies for talented newcomers, usually for a period of one or two years. Funding for the project was originally to come from a variety of sources, but it has since been assumed by the Exxon Corporation and the National Endowment for the Arts.

Both tiers of the program employ virtually the same annual selection process: a staged sequence that is rigorous, technical, and highly competitive. After an initial screening of career materials, applicants are interviewed and, whenever possible, observed in performance or audition. Selected candidates are then invited to audition for specific conducting posts. To qualify for a position, these candidates are interviewed and heard by the music directors, managers, and musicians of the participating orchestras.

From 1973 through 1984 a total of 33 conductors were placed in full-time residencies under the Exxon/Arts Endowment Conductors Program. An additional 8 conductors were awarded residencies through Exxon/Arts Endowment Conducting Assistantships in the period ending with spring season 1985.

Exxon/Arts Endowment Conductors Program Appointees

Name	Program Affiliation
David Agler	San Francisco Opera 1980, 1981
Christian Badea	National Symphony Orchestra 1978, 1979
Alan Balter	Baltimore Symphony Orchestra 1980, 1981, 1982
Victoria Bond	Pittsburgh Symphony Orchestra 1979, 1980
Catherine Comet	St. Louis Symphony Orchestra 1982, 1983, 1984
Myung-Whun Chung	Los Angeles Philharmonic/Young Musicians Foundation Debut Orchestra 1979, 1980, 1981
John Covelli	Milwaukee Symphony Orchestra 1974, 1975, 1976

Name	**Program Affiliation**
Enrique Diemecke	Rochester Philharmonic 1984, 1985
John DeMain	St. Paul Chamber Orchestra 1974, 1975
Raymond Harvey	Indianapolis Symphony Orchestra 1981, 1982, 1983
C. William Harwood	Houston Symphony Orchestra/ Houston Grand Opera 1978, 1979, 1980
Paulette Haupt-Nolen	San Francisco Opera 1978
Charles Ketcham	San Diego Symphony Orchestra 1974, 1975, 1976
Sung Kwak	Atlanta Symphony Orchestra 1978, 1979, 1980
Jahja Ling	San Francisco Symphony Orchestra 1983, 1984
Andrew Litton	National Symphony Orchestra 1983, 1984, 1985
George Manahan	New Jersey Symphony Orchestra 1982
William McGlaughlin	St. Paul Chamber Orchestra 1976, 1977, 1978
Thomas Michalak	Pittsburgh Symphony Orchestra 1975, 1976, 1977
Michael Morgan	St. Louis Symphony Orchestra 1981
Michael Palmer	Atlanta Symphony Orchestra 1975, 1976, 1977
Peter Perret	Buffalo Philharmonic Orchestra 1977, 1978, 1979
James Setapen	Denver Symphony Orchestra 1981, 1982, 1983
Murry Sidlin	National Symphony Orchestra 1974, 1975, 1976
Calvin Simmons	Los Angeles Philharmonic/Young Musicians Foundation Debut Orchestra 1976, 1977, 1978
David Stahl	Cincinnati Symphony Orchestra 1977, 1978, 1979

Name	Program Affiliation
Neal Stulberg	Los Angeles Philharmonic 1984, 1985
Clark Suttle	Buffalo Philharmonic Orchestra 1980, 1981, 1982
Carl Topilow	Denver Symphony Orchestra 1977, 1978, 1979
Kirk Trevor	Dallas Symphony Orchestra 1983, 1984, 1985
Christopher Wilkins	Cleveland Orchestra 1984, 1985
Hugh Wolff	National Symphony Orchestra 1980, 1981, 1982
Gerhardt Zimmermann	St. Louis Symphony Orchestra 1976, 1977, 1978

Affiliate Artists Conducting Assistants Project

Name	Program Affiliation
Neal Gittleman	Oregon Symphony Orchestra 1984, 1985
David Milnes	San Francisco Symphony Orchestra 1985
James Orent	Erie Philharmonic 1981
Stephen Stein	Indianapolis Symphony Orchestra 1984, 1985
Christopher Wilkins	Oregon Symphony Orchestra 1983
Antonia Joy Wilson	St. Louis Symphony Orchestra 1982, 1983
Rachael Worby	Spokane Symphony Orchestra 1983
Tsung Yeh	Saint Louis Symphony Orchestra 1985

Jesse Rosen, Director of both conducting programs for Affiliate Artists, was interviewed by Judith Zaimont for *The Musical Woman,* in December 1983 and February 1984 specifically to discuss the presence of women as applicants and appointees in these programs. A transcript of these interviews follows.

The Musical Woman: I am talking with Mr. Jesse Rosen of Affiliate Artists, the administrator and director of the Exxon/Arts Endowment Conductors Program as well as the Affiliate Artists Conducting Assistants Project. It really seems that the two programs operate in a very similar fashion, even though the Conducting Assistants Project came into being several years after the Conductors Program. Is this true?

Jesse Rosen: Absolutely. When we started thinking about [the Conducting Assistants Project] we were looking for an additional sponsor, a corporate or foundation sponsor, which led us to conceive of it as a separate program from the current Exxon/Arts Endowment Conductors Program. As it turned out, we wound up creating the Conducting Assistants posts through additional funding from the Exxon and the Arts Endowment, so there was no need, from a sponsor accrediting point of view, to think of it as a different program. It's really one mechanism for conductors and orchestras of varying ranges and sizes.

TMW: I noticed in the press material on James Orent, the first appointee under [the Assistants] program, that the funding was provided by the orchestra and the NEA. However, in the material about Antonia Joy Wilson, there was some mention of the Ford Foundation stepping in to fund her particular residency.

JR: The way that happened was that Ford was the foundation that we had in mind, initially, to fund a separate conducting assistants program. Ford approached us and said that they were interested in doing something for women conductors and would we consider the idea.

TMW: So Ford came specifically about women. Was it women and minorities or just women absolutely?

JR: First it was women, then it became women and minorities. We said to Ford, after having sort of general discussions about the problems of women entering the conducting field, that we know a number of women conductors who are wanting to enter the field who are not yet ready yet to go into our program, the Exxon Program. However, they *would* be ready for a program for conductors at the level before that, which up until that point we had been unable to work with. (The Exxon Program is set up for conductors who have been pretty much welcomed to a major orchestra—who do about 40, 50, 60 concerts a year usually including some subscription concerts and tours.) We were finding in our auditions conductors who were very talented but simply didn't have enough experience yet, and we were looking for some way to help them; and a number of those conductors that we were seeing who were talented but didn't have experience enough happened to be women. So we said to Ford, we could start a conducting assistants program and we could insure that a very high proportion of the participants would be women and minorities. Ford thought that was interesting, and then they came back and said, well, it really has to be only women and minorities or else we're not interested.

Because Ford felt very strongly that their interest really would be contingent on a program only for women and minorities, at the annual meeting of orchestra managers involved in the Exxon Program, we announced that there was a major foundation interested in working with us in a program for women conductors, and we asked very specifically what would the level of interest be if this program were only for women and minorities—unanimously, every manager said absolutely not.

TMW: I can understand that.

JR: They said they would be perfectly happy to have someone conducting their orchestra, but if the conductors come up here in a program that is named and designed and known as being only for women conductors, [the] immediate assumption is that they are not as good as other conductors, and they need some kind of remedial program.

TMW: As a service organization, Affiliate Artists obviously had to respect that reaction. I think that it sounds like your decision was a wise one, and you've certainly been able to incorporate a good number of women among the appointees.

JR: Yes, we have.

TMW: I notice in the material here, that your office sent me for the '82-'83 season, that two of the three conducting assistants were women. How about for '83-'84?

JR: Actually, there is only one woman in the [entire] program in '83-'84 and that's Catherine Comet in St. Louis. Antonia [Wilson] graduated after her two years from St. Louis and Rachael Worby's guest conducting quite a bit lately.

TMW: Well, since the two programs—stage two, very well established; and stage one, semiestablished now—are essentially of a single entity, maybe we can talk about the entire entity from now on and not have to backtrack to discuss the individual programs. The Exxon/Arts Endowment Conductors Program is concluding its tenth year now, is that correct?

JR: Well, this season that we are in now is the tenth season, '83-'84.

TMW: And so the word has really [already] gone out to all of the places around the country and abroad where likely candidates for those positions would be studying or working. Do you do any recruitment now? Do you have to do any recruitment, or do the applications just come to you?

JR: Yes and yes. We do recruit very actively and the applications do also just come to us.

TMW: About how many per year?

JR: Well, actually it seems to have been declining in the last few years, and I think that may be because in the last three or four years we have increased our dissemination of information about the program. We may have saturated the pool of aspiring conductors and potential participants in the Exxon Program. The American Symphony Orchestra League has the conductor category of "member," and there are seven or eight hundred conductor "members" of the League, and every year for the past three or four years we've done a direct mail[ing] to every one of those people, plus we do a mailing to all of the conservatories and schools of music around the country.

TMW: Aside from the emphasis in the Conducting Assistants Project, do you make any specific effort to recruit women or minorities as candidates in general?

JR: Yes . . . let me finish answering the previous question. The dissemination of information I suppose is somewhat active; it generates applications to us and we have no problem in terms of the quantity of applications. We usually have to review around 150 or 200 applications a year. However, the conducting field is not like wind players coming out of conservatories: of the 150 applicants, if there are *five* who possess the talent and the proficiency to have a professional career, that's a lot. The level of competence of young conductors seems extremely low in the United States, [among] people graduating from conservatories.

TMW: I was going to ask you about that because you are on the record as expressing that judgment for a number of years now.

JR: Consequently, what we do is we actively scout. I travel all over the country looking at conductors, and we go to conducting workshops and graduate programs all over the country and look at the people, and we'll invite people to apply, and we invite people to audition. A number of conductors who are in the program and have been in the program came through that way, rather than [formally applying by] writing up an application form and sending it in. There were people we saw in a workshop situation somewhere who we thought were talented, and we invited them to apply and then to go through the whole process. Now with women and minorities we have done that and we have just done it somewhat more extensively.

Before the Conducting Assistants Program started, if we would find a conductor who was very talented and not ready for the Exxon Program we would try to create an apprentice position for them. We would get funding elsewhere—usually the Martha Baird Rockefeller Fund was helpful with that. In two instances the conductors involved were minority conductors: Michael Morgan, who's from Washington (he's black), was placed in an apprentice position with the Buffalo Philharmonic, and he went from there to the St. Louis Symphony as

Exxon Conductor; and Charles Darden was another one (he's been working in London for the last few years)—I can't remember where we put him, but we were able to get funds from the Martha Baird Rockefeller Fund to create an apprenticeship for him. And for Victoria Bond, before she became an Exxon Conductor, we created an apprentice position for her with the Pittsburgh Symphony, which was funded by the Martha Baird Rockefeller Fund.

TMW: So that was prior to her appointment under the Exxon Program. I noticed St. Louis cropping up again and again with Michael Morgan, who you just mentioned, and Catherine Comet and Antonia Wilson. Are there other orchestras that take repeated advantage of the service that your program provides?

JR: You mean in terms of women and minorities?

TMW: No, just in general.

JR: Sure. The National Symphony has been in the program since it started in 1973. Well, Los Angeles. They began in 1976. Buffalo was in the program for six years; Denver was in the program for six years or so. St. Louis actually is not the longest—I think the National Symphony is the orchestra that has been in the program the longest. It's become a very highly sought after program for orchestras. In addition to the nine orchestras in the program, we have at least nine waiting to get in.

TMW: The application guidelines that are sent out to candidates describe a very rigorous selection process; however, there is some latitude left to have people filter into the auditions at various stages if they appear to be strongly sponsored candidates—especially, I would assume, if they are nominated directly from the orchestra. I notice that when the program began in 1973, for the first round it seems to have been people who were [already] in place who were funded.

JR: We had no mechanism to recruit or audition. It took a long time to get that started up.

TMW: In actual fact, since about 1980, for the last three seasons or so, have any of the candidates who have been placed been people who were brought to your attention by the orchestras themselves?

JR: Oh yes. The fellow we have in Washington now. . . . Actually none of them [that] have been brought to our attention [are people we] didn't know. There have been cases when the orchestra wanted someone in, who we would not have ordinarily recommended to them. A good case is Andrew Litton, who's with the National Symphony. Andrew had applied to us and I saw him conduct (I went to one of his concerts at Juilliard), and in my judgment he needed another year or two before we would look at him. But Rostropovich came to know him and became interested in seeing him audition, and he got the job . . . so.

TMW: Has that happened in the case of any of the women in the program?

Figure 3.1 Victoria Bond. Used with permission of Affiliate Artists Inc.

JR: Yes, as a matter of fact, with Antonia [Wilson]. I remember talking with Leonard Slatkin [music director of the St. Louis Symphony] about her before the audition, and Leonard had said that he had seen Antonia in Aspen and thought she should audition; I told Leonard that I'd seen her also, though I thought she was not ready yet to take the Exxon job and Leonard said "Well, I know that, but I'd like to give her a chance and just see what she does." So she auditioned, and after the audition . . . its very funny because Leonard said (Catherine [Comet] and Antonia auditioned at the same time) "I want them both; is there any way that we could take both?" and this was sort of fortuitous. It was a few months after the Ford Foundation had turned down our proposal for a conducting assistants program, and I said we might be able to do something with Ford, and I went back to Ford and said here is one situation with a woman conductor where the position could be very valuable, and the orchestra [is] very much behind her, the music director wants her: it's a situation we know—one where they will pay attention to her. So they said fine, and they funded her . . . so, yes that happens.

TMW: So it does happen.

JR: We are in a funny position because, on the one hand, we need to and want to maintain a certain sense of bureaucracy with regard to the application process—to keep it equitable and fair and give everyone a good shot at applying and interviewing and all that. But on the other hand, our primary objective in recruitment is to identify the best people. And if the best people haven't come through our process then we'd be foolish not to look at them just as well.

Catherine Comet is another good example. I had heard about Catherine, I believe, from Michael Steinberg [formerly music critic for the *Boston Globe*]. Michael heard a performance of hers at the New England Conservatory and had mentioned her to me once, and so I called her up; she was in Wisconsin at the time. She sent me a tape and some material, and I looked at her résumé and was amazed at her background. This was right around the time that we were organizing the final audition in St. Louis for the Exxon position, and I called Joan Briccetti to say I'd just gotten this tape and seen some interesting stuff on this woman Catherine Comet. I asked her to ask Leonard [Slatkin] and see what he thinks. Leonard said it would be great if they could get her; it would be terrific if she would want the job. (Leonard had gone to school with her, and they were contemporaries at Juilliard.) Anyhow, she was invited to audition; this was *after* we had already closed off the applications, reviewed them, and had done our preliminary auditions for that year.

TMW: Well, it does say in the guidelines "in addition, the music director of the orchestra may invite conductors to the final audition who have not participated in a preliminary audition." And now we know why that's there.

Could you give us something of an overview of the appointees to date—especially, how many of them have been women?

JR: I brought you some actual statistics. [See table 3.1]. They're more or less accurate; [but] I wouldn't say they're exactly the most scientifically arrived at, simply because there are a lot of aspects to our process that make it hard to view any of this activity scientifically. Although this particular question is easy to answer. Of the 30 total graduates of the program between 1973 and 1983, five, or 17 percent were women.

TMW: Five or 17 percent. It's a small sample, so that expressed as a percentage it's not an indicator of much.

What might be more helpful would be another statistic. I notice that a good many of the men appointed in the Exxon Program lasted for three years in their positions. Have any of the women in the program been hired or rehired for the full three years that the program can run?

JR: I guess Catherine Comet would be the only one.

TMW: We're going to get her here in Baltimore [as associate conductor of the Baltimore Symphony for 1984-85]. Many of the graduates of this

Table 3.1
Exxon/Arts Endowment Conductors Program
Percentage of Women Appointees

Season	Number of women/ Total Appointees	Percentage
1981-82	2/9	22%
1982-83	3/9	33%
1983-84	1/9	11%
1973-83 total	5/30	17%

program have gone on to permanent posts elsewhere. Have any of the women?

JR: Yes. Paulette [Nolan]; and Vicky [Bond] now is the music director of Empire State Youth Orchestra, which is in Albany. I know they're very pleased with her out there. And she's also the director of a small opera company [Bel Canto Opera] in New York City. [Since 1983, Bond is also music director of the Southeastern Music Center, a summer festival in Georgia.] And Paulette was music director of Opera Omaha for a couple of years, and now she's given that up and she has an affiliation with the O'Neill Theater Center in Connecticut [and is director of Lake George Opera].

TMW: Her original appointment had been with the San Francisco Opera, so that opera is her field. Have any other appointees, male or female, had appointments with opera companies, or is your program now strictly an orchestral one?

JR: No, we've had three others, John DeMain and C. William Harwood, with the Houston Grand Opera, and David Agler, with the San Francisco Opera.

TMW: Is any opera company presently participating?

JR: No, but we would like them to. We have had an inquiry from the Chicago Lyric Opera; they are interested in adding a young conductor to their composer-in-residence program, and they'd like to do it through the Exxon Program.

TMW: In your view, I imagine, the program would be thought of as very successful because most of the people are still active in their field; they haven't switched this profession for something else. Do you believe that it has been as successful for the women appointees as for the male appointees? [Referring to subsequent appointments for Victoria Bond and John DeMain] For instance, the Empire State Youth Orchestra is not exactly the Houston Opera!

JR: Well, I think the women who have graduated from the program to date have not assumed positions as significant in the professional world as the men have. You asked whether or not the program has been as successful for the women, I don't know.

TMW: As a springboard to attention maybe, or as a growth experience. . . .

JR: Actually, in terms of exposure and recognition in the last two years my impression is that the women who have been in the program have gotten a great deal of attention, probably more attention than the men. Actually Catherine and Paulette have really advanced on a par with the men, I would say. Rachael sort of has too; she left Spokane and has since guest conducted the San Francisco Symphony, the Los Angeles Philharmonic, where they immediately reengaged her, the Hartford Symphony, the Seattle Symphony—she's conducted some pretty good orchestras.

TMW: So. It's really been very helpful for her in terms of exposure.

JR: It has. And you know, we talk about the success rate being measured in terms of those with a permanent position, and that can be a major fallacy. There are many very, very successful conductors, in fact some of the most successful conductors in the world don't have permanent positions, they guest conduct all of the time. And I would say that Rachael, while she does not have a permanent post, is conducting very good orchestras.

By way of contrast, though, I should mention that Antonia, after being at St. Louis, decided to go to Yale to *study* some more, which was a good decision.

TMW: A very good decision, and not an easy one to make when you've been out in the field.

JR: So, I don't know. I couldn't generalize at this point really about them—what is happening, what will happen to the women—as they leave the program.

TMW: Is there any provision for a conductor who's done one, two, or three years in this program—presumably who would still fit your guidelines a year or two hence—to be engaged again by another orchestra? Would you permit that? Would the program permit that—a second residency for the same individual?

JR: After they've done three years or less than three years?

TMW: Whichever.

JR: Yes, I think we . . . well, we have done that, we keep conductors around. This isn't really the best example, but it's the most recent one. Christopher Wilkins, who was the conducting assistant with the Oregon Symphony, is now the Exxon Conductor with the Cleveland Orchestra, but he's staying within the program, he spent one year in Oregon and now he's in Cleveland. But John DeMain started out as an

Figure 3.2 Rachael Worby. Used with permission of Affiliate Artists Inc.

Figure 3.3 Antonia Joy Wilson. Used with permission of Affiliate Artists Inc.

Exxon Conductor with the St. Paul Chamber Orchestra, and I think he was there one year and then he went to Houston to the Grand Opera [where he's now the music director]. Again, we try to be flexible; if it makes sense, we'll do it. Michael Morgan, who was in St. Louis for only one year as an Exxon Conductor, was invited to audition this past spring for the Exxon position with the Rochester Philharmonic. So we really treat each case individually. Vicky, after leaving Pittsburgh where she spent two years, was in the same audition as Catherine Comet and Antonia Wilson in St. Louis. That was a very peculiar audition. There were seven conductors and we did it in two rounds, so in the finals the three finalists were the three women: Vicky, Antonia, and Catherine!

TMW: Let's turn now to an area where maybe the statistics would be a bit more accurate: not the pool of appointees, but the pool of applicants. If you get between 150 and 200 applicants per year, what percentage of those applicants are women?

JR: The first thing that I can tell you is that we actually have two categories of applicants. We have those which are new, newly received each year, and those that are *rereviewed* each year—and they're two different numbers. We always review many more than we receive in any given year, because people's files stay active with us often for three or four years. In any given year we might have 15 new applications, but we may have another 125 that were there from last year whose files are still open and active, and we look at them each year and try to make some determination. The best way to talk about it is [to discuss] the number of applications that we *review*, which would be a total, and that includes the new applications as well as the ones that we have on file. For the upcoming season, which is the 1984-85 season, 14 out of 97 applications were from women. [See tables 3.2-3.5].

TMW: So it's pretty consistent, and it's less than the 17 percent of appointees.

JR: That's right. Now the next significant number, I think, is how many women of the ones we review, we invite to audition. For the 1983-84 season, 31 applicants were invited to audition, representing 29 percent of 108 applicants. Six of these 31 were women, representing 19 percent of those applicants invited to audition and 50 percent of the 12 women applicants.

TMW: In other words, the percentage is still pretty steady. It's never as high as 20 percent of the applicants being reviewed, and it rarely gets as low as 10 percent, so it does correspond in a rough way to the 17 percent [figure] of women who are appointees.

According to these figures, there seems to have been a decline in the number of applications overall that have been reviewed in the last three seasons.

JR: It does seem that in the last few years there has been a steady decline—not dramatic, but nonetheless it has gotten less each year—in the number of new applications. My guess is that it's because we've just saturated the pool of potential applicants in the program. There's only a finite number of conductors out there, and within the whole group of conductors there is only a small grouping that falls within our guidelines, more or less.

Table 3.2
Women as a Percentage of the Total Applicant Pool

Season	Women/Total Applicants	Percentage
1982-83	20/195	10%
1983-84	12/108	11%
1984-85	14/97	14%

Table 3.3
Applicants Invited to Audition as a Percentage of the Total Applicant Pool

Season	Invitees/Applicant Pool	Percentage
1982-83	25/195	13%
1983-84	31/108	29%
1984-85	23/97	24%

Table 3.4
Women as a Percentage of the Applicants Invited to Audition

Season	Women Invitees/Total Invitees	Percentage
1982-83	4/25	16%
1983-84	6/31	19%
1984-85	4/23	17%

Table 3.5
Women Invited to Audition as a Percentage of Women Applicants

Season	Women Invitees/Women Applicants	Percentage
1982-83	4/20	20%
1983-84	6/12	50%
1984-85	4/14	28%

I think there was a point, oh, maybe five years ago or so, where we probably were not reaching all the potential applicants with our information. We stepped up the dissemination of the application information very substantially about four years ago. We started to mail directly, each year, to seven or eight hundred conductors; to all the member schools of National Association of Schools of Music; and we began to represent the program in person in various conducting schools and workshops. The immediate result was an increase in applications, which has now begun to fall off, and I think frankly we've just reached the other end; until some people drop out of the pool [of applicants] by virtue of either going through our process and being rejected or getting too experienced or too old, we'll probably stay this small.

TMW: And this is true even with the information going out about the Affiliate Artists Conducting Assistants Program?

JR: Yes; conducting is still a small—a relatively small—business.

TMW: Now, not being a conductor, all I know about your procedures are the qualifications I must have according to your guidelines, which include having a musical degree or the equivalent, proficiency in performance of a musical instrument, and mastery of ear-training skills, theory, etc. I should have "at least two but not more than ten years of experience conducting professional or professional level musical organizations," and I should have at my fingertips a command of standard orchestral repertoire. How closely do those guidelines match the profile of your average candidate?

JR: Well, I would say most of them . . . well, most of them have an advanced degree. Now, proficiency in performance of a musical instrument, that is something we frankly just don't test adequately and we should, because this is an area where many of them fall down; they're not good enough musicians.

TMW: Instrumentalists.

JR: Instrumentalists.

Ear-training. I would say about 90 percent of our applicants could not get through a freshmen level dictation course. They really [are not well prepared], you wouldn't believe it. You would faint.

TMW: I might, I teach solfège here [at Peabody Conservatory].

JR: The difference, though, is that these are people who say they want to be conductors and presumably they ought to be a little bit better at this than others, but they're not.

TMW: In the press clippings a couple of auditioners spoke about perfect pitch, and is it really a "leg-up" in this interview process? What would you say?

JR: I really couldn't say because the musical tests that we give the conductors are different at every place and at every session. It really depends on how we're doing it.

TMW: Yes. For instance, I think there was a twelve-tone excerpt played at one audition. And John Nelson [music director of the Indianapolis symphony] is quoted as commenting on perfect pitch, after the 1982 auditions in Indianapolis: "If you don't have it, you have to have very quick relative pitch—and very few in this group had it." [From an article by Betty Dietz Krebs, *Dayton Daily News,* May 30, 1982] But, overall, the candidates do seem to qualify?

JR: Yes, most of them meet the guidelines.

TMW: How about the women? Do they do as well in substantiating their credentials in the area of "two to ten years of experience conducting professional level organizations"?

JR: Yes. We interpret that, by the way, fairly loosely, to mean at the one extreme an orchestra which is paid and is made up of professional musicians who make their careers playing, and the conductor is paid. That is one end of the spectrum. All the way at the other end of the spectrum, maybe the conductor is the only one who is paid, and not even paid enough to make a living doing it, but they're being paid—and they have some ongoing relationship to the body of players that they're working with. Women do as well here. I think, on this score, women don't really have as much of a disadvantage as you might think. It becomes more problematic as they get higher up into the profession. For women to get jobs with amateur orchestras, with community based orchestras, choruses, and so on, my hunch is that it is perhaps no more difficult for them and possibly maybe easier than for men.

TMW: Do you find many of these women actually starting their own orchestras, like Catherine Overhauser here in Balimore started the Hopkins Symphony?

JR: Yes, many of them do. So do men, by the way.

TMW: How about the ages of applicants? Are the female applicants about the same average age as the males? To get that experience, do they wind up a couple of years older than their male colleagues?

JR: Oh, it's really hard to say. There's a woman, for example, who I saw about two years ago. She was a theory major in Manhattan and getting her masters, but she was an aspiring conductor, and I thought she was very good. Her name was Barbara Jahr, and she went to Stony Brook in a conducting program, and she was really not ready for us at either level, but she was very talented. When Max Rudolph (who is now teaching at the Curtis Institute) started teaching he asked us if there were any people we wanted to recommend to his class (which had just four people in it), and I said, well, this woman is really very good. She interviewed for Max and he was very impressed, and she is now in his class in Philadelphia. I mention her as an example because we try to maintain a relationship with young conductors—men and women—who are especially talented from our first contact with them, over a period of years, and up until the point where it makes sense for them to apply. [The women] are not any older or younger, I suppose, except in that the younger ones that come to our attention who we think are really talented we stay with, where we might not ordinarily do that.

And then at the other end of the spectrum we have auditioned some older women—one woman was about 55. She wanted very badly to audition and we said, "You know, it's unlikely you will be accepted. Even if you do very well, this is probably not the right program for you, it's not going to make sense," but we auditioned her anyway.

TMW: Staying with the applicants now, the application form indicates that applicants and candidates and appointees must be prepared to live and work in the United States, but they're not required to be United States citizens when they apply. What about the characteristics of the European applicants for the program, how do they stack up in comparison with their American counterparts?

JR: Well, that can be a very long answer.

TMW: How about a short answer?

JR: That's hard. A short answer would be that they stack up much better than the Americans do, in proportion. Of the Europeans that we audition, a higher proportion of them go on to final auditions and subsequent positions in the program than the Americans. Now that's a little deceptive because that doesn't mean therefore that the Europeans are better. It means the Europeans who have come from Europe to the United States are doing very well. It may well be that the sampling that we are looking at—of Europeans in America [who] are trying to build conducting careers here—is the cream of the crop, in Europe. The Europeans (that we see here), compared to the full range of young European conducting talent, may be the same as the best Americans measured against the full range of young American conducting talents. In other words, it's not a basis for comparison really, to say that Europeans do better than the Americans; we're comparing the Europeans against all Americans that we see.

TMW: I see.

JR: We're not comparing them against all Europeans, and it may be there are hundreds of average and below-average young European conductors who are staying in Europe. If you go to, let's say the Ruppert Competition, the conducting competition held in England, where last year [1983] first prize, second prize, [and] third prize winners were all Americans, what they were looking at there were the best, or among the best, young American conductors measured against all of the English conductors and people from all over the world. So, to the people in England judging that competition, I think it would be inaccurate for them to conclude that because the first three prize winners were Americans therefore America must be producing lots of good conductors in significant quantities.

TMW: A question about last year's [Ruppert] Competition. Were any of those three prize winners people who had gone through the Exxon Arts Endowment application procedure?

JR: Yes. The first-prize winner is an Exxon Arts Endowment conductor, Andrew Litton, and two of the three, [at least,] have been through our audition process.

TMW: Maybe my question about the Europeans was a little too broad. Naturally, when you go someplace else besides your own country, you're on your best footing, and you'd like to feel that you're best prepared. There's a little bit of a "routine" element in applying for any and all openings in your field within your own country, but if you're going to go into the expense of travelling overseas and through all the extras that that involves, there's a self-selection process there that only people with strong motivation and who think of themselves as well-credentialed will go through with.

JR: Yes.

TMW: What about the breadth and depth of their preparation as musicians? The European Conservatory training system—I know that France, for example, is extremely rigorous in the curriculum requirements [for] what we would call basics: theory and ear-training, and a lot of history, and solfège, and counterpoint studies, and fugue writing, and things of that sort. Do the Europeans show their strength more in [their] basic groundings as musicians? Is that where the difference is?

JR: I would say that the Europeans seen in our process are better trained as musicians than many of the Americans we see. We do see some Americans who are also very well trained, but they are by far a minority of the many American applicants. A higher percentage of [the Europeans] are better and more thoroughly trained as musicians than the Americans. A lot of the Americans decide to become conductors when they are maybe 20 years old, after they are enrolled in a conservatory as an instrumentalist—and, oftentimes, as a so-so instrumentalist; and they are able, because they are already in a conservatory, to go from their undergraduate degrees as instrumentalists and enroll in the conducting program without too much difficulty. And there they are, 21 years old, now graduates in a conducting program. They've devoted their studies so far to becoming, let's say, a clarinet player; they have not taken more than rudimentary keyboard harmony; they've taken only the required theory and history courses; they haven't read, they haven't thought about music in the way a conductor ought to think about music. There they are in the graduate conducting program, and they are so far behind already to begin conducting at that point, they have so much to make up—yet, in too many instances they're not required to make it up. For instance, their ear-training skills are just awful. I mean, when we audition conductors—you just wouldn't believe it—we give them a test, and they go into this panic beforehand, as though we were asking something horribly unreasonable. We play chorales on the piano, with just basic diatonic harmony, with maybe one augmented-sixth chord at the very worst.

TMW: Right.

JR: And they go into it, and they're just terrified! And these people want to be symphony conductors with aspirations to big careers.

TMW: Well, that seems to be a very sore point about the American preparation in general.

JR: It's just a shame, just a shame.

TMW: Let's go back now to the topic of women *applicants*. What sort of questions do they ask you in getting ready for an interview? Do they have concerns that seem to be other than, or in addition to, the male conductors'? For instance, for women the matter of dress has a lot more latitude to it, than [for] men, who will come in a business suit or a sports jacket and slacks; there's a vocabulary of dress, and women have a much wider one. Do [the women] have more personal concerns that they voice to you, or not?

JR: Only occasionally have any of those concerns been voiced. It's been apparent to me that they are concerns; once in awhile they've been voiced. For instance, "what should I wear to the audition," or "what should I wear to the concert?" It is something I've talked about with one or two women conductors, and I know that it's obviously a very real problem that women have and men don't have.

There was a woman applicant who came to see me last year; she was very well dressed, and she sat down and opened up a portfolio like a model carries, with a loose-leaf binder inside. She started flipping through the portfolio, which contained newspaper clippings; none of them reviews of concerts, but [just] photographs of her, for example, posing in mink stoles, because there was a promotional thing done between the local furrier and the orchestra; photographs of her at one promotional thing after another—all of the public relations functions that a conductor may perform with an orchestra—and *that's* what this portfolio consisted of.

TMW: Did she bring that to you because there were *no* reviews and she felt that she had to have something?

JR: Oh no, no, she was. . . .

TMW: Did she understand?

JR: I think she understood what she was doing, and I said to her afterwards, "You know I think this is very nice, but you know someone might get the wrong impression in looking through this. It doesn't convey that you are a *musician* particularly; it conveys that you are a good public relations asset for an orchestra."

TMW: Yes, but what would happen if she had no reviews? That's all too likely.

JR: Well actually even if she didn't (and I'm pretty sure she did, because I'm almost certain we have some here in our files), . . . to represent herself in this fashion, I thought was very detrimental to her. It's a tricky balance; it's a hard thing for men and women, but more so for women—but it's always hard. (For instance, a man who was in here last week said to me, "You know that I'm trying to build my career. I'm a very good teacher and lecturer, and I'm very comfortable with audiences. I like doing that kind of stuff. I like doing interviews, and when I apply for jobs, I let people know that." And I said, "Yes you should; but be very careful, because sometimes you don't want to give the impression that you are that first, and [only] secondarily a conductor. The primary thing that you want people to know is that you're a good conductor." I also said, "As far as we're concerned, we're not interested in that stuff at all, until you get to the stage where you're in a final audition; because there, in the face of all things being equal, if there are two conductors who are equally good musically, the one who will get the job is the one who is articulate, friendly, easy to work with, pleasant, etc., etc. So you should have those skills in your satchel but you don't want to make it sound as though that's your main thing.") And this woman, perhaps partially because she was a woman, got sidetracked in trying to present herself as a very good P.R. tool for the orchestra—and that's how she talked about herself. She said, "I want orchestras to know if they hire me, look at all the publicity I can bring them"; and she is anxious to promote the fact that as a woman she's a good publicity vehicle—and in a sense she's right.

TMW: But that comes as an "aura" after one is established in the job.

JR: That's right, that's how it should happen.

TMW: It seems as if, though, that part of her presentation must certainly have been motivated by the fact that she didn't have depth of credentials to show for herself in other ways—or not enough, or not recent enough. It's pretty sad if the local newspapers only take note of someone like that, who's developing, when that person does something that's extreme, or sort of catering to the media, or a real publicity stunt. It's hard to believe that that would happen now in 1984.

JR: Well, but she . . . I don't think it's right to lay it on the local newspaper because this gal chose to assemble the portfolio for herself; it's her decision.

TMW: True.

JR: She had the option, if she didn't have any reviews, of not doing this portfolio at all. It was totally beside the point to look at this volume that gave testimony to the fact that she got in the newspaper a lot. And I don't think it was because she felt she didn't have any other credentials. Anyone trying to make a career as a conductor grabs at anything they've got; because, even if they have the credentials, either there are other people who've got them too—or if they don't have them, then they have the right strings to pull, or whatever it is that makes it possible for the others to come out ahead. So you get as much ammunition as you can, and you get it from wherever you can.

TMW: Speaking of that, you talked earlier about the fact that the women appointees, perhaps in the last couple of years, may have gotten even more attention in the Exxon Arts Endowment Program than the men. Because this is the program's tenth year, the media might be looking for a fresh way to discuss the candidates. During the time of their tenure, what sort of functions did they fulfill with their participating orchestras? (I assume they were not publicity vehicles the way this other candidate seems to have been.) Were they regarded as fully, professionally part of their participating orchestra by all concerned; by the board members, by the orchestra? I assume the music director had no reservations, otherwise they wouldn't have been appointed to the orchestra; but what about the members of the staff and administration that they had to work with?

JR: As far as I've been aware, the experience of the three recent women members of the Exxon Program was pretty much, across the board—with music director, management, board and the orchestra members—a very, very supportive one. No one's ever told me of any kind of problem that arose out of the fact that they're women, that is, [of] there being resistance to them because they are women. To varying degrees, they all got a lot of publicity and were very active. Partially by virtue of their personalities, partially because they were women, and that was unusual (some people like to write about that, so they did); they got more than their fair share of publicity. It wasn't too much, but it was more than you otherwise would have expected; but I was never aware of any problems that arose specifically out of the fact that they were women.

One of the differences I think that there was with these three—Rachael Worby, Antonia Wilson, and Catherine Comet—is that they all have a different attitude toward youth concerts. To take it a step further, I think they have a different attitude about the [total] role of a conductor; for these three women the idea of teaching [as a component of conducting] is a quite comfortable and natural role in situations when they are on the podium conducting their big orchestra in a subscription concert and in youth concerts. In most cases, those three women were responsible for the youth concerts of their orchestras.

TMW: Didn't Catherine Comet's youth orchestra win first prize in the European Competition?

JR: That's right, first prize. Catherine is just totally, totally dedicated to youth concerts; she spends hours and hours thinking about them and trying to perfect them and make them better. Rachael Worby, the same way; Antonia Wilson to a somewhat lesser degree, partially just because of the difference in experience. But that's a difference between those three, set off from the men in the Exxon Program. I must say that, as a class, the Exxon Conductors tend to take youth concerts quite seriously.

TMW: They do form a significant proportion of the conductor's responsibility with the orchestra.

What about the earlier women appointees—or, for that matter, other women conductors who might not have been part of the program? Do you know of any who had particular problems with their orchestra's board or staff?

JR: There were, . . . I have to tell you to turn the tape off. [Jesse Rosen here related the story of a particular female conductor, appointed associate conductor to a municipal orchestra in the United States within the last 15 years. At the time of her appointment, she was already known to the orchestra's principal conductor, who felt she wasn't 100 percent ready but should be given the chance. The orchestra greeted her initially with a "wait and see" attitude—but when musical deficiencies and crucial lack of experience and knowledgeability became apparent over the course of time, latent skepticism about her as a "woman conductor" turned overt, and was voiced by members of the orchestra with growing frequency. Finally, after an almost two-year tenure with the orchestra, she was asked to leave. Rosen stressed that the basic reason behind her leaving was a musical one.]

TMW: So that the factor of bias on the part of the players or other people involved in decision making in the orchestra, *can* have an effect, even if it's something that's subterranean, let's say, and not overt. Do you feel that this has been a factor for any of the program's recent women appointees?

JR: I wouldn't put it the way you said it. What I would say is this: any man or woman that lives in the United States in the 1980s grows up with certain attitudes about sex roles, and I think most men have a hard time accepting women in the position of authority over them, in telling them what to do. And that's what a conductor does—they tell the orchestra what to do. I think that most men probably don't like that, just like most men probably don't like having bosses who are women. People do have these attitudes, and they remain [in force], although they may be latent.

TMW: For instance, do you think that Catherine Comet's going to have any trouble with the Baltimore Symphony Orchestra next year [1984-85]? She's coming in during an interregnum, before David Zinman gets his permanent, full-time appointment.

JR: I think it's possible. You know, often when orchestras are getting to know new conductors, they test them a lot; and it may be that some of the testing that goes on with Catherine takes on a coloring of an attitude about her being a woman. Although I don't know that orchestra well enough to say if they will or they won't do that, but I wouldn't be surprised. Orchestras do that. They test, and if it's a woman in front of them . . . if conductors present them with an opportunity to find ways to test them and get at them—and one way is if she's a woman—maybe they'll use it.

TMW: My next question is about family. Are any of the women who have been appointees concurrently mothers as well? How do they coordinate raising a family with a job that keeps them out nights and weekends and all sorts of odd hours—fund-raising times, dinners—and disrupts life in general?

JR: One of them is Catherine Comet, who has a husband and I think one young daughter.

TMW: Seven years old.

JR: Right. I'm pretty sure Catherine has a live-in housekeeper who stays and takes care of her child. Her husband . . . I know for a long time when Catherine was in St. Louis, her husband was living in [Madison,] Wisconsin, and they would commute somehow when they had free time and visit one another; but he did not move to St. Louis when Catherine went there from Madison. I'm not sure what the arrangement is going to be now between her and her family, with her appointment in Baltimore.

The first time I spoke to Catherine, when she was in Madison (I guess it was the second time that I had received her résumé in the mail), I called her up and I said, "You know, your credentials are rather extraordinary and yet you've been in Madison for six years and most people in the music business don't know who you are, that you exist."

TMW: I should tell you, we listened to "First Hearing" a [nationally syndicated] program hosted by Lloyd Moss, just last night, and there was a piece on the program by Michael Colgrass (New World Records) played by members of the St. Louis Symphony conducted, by Catherine Comet (Co-may). He said to his judging panel, "Does anybody know

Figure 3.4 Catherine Comet. Used with permission of Affiliate Artists Inc.

this woman, Catherine Kom-mêtt from St. Louis?" and they said, "No we don't know her, but we certainly know the St. Louis Symphony and wasn't the performance extraordinary?"

JR: No kidding, and it was a performance of the Colgrass piece?

TMW: Of the Colgrass piece, and I guess it was a recent recording because that's how they do it. I intend to phone him now and explain who she is and correct the pronunciation. But yes, there *is* a recognition problem, and it has nothing really to do with Madison, Wisconsin.

How about some broader comments, some of your perceptions on the general picture for women who are now in conducting programs all across this country: in conservatories; universities; summer programs, like Aspen's and Tanglewood's program; the Los Angeles Institute; and the ASOL Workshops. Do you think that they are present in about our "standard" 20 percent of those programs; do you think that their participation is growing and/or will in the future?

JR: I think their participation is growing, and I think it will continue to grow. Due, partly, just to the general change in our society over the last 40 or 50 years or so. I think there's just less and less resistance to women being conductors, as there is less and less resistance to women being lawyers, doctors, or any other kind of professionals.

TMW: Well, doesn't that resistance have to break down *within* the profession first? We're still dealing in many cases with maestros who have attitudes of a different stripe, representing the thinking of 40 years ago, let's say, or 30 years ago. Are these young women students being viewed and brought forward and carefully nurtured just like their male counterparts?

JR: Well, actually one of the leading conducting pedagogues in the United States, in my view and I think many others', is Otto-Werner Mueller who is of German origin and who must be a man in his middle 50s. He teaches the conducting program at Yale University and is someone who, if you were going to follow the expected stereotypes, should not be especially concerned or interested in women entering the conducting profession; and yet he—more than any conducting pedagogue I know—has had more women students and has really followed through with them and developed unusually strong and supportive and long-lasting relationships with them. Rachael Worby studied with him, and Antonia Wilson is studying privately with him now. There are, right now, two or three women in his conducting class, and there are other women that he is working with privately—so he defies the expected stereotype. So that's one way in which stereotypes don't always hold.

The second way is, even if they did, the world is changed. More and more music directors are not of European origin, and men in their 60s or 70s, but rather they are either Americans in their 30s and 40s (like Leonard Slatkin or John Nelson), or Europeans (Edo de Waart)—younger men, for whom I think it's less of a problem.

TMW: Speaking about American and European conductors, how far down the road are we yet from seeing a woman appointed as a principal music director of a *major* symphony orchestra?

JR: Oh I think a pretty long ways.

TMW: Is it before or after we'll get a woman president, do you think?

JR: Probably after.

TMW: So then there are still some obstacles?

JR: Yes. I think the obstacles begin at the very early stages, still, which are not places where there is either overt or covert discrimination, but rather the stage at which the overt career opportunities are allowed to be in the fantasy of young girls and boys. And still, I think, women by and large don't think about being conductors. Actually, little boys don't think about it either, but if they do think about it, they don't say, "Oh that's something that I can't do, because I'm a boy."

TMW: A question about that thought. There are a number of women who are noted as opera conductors: Sarah Caldwell, Eve Queler, Judith Somogi, and quite a few others. Admittedly just a few, in the opera world to date; but at least they're there, and we know who they are.

Why is it, that it seems to be more difficult for women to gain comparable positions in the realm of instrumental music?

JR: You know, I don't know. I have no idea why that is but it's true. Maybe it's because it's easier for women to get into the opera house.

TMW: You mean through coaching positions or choral directing, or something of that sort?

JR: Right, it's easiest for them to develop in those places so that's where their expertise winds up being used.

TMW: What additional general comments might you have for young people who are thinking of conducting as a career?

JR: One thing that ought to be said is that there is—in the United States anyway—amongst young aspiring conductors, a tendency to be preoccupied with career advancement, that is, to get a good job.

TMW: Sounds like ambitious M.B.A.'s [Masters of Business Administration].

JR: Right. To get a prestigious postion—to advance, and advance quickly—that's certainly a legitimate concern. It's also legitimate to want to be sure you get paid for what you've chosen to do for your livelihood. However, there is a tendency for young aspiring conductors—actually for all performing artists—to want that to happen very soon, and that tendency often interferes with the development of the long-term, regimented training and [artistic] development necessary to become really good at what you're doing. Hopefully, combining training, talent, and some savvy as to how to manage the practicalities of a career can yield a fruitful career. But today the tendency of young aspiring conductors is toward concentrating their efforts upon the advancement of their careers, often at the expense of developing their musicianship and talent. Obviously the ideal is to be able to be in a situation that does both, and sometimes that happens and sometimes one needs to be concerned about one or the other. But it's always useful to separate the two, that is, that which advances the career and that which develops. . . .

TMW: Develops the musician?

JR: Develops the musician.

TMW: Along with that, the problem of specializing at too early an age crops up. In the past we've had many people who've started going into conducting from other aspects of music, getting sort of a broad general music education and working on basic skills and musicianship and then winding up as conductors. Nowadays, people seem to be specializing in conducting at a very early stage (just like you see it in composing) and they do let the performance skills go, and they let other basic skills go. Do you think that too early a focus on conducting is necessarily going to make problems, or is that really not a part of this?

JR: Well actually, I haven't noticed that, so I don't know; well, maybe it's true. If it is, I think it's good. I think the problem is that people wait til too *late* to decide to become conductors. Max Rudolph (the music advisor for the Exxon Program) says that when he was 14 he could conduct by memory all nine Beethoven symphonies, and not because he's a genius. He doesn't have a photographic memory; he just worked at it, studying the scores until he knew them. And I think people wait too long. You know, in our audition people get up in front of a professional orchestra without knowing the many layers of basic fundamentals that they should have learned when they were 12 or 14 or 16, and it is a complete mismatch. [These young conductors] have this grandiose idea about how the music ought to go, which is often informed by very little more than their own impulses and how they happen to feel it—and that just "ain't good enough," unless you are a natural genius of interpretation. (Some people are, however. I'm not sure Klaus Tennstedt could justify his interpretations, based on any study or knowledge of the style or the intentions of the composers; and yet, no one quibbles if it's right or wrong, because his conducting makes an impact, and it's very compelling emotionally.) But this is rare. Most conductors, then ought to have something [concrete] that informs them how to treat the orchestra, and something to say about the music beyond how they just happen to "feel" it . . . that's so narrow.

When I was in high school in Pittsburgh, my father was the manager of the Pittsburgh Symphony, and he used to talk to me about [William] Steinberg. Steinberg was a very erudite, very well-read man, who knew about philosophy, about mathematics, about art. And I grew up always thinking that's what a conductor was supposed to be, someone who, by virtue of a broad view of history and of knowledge would be able to bring to the music something that sort of transcended [the "routine"] . . . not just a run-through of the notes on the page. Now we seem to come across very few aspiring conductors who have that perspective on being a conductor. Maybe that's just because the world is changed and the United States is not Germany, and the 1980s are not the 1860s; maybe that's not what is called for anymore.

TMW: But it seems like the question of specialization does creep in there—specialization as the sort of narrowing of things within a technological track. In other words, so many things nowadays are committee efforts (like our space program); we don't seem to be generating in this country the broad generalists, people who have the overview. And you're indicating that the overview—a sort of musical acculturation, or something that seeps out of the pores; a summation of knowledge and intuition and stylistic rightness—has to be part of what the conductor brings to his task.

JR: In that sense then, yes I do agree. Too many people are pursuing conducting, that is, the waving of the stick at the right time and the right place, in a very specialized way, as though conducting were a beginning and an end. In that sense, specialization too soon, I would agree, is the cause for some of the problems.

TMW: As an important coda to our discussions, we'd like to know more about Jesse Rosen as a musician. You certainly didn't early specialize in becoming director of a conductors program. How did you work your way to this position from Pittsburgh?

JR: Well, I was a trombone player, I went to a variety of schools (among them the Manhattan School of Music, where I got my Bachelor's degree, and Juilliard, where I did some masters work), and then I got to a point where I was absolutely miserable playing the trombone, so I decided to go into administration. It was a very easy thing for me to decide that I wanted to go into some administrative kind of work in the performing arts because my father was an orchestra manager for most of my life and most of his, and my mother is a dance teacher and administrator. Between the two of them I grew up hearing a lot about the arts from the managerial side of things, which was always very interesting, so I stopped playing trombone and I went to the National Endowment for the Arts (in a three-month Fellowship Program they have for people entering arts management) and, through various connections established there with Affiliate Artists, I wound up here in 1977.

TMW: Your career pattern, then, was almost a direct track from performing. Had you ever had the itch to conduct yourself?

JR: Oh no, never, absolutely never; the longer I do this, the less, the less of an itch.

TMW: Thank you very much.

JR: You're welcome.

EDITOR'S NOTE

None of the four women who made it to the audition phase received actual conducting appointments for the 1984-85 season, although two of them received favorable enough comment to have their applications reconsidered for 1986-87.

After two successful seasons (1984-86) as Associate Conductor of the Baltimore Symphony Orchestra (a Major orchestra), Catherine Comet was appointed Music Director of the Grand Rapids Symphony, a Michigan ensemble classed as a Regional Orchestra. With this appointment, effective for the 1986-87 season, Comet becomes the first woman to direct a regional American symphony orchestra. (For further information on orchestra classifications see Note 1 accompanying the Joan Briccetti interview, p. 89.)

4

My Life and Career with Young Concert Artists

SUSAN WADSWORTH

> Young Concert Artists, under its director, Susan Wadsworth, has made a remarkable reputation since 1961, when she had the quixotic idea of establishing a non-profit organization to help youthful musicians gain a foothold in the battlements of the concert world. Over the last twenty years it is extremely doubtful whether any management organization anywhere could have matched the YCA record for spotting great talent early and helping it along.
>
> —The *New York Times,* 2 June 1981

YCA TODAY: LAUNCHING MAJOR CAREERS

In the midst of the excitement, vitality, and achievements now generated by Young Concert Artists, it is sometimes hard to believe that it all began in 1961 as an experimental series of debut recitals in a Greenwich Village loft. Guided by the needs of the artists, Young Concert Artists has steadily grown into a thriving, professional, multi-faceted organization with an annual budget of almost one million dollars. And over the years YCA has gradually come closer and closer to realizing my goal: to discover major talents and to give great but unrecognized musicians every opportunity needed to launch their careers. The list of former YCA artists includes many who are now established: pianists Murray Perahia, Emanuel Ax, Ruth Laredo, Ilana Vered, Ursula Oppens, and Richard Goode; flutists Paula Robison and Eugenia Zukerman; harpsichordist Anthony Newman; trumpeter Stephen Burns; violinists Pinchas Zukerman, Ani Kavafian, and Ida Kavafian; the Tokyo String Quartet; sopranos Mrvis Martin and Dawn Upshaw; cellist Carter Brey; and many more.

In retrospect, it always seems surprising that any of the artists mentioned above ever needed help in establishing careers. But sometimes a special knack seems to be required to recognize a new talent. Even once an artist is "discovered," to develop an active concert career and be accepted into the busy music world takes a lot of work, time, love, money, skill, and dedication—all of which Young Concert Artists provides.

Career development quickly became a major focus of YCA's commitment to its artists. After the first debut Series in 1961-62, I realized that no matter how great any of those artists were, establishing a career required much more help. Little by little, I developed YCA's ability to give what was needed. Contrary to popular belief, just winning a competition does not make a career. It *did* happen once—to pianist Van Cliburn—and as a result the Cinderella fantasy shows no sign of losing its grip on our imagination. But in reality, a first prize brings a glorious moment in the spotlight that fades all too quickly, leaving the artist alone and needing to prove himself again. Winners of Young Concert Artists International Auditions, however, are not left holding a single prize. They get services and career guidance that lead to a solid career with commercial management, usually two to six years later. By then, the artist has given many concerts, gotten many good reviews, and made friends in the concert field. As Herbert Barrett of Herbert Barrett Management has said, YCA hands over its artists to commercial management on a silver platter!

The performing opportunities YCA offers its artists are many. Presenting the Young Concert Artists Series in New York City has always been the mainstay of our activities. The New York series has moved to various halls as its audiences have grown, and since 1976 the Series has taken place amidst the other prestigious cultural events in the Kaufmann Concert Hall of the 92nd Street Y. In 1979 we added the presentation of a second Young Concert Artists series in Washington, D.C., with the cosponsorship of the J. F. Kennedy Center for Performing Arts. These two showcase series, the only concerts that YCA actually sponsors, are presented because the press and audiences in these major cultural capitals are so important in launching new careers.

In addition to presenting solo recitals in the New York and Washington series, each artist also performs in many other engagements that have been booked by YCA, including concerto performances, recitals, and residency activities throughout the U.S.[1] In 1984-85, over 600 concert engagements were contracted by YCA for its roster of 20 artists. Booking engagements is an involved process at best. Basically, it involves persuading someone who presents concerts in another city that they want to pay your artist a fee to perform there. It is not an easy task to convince producers to pay for and present someone virtually unknown. However, YCA's track record of managing artists now recognized as "great" is a big help.

YCA's activities do not stop with the New York and Washington debuts and the booking of other engagements across the country. We also provide all professional materials such as photographs, biographies, and review reprints; we do publicity mailings and promotion through radio, television, and newspapers. All of these materials and services are provided *at no cost* to the artists.

I do feel, however, that it is important to establish a professional relationship with the artists by having them pay a small management fee when they earn money from concertizing, and so I've devised an unusual system for determining YCA's commission from concert fees. *After* deducting all of the artist's expenses (e.g., travel, living expenses, accompanist's fees, and accompanist's expenses), the artists pay a commission based on a sliding scale (5 percent to 20 percent) of the *net* fee. This token fee is paid when the artists are actually earning money by performing. In 1983-84, when the artists' total concert fees came to about $420,000, YCA's income from "commissions" came to about $60,000. This prepares the artists somewhat for the "real world" they will enter later, where commercial management will take a 20 percent commission "off the top" of their fee (i.e., *before* expenses)—*plus* charge the artists for all expenses on their behalf. But by then the artists can afford it!

Of course, once our artists become well known they can command fees that are quite substantial. People have often asked me why we don't hold on to the artists and make a commercial appendage to Young Concert Artists, letting the profit of the commercial part feed back into Young Concert Artists. We would certainly like that on a personal level, because we wouldn't have to let our beloved artists leave our hands; but the work of commercial managements is very different from ours. We specialize in helping unknown young artists become busy and recognized. We work hand in hand with commercial managements when it is time for a YCA artist to move on. Then they have to take over and build those careers into something even bigger. That is *their* expertise and their job. But we always have new artists who need our devotion and help—and that is *our* role and our mission. We are very proud to do it and to do our utmost. We are fortunate to be supported in our efforts by those individuals, corporations, and foundations who love music and want to help young artists to be heard, as well as by many of our former artists.

Each year we seem to get more applications for the YCA auditions. The auditions are open. We will hear almost anyone if they are not under management already. (If they already have a manager, they shouldn't need us.) Listening to hundreds and hundreds of auditions is a long, demanding process—but the hunt for those special talents is exciting, too. I have always had a sixth sense for spotting great musical talent, and listening to the auditions of talented young musicians has always been my favorite part of YCA. I often spot those who have been passed over by managers and competitions. One of my colleagues and I listen to *all* of the applicants in the preliminary round, either in person or on tape. We narrow the field to 50 or 60 people to be heard in the semi-finals by a jury of musicians. About 10 or 12 artists are selected for the finals, which are heard by a larger jury and an audience. The young artists are judged against the highest standards of excellence and potential—not one another. The criteria could be described as virtuosity, musicianship, individuality, and that special appealing presence and communicative power that cannot be easily defined. There is no set limit to the number of artists selected by the jury to join the YCA roster, and if none qualify, none are chosen. YCA can select three

Figure 4.1 Susan Wadsworth, Founder and Director of Young Concert Artists, Inc. Photograph by Christian Steiner.

violists as winners in one year and nobody else, or one pianist and two violinists—whoever projects those special qualities.

During their first year with YCA, the artists' sense of themselves often changes palpably. They usually start with an "Is this really happening to me?" kind of shyness. Then they begin to realize that YCA is theirs—that they can pop into the YCA offices and find somebody who will talk with them about an accompanist, a competition to enter, a recital program, a review, or the future. The whole team at YCA is working for them, and this gradually helps them to become very self-confident and eager to get started.

There is a lot for new artists to learn about performing: how to pace themselves physically; how to cope with travel; to learn whether they need a nap, and what and when to eat before they perform. They must learn how to respond to the people at the organization that is presenting them (i.e., the series, college, or orchestra) and how to be friendly, flexible, and appreciative of special efforts for them, such as a reception after a concert or being met at the airport.

The Young Concert Artists Series has never presented anyone who hasn't given me a thrill. Yet although the debuts are usually very exciting affairs for the audience, I often miss the special qualities that nerves have taken away: the inspiration that is too scared to emerge; that "something" that makes the music come to new life through the artist. Perhaps I am sometimes disappointed because I am the one who has the best idea of that which the artist is capable. I have learned that that special quality might not emerge again until years of performing have enabled the artist to communicate and reveal his feelings before an audience. But bringing the gifts of talented young musicians to fruition means providing each artist with belief, trust, maximum opportunity, and lots of time.

I always encourage the artists to enter competitions if they want to. Competitions can be wonderful stepping stones, chances to be heard, and sources of opportunities and cash. I don't believe that losing can hurt our artists' careers. YCA still believes in them. *If* they win, it's a great tool in addition to an accolade, because presenters do like to book competition winners.

Another part of YCA's management services, of course, is advising the artists—giving each one feedback and moral support. Each musician comes to us with different natural abilities. Some look wonderful on the stage, some look terrible. Some need a push when they really are ready for commercial management, but still think of themselves as struggling young artists needing our help. Sometimes we advise artists on programs or repertoire. Occasionally, artists fall in love with unusual repertoire and come up with deadly programs that audiences wouldn't be able to sit through. In such a case we might suggest that the artists consider making a change. But we don't dictate repertoire or say, "You should start out with this, and then you should play that." Musicians are taken on the YCA roster because they are artists; we respect their musical ideas while helping them to see themselves as performers.

It usually takes from two to six years until the artists "graduate" to commercial management; by that time they are self-assured and experienced performers. There are times when commercial managements are slow to respond, and often that has more to do with trends in the music business than with the talents of the artist. A case in point is Paula Robison. Now among the world's most prominent flutists, she remained with YCA for ten years. She had built a strong career and had many marvelous reviews, but it was a long time before we could persuade a concert manager that the flute could be a solo instrument. We are proud of our ability to stick with an artist for as long as it takes for them to achieve the recognition they deserve—even for "difficult" solo instruments such as winds or viola.

HOW IT ALL BEGAN

In retrospect it is easy for me to look back on my own life and see how everything was gradually leading up to the point at which I started Young Concert Artists. I saw my parents as enterprising, creative people who loved their work and loved nurturing other people, and both served as inspiring role models for me. My mother, Anne Popkin, had been working since the age of 14. As a child, I was regaled with funny stories of her escapades as a secretary, first to a wigmaker, then to a heavyweights' work-out gym, and finally to a successful real estate broker.The latter often left town, leaving his office in the hands of his supremely competent secretary who was then only 20 years old. By the time my mother was in her mid-twenties, she had started her own real estate company, which she ran with the same enthusiasm, zest, and brains she brings to everything—including motherhood and marriage.

My father, also an innovator and an independent person, had clerked in a law office for two dollars a week while putting himself through law school. Over the years I learned that as an attorney he had handled legal cases ranging from divorce, murder, and art fraud to real estate law, with properties managed by my mother's firm.

Music and playing the piano were always at the core of my life. I started to play the piano at the age of four, and from the age of 12 until my mid-20s I worked with the great Polish pianist and teacher, Mieczyslaw Munz. He became an inspiration, mentor, and close family friend. I also began studying the violin at the age of eight with Arlie Furman, a marvelous teacher who had been a student of the Roumanian violinist and composer Georges Enesco. When I was 12 years old I had one of the most unforgettable experiences of my life. I heard Enesco himself play an evening of unaccompanied Bach violin sonatas for a small private gathering in a New York hotel. He was very old and wizened and never rose from the chair in which he played. (Years later I realized that the "tickets" were sold to help Enesco pay medical bills and other costs; he was in dire need.) About six years later I had a similar experience. From a seat high up in Carnegie Hall I was held motionless throughout a recital of unaccompanied Bach played by Enesco's greatest student—Yehudi Menuhin. I remember sitting in my seat through the intermission, unwilling to break the spell by mingling the Bach in my mind with other sights and sounds. Once again I experienced the same laser-beam intensity generated by a great musical personality and hauntingly beautiful music-making. I loved the way that Yehudi Menuhin played—sinking his whole being into the music with deep concentration and a sense of peace. (For years my favorite recording was a performance of the Bach Double Violin Concerto Menuhin made at the age of 16 with his teacher Enesco.)

My family always encouraged me to develop my musical talent. I was drawn to the piano, and practiced every day but never had the drive to master the keyboard's complex demands. (Mr. Munz wryly called it "applying the seat of the pants to the seat of the piano bench.") It just wasn't what I wanted to do. My other interests—dance, language, literature and art—filled out my days after homework was done. My father always said I could do anything I wanted to, but for a long time I couldn't figure out what that was.

After graduating from The Brearley School, I decided to attend Vassar College and pursue liberal arts rather than just music. While there I continued to study both piano and violin, but I was most fascinated by my classes in English literature. When I eventually decided to major in English, my parents asked what *use* that would be. I tried to make a case for teaching English, but it didn't feel quite right to me either.

By the time I graduated with a degree in English, I had decided to try to pursue what I seemed best at—playing the piano—a decision made over the protests of my parents. They believed that the time for that decision had come and gone, and they worried, quite justifiably, about what my liberal arts education had prepared me to do. Nevertheless I entered the Mannes College of Music in New York City where I studied piano with Frank Sheridan, a kindly and lenient teacher. I felt comfortable with him, worked hard, and slowly began to feel my fingers improve. One day he told me that the Mozart concerto I was working on sounded so good that he wanted me to play it with the school orchestra. He was taking me seriously; I panicked. I really didn't want to pursue playing the piano as my life. So I left school and started to job hunt.

I tried to land a secretarial job in the concert management field, but without success. My first interview was with a man at Columbia Artists Management who was looking for a secretary. He told me I was overqualified, even though I knew nothing at all! He must have meant that my head was full of ideas, because he told me that I should try to work on my own. Another manager, Thea Dispeker, suggested that I "start something." I was puzzled and frustrated by their advice because I just wanted a job. I finally got a job in publishing as secretary to the children's book editor at Rand McNally, Lillian McClintock—a tough boss, but hardworking, intelligent, and talented. My two years with her proved to be invaluable, teaching me skills I needed to function in the world outside of school, skills that would be crucial for me later in establishing Young Concert Artists.

Eventually I wanted to try something other than being a secretary. While at Mannes I had come to know some extraordinary musicians, including the pianist Richard Goode (who was then 14), violinist Sanford Allen, and violist Jesse Levine. I conceived of starting a series of recitals as a showcase for young musicians whom I knew were special. It was an idea I thought would be off-beat and fun and would help musicians who would surely set the world on fire if they were heard. I really didn't see beyond that point; in fact, I didn't know whether the series would continue for more than a few months.

My parents were magnificently supportive of my new idea. My father assisted me in forming Young Concert Artists, Inc., as a nonprofit organization, and I was able to get enough contributions to start a series, presenting eight artists in recital from October through December of 1961. Our "concert hall" for those first concerts was a Greenwich Village loft restaurant. The owner of the restaurant thought it would be fun to have something going on on Monday nights when the restaurant was closed. Instead of paying rent, he asked me to buy the restaurant 300 second-hand chairs that were better than the old ones he had! We built a stage, put up lighting, hung a red velvet curtain as a backdrop, and moved in a seven-foot grand piano which Steinway let us use free for a year—a generosity for which I will always be astonished and grateful. Those first nine concerts went so well that I decided to extend the series, adding four more concerts in the spring of 1962. The expenses of the first season were about $8,000, including my salary!

I was—and still am—convinced that any great talent can entrance audiences, regardless of the instrument being played. I didn't hesitate to present a solo flute recital or a solo viola recital. This turned out to be helpful in attracting the attention of the press. During its first season the Young Concert Artists Series' first review from an "uptown" newspaper was a rave in the *Herald Tribune* on the debut of violist Jesse Levine. The second big break for the series that first year was a photo story that appeared in the *New York Times*'s Sunday Magazine section, which showed the restaurant turning into a concert hall on the night we presented the debut of flutist Paula Robison. It was a nice surprise that we were taken so seriously by the press. Of course I had sent out press releases about the concerts, but hadn't really expected anyone to come trekking down to the Village to cover them. Continued press attention, such as articles and reviews in the *Village Voice* and other papers, together with an enthusiastic subscription audience, encouraged me to go on with the series.

By the second year the whole project had taken on a life of its own. I realized that the artists needed a lot more than just one exposure, and I could think of lots of ways of helping them. Many people were interested in our artists and interested in Young Concert Artists, and I saw that I could expand the organization. Since our audiences had outgrown the loft's capacity, Leopold Mannes, then president of the Mannes College, allowed me to present our second season in the Mannes College Concert Hall. And most important for the future of YCA, I started booking additional concert engagements for the artists in the New York area.

For the first few years I invented everything as I went along, and did it all alone. I didn't know anything about the field; my style was—and still is—improvisatory. Fortunately, I worked fast and was able to avoid disasters. I booked concerts, wrote contracts, did fund-raising, handled correspondence, presented and promoted the Young Concert Artists Series, and selected the artists. Everyone in the traditional music establishment was very supportive from the start, and my professional colleagues continued to extend gratitude and camaraderie once the organization was well established. Particularly helpful was another nonprofit organization, the National Music League, whose director, Alfred Rossin, encouraged my plan to expand YCA's range of activities by providing additional management services. He even gave me the contract form that the National Music League used at the time, and said he had no objection whatsoever to my using it. So I just changed the top to read "Young Concert Artists" and used a photocopy of his contract!

Soon I found that I was receiving numerous requests from concert presenters who had heard about YCA's artists. In 1963 I was asked to take over a weekly radio program on New York's WEVD. For four years I presented and hosted a live weekly recital series called "Showcase for Young Concert Artists." I was soon deeply committed to providing as many opportunities for the artists as was humanly possible. Little by little the Young Concert Artists organization learned how it could successfully start and develop important new careers.

The first idea I had for expanding YCA's activities was to "sell" a complete YCA series to colleges. The first such series that I booked outside the New York City area was at Baltimore Junior College in 1964. There were many "firsts" connected with that series. The series had been planned because the college was building a new concert hall, but the hall wasn't finished in time for our opening concert of the season. So that September, a 16-year-old violinist named Pinchas Zukerman, accompanied by 21-year-old pianist Richard Goode, appeared in his first professional concert in the United States—in the college's cafeteria! I went down to Baltimore and turned pages for the concert. Pinky was as scared to play this cafeteria concert as any young debut artist could be. Just before he started, he turned away from the audience toward Richard and me and hissed in a stage whisper, "My knees are knocking together!"

It is hard to believe now how often Pinky questioned me and mused, "Do you think I'll make it?" I would always laugh, unable to take his question seriously, but he would persist until he got my answer: "Of course!" His technical ease and musical passion, even then, were breathtaking. But it took a lot of effort for me to book his first concerts, and it took a lot of playing for him to feel comfortable in performance.

I was able to book another series that year, this one presented by Hunter College-in-the-Bronx. Pinky started that one off, too—and with only about ten people in the audience. The route for an organization dedicated to helping unknown young artists to become heard was far from a smooth one.

The memories of those early years are many and special. I was young—as young as most of the artists. I sent Richard Goode on his first trip to Mexico to play with the National Symphony there. I kept Ilana Vered from getting too nervous before she played with an orchestra for a benefit concert in Madison Square Garden. I tried to calm Murray Perahia's nervous stomach, which reacted very badly to his first airplane flight to a concert in Ohio. And I remember sitting with the Tokyo String Quartet and an important Hollywood talent agent who had seen them on television in a Bartók Quartet performance shortly after they had won a chamber music competition in Los Angeles, and was so taken with the intense rapport between them while they played that he thought he could make them into superstars—glitzy suits, platinum records, personal tour manager, and all. It was too heady for us to turn down without listening to him for a bit; I know that we all got a kick out of his idea; besides, he only wanted them to play string quartets—no messing around with the music—except that they might have to be miked to reach the tens of thousands of people who would be clamoring to hear them in huge stadiums! I guess all of us in the classical music world wish that we could get across the excitement and beauty of classical music to a really vast audience—to create the stir and the crazed enthusiasm lavished on popular music's heroes, not to mention the monetary rewards. This imaginative producer was reaching for that, and we talked with him for as long as we could suspend our disbelief.

The New York series that YCA itself sponsored remained the most important focus for the early years. Here the artists were heard by an enthusiastic audience of friends, family, fellow students, and a small but devoted subscription audience. Our subscribers were people who were adventurous enough to take a chance on someone no one had ever heard of. They became good friends of the organization, and eventually began to send contributions that helped to make our work possible. Whenever the coffers were empty I would beat the bushes and go to people that I thought could help, and eventually we would pull out of it. Certainly it wasn't always a picnic, but I had reassurance every step of the way.

A significant turning point in YCA's development occurred in 1964. To help cover the artists' fees for that first series in Baltimore—then a mere $150 per engagement—I got YCA's first foundation grant of $5,000 from the Martha Baird Rockefeller Fund for Music. When Donald L. Engle, director of the Fund, told us that they were going to give us the grant ("us" then being me and a part-time secretary), he strongly recommended that I establish a Board of Directors "because other foundations might expect such a thing." I asked him, "What for?" and asked him what a Board was supposed to do. Gently, he tried to explain it to me. At the time I thought it sounded pretty peculiar and useless, but nonetheless I put together a bunch of friends and family and established a Board of Directors.

By that time I started to have broader aspirations of where the organization could go. For example, I realized that I wanted to be able not only to present the artists in New York, but also to book each for at least 20 concerts per year and have them become really well known in the field. I also wanted to have auditions that were more structured, as more and more people wanted to be heard.

By our fifth season, 1965-66, things were finally beginning to settle in. I had taken on a full-time assistant, we had a jury for the final round of our annual auditions, and my booking activities were steadily increasing. In addition to our official Board of Directors, I had gotten, gulping hard, several musical celebrities to join an Advisory Board, including Leopold Mannes, the pianist and head of the Mannes College of Music; Rosina Lhevinne, the great piano pedagogue; Van Cliburn himself; Alexander Schneider, the violinist—with whom I had briefly studied chamber music while I was still in high school; and the renowned conductor Leopold Stokowski. Stokowski asked me some odd questions. He ended up writing me a letter warmly agreeing to join our Advisory Board because we "spent our money on helping the artists and not on overhead." It seemed like a dull reason for lending his illustrious name, but I was overjoyed. I suppose he was impressed with all YCA was doing for the artists on such a shoestring budget.

When Young Concert Artists was celebrating its tenth anniversary, I felt established, settled, recognized, pleased. But when people asked who were some of the artists that Young Concert Artists had started on their careers, their names still weren't well known. Pinchas Zukerman had just won the Leventritt Competition, but his was still an unfamiliar name; Paula Robison had not yet emerged as a successful solo flutist; Ilana Vered had temporarily stopped pursuing her career while involved with marriage and family. It was only in 1981, when YCA's twentieth anniversary was celebrated, that names such as theirs had emerged and were even famous. By then YCA's reputation for its selection of musical talent had begun to take hold across the country and made our job of selling complete concert series much easier.

Nineteen seventy-eight was a landmark year for YCA. Young Concert Artists, Inc., was awarded a $125,000 Challenge Grant from the National Endowment for the Arts. I guess one of my proudest moments was reading a letter that said that the grants were awarded to organizations selected as "valuable to the nation as a whole."

As a woman who has created a successful organization, I frequently hear such questions as, "Did being a woman pose problems for you at the start or on the rise?" I am surprised that one doesn't hear answers more frequently that being a woman was a help rather than a hindrance! For me, if anything, being a woman was an asset. I find that women tend to be resourceful, cooperative, interested, and energetic. These qualities are a pleasurable part of our traditional role—to organize life for other people, to cooperate and deal with people. A woman's ability to beguile can be as effective as the ability to be forceful and persuasive, and women can express appreciation more freely than men can. So I have been successful while utilizing my "feminine" traits rather than copying "masculine" traits.

There are quite a few women in prominent positions in the field of artist management. Kazuko Hillyer is the head of one of the biggest artist management firms, which bears her name; Ann Colbert and Agnes Eisenberger run the distinguished Colbert management; and Thea Dispeker is the head of her own very prestigious firm.

Actually, arts management has become a recognized field only recently. Most people who are "arts administrators" like me got into it sideways because they were interested in the art form. For example, most artist managers were originally musicians who went into the field as managers instead of becoming professional musicians themselves. Now, of course, there are arts administrators getting Bachelor's degrees, Master's degrees, and, for all I know, Ph.D.'s. The things that we learned just by doing and figuring it out as we went along are now being taught in colleges. I think that this is a very positive development. The running of an organization such as YCA has become quite a complicated thing, involving fund-raising and general administration in addition to artistic concerns.

As one can see from my family background, my upbringing prepared me to expect to do what I wanted, to feel no worries or constraints because of being a woman. I expected to work—and to be a wife and mother, as my mother had done. And I *am* enjoying all three roles. My husband, Charles Wadsworth, is the pianist/founder/director of the Chamber Music Society of Lincoln Center and obviously we share an involvement in music.

Juggling the demands of career and family has been relatively easy for me, in part because in my career I have been my own boss. I had the freedom to be home with our daughter Rebecca when I wanted to be, and to be working when I wanted to work. Also, I had Rebecca quite late—not until Young Concert Artists was ten years old. So once Young Concert Artists was "grown up," I could concentrate on the next baby!

WOMEN AS PERFORMING ARTISTS: STILL A DIFFICULT ROAD

While I don't think that being a woman affected the pace or direction of my own career, I do see it affecting the lives and careers of the women artists on the YCA roster. There is still the prejudice that men are stronger as performers or artists—although when audiences *hear* a female artist I don't believe that they think about gender for a minute in their absorption of the music. The preconceptions come into play afterwards with compliments such as, "She plays like a man." This presumably means that the music communicated strongly instead of limply. But I can't think of any performing woman artist today who plays in that dainty, sensitive caricature of the "feminine" way. And while no man could communicate as an artist without an extraordinary amount of sensitivity, I have never heard a male artist praised for "playing like a woman." Also, when trying to book a female violinist on a series, for instance, it is not uncommon to be told, "Sorry, I can't use her this year; we already have a female violinist on the series." I would *never* be told, "No, we already have too many male artists on the series."[2]

And then there *is* an emotional difference between men and women—the difference that women in their struggle for equality have sometimes tried to dispose of, in one way or another. That is, that women are sharers and nurturers—a great gift that enriches their lives and the lives of the men with whom they share the world. Most women artists suffer from those two pulls that are rarely in the same direction: the love of music and the fulfillment of their careers as artists, and the love of their loved ones and their fulfillment as people involved with friends, children, husband, and home. Both cannot be enjoyed at the same time. And although some decisions can be easily made—because women of these gifts are generally not indecisive—they are not always easily lived with. For men, the role is traditional: to have a career and to catch what they can of their families. A career woman can happily give up housework and grocery shopping, but she cannot as easily cut off the pleasures of sharing and nurturing. As the women's movement achieves its goals, I hope that women will find what is of true value and accept their womanly strengths. Men and women should respect each other as human beings whose gender qualities are to be treasured and not homogenized.

I believe that even those former YCA artists not widely recognized at this time will come into their own in future years. I believe in their gifts, and know how hard they have worked to develop them. I can't believe that that motivation could be lost, even if it takes longer for the success to come. Two cases in particular come to mind, both of them involving women who temporarily gave up their careers to concentrate on marriage and family.

Toby Saks was an extraordinary cellist; by the age of 20 she had already won the Pablo Casals International Cello Competition. She was talked about by everyone in New York and performed extensively. But then she married, moved to the West Coast, and started a family. She dropped out of sight professionally and a decade passed. But now she has emerged again as a strong cellist and musical force as the founder and artistic director of the Seattle Chamber Music Festival. Saks is artistically responsible for its success. She performs extensively in it and selects all the other musicians who participate. While she may not have leapt back into her solo cello career where she left off, she obviously grew as a person and as a musician, and when she did get back into the field as an artist and a creator, she had a lot more to give. In the old days you either were a performer or you weren't. Fortunately the music field has really bloomed since then. One can be a performer and a creator and an arts administrator and a manager all at the same time, and this kind of career is a very rewarding one for many people.

Another interesting case is that of pianist Ilana Vered. She had had quite an early success, and a lot of people were very excited about her. But then she, too, got married and started a family, and she stopped playing in public for five or six years. When she did eventually return to concertizing, however, it was with even more enthusiasm and determination than before. At that point she had the security of a family and a life of her own making, and this added an extra depth and assurance to her musical personality.

I think that the stereotypes of how things have to be in order to succeed in the music world are slowly being proven irrelevant. The most important qualities to have are determination, self-confidence, and talent. If you've got all those things, you can pretty much do what you want to do. There are those who wait for "it" to happen, and there are others who keep searching, working, moving toward their goals. Those who don't keep their eyes looking *beyond* what is in sight are much less likely to succeed. A hard fact that took me many years to realize is that in addition to great talent, encouragement, and opportunities, the artist also must have an inner goal—and a drive to achieve it that never lets up. But bulbs can rest dormant for years without losing their life or their ability to bloom, and I like to think that each artist chosen and nurtured by YCA will eventually have his or her place in the sun.

Young Concert Artists is now on very secure footing. Over the years we have developed well-established systems that work effectively. In fact, a recent event underlines that point. In 1983 I was approached by Sir Ian Hunter, an important manager in London who manages artists such as Isaac Stern, Yehudi Menuhin, and Daniel Barenboim. He said that he had always wanted to do something to help young artists. He had heard a great deal about Young Concert Artists and decided that he wanted to establish an organization in London modelled closely after my own YCA to help young British musicians. Of course, I was delighted. He sent a representative to the YCA office who spent three days interviewing everyone on the staff and asking questions about how they did everything. He then went back to London, taking with him copies of all our forms and copious notes. And now there is a sister organization in London called Young Concert Artists Trust.

The Young Concert Artists staff now numbers six, including myself. I continue to guide the auditions, which involve a rigorous system of preliminary, semifinal, and final auditions, as well as a large and distinguished jury. While I still design and direct the Young Concert Artists series in New York and in Washington, D.C., the national concert bookings are now handled by YCA's associate director, who matches me in the enthusiasm and individualistic style of her work. If I have a gift for ferreting out talent, other YCA staff members have an extraordinary gift for making concert presenters around the U.S. *eager* to engage YCA's artists. In 1984-85 YCA booked and contracted not only 600 single engagements, but over 30 complete series throughout the country.

I am confident that YCA will go on after me. While I have certain special qualities, anybody who takes over will bring a new personality to the

ARTISTS LISTED BY THE YEAR THEY JOINED
THE YOUNG CONCERT ARTISTS ROSTER

1961
Sanford Allen, *violinist*
Shmuel Ashkenasi, *violinist**
Ruth Glasser, *cellist*
Richard Goode, *pianist*
Jesse Levine, *violist*
Paula Robison, *flutist*
Joel Shapiro, *pianist*
Ilana Vered, *pianist*

1962
Kenneth Goldsmith, *violinist*
Ruth Laredo, *pianist*
Robert Martin, *cellist*
Lawrence Smith, *pianist*
Margaret Strum, *flutist*
Inger Wilkstrom, *pianist*

1963
Luis Garcia-Renart, *cellist*
Yoko Matsuda, *violinist*
Satoko Takemae, *pianist*

1964
Edward Auer, *pianist*
Mauricio Fuks, *violinist*
Jung-Ja Kim, *pianist*
Mary Beth Peil, *soprano*
Toby Saks, *cellist*

1965
Paul Green, *clarinetist*
Ko Iwasaki, *cellist*
Max Neuhaus, *percussionist*
Michael Oelbaum, *pianist*
Murray Perahia, *pianist*
Lorraine Prieur, *pianist*
Paul Zukofsky, *violinist*

1966
Jonathan Abramowitz, *cellist*
Nerine Barrett, *pianist*
Christiane Edinger, *violinist*
Donald Weilerstein, *violinist***
Pinchas Zukerman, *violinist*

1967
Joan Benner, *soprano*
Nobuko Imai, *violist*
Joseph Kalichstein, *pianist*
Arthur Thompson, *baritone*
Marcus Thompson, *violist*
Hiroko Yajima, *violist*

1968
Jean-Jacques Kantorow, *violinist*
Joyce Mathis, *soprano*
Anthony Newman, *harpsichord*
Ursula Oppens, *pianist*
Fred Sherry, *cellist*
Michael Webster, *clarinetist*

1969
Gita Karasik, *pianist*
Jeffrey Solow, *cellist*

1970
Mari-Elizabeth Morgen, *pianist*
Thomas Simons, *pianist*
Eugenia Zukerman, *flutist*
The Tokyo String Quartet

1971
Joy Blackett, *mezzo-soprano*
Christoph Henkel, *cellist*
Rolf Schulte, *violinist*
Speculum Musicae

1972
Mona Golabek, *pianist*
Francoise Regnat, *pianist*
Peter Rejto, *cellist*

1973
Emanuel Ax, *pianist*
Ani Kavafian, *violinist*
Diane Walsh, *pianist*

1974
Heiichiro Ohyama, *violist*
Robert Routch, *French horn*
Jeffrey Swann, *pianist*
Ronald Thomas, *cellist*

1975
none

1976
Daniel Adni, *pianist*
Boris Bloch, *pianist*
Stephanie Brown, *pianist*
Sung-Ju Lee, *violinist*
Daniel Phillips, *violinist*
The Chilingirian String Quartet

1977
Steven De Groote, *pianist*

1978
Colin Carr, *cellist*
Lynn Chang, *violinist*
Robert Cohen, *cellist*
Ida Kavafian, *violinist*

1979
Franck Avril, *oboist*
Sergei Edelmann, *pianist*
Zehava Gal, *mezzo-soprano*
Beverly Hoch, *soprano*
Marya Martin, *flutist*

1980
Toby Appel, *violist*
Chantal Juillet, *violinist*

1981
Stephen Burns, *trumpeter*
Marvis Martin, *soprano*
Christopher O'Riley, *pianist*
Jean-Yves Thibaudet, *pianist*
The Endellion String Quartet
The Mendelssohn String Quartet

1982
Carter Brey, *cellist*
William Sharp, *baritone*
Dominique Weber, *pianist*

1983
Jaime Bolipata, *pianist*
Ben Holt, *baritone*
Benny Kim, *violinist*
Anne-Marie McDermott, *pianist*
Jeremy Menuhin, *pianist*
Christopher Trakas, *baritone*

1984
Douglas Boyd, *oboist*
Daniel McKelway, *clarinetist*
Paul Meyer, *clarinetist*
Dawn Upshaw, *soprano*

1985
Erik Berchot, *pianist*
Marc Laforet, *pianist*
Gary Schocker, *flutist*

1986
Jean-Efflam Bavouzet, *pianist*
Anthony DeMare, *pianist*
Yuval Fichman, *pianist*
Paul Shaw, *pianist*
Ory Shihor, *pianist*
Christopher Costanza, *cellist*
Marcy Rosen, *cellist*
Maurice Sklar, *violinist*
Eric Ruske, *French horn*

* *Vermeer String Quartet*, founder, *first violin*

** Cleveland String Quartet, founder, *first violin*

Figure 4.2 YCA Roster, 1962-1986 Winners.

organization and I am sure that it will thrive. Young Concert Artists now has a great Board of Directors, and we hope to raise a two-million-dollar endowment by the end of our 25th anniversary season, 1985-86.

It has been a gratifying musical career, indeed, to have played a part in the discovery and development of gifted musicians and to have had a part in bringing their music to those who are moved by it. I know now that YCA will go on. Its spirit and systems are well established, and the need for Young Concert Artists, Inc., seems as great as ever. I am certain that YCA will continue to meet the challenge that I took up in 1961: to give great young talents the opportunity to become known and to share their gifts and their music with us all.

NOTES

1. YCA's "mini-residencies" incorporate educational interactions with music students and community groups and often include special sessions such as master classes or lecture-demonstrations in addition to local performances.

2. To give special assistance to its outstanding female artists, YCA offers the Mortimer Levitt Career Development Award for Women Artists, which includes a special solo recital at the 92nd Street Y and a solo recording.

5

*Elizabeth Sprague Coolidge, Twentieth-Century Benefactress of Chamber Music**

CAROL NEULS-BATES

The proliferation of chamber music in the United States is a relatively recent phenomenon. As a young nation assimilating European art music in the course of the nineteenth century, America fostered first the more accessible genres of symphonic and operatic music. The beginnings of a chamber music tradition, by contrast, date from the World War I era, at which point Elizabeth Sprague Coolidge, in a unique exercise of patronage, lent both her financial support and her personal energies to its cultivation. Sometimes called the "patron saint" and the "Lady Bountiful of Chamber Music," Coolidge sponsored chamber music festivals and countless individual performances, she underwrote chamber ensembles, and she commissioned new works and organized composition competitions. Finally, to perpetuate her various aims, Coolidge endowed a foundation at the Library of Congress in Washington, D.C.

The details of Elizabeth Sprague Coolidge's life and work are not widely remembered and are indeed worthy of review, especially as we seek to broaden the inquiry about women in music beyond the compositional role. There is a striking dichotomy between Coolidge's late career as a patron in the public eye and her earlier private life as a wife and mother. For Coolidge undertook musical philanthropy only at the age of 50, when the deaths of her parents and her husband gave her a considerable fortune, as well as the need for new activity. Music, however, had been a central part of her life since childhood.

The Sprague family monies were made in the wholesale grocery business in Chicago following the Civil War—a time when Chicago was fast

---

*Elizabeth Sprague Coolidge's patronage was certainly not limited to chamber music; she was also a generous patron of other art forms and institutions (e.g., she commissioned dance works such as Stravinsky's *Apollon Musagète* [1928], and she built and endowed the music auditorium at the Library of Congress which bears her name). But it is her early support of chamber music that makes her a unique figure in musical history, and which shall be explored in this article.

—Editors' note.

becoming the major food distribution center for the western half of the nation. Coolidge's father, Albert Sprague, was a native Vermonter and a graduate of Yale College's class of 1859, who subsequently left the East for Chicago in 1861 and founded the partnership Sprague, Warner and Company with Ezra Warner, another Vermonter, and Sprague's younger brother, Otto. Albert Sprague credited Otto as being the "brains" of the business—for instance, Otto developed the plans to advance credit to grocers in Denver and Salt Lake City with the provision that these grocers handle *only* Sprague, Warner products. Within fifteen years Sprague, Warner and Company became one of the largest wholesale grocery businesses in the world, making fair-sized fortunes for the three partners. Meanwhile, Albert Sprague had married his Vermont fiancée, Nancy Atwood, a former school teacher, and brought her to Chicago. Their first daughter, Elizabeth, was born in 1864.

Elizabeth Sprague Coolidge grew up initially on Washington Avenue on the West Side of Chicago, when that area was considered the proper place to live, and later in the 1880s in a grand home on Prairie Avenue on the South Side, which had just become exclusive. Like many well-to-do girl children of the time, she was educated privately. At age eleven she started piano lessons with Regina Watson at Watson's "School for the Higher Art of Piano Playing."

Elizabeth's younger cousin, Lucy Sprague Mitchell—the daughter of Otto Sprague—recalls in her autobiography that, as a young girl, Elizabeth typically practiced long hours.[1] Coolidge herself stated later in life that besides the musical rewards she derived from extended practicing, her piano teacher's "extraction from me throughout my girlhod, of reverence for duty, of coordinated self-control and uncompromising fidelity to standards" developed great strength of character.[2] Coolidge's progress as a young pianist can be traced through Regina Watson's school programs—from Bach, Raff, Mendelssohn, and Hummel, to Chopin. She gave her first solo recital at age eighteen in 1882.[3]

All too little other information remains extant about Elizabeth Sprague Coolidge's formative years. She is known to have travelled abroad several times with her parents—to Bayreuth on one trip in 1882, presumably to attend the second Wagner festival, and as far away as Egypt and Russia.[4] Whether she considered attending college or not is a moot question.[5] Once in her 20s, she is described by Lucy as a "determined individualist, with 'social' leanings." Lucy also attests to Elizabeth's especially close relationship with her mother, a woman with an "abundance of executive energy and an uninhibited tongue."[6] These qualities Coolidge certainly inherited and manifested in her later work as a major patron. Likewise, the experience of being among the prominent families that founded the Chicago Art Institute in 1879 and the Chicago Symphony Orchestra in 1890 prepared her for a leadership role in disseminating the arts.

In 1891, at the age of 27, Elizabeth Sprague married Frederic Shurleff Coolidge, an orthopedic surgeon in Chicago. The couple spent the first year of their marriage in Vienna, where Elizabeth continued her piano studies. Returning to Chicago, she fulfilled the roles of wife to Dr. Coolidge and mother to her son Albert, born in 1894, but she also fostered music through the musicales she gave in her home. Two especially notable public performances came about in 1893, the first when Coolidge played the Schumann *Piano Concerto in A Minor,* op. 54, at the Women's Building of the Chicago Columbian Exposition, and secondly an engagement with the Chicago Symphony Orchestra under Theodore Thomas.

Such recognition suggests that Coolidge could have pursued a professional career as a pianist had she wished, although traditional views about the proper sphere of married, wealthy women were amply in force to restrain her. Similarly, when she began to compose—also in the 1890s—she appears to have regarded composition as a private hobby, to be enjoyed by herself and her family. Her output, over the many years of her lifetime, concentrated on songs, the most ambitious undertaking being her cyclic setting of Elizabeth Barrett Browning's *Sonnets from the Portugese.*[7] In the ultimate scheme of things, however, Coolidge's experience in performance and composition admirably equipped her to be a highly astute benefactress.

In 1902 Dr. Coolidge contracted an infection while performing surgery, and after his recovery the Coolidges relocated to Pittsfield, Massachusetts, in search of a climate that was beneficial to his health. He resumed practice, only to become ill with tuberculosis in 1911. During these years in Pittsfield, Elizabeth Sprague Coolidge's life was relatively quiet in a social sense, if emotionally turbulent because of her husband's decline and her own battle against increasing deafness.[8] But despite these health problems and the fact that her Pittsfield home did not have the space for her Chicago musicales of old, Coolidge continued to play music with her son Albert, who grew to be a fine amateur oboist and violist, and with her friend Gertrude Watson, also a pianist.

The deaths of her husband in May 1915 and of her father and mother in January 1915 and March 1916, respectively, brought about significant changes for Coolidge. She no longer was the wife of a man whose career and health determined her mode of existence, and she was a very wealthy woman with a free rein to proceed as she saw fit. Her initial moves were to establish memorials for her relatives: for her father (in conjunction with her mother while she still lived), $200,000 for the construction of Sprague Memorial Hall at Yale University to house the music department; for her husband, $100,000 to the Anti-Tuberculosis Association in Pittsfield; and finally in memory of both of her parents, the endowment of a pension fund for the Chicago Symphony Orchestra. She also agreed to contribute up to $50,000 a year for ten years to her cousin Lucy's Bureau of Educational Experiments, which later was chartered as the Bank Street College of Education. Lucy notes that Elizabeth decided to underwrite the Bureau because she recognized its value, and besides, "it would take time to develop her plans for music."[9]

As it happened, Coolidge moved fairly quickly with those plans. In May 1916, Hugo Kortschak, a violinist formerly with the Chicago Symphony Orchestra, wrote Coolidge about the string quartet he had formed and about the need for financial assistance that would allow all four of the players to give up other employment in favor of quartet playing. Coolidge replied immediately from her New York address in encouragement:

> My dear Mr. Kortschak: I was very interested in your letter received this morning, and the programs and notices which you enclosed. It is a strange thing that your proposition is exactly what I had been having in mind for some years, particularly since my mother died lately, and I have felt myself able to turn my attention more practically to helping the cause of good music. Ever since I have known the late Mr. E. J. de Coppet, and have had the wonderful privilege of listening to the Flonzaley Quartette both at his house and in public, I have wished that the time might some time arrive when I, too, might foster and develop a string quartette of finest quality, but it has always been very vague in my mind, chiefly, I suppose, because I did not feel that I could afford it. Now, however, I am disposed to investigate the matter and have been only recently intending to inquire of a few musicians . . . as I sought the material for forming and highly training such a quartette.[10]

String quartets of distinction in the United States in 1916 were few in number; namely, Franz Kneisel's quartet, which was founded by the former concertmaster of the Boston Symphony Orchestra in 1885; the Olive Mead Quartet, established by a former pupil of Kneisel's in 1903; and the Flonzaley Quartet—mentioned by Coolidge in her letter above—which was developed with the patronage of Edward de Coppet, also beginning in 1903. Initially the Flonzaleys played only in private for Mr. de Coppet, and when in time they performed publicly de Coppet still reserved a portion of the year for their performances in his music room. An invitation to one of de Coppet's "evenings" was highly prized among New York's musical and social circles early in the century; frequently Mrs. de Coppet, a fine pianist, would join the Flonzaleys for quintets. Such was the model Elizabeth Sprague Coolidge wanted to emulate when she assumed support of Hugo Kortschak's quartet. Her vision soon expanded, however, and her patronage became more ambitious and public in stature.

The agreement Coolidge made with Kortschak and his associates was that they were to play for and with her at her summer home in Pittsfield—hence the name the Berkshire Quartet—and at her New York City apartment in the winter. Secondly, they were not to play in public until, "by their concentrated practice, they had reached a satisfactory level of excellence." Coolidge was very much involved in the quartet's work, and she clearly found the experience exhilarating: "Their rehearsals, which I regularly attended, were held in my music room. You can imagine what an education this was for me, whose musical idiom had hitherto been so largely formed by keyboard standards. I had never before so well understood the possibilities of abstract music."[11] The Berkshire Quartet gave informal programs for the public during the summer of 1917, and during the 1917-18 season, two successful concerts in New York.

Meanwhile, Coolidge was evolving her plans for a major annual festival of chamber music at a music colony near her summer home in Pittsfield on South Mountain. This project began during the summer of 1917 when Frederick Stock, the conductor of the Chicago Symphony Orchestra and a longtime friend, took Coolidge to visit with Carl and Ellen Battell Stoeckel at their famous music shed in Norfolk, Connecticut. As a result, Coolidge decided to build a similar establishment on South Mountain.

Once again she acted quickly and was able to open the first Berkshire Festival of Chamber Music on September 16, 1918, with five concerts in three days for 250 invited guests, including many illustrious musicians. Her concert programs reflected a skillful blend of contemporary and classical repertory that became the festival's trademark, together with performances of very high quality. Coolidge herself played in this first festival with her so-called "Berkshire boys" in Ludwig Thuille's *Quintet* for piano and strings, op. 20, receiving good press as a "serious musician of broad attainments," and a "musicianly and brilliant pianist."[12] The Berkshire Quartet also performed the two prize-winning compositions that were selected from a total of 82 submissions, while the new Coolidge-supported Elshuco Trio made its debut.[13] Music critics were enthusiastic and quick to grasp the significance of the festival for stimulating chamber music competition and performance in the United States. For the participants, who represented many nationalities, their coming together in wartime had special meaning. Ugo Ara, the Italian violinist, some years later vividly recalled to Coolidge: "Who can ever forget the thrill received at that first 'historical' festival in 1918, when your temple of music was the *only temple of music in the world* in which Allies, Aliens, and Neutrals could come to worship at the same altar, ennobled by the same ideal and kindled by the same love."[14]

Between 1918 and 1925 Coolidge sponsored and ably presided over seven festivals of chamber music on South Mountain. They were all of increasing importance and reflected her ever widening contacts and musical experience. Her orientation was decidedly toward the European art product and European performer, a situation not uncommon for someone of her generation.[15] The prize competitions and commissions she planned resulted in many fine works by composers such as Barber, Bartók, Bloch, Britten, Honneger, Loeffler, Malipiero, Martinu, Ravel, Respighi, Schönberg, Stravinsky, and Webern. Soon the interest in Coolidge's Berkshire festivals became so great that she was urged to present similar programs in Europe. Her first foreign festival took place in Rome in 1923; others followed in Naples, Venice, Prague, Paris, London, and other cities.

In 1925 Coolidge's support of chamber music entered still another stage with the establishment of the Elizabeth Sprague Coolidge Foundation at the Library of Congress through plans she developed over some time with Carl Engel, Chief of the Music Division. She was motivated, she explained, by the need to "institutionalize and impersonalize" her activities begun at

Figure 5.1 Elizabeth Sprague Coolidge. Used by permission of Music Division, The New York Public Library at Lincoln Center/Astor, Lenox and Tilden Foundations.

South Mountain and to obtain "official recognition by the United States Government of the musical interests of our people." She also, at the age of 60, welcomed the opportunity of sharing her responsibilities with the leadership of the Music Division.[16] An initial gift of $60,000 for the construction of the Coolidge Auditorium at the library was later increased, while the foundation was endowed with an annual income of $25,000.

With the establishment of the foundation, Coolidge gradually transferred the major share of her philanthropies to Washington, although she also continued with independent philanthropic ventures until the Depression caused her to retrench in favor of the foundation. The Coolidge Foundation continued the music festivals, commissioned new works, and also developed new ways of disseminating chamber music, such as partially underwriting concerts at educational institutions on a matching basis and sponsoring radio broadcasts in the mid-1930s when "serious" music was not generally heard on the radio. The radio broadcast was a pet project of Coolidge's, and in general she kept in close contact with the foundation.[17]

Coolidge especially enjoyed working with Carl Engel, who as chief of the Music Division administered the foundation from its inception in 1924-25 until he left the Library of Congress in 1934 to head G. Schirmer's. The lengthy Coolidge-Engel correspondence attests to a growing, fine friendship and contains a number of interesting exchanges on the question of "Americanism." Engel, the European immigrant now associated with a national American institution, felt that Coolidge lacked a proper commitment to the American cause in music—a sensitive issue for many American composers and performers of the 1920s and 1930s. Coolidge, on the other hand, had an outspoken preference for European music and culture, as noted here previously, and she argued that being loyal to high standards was the only real way to be loyal to American music. Indeed, she wrote to Engel in an undated letter assigned to 1926, it was more patriotic to "supply the best than to protect the national infant [music] industry." "I like to put my shoulder to the American wheel when my artistic loyalty and self-respect do not forbid it," she continued, and then she reminded Engel of her contributions to the American cause, some not without irony:

> I have given, I should think, hundreds of free concerts to the colleges, libraries, and music-loving communities from Massachusetts to California, have started the career and maintained the existence of more than one American artist or organization; have included American composers in dozens of programs here and abroad (the latter not always to the advancement of their prestige), and have had very few but Americans in the juries which have awarded the prizes to Europeans.

And finally, in answer to Engel's implied criticism that she was spending too much on her festivals in Europe for European audiences, Coolidge noted that she felt she must satisfy "a spiritual need in Europe during the intervals of an American crusade."[18]

Elizabeth Sprague Coolidge was active as a benefactress of chamber music until the very end of her long life in 1953 at the age of 91.[19] In total, she devoted 41 years to this second career that combined music patronage with management, performance, and friendship. It is the many good friendships she had with her beneficiaries that makes Elizabeth Sprague Coolidge's work as a music patron unique. She was especially fond of the English composer Frank Bridge and his wife Ethel, and Anna and Gian Francesco Malipiero. Her assistance to both composers was considerable, while in turn Coolidge greatly valued the company of the two couples on various travels. Whatever the situation or the friendship, however, Coolidge never ceased to be less than circumspect about her philanthropy.

Near the end of her life Coolidge gave a talk about her work as a benefactress, and, among the few anecdotes that attest to her great satisfaction in being with creative people, she described a scene in Naples in 1931, where her guests included Malipiero, Casella, Respighi, Pizzetti, and other Italian composers less well-known today. The last day of the Naples festival fell on St. Elizabeth's day, and in honor of *their* St. Elizabeth these gentlemen communally wrote a "Farewell" piece, which Casella played at the piano just before Coolidge sailed for New York.[20] Coolidge concluded her talk with this moving summation of her career: "I have often felt that my work for chamber music has shaped my own course of destiny quite as truly as I have attempted to guide its course. It has given my life a significance which had not, before, been revealed to me."[21]

NOTES

1. Lucy Sprague Mitchell, *Two Lives: The Story of Wesley Mitchell and Myself* (New York: Simon and Schuster, 1953), p. 41.

2. Gillian Anderson, "Elizabeth Sprague Coolidge," *Notable American Women,* ed. Barbara Sicherman and Carol Hurd Green (Cambridge, Mass.: Bellnap Press, 1980), p. 161.

3. Coolidge surely inherited her musical talent in large part from her mother, Nancy Atwood Sprague, who describes her own musical upbringing and early activity in singing in her *Pleasant Memories of My Life*, ed. Elizabeth Sprague Coolidge (New York: privately published, 1916). Unfortunately Atwood sheds no light on her daughter's life and work. The present author extends many thanks to Frances Thompson McKay for reporting on Atwood's book.

4. Mary Tolford Wilson, "Elizabeth Sprague Coolidge," *Dictionary of American Biography, Supplement Five (1951-55),* ed. John A. Garraty (New York: Charles Scribner's Sons, 1977), p. 128.

5. The question is worth raising, however, because of Lucy Sprague Mitchell's experience. True, Lucy was 14 years younger than Elizabeth and greatly influenced by the example of Jane Addams, whose Hull House—a settlement house founded in 1889—was supported by Otto Sprague among others. Lucy entered Radcliffe College in 1896 and upon graduation pursued a life-long career as an early childhood educator, writer, and college administrator, in addition to marrying and raising a family. See Mitchell's *Two Lives* and Joyce Antler, "Lucy Sprague Mitchell," *Notable American Women: The Modern Period,* pp. 484-86.

6. Mitchell, *Two Lives,* p. 40.

7. Coolidge's compositions, the majority in manuscript, are listed in the Library of Congress *Catalogs,* vol. 27 (1953-57). The songs are chiefly children's songs, inspired in large part by her son and her grandchildren. Among them are the *After Supper Songs* and *Slumber Sonnets.* She also composed several instrumental chamber works, including a *Christmas Sextet,* a *String Quartet* in E minor (191?) and a *Sonata* for oboe and piano (1945), which was published by Carl Fischer. Cf.

Lubov Keefer, *Music Angels: A Thousand Years of Patronage* (Baltimore: privately printed, 1976).

8. In a letter of 18 February 1929 to Carl Engel, Coolidge recalled her husband's final illness. Engel was then at a difficult juncture in his personal life. "But no one knows better than I do the slow agony of witnessing a changed personality in one's dearest love. Mine was rather a *disintegrated* personality; I had to face a disintegrated life and fight against moral and emotional shipwreck—for two." See the Elizabeth Sprague Coolidge Collection, Library of Congress.

Coolidge was equally brave about her own deafness. She employed a variety of hearing devices over the years, which she took no special pains to conceal.

9. Mitchell, *Two Lives*, p. 273.

10. Letter dated 13 May 1916 in the Elizabeth Sprague Coolidge Collection, Library of Congress. Kortschak presumably approached Coolidge because of her endowment of the Chicago Symphony Orchestra's pension fund.

11. Elizabeth Sprague Coolidge, *Da Capo* (Washington, D.C.: Library of Congress, 1952), p. 2.

12. *Musical America* 28, no. 22 (28 September 1918), p. 3.

13. The first prize was awarded to Tadeusz Iarecki for his *Quartet*, the second to Alois Reiser for his *Quartet* in E minor.

14. Letter dated 2 August 1928 in the Elizabeth Sprague Coolidge Collection, Library of Congress.

15. Somewhat similarly, Coolidge promoted the work of male composers and performers, not women.

16. Letter from Coolidge to Herbert Putnam, Librarian of Congress, dated 23 October 1924 in the Elizabeth Sprague Coolidge Collection, Library of Congress.

17. For Herbert Putnam, she was sometimes in too close contact. See Coolidge's letter of 8 May 1934 to Carl Engel in the Elizabeth Sprague Coolidge Collection, Library of Congress.

18. Letter dated [September 1926] in the Elizabeth Sprague Coolidge Collection, Library of Congress.

19. The foundation endures to this day and continues to commission chamber music works as well as to present chamber music concerts of the finest quality in the Coolidge Auditorium at the Library of Congress.

20. To be quite technical, Coolidge specifies the date as November 26, while the feast days in November for two different St. Elizabeths are November 5 for St. Elizabeth, the mother of St. John the Baptist, and November 19 for St. Elizabeth of Hungary. It is, of course, the concept that counts.

Being the thorough archivist that she was, Coolidge naturally saw to it that this composite composition was deposited with the Library of Congress together with all other scores and papers in her possession.

21. Coolidge, *Da Capo*, p. 14.

6

Arthur P. Schmidt, Music Publisher and Champion of American Women Composers

ADRIENNE FRIED BLOCK

In 1958, when the publisher Summy-Birchard bought out the Arthur P. Schmidt Company, both principals agreed to donate the Schmidt papers to the Library of Congress. In the Arthur P. Schmidt Collection are about 100,000 items of correspondence, printed editions of music, photographs, business records from 1889 to 1950, and 113 boxes of manuscripts—a rich and important collection of musical Americana preliminarily assessed by Wilma Reid Cipolla in a paper read to the Sonneck Society in Boston on 26 March 1984 entitled "Arthur P. Schmidt, Champion of American Music."

Much work is still to be done in the collection. There is not yet a complete list of the composers whose manuscripts are included. The current list omits even the composers' names for several letters of the alphabet. A computerized list of musical manuscripts is still in its beginnings. Correspondence is filed by author, but nothing is catalogued. Therefore, what is written here is based on the author's examination of the letters and music of a select group of women composers: a preliminary evaluation of the Schmidt Collection from a special point of view. The aim of this paper is to examine Schmidt's relationship to the women who composed art music for publication by the Schmidt company, and to understand Schmidt's role in the development of these women composers and in the promotion of their music.

Arthur P. Schmidt occupies a special place in the history of American music because of his role in identifying, developing, and supporting through publication American composers of art music. Schmidt was the first to specialize in American music and to take on as his responsibility the development of an American school of composition. Beginning in 1880, Schmidt specialized in the Boston-based composers we now identify as the Second New England School. Later he included composers outside that circle as well. Among the composers he published were some of the leading women of the period, whose works he promoted as energetically as he did those by men.

Because recognition and support of native composers has frequently come too late and grudgingly, if at all, Schmidt's role as champion of American women composers must be seen in the context of his championing of American art music as a whole—at a time when American musical life was dominated by Germans and German music. His accomplishment is even more striking because he himself was German born and trained. What he did was to publish the bulk of his composers' works, often under exclusive contracts, and not just those works he expected would make a profit for the firm. This policy gave the composers support and legitimacy and made the complete range of their outputs available to the public. Although other publishers followed his lead, for many years Schmidt was virtually alone as a champion of American composers of art music.

Because of the primacy of German art music at this time, such support was most helpful to all composers in the United States. But to women composers it was crucial because of the double handicap they labored under as Americans and as women. Many believed at that time that women simply did not have the "scientific" turn of mind to produce great works.[1] But while the argument about whether women could or should compose art music heated up during the latter part of the nineteenth and the early twentieth centuries, Schmidt just went ahead and published music by Clara Kathleen Rogers, Helen Hopekirk, Amy Marcy Cheney Beach, Margaret Ruthven Lang, and later Mabel Wheeler Daniels, Florence Newell Barbour, Marion Bauer, Gena Branscombe, Radie Britain, and dozens of others. If, as John Tasker Howard wrote, Schmidt "deserves a monument for what he did to publish the larger orchestral works of our early composers," then he deserves a second one for his even-handed treatment of the women and men whose works he published.[2]

Schmidt certainly was not the first to publish American music. As music historian and critic Oscar Sonneck noted, "From the beginning the [American music publishing] industry divided its attention between native products and reprinted foreign music."[3] By "native products" read hymns, anthems, parlor songs, piano pieces, and selections from the musical theater; by "foreign music" read art music in the public domain. European imprints were not covered by United States copyright law until 1891; as a result, all earlier European publications could be reprinted freely by American publishers. Schmidt, however, stated that he was in business to publish, not to reprint, music. His catalogues, therefore, include primarily original imprints, whether of works by European or American composers.

Schmidt's predecessors in the field of art music include the American publishers Oliver Ditson and Gustave Schirmer. In 1835, when Ditson began publishing music, he specialized in sacred and school music.[4] Included in Ditson's catalogue were works by Americans George J. Webb, Thomas Hastings, Josiah Woodbury, George F. Root, William Bradbury, and especially Lowell Mason.[5] Ditson later published some large-scale sacred works, among them George Frederick Bristow's *Praise of God*

(1860), Eugene Thayer's *Festival Cantata* (1874), and John Knowles Paine's oratorio, *St. Peter* (1874).[6] Ditson's catalogue of 1872 included a number of his own reprints of European composers that were in the public domain, including Beethoven, Handel, Gounod, and others. However, in 1876 Ditson began an octavo series of choral music that included some American works.[7] While such publications were important to the history of American music, they were isolated and few in number in relation to Ditson's European offerings. Ditson did not specialize in American art music; rather, he offered a sprinkling of American art works in an otherwise European repertory. Nor did he help develop new American talent, as Schmidt did beginning circa 1880.

The second major publisher of art music, Gustave Schirmer of New York, began in 1861. A German immigrant as was Schmidt, Schirmer aimed to create an American Breitkopf and Härtel.[8] Although he too published an occasional large-scale work by an American—in 1865 Beer and Schirmer issued Paine's *Mass,* op. 10—until his death Schirmer imported and printed European music primarily. Schirmer's *New Music Catalogue* of 1889 is typical. Along with the overwhelming number of European works were short pieces by Americans, including songs by Victor Herbert, George B. Nevin, Harry Rowe Shelley, and Frank van der Stucken. The lone woman in that catalogue was the German composer-pianist, Marie Würm (1860-1938). Sonneck noted the increasing numbers of smaller works by American composers that appeared in the latter part of the nineteenth century and from then onward.[9]

After G. Schirmer's death, French art music began appearing in Schirmer catalogues.[10] But it was only under Sonneck's editorship (1917-28) that Schirmer's began issuing large-scale art works by Charles Tomlinson Griffes, John Alden Carpenter, Charles Loeffler, Ernest Bloch, Leopold Damrosch, and Amy Beach, among others.[11]

Works by American women composers began to be issued in the 1790s.[12] Their works were part of the same traditions as those by male composers: for the stage, the parlor, and the church, with an occasional concert piece by a pianist who needed a virtuoso flourish to spice up a program.[13] But it was only in the 1880s that women entered the field of art music in significant numbers, and Schmidt was in large part responsible for their entry.

Schmidt was born in Altona, Germany, near Hamburg, on 1 May 1846.[14] He probably received his musical training before emigrating to the United States. Settling in Boston in 1866, he worked as a clerk in George D. Russell's music store. In 1868 he married Helene P. Suck, sister of the cellist, August Suck. Ten years after his arrival in this country he established his own business as an importer of music. But within a year he began publishing music by Europeans, and three years later by Americans, especially by members of the Boston group with whom he had friendly personal relations.

In 1881 Schmidt issued *The Teacher's Guide: A Catalogue of Music Graded for the Use of Teachers and Students.* The catalogue offered songs by George W. Chadwick (4), Georg Henschel (11), Helen Hood (4), Clayton Johns (1), Horatio Parker (2), and Clara Kathleen Rogers (2). There were choral works by Chadwick (3), Louis C. Elson (3), and John Knowles Paine, whose three choral works were for soli, chorus, and orchestra. Among the composers of works for piano were Chadwick, Arthur Whiting, and Paine. This was a most impressive list for his second year of publishing American works. The balance of the catalogue included original imprints of foreign composers and imported editions from the foreign publishers Schmidt represented. Year by year the balance shifted as Schmidt issued more American works. A catalogue from circa 1894 has a large number of American works, with those by women prominently featured, among them Beach, Margaret Ruthven Lang, Helen Hood, Alice Locke Pitman, Rogers, Hattie P. Sawyer, and Irene Hale.[15] Schmidt's catalogue of piano music issued circa 1900 illustrates his fairness in promoting women's along with men's works: Edward MacDowell, Alice H. Baker, Beach, Stephen A. Emery, Foote, Henry Holden Huss, and Lang are all featured.

In 1891 a historical study dealing with women's entry into the professions appeared, *Woman's Work in America.*[16] This became a favorite title. *Etude Magazine* in 1901 put out the first of four issues dealing with "Woman's Work in Music."[17] The same year Schmidt issued his catalogue, *Woman's Work in Music*, which included the following women:[18] Alice H. Baker, Mrs. H. H. A. Beach, Mrs. C. F. Chickering, Mary B. Crowninshield, Eunice Dean, Louise Bryson Dougall, Ella M. Guyton, Mildred J. Hill, Helen Hood, Margaret Ruthven Lang, Mrs. M. T. H. Middlemore, Edna Rosalind Park, Alice Locke Pitman, Claire Ring, Clara Kathleen Rogers, and Mary Knight Wood. This catalogue is unique, at least among those in the Arthur P. Schmidt Collection. Otherwise Schmidt did not single out or isolate his women composers.

Schmidt did issue individual albums of works by single composers. In a catalogue entitled *Favorite Songs by American Composers* (1896) were announcements of song albums of works by Beach, John Hyatt Brewer, Chadwick, Foote, Hood, Lang, MacDowell, Pitman, Rogers, and others. He also put out a two-volume collection entitled *Lyric Fancies: Album of Songs by American Composers* that includes works by Beach, Lang, Hale, Rogers, and Hood among the women. Helen Hopekirk, who after about 1887 had her works published by others, disappears from Schmidt's catalogues about that time.

Schmidt's tenure as head of the firm (1876-1916) coincided with the Golden Age of music publishing. The tremendous numbers of people making music at home and singing in amateur choruses in turn were receptive audiences for concert artists in the decades before radio and recordings. Newspapers and music journals—and there were many at the time—are filled with information about the activities of performers, and the journals also had many paid advertisements with photographs and testimonials placed by innumerable singers and instrumentalists. All of these reflect the vitality of concert life at the time and the viability of music as a profession.[19]

This flourishing concert life meant that it paid publishers to offer singers ever more art songs and solo instrumentalists ever more novelties. It is significant that new music in the latter part of the nineteenth century was welcomed by public and performers alike; indeed, performances of new works by Beach and Lang, for example, made the headlines as items of exceptional interest. Changes of musical style that would have disturbed a person such as Schmidt did come, but not until after Schmidt's retirement. The Boston group, especially the second and third generations after Paine, took the advent of musical Impressionism in its stride, and in some cases—as with Loeffler and Griffes—cherished that change. The more shocking changes, to "survivors" such as Foote, came as aftermaths of World War I.[20]

The other significant aspect of the period to affect women was, of course, the First Feminist Movement. Women felt empowered, as they had not before, to enter fields such as medicine, law, sculpture, and especially music. Opera, which must have its quota of female singers, was by this time made respectable, while the concert stage was open to women and men capable of seizing the public imagination.[21] First rank professional orchestras, however, remained closed to all women except harpists until World War II.[22] But women crowded into music in ever-increasing numbers during this period, swelling the ranks of performers, teachers, students, and composers. Through the women's club movement, women participated in all-women's choruses, for which a new repertory had to be created, and women functioned also as patrons and concert managers. In addition, the women's club movement was supportive of women composers, even to the naming of clubs after women composers like Beach, Lang, and Cécile Chaminade.

Whether the feminist movement influenced Schmidt to include women among his composers is not known; when the huge volume of material in the Schmidt Collection is read we may know more. But the movement did encourage women to work in the larger forms of art music. The times were propitious.

To satisfy the enormous demand for music, Schmidt like other publishers issued school music collections, teaching pieces for instrumentalists, and art music for the well-trained amateur, the aspiring professional, and the finished performer. He also catered to a thriving business in church music, providing sacred vocal, choral, and organ music in large quantities. But unlike other publishers Schmidt provided this music mainly from his American composers.

In an expanding market such as this, opportunities for women expand as well. The incomplete list of composers and tally of works by each composer show that women constitute 12 percent of those published by Schmidt from 1876 to 1958, and their works make up 13 percent of the total. When the Golden Age was over, the market contracted sharply. In 1890, Ditson, for example, had 100,000 titles; by 1930 the number had shrunk to 30,000.[23] It is probable that Schmidt had a similar experience, although parallel figures are not yet available. As we shall see, toward the end of Schmidt's life a number of leading women were no longer under contract to his company.

During Schmidt's active years and as a direct result of publishing art works by Americans, the number of performances of American music reached a level probably not duplicated since. Lang's songs, for example, were featured by internationally known singers Alma Gluck, Johanna Gadski, Sophie Braslau, John MacCormack, and Ernestine Schumann-Heink, who regularly sang the *Irish Love Song* as an encore.[24] Beach's songs had even wider circulation and were sung by Emma Eames, Maria Jeritza, Gadski, Schumann-Heink, and many others.[25] Some works by Lang and Beach became standard repertory in churches, and Beach's instrumental and chamber works had frequent performances by violinists Maud Powell, Eugène Ysaye, Franz Kneisel, and by pianists Teresa Carreño, Olga Samaroff, Josef Hoffman, and others as well. Many orchestras and secular choral groups also performed works by the women composers Schmidt published.[26]

The Boston Symphony Orchestra (BSO), which evidently took pride in its local composers, was a leader in promoting American works during Schmidt's time. Between its establishment in 1881 and 1931, the BSO gave 255 performances of works by American composers, or an average of four to five works per season.[27] On the list are Beach's symphony and piano concerto, Lang's *Dramatic Overture*, op. 12, Hopekirk's *Concerto in D* and *Concertstück in D minor,* and Ethel Leginska's *Two Short Pieces* for orchestra. The year 1900 was a special year for women. The BSO played works by both Beach and Hopekirk as well as by Chadwick, Frederick Converse, and Rubin Goldmark. In 1917, the year after Schmidt retired, the BSO practically had an American festival. They played works by Edward Ballantine, Beach, Chadwick, Philip Greeley Clapp, Converse, Loeffler, and MacDowell. The high point was reached in 1927, when fourteen American works were programmed; although none were by American women, they did play a work by Germaine Tailleferre.

Arthur Foote stated that Schmidt "wished that no year should pass without one or more large-scale works appearing with his imprint."[28] Here is a list of major works by eight Americans that he published between 1880 and 1900:[29]

1880 John Knowles Paine, *Symphony no. 2,* "Im Frühling," Op. 34

1881 Paine, *Oedipus tyrannus,* op. 35 (rev. 1899; full score pub. 1908)

1882 Paine, *The Realm of Fancy,* op. 37, cantata

1882 Paine, *Phoebus, Arise*, op. 37, cantata

1883 Paine, *The Nativity*, op. 38, cantata (rev. in 1903 as op. 39; pub. in piano-vocal score)

1883 George Chadwick, *Thalia Overture*

1886 Horatio Parker, *King Trojan*, op. 8, cantata

1886 Arthur Foote, *The Farewell of Hiawatha,* op. 11

1888 Chadwick, *Symphony no. 2,* op. 21

1889 Chadwick, *Lovely Rosabelle,* cantata

1889 Edward MacDowell, *Etude de Conzert,* op. 36, for piano and orchestra

1890 Margaret Ruthven Lang, *The Jumblies,* op. 5 for male chorus and two pianos

1890 Amy Marcy Cheney Beach, *Mass in E-flat*, op. 5 for soli, chorus, orchestra (pub. in piano-vocal score)

1891 Chadwick, *Melpomene Overture*

1891 MacDowell, *Suite,* for orchestra, op. 42

1892 Beach, *Festival Jubilate,* op. 17, for chorus and orchestra (pub. in piano-vocal score)

1892 Foote, *Symphonisches Prolog: Francesca da Rimini,* op. 24

1892 Foote, *Serenade,* for string orchestra, op. 25

1895 Chadwick, *The Lily Nymph,* for chorus and orchestra

1896 Chadwick, *Symphony no. 3*

1896 Foote, *Suite,* for orchestra, op. 36

1898 Henry K. Hadley, *Ballade,* for chorus and orchestra

1900 Beach, *Piano Concerto,* op. 45 (pub. in two-piano score)

It was on works such as these that Schmidt took especial financial risks. In addition, he also published large-scale chamber, choral, and instrumental works without orchestra. Some instrumental works were so demanding technically, for example Beach's "Fireflies," op. 15, no. 4, that their market was limited to only the most accomplished performers. To balance these expenditures, however, Schmidt, who also was practical, was increasingly insistent that composers also produce educational music, on which the business increasingly depended.

Schmidt specialized in American music until his retirement in 1916. Correspondence shows, however, that his retirement was in some ways more nominal than actual for he was in constant touch with his firm and kept up a lively correspondence with his composers as well. After his retirement, the firm was headed by his long-term associates, Henry A. Austin, Harry B. Crosby (d. 1945), and Florence J. Emery (d. 1946), who collectively continued to publish many of the composers originally brought in by Schmidt himself.

Some indication of Schmidt's working methods can be gathered from correspondence with women composers and the actual record of publication. For Clara Kathleen Rogers (1844-1931), the first woman composer of art music published by Schmidt, there is unfortunately no correspondence for the latter part of the nineteenth century and only a few letters from the twentieth.[30] However, there is the music Schmidt published and the record of Rogers's involvement in Boston's musical life, a signal factor in her life as a composer.

Rogers was a generation older than Beach and Lang. When she settled in Boston in 1873 she already had an international reputation as a singer under her stage name, Clara Doria. Rogers was multi-talented, and her training at the Leipzig Conservatory—where, at age 12, she was the youngest student ever accepted—was in piano, voice, and theory. At that time composition classes were not open to females, even to those like Rogers, who had been composing since they were very young children.[31] Rogers came to this country in 1871 to sing her debut in New York with the Parepa-Rosa Company. Two years later Otto Dresel, the pianist, urged her to settle in Boston, and she then accepted a position as soloist at Trinity Church, where James Cutler Dunn Parker was organist and Phillips Brooks was minister. She quickly became part of Boston's musical elite. Among her close friends were John Sullivan Dwight, Paine, Longfellow, and Louis and Elizabeth Cary Agassiz of Harvard and Radcliffe, respectively. She also was close to the Langs, father and daughter, to Foote, Chadwick, Julius Eichberg, MacDowell, Hopekirk, and Beach. Rogers taught voice for many years, at first privately and from 1902, at Chadwick's request, at the New England Conservatory.

Rogers's output, except for a few instrumental works, consists entirely of art songs. In her memoirs, Rogers states that she wished she had had the training in orchestration that would have prepared her to write larger works.[32] From 1882, when Schmidt published her first set of songs, she composed steadily until 1906, and Schmidt just as steadily issued her works: 61 songs and two instrumental pieces. As Rogers noted, the assurance of regular publication was a catalyst for her. In the *Teachers Guide* of 1881 Schmidt listed five of Rogers's songs, among them "Clover Blossoms."

Subsequent catalogues regularly list her songs as they were published. After Rogers's appointment to the conservatory, she became increasingly involved with teaching and redirected her creative energies into the publication of books on voice culture.

Schmidt regularly sent out new music for review in music journals such as the *Music Review,* the *Musical Courier, Etude,* the *Musical Leader* of Chicago, and others, as well as notices of performances of his composers' works. Louis C. Elson wrote in the *Boston Musical Herald* in 1883 that Rogers's songs were "the most poetic and genuinely beautiful we have seen for a long time."[33] A half century later William Treat Upton wrote that as fine as were her early songs, her late songs, such as "Overhead the Treetops Meet," are her best.[34]

Schmidt's relationship with the Scottish-born pianist, composer, and teacher Helen Hopekirk (1856-1945), unlike that with Rogers, was neither as her first nor as her principal publisher; he was, however, her first American publisher. Schmidt issued a set of six songs and a choral work

Figure 6.1 "Clover Blossoms" (Oscar Leighton) by Clara Kathleen Rogers, No. 2 from *Six Songs*. © 1882 Arthur P. Schmidt Co.

(1886-87) early in her publishing career, thus helping to launch her as a composer in this country even before she settled here permanently.[35] Hopekirk came here on a concert tour and remained for four years. She made her United States debut as a pianist with the Boston Symphony Orchestra on 7 December 1883 and subsequently played 11 more concerts with that orchestra, as well as appearing frequently with other Boston-based groups including the Kneisel Quartet. When she returned in 1891 on her second tour, her first stop was again Boston, when she played the Tchaikovsky *Concerto* no. 1 with the BSO on 23 January 1891. Hopekirk settled in Boston permanently in 1897 after accepting Chadwick's offer of a teaching post at New England Conservatory. Like Rogers, Hopekirk's introduction to Boston's musical circles as a performer facilitated her transition to published composer.

A third composer Schmidt published was Margaret Ruthven Lang (1867-1972). Lang entered the circle of Boston's musical elite not as a

Robert Browning

Song from "Pippa passes."

Clara Kathleen Rogers

"Overhead the tree-tops meet"

Figure 6.2 "Overhead the Treetops Meet" (Robert Browning), op. 36, a late song by Clara Kathleen Rogers. © 1903 Arthur P. Schmidt Co.

performer but as the daughter of one of its established members. Her father, Benjamin Johnson Lang, was an organist, pianist, composer, teacher, and conductor of the Cecilia and Apollo Clubs; in short, one of the most influential people in Boston's musical life. Lang not only studied with her father, but she also relied on his opinions about her compositions, which she submitted to him for approval before sending them off to a publisher.[36] In addition, B. J. Lang introduced many of his daughter's compositions during concerts he conducted. For his daughter he was teacher, mentor, and sponsor. But Schmidt, by his publication of Lang's works, gave them wider circulation and availability.

Of Lang's 185 works, Schmidt published over 165, including songs, choral works, chamber music, and piano solos beginning in 1889 with her first published works. The song "Ojalá" was among the first of Lang's works Schmidt published. That same year, the song was given at a concert of American music at the Trocadero during the Paris Exposition.[37]

Andantino.
Con moto.
mp
Spring comes hith-er, Buds the rose;
mp
mp
Ro-ses with-er, Sweet spring goes, O-ja-là! Would she car-ry me.
ritard.
ten.
ritard.
mf
Summer soars, Widewinged day On-ward pours To the day; O-ja-là,
mf
ten.
Parlando.
mp
Would he car-ry me. Soft winds blow, West-ward borne,
mp

Figure 6.3 Margaret Ruthven Lang's song "Ojalá" (George Eliot pseud.). © 1889 Arthur P. Schmidt Co.

Lang composed a number of works that were not published, among them works for orchestra. Schmidt did publish two of the larger works, for chorus and orchestra, but in piano-vocal scores. The orchestration for one of these two, *The Heavenly Noël*, op. 57, still exists in manuscript.[38] The other orchestral works—three overtures, a ballade, incidental music to Rostand's *The Princess Far Away,* and four works for solo voice and orchestra—are lost, perhaps destroyed by the composer. It seems strange that Schmidt did not publish these works, considering the distinguished orchestras that performed them: the Boston Symphony, the Theodore Thomas Orchestra, and the Baltimore Symphony Orchestra, among others.

Figure 6.4 The Heavenly Noël (Richard Lawson Gales) by Margaret Ruthven Lang, piano-vocal score. Originally written for mezzo soprano solo, women's chorus, and chamber orchestra. © 1916 Arthur P. Schmidt Co. Used by permission of Summy-Birchard Music Division of Birch Tree Group Ltd.

When the Boston Symphony played Lang's *Dramatic Overture* in 1893, they were playing a work by a woman for the first time.

Lang stopped publishing and probably composing as well at age 50. Unfortunately, the Lang-Schmidt correspondence, which consists of letters written between the years 1901 and 1939, gives no clue to the omission of the orchestral works from among those Schmidt published. Judging by the wit, freshness, and craft of her songs and choral works, this is quite a loss. Nevertheless, without a contract with Schmidt, and given her propensity for harsh self-criticism, Lang might have allowed many fewer works to be published or even to survive than actually have.

Lang and Amy Marcy Cheney Beach were born the same year, but unlike Lang, Beach began to compose almost as an infant and continued almost to her death in 1944. The relationship between Amy Beach and the Schmidt Company was one of the longest lasting and most thoroughly documented; the correspondence it generated is important as a source of information on both Beach's life and works and Schmidt's methods and musical concerns.

We do not know when Schmidt and Beach met, nor when Schmidt became aware of Beach's compositions. She entered Boston's musical circles as Amy Marcy Cheney, the *Wunderkind*. From the time she was eight, Amy Cheney's progress as a young artist was monitored by an elite circle of composers, conductors, performers, critics, literati, and musical amateurs of Boston and Cambridge. Her autograph album, the earliest entry in which is 1878, testifies to those early connections.[39] For example, a letter from Longfellow dated 15 November 1880 and addressed to "Miss Amy" thanks her again for her beautiful piano playing and encloses the autograph she requested. In 1881, Rogers wrote in the same album: "Wishing you great happiness in the future, and that your artistic career may prove as brilliant in its fulfillment as it now is in promise." If most of the fuss was over her piano playing, it must be remembered that she was yet to prove herself as a composer.[40]

When Amy Cheney made her debut at the age of 16, interest in her was extremely high, the Boston music colony turned out to hear her, and the papers found the event noteworthy. Her marriage to Henry Harris Aubrey Beach, a surgeon on the faculty of the Harvard Medical School and personal physician to many Boston musicians as well as to Schmidt, merely reinforced her ties to that community. The year of Beach's marriage, 1885, was also the year of her debut with the Boston Symphony and the year Schmidt began publishing her works. Her professional and personal ties with the Boston community were so strong and her reputation as a pianist so well established that she could afford to curtail her playing and concentrate on composition, something that Henry Beach encouraged.

With the publication (under the name of Cheney) of her op. 1, no. 1, "With Violets," Beach began a relationship with Schmidt that ended only with the dissolution of the Arthur P. Schmidt Company. Between 1885 and 1944, Beach composed over 300 works; Schmidt issued over 200. This figure does not reflect the actual number of imprints. Typically, most songs appeared in at least two keys, and a number of works also appeared in more than one arrangement; in addition, Schmidt issued two albums of Beach songs. Thus the number far exceeds 200. The period during which Beach and Schmidt had the closest relationship was from 1885 to 1910—the years of her marriage—when Schmidt was Beach's exclusive publisher. During that period he issued all her works through op. 71, about 150 individual pieces.

Figure 6.5 "With Violets" (Kate Vannah), op. 1, no. 1 by Amy Marcy Cheney (Beach); facsimile of original manuscript. © 1885 Arthur P. Schmidt Co.

Many of Beach's large-scale works come from this period, among them the *Mass in E-flat*, op. 5 (1890), the *Gaelic Symphony*, op. 32 (1897), the piano concerto, op. 45 (1900), the violin and piano sonata, op. 34 (1899), the piano quintet, op. 67 (1909), and a large number of choral works including several with orchestra and the *Service in A*, op. 63 (1906). Schmidt published only one of these in full score, the symphony. The *Boston Herald* greeted its issuance with these words:[41]

> Mr. Arthur P. Schmidt has published the full orchestral score of Mrs. H.H.A. Beach's Gaelic Symphony, which was performed by the Boston Symphony last season. The score is beautifully engraved and printed in the style for which Leipsic has so long been famous. Again Mr. Schmidt distinguished himself as the only American publisher who gives encouragement to native composers by printing their large orchestral works and then giving them a permanent form and circulation they would not otherwise attain. Mrs. Beach's fine symphony merits the handsome form in which it has been issued, for it is prominent among the masterly works in its class that have been written by an American musician. It is a pity, however, that the title page was not couched in English instead of German.

Even though Schmidt's Leipzig branch printed the larger score, the *Herald* columnist suggests that the pride Bostonians felt in their own was to be not one whit diminished by a suggestion of German origin for the published score itself.

Henry Beach was both a close friend of Schmidt's and his physician, a relationship that probably predated his marriage to Amy Cheney. Some of the early Beach-Schmidt correspondence is signed by Henry Beach, although increasingly his wife took care of the business relationship with Schmidt. Among the letters from Dr. Beach to Schmidt is one that, while oblique, suggests the former's intense pride and belief in his wife's works. On 29 November 1901, Sigmund Beel and Henry Bird gave the London premiere of Beach's *Sonata*, for violin and piano, op. 34. The reviews, unlike those of the work's first performance in New York by Beach and Franz Kneisel in 1899, were enthusiastic. It is likely that Dr. Beach, having heard about the London reviews, asked Schmidt to get copies for him. On 19 December 1901, Dr. Beach must have received those copies, for he wrote to Schmidt: "The quotations appeared tonight thanks to your unfailing kindness and ready sympathy. It is a great satisfaction to have justice on our side once in a while and to be able to appeal to a friend for his kind offices, Be sure to let me know when I can reciprocate. You know I am *always* ready." Shortly after this letter was written, reprints of the London reviews appeared in the Boston papers. Major compositions such as this one or the symphony and piano concerto were considered by all, including the Beaches, as her most important works, and their critical reception was taken very seriously. The reprinting of the London reviews in Boston papers was a way of putting "justice" back on "our side" after the earlier poor reception.

In another letter (dated 4 January 1902), Dr. Beach thanks Schmidt for a

Christmas gift, a piece of sculpture called "The Nubian Minstrel." The same sculpture, along with a number of other gifts from Schmidt, is mentioned by Amy Beach in a letter to Schmidt written 13 February 1911, after the death of Henry Beach:

> There are several valuable gifts from you to my husband which he prized highly and which added much to the attractiveness of our home. It seems to me now a great pity that these should be idle in a storage warehouse when they might be giving so much pleasure. And it naturally occurs to me that you might like to have them back again, enriched as they now are by association with the life of your old friend.

Most of the letters from Amy Beach to Schmidt, however, are devoted exclusively to business matters. A typical example, a letter of 7 October 1901, opens: "The addition of new works to the contract are correct excepting that the edition of the "Hymn of Trust" *without* the violin obbligato is not mentioned. I return the contract, therefore, in order that both editions should be represented."

Beach was as meticulous in the preparation of scores for publication as Schmidt was in their issuance, a matter documented by their correspondence. It also shows the care with which Beach and Schmidt kept records of reviews, of performances, of professional copies sent out, and of advertisements and press releases announcing new works and reminding the public of those previously issued.

Shortly after Henry Beach died, Amy Beach wrote on 10 October 1910 in response to a letter from Schmidt offering to advance her money should she need it:

> You will understand how doubly dark my life seems when I tell you that my dear mother is *very* ill, and has been so ever since my husband's death. I live now for her, and must give her every comfort that can be furnished to help her bear her great pain and increasing problems. Of course, it all means a heavy outgo of money, and no brave husband to work and fight for me. Whatever can come from the sale of my compositions will be a great help to me until I am strong enough to take up other musical work. Therefore I shall appreciate any increase of advertising or other placing of my work before the public that you see fit to undertake. I should not have ventured to trouble you with these personal details save for the kind suggestion in your note.

Schmidt in response offered Beach advances on her royalties which she gratefully refused in the hope that increased sales would fill the breach.

Beach sailed for Europe in September 1911 several months after her mother died. Her plan was to rest and then embark on a European concert tour in which her works would be played, with herself at the piano wherever possible.[42] The purpose was to establish a European reputation that would help her build up her public in the United States. (This was necessary because she had stopped concertizing—except for occasional benefit programs—the year of her marriage.) Her plan worked out quite well. Her concerts in Europe were enthusiastically received by public and critics alike, and on her return in the fall of 1914 she was already booked for an extended tour of the United States.[43]

During Beach's European tour, her concern about sales came through in her correspondence with Schmidt. She was particularly vexed that Schmidt, despite his Leipzig branch, was not able to keep European dealers supplied with enough works to satisfy the demand that her concerts created.[44] Probably as a result of this dissatisfaction, she contracted with G. Schirmer to publish her future works beginning in 1914. Of course, this did not mean the end of her relationship with Schmidt or his firm, since they continued to handle the considerable volume of sales of works already published. In 1922, the year after Arthur Schmidt died, Beach returned to the firm, bringing a pair of her most successful works for publication, the "Hermit Thrush" pieces, op. 92, for piano. For the next 17 years she continued to have works published by the Schmidt Company but never again under an exclusive contract.

A number of composers under contract to Schmidt were writing works other than art music. Among them were Mary Turner Salter (1856-1938), whose "Cry of Rachel," the epitome of the sentimental song, enjoyed a tremendous popularity on the concert stage. Other writers of lighter songs included Emilie Frances Bauer (1865-1926), music critic, composer, and Marion Bauer's older sister and first teacher; Emilie Bauer wrote under the pseudonym Francisco di Nogero. There was also Edna Rosalind Park, Helen Hood, and Irene Hale (wife of the critic Philip Hale). Quite a few women wrote educational music for schools and instrumental and vocal students, among them, Juliet A. Graves Adams (1858-1951), Florence Newell Barbour (1866-1946), Edith Hatch and her sister, Mabel Lee Hatch, Mari Paldi, Mabel Madison Watson, and especially Anna Priscilla Risher, who wrote over a hundred works published by Schmidt.

In the next generation after Beach and Lang there were several composers of art music among the women, the most notable being Mabel Wheeler Daniels, Gena Branscombe, and Marion Bauer. All three were for a time under contract with Schmidt beginning in the years before Arthur Schmidt retired. Of the three, only Daniels (1878-1971) was a native of Boston. The Schmidt Company published most of Daniels's work written between 1905 and 1929, including songs and choral music, some with orchestra. (The company did not publish a sonata for violin and piano which remained in manuscript, nor did it publish her orchestral works, some of which later appeared under J. Fischer's imprint, following the termination of her contract with Schmidt.)

A singer, pianist, and conductor as well as composer, after graduating from Radcliffe in 1900, Daniels became a student and later a friend of George Chadwick.[45] She also studied composition in Munich, an experience she described in *An American Girl in Munich: Impressions of a Music*

Figure 6.6 From "A Hermit Thrush at Eve," op. 92, no. 1, by Amy Marcy Cheney Beach. © 1922 Arthur P. Schmidt Co. Used with permission of the MacDowell Colony, Inc., and Summy-Birchard Music Division of Birch Tree Group Ltd.

Student.[46] While early works like the song "Starlight" were tonal and consonant, her works became more dissonant and later moved toward atonality. Many of her works are for women's chorus, a reflection of her involvement with choral groups as a student and later as a conductor.

Her large-scale choral works with orchestral accompaniment appeared in piano-vocal scores, and Schmidt offered the manuscript scores and parts for rental. A work for baritone solo and orchestra, *The Desolate City,* op. 21, which was composed and first performed in 1913 at the MacDowell Festival, Schmidt also issued in a piano-vocal score.[47]

Allegro energico
ff
cres - cen - do
sfz
8va
f
ritard. molto
Molto moderato
(Horns)
Ped.
p con molto espr.
p
Dark to me is the earth.
Dark to me are the heav - ens.
dolce
Where is she that I loved, the wo - man with eyes like stars?
(Str.)
rall.
pp a tempo
Des - o - late are the streets.

Figure 6.7 *The Desolate City* (Wilfrid Scawen Blunt), op. 21, by Mabel Wheeler Daniels, opening section (piano-vocal score). Originally for baritone solo and orchestra. ©1914 Arthur P. Schmidt Co. Used with permission of the New England Conservatory of Music and Summy-Birchard Music Division of Birch Tree Group Ltd .

A letter from Daniels to Schmidt is typical of a number of exchanges between Schmidt and his composers and one that demonstrates his function as editor as well as publisher. On 12 November 1912 Daniels wrote: "As you see by the fresh appearance of the two part songs, I have acted on your suggestion and changed them somewhat. I have raised the low places in 'Secrets' (Op. 22 no. 1 for men's chorus and piano] and altered the tempo of the funny piece."

Schmidt published over half of Daniels's works; the remainder were published by J. Fischer and a scattering of other publishers. Her most important works, *Deep Forest,* op. 34, no. 1 for orchestra, and *The Song of Jael*, op. 37, for soprano soli, chorus, and orchestra appeared in 1932 and 1937, respectively, issued by J. Fischer. Clearly the Schmidt Company, especially after Schmidt's death, was no longer taking the same risks to bring major works to the public's attention, especially those by women.

The same pattern of lessened commitment held in the cases of Branscombe and Bauer. When Schmidt brought Gena Branscombe (1881-1977) onto his roster of composers, he reached outside the Boston circle. Branscombe was born in Canada and educated in Chicago; she taught at Whitman College, Washington, studied for a year in Europe, and married and settled in New York in 1910.[48] Schmidt, who had issued a single work of Branscombe's in 1905, offered her a contract in 1911 and put out her first sets of songs and instrumental pieces for violin and piano, including "At the Fair," op. 21 no. 2.

In the following undated letter to Schmidt, Branscombe is no doubt replying to a request that she change a piece to suit him. Her reply shows that, unlike Daniels and others, Branscombe did not welcome such requests. Nor was she pleased with the exclusive aspect of the contract:

> Shall see Mr. Farrell shortly. Don't see where "At the Fair" could be shortened or changed.
>
> About contracts—the waiting for an accounting until the entire edition is sold would not be a stumbling block to me. But I don't understand where the benefit comes from binding myself to show you all my things first. If you do not want them, you return them as any other publisher should. If you bind yourself to do special advertising—because of your right to my best things—that makes a difference. But at present I don't see how that clause has much bearing on the case. . . . If you like the things I'll send you, you'll take them anyway.

The record of publishing for the next ten years shows that Branscombe did sign the contract. She must have been satisfied with Schmidt's promotion of her works; indeed, a few years later Branscombe in a letter to Schmidt regrets ever having agreed to publish music elsewhere. However, after 1921, the year Schmidt died, the agreement was no longer in effect; her publishers then included not only Schmidt but also Boosey, Carl Fischer, and J. Fischer. The last work of Branscombe's that the Schmidt Company issued, *The Dancer of Fjaard*, for soloists, chorus, and orchestra, came out in 1926. The reason the company stopped issuing her works is unknown; the development of Branscombe's style was evidently not a key concern in this decision, as it is never mentioned as a problem.

Disagreements about musical style did become a problem between Schmidt and Marion Bauer (1887-1955). Like Branscombe, Bauer was not a Bostonian: she was born of French stock in Walla Walla, studied in New York, and in 1906 became one of Nadia Boulanger's first American students.[49] In 1910, Bauer went to Europe again, this time to study in Berlin with the German composer Jean Paul Ertel (1865-1933).

In 1912, Bauer signed a seven-year contract with Schmidt, and he subsequently published her songs and choral and instrumental works. Their correspondence shows unusually close relations between the two. However, at the time the contract was about to expire, Schmidt, who had retired but remained in contact with many composers, must have requested that Bauer, who had earlier assured Schmidt that a work was "*not* particularly modern,'' write in a more simple style.[50] Her reply is dated 10 May 1918: ''It is not stubbornness on my part not to write simple things. I can only write what I feel—and someday (soon I hope) I shall learn to do the *big simple* thing. I must do my work in steps—evolutionary, not revolutionary. I have so little time to write that naturally change of style is slow.''

A letter from Bauer to Schmidt dated 16 July 1918 signals the end of their relationship as composer and publisher:

> I take it for granted that you really don't want the manuscripts and that I am free to show them to anyone else. At any rate, I should like your permission to do so, for up to the present I have never submitted any of my work to any other publisher for any reason. . . . I would be glad to know just what kind of music you want to publish and whether or not you would like me to write a war song or so? I have steered away from them but if they would mean anything to you I would be glad to try.

Figure 6.8 The opening of Gena Branscombe's *The Dancer of Fjaard* (composer), for soprano and alto soli, women's chorus, and piano (also arranged for chamber and full orchestra). © 1926 Arthur P. Schmidt Co. Used with permission of Gena Tenney Phenix and Summy-Birchard Music Division of Birch Tree Group Ltd.

Schmidt's complaint may have been more a practical than a stylistic one. In 1922, the same year that G. Schirmer published Bauer's lush and technically demanding suite for piano, *From the New Hampshire Woods,* op. 12, the Schmidt Company issued her *Six Preludes for Piano,* op. 15. The latter set, while dissonant, has a pared-down texture that is relatively undemanding technically. Perhaps Bauer wrote these to please Arthur Schmidt, who had of course died the preceding year.

We do not yet know whether, from the 1920s on, the Schmidt Company had a lessened commitment to women as composers or to contemporary composers of both genders. For this information we must wait for the

Figure 6.9 Marion Bauer's "White Birches," no. 1 in the set *From the New Hampshire Woods* for piano solo. © 1922 by G. Schirmer, Inc. All rights reserved. Used by permission of the publisher, G. Schirmer, Inc., and Harrison Potter.

Figure 6.10 No. 4 of *Six Preludes for the Piano* by Marion Bauer. © 1922 Arthur P. Schmidt Co. Used by permission of Summy-Birchard Music Division of Birch Tree Group Ltd. and Harrison Potter.

completion of the cataloguing of the Arthur P. Schmidt Collection. But Arthur Schmidt's achievements during the Golden Age of the late nineteenth and early twentieth centuries were remarkable for his service to American music and especially to women composers.

There were many tributes at his death, each one stressing his role in the development of American art music. Beach's tribute to Schmidt is contained in a brief letter to the Arthur P. Schmidt Company dated 9 May

1921: "In the cultivation and diffusion—in the creation indeed—of American music, he has been a great force, by his interest and encouragement as well as by his good judgment and keen criticism."

Among the warmest tributes was Emilie Bauer's. Not only as a composer published by Schmidt, but as a critic for the *Musical Leader,* she was in regular contact with Schmidt and reviewed music the company published. Both of these functions are reflected in their correspondence. A letter addressed to Emilie Bauer from the Schmidt Company is dated 10 May 1921: "It was gratifying to us that Miss Marion Bauer was present at Mr. Schmidt's funeral on Sunday, as we know how close was the bond of sympathy between composer and publisher in this instance." Emilie Bauer's reply, addressed to Henry Austin, begins:

> I really could find no words with which to express the sorrow I feel for the loss of Mr. Schmidt. It was impossible to put into words one's feelings at a time like this. I take the liberty, however, of enclosing for you the carbon of what I wrote in the *Musical Leader* and beg you to appreciate that I refrained from extravaganzas because of the needs of journalism. I did not say one-tenth of what I felt and what I thought about Mr. Schmidt.

Her article in the *Musical Leader* says in part:[51]

> Throughout his musical career Mr. Schmidt devoted himself with energy and sympathy to the upbuilding of the American composer. . . . It was Arthur P. Schmidt who made possible the New England School of Composers for he worked with determination and published chamber music, orchestral scores and many works which he knew could not possibly defray their own costs. But to him it represented the creation of an American school of composition and out of his attitude and his kindly, financial, and moral support, America is able to boast of its MacDowell, Mrs. H. H. A. Beach, Arthur Foote, George W. Chadwick, Horatio W. Parker, Frederick Converse, John Knowles Paine, and in more recent days he gave the same support to the younger composers such as Gena Branscombe, Marion Bauer, Harold V. Milligan, and many others.

Emilie Bauer goes on to mention his importance in the publication of educational music and his "tremendous influence in developing composers of sacred music" as well.

Many of the tributes stressed Schmidt's role in the creation of American art music. Tributes came from foreign journals; from Bostonians Foote, Hale, and Chadwick; from the American Publishers Association; from journals such as *The Diapason* and *Musical America.*[52] An obituary in *Musical America* noted that Schmidt

> was the first to recognize the gifts of George Chadwick, Arthur Foote, and Amy Beach when they were youngsters in Boston. Mr. Schmidt also had the vision to appreciate the genius of Edward MacDowell at a time when MacDowell could find no New York publisher for his manuscripts. With the farsighted quality went a

> geniality, a rare kindliness by which every composer who knew him was stimulated. He saw a future for the American composer and he gave his best years to aiding in his development. . . . In the many years of his life he never failed to take a personal interest in the composers he brought forward. He consulted with them, they with him, to produce the best that was possible. It is a catalogue of copyright compositions containing no reprinted work, for Mr. Schmidt was willing to forego the money that reprinting copyright works would have brought him.[53]

Yet with all the tributes, none that I have seen mentions Schmidt's role as the first publisher and promoter of women composers. One can readily imagine Schmidt publishing only men and still earning the same encomiums for his assistance to American music. Possibly the presence in Boston of a number of gifted women who were an integral part of Boston's musical life was decisive. In his determination to develop an American School he chose all those with promise, and chose without concern for gender. Because of his publishing policies, American women composers from the 1880s on have had role models to follow, women whose achievements as composers are part of the public record and the American heritage. Because of Schmidt, women and men could give an affirmative answer when asked whether women could compose important works of art music. American women composers have a substantial debt to Schmidt, the extent of which is most clearly grasped when seen in the context of feminist history and of women's long and still unfinished struggle for acceptance as composers.

NOTES

1. See Edith M. Brower, "Is the Musical Idea Masculine?," *Atlantic Monthly* 73 (March 1894), pp. 332-39. Other opinions can be found in Adrienne Fried Block and Carol Neuls-Bates, *Women in American Music: A Bibliography of Music and Literature* (Westport, Conn.: Greenwood Press, 1979), nos. 177, 652, 659, 725, 727, 1168, and 2052.

2. John Tasker Howard, *Our American Music: Three Hundred Years of It,* 3rd ed., rev. (New York: Thomas Y. Crowell, 1946) p. 301.

3. Oscar Sonneck, "The American Composer and the American Music Publisher," *Musical Quarterly* Vol. IX no. 1 (January 1921), p. 128.

4. William Arms Fisher, *One Hundred and Fifty Years of Music Publishing in the United States 1783-1933* (Boston: Oliver Ditson, 1933) p. 60.

5. Ibid. p. 55.

6. Ibid. p. 57.

7. Ibid. p. 60.

8. Paul Henry Lang, ed., *One Hundred Years of Music in America,* "Introduction" by Lang (New York: G. Schirmer, 1961), p. 12.

9. Sonneck, "The American Composer," p. 128.

10. Lang, *One Hundred Years of Music,* p. 15.

11. Ibid. p. 17. Beach, however, began composing under contract with G. Schirmer in 1914, three years before Sonneck became editor at Schirmer's.

12. See, for example, *Six Songs, composed by Mrs. Pownall and J. Hewitt* (New York, 1794), among many other listings of early works by women in Block and Neuls-Bates, *Women in American Music,* p. 19.

13. See, for example, Adele Hohnstock's *Hohnstock Concert Polka with Variations for the Pianoforte* (Philadelphia: A. Fiot, 1849).

14. Biographical information about Arthur P. Schmidt is in the scrapbook in the Arthur P. Schmidt Collection at the Library of Congress, Washington, D.C., Music Division, hereafter referred to as APS-DLC.

15. *Supplement to Graded Catalogues of Music* (Boston, n.d.). All Schmidt catalogues cited are in APS-DLC.

16. Ed. by Anne Meyer Nathan, forward by Julia Ward Howe (New York: H. Holt, 1891).

17. *Etude Magazine* 19, no. 9 (September 1901), pp. 310-49. Earlier, *Etude* instituted a Woman's Page that was a regular feature from 1897 to 1903.

18. The catalogue is not dated. However, it is possible to assign a date based on the latest works by Lang and Beach that are listed.

19. On the entry of women into music, see Judith Tick, "Women as Professional Musicians in America, 1870-1900," *Yearbook for Inter American Musical Research,* Vol. 9 (1973), pp. 95-133.

20. Arthur Foote, in an undated letter to Beach, probably written just after his 80th birthday in 1933, talks nostalgically of the "golden time" from 1880 to 1900 and complains that he has "dried up" and is no longer composing. The letter is in the Amy Beach Collection, University of New Hampshire at Durham, hereafter referred to as AMB-UNH.

21. Emma Eames in *Some Memories and Reflections* (New York: D. Appleton, 1927; reprint ed., New York: Arno Press, 1971), p. 41, states the prevailing attitude about the operatic stage and its moral hazards for women. Eames overcame the strictures only with difficulty. Jenny Lind was in part responsible for a change in attitude about the respectability of opera for women singers.

By this time, women like Teresa Carreño, Camilla Urso, Teresa Liebe, and Clara Schumann had set the precedents for women as concert artists.

22. But note that Elsa Hilger, cellist with the Philadelphia Orchestra, 1935-69, was the exception, the first woman other than a harpist to be hired by a major orchestra. See also William J. Henderson, "Music and Musicians," *New York Sun*, 16 November 1935, p. 8.

23. Fisher, *One Hundred and Fifty Years*, p. 75.

24. Information about performances of Lang's works is in her four scrapbooks in the Rare Books and Manuscripts, Research Division, Boston Public Library.

25. Information about Beach's performances is in the Beach correspondence, APS-DLC, and AMB-UNH.

26. See, for example, the programs of the St. Cecilia Society of New York, an outstanding woman's chorus conducted by Victor Harris, 1906-36, in the Music Division, New York Public Library.

27. This information is based on the listings in Mark A. De Wolfe Howe, *The Boston Symphony Orchestra, 1881-1931* (Boston and New York: Houghton Mifflin, 1931).

28. Foote is quoted in "A.P. Schmidt, Pioneer Publisher of American Music, is Dead," *Musical America* 39, no. 3 (14 May 1921), p. 55.

29. Sources of information about the published music of Paine are in John C.

Huxford, "John Knowles Paine: His Life and Works" (Ph.D. diss., Florida State University, 1968). The catalogue of works is on pp. 176-93. See also John C. Schmidt, *The Life and Works of John Knowles Paine* (Ann Arbor: UMI Research Press, 1980). On Foote's works, see Wilma Reid Cipolla's *A Catalog of Works of Arthur Foote* (Detroit: Information Coordinators, 1980). On Hadley, see "Henry Hadley, An American Composer and Conductor," *Musical Courier,* 76, no. 19 (9 May 1918), p. 18. Detailed information about MacDowell's works can be found in Otto Strunk, ed., *Library of Congress: Catalogue of First Editions of Edward MacDowell* (1861-1908) (Washington, D.C.: Government Printing Office, 1917). On Chadwick, see Douglas Graves Campbell, "George W. Chadwick: His Life and Works" (Ph.D. diss., University of Rochester, 1956), list of works, pp. 150-58. On Parker, see David Stanley Smith, "A Study of Horatio Parker," *Musical Quarterly* 16, no. 2 (1930), pp. 153-69. The author has compiled works lists for Beach, Lang, Rogers, and Hopekirk for the forthcoming *New Grove Dictionary of Music in the United States,* ed. by H. Wiley Hitchcock and Stanley Sadie, 1985. Hopekirk's works and scrapbooks are in the Library of Congress, Music Division. For information about Hopekirk, see Constance Huntington Hall and Helen Ingersoll Tetlow, *Helen Hopekirk, 1856-1945* (Cambridge, Mass.: Privately printed, 1954). For the most complete listing to date of Beach's works, see Myrna Garvey Eden, "Anna Hyatt Huntington, Sculptor, and Mrs. H. H. A. Beach, Composer" (Ph.D. diss., Syracuse University, 1977). Block and Neuls-Bates, *Women in American Music,* list most published works of Lang, Beach, Hopekirk, and Rogers.

30. The Schmidt-Rogers correspondence is in APS-DLC. Hereafter, any correspondence not otherwise located will be part of the APS-DLC collection.

31. Clara Kathleen Rogers, *The Story of Two Lives* (Norwood, Mass.: Privately printed, 1932), pp. 80-81. Rogers's autobiographical account of her later years is a sequel to *Memoirs of a Musical Career* (Norwood, Mass.: Privately printed, 1932).

32. Rogers, *The Story of Two Lives,* p. 80.

33. "Review of New Music: Mr. Arthur P. Schmidt," *Boston Musical Herald* (January 1883) p. 24.

34. W. T. Upton, *Artsong in America* (Boston: Oliver Ditson, 1930; reprint ed., New York: Johnson Reprint, 1969) p. 110.

35. See Hall and Tetlow, *Helen Hopekirk,* pp. 8-9.

36. See, for example, Lang's letter to Schmidt dated 9 February 1906 in APS-DLC.

37. The program, which took place 12 July 1889, is in Lang's Scrapbook (1887-1904) in Rare Book and Manuscripts, Research Division, Boston Public Library.

38. *The Heavenly Noël,* published in piano-vocal score by Schmidt in 1916, calls for women's chorus, mezzo solo, organ, and chamber orchestra; also with voices and string quartet, harp, piano, and organ. The orchestration is at the New England Conservatory of Music, Boston.

39. The autograph album is in AMB-UNH.

40. A juvenile work of Amy Cheney's, "The Rainy Day" to a text by Longfollow, was written in 1880 and published by Oliver Ditson in 1883. This work was the only one published prior to 1885.

41. This clipping is in the Beach Scrapbook (1890-1909), p. 32 in AMB-UNH.

42. See the letter from Beach to Schmidt dated Munich, 30 November 1912, which outlines her plans. The letter is in APS-DLC Correspondence.

43. A clipping in the Beach file of the Music Division of the New York Public Library, from the *Musical Courier,* 9 December 1914, reports that Beach had 30 concerts booked on her return to the States.

44. See, for example, Beach's letters to Schmidt dated Munich, 5 October 1912, and 2 February 1913, APS-DLC.

45. Howard, *Our American Music,* p. 395.

46. Boston, Little Brown, 1905.

47. Howard, *Our American Music,* p. 395; Christine Ammer, *Unsung: A History of Women in American Music* (Westport, Conn.: Greenwood Press, 1980), p. 89.

48. Ammer, *Unsung,* pp. 160-61. For full information, see Laurine Elkins-Marlow, "Gena Branscombe, American Composer and Conductor" (Ph.D. diss., University of Texas at Austin, 1978).

49. Ammer, *Unsung*, p. 124.

50. Howard, *Our American Music*, p. 435, states that Bauer "was considered somewhat radical in the 1920's," but by the mid-1940s her impressionist style was "almost conservative."

51. "Arthur P. Schmidt Dies in Boston Home," *Musical Leader* 41, no. 19 (12 May 1921), p. 455. The article is unsigned.

52. A number of tributes are in the Schmidt scrapbook, APS-DLC. *The Diapason* has an obituary in 12, no. 7 (1 June 1921) p. 16.

53. "A. P. Schmidt, Pioneer Publisher of American Music, Is Dead," *Musical America* 39, 10.3 (14 May 1921), p. 55.

I wish to thank Wilma Reid Cipolla and Catherine P. Smith for reading this article in typescript and for their helpful suggestions.

I gratefully acknowledge the help and cooperation of Gillian B. Anderson and Wayne Shirley, Music Division, Library of Congress; of Barbara White, Special Collections, University of New Hampshire Library, Durham, N.H.; of Kathy Sherman, Special Collections, University of Missouri Library, Kansas City, Mo., and of Karin Pendle, University of Cincinnati, Cincinnati, Ohio.

Excerpts from Amy M. C. Beach's correspondence in the Arthur P. Schmidt Collection, Music Division, Library of Congress, and from her correspondence in Special Collections, University of New Hampshire Library, Durham, are used with the kind permission of The MacDowell Colony, Inc.

Excerpts from Mabel Wheeler Daniels's correspondence in the Arthur P. Schmidt Collection, Music Division, Library of Congress, are used with the kind permission of the New England Conservatory.

Excerpts from Gena Branscombe's correspondence in the Arthur P. Schmidt Collection, Music Division, Library of Congress, are used with the kind permission of Gena Tenney Phenix.

Excerpts from Marion Bauer's and Emilie Frances Bauer's correspondence in the Arthur P. Schmidt Collection, Music Division, Library of Congress, are used with the kind permission of Harrison Potter.

7

Germaine Tailleferre: Before, During, and After Les Six

LAURA MITGANG

INTRODUCTION

Many articles and books tell the story of *Les Six*, but no lengthy study has been devoted to its only woman member, Germaine Tailleferre. Early critics set a precedent for ignorance about her music and her life. In 1927, the British musicologist, Cecil Gray, wrote:

> Of Mlle Germaine Tailleferre one can only repeat Dr. Johnson's dictum concerning a woman preacher, transposed into terms of music: "Sir, a woman's composing is like a dog's walking on his hind legs. It is not done well, but you are surprised to find it done at all." Considered apart from her sex, her music is wholly negligible.[1]

And in France, where women did not cast their first ballots until 1945, Tailleferre repeatedly encountered professional and personal obstacles. Seldom, though, did she become active in political or social issues. Outwardly, she avoided conflicts at all costs, sometimes even at the sacrifice of her own advancement. Music, throughout her life, was her main motivation, her support, her greatest pleasure.

Germaine Tailleferre's life spanned almost a century (1892-1983). She witnessed many developments in music and art, having personally known Maurice Ravel, Igor Stravinsky, Erik Satie, Pablo Picasso, Guillaume Apollinaire, Charlie Chaplin, and many others who helped to move aesthetics into new realms. Tailleferre herself admired and explored musical ideas that went beyond the staid conventions she so ably mastered during her training at the Conservatoire.

Just after World War I, Tailleferre, her friends in *Les Six* (Darius Milhaud, Arthur Honegger, Francis Poulenc, Georges Auric, and Louis Durey), and other young composers aimed for a new, pared-down French style, which would not take itself too seriously and did not pretend to have a profound intellectual message. But just as the grouping of *Les Six* was more an invention of critics than a deliberate movement, so is it misleading to mention the widely differing music of these composers in one breath.

An exceptionally gifted pianist, Tailleferre wrote many works for her own instrument. She also composed orchestral music such as an overture, ballets, concertos, film scores, and, in later years, music for band. Her vocal works include a cantata, chamber operas, concertos for voice and orchestra, and a few songs. Finally, among her chamber music pieces are two violin sonatas, a string quartet, a piano trio, and other small-scale works.

Those who do not like her music have often termed it "feminine," implying frivolity, weakness, passivity. Yet some of her better-known colleagues, such as Darius Milhaud, considered this so-called femininity a positive trait. He would say she wrote "the music of a young girl full of freshness," which she always took as a compliment.[2] Georges Auric, in an interview one year before his death in 1983, explained that she had always been quite independent, that she wrote "the music of Germaine Tailleferre." On the subject of feminine music, he commented:

> I do not know what feminine music is. One would have to be a woman to try to understand. I don't know if there is masculine music, feminine music, androgynous music, lesbian music, or pederastic music. For me, there is music, and that is all. If I listen to a work of Germaine Tailleferre's that I consider to be successful, I do not ask if it is masculine or feminine. It is music, and good music—that is enough for me.[3]

And Roland-Manuel, often called the "seventh" composer of *Les Six,* wrote in 1933:

> The misogynists of the aesthetic habitually defy women to triumph consistently where men sometimes succeed. How do they not see that [women] are made to succeed in some areas where we always fail? The divorce between ingenuity and intelligence is just the ill from which music is presently suffering. Germaine Tailleferre, spiritual daughter of Domenico Scarlatti, practices a light art, playful, fugitive, a mixture of alert discrimination and simplicity.[4]

With the repeated surfacing of this issue, it seemed crucial to seek the composer's own assessment. Tailleferre's response lays to rest the question of whether her music can accurately be labeled "feminine":

> What difference does it make? The essential thing is that it be music. I do not see a reason why I shouldn't write what I feel. If it gives the impression of being feminine, that is fine. I was never tormented by explanations. I tried to do the best I could, but I never asked myself if it was feminine or not. You can say that my music is neither masculine nor feminine. It is just plain music. That is what I try to do: I do what I want.[5]

Granted that we can dismiss this irrelevant terminology, yet, we are still left with the problem of assessing Germaine Tailleferre's music, both in relation to the other music of her time and taking into consideration the fact

Figure 7.1 Germaine Tailleferre. Used by permission of Patricia Adkins Chiti and Donne in Musica.

that she was a woman. As we shall see, this undeniably set her apart from almost all of her colleagues and had bearing on her training, her opportunities, and her way of life.

1892–1918: YOUTH AND MUSICAL BEGINNINGS

Germaine Marcelle Tailleferre (née Taillefesse) was born on 19 April 1892 in Parc Saint-Maur outside of Paris. She was the youngest of three girls and two boys. The unhappy marriage of her parents shadowed her childhood, but while her father was strict, conservative, and often cruel, her mother quickly sensed Germaine's artistic sensitivity and fought to give her an opportunity to develop her talents.

Madame Tailleferre played the piano well enough to teach one of her older daughters. During these lessons, Germaine would listen closely and was soon playing *Au Clair de la lune* and other songs by ear on a toy piano. In addition to composing short piano pieces, as a young girl she showed facility in drawing, needlework, and design. Mme. Tailleferre, without consulting her husband, arranged for Germaine to play for one of the teachers at the Conservatoire de Paris. When Mme. Sautereau-Meyer accepted the gifted child, Tailleferre's parents quarreled bitterly over allowing her to attend. Her mother helped her to practice secretly while her father was at work.

In 1904, Tailleferre entered the Conservatoire, where she studied solfège with Mme. Sautereau-Meyer through 1906. Her father continued to object and finally sent her to a convent school. In spite of this, Tailleferre earned a first prize in solfège and began to teach to earn money for her clothes and tuition.This was the first of many times in her life when she would work to support herself and her art.[6]

A brilliant student at the Conservatoire, Tailleferre earned more first prizes than the other future members of *Les Six*. Gabriel Fauré, the school's director, often attended the annual examinations with Maurice Ravel, Claude Debussy, Charles Koechlin, and Florent Schmitt. In 1913, she received first prizes in harmony and counterpoint and two years later first prizes in fugue (under Charles-Marie Widor) and piano accompaniment, one of the most difficult courses.[7] Among her classmates were Darius Milhaud and Arthur Honegger. They were the same age as Tailleferre; Georges Auric also attended the Conservatoire but, being seven years younger, he was not yet one of their *camarades*.

During these prewar years, Tailleferre broadened her milieu to include young painters and poets such as Fernand Léger, Robert Delaunay, Albert Gleizes, André Lhote, Jean Metzinger, André Salmon, Paul Fort, Guillaume Apollinaire, and Marie Laurencin.[8] She became familiar with Cubism and also had her first exposure to the music of Stravinsky and other contemporaries.

When war broke out in 1914, the Conservatoire lost many of its students. Tailleferre continued to teach private lessons and also helped her mother, who suffered from phlebitis; her father had a serious accident and died later that year. She also attended Charles-Marie Widor's composition class once a week, where her only classmates were Darius Milhaud, Arthur Honegger, and Henri Cliquet-Pleyel.[9]

This was the beginning of a long friendship with Darius Milhaud. Tailleferre would later recall his sensitivity, taste, and musicianship. Milhaud recognized her gifts and encouraged her to continue composing. He lived in the Montmartre area in a small apartment on rue Gaillard, where young composers, musicians, and poets gathered regularly on Saturday nights. Ties formed between some of the future *Six* and others who were as much a part of the group, though not thus labeled. Evenings "chez Darius" were a welcome distraction from troubles on the front. The friends would recount anecdotes, caricaturize people, share meals; it was not a time for serious intellectual pursuits.[10]

In 1917, Darius Milhaud and poet Paul Claudel left for Brazil, and Widor suspended the composition class. With few diversions remaining to her, the war weighed more oppressively. Tailleferre left with her mother and sister for Pestin-les-Grèves in Brittany, then went for a short time to Barcelona and also traveled to Biarritz.

Upon returning to Paris, she lived in the Montparnasse quarter on rue Notre-Dame des Champs. At "La Rotonde," a now-famous bistro, she met Modigliani, Picasso, and others. The artistic surroundings rekindled Tailleferre's earlier desire to draw. She began to study at l'Académie de la Grande Chaumière and l'Académie Ranson, though she continued to give music lessons in order to support her mother and herself.

1917 was a very important year in Parisian artistic life. On May 18, Serge Diaghilev's Ballets Russes performed *Parade,* conceived by Jean Cocteau, designed by Picasso, with music by Erik Satie. To the impresario's delight, the innovative combination of larger-than-life cubist costumes and a score that requires typewriters, sirens, and airplane sounds inspired a *succès de scandale* that recalled Stravinsky's *Le Sacre du Printemps* of 1913.

Satie's capricious manner attracted young composers, and some who frequented Montparnasse—where many visual artists lived and worked—decided to introduce music into the artistically exclusive quarter. Satie wanted to combine an art exhibit with unimposing, light background music, music that one could "sit on" like furniture: *musique d'ameublement.* The first concert took place on 6 June 1917 at a painter's studio on the rue Huyghens and included Georges Auric's *Trio,* Arthur Honegger's *Six Poèmes d'Appollinaire,* Louis Durey's *Carillons,* and *Parade* performed in a four-hand version by Satie and Juliette Méerowitch. Tailleferre, who by then was repelled by the rigidity of the Conservatoire, welcomed the opportunity to explore new paths.

Shortly after the initial Montparnasse concert, Satie heard Tailleferre reading through one of her own compositions for two pianos at the home of Marcelle Meyer. Immediately proclaiming Tailleferre his *fille-musicale,* he decided to include her music at the informal concerts that were continuing. Satie named his young followers *Les Nouveaux Jeunes.* To describe the musical ambiance, Louis Durey wrote:

> We had to escape from the dangers of impressionism, of the pursuit of Debussy and Ravel, chasing away those who were too easily seduced by the magic of colors and sounds; and on the other hand, the excess of a romanticism that we considered to be seriously outdated. We felt a need for a less ethereal music, closer to the realities of life, of our daily life, for a cutting, biting music, [*musique a l'emporte-pièce*] as we used to say.[11]

The first more formal concert of works by *Les Nouveaux Jeunes* took place on 15 January 1918 at the Théâtre du Vieux-Colombier. Jacques

Copeau, who was in America, entrusted his theater to the singer, Jane Bathori, and to Pierre Bertin, an actor and singer.[12] The program opened with Germaine Tailleferre's *Sonatine pour cordes* (the first two movements of her yet unfinished *String Quartet*), performed by four women: Hélène Jourdan-Morhange (a close friend of Ravel's), Fernande Capelle, Marguerite Lutz, and Adèle Clément. The other works were by Honegger, Auric, Roland-Manuel, Durey, and Poulenc.[13]

This *Quatuor*, which Tailleferre completed in 1919 and published two years later, was dedicated to Arthur Rubinstein, who would become a good friend. Certain stylistic tendencies are already evident in this early work. The balanced, mostly stepwise four-bar motive, stated first by the cello, is picked up and repeated on different levels by each instrument. Harmonically, melodically, and rhythmically uncomplicated, the work flows with great smoothness and ease, while never becoming stagnant. The

Figure 7.2 Tailleferre's *Quatuor*.

use of repetition, both of the motive as a whole and within itself, occurs frequently in later works.

In just a few months, the popularity of *Les Nouveaux Jeunes* grew, largely because of Jean Cocteau. Cocteau knew *tout-Paris*, and soon Misia Edwards, the Princess of Polignac, the Princess Violette Murat, the Count of Beaumont, and the Duchess of Clermont Tonnerre, important patrons, began to attend these concerts.[14] But Cocteau did more than promote. He was a poet, an artist whose cultured imagination reflected, shaped, and articulated the period's aesthetics. In 1918, in his apartment on rue d'Anjou, he assembled his friends for a first reading of his short book of "notes about music," *Le Coq et l'Arlequin,* which he dedicated to Georges Auric. Here he heralded a new, simplified French sound and named Satie to lead the young away from Debussy's hazy pastels:

> Yet while Debussy was delicately expanding his feminine grace, displaying Stéphane Mallarmé in "Le Jardin de l'infante," Satie was continuing along his little classical route. He finally reaches us today, young among the young, at last finding his place after twenty years of modest work. . . . Satie rarely looks at the painters and does not read the poets, but he loves to live where life rumbles; he instinctively knows the good taverns. . . .[15]

Le Coq et l'Arlequin touched the sensibility of many young composers. Germaine Tailleferre, for one, would seldom wander from a frank simplicity of musical style.

1918–1923: IMPACT OF *LES SIX*

With the Armistice of 11 November 1918 came a vital necessity to laugh, to rebuild, and to celebrate a youthful French spirit. The arts ridiculed a pompous nobility that had been debased in the trenches. Seeds of modernism sown before the Great War were harvested with desperate hunger in the 1920s. Automobiles honked on the streets, the motion picture industry flourished, dresses rose above the knee, cafés overflowed—in short, Paris was intoxicated.

The public begged to believe in fresh artistic ideals. Literally overnight, a group of six friends found themselves at the helm of an illusory musical movement. The events leading to the birth of this "movement" are easily described. In early January 1920, the critic Henri Collet attended one of the studio concerts on rue Huyghens. That night he heard pieces by Georges Auric, Darius Milhaud (recently returned from Brazil), Louis Durey, Francis Poulenc, Arthur Honegger, and Germaine Tailleferre. On 16 and 23 January 1920, Henri Collet wrote articles for *Comoedia* in which he compared the "French Six," led by Satie, to the "Russian Five."[16]

Sixty-two years later, Georges Auric would retell this story of the critic who, by creating a legend, changed their lives:

Henri Collet came and he wrote an article. He called us *Les Six*, but that's his find: we had never thought of calling ourselves the Six or the Seven or the Five. When you have labels, it is very hard to take them off. We were not the ones who wanted to keep them, but it was the press, the articles—the public was calling us that, and there was nothing to be done about it.[17]

It was not chance that put the music of these six composers on the same program—each had already been regularly accepted in Satie's amicable circle. Yet no true philosophy united the composers, nor could they pretend to integrate their styles. One may wonder why, then, they did not deny this allegiance from the start. Madeleine Milhaud, Darius Milhaud's widow, responded in an interview in 1982:

Why they decided to keep this on? Because they thought it was, perhaps, convenient. After all, as long as they decided we're "the Six," we shall be "the Six"—then we give concerts and we are called the Six. It makes things easier, perhaps as when you have writing paper with the name of a society, association, you feel more able to ask a favor than if you ask it in your name.[18]

In an interview 12 days later, Georges Auric answered similarly, "Labels in concerts as in industry are very important. If one puts a label on a can of Coca-Cola, it sells much better than if one does not."[19]

This label helped launch Germaine Tailleferre's career, and it did the same for the other five composers. During the two years before, she had completed her *String Quartet* and composed *Images* for eight instruments, works that show the influence of Ravel and Satie. Durand published her *Jeux de plein air* for two pianos in 1919. These "Outdoor Games," which first brought Tailleferre to Satie's attention in 1917, evoke a child's spontaneous imagination. The first movement, "La Tirelitentaine," is marked "Pas trop vite." On the other hand, the second movement, "Cache-cache mitoula" (a hide-and-seek game), is marked "Très vite (décidé)," and begins in a *fortissimo* that contrasts with the previous *piano*.

These examples, taken from the second movement, show the unsophisticated, childlike opening motive that, characteristically, is scalar, symmetrical, and repetitive. Always audible, this same simple line develops with harmonically surprising quirks that catch the listener off guard. The dissonances caused by a flirtation with polytonality are never abrasive but add a spicy quality to an otherwise deliberately straightforward melodic idea. At the apparent moment of discovery during this game of hide and seek, Tailleferre playfully builds toward a long glissando that then descends abruptly to the lowest notes of the instrument.

On 14 April 1919 Cocteau wrote, "'*Jeux de plein air*' makes one think of a horse by Irène Lagut, a neighbor of Tailleferre's boulevard Raspail. The country. Window open. One is raking. The scales go and come. It is a vacation piece."[20] This work was one of the great favorites during the early part of Tailleferre's career. She also dedicated a short *Pastorale* to Darius

Figure 7.3 Three excerpts from *Jeux de plein air* for two pianos, by Tailleferre: mms. 1-6, 19-22, 39-42. Published by Durand S.A. in 1919; subsequently reprinted. Used by permission of the publisher.

Milhaud for the 1920 publication of *Album des 6*, to which each composer contributed. This little collection of piano pieces stands as the sole product of the entire group.*

Clearly, this Parisian musical circle included and appreciated Tailleferre's music, and her renown began here. Henri Sauguet (a composer who, with Roger Désormière, Henri Cliquet-Pleyel, and Maxime Jacob formed a group called *L'Ecole d'Arcueil* in 1923) remembers frequent performances of Tailleferre's music and recalls Poulenc and Milhaud asking her for compositional advice. In his opinion, affiliation with *Les Six* both advanced her career by giving her early recognition and became a stifling hindrance that she would always struggle to overcome: she could no longer be viewed purely as a composer but rather as the woman member of *Les Six*.[21]

At the group's height, Tailleferre appeared happy and sociable to such friends as Hélène Jourdan-Morhange, who later would write: "A delicate complexion, a laughing eye, a blond lock covering half her forehead, she was truly 'the princess of the Six' and that was very pleasing to us other women, to see one of ours emancipate herself (for the period) to the height of possibilities."[22]

And in 1954, Poulenc who, with Milhaud, remained one of Tailleferre's closest friends, recalled to Claude Rostand:

> How ravishing our Germaine was in 1917, with her school girl's satchel full of all the Conservatoire's first prizes! How kind and gentle she was! She still is, but I regret some that, through an excess of modesty, she did not draw from herself all that a Marie Laurencin, for example, knew how to extract from her feminine genius. Be that as it may, what a charming and precious contribution her music makes! I am delighted by it each time![23]

Tailleferre remembered herself not as a "princess," but rather as an introverted, naïve young woman who often felt overwhelmed by the glamorous milieu. Then, as throughout her life, she did not want to exploit

---

*The *Album des 6* brings up a most troubling and yet unanswered question. When relating the origin of *Les Six*, historians and even members of the group point to the two articles in *Comoedia* and attribute both the official linking together of these particular composers and the naming to Henri Collet, the music critic who wrote them. According to all sources, the formation of *Les Six* took place rather arbitrarily, without solicitation from those who were to be included. Why, then, does Henri Collet, in the fifth and sixth paragraphs of his initial article of January 16 make specific reference to "the curious collection '*du groupe des Six*'"? He calls this a *Suite* of six pieces, and lists the very music included in *Album des 6,* which seems to be the collection in question.

The implication here is that *Album des 6*, which was published by E. Demets in 1920, had to have been conceived, if not printed, before January 16 of that year—that is to say that these specific six composers (and not other members of *Les Nouveaux Jeunes*) joined themselves previous to the citation in *Comoedia*. Perhaps they were even already "*Six*!"

This raises other questions and is a topic too large for discussion in the present study. However, in recounting the birth of *Les Six*, I feel it essential not to reiterate the traditional story without making mention of this puzzling discrepancy.

her talents or her situation; she had little flair for the politics of success. For the most part, those around her were quite sensitive to this "excess of modesty." Madeleine Milhaud explained: ". . . but what I want you to understand and feel is that Germaine was so perfectly decent and pure that if she had met what you call in American 'wolves,' they would not have taken advantage of her—or they would have been very badly treated by other wolves who were more decent than they were."[24]

Maurice Ravel inspired Tailleferre and provided subtle guidance and encouragement. Indeed, some sources mistakenly call Ravel her teacher, although she never studied composition under him. Stylistically, she did pay tribute to his textures, melodic contours, and accomplishments, particularly in her early works, such as her *Quatuor*. To Satie's displeasure, she and Hélène Jourdan-Morhange would visit Ravel in Monfort l'Amaury once a week. There, Tailleferre remembered seeing Roland-Manuel, Maurice Délage, and other young musicians who respected the already established composer. They would walk together for hours in the country near his home. On one occasion, he asked Tailleferre to play *Petrouchka* from memory, which she did flawlessly, putting aside her inhibition while at the piano.

Tailleferre's talent pleased Ravel, and he encouraged her to enter competitions to win the badly needed prize money. Attuned to her sensitivity, he wrote the following letter to Roland-Manuel on 10 April 1924:

> Dear Friend, If you have occasion to see Tailleferre, let her know gently that she had but one vote, you can imagine whose. I do not dare to write to her: my letter's envelope would give her a false joy.
>
> I return pretty disgusted from this session. I came too young into too old a generation, excluding at least Widor. . . .
>
> Excuse the unpleasant mission, and believe I am most affectionately yours, Maurice Ravel.[25]

Tailleferre later thought nostalgically of this period of the early 1920s when the group became one of the centers of postwar Parisian social life. During the first year of *Les Six,* Milhaud's good friend Jean Wiéner, a pianist, arranger, and composer of predominantly jazz and popular music, proposed a bistro exclusively for the group. "Le Gaya" was a tiny bar on rue Duphot, but *Les Six* and their friends made it their home; Cocteau, as ever, knew how to attract the choicest guests.[26]

In 1921, Le Gaya's proprietor, Louis Moysès, found a larger location on rue Boissy-d'Anglas, and in December he opened the famous *Boeuf sur le Toit*, named after Milhaud's ballet. One of Francis Picabia's Dada canvases hung on the wall with senseless inscriptions by Milhaud, Poulenc, and even Isadora Duncan.[27]

Tailleferre first met Arthur Rubinstein at the Gaya. In one of his autobiographies, he remembers when Milhaud brought him to rue Duphot:

Inside I was greeted by a display on three walls of posters in different colors saying: "Bienvenue à Arthur Rubinstein" . . . I embraced Milhaud, obviously the instigator of this lovely welcome. Auric, Poulenc, Honegger, and the lovely Germaine Tailleferre were there. They were a young and eager lot, all babbling at the same time, calling "*pompier*" all the prewar masters, including even Ravel, and promising a new world of music.[28]

Rubinstein and Tailleferre became good friends. His seductive charm was no secret, but he quickly sensed Tailleferre's insecurity and treated her as a younger sister. He helped to promote her music and later advised her as a confidant. Rubinstein brought her music on tour to Brazil, played *Jeux de plein air* with Risler, took her *String Quartet* to other countries, and proposed that she play *Jeux de plein air* with him in one of his London recitals.

Despite self doubts during this period, due, in part, to her sudden fame, Tailleferre continued to compose and play the piano. She must have performed her transcriptions of Stravinsky's music with great enthusiasm because they were popular not only with Ravel but at the afternoon gatherings at the home of the Princess of Polignac. Tailleferre admired Stravinsky, thinking of him as "Bach in person" and, since *Les Six* had free passes to rehearsals and performances of the Ballets Russes, she was able to meet him for the first time after one of these rehearsals.

In addition to composing, she continued to give lessons and learned to be a milliner in order to earn a living and support her mother. In late 1920, Tailleferre completed her *Ballade* for piano and orchestra and dedicated it to the pianist Ricardo Viñes.[29] Alfred Cortot rhapsodized over the piece:

the principle of bitonality, hardly arbitrary, that governs the exposition of the first section passes on to the expression of a sensitive and penetrating poetic feeling, and it is fitting even today, to allow oneself to be surprised by the seductive fertility of that imaginative resource which, in each bar, proposes in the development of musical discourse, the surprise of an unusual dialectic, and of a technical means to which it is hard to assign the reference of a valid predecessor.[30]

The *Ballade* exemplifies the composer's natural understanding of her own instrument and a transparent quality of orchestration. The piano solo contrasts textures of harplike arpeggios, more languorous melodic lines, and simple dance patterns. The sections flow freely from one to the next, with a recapitulatory rounding-off at the end. There are notable similarities to Debussy, Fauré, Ravel—certainly in 1920 their influences remained imposing. In the *Ballade,* Tailleferre seems to pay homage to these masters who had judged her at the Conservatoire.

The piece begins with arpeggios in the piano and a rhythmically slower scalar line in the oboe. This gradually leads to a second theme stated first by the piano.

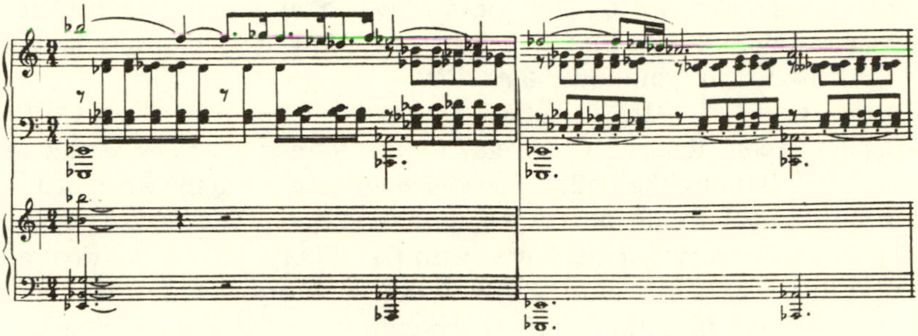

Figure 7.4 *Ballade* for piano and orchestra (piano reduction by the composer), mm. 42-43. © 1925 J & W Chester/Edition Wilhelm Hansen London Ltd. Reproduced by permission.

The pulsating accompaniment in the left hand recalls a similar figure in Fauré's *Ballade* for piano and orchestra, op. 19. The end of Tailleferre's *Ballade* resembles the end of the earlier work as well.

Following a cadenza, we arrive at a "Valse," whose pentatonic theme calls to mind Ravel—as does another pentatonic section further on, "Lent"—both in melodic line and in orchestration.

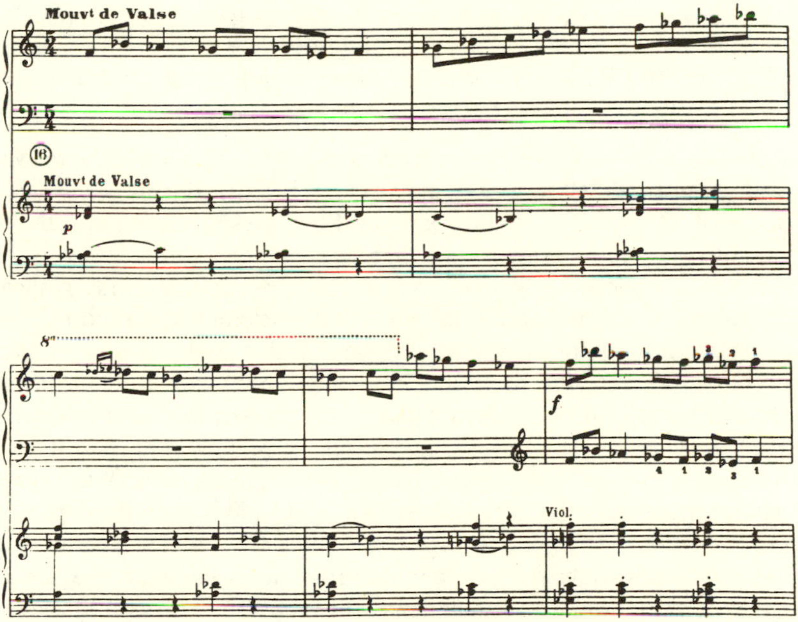

Figure 7.5 Tailleferre's *Ballade*, mm. 100-104. © 1925 J & W Chester/Edition Wilhelm Hansen London Ltd. Reproduced by permission.

When asked for her opinion of *Ballade* in an interview, Tailleferre answered, "No, I don't like it. When I wrote it I liked it, but everything has changed since then, you understand?"[31]

In the spring of 1921, Tailleferre received a letter from Jean Cocteau asking her to contribute a "Quadrille" to his production of *Les Mariés de la Tour Eiffel*. Because the Ballets Suédois wanted to stage the work in June, Cocteau decided to divide the composing among *Les Six*. The script parodies a bourgeois wedding party, with frivolity typical of the twenties.[32] Cocteau poses mirage against reality, mocks authority figures, and gently criticizes modern inventions such as the camera, the phonograph, and the Eiffel Tower itself.

Four days before the opening, Louis Durey decided not to participate, and so Tailleferre wrote the "Valse des dépêches" ("Waltz of the Telegrams") in his place. As she scribbled furiously, Darius Milhaud orchestrated. Both the "Valse" and the "Quadrille" are light-hearted dances, full of charm and vigor in the spirit of the work. *Les Mariés* opened on 18 June 1921 at the Théâtre des Champs-Elysées. As was typical of the period, the audience reacted with a mixture of outrage and glee.

In September of that year, Paul Landormy wrote an article on *Les Six* for *La Revue de Genève*. He commented:

> Germaine Tailleferre seems gifted with an amiable and delicate talent. She has none of her friends' aggressive humor. Neither too much violence nor rash audacity. It is not she who leads the band: she rather follows it with a sometimes timid step.
>
> But let us not risk marking with too much precision the traits of a countenance that is not yet definitely settled. Germaine Tailleferre surely has so far confided in us very little of her most intimate secret.[33]

A month later, she completed her *Sonata for Violin and Piano,* which Durand would publish in 1923. She wrote this work during a visit to the Princess of Polignac in Saint-Jean de Luz. Despite apparent melodic simplicity, analysis reveals a subtle and sophisticated construction.

The first movement, *Modéré sans lenteur*, seems, on first glance, a straightforward sonata form with two thematic elements, but complexities and ambiguities present themselves. It opens with a C-sharp aeolian theme, predominantly in scalar motion. This leads to a stepwise but broader secondary theme in E (starting in measure 11), underpinned by a seemingly contradictory F_7 in the accompaniment. A surprising restatement of the first theme follows, deformed and fragmented, and an equally unexpected repetition of the secondary theme in the key of C major ends the exposition. Tailleferre then writes out a repeat of the entire section. Thus primary and secondary themes are heard no fewer than four times each in the exposition. In the recapitulation, the initial appearance of the secondary theme is eliminated, although the concluding statement comes in the tonic key, as expected.

In the middle section, more episodic than developmental, Tailleferre introduces new thematic material based on the G major triad, later transposed to D major. Certain rhythmic patterns recall the exposition, but there appears to be no true melodic or harmonic development.

The bitonal aspect of this movement is one of its most distinctive traits. Henri Sauguet, however, characterizes Tailleferre's temperate use of bitonality as a "flavoring" or a "spice" rather than a system. Although the accompaniment seems tonally to contradict the key of the melody, it often happens, as already mentioned, that the two "conflicting" chords are reconcilable within a broader structural context, in this case, E major as the expected key of resolution.

The second movement, a scherzo, dances rhythmically in 5/8, a meter Tailleferre often employs. Playful glissandos and chromatic slidings hint at a jazz influence, particularly in the smooth piano statement. The undevelopmental trio changes to 3/8, and the scherzo soon returns to round off the movement.

The third movement, marked "Assez lent," leads directly into the finale, which refers back to the scherzo and includes a fugato. The bass line near the end suggests the primary theme of the first movement. The piece concludes with vigorous staccato.

This *Sonata,* once again, reveals the composer's maturing characteristic sounds. The melodies are diatonic, accessible, and sometimes modal. They are symmetrically formed and often contain repeated notes or fragments. From the beginning, there are clear motivic interrelationships. Tailleferre occasionally refers to a pentatonic or whole-tone sound, but, as with bitonality, only for flavoring.

Jacques Thibaud, to whom the *Sonata* is dedicated, and Alfred Cortot premiered the piece in June 1922. *Comoedia* reviewed this concert on June 26:

> The same qualities are found in her Sonata [as in her String Quartet] which entices with rhythms, melodic playfulness, orderly and concise elegance of construction. Mlle. Tailleferre's audacities of writing are in the best taste and never shock the senses by using aggressive methods. In her Sonata, Mlle. Tailleferre reveals a temperament where tact and moderation dominate. Her music, sincere without emphasis, shivering with youth, and hardy without any pedantry, found an excellent welcome from its listeners.[34]

A commission from the Ballets Suédois came in March 1923. Tailleferre completed her first ballet with characteristic rapidity, and it opened to rave reviews on May 25 of the same year.[35] *Le Marchand d'oiseaux* begins with an overture and continues without a true break through a number of different sections that announce and define the various characters on stage.

She wrote an article on the work and on her composing for *l'Intransigeant.* Here she states that she made deliberate allusions to Chopin and to older music of the eighteenth century. In step with her friends, she does not acknowledge a strict intellectual approach but rather a

Figure 7.6 *Sonate for Violin and Piano*. First movement, mm. 1-12. Published by Durand S.A. in 1923. Used by permission of the publisher.

Sonate for Violin and Piano. Second movement, mm. 31-40. Published by Durand S.A. in 1923. Used by permission of the publisher.

spontaneous choice of sounds that happened to please her. She also mentions how lucky young composers are to benefit from postwar opportunities. Summing up, she writes:

Having recently very much attached myself to old music, I colored, here and there, my little work with faded tones taken from old palettes, without thinking for one second of an evolution in my temperament and my instincts. . . . The "six!" Still a school, are you going to say? No. Six good friends, quite simply.[36]

All of the many reviews of *Le Marchand d'oiseaux* lauded the work as one in which Tailleferre truly affirmed her position as a serious composer. Some see Bach in it, others Scarlatti, Rameau, or Chabrier—the composer claims consciously to have made many references.

The Ballets Suédois's records show that in its three seasons, from 1923 to 1925, *Le Marchand d'oiseaux* was danced 94 times, while *Les Mariés de la Tour Eiffel*, from 1921 to 1925, had only 50 performances.[37] *Le Marchand d'oiseaux*, which has not been performed since 1925, contains an overture that pleased Diaghilev, and he used it as an interlude when the Ballets Russes went on tour. Because he was always looking for new works and Tailleferre was such a facile sight-reader, they went through scores together at the Bibliothèque de l'Opéra. He later commissioned a work from her called "La Nouvelle Cythère" based on extracts from Bougainvillier's *Voyages autour de la terre*. But Diaghilev died before presenting it.[38]

With *Le Marchand d'oiseaux,* Tailleferre asserted her capacity as a composer. Although she would never flaunt her natural talent, she felt more encouraged to share it and began to show a new ease before the public eye.

1924–1931: UNITED STATES AND RALPH BARTON

By 1924, few still believed in *Les Six*. The critics and the public felt misled by a label that the composers themselves had begun to disclaim. Emile Vuillermoz, in particular, wrote biting articles on "The Legend of the Six," protesting that "publicity takes rank above art."[39]

Louis Durey had retreated to St. Tropez shortly after *Les Mariés de la Tour Eiffel*. Despite the dwindling of her circle, in early 1924 Tailleferre completed a *Piano Concerto in D Major* that the Princess of Polignac had commissioned. Of this work, Stravinsky said, "C'est de la musique honnête!"[40]

In program notes, Tailleferre describes the *Piano Concerto* that Cortot, among others, compared to Scarlatti:

The classic form which I have used in this work may be regarded as in a way a reaction against Impressionism and Orientalism, and as an indication of an attempt to find an expression purely musical, exempt from all literary implications.

> It is written in three parts. The first movement (*Allegro*, D major, 4/4) begins with two themes, exposed concurrently by the orchestra and the piano, but developed separately. The second movement is an *Adagio* in B minor, 3/4 time. The songful theme is announced at once by the solo instrument and is taken up at the fourth measure by the flute. The Finale (*Allegro non troppo*, D major, 6-8) opens with a pianissimo statement of the chief theme, of a more flowing nature, stated by the piano alone. The development section of this movement requires no special comment.[41]

Yet Tailleferre felt the need for a change. Fortuitously, an American friend introduced her to Leopold Stokowski and invited her to visit New York. Troubled by continuing financial difficulties and added expenses incurred because of her mother's poor health, Tailleferre accepted. As Stokowski had booked Alfred Cortot to perform her new *Piano Concerto,* the composer hoped the United States would offer further performance opportunities and speaking engagements.

On 14 February 1925, she made her first appearance in Aeolian Hall in New York. Here she and Robert Imandt played the *Sonata for Violin and Piano* in the second "Referendum" concert of the Franco-American Musical Society.[42] On March 20-21, the Philadelphia Orchestra premiered her *Piano Concerto,* probably with Cortot as soloist.[43] And on April 2-3, Tailleferre herself played the *Concerto* in New York with the Philharmonic Society under Willem Mengelberg, while Cortot performed it in Boston on April 3 under Serge Koussevitzky.[44] Shortly thereafter, Tailleferre returned to France and performed the *Concerto* once again in Paris under Koussevitzky on May 30. On 1 July 1925, the death of Erik Satie brought a more definitive end to *Les Six.* Paul Collaer, a highly respected friend of Satie and other composers would write, "Satie was more 'Six' than the Six."[45]

The following September, Tailleferre made a second, more determinative trip to America. This time she met Ralph Barton, a famous caricaturist who spoke French fluently and possessed a spontaneous charm and wit. Their marriage, Barton's fourth, followed shortly, and the couple settled in Manhattan.

Barton's wedding present to Tailleferre of a player piano illustrates his perverse sense of humor. She recalled that he did not want her to play or compose on the real piano, that rather she was to prepare savory French dishes while he worked in his study. The arrival of Charlie Chaplin, a good friend of Barton's, began a brief period of happiness for Tailleferre, because it meant improvising musical accompaniments for his film characters. Chaplin at one point proposed she join him in Hollywood to work on *The Circus*, but Barton objected.

Despite her new, rather prestigious circle, which included Sinclair Lewis, Ethel Barrymore, Somerset Maugham, Loretta Young, and Paul Morand, life in New York gave Tailleferre little pleasure. During this time, the

Boston Symphony premiered an orchestrated version of *Jeux de plein air* and her new *Concertino* for harp and orchestra.

Barton began almost immediately to resent his wife's success and would say he felt like "Monsieur Tailleferre." Tailleferre later encountered a similar reaction from her second husband. She could not reconcile men's conflicts toward her: though attracted at first by her renown, they would eventually become threatened and try to prevent her from working. Only later on did she realize that, for her, married life and composing were incompatible. At the age of 89, she responded to a question about whether she had encountered many obstacles in her musical life:

> Yes, yes, yes, yes, yes. I married a well-known American who went mad. The first thing he did was to buy me a player piano. And then the second husband, when I was writing the *Cantate de Narcisse* with Paul Valéry, which was a very important thing for me, he constantly prevented me from working. Perhaps it is jealousy because men never like it that women . . . I began to be famous rather quickly because of the *Groupe des Six,* and so that annoyed them. I have had a very difficult life, you know. Only I do not like to talk about it, because I write happy music as a release. But anyway, things were always against me. Whatever happened, it was against me.[46]

In 1927, Barton decided that they should move to Paris for good. This pleased Tailleferre immensely, as she had not adjusted to Barton's way of life in America. On the boat trip back they met Paul Claudel, who Tailleferre knew from the Ballet Suédois's rehearsals of Milhaud and Claudel's *L'Homme et son désir*. The playwright was working on an homage to celebrate the centenary of Marcelin Berthelot's birth.[47] Although Claudel wrote this "philosophical dialogue" in prose, it has a poetic rhythm that he envisioned as incidental music.

When asked to collaborate, Tailleferre hesitated with characteristic deference and modesty. Rather than leaping at the chance to work with this famous poet, she immediately thought of Darius Milhaud, who had often collaborated with Claudel in the past, and felt she should ask his permission. Milhaud encouraged her to accept and said that her music would be well suited to Claudel's conception. Thus, once settled in Paris, Tailleferre composed *Sous les remparts d'Athènes*. The work would be performed only once, and its score is now lost. Paul Claudel, who became ambassador to Washington just afterward, ironically named Barton to the Légion d'Honneur in foreign affairs to thank Tailleferre for this music.

Tailleferre and Barton lived on rue Nicolo. Barton did much of the decoration himself and designed large tapestries for his wife to sew. As their lives stabilized, Tailleferre found it easier to work, but Barton restlessly divided his time between Paris and New York.

In 1928, Tailleferre composed *Deux Valses* for two pianos, *Pavane, Nocturne, Finale* for orchestra, and two other piano pieces, a *Sicilienne* and a *Pastorale in A-flat* (another work in 5/8 meter) dedicated "à Ralph."[48]

Barton was writing *God's Country*—dedicated "to Germaine"—a satirical history of America with his own illustration, to be published the following year.

In the summer of 1929, Tailleferre wrote her modal *Six Chansons Françaises,* using fifteenth-, seventeenth-, and eighteenth-century texts. During an interview years later, she delighted in the memory of these songs, which she termed "*très drôles.*" She wanted to write something "more gay than tedious" to counteract domestic problems she and Barton were facing. Most of the texts boldly glorify infidelity. In the first song, "Non, la fidélité . . . ," a man celebrates constant change. In the third, "Mon mari m'a diffamée," a woman laughs at her husband's worthlessness and praises her lover's strength. In the fourth, a woman mourns having been forced to marry an old man who sequesters her; she dreams of joining a young lover in the woods.[49]

Three of the songs are fast, light, and staccato, while the alternating three are slower and more legato.

Figure 7.7 "Non, la fidelité . . ." from *Six Chansons Francaises,* mm. 1-8. Reprinted by authorization of Alphonse Leduc—Paris, owners and publishers for all countries.

This example from the first song has a comfortable octave range and is confined to tonal intervals, with mostly scalewise movement. The accompaniment rocks repetitively between two chords, with mild dissonances.

The sixth song, "Les trois présents," also begins with a straightforward diatonic melody in an octave range. Here the accompaniment doubles the melody and combines uncomplicated harmonies with a constant dominant pedal. The rest of the song moves into a "B" section, and then back to "A," ending with a conventional V-I in the original C major.

Tailleferre did not write these texts herself—she chose them. But they reflect her dwindling faith in marriage. Bored and restless, Barton was seeing other women. According to Tailleferre, he needed a more exciting life of arguments, tears, and reconciliations, which she did not provide. After growing up in a home full of marital tensions, she thought it best to remain conciliatory. This only aggravated Barton further. After a series of distressing incidents, Tailleferre filed for divorce and Barton left for New York. She would never see him again.

In 1930, Tailleferre's mother, whom she had supported for years and who had encouraged Tailleferre from the start, died. The divorce from Barton came through on 20 April 1931, and on May 20 Barton committed suicide in New York—a dramatic event that made page one of the *New York Times* the following day. "I did it because I am fed up with inventing devices for getting through twenty-four hours a day and bridging over a few months periodically with some beautiful interest, such as a new gal who annoyed me to the point where I forgot my own troubles."

That same year, Tailleferre married a young French lawyer named Jean Lageat and gave birth to Françoise, her only child.

Figure 7.8 "Les trois présents" from *Six Chansons Françaises,* mm. 1-8. Reprinted by authorization of Alphonse Leduc—Paris, owners and publishers for all countries.

1931–1946: JEAN LAGEAT AND WORLD WAR II

During the first year of their marriage, politics dominated Lageat's and Tailleferre's lives. They followed their friend Gaston Bergery (who had introduced them) on his electoral campaigns. Bergery was deputy of Mantes, a small city just west of Paris, where Tailleferre played a movement of her *Piano Concerto* with local amateur musicians. She rejoiced to be back among her countrymen and married to a man she hoped would bring her greater happiness and stability.

But the new household brought problems of its own. Friends of the composer later recalled that Jean Lageat spoke publicly with a pretentious elegance that did not entirely camouflage his unpleasant personality.[50] A serious illness, of which he was not yet aware, aggravated his moods. Tailleferre began to write film music to supplement their income; she later had few fond memories of these times, aside from the joy of her baby daughter Françoise.

Despite problems, in 1932 Tailleferre composed an exuberant *Ouverture*, first conducted by Pierre Monteux on 25 December 1933.[51] Many point to this lively piece as one of Tailleferre's finest. It calls for two flutes, piccolo, two oboes, English horn, two clarinets, two bassoons, four horns, three trumpets, three trombones, tuba, percussion, strings, and harpsichord. The harpsichord solo refreshingly alters the texture and echoes the composer's affinity with things classic.

Two years before, Tailleferre made a statement that has often been quoted since: "I do not have a lot of respect for traditions. I make music because I enjoy it. I know that it is not *grande musique*. It is light and gay music, which explains why sometimes I am compared to the *petits maîtres* of the eighteenth century, and I am very proud of this."[52]

Because of the tension between them and Lageat's growing envy of her career, Tailleferre could not entirely enjoy the acclaim that accompanied the *Ouverture*. By 1934, the year she wrote and performed her *Concerto for Two Pianos, Chorus, and Orchestra,* doctors diagnosed Lageat's tuberculosis. Tailleferre's work suffered when they were thus obliged to move to Leysin, Switzerland, where Lageat spent three years in a sanatorium.

To enliven this stagnating existence, Tailleferre invited friends from Paris. Between March and October of 1936 she composed her *Violin Concerto*. During that summer, Igor Markevitch, the Russian composer and conductor, stayed at their house in Leysin. At 24 years old, he had just married Kira Nijinska. Markevitch orchestrated the second movement, the *Largo*, of Tailleferre's *Violin Concerto*. Asked why this happened, she explained:

> He said to me, "I feel like orchestrating that one!" And I was enchanted—it was a good transaction for me. Why not? It was an experience. When Monteux played it,

he asked, "Why did you do that?" "Because it was fun to see what he would make of it," I answered. One has to have some fun in one's profession, not be rigorous all the time.[53]

The *Violin Concerto* was written for Yvonne Astruc, who gave the first performance on November 22 under Pierre Monteux.[54]

During these years, Tailleferre also composed music for a number of films, and in 1935 she helped launch a new group composed of Olivier Messiaen, André Jolivet, Daniel Lesur, and Yves Baudrier, *La Jeune France.*

For the Paris Exhibition of 1937, Tailleferre wrote "Le Marin de Bolivar," her first collaboration with Henri Jeanson. In addition, she and other composers produced *A l'Exposition.* Lageat and Tailleferre had returned to Paris, where for a few months life seemed brighter. But Lageat's tuberculosis returned, and they had to move south to Grasse, where his father owned a perfume factory.

Fortunately, a number of old friends now lived in Provence, most significantly Paul Valéry, who taught once a week in Nice. Tailleferre received a twenty-thousand-franc commission from the "Direction des Arts et Lettres" to write a lyric piece, preferably a cantata, for which she could freely choose the text and librettist. Valéry expressed interest in collaborating on a setting of his *Narcisse.* As in the case of Paul Claudel, Tailleferre initially hesitated to work with so great a poet. But Valéry encouraged her to compose this music in the style of Gluck, and she realized she was quite capable of doing so.[55]

Tailleferre was very proud of this collaboration. She fondly remembered walking beneath the olive trees in the south of France as Valéry related the story of Narcissus. Each week he would bring a new scene. Like Claudel, Valéry had precise ideas, and sometimes he would ask Tailleferre to rewrite sections. The third scene gave her particular trouble; after trying a number of versions, she lost all perspective. Valéry admitted that he had rewritten these verses many times himself. To facilitate her work, he read the poetry aloud as she took down rhythmic dictation. This elucidated for Tailleferre precisely what the poet had in mind, and she immediately composed the music according to his conception. The result pleased them both, despite the personal hardships Tailleferre endured during its composition.[56]

The "Cantate du Narcisse" for four women's voices, tenor, and orchestra had its first performance in Marseilles by l'Orchestre de la Radio in 1942. It did not receive great critical acclaim and was never published. On 14 January 1944, Alfred Cortot conducted it in Paris. Tailleferre had left again for the United States by that time, but Valéry wrote to her from occupied France, "I am thinking of our child 'Narcisse.' . . . What a time for this beautiful son of music and of poetry."[57]

After completing the "Cantate," Tailleferre continued to write film music. She worked with Maurice Cloche on *Provincia, terre d'amour* and *Ces Dames aux chapeaux verts,* whose score was well received.[58] But the presence of the enemy on French soil brought this work to a halt. Indeed, life became intolerable, even in Grasse, which inevitably grew dependent upon Vichy's Nazi rule.

Tailleferre saw Valéry for the last time in 1941 in Paris where he insisted that she play the entire "Cantate." Before her departure for the United States in 1942, she composed a *Pastorale* for flute and piano. This direct

Figure 7.9 Manuscript copy of the violin version of *Pastorale*, in Tailleferre's own hand. Reprinted courtesy of Yvonne de Casa Fuerte.

and simple work exemplifies Tailleferre's mastery of melody and her ability to affect the listener through understatement. Though short, the *Pastorale* is performed rather often on recitals devoted to the flute works of *Les Six*. Tailleferre wrote out the manuscript version for Yvonne de Casa Fuerte, a violinist who lived in New York during the war, and whom she knew from her years at the Conservatoire.

Tailleferre left Marseilles in late September 1942, crossed Spain, Portugal, and finally the Atlantic. Thirty-three days later, she disembarked in New York, where she had not been since her years with Barton. In the November-December issues of *Modern Music*, she published an article on France's cultural life under the Germans. She wrote that conditions prevented her from working, that she searched for over a year to find music paper in Lyons, Marseilles, and Nice. Citing conductor Paul Paray, she praised those who refused to obey such anti-Semitic rulings as discharging Jewish instrumentalists and removing music by Paul Dukas from a concert. Tailleferre described the struggles in the cinema industry, radio, and concerts. She concluded:

> Two years of experience under German rule have taught me that all expressions of pride, dignity, spirit, aspiration of the human will, in one word, all the effort of the free mind, can be made only clandestinely. The artist and the intellectual in general have a bitter choice. They must be silent, pursue the most discreet opposition or else collaborate, even for publication of their most abstract works. German rule, faithful to the tradition of totalitarian regimes, strangles the spirit. It is a historical truth that the human mind makes its greatest progress under freedom. Under servility, its concessions to the ruling power have always debased it, without even helping to consolidate tyranny.[59]

Lageat had already settled in the United States when Tailleferre and Françoise arrived. But he remained primarily in Washington, D.C., where he worked on international affairs between the United States, France, and England. Tailleferre lived first in New York; here she met Igor Markevitch's mother, who was teaching at Swarthmore. Tailleferre then rented a small house near Philadelphia, which she much preferred to Manhattan, and Françoise, now about 11 years old, studied with Mme. Markevitch.

Tailleferre never felt at home in the United States. She did, however, find a number of compatriots who, like herself, had fled their occupied homeland. The Milhauds and Stravinsky lived in California but sometimes visited the East Coast. She would see poet Philippe Soupault and composers Marcelle de Manziarly and Vittorio Rieti.

She did not write during the war years, although she taught a few music students. One former student remembers that in teaching composition, fugue, and counterpoint, Tailleferre emphasized the strict rules that she had mastered years before at the Conservatoire. But the composer also conveyed that those who are gifted will surpass conventions. A stylish woman with a joie de vivre and an "acid sense of humor," she taught with great patience and treated her students as apprentices in the French artistic tradition. She would play her music on the piano, but she did not then wish to analyze it intellectually.[60]

Tailleferre recalled that in America her work suffered, and she constantly worried about family and friends who remained in France. As when she had lived in New York with Barton, she felt physically and emotionally estranged. She socialized mostly with French friends and never learned to speak English well.

She returned home to France in the spring of her 54th year. Though the enemy had been defeated, France was no victor. Tailleferre discovered that many friends of hers were gone and that the Germans had occupied and pillaged her home in Grasse.

1946–1968: TIES FORMED AND SEVERED

Tailleferre did not take up composition again immediately after the war. In Grasse she tried to restore her household to normal, though Lageat and his mistress only contributed to the disarray. Many guests visited them in the south, including Grant Johannesen, the Casadesuses, and often Poulenc.

In the spring of 1948, the American duo-pianists Arthur Gold and Robert Fizdale made their first trip to Paris with a package for Germaine Tailleferre: the score to Virgil Thomson's opera *The Mother of Us All.* When Gold and Fizdale arrived at Tailleferre's, they found an animated luncheon in progress. Fizdale remembers Lageat's pompous English welcome speech, to which Tailleferre added simply "me too," a coda that won the Americans' hearts.[61] In their biography *Misia* they write:

> After lunch Georges Auric sat at the piano, carefully turned the music upside down, and improvised a Thomsonesque accompaniment while Francis Poulenc "created" the roles. He sang a nonsense-syllable imitation of Gertrude Stein's English in a hilarious falsetto, and was especially compelling in the role of America's pioneer suffragette Susan B. Anthony. Thus on our first day in Paris we were entertained by three of *Les Six.*[62]

When Gold and Fizdale returned to the United States, they introduced some of Tailleferre's newer works without remarkable success. In fact, of the *Valse lente*, performed on 14 November 1948, the *New York Times*'s Noel Strauss commented, "Exceedingly feminine and unimportant."[63]

In the next few years, the Opéra-Comique staged her "Paris-Magie" and "Le Petit navire," neither of which inspired much public acclaim. "Paris-Magie" opened on 13 May 1949 and closed at the end of the season, June 3. "Le Petit navire" had only two performances. The premiere evoked memories of *Les Mariés de la Tour Eiffel*, which had sent Tailleferre and her mother to huddle in the rear of their theater box. Critic Henri Barraud writes that the opening on 9 March 1951 was the most exciting first performance that Paris has seen in many, many years. The gallery let loose with a storm of invective against the authors and actors, shouting disapproval and demanding its money back. The people in the orchestra and the first balconies, fortified by a large group of invited guests, tried to offset the hostile outcries with their applause.[64]

Tailleferre and librettist Henri Jeanson had begun this work in 1948. The composer felt some frustration at Jeanson's irregular output, which arrived in spurts for two years. Their first complete version, entitled "Il était un petit navire," pleased the Opéra-Comique's director, Henri Malherbe, who insisted they expand it from one to three acts. This, Tailleferre and critics felt, was a grave mistake. In addition, although the music itself contained nothing jarring or radical, Jeanson's words left the public outraged. In the same review quoted above, Barraud comments:

In curious contrast, Germaine Tailleferre has the gentlest, most inoffensive personality possible. A charming and delicate artist, how could she find the deliberate truculence to illustrate musically the unbelievable jibes and provocative attacks that Janson [*sic*] has scattered liberally throughout his text?

Following the war years, Tailleferre and her early companions again drew close to each other. Neither their own increasing age nor a radically altered France could destroy the friendship that bound Satie's *Nouveaux Jeunes*. In 1952, the International Council of Music sponsored an exhibit of their manuscripts, stage sets, letters, and mementos. The composers and Jean Cocteau each wrote a brief statement for the occasion. Tailleferre's read: "In the breast of the *Groupe des Six,* I have found an atmosphere of participation which has permitted me to be associated with the first manifestations of today's greatest composers. Their friendship has been determinative for me."[65]

Tailleferre also joined Auric, Honegger, Henri Sauguet, Roland-Manuel, and Daniel Lesur in *La Guirlande de Campra,* an orchestral work to which she contributed a "Sarabande." Hans Rosbaud conducted this in Aix-en-Provence on 30 July 1952.

On 4 November 1953, *Les Six* celebrated their 35th anniversary in a gala concert at the Théâtre des Champs-Elysées. Honegger was too ill to attend, and Milhaud was confined to a wheelchair. With characteristic eloquence, Jean Cocteau made an introductory speech on the group and its members. Of Tailleferre, he said:

Our group had its flower in a woman, a girl, a musician. Strange as it may seem (since every woman is sensitive and good at figures), although there are many composers with feminine souls—Chopin remains the best example—there is, so to speak, no real woman composer. I salute Germaine Tailleferre as a charming exception.[66]

Approximately three thousand people filled the theater. Georges Tzipine conducted the Orchestre de la Société des Concerts du Conservatoire in works by each composer, beginning with Tailleferre's *Ouverture* of 1932. Janet Flanner ("Genêt") devoted a "Letter from Paris" in the *New Yorker* to this event: "None of the young Paris intellectuals attended. The enormous audience was composed of people who were young thirty-five years ago. . . . It recalled the wonderful first postwar Paris, when the Kaiser's Germans had just been defeated and Lenin's Russians worried no one yet.[67]

At about that time, Tailleferre completed a new *Piano Concerto* for her daughter, who performed it in Cannes with Georges Tzipine, again conducting; Tailleferre would also dedicate a *Partita* to her in 1957. But Françoise had been severely affected by her father's violent nature, with resulting emotional damage. Almost from the start, the unusually complicated demands of her family life troubled and distracted Tailleferre. She often chose to put these problems ahead of her work.

Françoise married Jean-Luc de Rudder in her early 20s, but they were subsequently divorced. Germaine Tailleferre raised her only granddaughter, Elvire, who was born in 1955. The composer, too, filed for a divorce from Jean Lageat and received a meager settlement, which she invested in a house in Saint-Tropez. There, once again lacking financial security, she did *trompe-l'oeil* paintings and restored antique furniture. She lived near Louis Durey, who had retreated to the south more than 30 years before, but they were never very close personal friends, apart from their mutual affiliation with *Les Six*.

Of the group, Tailleferre was probably closest to Francis Poulenc, "Poupoul," who called her "Bidulette" (*bidule* means "thingamajig"). During these postwar years, Georges Auric and she collaborated on a film entitled *Torrents*.

Tailleferre composed a number of new works in the 1950s: a *Second Sonata* for violin and piano, a *Sonata* for harp, a *Concertino* for flute, piano, and chamber orchestra (in which she and Jean-Pierre Rampal performed), and a *Concertino* for soprano. But she based this last largely upon her *Sonata* for harp. Similarly, she derived the "Concerto des vaines paroles," with a text by Jean Tardieu, from her earlier *Concerto for Two Pianos*. Tailleferre wrote this piece for the baritone Bernard Lefort, whom she accompanied on highly successful concert tours across Europe after her divorce, much as Poulenc had done with Pierre Bernac. Lefort, who later headed the Paris Opera, helped Tailleferre in her later years to receive commissions and to have her works published or reissued. He recalls her excellence as a pianist and a musician, but also her refusal to promote herself or to make any demands, even for well-deserved compensation.[68]

Her ballet "Parisiana" was first performed in 1953 in Copenhagen. Jean-Luc de Rudder, Françoise's husband, designed the sets. At the 1954 Edinburgh Festival, where Tailleferre and Lefort gave a concert, "Parisiana" was staged again. The French Radio also commissioned a number of small-scale chamber operas from her, including settings of George Huguet's "La Voix," Philippe Soupault's "La Petite Sirène," and Ionesco's "Le Maître." Her "Au Paradis avec les ânes" was presented at the Prix Italia.

Arthur Honegger, who had suffered a serious heart attack eight years before, died in 1955. That same year, Tailleferre commented to Hélène Jourdan-Morhange, "My music doesn't interest me anymore and twelve-tone music, which attracts me, represents such a task that I no longer have the strength to undertake it. It would almost be like wanting to express myself in Chinese! It is a bit too late to learn."[69] In 1957 she did, nevertheless, experiment with serial techniques in her three-movement *Sonata for Clarinet Solo*. Despite its chromaticism and frequent metrical shifts, the piece reflects Tailleferre's affinity for accessible melodic lines, phrase repetition, and minimal development. This work, while an attempt to be open to other modes of expression, could not be called one of Tailleferre's finest.

Figure 7.10 *Sonata for Clarinet Solo* (1975), in which Tailleferre experimented with serial techniques; movement one, mm. 1-12. © 1959 by Rongwen Music, Inc. Reprinted by permission of the publisher.

In 1961, *Les Six* (now five) and Cocteau celebrated the 40th anniversary of *Les Mariés de la Tour Eiffel* at the Hôtel de Ville, where they received the Medal of the City of Paris. Two years later, first Poulenc and then Cocteau died, leaving four deeply saddened friends.

By this time a woman in her 70s, Tailleferre was nonetheless raising her young granddaughter. Some have suggested that bringing up Elvire rejuvenated Tailleferre. Of her grandmother, whom from childhood she called "Baboum," Elvire said, "She was born a musician just as she was born with blue eyes." Elvire remembers with admiration her grandmother's tremendous facility and grace at the piano and her love of orchestration. "Baboum" would orchestrate the way she would fill in the colors on her tapestries—with subtlety and balance. She also recalls Tailleferre's outer naïvete and simplicity that, in her view, was a deceptive protection for the inner strength and equilibrium that sustained her.[70]

In sympathy with the student riots of 1968, Tailleferre joined the Communist Party. Frédéric Robert, Louis Durey's biographer, said in an interview that although Tailleferre felt strongly enough to take action, she did not have the intellectually rooted political convictions of Durey, a longtime member. Madeleine Milhaud even remembers that, just as Tailleferre would minimize things by saying "my little piano" or "my little sonata," she would say, "my little Communist Party!"[71] Years earlier, Tailleferre had remarked in an interview, "I continue on: is life not an eternal new beginning?"[72]

1969–1983: FINAL YEARS

Tailleferre's old age brought a few tributes but no great comforts or compensations. With characteristic quiet resiliency, she remained active as long as she was physically able, accepting any commissions that came her way, though without seeking them herself. Late in life, she said:

> It is very difficult to write music if one does not have some sort of goal. I have really gotten the better of interviewers who ask me, "Why do you write music?" "For money!" I say. It has always been that way. Each time I received a commission, whatever it was, I was glad to have earned a little bit more money. What do you want? One has to live.[73]

An energetic but elderly woman, Tailleferre had little financial security and would not keep track of royalties or to whom she lent her manuscripts. Consequently, many of her works are incomplete or lost. Nevertheless, thanks to a few friends who helped look after her, Tailleferre's name and her music sometimes resurfaced. An "Association Germaine Tailleferre" was even formed six years before her death.[74]

From 1970 to 1972, she taught accompaniment at the Schola Cantorum, and in the following years she prepared students for the baccalaureate through private harmony and counterpoint lessons. In 1973, Lemoine published a significant number of her newer chamber works, and she won the *Grand Prix Musical* from the Académie des Beaux Arts. Five years later, the City of Paris also awarded her the *Grand Prix Musical.*

Still living with her granddaughter in a very modest apartment, Tailleferre began in 1975 to work at the Ecole Alsacienne for a few hours a day. There, she improvised piano music for children between five and eight years old who would move and react freely to the varying rhythms and styles she played. Georges Hacquard, director of the school, remembers how much the children loved "Madame Tailleferre," and how her music inspired them. In a video tape of one of these rhythm classes made in 1980, one can see her pleasure and theirs as she switched from well-known children's songs to touches of *Petrouchka*, to melodies in the style of Kurt Weill.[75]

The same year she joined the Ecole Alsacienne, she met Désiré Dondeyne, conductor of a prestigious concert band and director of a conservatory. He not only introduced her to music for band, but also became her orchestrator when she could only write out piano scores. According to Dondeyne, music was not a complicated matter for Tailleferre—she was very flexible and open to suggestions and changes and was no great philosopher on musical aesthetics. Yet she was always full of new composing projects and, in spite of a childlike personality, knew what she wanted.[76]

She continued composing despite arthritis and worked a few hours a day. Some of her very late works include a piano trio, a woodwind quintet, songs, piano music, and some earlier pieces reorchestrated for band. No extreme stylistic changes are evident in her work as a whole, although she did occasionally experiment. She mainly clung to her belief in simplicity, that "music is an expression, it is a way to express something in notes. If one expresses in an incomprehensible way, what purpose does it serve?"[77]

Georges Auric, in an interview one year before his death, commented: "Obviously she has not changed her vocabulary. But one can keep the same vocabulary and, with age, subtly transform what one writes to give it more weight, more gravity, more importance. And I find that her recent works, in that sense, are remarkable."[78]

Madeleine Milhaud, on the other hand, noted:

> I don't think that Germaine's talent could have been more rewarded than it was according to the fact that it was charming and elegant but did not change things. That's the only point. There are many composers who are like that. Now these, perhaps, will be lucky enough to have an official position and therefore will be able to push their music through contacts and exchanges. I don't think Germaine is able to do that type of dirty work. She is too honest, too upright.[79]

As mentioned before, Madeleine Milhaud also pointed out that Tailleferre tended both to minimize her ability and to be easily satisfied. "She would say 'my little symphony,' 'my little quartet,'—it was her way of thinking and doing."[80]

On 4 March 1982 Tailleferre attended a performance at the Paris Opera of her "Concerto de la Fidélité," written the year before for high voice and orchestra. The evening, which Bernard Lefort was influential in arranging, paid tribute to Germaine Tailleferre and the deceased André Jolivet, who had been a member of *La Jeune France*. One person who attended commented that this beautiful and "serene music" could have been written when she was 25 years old, that it is "eternally youthful."[81] Similarly, a critic from *Le Monde* wrote: "The carefree freshness of the *Groupe des Six*, sixty years ago, perfumed this work by a woman soon to be ninety years old, who responded, very moved, to the applause of a large audience come to salute two engaging personalities of French music."[82]

To a question posed not long before that performance on whether she had achieved what she set out to accomplish as a composer, Tailleferre answered forthrightly, "I have no idea. None. I was trying to earn my living."[83]

Germaine Tailleferre died on 7 November 1983 at the age of 91—the last of *Les Six*—and was laid to rest with quiet ceremony. The international papers noted her passing, though many people, even in France, had long forgotten the woman who once added a striking dimension to *Les Six*.

OBSERVATIONS/EVALUATIONS

Germaine Tailleferre is not an undiscovered master of legendary proportions, and she cannot even be called an influential innovator. She was an enormously gifted artist whose natural talent flowed freely from her long, graceful fingers (which many who knew her have recalled), whether she was playing, improvising, or accompanying at the piano; composing; or designing and sewing large tapestries. Her appreciation of the subtleties of visual and aural color produced delicately balanced works of great beauty, works that are thoughtfully structured and which are moving because of their directness and honesty of expression.

While Tailleferre certainly did not change the twentieth-century musical world, or even imitate consistently those who did, she insisted on going her own way and writing music that pleased her. Integrity, honesty, taste, and technical excellence marked her style. Her statement was small in scale and very personal, but not inconsequential. Regardless of an eventful and often painful life, she did not dramatize her condition but rather persevered. Her music reflects her grace, her sense of proportion, her admiration for predecessors and contemporaries, and her innate ease of artistic expression.

Germaine Tailleferre had no problem—musically, at least—in saying, "I do what I want." And if she wanted in her early years to pay homage to Ravel, whom she admired and enjoyed, she did so without pretense and without excusing herself. She claimed a proud affinity with the *petits maîtres* of the seventeenth and eighteenth centuries and enjoyed the tradition of smooth structures, lighthearted spirit, and frankness. Even when she experimented with 12-tone techniques at one point, she retained a lyric accessibility and an appreciation of line. In general, though, it was difficult to lure the composer herself into discussion of these stylistic qualities: "I do not analyze those sorts of things. Either music happens naturally or it should not happen at all."[84]

As we examine Germaine Tailleferre's life, certain personality traits emerge, as well as certain events, which help explain why the young woman, whose public career pointed toward such a promising course when she was associated with *Les Six*, did not go as far as some of the other composers in the group.

Tailleferre tried very hard to embrace a tradition that repeatedly conflicted with her desire for a composing career. She was raised in a family where her father had little respect for his wife or daughters, and he opposed her musical training at the Conservatoire. Later, both her first and second husbands, rather than supporting her in her work, considered themselves and their careers to be primary. She tried hard, in both cases, to live up to their expectations of her as a wife and consequently lost time that probably would have been devoted to her profession. She missed opportunities for film contracts and other commissions and drifted from the artistic mainstream during the period when her second husband had to move to Switzerland, Grasse, and the United States.

What's more, because of a modest disposition and her own self-doubts, combined with being told by her father and both husbands that her talent should not be exploited, she made few of the demands that her colleagues did upon conductors, publishers, and "connections." The thought of self-promotion horrified her. She preferred, in many situations, to remain silent and avoid conflicts than to stand up for the credit she deserved.

Tailleferre's inclusion in *Les Six* followed brilliant studies at the Conservatoire, Satie's recognition of her talent, and musical activity in his *Nouveaux Jeunes*. It furthered her career by connecting her to the center of the postwar cultural surge and facilitating performance of her music. But this sudden public acclaim arrived at a time in her personal and professional life when she lacked confidence and felt undeserving of such attention. She developed a habit of minimizing herself to convey an awareness of her own faults. She perceived a misalliance between her "small talent" and some of the period's more influential artists and suspected others did, too.

She may have been right that, initially at least, her work was not yet ripe. And she recognized, as soon as she met Stravinsky and heard and played his music, that they were in different leagues. Yet even when she matured as a composer, she continued this self-deprecation and deemed it inappropriate to insist upon recognition. And because the public would forever associate her with *Les Six,* critics even viewed later pieces as having been written by "the only woman member" of the group, rather than by Germaine Tailleferre, composer.

In her married life, Tailleferre indulged her first and second husbands' egos at her own expense until, at last, the marriages became intolerable. It was this very conforming quality that the poets Paul Claudel and Paul Valéry appreciated in their collaborations with her. Said the former, "Women are much more supple than men and they do what I want."[85] Tailleferre sympathetically deferred to men's needs, as she had been taught to do by her family and her society. Always careful to keep a necessary sense of humor and not to become "emotional," she accepted a secondary position and knew that, even if she thought otherwise, she had to allow men to have a sense of power and control. Not until much later did she finally say, "It would be better to marry music because men never understand that it takes a lot of reflection, of work, that it is not easy."[86]

An evolution in Tailleferre's personality allowed her finally to decide that marriage was not compatible with a composing career. The early insecurities made her feel she neither could nor should stand alone, that she ought to sacrifice for a husband, to consider her own career a "hobby." The ungenerous men she chose, however, not only could not encourage and share her modest successes, but wanted to smother her creativity entirely, as it threatened their own shaky self-images. For years she tolerated this castigation, perhaps feeling that it was somehow deserved.

Given that time and circumstances prevented Tailleferre from obtaining greater personal freedom, one still cannot assume that she could have been more professionally successful. To label her simply the product of her era would be to ignore what we know about her as an individual. In spite of a male-oriented social structure, many women have, historically, overcome obstacles with their own inner strength and drive. Had Tailleferre proclaimed that "it would be better to marry music" at the age of 20 rather than she did in an interview at the age of 90, she would not necessarily have gone further, except on a superficial level.

Again, we come to Tailleferre's personality—the simplicity, modesty, lack of pretension, and honesty that all who have known her seem to remember. This was a woman of tremendous natural ability, both in art and in music. And yet she, as a creator, lacked a fundamental quality: egotistical, all-consuming, obsessive artistry.

Tailleferre undeniably possessed a creative talent and the ability to express it, both through notes and through colors. Without this inspired gift, she could not have generated all she did. A love for music, more than an ambition, made Tailleferre want to create. She used her power practically, to earn a living, and to fulfill the more intimate purpose of consolation. She did not feel the driven obligation to make a "statement."

I last saw Germaine Tailleferre in the summer before her death, when it was clear that her world was becoming smaller each day. She no longer musically illustrated anecdotes with constant trips to the piano, as she had done during past visits, but she continued to speak of friends and music with great lucidity and detail. For the first time, she characterized each of *Les Six*: Auric as the most intellectual, Honegger as independent, Milhaud as goodness personified, Durey as removed and shy, and Poulenc, fondly, as a spoiled child.

It was not Germaine Tailleferre's style to include herself in such an analysis. Instead, she would refer us directly to the most personal and open statement she left—her music.

NOTES

1. Cecil Gray, *A Survey of Contemporary Music,* pp. 245-46. Virginia Woolf cites this quotation on Tailleferre in *A Room of One's Own.*

2. This is a rather free translation of Milhaud's original words, "la musique d'une jeune fille qui sent bon."

3. Interview with Georges Auric, 19 Jan. 1982.

4. Pierre du Colombier and Roland-Manuel, *Les Arts, la musique et la danse 1900-1933* (Paris: Les Editions Denoël et Steele, 1933), p. 338.

5. Interviews with Germaine Tailleferre, 13, 15, and 27 January 1982.

6. The records at the Archives Nationales in Paris include biannual remarks by Mme. Sautereau-Meyer. Typical of these are, "a musician and a hard worker," "very talented and a hard worker," "admirably talented and very much a musician."

7. The test that year was as follows: a) realization of a figured bass; b) improvisatory accompaniment of a song at first sight; c) transposition down a step of a fragment for piano and voice from Mozart's *The Magic Flute*; d) execution at first sight of a fragment from Haydn's sixth Sonata; and e) reduction at first sight of a fragment from the orchestral score to *The Magic Flute.* (Archives Nationales)

8. Marie Laurencin, a painter who designed the sets and costumes for Francis Poulenc's *Les Biches*, is often called "Apollinaire's Muse." Jean Cocteau and others would later proclaim Germaine Tailleferre "a Marie Laurencin for the ear." This idea probably stems less from a similarity in their work (Tailleferre being more "classical," or as she said, "less original") than from their both being women in a milieu of men. In an interview, the composer was pleased to be associated with her friend, but saw absolutely no artistic validity in the comparison.

9. In 1923, when *Les Six* were already past their height, Milhaud introduced another group of four young composers to Erik Satie, who promoted them. These, Henri Cliquet-Pleyel, Roger Désormière, Maxime Jacob, and Henri Sauguet, were known as *l'Ecole d'Arcueil,* after the suburb where Satie lived.

10. Some historians seem to portray these evenings almost as a *camarata.* Madeleine Milhaud, Georges Auric, Yvonne de Casa Fuerte (a violinist at the time), and Germaine Tailleferre all stressed in interviews the informal, anti-intellectual atmosphere.

11. See Frédéric Robert, *Louis Durey, l'aîné des Six,* p. 30.

12. Pierre Bertin and Marcel Herrand would read Cocteau's text in *Les Mariés de la Tour Eiffel*, 1921. The former's voice can be heard on the 1966 recording (see Discography). See Bertin, "Erik Satie et le Groupe des Six."

13. As his inclusion in this concert demonstrates, Roland-Manuel was very much a part of the musical circle. He is often called the "seventh" of the group and went on to become a critic and an author.

14. See Pierre Bertin, "Erik Satie et le Groupe des Six," p. 56; for a sense of the milieu, see Arthur Gold and Robert Fizdale, *Misia.*

15. See Jean Cocteau, *Le Coq et l'Arlequin* (1918; rpt. Paris: Stock/Musique, 1979), pp. 58-59.

In an interview on Jan. 26, 1982, Arthur Hoerée, who knew Debussy, Satie and Cocteau, said the pamphlet leaves a false impression that its author does not recognize Debussy's genius. In 1942, for the fortieth anniversary celebration of *Pelléas et Mélisande* by the Réunions des Théâtres Lyriques Nationaux, Cocteau wrote this *Hommage*: "If, long ago, I told the young to be guarded against Claude Debussy, it is because such a genius opens the door and closes it behind him. One would be lost in wanting to follow him."

16. For general information on *Les Six,* see James Harding, *The Ox on the Roof*; Paul Collaer's articles in *Revue Générale* vols. 5, 6, and 7 (May-July 1974) (also translated in Italian in *L'Approdo musicale*, nos. 19-20 [1965]); and Pierre Bertin in *Les Annales Conferencia* 58, no. 4 (1951), pp. 46-60.

17. Interview with Georges Auric, 19 January 1982.

18. Interview in English with Madeleine Milhaud, 7 January 1982.

19. Interview with Georges Auric, 19 January 1982.

20. Irène Lagut would later design the sets for *Les Mariés de la Tour Eiffel.* For another discussion of *Jeux de plein air,* see Alfred Cortot, *La Musique Française de Piano*, p. 24.

21. Interview with Henri Sauguet, 12 January 1982.

22. H. Jourdan-Morhange, *Mes Amis Musiciens,* p. 153.

23. F. Poulenc, *Entretiens avec Claude Rostand*, pp. 31-32. Note here, again, the reference to Laurencin discussed in note 8.

24. Interview with Madeleine Milhaud, 7 January 1982.

25. René Chalupt, ed. *Ravel au miroir de ses lettres,* pp. 207-8.

26. See Jean Wiéner, *Allegro Appassionato*, pp. 42-49. Wiéner also organized a concert series from 1921 to 1923. On page 52, he includes a program with Tailleferre and Robert Soëtens performing her *Violin Sonata* on 29 January 1923 at the Théâtre des Champs-Elysées.

27. See James Harding, *The Ox on the Roof*, pp. 82-84.

28. See Arthur Rubinstein, *My Many Years,* p. 100.

29. Chester published a version for two pianos in 1925. The *Ballade* was first heard on 3 February 1923 with Rhené Baton conducting and Viñes at the piano.

30. Alfred Cortot's description continues in *La Musique Francaise de Piano*, pp. 78-80.

31. Interview with Germaine Tailleferre, 13 January 1982.

32. See *Les Mariés de la Tour Eiffel* in Jean Cocteau, *Théâtre*, vol. 1, pp. 41-67. The musical scores disappeared until Cocteau's trip to Sweden, where he discovered them in the Ballet Suédois's files. In 1966, Darius Milhaud conducted the reconstruction. See Discography.

33. See Paul Landormy, "Le Groupe des 'Six'" in *Revue de Genève* (September 1921), pp. 393-409.

34. See *Comoedia,* 26 June 1922.

35. Heugel published a piano reduction of *Le Marchand d'oiseaux* in 1923. For reviews of the opening, see *Comoedia* (5/24 and 5/27), *Liberté* (5/29), *Oeuvre* (5/28), *Eclair* (5/28), *Excelsior* (5/30), *Figaro* (5/28), *Echo de Paris* (5/28), *Echo National* (5/28), *Petit Parisien* (6/4), *Avenir* (5/28), *l'Intransigeant* (5/27), and *Bonsoir* (5/22 and 5/27).

36. See G. Tailleferre, "Quelques mots de l'une des 'Six'" in *l'Intransigeant,* 3 June 1923.

37. Bibliothèque de l'Opéra in Paris. See *Les Ballets Suédois dans l'art contemporain* for photographs of sets, performance records, and summaries of ballets.

38. See José Bruyr, *L'Ecran des musiciens,* p. 97, and *Musica Disques* no. 36 (March 1957), p. 32.

39. See *Modern Music* (February 1924), pp. 15-19. Roland-Manuel later answers

Vuillermoz in "Ravel and the New French School," *Modern Music* (January 1925), pp. 17-23.

40. Interview with Germaine Tailleferre, 15 January 1982.

41. Lincoln Center Library, New York, dossier of clippings on Tailleferre. Many of the items, including this one, are not labeled with dates and exact references. That these are the notes for her performance in New York is a most likely assumption. See, in addition, Cortot, *La Musique Française de Piano,* pp. 76-78, for a more detailed discussion of the *Concerto*. Cortot would perform it again in London on 18 July 1925 with the British Women's Symphony Orchestra and later at Queen's Hall under Sir Henry Wood.

42. Notes from Carnegie Hall Season, 1925-1926.

43. See Frances Anne Wister, *Twenty-Five Years of the Philadelphia Orchestra 1900-1925,* p. 233. The pianist is not listed here, but quite likely Cortot played the *Concerto.*

44. See John Erskine, *The Philharmonic-Symphony Society of New York, Its First Hundred Years,* p. 93, and H. Earle Johnson, *Symphony Hall, Boston.*

45. See Collaer, "La fin des Six et de Satie" in *Revue Générale*, vols 6-7 (June-July 1974), p. 25.

46. Interview with G. Tailleferre, 13 January 1982. The ellipsis after the word "women" indicates Tailleferre's trailing off, leaving the thought incompleted.

On January 7, Madeleine Milhaud spoke of Barton and of Tailleferre: "He was an artist, a cartoonist for the *New Yorker*—of a certain talent. He drank heavily. Germaine is a person who never had any luck. I know a few women like that. They deserve luck because they are good. Germaine never had luck. And she's not demanding. I mean anything pleases her."

47. Marcelin Berthelot (1827-1907) was a famous scholar, historian, scientist, and philosopher.

48. The *Pavane, Nocturne, Finale* was first heard on 8 December 1929. See L. Aubert's review two days later in *Paris Soir,* and *Revue Musicale* (January 1930), p. 69. For comments on a performance of *Sicilienne* and *Pastorale,* see *Revue Musicale* (February 1930), pp. 156-57.

49. These songs were performed on 2 September 1930 at the Eighth Festival of the International Society of Contemporary Music in Liège. Claude Chamfray also lists Jane Bathori as having sung them on 6 May 1930, accompanied by the Orchestre Symphonique de Paris. See *Revue Musicale* (February 1930), pp. 156-57.

50. Interviews with Madeleine Milhaud, Robert Fizdale, and Nina Garsoian.

51. See *Revue Musicale* (February 1933). Heugel published the score in 1934. Tailleferre originally wrote the *Ouverture* for a comic opera whose libretto did not please her (probably Charles-Henri Hirsch's "Zuleïna"—see *Candide* 19 November 1931, and Bruyr, *L'Ecran des musiciens* [1933]. In 1937, she used the same overture for "Le Marin de Bolivar" with a new libretto by Henri Jeanson. The *Ouverture* alone was broadcast in the United States by the NBC Symphony Orchestra under Monteux on 11 November 1937. In 1953, Angel recorded a special reunion concert of *Les Six* at which the *Ouverture* was played (see Discography).

52. See *Candide,* 19 November 1931.

53. Interview with Germaine Tailleferre, 15 January 1982.

54. See *Le Figaro* 8 December 1936. Astruc played the *Concerto* with the New York Philharmonic in 1938. See *Musical America,* 25 January 1938, and the *New York Times,* 9 January 1938.

55. The date of the resulting "Cantate du Narcisse" is uncertain. A review in *La*

Gerbe (3 February 1944) cites 1938, yet the *New Grove* and *Courrier Musical* list 1937. The more likely possibility is 1938 because in the May-June 1939 issue of *Modern Music*, pp. 236-37, Virgil Thomson announces that "last spring" the French government, to relieve unemployment among composers, commissioned works from Charles Koechlin, Darius Milhaud, Germaine Tailleferre, Marcel Delannoy, Yvonne Desportes, Henri Barraut, and Elsa Barraine.

56. In an interview on 27 January 1982, Tailleferre spoke of Lageat's behavior during her collaboration with Valéry. In front of the poet he was extremely polite, but to Tailleferre and Françoise he spoke brutally. She remembered that while he lay upstairs ill he would frequently call to her for no reason, and that after she had climbed the stairs a number of times, she no longer could concentrate on her work.

During the same interview, the composer played parts of the "Cantate" from memory. When she finished, though, she perhaps unconsciously mimicked the "Germaine!" that Lageat would shout, as if it was permanently linked to the music.

57. See *Comoedia* (5 February 1944) and *La Gerbe* (3 February 1944).

58. See *Revue Musicale* (February 1938), pp. 158-59.

59. See *Modern Music* (November-December 1942), p. 16.

60. Interview with Nina Garsoian, 23 December 1981.

61. Interview with Robert Fizdale, 2 February 1982.

62. Gold and Fizdale, *Misia*, p. 306.

63. *Music News*, vol. 41 (1949), p. 46.

64. H. Barraud, "The French Lyric Stage: It Must Grow a New Skin or Rejuvenate the Old." In *Musical America*, 15 April 1951, p. 9.

65. See "Les Six" in *C.D.M.I. Bulletin*, no. 3 (January 1952), p. 14. See also Ernest Lubin, "The Six Return to the Limelight in Paris," *New York Times*, 13 January 1952.

66. Ned Rorem's translation, *Keynote* (February 1982), p. 13. In 1954, Angel Records released this speech and the concert that followed. See Discography. For a review of the record, see Harold Schonberg, "'Les Six' Once More." *New York Times*, 13 January 1952.

67. Janet Flanner, *Paris Journal 1944-1965* (10 November 1953), pp. 218-19.

68. Interview with Bernard Lefort, 23 October 1984.

69. Hélène Jourdan-Morhange, *Mes Amis Musiciens*, p. 160.

70. Interviews with Elvire de Rudder, 17 December 1983, 25 November 1984.

71. Interview with Madeleine Milhaud, 24 November 1984.

72. José Bruyr, "Germaine Tailleferre," *Musica Disques*, (March 1957), p. 33.

73. Interview with Germaine Tailleferre, 15 January 1982.

74. Founded in 1977, the "Association Germaine Tailleferre" seeks to have works by Tailleferre and other French composers be performed. Though a few concerts have taken place, this has not been a highly active organization.

75. Interview with Georges Hacquard, 15 December 1983. Video tape, "Une heure avec Germaine Tailleferre" by Daniel Faugeron, 1980.

76. Interview with Désiré Dondeyne, 19 December 1983.

77. Interview with Germaine Tailleferre, 15 January 1982.

78. Interview with Georges Auric, 19 January 1982.

79. Interview with Madeleine Milhaud, 7 January 1982.

80. Ibid.

81. Interview with Georges Hacquard, 15 December 1983.

82. Jacques Lonchampt, *Le Monde*, 9 March 1982.

83. Interview with Germaine Tailleferre, 27 January 1982.
84. Interview with Germaine Tailleferre, 15 January 1982.
85. Germaine Tailleferre, edited interview, "Musique pour Claudel." *Sang Neuf*, no. 43 (January-October 1980), pp. 10-11.
86. Interview with Germaine Tailleferre, 15 January 1982.

SELECTED LIST OF PUBLISHED WORKS

The following list is, of necessity, limited to Germaine Tailleferre's published pieces and does not claim to be final. Because the composer did not keep close track of her work during her lifetime, the task of assembling a complete catalogue will not be easy. In November 1984, Elvire de Rudder, Frédéric Robert, Désiré Dondeyne, and I opened boxes of published and unpublished scores, many of which were previously unknown. Thus, for the sake of accuracy until all is put in order, I have chosen only this partial list, which does not reflect the entire body of Germaine Tailleferre's work. It has been compiled with the help of the Library of Congress; the Bibliothèque Nationale; Editions Lemoine, Durand, Heugel, and Salabert; various reference sources; Frédéric Robert, and Germaine Tailleferre.

*indicates composer's arrangement for two pianos, or piano reduction of orchestral score.

†Indicates composer's transcription and realization of figured bass; project directed by Henri Prunières (see *Revue Musicale*, February 1925, p. 199).

The list is arranged chronologically according to the date of composition.

Date of Composition	**Title**	**Date of Publication**
c 1917	*Jeux de plein air* (2 pianos)	Durand, 1919
1918	*Quatuor* (*String Quartet*)	Durand, 1921
November 1918	*Image* for 8 instruments	Chester, 1921*
4 September 1919	*Pastorale* (in *Album des Six*)	E. Demets, 1920
1920	*Ballade* for piano and orch	Chester, 1925*
1921	*Les Mariés de la Tour Eiffel* ("Quadrille," "Valse des Dépêches")	Salabert, 1962
October 1921	*Sonate* [No. 1] for violin	Durand, 1923
April-May 1923	*Le Marchand d'oiseaux*	Heugel, 1924*
1924	*Adagio* from the *Concerto* for piano (arr. for violin and piano)	Heugel, 1924
c. 1924	*Airs de Lully* (*Les Maîtres du Chant* Vol. 1)	Heugel, 1924†
January 1924	*Concerto* for piano	Heugel, 1925*
11 October 1924	*Romance* (piano)	Eschig, 1924

Date of Composition	Title	Date of Publication
c. 1925	*Airs de Lully* (Vol 2)	Heugel, 1925†
c. 1926	*Concertino* for harp	Heugel, 1928*
c. 1927	*Maîtres du Chant* (3 vols)	Heugel, 1928*
1928	*Deux Valses* (2 pianos)	Lemoine, 1928, 1962
December 1928	*Pastorale in A-Flat* (piano)	Heugel, 1929
December 1928	*Sicilienne* (piano)	Heugel, 1929
July-August 1929	*Six Chansons Françaises*	Heugel, 1930
September 1929	*Pastorale in C* (piano)	Heugel, 1930
1932	*Ouverture* for orch	Heugel, 1934
c. 1937	*A l'Exposition*	Salabert, 1937*
1942	*Pastorale* for flute and piano	Elkan-Vogel, 1946
7 March 1946	*Pastorale* for violin and piano	Elkan-Vogel, 1946
c. 1951	*Scènes de cirque* (piano)	Philippo, 1953
24 September 1951	*Deuxieme Sonate* [*Sonata No. 2*] for violin	Durand, 1951
1951	"Sarabande" for orch (from *La Guirlande de Campra*)	Salabert, 1954
c. 1952	*La Forêt enchantée* (piano)	Philippo, 1952
c. 1952	*Concertino* for flute, piano and chamber orchestra	Philippo, 1952
c. 1952	*Sonate* for harp	Nouvelles Editions, Meridian, 1957
1955	"Premieres Prouesses" (In *Pages choisies d'hier et d'aujourd'hui*) (piano 4 hands)	Lemoine, 1955
c. 1956	*La Rue Chagrin* (voice and piano)	Ed. Tropicales, 1956
1957	*Sonata for Clarinet Solo*	Broude Bros., 1959
1957	*Partita* (piano)	Broude Bros., 1964
c. 1958	"Seule dans la forêt" (In *Printemps musical*) (piano)	Lemoine, 1958
c. 1959	*Le Maître* (chamber opera)	Editions françaises de musique, c. 1974
c. 1961	*Fleurs de France* (piano)	Lemoine, 1962
c. 1962	*Deux pièces* (Larghetto, Valse lente) (piano)	Lemoine, 1963
1969	*Etonnement* (ob, hp, pno, vln, vc)	E.F.M. Technisonor, 1969

Date of Composition	Title	Date of Publication
1969	*Jacasseries* (fl, ob, cl, hp, celeste, 2 vlns, vla, vc, cb)	E.F.M. Technisonor, 1969
1969	*Amertume* (fl, ob, cl, cor, hp, 2 vlns, vla, vc, cb)	E.F.M. Technisonor, 1969
November 1972	*Forlane* (fl, pno)	Lemoine, 1973
c. 1973	*Rondo* (ob, pno)	Lemoine, 1973
c. 1973	*Arabesque* (cl, pno)	Lemoine, 1973
c. 1973	*Choral* (tpt, pno)	Lemoine, 1973
c. 1973	*Gaillarde* (tpt, pno)	Lemoine, 1973
1978	*Trio* (pno, vln, vc)	Lemoine, 1980
c. 1980	*Suite burlesque* (2 pianos)	Lemoine, 1980
1981	*Concerto de la fidélité* (high voice and orch)	Lemoine, c. 1982
c. 1982	*20 Leçons de solfège en clé de sol, avec et sans accompagnement de piano, pour les débutants (20 Solfège Lessons in G Clef, with and without Piano Accompaniment, for Beginners)*	Lemoine, c. 1983

FILM MUSIC

Bretagne (c. 1940, arr. for piano: Salabert)

Caroline au pays natal

Ces Dames aux chapeaux verts (c. 1973-83)

Cher vieux Paris

Coïncidence (with Georges Auric)

Les Grandes personnes

Homme, notre ami

Marche du Sud

Le Petite chose (c. 1939, arr. for piano: Choudens)

Les Plus beaux jours

Provincia, terre d'amour (before 1937)

Torrents (with Georges Auric, c. 1952)

[N.B.: Many dates not known]

DISCOGRAPHY

Tailleferre, Germaine. *Ballade.* With Rosario Marciano, piano. Turnabout TV 34754, 1980.

Concertino for Harp. With Nicanor Zabaleta, harp; cond. Jean Martinon. Orchestre ORTF. Deutsche Grammophon 2530008, n.d.

Concertino for Harp. With Susan Allen, harp; cond. Dr. Antonia Brico, The New England Women's Symphony. Galaxia, 1980.

Fleurs de France, Pastorale in D, Sicilienne, Valse lente, Jeux de plein air. With Leigh Kaplan and Susan Pitts, piano. Cambria Records, C-1014, 1979.

Jeux de plein air, Deux valses. With Eugene Hemmer and Leigh Kaplan, piano. Charade Records, CH 1012, 1975.

Ouverture. Cond. Georges Tzipine, Orchestre de la Société des Concerts du Conservatoire. On "Le Groupe des Six," Angel Records 35117, in set 3515 B, 1954.

Pastorale for Flute and Piano. With Katherine Hoover. Leonarda LPI 104, 1980.

Sicilienne. With Rosario Marciano, piano. Turnabout TV 34685, 1979.

Six Chansons Françaises. With Carole Bogard, soprano, John Moriarty, piano. On "Songs by Le Groupe des Six," Cambridge 2777, n.d.

Sonate pour harpe. With Nicanor Zabaleta. Deutsche Grammophon, 2531 051, n.d.

String Quartet [*Quatuor*]. With the Vieuxtemps Quartet. Gemini Hall Records, RAP 1010, 1975.

Violin Sonata [No. 1]. Joseph Roche, violin, Paul Freed, piano. Vox SVBX 5112, 1979.

Violin Sonata [No. 1]. Arnold Steinhardt, violin, Virginia Eskin, piano. Northeastern Records, NR 222, 1986 (NR 222-C for cassette)

Le Groupe des Six. *Les Mariés de la Tour Eiffel.* Cond. Darius Milhaud, Orchestre National de l'O.R.T.F. Adès 14.007, 1966.

A SELECTED BIBLIOGRAPHY

Books

Auric, Georges. *Quand j'étais là. . . .* Paris: Bernard Grasset, 1979.

Les Ballets Suédois dans l'art contemporain. Paris: Editions du Trianon, 1931.

Bruyr, José. "Germaine Tailleferre." In *L'Ecran des musiciens.* Seconde série. Paris: J. Corti, 1933. Pp. 91-98.

Chalupt, René. *Ravel au miroir de ses lettres.* Paris: Robert Laffont, 1956.

Cocteau, Jean. *Le Coq et l'arlequin.* Rpt. Editions de la Sirène, 1918. Paris: Stock/Musique, 1979.

______. *Les Mariés de la Tour Eiffel* [1921]. In *Théâtre,* vol. 1. Paris: Gallimard, 1948. Pp. 41-67.

Colombier, Pierre du, et Roland-Manuel. *Les Arts, la musique et la danse 1900-1933.* Paris: Les Editions Denoël et Steele, 1933.

Cortot, Alfred. *La Musique Française de piano.* Vol. 3. Paris: Presses Universitaires de France, 1944.

Erskine, John. *The Philharmonic-Symphony Society of New York: Its First Hundred Years.* New York: Macmillan Co., 1943.

Flanner, Janet ("Genêt"). *Paris Journal 1944-1965.* Ed. William Shawn. New York: Atheneum, 1965.

Gold, Arthur, and Robert Fizdale. *Misia.* New York: Morrow Quill Paperbacks, 1981.

Gray, Cecil. *A Survey of Contemporary Music.* London: Oxford University Press, 1927.

Harding, James. *The Ox on the Roof.* New York: St. Martin's Press, 1972.

Johnson, H. Earle. *Symphony Hall, Boston.* Boston: Little, Brown and Co., 1950.

Jourdan-Morhange, Hélène. *Mes Amis Musiciens.* Paris: Les Editeurs Français Réunis, 1955.

Milhaud, Darius. *Notes sans musique.* Paris: René Juilliard, 1949, 1963.

Poulenc, Francis. *Entretiens avec Claude Rostand.* Paris: René Juilliard, 1954.

Robert, Frédéric. *Louis Durey, l'aîné des Six.* Paris: Les Editeurs Français Reunis, 1968.

Rubinstein, Arthur. *My Many Years.* New York: Alfred A. Knopf, 1980.

Wiéner, Jean. *Allegro Appassionato.* Paris: Pierre Belfond, 1978.

Wister, Frances Anne. *Twenty-Five Years of the Philadelphia Orchestra 1900-1925.* Philadelphia: Edward Stern & Co., Inc., 1925.

Articles and Reviews

Aubert, L. Review of *Pavane, Nocturne, Finale. Paris-Soir,* 10 December 1929.

Aubin, Tony. Review of "Cantate du Narcisse." *Comoedia,* 5 February 1944.

"Les Ballets Suédois au Théâtre des Champs-Elysées." Review of *Le Marchand d'oiseaux. Comoedia,* 24 May 1923.

Barraud, H. "The French Lyric Stage: It Must Grow a New Skin or Rejuvenate the Old." *Musical America,* 15 April 1951, p. 9.

Bertin, Pierre. "Erik Satie et le Groupe des Six." *Les Annales Conferencia* 58, no. 4 (1951), pp. 49-60.

Boissy, Gabriel. Review of *Le Marchand d'oiseaux. Intransigeant,* 27 May 1923.

Borne, F. le. Review of *Le Marchand d'oiseaux. Petit Parisien,* 4 June 1923.

Boschot, Adolphe, Review of *Le Marchand d'oiseaux. Echo de Paris,* 28 May 1923.

Bruyr, José. "Germaine Tailleferre." *Musica Disques* (March 1957), pp. 29-33.

"Les Six." *Centre de Documentation de Musique Internationale* [*C.D.M.I.*] *Bulletin,* no. 3 (January 1952), pp. 9-15.

Chamfray, Claude. "Germaine Tailleferre." *Le Courrier Musical de France,* no. 9 (1965).

______. "Hommage à Germaine Tailleferre." *Le Courrier Musical de France,* no. 29 (1979), p. 119.

Charpentier, Raymond. "'Marchand d'oiseaux' Ballet de Mme Hélène Perdriat, Musique de Mlle Germaine Tailleferre." *Comoedia* 27 May 1923.

Collaer, Paul. "I Sei." *L'approdo musicale,* nos. 19-20, Torino (1965), pp. 11-78.

______. "La Musique française de 1917 à 1924, Le Groupe des Six." *Revue Générale,* Vol 5 (May 1974), pp. 1-27.

______. "La Musique française de 1917 à 1924, La fin des Six et de Satie." *Revue Générale,* vols. 6-7 (June-July 1974), pp. 1-25.

Daven, André L. Review of *Le Marchand d'oiseaux. Bonsoir,* 22 May 1923.

Le Figaro. Review of Violin Concerto. 8 December 1936.

"How NY Critics See New Works by Living Composers." Review of *Valse lente. Music News,* vol 41, (January 1949), p. 46.

Lonchampt, Jacques. "André Jolivet et Germaine Tailleferre à l'Opéra." Review of "Concerto de la fidélité." *Le Monde,* 9 March 1982, p. 20.

Lubin, Ernest. "The Six Return to the Limelight in Paris." *New York Times,* 13 January 1952.

Lyon, Raymond, "Visite à Germaine Tailleferre." *Le Courrier Musical de France,* no. 61 (1978), pp. 3-4.

Merry, Jean de. "Pour les féministes." Review of *Le Marchand d'oiseaux. Eclair,* 24 May 1923.

Messager, André. Review of *Le Marchand d'oiseaux. Le Figaro* 28 May 1923.

Mitgang, Laura. "One of 'Les Six' Is Still at Work." *New York Times,* 23 May 1982.

Moreux, Serge. Review of "Cantate du Narcisse." *La Gerbe,* 3 February 1944.

Moulin, Albert du. Review of *Le Marchand d'oiseaux. Bonsoir,* 27 May 1923.

Musical America. Review of *Violin Concerto.* 25 January 1938.

New York Times. 21 May 1931, pp. 1, 16. [Ralph Barton suicide]

______. Review of *Violin Concerto.* 9 January 1938.

Pannetier, Odette. "Avec Germaine Tailleferre." *Candide,* 19 November 1931.

Revue Musicale, Review of *Le Marchand d'oiseaux.* (August 1923), p. 92.

______. Review of *Sicilienne, Pastorale,* and *Six Chansons Françaises.* (February 1930), pp. 156-57.

______. Review of *Ouverture.* (February 1933), p. 133.

______. Review of *Ces Dames aux chapeaux verts.* (February 1938), pp. 158-59.

Robert, Frédéric. "Cinquante Ans Après . . . A Propos du Groupe des Six." *Journal Musical Français,* nos. 193-94 (1970), p. 29.

Roland-Manuel. "Ravel and the New French School." *Modern Music,* (January 1925), pp. 17-23.

Rorem, Ned. "Cocteau and Music." *Keynote* (February 1982), pp. 8-15.

Schonberg, Harold C. "'Les Six' Once More—Famous French Group Reunited in Album." *New York Times,* 23 January 1955.

Sordet, Dominique. Review of *Le Marchand d'oiseaux. Echo National,* 28 May 1923.

Tailleferre, Germaine. "Quelques mots de l'une des 'Six.'" *Intransigeant,* 3 June 1923.

______. "From the South of France." *Modern Music* (November/December 1942). pp. 13-16.

______. "Musique pour Claudel." *Sang Neuf,* no. 43 (January-October 1980), pp. 10-11.

Thomson, Virgil. "More and more from Paris." *Modern Music,* (May/June 1939), pp. 236-37.

Vuillermoz, Emile. Review of *Le Marchand d'oiseaux. Excelsior,* 30 May 1923.

______. "The Legend of the Six." *Modern Music* (February 1924), pp. 15-19.

Privately Owned Material in Libraries

Archives Nationales, Paris. Records of studies at Conservatoire de Paris, 1904-1916.

Bibliothèque Nationale, Paris. Dossier of press clippings and programs.

______. Dossier of letters.
New York Public Library at Lincoln Center. Dossier of press clippings and program notes.

Interviews

Auric, Georges. Personal interview, 19 January 1982.
Casa Fuerte, Yvonne de. Personal interview. 21 January 1982.
Dondeyne, Désiré. Personal interviews. 19 December 1983; 21 December 1983.
Fizdale, Robert. Personal interview. 2 February 1982.
Garsoian, Nina. Personal interview. 23 December 1981.
Hacquard, Georges. Personal interview. 15 December 1983.
Hoérée, Arthur. Personal interviews. 8 January 1982; 26 January 1982; 29 June 1983; 15 December 1983.
Lefort, Bernard. Personal interview. 23 October 1984.
Milhaud, Madeleine. Personal interviews. 7 January 1982; 20 December 1983; 24 November 1984.
Rieti, Vittorio. Personal interview. 6 January 1984.
Robert, Frédéric. Personal interviews. 11 January 1982; 27 January 1982; 29 June 1983.
de Rudder, Elvire. Personal interviews. 17 December 1983; 25 November 1984.
Sauguet, Henri. Personal interviews. 12 January 1982; 20 December 1983.
Tailleferre, Germaine. Personal interviews, 13 January 1982; 15 January 1982; 27 January 1982; 27 June 1983.

All translations from the original French are by the author unless otherwise indicated.

8

The Vocal Chamber Music of Miriam Gideon

BARBARA A. PETERSEN

Forty years ago Miriam Gideon was considered a pioneer among women composers in America. Today she continues to create new works, teach composition, and enjoy a growing number of performances and recordings of her music. She shows no inclination to retire from her active career. Concentrating on chamber music for instruments both with and without voice(s), she has written approximately 55 compositions (excluding student works prior to the 1940s). Gideon's personal musical style is essentially expressionistic with a pleasing balance of dramatic and lyrical elements. Her works are immediately engaging but not without strong elements of dissonance and chromaticism. Economy of musical materials and clarity of design also characterize her music, providing features in common with the works of other composers who are her approximate contemporaries in age and colleagues in aesthetic. Among them might be mentioned Hugo Weisgall, George Perle, Roger Sessions, and Milton Babbitt.

Composer Lester Trimble summarizes her style most astutely in a statement made over a decade ago: "This has always seemed to me one of Gideon's particular strengths as a composer: her ability to take both the refractory twelve-tone method and Expressionism in hand and make them the servant of a very personal imagery. Hers is *American* Expressionism, not Central European."[1] Without categorizing it too strictly, perhaps we might describe her style as "Expressionismus ohne Angst."

Technically speaking, Gideon's working method is neither rigorous nor dogmatic. She does not make impossibly difficult demands on her performers or audience and has not attempted to extend the techniques or resources of virtuoso instrumentalists. Her initial inspiration often comes from extramusical ideas or events, not from the desire to apply any strict process of composition. (This approach to composing may well explain the absence of any tape or synthesizer music in her catalogue of works.) Gideon's desire is to create works that communicate her musical personality to performers and audiences alike. An all-important aspect of this musical profile is her use of words, either as literary background for instrumental compositions or as poetry in vocal settings. The dual settings of a single poem in two different languages within one composition constitute a unique expression of her continuing exploration into the realm of combining language with tones.

Gideon's most significant contributions to twentieth-century music are her dozen works for chamber ensemble and voice. This essay concentrates on these works, most of which are available in published scores and recordings, in an attempt to illuminate her approach to composing.[2]

Miriam Gideon was born in Greeley, Colorado, on 23 October 1906 to a family of German-Jewish extraction. Her father, Abram Gideon, was a distinguished scholar and professor of philosophy and modern languages at Colorado State Teachers' College; her mother, Henrietta Shoninger Gideon, was an elementary school teacher. Even though her parents had no music or musical instruments in their home, they were creative and intellectual and encouraged Miriam's musical inclinations. She began to take piano lessons at age nine.

In a gradual eastward pilgrimage, the Gideon family moved to Chicago in 1915, then to New York in 1916. For three years young Miriam studied with Hans Barth, a German-born pianist and composer, at the music conservatory in Yonkers, where she gave her first solo recitals. In 1921 her parents agreed to let her move to Boston and study music with her uncle, Henry Gideon, the music director of Temple Israel, the largest reform synagogue in Boston. Community choral, solo, and chamber concerts presented by her uncle offered Miriam opportunities for performance while she attended Girls High School in Boston. Enrolling at the College of Liberal Arts of Boston University, she continued her piano studies with Felix Fox, received solid training in music theory, and developed an interest in composition that would soon relegate performance to secondary importance. These musical experiences—particularly with choral and song literature and the great tradition of synagogue music under the guidance of her uncle and his colleagues—profoundly influenced her future. Her early exposure to the combination of words and music had a powerful and lasting influence on her work as a composer.

After graduation from Boston University, Gideon left Boston for New York, where she has resided ever since. (Her sister, Judith, also lives nearby in New York.) Miriam continued to study. She also worked briefly in the late 1920s with Marion Bauer, Charles Haubiel, and the French composer Jacques Pillois at New York University, and from 1931 to 1934 with Lazare Saminsky, the Russian-American composer, conductor, and author who held the prestigious post of music director at Temple Emanu-El in New York. Saminsky encouraged her to work further with Roger Sessions, who had recently returned from several years in Europe. This was a recommendation that she pursued with eagerness and concentration from 1935 to 1943.[3]

Always a scholar with a mind for the historical and literary, Gideon entered graduate school at Columbia University in 1942 to study musicology with such noted scholars as Paul Henry Lang and Erich Hertzmann. In 1944 she was appointed to the faculty of Brooklyn College and began a decade-long association with that school. While at Brooklyn she taught harmony, composition, and music history. And she also met Frederic Ewen, a member of the English department, whom she married on 16 December 1949.[4] Her next academic appointment came in 1947 at City College, where she taught harmony, counterpoint, composition, and period courses in music history until 1955. In 1971 she returned to the City College faculty and achieved the rank of full professor before becoming professor emeritus in 1976.

Being named to the teaching staff of the Cantors Institute of the Jewish Theological Seminary of America in 1955 encouraged Gideon's involvement with synagogue music, which would more than once result in commissioned compositions for Jewish services. In 1970 the Jewish Theological Seminary granted Gideon the degree of Doctor of Sacred Music in Composition. At present she is an associate professor in the Cantors Institute of the Seminary, a faculty member at the Manhattan School of Music, and a private teacher of composition. Being a teacher as well as a composer has always given her great satisfaction. Unlike those composers who find teaching a financial necessity but a hindrance to their creativity, Gideon has welcomed the responsibilities and involvements of her teaching positions. She finds that they grow from and are nourished by her being a composer in the first place, and she encourages her students to create music by the same principle she applies to her own work, that of writing what one really feels, regardless of current fads.

With over 55 compositions to her credit and new ones always in progress, Gideon is especially fortunate in having a large number of works published and recorded. Live performances of her compositions have been heard not only in the United States but also in Europe, the Far East, and South America. Symphony orchestras in Prague, London, Zurich, and Tokyo have played her works—along with many chamber ensembles, choruses, and soloists throughout the world, including such noted singers as Jan de Gaetani, Phyllis Bryn-Julson, Judith Raskin, Evelyn Mandac, Elaine Bonazzi, Paul Sperry, and Constantine Cassolas. Greatly to her credit is the fact that these same soloists and ensembles are eager to go beyond premiere performances to give second and third hearings, to record her works, and to request new compositions from her.

Miriam Gideon is a woman of strong convictions with a refreshingly frank way of expressing them. She shies away from overly analytical or thoughtlessly superficial labels—in both human and musical spheres—and does not hesitate to speak her opinions. Gideon prefers to be known as a

Figure 8.1 Miriam Gideon. Photograph by Judith Leigner.

composer, not as a *Jewish composer* (although she has set Hebrew texts and written two Sacred Services) or as a *woman composer* (although her works have sometimes been performed by all-women groups or discussed, published, or recorded with compositions exclusively by women).[5]

Gideon feels that earlier in this century composers who happened to be women did not worry needlessly over the issue of male or female composers. She cites, for instance, the number of women who were residents with her at the MacDowell Colony in 1936, among them Marion Bauer, Amy Beach, Mabel Daniels, and Mary Howe. As early as 1946, the year of the completion and premiere of her *Quartet for Strings*, Gideon was considered one of the most accomplished of women composers, and nearly 25 years later much was made of her being the first woman ever commissioned to write two full synagogue services. In 1975 she was the second woman composer elected to membership in the American Academy and Institute of Arts and Letters. (The previous year her good friend and colleague Louise Talma had been the first; since then Vivian Fine and Betsy Jolas have also joined these distinguished ranks.)

Since the rise of feminism in the 1960s, Gideon has, of course, developed her own opinions and attitudes about male versus female composers. She recognizes that discrimination against composers who happen to be female has long existed, but she feels that there is less of it now than in previous decades. With firm conviction Gideon has stated: "I strongly believe a woman composer can have something special to say, in that there is a very particular woman's way of responding to the world—and this in some basic way is quite different from and yet no less important than a man's."[6]

While Gideon feels that creative women have something special to say, she does not believe in having to direct it toward a separate audience: "I consider it a tactical mistake to isolate women in concerts, broadcasts and publications. While to do so may attract attention in the way a mixed concert might not, at the same time it makes it difficult to judge the music on its own merits."[7]

In line with this thinking, Gideon has not joined any groups of women composers, although she is personally supportive of other women composers and applauds their successes. As a self-aware and reflective creative artist, Gideon prefers to be—and feels that she almost always has been—treated impartially and judged on her own merits, not within categories, be they of gender, school of composition, or religious heritage. Concerning the last of these, she recognizes that the epithet "Jewish composer" might be important to a "certain type of composer as a form of symbolic reference," although she herself would not need such a point of reference. To Gideon, singling out a creative artist as Jewish or as a woman "implies in my mind, at least, some limitation" in the consideration of the artist's works.[8] Certainly, then, she was glad to see this implicit limitation acknowledged and set aside in remarks such as this: "It would be easy to begin a review of Miriam Gideon's music by saying that she is one of the United States' finest women composers. It would be more accurate to say simply that she is one of our most gifted and accomplished composers, period."[9]

Gideon is definitely now considered one of the distinguished "elders [with George Perle] of the contemporary music scene who have arrived at positions of respect through years of steady work as composers and teachers."[10]

The late Margaret Jory, former executive director of the American Music Center, noted also that Gideon is "held in high esteem by the East Coast musical establishment, a fiercely competitive and discerning bunch."[11]

Gideon can frequently be seen at concerts of contemporary music in New York. She enjoys getting acquainted with "the competition" and is not concerned that hearing too much music by other composers will affect her own style. That style has not changed radically since her first representative compositions, which she wrote while studying with Roger Sessions, her most influential teacher. Milton Babbitt (another former Sessions student) has said of Gideon, "I've known Miriam for 35 years and hers is a very distinguished music. It's always struck me that she has developed her own musical line, a well-defined line, so consistently over the years."[12]

Although the first public performance of a Gideon composition took place as early as 1933, today she prefers to begin her list of works with the *Lyric Piece for String Quartet* (1941). (Readers will note the inclusion in the List of Works of one even earlier piece, *Hommage à ma Jeunesse*, a suite for two pianos dating from 1935. Since this work has been published, it cannot really be withdrawn.) Already in *The Hound of Heaven* (1945) the most important features of her style are set. According to George Perle, this music is "strikingly personal, characterized by lightness, the sudden exposure of individual notes . . . a technique that imposes economy and the exclusion of irrelevancies—a technique that may be indefinitely expanded and within which a composer may grow."[13] This last factor is a key to the success of her method. As a student, she was clearly influenced by expressionism and by the 12-tone method, but whatever she learned from the styles and techniques of her predecessors and mentors she has made her very own.

Gideon's refusal to have labels—other than a vague one such as "free atonality"—applied to her music has given her enough space to explore freely within her musical language. Repeatedly, critics have applied adjectives such as lean, laconic, terse, economical, and concentrated to her instrumental and vocal scores. Other writers have praised her works as highly charged and strongly communicative. Reviewing the recording of her *Symphonia Brevis* (1953), Arthur Cohn remarked, "Her music has a succinct way about it that makes one anxious to hear more of her output."[14] Indeed, Gideon rarely indulges in literal repetitions, never in too obvious or aimless transitional material; her works never seem longer than they should be. In actual fact, her chamber pieces rarely exceed twenty minutes' duration, the average being ten to twelve.

The obvious economy in Gideon's musical style is reflected on a larger scale in her total output, which is not extensive in comparison with the catalogues of some composers of today or in the past. She explores in her compositions the fusion of abstract ideas with subjective emotional experience; she is more concerned with "illuminating her inner feelings in a way particular to herself" than with following the dictates of any rigid compositional system.[15] Gideon puts much of herself into each of her new works and has created music of a wide emotional range. In the words of her own personal credo, "What I write has to *mean* something to me." Her new works evolve from both musical impulses and human responses to her environment or personal experiences, not from mechanical application of arbitrary rules or precompositional devices. Her stimulus and goal are the bringing to life of what she has so carefully crafted on the page, the fulfillment of the score in performance.

In 1985, in her cozy and crowded 17th-floor studio overlooking New York's Central Park, Gideon completed her 14th composition in the genre that is here referred to as vocal chamber music. Before this essay is printed, she will have completed and had premiered yet another, a setting of poems in Italian and English commissioned by Musicians Accord.[16]

Each of these works for solo voice(s) and three to eight players uses a different combination of instruments. The ensembles range from the homogeneous string trio of *Three Sonnets from "Fatal Interview"* to the mixed string/wind/percussion timbres of *Rhymes from the Hill* or *Nocturnes*. Often the choice of instruments is suggested by the poetry itself: for instance, the percussive marimba, ticking away with clocklike regularity in "Die Korfsche Uhr" (no. 3 of *Rhymes from the Hill*) or the jubilant trumpet in "Hallelujah," the third song of *The Resounding Lyre*.

Only once has Gideon felt that her initial choice of vocal and instrumental media should be improved upon. Her *Spiritual Madrigals* (1965) for TTB chorus, viola, violoncello, and bassoon was reworked in 1979 for tenor solo with seven instruments (trios of strings and woodwinds with trumpet added in the final song). The change from choral to solo voice as the vehicle for the text caused her to retitle the work *Spiritual Airs*. Upon further consideration, she altered this to *The Resounding Lyre* "as a metaphor for the human heart," which figures in each of the cycle's poems. Although reviews of the original composition praised the distinctive sound world created by the dark-hued low register instruments in combination with male voices, in the new version Gideon has created an even more impressive setting by using varied timbres. She also added two to three minutes of new music, in the form of instrumental introductions to each song and a few cadential bars between some of the verses.

Although none of her other chamber works has been recomposed this extensively, Gideon is always open to suggestions from performers and to reevaluation by her own ears and those of trusted colleagues; she often makes minor adjustments, especially in rehearsal or after a first performance. The goal of her composing is, of course, the performance, and only after this has been achieved can certain details of the manuscript be finalized. Typical changes in one of her new scores are for the sake of sonority: adjustment of a dynamic marking, transfer of individual notes or whole phrases from one octave or even instrument to another, new bowing or muting instructions. Less frequently is there an actual alteration of pitches. The composer is thinking always of how to perfect the statement at hand. She studies tapes between performances of her works and may alter earlier decisions based on what she hears.

In line with this approach to her music, Gideon prefers that listeners have multiple opportunities to hear her works; she would no doubt agree with Andrew Porter that the most useful evaluation one can make after a single hearing is simply whether one would care to hear the work again or not. With Gideon's music we are fortunate to have the opportunity for frequent rehearings through recordings. About the many recordings of her music, the composer notes:

> I am especially gratified by the response made by people who have listened to my recordings, since they have had the opportunity of hearing my music more than the one time a live performance provides. One performance, even though it may generate a warm reaction in the listener, does not really provide a key to what the composer is saying. Only repeated hearings can do that. I am fortunate in having had excellent performers for my recordings—the finest soloists and chamber players a composer could wish for.[17]

Music with text has always been significant in Gideon's oeuvre, but it has become especially so in the last decade. It is not surprising to hear her declare "I am moved by poetry and great prose almost as much as by music," or to admit, "It takes me a long time to find the right texts."[18] The importance of words to Gideon's musical inspiration is not limited to her vocal chamber works. In studying or listening to her other compositions, we are soon alerted to the repeated connections between words and music. Among the solo piano pieces are two particularly good examples with their origins in the world of words, *Of Shadows Numberless* (1966) and the *Sonata for Piano* (1977). *Of Shadows Numberless* is a mood piece suggested by Keats's "Ode to a Nightingale." Peter G. Davis has called this six-part suite "an effective, expressively generous piece of musical poetry in its own right."[19] The *Sonata for Piano* has an even more intricate conjunction of words and music. The descriptive titles of its three movements are phrases drawn from Swinburne's choruses in his play *Atalanta of Calydon* (1865):

1. "Veiled Destinies"
2. "Night, the Shadow of Light"
3. "Rapid and Footless Herds."

Equally significant, the musical germ of the outer movements is a single harmonic cell from a Mörike song by Hugo Wolf; in the middle movement another cell is similarly borrowed from a Schumann lied on Friedrich Rückert's verses.

Gideon's choice of texts for her vocal works ranges from ancient Greek and Japanese poems to the second half of the twentieth century, and from America to Europe and the Orient. English, German, Latin, Italian, Japanese, and French are used in her works for voice and chamber ensemble, four of these in *The Condemned Playground* alone. Her libretto for *The Adorable Mouse* is from a French fable of La Fontaine; that for her opera, *Fortunato*, comes from a Spanish play by Serafín and Joaquín Quintero. Her two synagogue services and the prayer *Adon Olom* employ traditional Hebrew texts.

To appreciate Gideon's music, one must recognize not only the diverse historical periods and cultures on which she draws but also that she uses texts in various languages. The ages from which her poetic choices come have expanded with her two recent cycles, *Voices from Elysium* (translations of Greek poetry from as early as the sixth century B.C.) and *Spirit above the Dust* (in which two of the poems by Norman Rosten were copyrighted in 1979). Not only her texts but also other aspects of her compositions reveal a worldwide and centuries' deep interest in different cultures and how elements from them may be incorporated into a modern musical idiom. Among Gideon's instrumental works with "ethnic" sources are the *Fantasy on a Javanese Motive* (1948), which uses the structure of a gamelan melody and, in its delicate scoring for violoncello and piano, evokes the sonorities of a gamelan orchestra, and the *Fantasy on Irish Folk Motives* (1975). *Fortunato*, incorporating tunes native to its Madrid setting, also draws on folk songs. The Friday Evening Service *Shirat Miriam L'Shabbat* uses cantillation motives; other such motives from the Book of Esther appear in an earlier instrumental work, *Three Biblical Masks*, where Gideon paints in music portraits of the main characters in the Purim story.[20]

A particularly interesting example of Gideon's crossing of cultural boundaries is *The Hound of Heaven* (1945). This composition was commissioned by Lazare Saminsky to celebrate the centenary of the founding of Congregation Emanu-El in New York and was first performed there on 23 March 1945. One may at first be surprised to find Gideon using such an overtly Roman Catholic poem for the occasion. Perhaps the most famous poem by Francis Thompson (1859-1907), "The Hound of Heaven" is fashioned after the style of seventeenth-century devotional poetry written by Richard Crashaw and other metaphysical poets. An English poet and essayist, Thompson was himself a devout Catholic. This poem records his experiences and thoughts after he was rejected both for the priesthood and for the practice of medicine. The composer has explained her choice by pointing out that the verses she selected from this lengthy poem evoke the purification through suffering underlying the Jewish experience. Indeed, such poignant lines as "Yea faileth now the dream the dreamer, and the lute the lutanist" or "Designer Infinite! Must Thou char the wood ere Thou canst limn with it?" reflect the suffering in the life experience of all humankind.

Concerning the diversity of languages used in her works, Gideon frankly admits to not knowing all of the languages she sets (for example, Japanese), but she does become intimately familiar with the sound and meaning of all words in any poem she intends to use. In some cycles and individual songs she combines English with another language and experiments with different approaches to the fusion of words and music:

a) entire poem set first in English then in the other language (*The Condemned Playground,* nos. 1 and 2, or *Songs of Youth and Madness,* nos. 2-4);

b) sections alternating between the two languages (*Songs of Youth and Madness,* no. 1);

c) most of the text in one language with refrains in the other (*The Condemned Playground,* no. 3).

Her earliest song to use two languages is the 1957 *Mixco*, a setting in both Spanish and English of a poem by Miguel Angel Asturias, the Guatemalan poet. The procedure she followed here was to set each stanza first in English translation then in the original Spanish, with a different musical framework for each.

One of the most fascinating aspects of these bilingual settings is the contrast between the music written for one language and that for the other. Gideon knows that she has come under attack for—as her detractors might claim—prolonging a work this way, but her method is no mere repetition for the two settings. On this issue, the composer has said:

> One aspect of my music that has aroused interest and at times controversy is my dual setting within the same work of poems in the original language and in English translation. I can explain my attraction for this way of composing by my fascination with language as such, and by the challenge of finding an appropriate musical garb for the same poetic idea in a different language, at the same time resolving this diversity into an integrated whole.[21]

Perhaps Gideon's most important bilingual—actually multilingual—work is *The Condemned Playground* (1963). The title is also the title of a series of essays by the late British critic Cyril Connolly. Connolly's reference was to Art—"Man's noblest attempt to preserve Imagination from Time." In spite of the permanence and authority granted to masterpieces of art, he argued that all art is doomed to decay. Gideon has applied this notion of the "impingement of the sinister upon the pleasurable" to Love, Life, and Knowledge in her three settings.[22]

The first song, "Pyrrha," is a setting of Horace's Book I, Ode 5. The tenor begins with John Milton's English translation; then to new music the soprano sings the original Latin, with the tenor joining in (also now in Latin) midway through. The second song continues the vocal duet with the modern English poem "Hiroshima" by Gary Spokes. After the entire poem is sung, the soprano continues alone with its Japanese rendering by Satoko Akiya. For the third song, "Litanies of Satan," Gideon uses a different textual procedure in setting a poem from Baudelaire's *Les Fleurs du Mal* (1857) and its English translation by Edna St. Vincent Millay. Only the original French refrain, "O Satan, prends pitié de ma longue misère!" survives. Gideon divides the poem into five stanzas and an *envoi*, with the refrain following four of the stanzas but not the *envoi*. At first the refrain is sung in English, then French, but after subsequent stanzas in French only. Soprano and tenor alternate in the five stanzas, joining together for the final doxologylike verse ("Praise to thee, Satan, in the most high,/where thou did'st reign;/and in deep hell's obscurity . . ."). The composer has condensed the litany form of the original (15 couplets, each with refrain, and the concluding 6-line *envoi*)—probably to good advantage lest the musical setting become overlong.

Gideon's success in setting two versions of the same poem, finding "an appropriate musical garb" for each, is especially obvious in "Pyrrha." The English version is rhythmically and metrically complex for both voice and instruments—not unlike much of her music in the 1960s. The slower and smoother pace of the Latin poem at once suggests an ancient music, perhaps Gregorian chant.

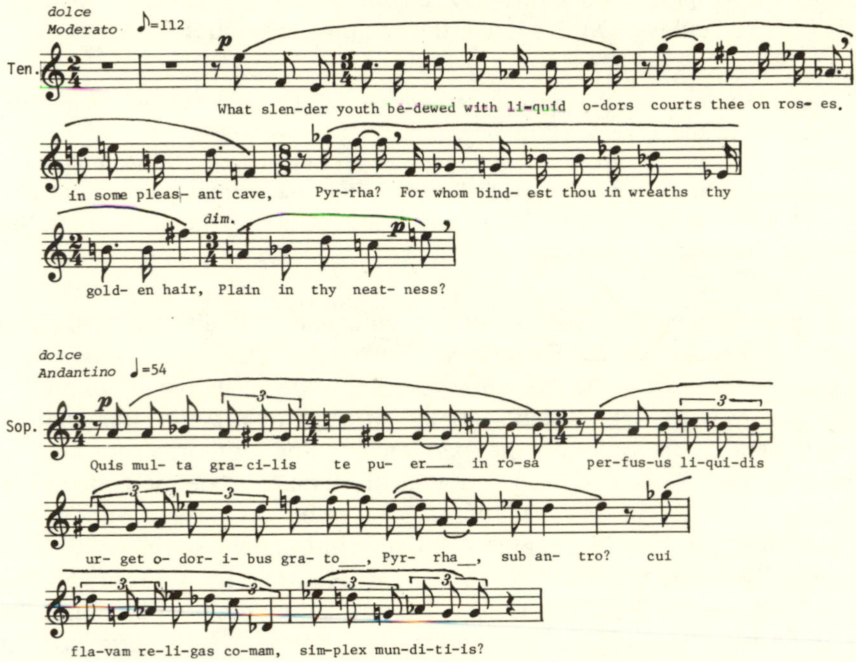

Figure 8.2 *The Condemned Playground:* No. 1, *Pyrrha* (tenor, mm. 1-9; soprano, mm. 31-38). © 1980 by Mobart Music Publications, Inc. Used by permission.

To a scholar (and former language major) such as Gideon, Latin probably has unavoidable musical connotations. Hints of medieval compositional techniques in this movement include the use of canon and organumlike motion of the voices. Though the lines are not always parallel, between them they sound many perfect fourths and fifths.

The music of "Hiroshima" is equally evocative of its text, particularly in the interlude between the English and Japanese poems, where flutes in the high register and violoncellos playing harmonics prepare an otherworldly atmosphere for the Japanese. The English version begins with seven bars of long-lined alternating entries for the two voices, then continues in more static homophonic style. The Japanese version contrasts greatly with the two parts of the English; it begins as unaccompanied recitative in short phrases to which trilling flute and tremolo strings are gradually added. In both versions the text is sung primarily in eighth notes, but the two versions are nonetheless totally different.

In "Litanies of Satan," Gideon sensitively varies the pacing on a small scale in the increasingly dramatic refrains and on a larger one as well. The rapid "mad gait" of hope ending the soprano stanza, for example, contrasts strongly with the ending of the slower tenor stanza that follows:

Figure 8.3 *The Condemned Playground:* No. 3, *Litanies of Satan* (mm. 43-47 and 56-62). © 1980 by Mobart Music Publications, Inc. Used by permission.

The concluding duet or *envoi* has hints of parallel organum, recalling "Pyrrha" and underscoring the mock liturgical text of the litany.

More than a decade after writing *The Condemned Playground,* Gideon created another remarkable bilingual composition, *Songs of Youth and Madness* (1977) for high voice and chamber orchestra. Perhaps her most important orchestral composition, the *Songs of Youth and Madness* are settings of four German poems by Friedrich Hölderlin (1770-1843), with English translations by Michael Hamburger. The youth of the title refers to the first three poems (*An die Parzen*, *An Diotima*, and *Der gute Glaube*), which are passionate, sorrowful writings from the early period of Hölderlin's overwhelming love affair with Susette Gontard (i.e., Diotima). For the song of madness, Gideon set *Der Spaziergang*, a poem Hölderlin wrote after Madame Gontard's death, when he suffered from insanity, depersonalization, and bitter pain. The English and German versions of the first poem are divided into two parts: the first four-line stanza is sung in English, then German, and the remaining eight-line unit of the poem is treated the same way. Each of the other poems is sung in its entirety first in English then in German. Each musical rendering of these poems is distinct, with its own emotional depth, color, and impact. On the surface, twice as much music is offered as in a single-language setting; the total effect, however, is much more than that. The listener experiences not only the contrasting settings, but also the convincing unification of their diverse elements.

After the premiere of *Songs of Youth and Madness,* one reviewer summarized the contrast of the English and German settings by describing the English as mainly dramatic and declamatory, the German as soft and reflective. Others have felt that the music is intensified in the German sections. These examples of the vocal line represent only a few of the many instances of contrasting styles:

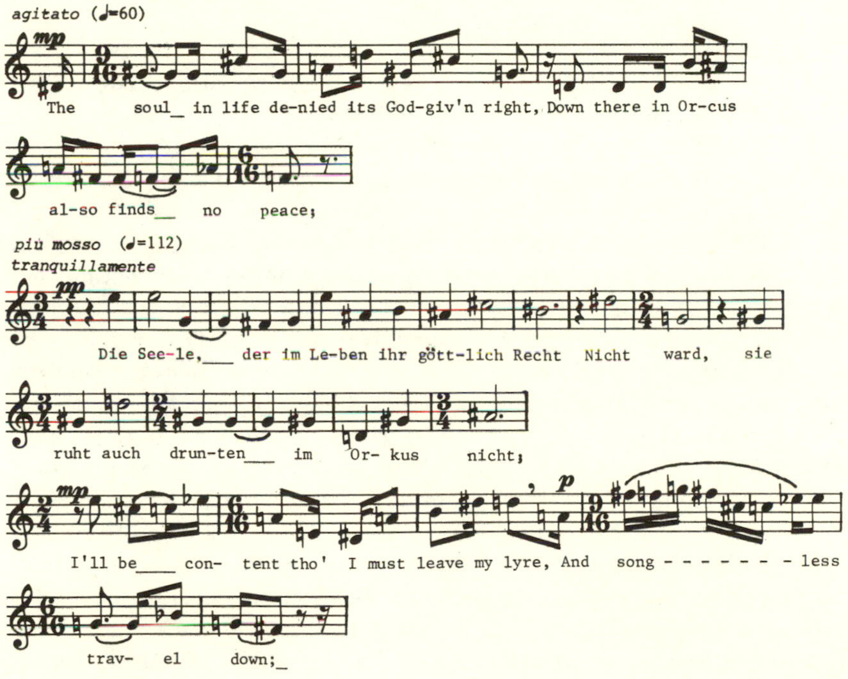

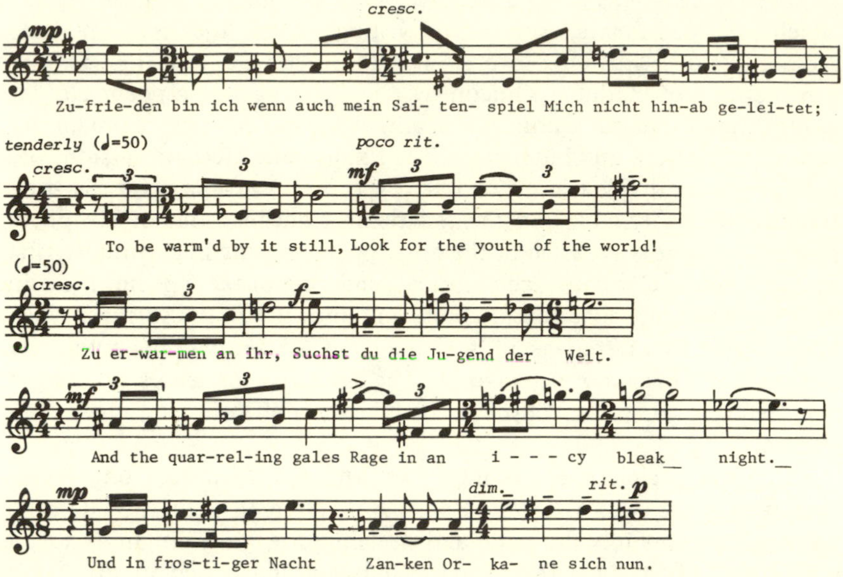

Figure 8.4 *Songs of Youth and Madness*: Nos. 1 and 2 (a) *An die Parzen* (voice, mm. 45-49 and 60-65 in English; mm. 71-84 and 99-103 in German) (b) *An Diotima* (voice, mm. 13-16 and 22-29 in English; mm. 50-54 and 59-62 in German). © 1980 by Mobart Music Publications, Inc. Used by permission.

The instrumental writing, of course, is an equally important reinforcement of the different moods.

Besides using a poem in two different languages, Gideon recurrently reveals a preference for assembling the poetry for multi-movement pieces from disparate sources. There is always a unifying theme that makes her combination of poems convincing. In *Spirit above the Dust* she set poems by three sharply contrasting Americans, including a seventeenth-century woman (Anne Bradstreet), a former Librarian of Congress (Archibald MacLeish), and a contemporary writer (Norman Rosten). The selection of all Americans—and of MacLeish in particular—is appropriate since this work was commissioned by the Elizabeth Sprague Coolidge Foundation in the Library of Congress to celebrate the fiftieth anniversary of the founding of the Music Library Association. Gideon has here set seven poems that express a wide range of human expression, from anguish to quietude.

The Resounding Lyre and *Voices from Elysium* also each have poems from a single culture (German and Greek, respectively) but different centuries. The three German poems of *The Resounding Lyre* range from contemporary (Frederic Ewen's "Mutterbildnis"), back through the nineteenth century (Heinrich Heine's "Hallelujah"), to the thirteenth-century Jewish minnesinger Süezkint von Trimperg's lament "Wähebûf und Nichtenvint.'' The oldest poem, in Middle High German, tells of the minnesinger's poverty and persecution, of how he will no longer sing for those unworthies at court who disdain his talent and his person. ''Mutterbildnis'' is the portrait of a mother as a symbol of compassion for all humanity. ''Hallelujah'' is an exuberant poetic outburst, which Gideon translates into music by adding a trumpet to the previous trios of strings and winds. This poetic celebration of glory and wonder at ''the masterpiece of creation—the human heart'' demands the regal musical interpretation she has given it. Examining these poems closely, it is easy to see why she expanded the earlier instrumental trio of *Spiritual Madrigals* into a septet.

The Resounding Lyre is unified textually because the subject of all three poems is the heart of mankind, for which the ''resounding lyre'' is a metaphor. In contrast, the seven texts of *Voices from Elysium* vary in subject matter, ranging from a down-to-earth prayer to a luxurious evocation of nature, a sombre epitaph, and an ancient tale of children welcoming the spring. The sources are Greek poetry between the sixth century B.C. and the seventh A.D., translated into English by three different scholars of the nineteenth and twentieth centuries. Gideon has summarized this composition as ''an evocation of Greek antiquity as it reflects tenderly and at times whimsically upon life and death.''

Ultimately, all of the texts Gideon sets in her vocal chamber works are about the experiences of human life. The interaction of life and nature is the theme of such works as *Nocturnes,* which was commissioned for the eighteenth birthday of Rena Siegel by her parents. The three poems describe nature at night, with moonlight figuring in all of them. Gideon chose these poems believing that they are ''an appropriate evocation of youth and its awakening to the magical forces of nature.'' In *Questions on Nature* the first six songs dwell on physical aspects of the earth, sun, planets, winds, stars, animals, the phenomena of echoes and light. But the final text concerns man himself—his emotions, spiritual existence, and death. Naturally, the musical setting that concludes this cycle is the most dramatic and emotional because of its intense subject matter.

Whether their texts are bilingual, in one language by a single poet, or in one language by many poets spanning the centuries, Gideon's works always reveal her fascination with both the sense and sound of language. The lyric intensity and aural sensitivity of her music are made possible by a successful synthesis of words and tones.

This synthesis is built upon the interactions of poetry in different languages with the colorations of diverse chamber ensembles. Her large-scale palette of instrumental colors is a more identifiable characteristic of her music than is small-scale painting of individual words (although the latter too can be found and is certainly worthy of mention).

For *Questions on Nature,* Gideon carefully chose the instrumental ensemble of oboe, piano, glockenspiel, and tam-tam to accompany the voice: ''The instrumental sonorities as well as the character of the vocal line are intended to convey the mystery and the childlike directness of the topics contemplated."[23]

The texts of the seven miniature songs are cast as questions—every line begins with "how," "if," "why," "whether," "what," or "whence". The instruments end most of the movements questioningly, with inconclusive sounding phrases and intervals. In these songs Gideon indulges in rather more individual word painting than usual, perhaps taking her cue for this from the naïveté of the questions, which come from a textbook the twelfth-century Adelard of Bath wrote for an inquisitive nephew. In the sixth song the phrase "Why we hear echoes" invites her to repeat the text (a rarity in her vocal works) and indulge in repetitive instrumental word painting. In the seventh song a jubilant outburst and repetition on the word "joy" is striking. The entire third song, with questions of wind, air, and motion, is mostly a duet for voice and oboe, with the oboe constantly moving in trills and other rapid figurations.

A critical assessment of the premiere of *Questions on Nature* indicates the success of her musical treatment: "Miriam Gideon's vocal line was refreshingly idiomatic, and with the surrounding evocative instrumentation carried the intimations of wonder in the text."[24]

Like *Questions on Nature, Rhymes from the Hill* (1968) is based on a single work by one writer, the *Galgenlieder* (*Gallows Songs*, 1905) of Christian Morgenstern. The poems selected by Gideon have rhyme, repetition, alliteration, and assonance; their moods include the humorous, satirical, burlesque—even nonsensical and gruesome. Colorful in subject matter as well as in diction, they invite coloristic and descriptive musical settings. For these five musical portraits Gideon effectively combined a mixed ensemble of medium voice, clarinet, violoncello, and marimba. "Zwei Uhren," the third and fourth songs, are delightful portrayals in music of clock mechanisms. The first, created by Herr Korf (an inventor who appears in many of Morgenstern's humorous poems), has hands that mirror one another. As one goes forward, the other moves backward, thus nullifying time. For the clock's action, Gideon uses the marimba in metronomic, staccato eighth notes. The ironic twist in the text is echoed musically by almost constant half-step dissonances or clusters of three adjacent half steps. The next poem is about Palmström, another of Morgenstern's recurring inventors (in another poem he invents an olfactory organ on which to play sonatas!). Here Palmström has created a clock quite in contrast to Korf's. It runs not mechanically or by the rules, but from the heart—impulsively, sympathetically, reacting with a "mimosa-like delicacy." The contrast with "Die Korfsche Uhr" is reflected musically, for here there is no metronomic regularity. The rhapsodic mood set up in the introduction continues with many suspensions, syncopations, and other patterns that give rhythmic variety. Echoing the final line, "Doch zugleich ein Werk mit Herz," Gideon has this song cadence with one of her rare quotations—a hint at the "Tristan" progression.

Each of the other songs in *Rhymes from the Hill* has a single dominant mood, which she illustrates in both instruments and voice. Textually the first song, "Bundeslied der Galgenbrüder," sets a gruesome, haunted scene with spiders, toads, and screech owls. Morgenstern's rhymes and repetitions ("Unke unkt," "Spinne spinnt," and "Greule" used six times and rhyming with "Eule" and "Silbergäule") give a haunted character to the text that Gideon transfers well into the music. In the last two lines the hard consonants and twisting vocal line add to the imagery.

Figure 8.5 *Rhymes from the Hill*: No. 1, *Bundeslied der Galgenbrüder* (voice, mm. 31-37). © 1978 by Mobart Music Publications, Inc. Used by permission.

The contrasting "Galgenkindes Wiegenlied" is slower, muted and legato—if not without some bizarre and gruesome hints of text and tone. The ironic and fanciful fifth song, "Der Seufzer," paints yet another scene of fantasy with a touch of irony. Gideon begins and ends this song with intentional fragmentation of the vocal line (frequent rests and staccato eighth notes). "Ein Seufzer" (a sigh), which has gone ice skating at night, turns human as it dreams of a maiden in a lyrical phrase marked *con amore*; all aglow (melisma on "glühend"), it remains in one spot that melts the ice:

Figure 8.6 *Rhymes from the Hill*: No. 5, *Der Seufzer* (voice, mm. 1-9 and 19-24). © 1978 by Mobart Music Publications, Inc. Used by permission.

The texts of *The Seasons of Time*—ten Tanka poems of ancient Japan—are quite a contrast to the simplicity and humor of *Questions on Nature* or *Rhymes from the Hill.* Considered "the classical Japanese form" from the seventh century, Tanka poems are in five lines of 5-7-5-7-7 syllables and usually concern nature, love, laments, or special occasions.[25] Their diction is traditional and elevated. Gideon has chosen poems (which in translation do not adhere strictly to the original structure) moving from spring through summer to autumn, commenting on the passage of time in human life as well as the changing seasons in nature. In this poetry it would not be suitable to introduce overt orientalisms or too-obvious quotations of birdsong at the mention of warblers, cuckoos, and nightingales. Rather, by subtle instrumentation Gideon has created an appropriate sound world: "The delicacy of the texts, from ancient Japanese poetry, is mirrored in the sounds of flute, pianoforte, cello—each used with a shimmer like that of silk screening."[26]

Throughout this cycle Gideon varies the instrumental textures and density with considerable imagination. The second song is a duet for voice and flute; five others are trios, and the remaining four use all three instruments and voice. The fifth song, the longest and most fully scored in the cycle, is a rich outpouring of passionate music. Here and in the ninth song instrumental interludes develop dramatic tension and propel the listener forward to the next line, but also give a respite from the text so that words are not lost by too many of them coming too rapidly.

The desire to ensure that the text is absorbed and not spun out in too rapid delivery is probably one of the reasons that Gideon uses both instrumental passages within vocal movements and also separate instrumental movements in her vocal chamber works. In the early *Hound of Heaven* she wrote a striking interlude (bars 77-86) that builds to a dramatic climax with fortissimo octave doublings before a varied return of the opening instrumental material. When she reworked *Spiritual Madrigals* into *The Resounding Lyre*, one of her most effective additions was the eight-bar instrumental interlude dividing the two halves of "Hallelujah." Gideon first used separate instrumental movements in *Sonnets from Shakespeare,* where three *ritornelle* (of different length and consisting of different music) are strategically placed after the second, third, and fifth songs. The final (and longest) *ritornelle* is well placed and well timed after the dramatic intensity of the final couplet of "No! Time, thou shalt not boast that I do change!"

Two separate instrumental movements appear in *Nocturnes,* an opening *Prelude* and an *Interlude* before the final song. After its world premiere, *Nocturnes* was claimed to be

> a lovely, sensitive chamber piece. The vocal part moves mostly in smoothly lyrical lines and is admirably attuned to both inflections and sense of texts. The instrumental setting is firmly and delicately woven through the vocal lines, and its colors beautifully evoke the atmosphere and imagery of the poetry.[27]

Indeed, the interweaving of instrumental and vocal lines in Gideon's vocal chamber works deserves further comment, along with the style of her vocal writing in general. For the most part she sets her texts syllabically, in short note values, and without repeating words. The exceptions to this rule are always for dramatic purpose or descriptive musical interpretation of particular words. Often Gideon's vocal phrases are of narrow range, with close-knit intervals (second, thirds) or repeated notes. A favorite phrase-ender is the half step, either ascending or descending as appropriate to the text. Her breaking up of vocal lines with rests may at first suggest recitative, but further analysis reveals carefully shaped directional phrases, with larger intervals (especially sevenths and ninths) used sparingly and for expressive effect. Some critics have—and I think wrongly—emphasized the fragmentation of her vocal lines rather than their continuity. Hans Nathan, for example, points out the angularity, recitative-like, and chromatic aspects of works from *The Hound of Heaven* through *To Music.*[28] (A short rest, of course, need not be the end of a phrase, either in Gideon's music or that of any composer in any century!).

A brief example from *The Hound of Heaven* illustrates Gideon's typically sinuous line, with gradually expanding intervals, fluctuating meters, and obviously directional phrase endings (rising from "fled"/"stars" to "bars," "chatter," and "moon").

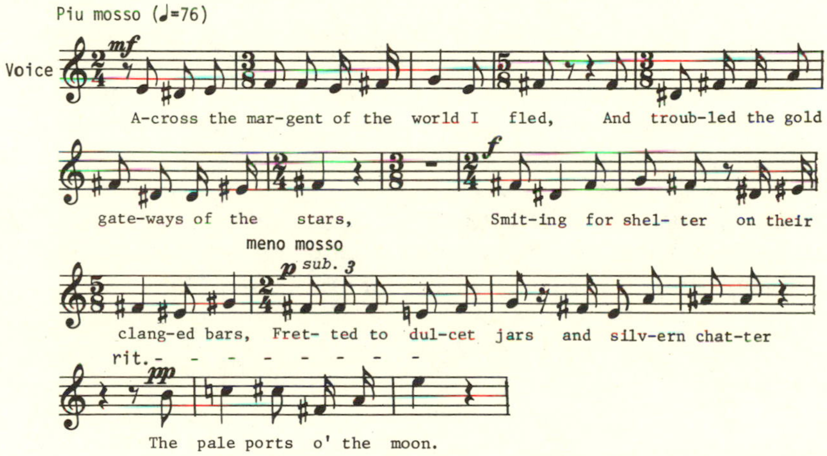

Figure 8.7 *The Hound of Heaven* (voice, mm. 14-30). © 1975 by Columbia University Music Press. Used by permission.

In a section such as this we must look also at the text—the urgency of the first three phrases and then the contrasting calm of the next two. Thompson's very choice of words ("clanged bars" then the contrasting image of "The pale ports o' the moon") is reinforced here by the instruments, with driving, accented tremolos through "bars" followed immediately by slower moving legato phrases.

In crafting her vocal lines, Gideon considers carefully the rhythms of individual words in the text as well as the flow of entire lines and the contrast of poems within a group. In *Nocturnes,* for example, "To the Moon" is a peaceful, shimmering, and impressionistic song; "Witchery" evokes the magical and mysterious aspects of the night. Compared to these two surrounding songs, the first half of "High Tide" has a more dramatic and forward-driving declamation entirely appropriate to the text ("I edged back against the night/The sea growled assault on the wave-bitten shore"). The second half of the song is much more serene and ends with a delicate and lucid setting of the lines "as, calm and unsmiling, she [the moon] walked the deep fields of the sky." Gideon later extracted the final dissonant five-note chord on "sky" and used it as the harmonic basis of "The Snow Ball," the final song in *Spirit above the Dust.* By repeating this chord again and again in various transpositions, she enhances the poetic image of quiet solitude.

The contrasts explored on a small scale in the preceding example of *The Hound of Heaven* are evident in a larger dimension in *Spirit above the Dust.* Of the many musical high points that we might single out in these seven poems, one of the most striking is the contrast in sound of both words and music between the fourth (MacLeish's "The Linden Branch") and the sixth (Rosten's "Caliban"). Not only is the sense of "The Linden Branch" musical, but the sound is lyrical, legato, and full of the softer consonants (e.g., abundant liquid *l*s). The dreamy nature world of the German romantics is not far from MacLeish's mind, and Gideon echoes this in a richly melodic and lush setting for string quartet and voice. "Caliban," on the other hand, uses all eight instruments of the ensemble to support the wild and vivid images in the poetry. The poem is full of percussive consonants, particularly the hard *c* of Caliban and other *k* sounds. The vocal line here is appropriately accented and dramatic, even sometimes wild and reckless. Here are examples of the contrast between these songs:

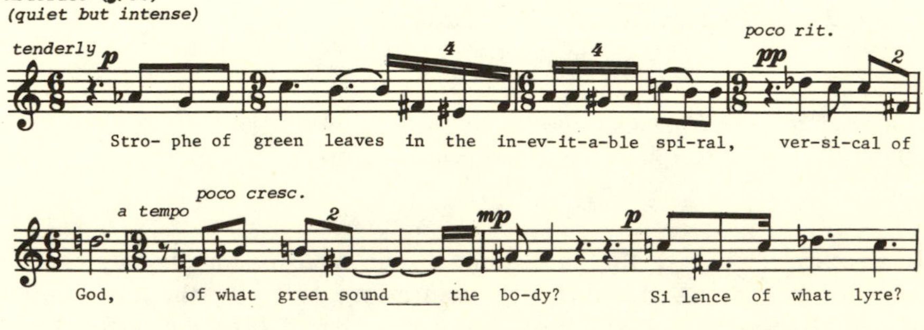

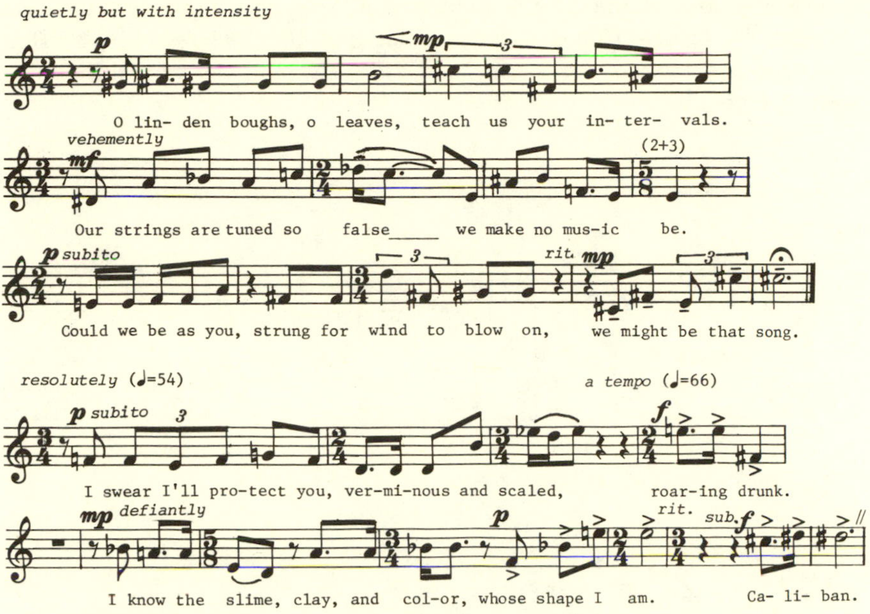

Figure 8.8 *Spirit above the Dust*: Nos. 4 and 6 (a) *The Linden Tree* (voice, mm. 5-13 and 16-28) (b) *Caliban* (voice, mm. 33-43). © 1981 by C. F. Peters Corporation. Used by permission.

Throughout her vocal chamber works, Gideon avoids exact doubling of the voice by the instruments. But she often creates a subtle heterophony, with the singer's notes scattered among different instruments or octaves. This technique is already established in *The Hound of Heaven:*

Figure 8.9 *The Hound of Heaven* (mm. 51-55). © 1975 by Columbia University Music Press. Used by permission.

Another good example appears in the second song of *The Seasons of Time,* a delicately scored 13-bar duo for voice and flute. Here wisps of flute arabesques surround the poem, and for five bars the two lines move heterophonically:

Figure 8.10 *The Seasons of Time*: No. 2 (mm. 5-9). © 1971 by Joshua Corporation. Used by permission.

Equally characteristic of Gideon's style as such simultaneous interaction of vocal and instrumental lines is her treatment of one as an extension of the other. Particularly striking in this regard are the interactions of voice and trumpet in the middle three *Sonnets from Shakespeare* and of voice and oboe in *Questions on Nature.* In the sonnets Gideon treats the voice and its companion instrument sometimes in unison or heterophonically and other times contrapuntally, with one growing out of the other as an extension of its phrase. In the opening song of *Questions on Nature,* she has the oboe begin with rapid moving figures that eventually become counterpoint to the voice. They continue on after the voice, ending the song inconclusively but appropriately, since the entire text is built on open-ended questions. In the sixth song, the text itself invites interplay:

Figure 8.11 *Questions on Nature*: No. 6 (voice and oboe, mm. 1-4). © 1978 by Mobart Music Publications, Inc. Used by permission.

In the Shakespeare cycle also, text gives rise to the music. The opening sonnet, "Music to hear, why hear'st thou music sadly?" is one of Gideon's most lyrical compositions. It begins and ends with four well-crafted phrases for the singer alone. The blossoming of the instrumental parts for lines 5 to 10 of the poem is evidence that she has delved into the text and discovered its most fitting musical counterpart. It is regrettable that this collection is one of her least frequently heard vocal works. It is available in versions for either high or low voice, with accompaniment for trumpet and string quartet or string orchestra. Perhaps a reiteration of George Perle's 25-year-old appraisal of this opus will encourage some potential performers:

> The intimate atmosphere of these songs, the absence of rhetoric and gesture, the spontaneity, variety, and compelling beauty of the melodic ideas, the incomparable fusion of word, sound and sense, make this work Miss Gideon's supreme accomplishment. . . . a work whose every page bears the stamp of a masterpiece.[29]

In all of these vocal chamber works, Gideon has created vocal lines that are, above all, singable. In spite of occasional dissonances with the instrumental lines (half steps or clusters of three adjacent pitches), the notes always seem to flow logically from one to the next. Gideon avoids wordiness and text repetition, always calling for simple and clear declamation with special regard for poetic meters and accents. A good example of her vocal lines is the first of the *Sonnets from Shakespeare*, where the voice moves predominantly in eighth notes—unmetered when unaccompanied and mostly in 2/4 with the instruments—with an occasional brief but expressive melisma:

Mu-sic to hear, why hear'st thou mu-sic sad-ly? Sweets with sweets war not,
joy de-lights____ in joy. Why lov'st thou that which thou re-ceiv-est not
glad - - - - ly, or else re-ceiv-est with plea-sure thine an- noy?

Figure 8.12 *Sonnets from Shakespeare*: No. 1 (opening). All rights reserved by Miriam Gideon. Reprinted by permission of American Composers Alliance, New York.

Regardless of whether she is writing sinuous chromatic lines or wide-ranging passages with large intervals, Gideon always suits the music to the words and the notes to the capabilities of the human voice. In spite of their highly chromatic nature, her vocal lines could never be called disjunct or awkward to sing. She does not always specify precise voice ranges for the chamber works; when she does indicate a high, low, or medium range, it is usually not further restricted to male or female. (Her designation "medium voice" can, I think, be interpreted quite freely. The score of *Spirit above the Dust*, which merely indicates "voice" has been sung by both baritone and mezzo-soprano. While the range [c-sharp^1 to f-sharp^2], an eleventh, seems most suited for medium voice, it would not be impossible for either higher or lower voices. *The Hound of Heaven* has a similar range [c^1 to f^2] and could likewise by sung by any voice type comfortable with its range and tessitura.) *The Condemned Playground* is the only one of her vocal chamber works that specifically calls for tenor and soprano voices. Several of the songs with piano accompaniment are available in transpositions for different voice categories.

While not wishing to deny the importance of Gideon's other compositions—especially the keyboard works and sacred services—I find that among all her compositions it is the vocal chamber works that stand out as unique contributions to contemporary musical literature. The high quality and lasting significance of her compositional activity is attested to by this citation, read and presented to Gideon at her induction into the American Academy and Institute of Arts and Letters on 21 May 1975:

Miriam Gideon, composer. For many years she has worked to build in her music a gracious, delicate and thoroughly convincing personal style. Every aspect of her work displays deep insight, as to her inspiration and her accomplishment. Her musical-poetic nature is both original and definitive.

Figure 8.13 At the final rehearsal for the world premiere of Gideon's *Spirit Above the Dust* (Yale School of Music, New Haven, Connecticut), February 11, 1981: seated: Arthur Weisberg, conductor of Yale New Music Ensemble, and Miriam Gideon, standing: Nathaniel Watson, baritone singing the premiere performance, and Barbara Petersen.

NOTES

1. Lester Trimble, review of *Rhymes from the Hill recording on CRI SD 286, Stereo Review* (November 1972), p. 112.

2. Much of the biographical and a little of the analytical material in this essay derive from the author's brochure on Miriam Gideon printed by BMI in 1980. The list of works and discography found in that publication are here expanded and brought up to date as of June 1986.

3. In 1939, Gideon (as Sessions and so many other American composers of his generation had done) headed for France and Switzerland to pursue her art. Her

original plan to stay in Europe indefinitely, if the cultural climate proved conducive to her creative activity, was frustrated by the outbreak of World War II, and she returned to New York.

4. A European born literary critic, translator, and historian, Frederic Ewen is the author of widely used books on Schiller, Heine, and Brecht. He has recently completed a monumental study of European literature of the nineteenth century.

5. Three of Gideon's songs are listed and described in Miriam Stewart-Green's article "Women Composers' Songs: An International Selective List, 1098-1980," *The Musical Woman: An International Perspective, 1983,* ed. Judith Lang Zaimont, vol. 1 (Westport, Conn.: Greenwood Press, 1983). The songs are "The Bells," "Little Ivory Figures Pulled with String," and "Farewell Tablet to Agathocles" from *Songs of Voyage.* (Contrary to Green's comment, "Little Ivory Figures" is not "aleatory music.") *The Bells* will be printed in Stewart-Green's future anthology *Art Songs by Women: Across Time.* The Desto 7117 recording, which includes Gideon's *Seasons of Time,* is devoted exclusively to works by women.

6. From Albert Weisser, "An Interview with Miriam Gideon," *Dimensions in American Judaism* (Spring 1970), p. 39.

7. Hannah Hanani, "Portrait of a Composer," *Music Journal* (April 1976), p. 24.

8. Weisser, "An Interview with Miriam Gideon," pp. 39, 40.

9. Trimble, review, p. 112.

10. Allen Hughes, "Works by Gideon and Perle Heard in League Series," *New York Times,* 18 December 1976. George Perle has written most perceptively about Gideon's music in "The Music of Miriam Gideon," *American Composers Alliance Bulletin* 7, no. 4 (1958), pp. 2-6. This article includes analyses of *The Hound of Heaven, Quartet for Strings, Sonnets from Shakespeare,* and *Sonnets from "Fatal Interview."*

11. Quoted in Lesley Valdes, ". . . women composers, Miriam Gideon among most honored," *The Sun* (Baltimore), 27 September 1981, p. D1.

12. Ibid.

13. Perle, "The Music of Miriam Gideon," p. 4.

14. Arthur Cohn, review of CRI 128, *American Record Guide* (November 1960), p. 218.

15. Burt Korall, "Miriam Gideon," *BMI News* (June 1963), p. 31.

16. The work, for high voice, flute, oboe, violoncello, percussion and piano, is scheduled for first performance in January 1987.

17. Miriam Gideon, as quoted in Jane Weiner LePage, *Women Composers, Conductors and Musicians of the Twentieth Century: Selected Biographies,* vol. 2 (Metuchen, N.J.: The Scarecrow Press, 1983), p. 125.

18. Korall, "Miriam Gideon," pp. 32, 33.

19. Peter G. Davis, "Pianist: Elisha Gilgore On Estonian Instrument," *New York Times,* 21 September 1980.

20. For further thoughts on the national identities in Gideon's works, see David Ewen, *American Composers: A Biographical Dictionary* (New York, G. P. Putnam, 1982), pp. 258-59.

21. Ibid., p. 260.

22. Prefatory comments to the score of *The Condemned Playground* (Hillsdale, N.Y.: Mobart Music 1980), p. [1].

23. Miriam Gideon quoted in notes to CRI SD 343.

24. Raymond Ericson, "Music in Our Time Winds Up Season," *New York Times*, 27 April 1964.

25. For more on Tanka poetry, see Alex Preminger, ed., *Princeton Encyclopedia of Poetry and Poetics,* enlarged edition (Princeton, N.J.: Princeton University Press, 1974), pp. 842-43.

26. Paul Hume, "Four Women and One Violin," review of Desto 7117, *Washington Post*, 24 March 1974. (The piano referred to in this review alternates with celesta in some of the songs of this cycle.)

27. John Harvey, "Three Help Achieve Triumph," review of soprano Judith Raskin and members of the St. Paul Chamber Orchestra, *St. Paul Pioneer Press,* 23 February 1976.

28. Hans Nathan, chapter on U.S.A. in *A History of Song,* ed. Denis Stevens (New York, W. W. Norton, 1961), pp. 452-53. Although I do not agree with much of Nathan's analytical commentary, I recommend reading it. In discussing Gideon's vocal works, he makes rather thought-provoking comparisons to works as divergent as Wagner's song "Im Treibhaus" and Bartok's String Quartet No. 6!

29. Perle, "The Music of Miriam Gideon, p. 6.

CURRICULUM VITAE

Degrees

B.A., Boston University, 1926 (major in French, minor in mathematics)

M.A, Columbia University, 1946 (musicology)

D.S.M., Jewish Theological Seminary of America, 1970 (composition)

Fellowships, Awards, and Honors

Ernest Bloch Award for choral work, 1948

National Federation of Music Clubs/ASCAP Award granted to an American woman composer for notable contributions to the symphonic literature, 1969

National Endowment for the Arts, grant for an orchestral work, 1974

Recording grants from N.F.M.C./Ford Foundation Recording-Publication Program, Martha Baird Rockefeller Fund for Music, Inc., the Tyrrel Fund, and others.

Doctor of Music *honoris causa*, Jewish Theological Seminary, 1981

Doctor of Humane Letters *honoris causa,* Brooklyn College, 1983.

Memberships

Collegium of Distinguished Alumni of Boston University, 1974

American Academy and Institute of Arts and Letters, 1975

Honorary Phi Beta Kappa, Boston University, 1975

American Composers Alliance, American Music Center, Broadcast Music Inc., League of Composers-ISCM; has also served on the board of directors, judging or evaluation panels or committees for these and numerous other organizations.

Commissions

Herman Berlinski; City College Orchestra; Da Capo Chamber Players; Irwin Freundlich; Meyer Kupferman; Library of Congress; 92nd Street YMHA; New York New Music Ensemble; New York State Music Teachers Association; Sigma Alpha Iota; Mr. and Mrs. Sidney Siegel; temples in Baltimore, Cleveland, and New York.

LIST OF WORKS

Orchestra

Lyric Piece (1941). ACA (9 min.). String orchestra; also available for string quartet.

Songs of Youth and Madness (1977). MOB (15 min.). Poems by Friedrich Hölderlin and translations by Michael Hamburger. High voice and orchestra of 1-1-1-1, 1-1-0-0, timpani, percussion, strings. 1. *An die Parzen;* 2. *An Diotima;* 3. *Der gute Glaube;* 4. *Der Spaziergang.*

Sonnets from Shakespeare (1950). ACA (18 min.). High or low voice, trumpet, string orchestra; also available for voice, trumpet, string quartet. 1. "Music to hear, why hear'st thou music sadly?" (Sonnet VIII); 2. "Devouring Time, blunt thou the lion's paws" (Sonnet XIX); Ritornelle; 3. "Full many a glorious morning have I seen" (Sonnet XXXIII); Ritornelle; 4. "No longer mourn for me when I am dead" (Sonnet LXXI); 5. "No! Time, thou shalt not boast that I do change!" (Sonnet CXXIII); Ritornelle

Symphonia Brevis (1953). ACA (8 min.). Two movements for orchestra of 2-2-2-2, 4-2-2-0, timpani, strings.

Where Wild Carnations Blow: A Song to David (1983). ACA (12 min.). Text by Christopher Smart. For SATB soli, SATB chorus, flute, oboe, trumpet, timpani, strings.

Chorus

Adon Olom (1954). ACA (6 min.). SAT soli, SATB chorus, oboe, trumpet, and string orchestra; also available for soli, chorus, pianoforte, or organ.

The Habitable Earth (1965). ACA (12 min.). Cantata based on the Book of Proverbs for SATB soli, SATB chorus, oboe, pianoforte, or organ.

How Goodly Are Thy Tents—Psalm 84 (1947). TMP (5 min.). SSA or SATB chorus, organ or pianoforte.

Sacred Service for Sabbath Morning (1970). TMP (30 min.). Cantor, SATB soli, SATB chorus, flute, oboe, bassoon, trumpet, organ, viola, violoncello.

Shirat Miriam L'Shabbat—Miriam's Song for the Sabbath (1974). CFP (30 min.). Friday Evening Service for cantor, SATB chorus, organ.

Slow, Slow Fresh Fount (1941). ACA (5 min.). Poem by Ben Jonson. SATB or TTBB.

Spiritual Madrigals (1965). MOB (9 min.). Texts by Frederic Ewen, Süezkint von Trimperg, Heinrich Heine. TTB, bassoon, viola, violoncello; also see *The Resounding Lyre* in next section. 1. *Mutterbildnis;* 2. *Wähebûf und Nichtenvint*; 3. *Hallelujah.*

Sweet Western Wind (1943). ACA (3 min.). Poem by Robert Herrick. SATB.

Voice with Piano or Chamber Ensemble

The Adorable Mouse (1960). JOS (11 min.). Libretto by the composer after a fable of LaFontaine. Voice (sung and spoken), flute, clarinet, bassoon, horn, timpani, harpsichord; also available in manuscript for narrator, flute, clarinet, 2 horns, pianoforte, timpani, strings.

Ayelet Hashakhar—Morning Star (1981). ACA (8 min.). Songs of childhood on Hebrew texts. Medium voice, pianoforte.

The Bells (1966). ACA (3 min.). Text by Marvin Hays. Low voice, pianoforte.

The Condemned Playground (1963). MOB (14 min.). Texts by Horace, Milton, Spokes, Akiya, Baudelaire, Millay. Soprano, tenor, flute, bassoon, string quartet. 1. *Pyrrha;* 2. *Hiroshima;* 3. *Litanies of Satan.*

Creature to Creature (1985). MOB (10 min.). Text by Nancy Cardozo. High voice, flute, harp.

Four Epitaphs from Robert Burns (1952). ACA (6 min.). High or low voice, pianoforte (no. 3 also available for medium or medium-low voice). 1. *Epitaph for a Wag in Mauchline;* 2. *Epitaph for Wee Johnnie;* 3. *Epitaph on the Author;* 4. *Monody on a Lady Famed for her Caprice.*

Gone in Good Sooth You Are (1952). HG (3 min.). From *Sonnets from "Fatal Interview"*, text by Edna St. Vincent Millay; in *American Artsong Anthology*, ed. John Belisle. High voice, pianoforte.

The Hound of Heaven (1945). COL (7 min.). Text by Francis Thompson, excerpts from "The Hound of Heaven." Medium voice, oboe, violin, viola, violoncello.

Lament for a Wag in Mauchline (1952) SCH (2 min.). From *Four Epitaphs from Robert Burns;* to appear in 1984 in an anthology of songs by women edited by Cathy Berberian.

Little Ivory Figures Pulled with String (1950). ACA (4 min.). Text by Amy Lowell. Sprechstimme; medium or low voice, guitar (or pianoforte).

Mixco (1957) ACA (5 min.). Poem by Miguel Angel Asturias. High, Medium or low voice, pianoforte.

Nocturnes (1976). MOB (8 min.). Poems by Percy Bysshe Shelley, Jean Starr Untermeyer, Frank Dempster Sherman. Medium voice, flute, oboe, vibraphone, viola, violoncello. 1. *Prelude;* 2. *To The Moon;* 3. *High Tide;* 4. *Interlude;* 5. *Witchery.*

Questions on Nature (1964). MOB (10 min.). Texts by Adelard of Bath (12th century). Medium voice, oboe, pianoforte, tam-tam, glockenspiel. The seven movements are numbered, not titled. Their opening lines are "How the earth moves," "Why the planets," "Whence the winds arise," "Whether the stars fall," "Whether beasts have souls," "Why we hear echoes," and "Why joy is the cause of weeping."

The Resounding Lyre (1979). MOB (12 min.). Texts by Frederic Ewen, Süezkint von Trimperg, Heinrich Heine. High voice, flute, oboe, bassoon, trumpet, violin, viola, violoncello. (See Chorus listing for *Spiritual Airs.*).

Rhymes from the Hill (1968). MOB (8 min.). Christian Morgenstern, from *Galgenlieder*. Medium voice, clarinet, marimba, violoncello. 1. *Bundeslied der Galgenbrüder*; 2. *Galgenkindes Wiegenlied*; 3. and 4. *Zwei Uhren: Die Korfsche Uhr, Palmströms Uhr*; 5. *Der Seufzer.*

The Seasons of Time (1969). JOS (17 min.). Ten Tanka poems of ancient Japan.

Medium voice, flute, pianoforte (cello), violoncello; also available for voice, pianoforte. The movements are numbered, not titled. The texts begin: "Now it is spring," "The wild geese returning," "Can it be that there is no moon," "Gossip grows like weeds," "Each season more lovely," "In the leafy treetops," "A passing shower," "I have always known," "To what shall I compare this world?" and "Yonder in the plum tree."

Songs of Voyage (1961). ACA (8 min.). Texts by Josephine Preston Peabody and Florence Wilkinson. High or low voice, pianoforte (no. 1 also available for medium voice, pianoforte). 1. *Farewell Tablet to Agathocles;* 2. *The Nightingale Unheard.*

Sonnets from "Fatal Interview" (1952). ACA (10 min.). Edna St. Vincent Millay, from "Fatal Interview." High voice, pianoforte, or string trio. 1. "Gone in good sooth you are"; 2. "Night is my sister"; 3. "Moon, that against the lintel of the west."

Sonnets from Shakespeare (1950). ACA (18 min.). High or low voice, trumpet, string quartet. (For details, see listing under Orchestra.).

Spirit above the Dust (1980). CFP (15 min.). Poems by Anne Bradstreet, Archibald MacLeish, and Norman Rosten. Medium voice, flute, oboe, bassoon, horn, string quartet. 1. *Prologue* ("To sing of Wars, of Captains, and of Kings"); 2. *Know the World*; 3. *The Two Trees*; 4. *The Linden Branch*; 5. *Black Boy*; 6. *Caliban*; 7. *The Snow Fall.*

To Music (1957). ACA (5 min.). Poem by Robert Herrick. High, medium or low voice, pianoforte.

Voices from Elysium (1979). ACA (12 min.). Various Greek poets and translators. High voice, flute, clarinet, pianoforte, violin, violoncello. 1. *The Swallow* (Children's Song); 2. *Cicada*; 3. *Prayer to Hermes*; 4. *Epitaph of a Sailor*; 5. *Of the Sensual World*; 6. *Hesperos*; 7. *Rest.*

Winged Hour (1984). CFP (10 min.). Texts by Dante Gabriel and Christina Rossetti and Walter de la Mare. Voice, flute, oboe, violin, violoncello, vibraphone.

Woman of Valor (1982). ACA (5 min.). Hebrew texts from Psalms and Proverbs. Voice, Pianoforte.

Instrumental Chamber Music

Air for Violin and Piano (1950). ACA (5 min.).

Biblical Masks (1960). ACA (9 min.). Violin, pianoforte; also available for organ.

Divertimento for Woodwind Quartet (1948). ACA (10 min.). Flute, oboe, clarinet, bassoon.

Fantasy on Irish Folk Motives (1975). ACA (13 min.). Oboe, bassoon, vibraphone, glockenspiel, tam-tam, viola.

Fantasy on a Javanese Motive (1948). HG (3 min.). Violoncello, pianoforte.

Lyric Piece for String Quartet (1941). ACA (9 min.). Also available for string orchestra.

Quartet for Strings (1946). ACA (12 min.).

Sonata for Violoncello and Piano (1961). ACA (13 min.).

Sonata for Viola and Piano (1948). ACA (17 min.).

Suite for Clarinet or Bassoon and Piano (1972). ACA (10 min.).

Trio for Clarinet, Violoncello and Piano (1978). ACA (7 min.).

Keyboard

Biblical Masks (1958). ACA (9 min.). Organ; also available for violin, pianoforte.
Canzona for Piano (1945). NME (6 min.).
"*Hommage à ma jeunesse*"—*Suite for Two Pianos* (1935). ACA; formerly MER, now out-of-print (10 min.).
Of Shadows Numberless—Suite for Piano (1966). ACA (12 min.). Based on lines from Keats's "Ode to a Nightingale."
Piano Suite No. 3 (1951). LG (4 min.).
Six Cuckoos in Quest of a Composer (1953). ACA (15 min.). Suite for keyboard in styles from the Renaissance to the present.
Sonata for Piano (1977). ACA (11 min.).

Opera

Fortunato (1958). ACA (60 min.). Opera in 3 scenes, libretto by the composer based on the play by Serafín and Joaquín Quintero. Soprano, mezzo-soprano, tenor, and 2 baritone soli with orchestra of 1-1-1-1, 1-1-0-0, timpani, percussion, strings.

Abbreviations and Addresses of Publishers

ACA—American Composers Alliance
170 West 74th Street/New York, NY 10023

CFP—C. F. Peters Corporation
373 Park Avenue South/New York, NY 10016

COL—Columbia University Press
c/o Galaxy Music Corporation/131 West 86th Street/New York, NY 10024

HG—Highgate Press
c/o Galaxy Music Corporation/131 West 86th Street/New York, NY 10024

JOS—Joshua Corporation
145 Palisade Street/Dobbs Ferry, NY 10522

LG—Lawson-Gould Music Publishers
c/o G. Schirmer, Inc./866 Third Avenue/New York, NY 10022

MER—Merrymount Music
c/o Theodore Presser, Inc./Presser Place/Bryn Mawr, PA 19010

MOB—Mobart Music
Hillsdale, NY 12529

NME—New Music Edition
c/o Theodore Presser, Inc./Presser Place/Bryn Mawr, PA 19010

SCH—G. Schirmer, Inc.
866 Third Avenue/New York, NY 10022

TMP—Transcontinental Music Publishing
838 Fifth Avenue/New York, NY 10021

DISCOGRAPHY

The Adorable Mouse. Reardon, Heller, Ariel Quintet. Serenus 12050.
The Condemned Playground. Bryn-Julson, Cassolas, Jahoda. CRI SD 343.
Fantasy on a Javanese Motive. Barab, Masselos. Paradox X-102 (out of print); Rudiakov, Wright. Golden Crest (not yet released).
The Hound of Heaven. Metcalf, Jahoda, Cohen, Phillips, Sherry. CRI SD 286.
How Goodly Are Thy Tents. Choral Society of Chizuk Amuno Congregation. Baltimore, Weisgall. Westminster XWN 18857 (out of print).
Lyric Piece for String Orchestra. Strickland, Imperial Philharmonic Orchestra, Tokyo. CRI 170.
Nocturnes. Raskin, DeMain, Da Capo Chamber Players. CRI SD 401.
Piano Suite No. 3. Helps. CRI SD 288.
Questions on Nature. De Gaetani, West, Lipman, Jekofsky. CRI SD 493.
The Resounding Lyre. Cassolas, Speculum Musicae, Black. CRI SD 493.
Rhymes from the Hill. De Gaetani, Gilbert, Bloom, Sherry, Des Roches. CRI SD 286.
The Seasons of Time. Chamber version: Mandac, Arico, Jahoda, Kraber. Desto 7117; voice and piano version: Sperry, Muraco. Serenus SRS 12078.
Slow, Slow Fresh Fount. Ericsson Bushnell Choir, Dashnaw. Golden Crest CRS 4172.
Sonata for Piano. Black. CRI SD 481.
Songs of Youth and Madness. Raskin, Dixon, American Composers Orchestra. CRI SD 401.
Sonnets from Shakespeare. Sharp, Prism Orchestra, Black. CRI SD 527.
Spirit above the Dust. Bonazzi, Contemporary Chamber Ensemble, Weisberg. CRI SD 493.
Symphonia Brevis. Monod, Radio Orchestra of Zurich. CRI 128.
Voices from Elysium. Cassolas, Da Capo Chamber Players. New World Records 317.
Winged Hour. Cassolas, Prism Ensemble, Black. CRI SD 527.

BIBLIOGRAPHY

(See also several performance or record reviews and short articles cited in the Notes.)

Anderson, E. Ruth, comp. *Contemporary American Composers: A Biographical Dictionary.* Boston: G. K. Hall, 1976. Pp. 160-61; also second edition.
Baker's Biographical Dictionary of Musicians. 6th ed. Ed. Nicolas Slonimsky. New York: Schirmer, 1978. Pp. 596-97.
Ewen, David. *American Composers: A Biographical Dictionary.* New York: G. P. Putnam, 1982. Pp. 257-60.
______. *Composers since 1900.* New York: H. W. Wilson, 1969. Pp. 221-23.
Gideon, Miriam. "The Music of Carlos Chávez." *New Book of Modern Composers,* ed. David Ewen. New York: Knopf 1961. Pp. 122-30.

______. "The Music of Mark Brunswick." *American Composers Alliance Bulletin* 13, no. 1 (1964), pp. 1-10.

Kamien, Roger. *Music. An Appreciation.* 2d ed. New York: McGraw Hill 1980. Pp. 474-75.

Korall, Burt. "Miriam Gideon." *BMI News* (June 1963), pp. 31-33.

LePage, Jane Weiner. "Miriam Gideon." *Women Composers, Conductors, and Musicians of the Twentieth Century: Selected Biographies.* vol. 2. Metuchen, N.J.: Scarecrow Press, 1983. Pp. 118-41.

Machlis, Joseph. *Introduction to Contemporary Music,* 2d ed. New York: W.W. Norton and Co. 1979. P. 552.

Perle, George. "The Music of Miriam Gideon." *American Composers Alliance Bulletin* 7, no. 4 (1958), pp. 2-6 (followed by list of works on pp. 7-9).

Petersen, Barbara A. "Miriam Gideon," 12-page foldout brochure issued by Broadcast Music Inc., New York, 1980.

Rosenberg, Deena, and Bernard Rosenberg, eds. "Miriam Gideon." *The Music Makers.* New York: Columbia University Press, 1979. Pp. 61-69 (from an interview with M. G. in April 1976).

Saminsky, Lazare. *Living Music of the Americas.* New York: Crown, 1949, pp. 106-10.

Stewart-Green, Miriam. "Women Composers' Songs: An International Selective List, 1098-1980." *The Musical Woman: An International Perspective, 1983.* Vol. 1. Westport, Conn.: Greenwood, 1984. Pp. 283-381.

Trimble, Lester. "Miriam Gideon." *The New Grove Dictionary of Music and Musicians.* Ed. Stanley Sadie. London, Washington, and Hong Kong: Macmillan 1980). 7: 362.

Tucker, Tui St. George. "Miriam Gideon." *EAR Magazine East* 6, no. 3 (April-May 1981), p. 3.

Vinton, John, ed. *Dictionary of Contemporary Music.* New York: Dutton 1974. P. 269.

Weisgall, Hugo. "Miriam Gideon's 'Shirat Miriam L'Shabbat.' A Sabbath Evening Service." *Musica Judaica* 3, no. 1 (1981), pp. 80-82.

Weisser, Albert. "Interview with Miriam Gideon." *Dimensions in American Judaism* (New York) (Spring 1970), pp. 38-40.

______. "Miriam Gideon's New Service." *Congress Bi-Weekly* 39 (30 June 1972), pp. 22-23; reprinted in LePage, pp. 131-32.

______. "Review of New Music." *Journal of Synagogue Music* 9, no. 3 (November 1979), pp. 87-88; reprinted in LePage, pp. 133-34.

9

Toshiko Akiyoshi: Jazz Composer, Arranger, Pianist, and Conductor

LAURA KOPLEWITZ

> Jazz is still thought of as a very masculine music, and men don't like to see women involved in it. But my musicians respect me. They know what I am trying to do. I want to keep on creating sounds that will add something to the American tradition, without distorting its basic character.
>
> —*Ms. Magazine*, November 1978, p. 35. Interview by Leonard Feather.

> And yet, I realize that it [jazz] is purely American music, and since I am Japanese, what is my position in the jazz world? . . . Am I taking from jazz and giving nothing back? . . . The only way I am able to resolve this dilemma is to give what I am back to jazz by composing. If I have developed my music to the point where a listener can sense my attitudes—that is, my history as it reflects Japan and as it reflects what I've learned of America in the past 20 years—if the listener can hear my history and my individuality, then I have accomplished the solution.
>
> —Toshiko Akiyoshi, Introduction to "March of the Tadpoles," Toba Publishing Co., 1983.

BACKGROUND AND CAREER

Toshiko Akiyoshi is the first person of Japanese descent to have created a sensation in the world of jazz. The first woman to have created an entire repertoire for her own big band, she has consistently brought that band into the limelight in America, Europe, and Japan by the excellence of her musical craft and her extraordinary determination to succeed. Since the 1950s Akiyoshi has recorded a total of more than 30 albums, including solo piano, trios, quartets, combos, and over a dozen albums of her own compositions for big band. Her music, derived primarily from the 'be-bop' tradition in jazz, is hard-driving, with subtle, unique orchestral colorations. In recent years she has frequently experimented by combining music from the Japanese cultural tradition (Noh theater, for example) with the music of jazz. Her recordings have consistently received the highest acclaim both in the United States and in her native country.

Akiyoshi was born in 1929 in Darien, Manchuria, a portion of the Asian mainland then under Japanese rule. Her father owned a textile company and a steel mill; the family was fairly well-off financially. It was expected that Toshiko, the youngest of four daughters, would study to become a doctor. She says of her family's plans for her future: "I suppose my father was disappointed that he never had a son, and for some reason he thought I would be the one to accomplish something."[1] The educational system and family life in Manchuria were very strict. As part of their upper-class female acculturation, the Akiyoshi daughters were expected to learn to play music. Toshiko developed an immediate love for the piano from the time she began her training in Western classical music at the age of seven.

Having lost their business and all their possessions and been forced to leave amidst the post-World War II political and economic disenfranchisement of Japanese people, the Akiyoshi family moved to Japan in August of 1948. Toshiko was to begin medical school in Japan in March of the following year, just six months after the family's arrival in Japan. Her own private goal was to continue to study the piano. She practiced whenever possible, but since her family was in dire economic straits, a piano at home was an unaffordable luxury. Says Akiyoshi, remembering post-World-War-II Japan,

> Japan was still heavily occupied then and our resort city of Beppu was flooded with soldiers. . . . I spent a lot of time wandering around the city, looking at the shops and the people. I was still too young to understand my family's financial disaster, and I think more than anything I missed my piano. One day, I happened to pass one of the many dance halls that were set up for the occupation soldiers, and I noticed a sign—"Pianist Wanted." I couldn't think of anything but how much I wanted to touch that piano, so I went in.[2]

Akiyoshi auditioned that day to play with an army dance band. Her audition consisted of a Beethoven piano concerto performance for the manager of the dance hall; he told her to begin that evening at six.

The band, led by an ex-Navy orchestra leader, included violin, saxophone, accordion, drums, and Akiyoshi at the piano. "They were really bad!" says Akiyoshi.[3] "We played from a 'Hit Kit' of basic arrangements of standard tunes, including some current popular music of the time. The book was published and distributed by the U.S. Military Special Services."[4] Having never heard real jazz (which was not available in Manchuria), Akiyoshi assumed that the popular arrangements performed by the dance hall band were the fundamental sounds of jazz. Such tunes as "Sweet Jenny Lee," "Sweet Sue," and other placid melodies were, to the teenage piano player, "jazz," and she remembers, "Boy did I hate it. All that mattered was that I could use the piano in the afternoon."[5]

Akiyoshi did not inform her parents about her job at the dance hall, and when she was finally found out there was a family uproar. At first, her father wouldn't even give her the identification card that she was required to have for the state records. But finally it was agreed that she could continue to play until medical school began. That date came and went, but she never did begin her studies at medical school. Since World War II had interrupted her high school studies (she was drafted into the army in Manchuria, but the war ended before she was placed on active duty), and reconstruction in Japan after the war was a hardship, medical school studies were indefinitely postponed. Instead, Akiyoshi continued to practice an extensive classical music repertoire and began to think about music as a possible career.

One day a record collector played several albums for her including Teddy Wilson's "Sweet Lorraine," and the musical realm of genuine American jazz music was revealed to her. Overnight, Akiyoshi fell in love with this new musical repertoire. She devoted herself to learning as much of it as she could, spending hours copying the music from recordings and trying her hand writing original tunes. Soon she grew restless and felt the impetus to continue with her musical education. Against family wishes, Akiyoshi moved from the provincial southern region of Japan to metropolitan Tokyo.

Remembering her formative years as a jazz musician, Akiyoshi has commented,

> The most important developmental years in anyone's life are, I think, between 16 and 25. That is the time when your character is built, when what you are as a human being is defined. My whole life was jazz during those years, so I really became an adult through jazz music. To me, jazz is mine. I can't pretend that it's someone else's music, or that I just play it because I love it—I can't separate myself from it at all.[6]

In the early 1950s Akiyoshi began to play in Tokyo coffee-houses and gained experience playing with the Mori Orchestra, the Tokyo Jive Combo, Matsumoto and His Combo, the Blue Coats Orchestra, the Victor All Stars, and the Six Lemons. In 1951, she departed from the role of sidewoman to form her own jazz combo.[7]

Listening to all the jazz music that she could find, Akiyoshi absorbed the sounds of Harry James, Gene Krupa, Teddy Wilson, and Bud Powell. Powell, associated with the development of be-bop music in the United States in the 1940s, is the pianist that she feels most strongly influenced her early style of jazz piano playing.[8] Toshiko Akiyoshi's piano style developed to include a strong, sinewy right-hand capable of spinning out long melodic improvisations, accompanied in the left hand by light, sparse chord punctuations. This general playing ability, matched by clear articulation and fluid improvisatory concepts, was extremely effective both in the context of solo playing and in an accompaniment function in jazz combos.

When the Canadian-born jazz musician Oscar Peterson arrived in Tokyo

Figure 9.1 Toshiko Akiyoshi. By permission of Akiyoshi.

in 1953 to perform as part of a "Jazz at the Philharmonic" tour managed by Norman Granz, he heard Toshiko Akiyoshi. Peterson pronounced her to be "the greatest female jazz pianist he had ever heard" and recommended to Granz that Akiyoshi be recorded.[9] That year Granz recorded her on his "Verve" label, employing Oscar Peterson's rhythm section (supplemented by J. C. Heard on drums) as her back-up band.[10] The album was released in the United States and was an overnight success.

In 1954 Akiyoshi reorganized her own ensemble and formed an octet. Then considered to be Japan's leading jazz pianist, she was frequently in demand for radio and television appearances. To satisfy again her desire for musical growth, Akiyoshi had begun to write and to arrange music for her ensembles. By the mid-1950s she had become the highest-paid jazz musician in Japan.[11]

At this point Akiyoshi decided to further broaden her horizons. She applied to the Berklee School of Music, well known for its outstanding professional jazz curriculum, and sent them a copy of her Granz recording. The school, recognizing that she would provide Berklee with significant media attention, was pleased to accept her. Only when Akiyoshi arrived in Boston in 1956 did she discover that although Berklee offered her the chance to expand her skills in arranging and the opportunity to be exposed to a great variety of jazz music, as a scholarship student her musical performance work was indentured to Berklee for the term of her three-and-a-half years of study. Since it was difficult for a person of Japanese descent to obtain a visa or permanent resident status, she was required to accept the compromise situation as her only opportunity to remain in the United States. Akiyoshi led a jazz trio that was sent to clubs such as the Hickory House in Boston under the auspices of the Berklee School of Music. She received considerable attention from the critical press and appeared on radio and television shows, including "What's My Line," playing be-bop piano dressed in a traditional Japanese kimono.[12]

Audiences in the United States had accepted Akiyoshi initially as an accomplished jazz player on the basis of her Granz-initiated recording. But when Akiyoshi began to make personal appearances in this country she was regarded more often as a curiosity and felt keenly the problem of being an outsider in the American jazz scene both because she was Japanese and because women in jazz were considered second-class citizens, regardless of nationality or race. (According to Sally Placksin, in her book *American Women in Jazz*, a 1957 survey of a college psychology class that assessed the most and least acceptable roles of men and women in music, placed women performers of jazz in the least favorable category. Placksin concluded that women's activities as jazz performers were, in the 1950s "far from a realistic option.")[13]

Toshiko Akiyoshi persisted and, despite the odds against success, continued to perform and compose. But at the same time, the initial impact of her recordings and appearances in the United States began to fade as audiences tended toward the latest fashion, the rock n' roll explosion of the late 1950s and early 1960s. Although Akiyoshi worked four nights a week at the "Storyville," George Wein's club in Boston, and debuted at the Newport Jazz Festival in 1956, she was dismayed by the restrictions of racial and sexual stereotypes in the jazz arena.[14] She left Berklee in 1959 and struck out on her own, hoping to earn a living as a performer, composer, and arranger. She preferred to avoid the label of "woman musician" and simply desired to play music and be judged in the same league with the best musicians, male or female. But audiences did not comply with this plan, and when Akiyoshi appeared at jazz clubs intending to play hard and fast be-bop, listeners insistently requested "light patter-music and background music" according to Akiyoshi.[15] Even so, she was able to make several recordings, and other talented (male) jazz musicians continued to recognize her abilities. She played frequently with Charles Mingus and with her own quartet and trio. Her early recordings in the United States were on such labels as Norgran, Verve, Storyville, Metrojazz, Candid, RCA, Vee-Jay, and Concord.

After leaving the Berklee School of Music, Akiyoshi spent a discouraging year in Boston. At the same time, however, her personal life took a more fortunate turn; she met Charlie Mariano (a saxophonist who had developed a strong reputation during the 1950s performing with Stan Kenton and others), and they were married in November of 1959. Charlie Mariano and Toshiko Akiyoshi formed the Toshiko-Mariano Quartet, and both contributed arrangements to the group's repertoire, primarily using Akiyoshi's original compositions as the foundation for the group's sound. Mariano eventually recorded with Akiyoshi and Charles Mingus, Elvin Jones, and McCoy Tyner on Impulse Records and produced his own LP, "A Jazz Portrait," on Regina Records.[16]

Akiyoshi gave birth to a daughter, Michiru Mariano, in Japan in August of 1964. She remained in Japan for several months, and then moved to New York. While caring for her young daughter, she continued to perform and compose. During her first few years in New York, it was difficult to balance the demands of motherhood with her dedication to the development of her professional career. Akiyoshi was able to find jobs playing solo piano at clubs such as the Five Spot and the Village Gate. But although she received critical attention in the press, she more often than not was considered a phenomenon on the fringes of the jazz scene, and opportunities to perform were limited even if recognition of her talent was widespread within the relatively small circle of jazz musicians and aficionados in Boston and New York. A typical form of recognition during the mid-1960s, for example, was a *New York Times* article featuring Akiyoshi entitled "Tokyo Jazz Pianist Plays Here."[17] Publicity continued to focus on her nationality rather than her musical personality.

In the mid-1960s Akiyoshi's marriage to Charlie Mariano ended, and she found that there was sufficient interest in her music in Japan for her to divide her time between Tokyo and New York. She performed with several Japanese symphony orchestras and in the United States received recognition from *Mademoiselle Magazine* as one of the top ten "Women of the Year" for her composition titled "A Jazz Suite for String Orchestra."[18]

In 1963-1965, Akiyoshi spent the majority of her time touring Japan and Europe. In 1963 she was commissioned to write a work for the Tokyo International Theater, and in 1964 she wrote the music for a Swedish movie, "The Platform." She toured Japan with the J. J. Johnson Sextet in the summer of 1964 for an international jazz festival. In 1965, Akiyoshi returned to the United States to teach piano at summer jazz clinics in Reno,

Nevada, and Salt Lake City. The Japanese jazz magazine *Japan Swing Journal* had contracted her to write articles on a monthly basis, in addition to her other work.[19]

Akiyoshi's compositional interests eventually turned toward writing for big bands, perhaps fueled by the alternation between performances with orchestras and solo "gigs" during the early 60s. While the opportunity to fully explore her talents in this area was not to come for several years, the impulse to write music for big bands evolved into a determination to have her own debut in New York City. She had been in the United States for a decade (1956-1966), and felt that the time was ripe for a presentation of her work. Akiyoshi spent a year setting aside a modest portion of her earnings from club and hotel lounge performances, to underwrite the costs of the debut from her own finances. Town Hall was the location she selected for the concert; the format would include solo playing and trios, with premieres of several new works for big band as the grand finale. Hoping that she could generate support from the New York Japanese community for her concert, Akiyoshi went door-to-door to businesses in order to sell tickets. As she explained at the time, "They will only buy if I come to them in person. I have spent many days going to businessmen and the nights working on my music. It is very tiring, but it must be done this way. Otherwise it is not proper."[20]

The Town Hall debut in 1967 was a critical success, but the financial problems of rehearsing and performing with a big band (particularly in a period two decades past the prime of the big band era) limited Akiyoshi's future prospects for continuing to develop her compositional skills in big band writing. In turmoil over this state of affairs, she considered quitting her musical career entirely. But once again a new development in her personal life provided crucial support. She met saxophonist Lew Tabackin, who recognized that Akiyoshi had the potential to make major contributions to jazz as a composer and encouraged her to continue her career. In 1969 Toshiko Akiyoshi and Lew Tabackin were married, and they moved to Los Angeles to explore performance possibilities there.

Tabackin became a member of Doc Severinsen's band on television's "The Tonight Show." Together Akiyoshi and Tabackin formed a quartet and played at clubs in the Los Angeles region. They then decided to try out a "workshop" situation with a big band. They organized a group for the purpose of practice sessions but for the moment did not consider the big band as a performing ensemble. The band rehearsed weekly, and Akiyoshi's portfolio of big band pieces began to grow. After a year of diligent workshop sessions, a decision was made to try to contract the band for performances. The big band played at a small club in Pasadena for little or no money, taking home whatever income was generated at the door. Akiyoshi and Tabackin financed a concert of the band in Los Angeles, and although they drew an ample audience, concert producers and club owners were still more interested in either smaller, less expensive ensembles or in "all-star" bands comprised of jazz performers who were recognized figures on the L.A. jazz scene.[21]

Akiyoshi again turned to Japan for support, and found sufficient interest in big bands there to convince backers to invest in a recording of her band. In 1974, on a tiny budget, and under primitive recording conditions in a small Los Angeles studio, the album "Kogun" was recorded and then sent to Japan for release there. The album became one of the biggest all-time jazz hits in Japan, selling an immediate 30,000 copies when it first appeared and tens of thousands of additional copies to date.

Since the mid-1970s Toshiko Akiyoshi has become established as a big band composer, arranger, and conductor, in addition to her renown as a jazz pianist. In 1976 the Akiyoshi-Tabackin Big Band placed first in a *down beat* critics' poll; in the same year the album *Long Yellow Road* was named best album of the year by *Stereo Review* Magazine, and the album *Insights* was voted Jazz Album of the Year in Japan. Akiyoshi has received six Grammy Award nominations since 1976 for her big band albums.

Further accolades for Akiyoshi arrived in 1978. The *down beat* critics' poll selected *Insights* as Record of the Year, the same poll awarded first place to Toshiko Akiyoshi as a jazz arranger, and her big band was voted number one in the big jazz band category. This marked the first time in the history of jazz that a woman had received these top honors in *down beat*'s composer/arranger and big band categories. Since these first awards, Akiyoshi has been repeatedly cited in the magazine's Critics' and Readers' Polls, earning two or more awards for both the band and herself in 1979, 1980, and 1981.

Toshiko Akiyoshi formed her own jazz recording label, Ascent, in the late 1970s. She has released three albums on her own label to date, including *Salted Gingko Nuts, European Memoirs,* and her most recent release, the 1984 album *Ten Gallon Shuffle*. The latter recording was the first to feature her big band titled solely with her own name, as the "Toshiko Akiyoshi Jazz Orchestra."

MUSICAL PERSONALITY

Akiyoshi's recordings reveal that the early years of her musical growth were concentrated on an attempt to simply expand her prowess as a piano player in the jazz idiom. In the 1950s she worked exclusively with small ensembles—trios, quartets, and jazz combos. She familiarized herself with be-bop, swing, Latin-influenced jazz (sambas, etc.), ballads, basic jazz blues, and the essential technical equipment of a jazz piano player; her ability to "solo" in the jazz tradition was well established by the mid-1950s. Her voice as a composer began to develop at that time as well.

Toshiko Akiyoshi may initially have simply sought acceptance in the American jazz community in the 1950s, but once she had proven herself able to perform in the ranks of the best American jazz players (her recordings on the Storyville, Verve, Metro Jazz, Concord Jazz, Inner City, and other eminent jazz labels are a testament to this achievement), the question of developing a greater individuality as a performer and composer arose. Although it seemed in the 1950s that her compositional interests were confined to the arena of small-ensemble, Akiyoshi's interest in exploring a wider textural and timbral pallete was slowly infusing its presence into her ensemble activities. The colors of small-ensemble jazz sounds were becoming a limitation. And, too, during her first ten years in the United States, American jazz was not the only music to which Akiyoshi was exposed. It gradually became clear that finding a musical identity solely within an American-based idiom was no longer of exclusive importance to her. Akiyoshi "began to think that instead of always following the American jazz styles, perhaps I could bring some new elements into the tradition to make it a little richer. That's when I became very serious about infusing some of my Japanese heritage into American jazz."[22] She began to incorporate Japanese musical elements into her jazz compositions in the early 1970s, and this effort resulted in significant expansions in the artistic purposes and structural functions of her music.

The best early example of these changes is the album *Kogun*, which was released in Japan in 1974 and in the United States four years later. The title piece "Kogun" was inspired by a story Akiyoshi had heard in the international news: a Japanese soldier had been found in the Philippines, who had been in hiding and did not know that World War II was over. Thirty years after the close of World War II, the soldier decided to give up his sword in the traditional Japanese manner of surrender. The title "Kogun" means, according to Akiyoshi, "forlorn force," or "one-man army."[23] In "Kogun" the composer made use of the traditional *tsuzumi* drum of the Japanese Noh drama, setting a precedent for future inclusion of other traditional Japanese instruments in her works of the late 1970s and 1980s.

"Kogun," which lasts nearly seven minutes, is described in the published score as "Oriental/Swing." (The work is recorded on the albums *Kogun* and *Road Time*.) It opens with the solitary sounds of a *tsuzumi* drummer; before striking the *tsuzumi* drum, the musician utters a throaty, gutteral cry whose quavering tone creates an atmosphere of urgency and a sense of distant sorrow. A flute enters, imitating the fluid, bending tones of the voice and playing a plaintive melody. On the heels of the flute, an ensemble of saxophones, trumpets, and trombones commences playing and amplifies the sounds of the *tsuzumi* player's voice with a downward glissando of instruments fading into silence. The ensemble slowly builds in intensity until a clear-cut swing jazz momentum emerges. The players punctuate melodic phrases and chordal breaks with the snappy articulations of upbeat swing. This ends abruptly when the solo flute reemerges, imitating the breathy tones and bending notes of the *tsuzumi* player's voice and the hollow tones of his drum. The tempo swiftly charges ahead a second time, and the improvisatory lines of unison melodies among the winds and brasses become more highly embellished until the momentum peaks, allowing the

Figure 9.2 Conclusion of "Kogun." © Toba Publishing Company. Used by permission.

flute to take a "shakuhachi"-style solo. The coda to the piece is the reentrance of the *tsuzumi* drummer, whose voice sounds a quavering, brief cry to close the work.

Eastern and Western sounds are juxtaposed in "Kogun," but rarely do the crosscultural musical concepts actually merge. Their closest alliance is at the opening; thereafter the piece progresses toward a greater and greater independence of sounds in terms of the Eastern and Western influences. The jazz ensemble becomes more "jazzy," building excitement and strength with each refrain, while the solo flute takes on a stronger "shakuhachi" character. Only the character of the *tsuzumi* drummer's vocal cries does not change, seeming to represent the sense of timelessness or time forgotten that was the crux of the story on which "Kogun" was based.

Both the programmatic nature of Akiyoshi's music and her interest in combining Eastern and Western musical sounds into essentially jazz music continued to expand. The theme/programs extended beyond individual pieces, evolving into entire album concepts. The composer explained her primary themes for the album *Kogun,* for example, when discussing another work on *Kogun*, a piece titled "Memory."

> I consider this to be an important piece because it introduced a new element that I wanted to bring in. Memory is something we all wonder about—as time goes by, what one remembers or wants to remember may be different from what really happened. I have tried to capture that feeling of distance from reality, to crystallize that abstraction in a certain way, and I orchestrated it in what I felt would be a beautiful, traditional style using four flutes and one bass clarinet, and putting the trombones in bucket mutes to soften their sound.[24]

Compositional manipulation of *sounds* had begun to interest Akiyoshi, marking a radical departure from the traditional perspective she had carefully nurtured in Japan and during her days at Berklee. While in the 1950s and 1960s she had developed a secure sense of jazz forms and structures, in the 1970s she was able, as on *Kogun*, to incorporate spoken vocal effects into a piece in such a manner that the vocal origins of the sounds were obscured and absorbed into the overall coloristic effects of her jazz orchestrations. As she described the creation of "Memory," "I had Scott (the speaker) pick up some lines from the poetry of D. H. Lawrence—I asked him to read them, and from that I picked words that I thought appropriate for this piece. I cut the tape and kind of messed them up, wrinkled them, used echo on some, and rerecorded it."[25]

The musical characteristics established in the album *Kogun* were foremost in Toshiko Akiyoshi's thoughts in the mid-1970s, when she created the albums *Long Yellow Road* (1975), *Tales of a Courtesan* (1975), *Road Time* (1976), and *Insights* (1976). The composer's fascination with sound sources and extramusical themes took another step forward with the making of the album *Insights*. The thematic story of *Insights* was represented in the extended musical work "Minimata," which comprises the entire second side of the album and lasts about 21 and a half minutes. As jazz critic and historian Leonard Feather commented in the liner notes for *Insights*, "The album marks a significant stepping stone. . . . In it, Toshiko makes her most ambitious and, it seems to me, most artistically impressive statement to date; Minimata, an extended composition that might be called a suite, offers inspiring evidence of her ability to use the orchestra as her instrumental palette."[26]

Composed in three parts titled "Peaceful Village," "Prosperity and Consequence," and "Epilogue," the work presents the story of a small fishing village in Japan that is brought to ruins by the devastation of toxic poisoning of the fish that provide the people with their daily food and their livelihood. It is a story about the consequences of human greed and the destruction of the balance that nature has created between humanity and the environment. "Minimata" opens with a child's voice, that of Akiyoshi's daughter Michiru Mariano, singing quietly as if musing to herself while playing a childhood game. The music slowly evolves into a mournful, elegiac melody, spun out in solo brass lines supported by single notes suspended in the air from the woodwinds and brasses. The quiet sounds of a cymbal softly rustle and tremble in crescendo as if the waves of time were passing by in billows in one's memory. In the second section, "Prosperity and Consequence," there is an immediate, surprising shift of mood as the ensemble jumps into a rhythmic, up-tempo, swing-style section dominated by tenor saxophone solos supported by background saxophone choruses. The mood of the music is optimistic and slightly headlong in its quick pace, implying perhaps a certain recklessness in the ever-increasing prosperity of the village of "Minimata." The celebrations are suddenly undermined by the introduction of the voice of a Noh vocalist intoning low, long phrases that might be words of warning but are not decipherable. There is an ominous tone to the voice. Yet the orchestra continues its quickening pace, seemingly unaffected by the moody, sonorous element. Suddenly the ensemble comes to a halt with a series of staccato chords that hold a fateful, final ring. The Noh vocalist continues his solitary lament, casting a sombre mood to the "Epilogue" of "Minimata." The music presents a discomforting yet poignant sound of a village in mourning, represented by the Noh voice.

The cross-rhythms of the up-tempo jazz sections of "Minimata" overlaid by the Noh voice have the effect on the listener of dislocating the rhythmic meter and bar line of the music. This amounts to a compositional technique of "layering" musical styles and sounds that are fundamentally opposed in their musical languages. The compositional characteristic found in "Minimata" is a more pronounced version of Akiyoshi's earlier East-meets-West experiments on the album *Kogun,* but the musical and programmatic effects are more fully refined and realized in "Minimata."

Only two years after the composer's discovery of a new fundamental concept for her writing, the intense drama—created by use of the Noh voice, *tsuzumi* drums, and by the expansion of orchestrations to achieve greater coloristic effects—clearly revealed on *Insights* that Toshiko Akiyoshi had disallowed herself a comfortable stylistic niche in traditional jazz forms and was pushing the outer limits of jazz and creating music of great originality. While not all of her subsequent albums beyond *Insights* include direct musical borrowings from traditional Japanese culture, the changes effected by her experiments incorporating Japanese elements into jazz are far-reaching, even in her more traditional-sounding jazz compositions of recent origin. In particular, the use of instruments of one class (such as four flutes or five saxophones) in a soloistic context is a favored characteristic of Akiyoshi's compositions of the late 1970s and 1980s. This perhaps represents a search for a wider spectrum of sound-qualities derived from the traditional jazz instruments. The search seems to have begun on *Insights* with a piece titled "Sumie," which makes use of five flutes in complex part-writing. The piece "Elusive Dream" on the album *Salted Gingko Nuts* (recorded in 1978 and released in the United States in 1982) makes use of four flutes and bass clarinet in a similar fashion; "American Ballad" (1974) features two flutes and three clarinets.

The harmonic context of Akiyoshi's writing has evolved in like manner. The voicings of chords and the intervals of melodic lines have taken on a slightly dissonant character, which seems to have a strengthening effect on the nuances of mood in her compositions. The chorus-solo interaction in her works is always very energetic, with frequent meter changes, careful balancing between rhythmic tension and release, and continual successive variations of the motifs of any given piece. Although Akiyoshi's compositions retain the standard jazz-tune format, with clearly demarcated introductions, statements of theme, and motivic development, including a sequence of soloists, refrains, repeats, endings, and codas, the complexity of her compositional forms often defies the traditional jazz formats. A piece may have an apparent "coda" and suddenly gallop off in a new direction, as happens in "Kogun," for example. Certain orchestrations may be due to the influence of the human voice derived from the Japanese Noh drama. For example, the composer frequently employs the piccolo and the bass clarinet simultaneously to outline melodic passages—exploiting the high-range and whistling timbres of the piccolo and the low, rumbling, throaty sounds of the bass clarinet.

Akiyoshi's musical "charts" or scores are written in standard jazz notation. She writes according to a concept of layering different melodies and rhythms on top of one another so that complex counterpoints and syncopations result. Her refined compositional style reflects a preference for creating dramatic essences in each piece. Although her works are lush and thickly textured, the writing is concise. There are no extraneous musical lines. Her music features frequent and abrupt tempo changes, which create an obvious breaking point between jazz-oriented and nonjazz musical materials in a single piece. The juxtaposition of Japanese and American jazz idioms in her recent music seems to be the sowing of a new conceptual

Figure 9.3 From "American Ballad" by Toshiko Akiyoshi. © Toba Publishing Company. Used by permission.

1st Alto
2nd Alto
1st Tenor
2nd Tenor
Baritone
Saxes
Trpts
Trbs
Bass
Drums
Guitar
Piano
E
Fmi
Bbmi
Db
Dbmi

1st Alto
2nd Alto
1st Tenor
2nd Tenor
Baritone
Saxes
Trpts
Trbs
Bass
Drums
Guitar
Piano
TO SOPRANO
TO CLARINET
TO PICCOLO
TO BASS CLARINET
(TRB. SOLO)
Cmi7
Bmi7
Bbmi7
A7 Ab7
(TIME - 36 BARS)
(TB SOLO - COMP)

Figure 9.4 Orchestration featuring close part-writing for trombones, from "March of the Tadpoles" by Akiyoshi. © Toba Publishing Company. Used by permission.

Figure 9.5 Coloristic use of winds in "March of the Tadpoles." © Toba Publishing Company. Used by permission.

field that Akiyoshi has yet to plumb to its fullest depths. Her music reflects an apparent desire to both expand and clearly demarcate the boundaries of her two strongest voices: traditional Japanese music and traditional jazz. It seems that the composer continues to experience Western and Eastern idioms as separate voices that can converse within a given work but cannot fuse to become a single musical voice. The two separate idioms seem to weave in and out of her compositions intact, without changing their essential forms or identities. Their intermingling in any given work may be at times uneasy, restive; it is always, in Toshiko Akiyoshi's music, meaningful and profoundly evocative.

Independent of her cross cultural musical experiments, Toshiko Akiyoshi is by no means a conventional composer within the jazz idiom, even in her most traditional works. Rather than being caught within the confines of a particular period of jazz stylization, Akiyoshi prefers continually to expand her definition of jazz as contemporary music. Her music crosses over between "through-composed" and improvised scores. A steamy, slow ballad unreels with as much color and momentum as does a racy, staccato swing tune. Akiyoshi's attachment to the jazz idiom constitutes her personal credo and directive and involves a lifelong commitment to the music that she feels is her own by an artistic, if not a cultural, birthright.

Since Akiyoshi presides over the big band that performs her music and conducts it herself, she can articulate her musical objectives and key elements of her style in person. The effect of this continuing personal contact with the performers has given her an important tool for fine-tuning her compositional ideas, and this experience is reflected in her writing. Lew Tabackin, a frequent featured soloist, comments,

> What Toshiko notates is very important, but she really works hard to personally communicate the mood of each piece to the band. The band has always worked hard to maintain a high level of performance. In other people's music, you can often hear that the germ of the musical idea is really great, but the execution leaves a lot to be desired. We compete with ourselves as a band, really, because if we give a good concert or make a great record, then it is there as a standard when we make the next recording. In rehearsals, we try to narrow the gap between what's written and what is actually being played. This means improvising in the spirit of the piece, at times going beyond the music itself, to try to express feelings that are extra-musical but can't really be analyzed. Toshiko conducts all of her own pieces, and her presence is crucial to the sound of the music. It really is "Toshiko's band." But she doesn't consider herself a "band leader." She feels she is just doing what needs to be done to get the music played, as an extension of her work as a composer. There are many "band leaders" who strive to create a special image and stage personality in front of a band. Toshiko considers this a form of "show business"; most of the time it is not necessary and detracts from the music. In Toshiko's case, she is in front of the band because of artistic, musical things that need to be communicated."[27]

Familiarity with the individual personalities of the band members influences Akiyoshi's compositional techniques. She writes parts with specific players in mind. Says Tabackin, "Toshiko always tries to write a little bit beyond someone's playing level—so the player always has to be on the edge of the chair, learning how to play the piece. Then there is progress and growth. And since she writes for the individual players, the musical materials change as the players change; Toshiko writes for the colors that are available to her."[28]

It is interesting to note that Lew Tabackin's presence in Akiyoshi's band has frequently inspired audiences and critics to attribute her contributions to him. Often Tabackin has found himself explaining to audiences following a performance that the compositions are, indeed, entirely the creations of Toshiko Akiyoshi.

Strongly affected by the politics of cultures as well as by the more immediate presence of her band, Akiyoshi has determined that extra-musical elements play a particularly significant role in her current creative explorations. According to Lew Tabackin,

> About half of the music she is writing deals with something outside of the music itself, and tries to musically tell a story. This seems to go in cycles in her writing. She will work on a story concept and create an extended musical work, such as "Minimata," followed by what we call "relief pieces"—shorter, "lighter" pieces that do not have a poetic storyline. As a player, I have often asked Toshiko to tell me as much as possible about the story concepts of her larger works, so that I could come up with the right kinds of musical interpretations as a player. I wanted to absorb the information and transform those abstract ideas into a different abstract form, in music.[29]

Akiyoshi's program notes for her programmatic works reveal the detail and clarity of her philosophical-musical interests in more extended works. For example, the notes about "Two Faces of a Nation" on the recently released *European Memoirs* album (1983), describe the composer's coming-to-terms with post-World-War II German society.

> On this tour we played several small, old cities of Germany. . . . The charm of these picturesque towns and the warmth of the people conjured up visions of an old, innocent, carefree Germany. How in this setting could events have taken such a tragic, inhuman turn? This piece reflects the universal duality of man. All nations have potential for great achievements, but also for incredible evil. The composition ["Two Faces of a Nation"] is in two parts. Part one expresses happier, carefree times. Part two, the tragic horror to follow . . . use of Japanese Noh voices emphasizes the universality of the message.[30]

As Lew Tabackin sums up Akiyoshi's constant frame of reference, "She doesn't write in a vacuum."[31]

The complexity and virtuosity of Toshiko Akiyoshi's music present many challenges to performers. At a panel discussion Akiyoshi and Tabackin were asked, "How come your music is so damn hard?" They responded, "It is just a matter of the time and effort you put into it: today it's difficult;

Figure 9.6 Toshiko Akiyoshi in performance. By permission of Akiyoshi.

tomorrow it's easy."[32] Also commenting on the difficulty of her music, Akiyoshi says she considers herself to be "a musical amateur in the true sense of the word, because I do music for the sake of the music, and try to have the practical considerations at a minimum, spending as much time as is needed rehearsing a piece. If the music doesn't sound right, it is better to put it away for a while, and then go back to it, and it will sound better."[33]

Akiyoshi's path is clearly on an open road into the future of music toward yet more innovative jazz and a further integration of her multicultural identity into her musical works. She looks forward to expanding the multi-media aspects of composition in future works and hopes to write music for dance companies and other artistic collaborations. In the meantime, Akiyoshi has frequent tours to Europe and Japan, and she performs in the United States at jazz festivals and in jazz clubs. Her record company, Ascent, is an ongoing project, and she is encouraged that she has been able to generate enough income from record sales and concerts to continue to create albums. Although big band music is currently at a low ebb in terms of its general popularity in America, Akiyoshi's popularity in Japan and in Europe is steadily escalating. It is inevitable that she will continue to achieve recognition and success in a musical arena where few women have ventured.

Toshiko Akiyoshi's musical work constitutes her lifelong personal credo and directive. And jazz is the music that is her own, by her artistic birthright. Her work has spanned nearly four decades, and yet, as the composer notes, "I think the music in our (the band's) library has an advantage in being all the work of just one writer. It has its own character, so that regardless of age, it sounds as though it could have been written today."[34]

NOTES

1. Material from author's interview with Toshiko Akiyoshi and Lew Tabackin, February 1984.

2. Ibid.

3. Ibid.

4. Bill Hochkeppel, "Tasteful Sounds: The Toshiko-Tabackin Big Band," *The Instrumentalist* (April 1984), p. 22.

5. Material from author's interview with Toshiko Akiyoshi and Lew Tabackin, February 1984.

6. Hochkeppel, "Tasteful Sounds," p. 21.

7. Leonard Feather, *The New Edition of the Encyclopedia of Jazz* (New York: Horizon Press, 1960), p. 98.

8. Hochkeppel, "Tasteful Sounds," p. 23.

9. Material from author's interview with Toshiko Akiyoshi and Lew Tabackin, February 1984.

10. Author interviews with Lew Tabackin, winter 1984-85.

11. Leonard Feather, "Toshiko Akiyoshi: The Leader of the Band," *Ms. Magazine,* November 1978, p. 35.

12. Author's interviews with Lew Tabackin, 1984.

13. Sally Placksin, *American Women in Jazz: 1900 to the Present* (New York: Wideview Books, 1982), p. 222.

14. Author's interviews with Lew Tabackin, 1984-85.

15. Ibid.

16. Leonard Feather, *The Encyclopedia of Jazz in the Sixties* (New York, Horizon Press, 1966), p. 204.

17. John Wilson, "Tokyo Jazz Pianist Plays Here," *New York Times,* 27 April 1961.

18. Author's interview with Toshiko Akiyoshi and Lew Tabackin, February 1984.

19. Feather, *The Encyclopedia of Jazz in the Sixties,* p. 51.

20. Bryna Taubman, "Jazz is Her Way of Life," *New York Post,* 4 October 1967.

21. Author's interviews with Lew Tabackin, 1984.
22. Hochkeppel, "Tasteful Sounds," p. 23.
23. Leonard Feather, record liner notes, *Kogun,* New York, RCA Records 1978.
24. Ibid.
25. Ibid.
26. Leonard Feather, record liner notes, *Insights,* New York, RCA Records, 1978.
27. Author's interviews with Lew Tabackin, 1984-85.
28. Ibid.
29. Ibid.
30. Record liner notes, *European Memoirs,* Ascent, 1983.
31. Author's interviews with Lew Tabackin, 1984.
32. Ibid.
33. Author's interviews with Toshiko Akiyoshi and Lew Tabackin, 1984.
34. Akiyoshi quoted by Leonard Feather in record liner notes, *Kogun,* RCA Records, 1978.

SELECTED DISCOGRAPHY

The task of compiling a complete Akiyoshi discography is particularly complex due to the numerous reissues of her work on various labels in both Japan and the U.S.A. The present discography was compiled by Catherine Overhauser, with the assistance of Laura Koplewitz, Lew Tabackin, Dan Morgenstern (Director, Institute of Jazz Studies at Rutgers University), and Jan Leder (*Women in Jazz,* Westport, CT: Greenwood Press, 1985). Much of the information from this discography was drawn from Walter Bruyninckx's ongoing work, *Jazz Discography: Modern Jazz: Be-Bop/Hard Bop/West Coast.* Vol. I, A-D (Project: Mechelen, Belgium, 1984).

Japanese releases are indicated by (Jap) immediately preceding the record number. Recording dates and places refer to the actual recording session(s), *not* the eventual release(s).

Solo and Small Ensemble

Amazing Toshiko Akiyoshi. Verve MGN22, (Jap)MV2579; Norgran EPN-47, EPN-48. Tokyo, 1954.

The Toshiko Trio. Storyville SLP912, SLP916; Trio (Jap) PA6133. Boston, 1954.

Jam Session for Musicians III: The historic Mocambo Session '54 Vol. 3: Toshiko at Mocambo. Polydor (Jap)MPF1029. Yokohama, 1954.

Jam Session for Musicians III: The historic Mocambo Session '54, Vol. 4. Polydor (Jap)MPF1070. Yokohama, 1954.

Toshiko, Her Trio and Quartet. Storyville SLP918; Trio (Jap)PA6134. Boston, 1956.

Amazing Toshiko Akiyoshi (also *Newport '57*). Verve MGV8236; Col (E) 33CX10110, (Jap)MV2579. Newport, 1957.

The Many Sides of Toshiko. Verve MGV8273, (Jap)MV2567; Col (E)LB10098; SEB10107. New York, 1957.

United Notions (also *Toshiko and Her International Jazz Sextet).* Metrojazz E1001; MGM (Jap)MM2087. New York, 1958.

Toshiko-Mariano Quartet. Candid CM8012, CS9012; Jazzman 8000. New York, 1960.

Long Yellow Road. Asahi Sonorama E23. Tokyo, 1961.

Toshiko Meets Her Old Pals. King (Jap)SKC3, K20P6104. Tokyo, 1961.

Untitled. United Artists VAJ14024. New York (Town Hall), 1962.

Untitled. Vic (Jap)JV5084. Tokyo, 1963.

Country & Western Jazz Piano's Toshiko Akiyoshi-Steve Kuhn [also *Together*] Dauntless DM4308, 6308; [Chi CR 2026]. New York, 1963.

West Side Story: Toshiko-Mariano Quartet. Takt Jazz 12. Tokyo, 1963.

Untitled. Vee Jay VJ2505. Tokyo, 1964.

Buddy Rich & Louis Bellson Accompanied by the George Kawaguchi Orchestra. Roost (S)LP2263. Tokyo, 1965.

Toshiko's Lullaby. Col (Jap)PS1185. Tokyo, 1965.

Toshiko at Top of the Gate. Col (Jap)XMS10008CT; Takt XM510008CT. New York, 1968.

Untitled. Liberty (Jap)LPC8049. Osaka, 1970.

Untitled. Dan (Jap)VC6001. Tokyo, 1971.

Sumie. Vic (Jap)CD4B-5007. Tokyo, 1971.

Toshiko Akiyoshi: Solo Piano. RCA (Jap)6270, JPL1-0399. Tokyo, 1971.

Dedications. Disco Mate (Jap)DSP5001. Hollywood, 1976.

Dedications II. Disco Mate (Jap)DSP5006; Inner City IC6046. Los Angeles, 1977.

Toshiko Akiyoshi Plays Billy Strayhorn. Disco Mate (Jap)DSP5001; Jazz American Marketing JAM-5003. Los Angeles, 1978.

Finesse. Concord Jazz CJ69. Hollywood, 1978.

Notorious Tourist from the East [also *Toshiko Plays Toshiko*] Inner City IC6066; [Disco Mate (Jap)DSP5014]. Hollywood, 1978.

Just Be-Bop. Disco Mate (Jap)DSP8102. 1980.

Tuttie Flutie. Disco Mate (Jap)DSP8107. Hollywood, 1980.

Toshiko Akiyoshi Trio. Toshiba EMI. 1983.

Time Stream. Toshiba EMI. 1984.

Women in Jazz: Vol. 2: Pianists. Stash ST112. No date.

Toshiko Akiyoshi-Lew Tabackin Big Band

Kogun. RCA JLP1-0236, AFL1-3019, RCA 6246. Hollywood, 1974.

Long Yellow Road. RCA JLP1-1350, AFL1-1350, RCA 6296. New York, 1974 and 1975.

Tales of a Courtesan. RCA JLP1-0723, AFL1-0723; RCA (Jap)RVP6004. Los Angeles, 1975.

Road Time. RCA CLP2242; RCA 9115. Tokyo, 1976.

Insights [also *Sumi-e*]. Vic AFL1-2678; RCA (Jap)RVP6106; [Baystate (Jap)RVJ6061]; [RCA (F)PL45363]. Hollywood, 1976.

March of the Tadpoles. RCA (Jap)RVP6178. Hollywood, 1977.

Toshiko Akiyoshi-Lew Tabackin Big Band Live at Newport '77. RCA

(Jap)RVJ6005; RCA (F)PL40821. Newport Jazz Festival, 1977.

Live at Newport II. RCA (Jap)RVJ-6088. Newport Jazz Festival, 1977.

Salted Gingko Nuts. Insights (Jap)RVJ-6031. Los Angeles, 1978.

Sumi-e. Insights (Jap)RVJ6061; RCA (F)PL37537. Saitama, 1979.

Farewell to Mingus (also *Farewell*]. RCA (Jap)RVJ-6078; Jazz America Marketing JAM-003; [Ascent ASC1000]. Los Angeles, 1980.

From Toshiko With Love. Baystate (Jap)RJL8016. Los Angeles, 1981.

Tanuki's Night Out. Jazz America Marketing JAM-006. Los Angeles, 1981.

European Memoirs. Baystate (Jap)RJL8036. Los Angeles, 1982.

Ten Gallon Shuffle (Toshiko Akiyoshi Jazz Orchestra Featuring Lew Tabackin). Ascent ASC1004. Los Angeles, 1984.

My Elegy. Pioneer Electronic Corp. (Jap)SM068-0031 (Laser Disc). Tokyo, 1984.

BIBLIOGRAPHY

Akiyoshi, Toshiko. Press Biography furnished by Toshiko Akiyoshi/Lew Tabackin.

Bruyninckx, Walter. *Jazz Discography: Modern Jazz: Be-Bop/Hard Bop/West Coast, Vol. 4, A-D.* Mechelen (Belgium), Project, 1984.

Corry, John. "Portrait of a Japanese Woman And Her Life in Jazz." *New York Times.* 22 December 1985.

Dahl, Linda. *Stormy Weather, The Music and Lives of a Century of Jazzwomen.* New York, Pantheon Books, 1984.

Feather, Leonard. *The Encyclopedia of Jazz in the Sixties.* New York, Horizon Press, 1966.

______. Liner Notes. *Kogun.* New York, RCA Records, 1978.

______. Liner Notes. *Salted Gingko Nuts.* New York, Ascent Records, 1982.

______. *The New Edition of the Encyclopedia of Jazz.* New York, Horizon Press, 1960.

______. "Toshiko Akiyoshi: The Leader of the Band." *Ms. Magazine.* (November 1978), pp. 34-40.

Hochkeppel, Bill. "Tasteful Sounds: The Toshiko-Tabackin Big Band", *The Instrumentalist* (April 1984), pp. 21-26.

Keepnews, Peter. "Personality Would Help This Band." *New York Post.* 27 June 1983.

Leder, Jan. *Women in Jazz: A Discography of Instrumentalists, 1913-1968.* Westport, Conn., Greenwood Press, 1985.

Lynch, Kevin. "Best Big Jazz Band Off To a Slow Start." *Milwaukee Journal.* 5 April 1983.

Pareles, Jon. "Pop: Piano Solos by Miss Akiyoshi." *New York Times.* 2 September 1983.

Placksin, Sally. *American Women in Jazz: 1900 to The Present.* New York: Wideview Books, 1982. Pp. 222-23, 250-51.

Tabackin, Lew. Three Interviews in New York City with Laura Koplewitz. Transcripts of approximately 75 pages, 1984.

Taubman, Bryna. "Jazz is Her Way of Life." *New York Post.* 4 October 1967.

Wilson, John S. "'New' Band in Debut at Carnegie." *New York Times.* 27 June 1983.

Wilson, John. "Tokyo Jazz Pianist Plays Here." *New York Times.* 27 April, 1961.

10

Composers Speaking for Themselves: An Electronic Music Panel Discussion

JUDITH ROSEN

On Saturday, 28 March 1981, a group of women active in the composition of electronic and computer music formed a panel of speakers at the First International Congress of Women in Music, held at New York University. The panel, moderated by composer Ruth Anderson, consisted of composers Tera de Marez Oyens, Liz Phillips, Alice Shields, Daria Semegen, Maryanne Amacher, Beverly Grigsby, and Laurie Spiegel, who were joined by Otto Luening, a pioneer in the field. Together these composers represented a microcosm of the history of electronic music, presenting a variety of approaches to the medium spanning the range of techniques used over the past 30 years.

During this time electronic music has developed into a viable art form, which has advanced rapidly. It continues to grow at such a fast rate that some of the techniques discussed in early 1981 are already outdated. Similarly, many of the panelists' hopes, projections, and even fantasies for improved systems have now become reality. Each of these composers has gone on to perfect her craft and her art, and just as they represented the variety of methods used by composers of electronic music in 1981, they are equally representative now.

In trying to recapture the spirit and enthusiasm generated that day, I have tried to stay as close as possible to the spoken word, in some cases choosing context and content over written form. While this sometimes may have resulted in either a more simplistic or a more verbose treatise than would have been the case had the panelists not spoken extemporaneously, I believe it has helped to preserve the individuality of each speaker's personal "voice" as well as the flavor of that historic day.

Ruth Anderson: I want to welcome all of you to this forum on electronic music. First, I want to tell you something of our panel members, and then I'll just briefly ask them to tell two things: first, something about the equipment with which they work or the studio where they are working; and second, something about their own work. We have represented here an extraordinary variety of electronic resources and compositional concepts and a remarkably distinguished panel. But before we begin, I want to introduce to you our very honored guest, Otto Luening. [Applause]

Otto Luening: I am very happy to be here for various reasons. In the first place it's really nice to see how successfully this Congress has been going. I feel it very strongly because I have been in the business for a long time (since the thirties) of educating women, both in college and in private study. Many things that are represented by this Congress were not so easy to achieve in the thirties. So I want to say just a word or two about it, because I think you'll feel very much encouraged.

The history of music and the arts in this country would be a sad commentary had it not been for the women of our nineteenth century and early twentieth century. The country needed their vision in order to achieve certain things at that time. Of course, these things become a habit, but in the thirties, when I used to work with the young students at Bennington and try to get them to write music, although they could recognize some of the classical women composers: Mrs. Beach, Dame Ethel Smyth, Augusta Holmès and people like that, they were afraid to tackle this field themselves. Finally, I got them going by example: reading poetry by Emily Dickinson and Edna St. Vincent Millay; showing them pictures that had been done by women painters; and so on, and explaining: "Look, they have something to say. I think that you should just look to them – and you'll get going." It wasn't too long before they began accepting the writing of music as another way of communication. And, of course, from this momentum, then gradually things emerge and talents come and people develop, and so on. Of course this happened in a broad sense all over the place. I recall also when I got my diploma way back in 1919 at the Zurich Conservatory, one of the pieces that I played with the Zurich Orchestra was Chaminade's *Concertino* for flute. It was a risky thing to do, you know, but it was a very good flute piece. I played it based on that, and my teacher backed me up.

Since that time things have improved enormously. We are now at the point—a very good point here at this conference and with this panel—where in the new field of electronic music and computer music, we can see the results of what has been done in the last 25 years. Again, it started with nothing and look at where we are now; so it's most encouraging, and one feels good about it. And *particularly* at this stage, the women at this Congress had the brilliant concept of exchanging ideas and telling each other what they have done, and what they are looking for, and giving some examples of these things. That was the kind of communication that we had in the twenties and thirties after the First World War, and it made contemporary music really work and really live. I think you should be congratulated on the fact that you've done this; that you're willing to talk to each other and you're willing to discuss these things, instead of everybody crawling into his or her own corner and producing masterpieces (or maybe not masterpieces), but suffering through this whole thing without having the benefit of mutual experience and an exchange of ideas. I know that I'm going to learn a great deal here this afternoon. [Applause]

RA: You well understand that Otto Luening is a feminist who is a humanist. . . . This is the way this remarkable man has lived his life—in generous support of other composers and of musicians. And I am sure very often he sacrificed his own time from his own elegant and fascinating and living composition. I am deeply grateful that you are here.

OL: Thank you very much.

RA: I want to introduce next Tera de Marez Oyens who has come from Utrecht and who has worked at the Institute of Sonology [Instituut voor Sonologie]. She is going to talk about writing for electronic and acoustic instruments. I'll bring your voice to you. [Moves microphone closer.]

Tera de Marez Oyens: Thank you. I studied indeed at the Institute of Sonology in Utrecht, but at that time it was still called the Studio of Electronic Music of the University of Utrecht. I studied with Gottfried Michael Koenig, and he was a very fine teacher. The Institute was founded afterwards. It is a very well-equipped institute, and composers from all over the world come there to work or to study. There are four or five studios, a computer center, and a technical staff for repairs, for services, and also for new inventions. This, because it happens sometimes that a composer wants a special sound or a special process that doesn't exist yet and the staff is so—it's difficult to find a word in English—versatile in finding the particular sound the composer wants, even if this requires a new apparatus.

I started by composing pure electronic music, and I must admit something. I must tell you a secret, but don't tell it to anybody else. I make electronic compositions the way I drive a car. People say I'm a very good driver, but if the car should break down and stop, I have to walk because I don't know what to do. I have no idea what's going on in the car. The same is true of my electronic compositions. I know which knob to turn. I know what to plug in to get the sound I want—but don't ask me what the name of the apparatus is and what is happening inside because I don't have the faintest idea! I'm not technically minded at all.

I switched to a combination of electronics and acoustical instruments for a practical reason. I don't know how it is here, but in Holland electronic concerts were a very dangerous adventure. You would have to do your very best to get people interested in going to an electronic music concert, and, when they were finally in the concert hall, there was a lot of embarrassment and hilarity. First of all the sounds were very new and, secondly, where were they to look? There was no orchestra, no soloists; so they looked at the ceiling, at the floor, and at each other. They would close their eyes to be very concentrated, or they read the program over and over. So I thought we must make it a little bit easier for them. We must help them to focus the eyes and to let the eyes participate with the ears. The first work that I made to help them a little bit was called *Photophonie.* In that work I used eight light sources together with an electronic tape. There was also a score for the light sources. You could not just switch them on the moment you wanted; you had to do it slowly and go back so that every sound of the music was congruent with a light pattern. It went well; people had something to look at, and they liked it. Then I started other electronic works. One, for instance, was in combination with a choir. I did this as follows: I first made a recording of the choir performing a whole composition. Then I took the recording of that choir and reworked it electronically and also added some electronic sounds—but it was still not ready. Then I had the choir situated on the stage, and from four sides they got the sounds over them and had to react to that while singing again what they had already sung. Can you follow me? It's a little bit complicated to tell; for me it's very clear.

I made some other electro-acoustic compositions: a combination with percussion and a work that's called *Trio* for bass clarinet, percussion, and tape. The latest I wrote was a work for horn and tape. I knew very little about the horn, so I studied very hard to know what you can do with this instrument. It was a horn player who had asked me to compose this work. He gives a lot of solo concerts, and he said you have to play and play and play and your lips get tired, and you have no more breath, so I wanted to give him pauses. I made a tape for him so that he could catch his breath. I did a little bit of the same process as with the choir piece. I recorded some sounds of the horn and rewrote them electronically, and the horn player had to react to that. But in this case the score was exactly notated. Maybe I have talked too long already. [Applause]

RA: No, this is wonderful. Thank you, thank you very much. Liz Phillips is sitting here, and she is going to speak about [sound] installations.

Liz Phillips: Thank you. I make installations using sound. Originally, I started in sculpture, making traditional sculpture and then environmental sculpture; I started to use electronic sound when I wanted to change spaces over time and have a concept of three-dimensional space in the piece, but also a concept of actual time spans built into the work. So I make pieces that are as much sound sculpture as music. The way they work is that there are metal plates in a room that are shaped, and they project fields into the space. People moving in those fields—like the way the old Theremin worked, but very much expanded fields—change sound depending upon where they are in the space and how long they are in the space and how fast they are moving. The sounds they change are electronic or processed sound from the environment.

I've always worked that way, never with tape and very little with instruments.

OL: Do you work this way with dance too?

LP: Yes, sometimes, but mostly with audience. When I began this work, my ideas were to describe certain three-dimensional spaces and to use sound as a material: sound as a signal, but as a signal that you could listen to over a long period of time and sounds that would change over time. Electronic sound and these electronic fields were the only method of working this way, and so I almost came to music via a back door.

As I've used sound—and it's the material I use—I've learned more and more about how to make pieces work in [dimensional] space and in acoustic space. The electronics I've used specifically are often homemade, custommade circuits that sense the environment. Then to those I add traditional synthesizer modules. I first built them all myself, but now I have most of them built for me by Serge Modular. (Serge Tcherepnin is a composer, and his father was also a composer.) He builds beautiful electronics for composers to use, so when I can afford to, I order from him; otherwise, I build it myself. But it's very simple synthesizer stuff. I've been working with electronic music technology since I was 19, and I feel that it's just another tool. Technology is just technique, and I feel very comfortable with it. I think anybody can use electronics. What you're dealing with is a potential energy all the time, and in my pieces, which are always open to the environment, you're just channelling into that energy.

Lately, I've been working on a piece—a permanent installation—that will be in a windmill and is not audience-activated but wind-activated sound. The windmill is in the South Bronx on an alternative energy site. The piece is wind-powered and wind-activated; there are little anemometers that are like small windmills and generate tiny bits of power depending upon the wind speed, and there are weather vanes that pick up the wind direction at different levels, different heights, in the air. I use those changes to change sounds that radiate from the 60-foot-high steel tube that holds up the windmill. So it's tuned; it's like a giant instrument. It fades on in the morning with the sun and it fades off in the evening with the sun. The permanent piece opens May thirteenth. [Applause]

RA: I want to introduce one of the first people I met in the Columbia University electronic music studio, Alice Shields.

Alice Shields: I work at the Columbia-Princeton Electronic Music Center where I teach electronic music one-to-one. To describe the studio is a little difficult. There are actually three studios at Columbia—more or less with the same equipment—and they each have four stereo tape recorders, four loud speakers, a large mixing panel, and various pieces of synthesizer equipment like Buchla synthesizers.

There's obviously a great variety of equipment there, but what I've found in working with electronic music is that it's not so much what you have in the way of equipment, it's what you do with it. This becomes very plain when you hear a lot of computer music. Many things can be done with it, but as it is now, in my opinion, it's still very limited aesthetically. We're only just now getting to the point where we can use this kind of technology, not to overwhelm or negate the existence of ordinary instruments but as an addition to them. And that's the way I think of electronic music, particularly the use that I've made of the voice in electronic music.

I've tried to extend the capacity of the human voice electronically by varying tapes of myself singing, speaking, screaming. My specialty, I guess you could say, is the voice and the use of the voice electronically. I made one piece called *The Transformation of Ani*, which uses only my own voice speaking and singing the words of the text, and I chopped up my voice—sustaining tones through the Buchla Synthesizer—and made attacks that no human could impose upon his or her voice—very percussive attacks—and transposed these sounds down through the use of speed variation equipment so that they would become like drums or like bass brass instruments of some sort. I also use instrumental sounds. I'm fonder of using nonelectronic sound sources. To me electronic sounds don't have enough richness in them.

In one piece, *Coyote*, which is in the installation here [a continuous program of taped and recorded works by women was part of this Congress], I've used the prelude from *Lohengrin* backwards and slowed it down to give a very mysterious string-type effect. I'm particularly interested in the ritualistic aspects of music and how these can be gotten at electronically. In *The Transformation of Ani*, I've taken the scribe Ani's words from the *Egyptian Book of the Dead* and have a voice read them in a very dead tone surrounded by multiple voices singing and speaking and responding to these words. What takes place during this piece is that the scribe Ani translates himself from corporeal form to spiritual form by chanting these words. In *Coyote*—this is part of my opera, *Shaman*, which is for live voices and electronic tape that I have an NEA grant to write—a shaman translates himself from human form to coyote form and back again. In the middle of the piece I have some coyote yells which I took from a particular coyote I found in Utah—a very cute doglike creature who was chained in the desert and cared for by his master. Anyway, this coyote screams in the middle of my piece as the shaman translates himself into coyote form.

I've been a professional singer myself, and I feel that electronic music has something to offer the instrumentalist as an extension of the instrumental technique. I believe this is electronic music's very important role in contemporary music. [Applause]

RA: Next, I want to introduce Daria Semegen who is going to talk about hybrid studios and her own work.

Daria Semegen: At this time I'm teaching at Stony Brook [State University of New York at Stony Brook], and I also work there in the electronic music studio. We have recently acquired, in addition to our basic set-up of about five studios, three large studios and two smaller studios which are analog studios using typical synthesizer and classic studio equipment of the analog sort. We also have a hybrid system which [Donald] Buchla had installed last April. We've been fortunate to have this latest model; it's a knock-out unit. We've gotten tremendous results from this system, and we hope to expand upon the types of things we can do with it year by year.

It's a system with a tremendous amount of growth potential. With the digital-analog hybrid system, it's possible to hear the sounds immediately and have some improvisatory control as well as a tremendous amount of accuracy in terms of pitch and rhythmic patterns and so on. I think that anyone who has worked with computers can appreciate the amount of accuracy and precision one can get, and also the scope of control, in that sense. The analog portion also provides the possibility of improvising to some extent, perhaps in real time performance. Since we don't really do any live performance, most of the work done in our studio ends up on tape simply for the sake of being distributed for performance at other schools or for radio broadcasts.

As for myself, I became interested in electronic music without actually knowing it. This was around 1965 as an undergraduate student at the Eastman School of Music, which is a fairly conservative place—at least it was at that time. I had met a guy who was involved in doing recording sessions and who is now a professional recording engineer in New York City. He had a tape recorder, and I had an idea of recording sounds from instruments on tape and then manipulating the tape: having the live ensemble play against a kind of modified or metamorphosed version of itself with different kinds of rhythms, and speeding up and slowing down the instruments to such an extent that they would be extensions or compressions of what the live instruments could actually do. Well, I remember we put this on a concert at Eastman in '65 and our audience walked out! I wasn't discouraged at all by this because it was an extremely fascinating sort of thing to get involved in. When I got to Columbia-Princeton, I worked on electronic music and used classic studio techniques primarily (which, at that point, was without a synthesizer). Later I did introduce some synthesizer sounds into my music.

To me, there is one very interesting aspect of electronic music, and that is regardless of where my source material comes from—whether it's a computer source, or it's purely analog from old oscillators using source material, or synthesizer—I still feel that the composer has to have poetic license in being able to take the tape that the material is recorded on and being able to splice it. I still have an approach that the razor blade is very much like a painter's brush, so that I'm able to change sounds around. I'm less of a purist than some people might be in that if there's a computer program, the whole thing ends up on tape: both the music resulting from the creation and from the program; one has a tendency not to want to touch the tape. I like to get my hands on it. There's always something I want to punctuate, to change around. I think it's very important. Also, this way it's possible to create hybrid sounds, which do not exist, coming from a gadget. Any kind of gadget unit, no matter how sophisticated it is itself, and in the way it's used, still produces a certain type of sound. And if you're interested in expanding, you might be doing a lot of mixing, or juxtapositioning different kinds of sounds which ordinarily would not occur coming out of a machine. So this is a very interesting idea for me, personally, to use in working with a source material and doing electronic music composition.

Most of my work so far has just been in pieces without any particular kind of program, except for one piece [*Arc*] which was done for dance. That was a very, very specific sort of piece, as I was working from a choreographer's score. The choreographer actually had graph paper and had worked out beats and tempos, including a computer-driven and computer-synchronized lighting system for the various pulsations of the dance. The music came after the choreography was done and was basically background enhancement to what was going on in the choreography. This was quite a feat to do for me, not having had to do music beat by beat, so it took much work with the synthesizer and also lots of splicing to make things extra accurate. Boy, did I wish I had a computer at that point! It would have given me all those pulsations with a high degree of accuracy.

Currently, I'm working on a piece for live performer, viola, and electronic music sounds. In this piece I have a tendency to use very large, almost orchestral sounding, background layers of music. So rather then, perhaps, having an attitude that the instrument is being extended by using electronic music sounds, the electronic sounds are kind of a background (though sometimes they come into the foreground) and the instrument is weaving in and out of the material in a very luxurious kind of way. At this point my feeling about the expression of the string instrument that is involved in this piece concerns itself with long lines as opposed to very active, maybe neurotic-sounding material which one can also get out of string playing. So it's interesting to work with this sort of situation. Having done only instrumental pieces and then only electronic pieces without any performer, I have found that there is a tremendous difference psychologically for me. Usually, I go into the studio. There are four walls; there is equipment; there's no feedback from a person; there's no performer; there's no interpreter involved in having to play my electronic music. I do the pieces very much as a sculptor may sculpt a work or a painter might paint a painting.

I refer to the electronic music work that I do as more "plastic arts" than something which is a performance: a musical performance that involves perhaps doing the instrumental music score with a lot of consideration for the types of notation to be interpreted by the performers. So it's a different sort of thing. You're not involved with performers in doing just straight tape music, whereas in instrumental music you do have a communication, and I feel this is a constantly variable situation from performance to performance. You have different players; perhaps, it's a different day. Even with the same players, they can feel differently, so the performance is slightly different. With a piece on tape it's very much like a painting, so I have a different relation to it. Anyhow, that's the way I feel at this point about what's going on in my work. [Applause]

RA: Next, we have Maryanne Amacher who will talk about "perceptual geography."

Maryanne Amacher: For me, one of the very useful features of working with electronic instrumentation has been the opportunity of hearing sounds experientially and working with them in real time. Except for my early composing years, all my work—both research and composition—has developed from direct listening experiences—hearing, observing, studying actual acoustic phenomena, and in some cases, the so-called "psychoacoustic" effects on the listener.

In this work, listening and observing sound structures is very much like that of a microbiologist observing cell structures for many, many hours—looking at "life within," to discover and understand its special features, order of shapes, and unique intelligence before composing new theories or rearrangements. This has been much easier to accomplish then if I were to attempt to carry out this kind of work with instrumentalists. Time is mine this way. And I need it. That I could actually spend, if I wanted, ten to a hundred hours in real time listening and trying to understand things, has been vital to almost everything I've done.

I'm deeply intrigued by what I do not understand. And there is much I do not understand about music. Very basic questions concern me. Sometimes I believe that I really am a composer because I am trying to do just this—to understand what I do not as yet understand, but am deeply intrigued by: the attraction of music to minds' responses. In composing I am really pursuing "the study of music;" through music I am able to observe many facets of human sensitivity.

For instance, as I was coming here today in a taxi, the cab driver was playing the radio and this incredible music was coming out—all tinkling bells and little rhythms. The assumption in this society that we have to have music everywhere, or in fact that people need it, is something that I guess I have never understood. Even as a child, I never understood why they played nursery rhymes because I really didn't like them!

Later, when I started studying harmony, what I really wanted to know was what was *inside* the sounds. Knowing the name and recognizing that it was a V or a IV chord wasn't enough. Names were not enough. I really wanted to know what the chords were made of; to describe them *physically,* and I never learned that in my musical background at all. I later learned that this information was found in the field of acoustics, not music. I felt that much of my musical background and often music, itself, obscured much of the physical nature of sound that I wished to know about. I needed to crack the cover. So it was really exciting for me when I first could go into [an electronic music] studio and listen and be able to try [sound] combinations and to study acoustics. I developed my first pieces after understanding some of these things, and it still goes on and on.

Human beings respond to music in many ways which are now known. These may have been a mystery or considered subjective some years ago, but no longer. Yet, to be familiar with such known responses to music and sound is considered the domain of the psychoacoustician, not the composer!

The terrible truth is, we live in a time that calls *human response tones* "psychoacoustic phenomena!" That tells a lot about us! Such tones and patterns originate and "sound" *within* the listener's ear and mind in response to tones sounding in the room. They are tones the listener *creates*, like another instrument joining the orchestra. Although everyone experiences them, usually they are not consciously acknowledged by composers or listeners. They are still considered "mysterious," psychoacoustic phenomena—something for psychoacousticians to know about, not for composers or listeners to recognize *consciously* and enjoy *creating*!

Composers are supposed to know how to move their tones around successfully, but act dumb while unconsciously manipulating the minds and feelings of others. The advertising industry at least owns up to this—acknowledges mind's sensitivity. Like the idiot savant, a composer need not understand too much, only proceed with whatever programs are "learned by heart." It is assumed that professional musicians and composers need only know how to count; to recognize and name notes, tones, and chords, etc., but really not be concerned with their physical making: what they are as energy; all the complex and beautiful events taking place within the timbres. In truth, what composing usually amounts to is really nothing more than a rearranging and modifying of musical patterns, i.e., "other men's tunes," and giving them a *personalized sequence in time.* The silicon composers will very soon be doing this—and much better and faster!

Today in the adult professional world we still identify music as thinking of it as "electronic, instrumental, concrète, computer, pop, minimal, expressionist." All names and procedures again! It's about imitation really! They tell little! Did you know—someone told me—Stravinsky identified himself on his passport as a "professional translator"!

Why not descriptions about the energy or physics of the music? We are dealing with the spectrum and its energies. The wave length we feel in air for middle C is 4 feet BIG, and 19 feet BIG in water. Why don't we begin here with the spectrum itself, probe more deeply its energies, and create our shapes from this basis instead of snatching the figures of "other men's music"?

I wanted to learn more about "ways of hearing," i.e., the many ways we hear and perceive sound and light in open space. For example, hearing sound far away, close up, very near beside our nose, etc. And what seems to be "sounding" in our mind after the sound disappears—the effects of aftersound, the tunes you remember, the ones you forget.

The object of this was to learn to compose spatial dimensions in my music—the kind we experience in life—but usually not in music. There really do not exist many musical models for this. Usually musicians are in one place, on the stage, or together in one spot, whereas in an outdoor environment we hear sound from many directions and in many different ways and thus perception has many modes which trigger a great variety of different mental states.

To study this I install microphones in outdoor and sometimes indoor environments which have a special acoustic, and I arrange for the sound to come "live" directly to my studio through open 15 kc [kilocycle] high-fidelity telephone lines. This way I can listen under many different circumstances—concentratedly, casually, while resting, eating, just living with these acoustic spaces. For three years I had a microphone installed at the Boston Harbor, and most of the good work that I was able to do there was late at night, when things would really quiet down, and it was possible to hear very clearly some of the special spatial dimensions that interested me. I learned much about time and structure that way, which I had wanted to examine more deeply. Why we choose to have one sequence follow another one in music, and not a different one, always puzzled me. I wanted to probe past what I knew from [already-identified] musical styles and my musical background. I could now relate these observations to more basic responses.

I should make it clear I did this work not because I was interested in environmental sound nor that I wished to create what it is like at the

Boston Harbor, nor was I particularly interested in the kinds of sounds that I would receive from places like this. But what I did want was to observe the many different ways of hearing and what they created perceptually—observing my own mind and interpreting this energy over time and in a variety of conditions.

My orientation has always been more like Varèse, starting with the physical nature of sound. This led me to continue working with electronic instrumentation. I wished to further investigate difference tones: beat patterns at the unison, octave, fifth, which I found to be very powerful. These were the early days of my work, and I would go from studio to studio attempting to tune these intervels with oscillators, which were always slipping out of tune. (I now have my own instruments to do this work.) Also then, working such long hours examinining the effects of these tunings, I was not sure if some of these effects that I was hearing were actually coming from the loud speakers or were in my head.

It was not until later that I discovered a wonderful article by Gerald Oster in *Scientific American* called "Auditory Beats in the Brain" [October 1973, volume 229, no. 4] describing how we respond to such intervals. That, in fact, these beat patterns do not exist in the room, but originate in the brain. The mind responds by putting the information together. What I would refer to in my notes by a variety of curious names (to facilitate my composing), such as "the melody within," "the coast," "the drift," were referred to by Oster as pattern modulations which are created in the mind. With pattern modulation we have a shape, or in other words, a melody, often in contrast to difference tones which arise in the cochlea of the ear and not in the brain. So though I had no knowledge of the psychoacoustic explanation for these at the time, now there was a reason for what I had heard.

I think it's extraordinary that we respond to music by creating new tones and shapes within our ears and brains. The simplest case is demonstrated when two sine waves sound, and we respond by creating three more tones in our ears. Such "tone sensations," created in our ears and brains, in response to many of the intervals in music, are known as "additional" tones because they are not the given acoustic tones sounding in the room, nor are they traditionally written in the score. However, because we "hear" and perceive them along with the given acoustic tones, they have long been a major part of our musical experience. In some cases difference tones are usually regarded as phenomena rather than tones the composer is consciously inducing with the pitches he selects. Traditional music theory acknowledges such "additional" tones merely as accidents, fall-outs of the real tones sounded by the instruments. Although their existence is well established by modern psychoacoustics, "additional" tones are still regarded as a subjective aspect in musical composition: something the listener creates, but not the composer, who, in fact, induces the existence of these tones intentionally or not by the acoustic intervals he selects for his music.

My music reinforces such "additional" tones consciously and cultivates interplays between tones that originate in the ears, the brain, and in the room. This is what I call "perceptual geography." My recent work is dedicated to finding ways to enhance such features in my music in the hope of creating a more conscious experience in the listener's creative response to music.

I also wonder why human beings seem to need music? Animals don't seem to need music as we do. Such questions as what is attracting us to music as a species—being fulfilled, satisfied, excited, dulled as we perceive music—probably underlie everything I'm pursuing.

When in the presence of music we seem biologically endowed with the need to create, to respond, by making response tones and shapes almost as if another instrument were joining the orchestra. Coded to respond this way to music, we need now to create new codes that will help us to respond consciously and find new energy through releasing what has been so long suppressed within our subliminal perception. Perhaps it is this creative role we play when experiencing music that is one of the reasons why the taxi driver and all of us seem to have a need for music. [Applause]

RA: Fascinating people. I want to introduce next someone I met in 1976 at the International Computer Music Conference in San Diego. A woman. There weren't many there, Laurie [Spiegel], as you commented about the last computer conference.

Laurie Spiegel: There were 65 papers [given] and 30 composers [represented], and not a single presentation by a woman. It was just really mind-blowing to me, but this is a topic which I may touch on afterwards.

RA: At that time this next composer had just started a very exciting program which she was ecstatic about (and which I think all teachers would be ecstatic about) called computer assisted instruction: CAI. Beverly Grigsby.

Beverly Grigsby: Thank you very much, Ruth.[1] Among the many programs that have been activated in the music department at California State University, Northridge [CSUN] are programs in computer assisted instruction in music. Incidentally, I was very happy to hear Maryanne's discussion, because we, in computer music composition, do work with perception and psychoacoustics. We study the basilar membrane; that is to say, we go into a whole study of the ear. We are doing quite a bit of work in space and location; some of the things that you were discussing, we are doing, and it's producing incredible compositions.

In 1977 I had the good fortune to win many grants. One of them, The California State University Chancellor's Maxi-Grant, financed a computer music studio at CSUN. At that time we were able to acquire a

Nova 3/12 with storage of five mega-bytes of memory that powered a synthesizer developed at Dartmouth. We have put together a studio which runs programs based on a hierarchy of three author languages. The simplest and most structured language called PLAY deals mainly with programs for nonmusic majors, and we are capable of inviting students in such courses as music appreciation and music involvement to participate and literally begin to work in composition and sound manipulation. Even though the students do not read music and have no ability to perform on any instrument, within a matter of a week or two they are "making music." And by the time the course is completed, they have a very good concept of rhythm, meter, time, pitch association, and the many parameters of sound. It's quite an exciting program. At first it was just experimental, but it is more and more apparent that it will eventually become a part of the music involvement program at CSUN.

We find that our TEACH language, the second in the hierarchy, gives our professors the ability to create tutorial programs in course form. Students taking such courses as ear-training, theory, and counterpoint on the computer (CAI), find the procedure very valuable for several reasons. For example, such self-paced programs take the pressure off the students by allowing them to work at their own level of competency. There's a tremendous dread among musicians when they are, so to speak, "put on the line" with sight-singing and dictation. There are people that can work very rapidly and have a natural gift; others find it very difficult, and the more pressured they become, the more difficult it becomes for them to respond in a positive fashion. With computer assisted instruction the ear-training programs we have developed are proving their worth by their efficiency, time-saving, and motivating factors. We find that within a matter of weeks the student can take dictation very fluently, because they are given time to just sit and work without any sort of pressure or condemnation. They are not put up against anybody else; they just work at their own speed. The entire fundamentals program has become so exciting that what we are doing at Northridge has now interested the Chancellor's Office.

The University group in experimental instruction, which presented my efforts with a grant in 1977-78, now, after three years, sees it as a very rewarding program. And we are beginning to move throughout the state of California with computer assisted instruction. We'll be meeting on April 24 at one of the universities as a group to form a council, and we hope within another year or so to have a network through our great CYBER unit. We have been fortunate enough in the state university system of California to acquire one of the most powerful computer networks outside of military installations in the country. We hope now to be able to run programs from each of our 19 universities. That's one of our dreams. We've worked very hard for it, and I think we are accomplishing it at this very moment.

Beyond our tutorial TEACH language and its programs, we have our SING language. All of these languages were more or less prototype situations, as was our hardware when it first came in. We've been developing it over the past three, four years, and it has reached a point now where we are about to make some big hardware and software changes—which is a mind-boggling situation. After you've settled down with one series of ideas, and it's time to move on, it means a tremendous number of hours of rehashing and transferring programs; just the thought of it gives me quavers and quakes. (I see someone smiling back there; he must know what it's like to change hardware and software along the line.) But at any rate we're looking forward to it because it will give us even more power to do what we are attempting to do to expand and improve our programs.

Our SING program, which is the highest in the hierarchy of author language, is devoted to computer composition. In teaching computer composition, the involvement in the parameters of sound that Maryanne referred to is intense. Interestingly enough, students come into the class preoccupied with writing notes and rhythms into the system, but before a few weeks are up they have grown tremendously interested in timbre and the ability to create "instruments": that is, producing combined colors that imitate acoustical instruments (but not necessarily), as well as timbres that go beyond acoustical sound. Also, there is involvement with the whole idea of space and location—to make sound come up to the middle of one's face, maybe sit on one's nose or move around in controlled space. Our studio houses a quadraphonic system.

At this particular time, we have a time-sharing unit of four terminals—actually five, one is a hard-copy terminal. We have ambition to move from here to 16 or 32 units. That will be, of course, for our CAI. But at the moment the composer has the utilization of all of this equipment and can run on 16 channels of information. The system uses John Chowning's algorithm—his procedure, which is a simple mathematical formula to create what we call FM. This produces a very complex sound-spectra which facilitates an emulation of acoustical and nonacoustical sound. The system also utilizes additive-synthesis and, of course, we can go on to do (with the great CYBER) direct synthesis—but mainly additive-synthesis and our FM are very useful in producing these wonderful timbral materials. Interestingly enough, in the few years that we have been working in FM and additive-synthesis, there has not been as much time spent in experimentation as in composition. I am very proud of that. Most studios, when they do have the facilities for experimentation, wind up extremely experimental and nobody composes. They just sit around experimenting with sound.

There is some experimentation at CSUN. At present the psychology department is extremely interested in two young men who are doing a very intuitive research project in perception. They are using the studio for their experimentation and will write a thesis based upon this work. But the composers in the studio are not experimenting, they are composing, and that thrills me. They already have been moving out into the nation, so to speak; one of the students has had his computer music presented at Festival Eight in Memphis, Tennessee, and last November another student was part of the conference on computer music held here in New York. So in just a few years their work in computer music has progressed sufficiently to be accepted at these festivals, and I'm very proud of what they are doing. We will present a big concert on the campus in May to display their efforts. There are several women who are in the compositional group that I expect to see at the next conference—their music, hopefully, will be accepted.

In general, I feel that Northridge has been very fortunate to have acquired a system that allows us not only to compose, but to work in computer assisted instruction and to have interdisciplinary action with psychology, digital engineering, and computer science. [Applause]

RA: This is a very high-powered panel. I wish I knew everything that everyone on it knows. I love the diversity, the different concepts, the different equipment.

Next is Laurie Spiegel who has done remarkable work at Bell Labs. . . . She'll use anything: ElectroComp analog, Apple Computers, and various digital synthesizers. She has also worked in video.

LS: A point was briefly raised here earlier which is a very important one. It's not the equipment; it's what you do with it that's important. We do have Otto Luening here, and if you're familiar with his works, like some of the very early tape delay things that he did with the flute in the early fifties which are still some of the nicest things in the idiom, and you compare them to the works that were done with the giant RCA later. . . . It's what you do musically that's important. I've worked with a lot of different kinds of musical technologies, and I still do. I still use paper; I use analog synthesizers . . . it depends upon what I'm trying to do. I get an idea musically and then I find the best way of realizing it. I went into music because I *heard* music, and it moved me, and it grabbed me, and I loved it; and I love counterpoint and rhythm and harmony and timbre, and sometimes I really get into one or another of them. I probably love counterpoint the best (although I'm beginning to get more and more interested in harmony again). But timbre, of course, is extremely important; it always has been for me.

I always would make things up whenever I had access to any instrument. Then as soon as I began learning notation, I began writing things down. As long as I could read it, I might as well write it. I went to Juilliard, and they had us sitting there with these big pieces of paper writing down all these symbols. I was writing orchestral scores that I knew I would never ever hear—and if you can't hear, you can't learn, because you've got to hear what you write and then you can learn much, much better and faster.

Then I was lucky to get access to the early hand-soldered, original Buchla Synthesizer that Mort Subotnick had set up at NYU [New York University] in the late sixties. I had some electronics background, maybe because my father really wanted a son. When I was nine he gave me a soldering iron, when all the other girls were getting dolls. And I was *really* glad I got the soldering iron. Anyway, when I got my hands on the synthesizer, music sort of went from black and white to color—literally—and I began composing with sounds directly. Then after several years I got very, very fed up with the kinds of problems Maryanne was talking about. Everything drifted. The main problem, of course, with analog equipment is that it has no memory, which means that in essence you have to do an improvisation and record it. Then you can edit it a little bit on tape, but you don't have the facility of really composing and working on something where you can go back and change one little note the way you can on paper. There you've got an eraser on the other end of the pencil, and you can erase one flag off that 64th note or whatever you want. With analog equipment (with tape as a storage) once eight voices are mixed together you can't go in and rebalance them just a hair; you can't decide this one should have been an F-sharp. You're stuck with it. Also, the kinds of logic and musical relationships you can work with on analog systems are very simplistic compared to what you can do with digital systems.

But, I was very fortunate. Having previously known Emmanuel Ghent and Max Mathews at The Kitchen in New York, I was permitted access to the computers of the acoustic and perceptual research department at Bell Labs. For seven or eight years I was out there, almost all the time. I used to take naps in the anechoic chamber and just stay all weekend, and it was so quiet. Anyway, I worked with the GROOVE hybrid system there, chiefly because I wanted to be able to use real time interaction with sounds.

I also began to be very interested in creating visual representation. I'm one of those sort of synesthetic types—I've always seen visual patterns in my mind when I've heard music. So I began to work on trying to realize them; I adapted the software for the computer music system I was using there to run real time visual displays and then was able to use musical time structure to compose images (to a certain extent) and do some video tapes. In 1977 it became possible for the first time to do digital synthesis interactively in real time. Then things began happening very quickly. I was hired there as a consultant on a very large digital synthesizer built by Hal Alles, which pioneered some of the kinds of technology which later turned up in some of the digital synthesizers that are available now.

Then I stopped for a while, and I decided that I wanted to really hone in on my aesthetic values. I was going to draw, if I wanted to do images, and I was going to write, if I wanted to do music. I did that for about a year, just to kind of get back to myself in some ways and become sort of aware of the biases that technology had had. And I realized there were certain biases toward processes which are harder to break out of. On paper the hard part is keeping something up because you're building up something out of a lot of little particles. But with machines it's harder because you've got too much inertia in a logical system to say, just at any given moment, "Oh wow, I think I'll do this." So I decided to try to get something together, where I had all the freedom of paper and all the freedom of sustained process too. Basically the ideal of the computer was initially a labor saving device; so you wanted it to be able to take care of all the redundancies for you and the busy work, but not to impede your freedom in any way nor to limit the information you were creating.

At that point I met the head of research at Apple computers, Jef Raskin, who also composes and is a very, very fine musician—one of the few people I know who can always improvise a fugue if you ask him. There are a lot of really, really very musically adept, talented, and educated people out there in the world who are not in "new music" because they didn't like a lot of the stuff that happened during this century. They dropped out because they didn't like the atonal music, or art world politics, or were also very involved in other creative areas, such as science. So I have been more and more involved working with people who love music, but are outside of the "new music" world; there are many of them in the computer world. I've been working with a variety of individuals, mostly on the West Coast. I'm getting together very, very low cost music systems that people can afford that are, like, this big [hand span depicts small size], and that you can really use. At this point I have a prototype system in my loft which I'm working on that's an Apple Computer with 16 voices of digital waveform synthesis where you can describe any waveform you want. It's got light pen input. It's got keyboard stuff that you can play. It's got a full graphic notation thing where you hit the right point with the light pen and it puts up an alto clef or a tenor clef—or you can do standing notational work with it if you want, or you can use other graphic representations. You know, it's free; it's reconfigurable. You can use it like paper or you can use it like an analog synthesizer because it's real time interactive. [Spiegel was one of the originators of the Apple II music system which was later marketed as the AlphaSyntauri; she also consulted on other personal computer music systems.]

You shouldn't be locked into one thing or another. I've been working very hard on debugging software and hardware and in research and development. The music that I do is highly varied, so some of the pieces are visual; some are entirely structured; some of them are totally intuitive. Sometimes I write eight-voice cancrizans canons; sometimes I just put down a note, and then I put down the one that feels like it's right to go after it. Sometimes I do things that are atonal that work with motivic shapes, and sometimes I do things which are modal and come out of banjo music. (One of the instruments I play is the banjo.) My music is highly varied, and I want an instrument which can do all of it—or help me out with the parts of all of it which get in the way of the music. I want the machine to permit me to concentrate on the musical content as much as possible and do all of the busy work for me.

I'm also very interested in studying perception because perception *is* aesthetics: how we derive meaning from the sounds that we hear, and how we can understand how music affects us. There's never been a human society that doesn't have music; it's obviously something that's essential to people. Yet we don't know anything about it, not how it works, why we want it, or anything. So I'm interested in just about everything about music; music tells us a lot about ourselves.

The computer thing is very promising, and it's at a point where I would anticipate that within the next ten years it will be extremely common for every junior high school to begin having at least computer-aided education. Incidentally I should say that when I wanted to brush up on my own ear-training skills last year, I wrote a little program for myself which would just continue dictating melodic lines, and I could sit there and practice taking them down.

MEMBER OF THE AUDIENCE: Did it work?

LS: Yes, it's very, very handy, because there are a few things in music education that you can't study on your own; you have to go there and work with somebody. Computers are absolutely wonderful because they can handle a lot of complex logic, and they increasingly are having *all* the flexibility of analog synthesizers or older musical instruments. But the fact that they have memory means that you can work on a very intricate polyphonic piece for months, and you don't lose anything. It's all stored. You can store many, many multiple versions; and you can also distribute them. As little machines become more standardized and widespread and there get to be hundreds of systems out there, you could send music around on a mini floppy disk or over the telephone wire via modem [a signal converter] for other people to play on their own little computers. I've done this, and it's wonderful! I have put some music in a software library (amateur computer library), and every once in awhile I run into somebody whose seven-year-old kid was playing with it and modifying it, and it's really wonderful! It's another world. [Pause] I still use paper sometimes. [Laughter]

MEMBER OF THE AUDIENCE: You were talking about an Apple Computer that you were working on. Have you got any price tag on it for mass production?

LS: Well, an Apple Computer sells for, like, $1,100; you can buy 16 voices of digital waveform synthesis for 545 bucks—I think that's what they are selling for now—[By the next year it was $385 and technology continues to get cheaper and cheaper] with a visual notational display. It's very cumbersome; I'm constantly pounding on it. You see most of the people who are writing software for these things don't know as much about music as about computers. But, potentially, computers are going to be very important for music. They're going to enable a lot of people to do music who didn't have a way of doing it before, because the technique of composing has always been *extremely* cumbersome and taken many years of study, whereas the technique of writing is easy—everybody can sit down with a pen or a typewriter. Composing has been the most difficult of the arts because the only technique for it has always been an extremely difficult technique dealing with symbolic notation for sound. I think that computers can mean a real revolution because new techniques are evolving, but they need to be very carefully thought out. There are many, many possible ways that you could put together a composing machine, but one that gives as much freedom of musical expression as possible is an extremely difficult problem. That's going to take many years to work out. So I'm working with a variety of people along a variety of lines; the ultimate goal is that it should become easier for people to make good music and to really concentrate on the musical part of it.

I did one test piece last year, for example; I decided if this machine is good for writing music, you should be able to write in any style. So I did *A History of Music in One Movement* on this little computer in one of these systems: I started with chant, and I wrote a little Dowland, and a little Bach, a little Mozart, and a little Brahms, and a little this and—just, you know—evolving on up and a little timbral stuff at the end. I found it was certainly more flexible than some of the other computer systems I've worked with but it still wasn't anywhere near good enough. That is, not as good as a piece of paper in terms of the freedom you have; but because you're working directly with sound, it's better in other ways. If you could get to work with the sound with the same kind of freedom that you have with a piece of paper, then that would be very good—but we're not there yet, though it's all very, very exciting. There are a lot of people that really love music and haven't had any way of doing it. Musically sensitive people have been filtered out from being composers, not on the basis of how they relate to sounds, but on the basis of their ability to use an abstract symbolic language and to be physically coordinated. Those are both very unmusical criteria for the selection of composers. I think computers are going to change this a lot. [Applause].

RA: We had one more panelist who is unable to be here, Annea Lockwood. She is over at Washington Square Church setting up all the equipment for her piece which is to be performed tonight. I think all of us have done well to resist the tendency toward curvature of the spine in our particular field because of toting speakers, tape recorders, cables, and what not.

I'm sure there are questions that you would like to ask a few of our panelists. Is there anyone who would like to ask a question?

[The author later interviewed both Annea Lockwood and panel moderator Ruth Anderson on their work in the electronic medium. These interviews follow the transcript of the Congress panel discussion.]

OL: I would like to make a comment that I think may be of interest to everybody here. It's about the very early start of this whole electronic music business. It wasn't discovered in 1950; it wasn't even discovered by Busoni in 1907.

My first memories of it were just after Cahill had his experiment here with the Dynamophone [1906]. It was widely publicized in all of the magazines at that time, and I remember my father on the farm in Wauwatosa, Wisconsin, talking about it. There were big headlines all over, "electric music, a new type of thing is coming." There was a big noise about it, and my father would say, "You'll see, there will be electric music." The other side of it was that the magazines were very careful to say, "this will not destroy the old music, but it will enhance it," and so on.

Well, it was Busoni—that remarkable, prophetic mind—who picked that up. Then he wrote in his "New Aesthetic" ["Sketch of a New Esthetic of Music" translated from "Entwurf einer neuen Asthetik der Tonkunst," 1907] that this was indeed a way of finding certain new things, particularly in the department of timbre and extension that we didn't have. That just trying to extend Wagner and Mahler and Strauss wasn't the way to go, but that we'd have to get back to this reevaluation, which we're talking about today. Now Busoni was the first big influence on Varèse, and Varèse moved along in that direction very much.

By the time I got to Busoni there was another element that I feel needs stating here. Busoni said that only a long period of ear-training on the part of those who use this material will make it plastic and useful for artistic purposes. Now that was said in 1907, but there was another thing that Busoni was talking about in 1917 that I think comes in right now. He said that no matter what style you use, no matter what sounds you use, no matter what, you have the problem of the form: the shape of the piece, the Gestalt of the piece. What are you trying to do? What reason? What are you trying to project? This was one very powerful influence at that time. Also, there was the influence of Carl Jung where the whole matter of the fantasy world—the world of the imagination—

came in. When is it sick and when is it art? And this is still an open question today.

One other thing came into this much later and that was the responsibility of the composer to check on his or her own hearing. Along these lines, I would like to be just a bit personal, and then I'll shut up! In my case I have my hearing tested once a year to see what has happened to my ears and the possible decline that, unfortunately, may come with the years. I don't want to pass off whatever that may be as the norm.

Also I have a new post-graduate course: I've been appointed to the Mayor's Committee on noise control. I want to find out where the areas of noise are. Where is it "destructive," where is it "useful" for artistic purposes? These are sort of the real human areas, because if you go further into the psychological realm you find this enormous unconscious volcano that we have in us. We have a subconscious filter before we even get to the conscious job that we have talked about so much. Now we are at the point where we can begin to communicate in all of these areas, which will probably bring the whole business to the point where it reaches people in a certain way that is neither technical nor experimental (those things we've been accused of), but it will make an impact—a human impact. I think that we're just about around to that point I'll shut up now. [Laughter, Applause]

RA: I want to thank all of you for coming and to thank this really brilliant panel, and in particular Otto Luening. [Applause]

End of the Congress Panel

INTERVIEWS WITH ANNEA LOCKWOOD AND RUTH ANDERSON, APRIL 1984

Judith Rosen: Annea, instead of being able to participate as a panelist, you were most occupied—and preoccupied—with the setting up of your piece *World Rhythms*. Could someone else have set it up equally well with your directions?

Annea Lockwood: At a certain point I would have to set up. . . . *World Rhythms* is a complex piece, really. It is a ten-channel piece, with an environmental sound on each channel. Even if there had been enough money to have someone else do the technical set-up (and I did have some help with it), I decide which of the ten different tracks is going to come through each speaker according to the acoustics of the building in which it's being done. So at a certain point I am trying different tracks on different speakers, each of which has its own specific location in the space, and listening to how that sound travels in the space coming from that particular location.

JR: So, you would have to be on the premises to make those final decisions. Let's talk about concrète music which is so well represented by *World Rhythms*.

AL: Well, originally, musique concrète involved working with what I would now call acoustic sound, recording such material as urban sounds, live speech, live music performance, that sort of stuff. These sounds were then manipulated, using collage techniques as applied to sound instead of visual images: collaging, editing, juxtaposing the sounds, and modifying them in terms of tempo and the various techniques that were available in the forties, which were mostly speed modification or editing techniques (such as cutting out a piece of tape and slipping it in backwards, reversing the direction of the tape so that the sound was reversed, so that what was once a crescendo becomes a diminuendo and vice versa). Though a separation grew between the aesthetics of musique concrète and the aesthetics of other forms of electronic music in which the sound was generated electronically, fortunately, these two ideologically different approaches began to merge. So at this point, it's not quite so easy to talk about musique concrète in the sense that a lot of electronic music incorporates acoustic sound. Personally, I happen to prefer still to work purely with acoustically derived sounds: sounds that I record through a mike as opposed to electronically-generated sounds.

The difference, perhaps, between my approach to musique concrète (if it can still be called that) and that of many other people is that I do very minimal manipulation of the sounds. I feel that the intrinsic structures of sounds are very interesting, so that I edit them relatively little—only as much as is needed for the pacing and flow and timing of a piece essentially and the flow of one type of sound into another type of sound. That is a little different from most other composers working with environmental sounds, for whom it is usually a raw material to be treated and manipulated and rather heavily treated quite often as are other sound sources. I don't see it as a raw material. I see the sound almost as a fine product, the thing itself.

JR: And *World Rhythms* represents your use, or processing, of sound sources.

AL: Yes, very much so. I think it is one of my best concrète pieces. It is a live improvisation, not a set piece; I am running ten channels of sound throughout the performance and I'm mixing them up and down, and fading one sound in and out, and bringing another in, and making different combinations. The sources are tree frogs, rivers, a lake on a calm day and with wave action in a storm, volcanos, earthquakes, a star (radio wave emissions from a pulsar), a fire with crows circling it, human breathing—very slow, calm, human breathing—and somebody sitting live during the performance playing a gong in a biorhythm.

Apart from the gong player, who operates on free will, I control the mixtures of all the other sounds as a live improvisation. I like that very much: a combination of being able to bring the sounds of the exterior world into any space and being able to work with them as an improvisation *live* and to choose the structure night by night instead of having it sort of permanently sitting on the tape in a form which is unchangeable.

JR: You say the gong player operates on free will, and I remember, having seen the piece, that the gong was struck not as a response to the music, but as a response in some way to her own inner feeling, or I guess you would say, rhythm. But don't you regulate that response by your very selection of the sounds, so that it is only free will to the extent that the music allows it to be?

AL: Oh, of course, Sure. It is limited. The gong player has to work within the restrictions of his or her own biological rhythms, responding to any action he or she may make.

JR: Oh, so this, then, is the human rhythm that is added to all the environmental ones. Does this rhythm come across differently each time the piece is performed, or if there is a different gong player? Would the change be obvious?

AL: It's a matter of temperament with the gong player, but one of the basic aesthetics of the piece is that all the changes are slow except when the volcano or a geyser goes off suddenly. I try to cross-fade the sounds with one another so that the audience isn't aware of the cross-fading going on until the sound reaches a certain point—either disappearing beyond the point of hearing or suddenly becoming obviously present. But I try to do it imperceptibly, so that this gives the whole piece a slow rhythm of change, a slow rate of change, and that is constant from evening to evening. Other than that, one of the other rhythms is my own rhythm of response, evening by evening, and that modifies how many combinations I use.

JR: What is the general duration for this piece?

AL: It is about an hour long. It's intended as a whole evening's performance, and usually it's the entire concert when I do it.

JR: Could it run longer than that amount of time?

AL: Yes. I did it a couple of times with Merce Cunningham and his company. He wanted an hour and a half performance, because that was the length of his program, so we did an hour and a half, but usually about an hour and ten minutes is as long as I like to do it for. That gives people's own rhythms time to slow down as the audience gets very relaxed and involved with the piece.

JR: Is it recorded?

AL: There is a 20-minute version of it on a commercial cassette called "Audiographics" put out by New Wilderness, which is under the auspices of *EAR* magazine. There is also a short ten-minute version on 1750 Arch Records, which is called "New Music for Electronic and Recorded Media," and is in fact an anthology of music by women composers.

JR: Laurie Spiegel and Ruth Anderson have their music on that recording also, and . . .

AL: Pauline Oliveros, Johanna Beyer (a German composer, who is now dead), Laurie Anderson, Megan Roberts, and I think that is everybody.

JR: *World Rhythms* is just one work of yours, but you have been a composer for a long time. Have you worked primarily in the electronic music medium?

AL: Yes. I have been working with tape for years and years and years, and I have been working with environmental sounds on and off for many, many years.

JR: Your "purist" attitude toward environmental sounds is really quite different from that of other composers. If you don't tamper with it, how do you determine where and how a sound will be used in a composition?

AL: It's a matter of listening and listening. It's as if each sound has its own time—needs its own time—to display itself, or complete itself, or complete some phase of the changes it goes through. I try to figure out what that time is and give the sound all the time it needs. Mine is a contemplative attitude towards sound, actually; contemplating it more than shaping it, perhaps. I think Cage was really useful to me when I was a kid. Very helpful.

JR: What specifically about Cage?

AL: Just reading Cage; all his attitudes towards sound. His noninterference attitudes were very revealing.

JR: Tell me about your composition, *Delta Run,* which was played at the First Congress.

AL: Yes, that piece combines two forms of material I have used for a long time: natural sounds and human speech. This has also been a preoccupation of mine: recording people talking about strong experiences in their lives, and then working with that material. I started doing that in about 1975, and I did it quite intensively through to 1981.

Delta Run is about the experience of death or one's feelings about death. It combines environmental sounds and a monologue on the subject of his own coming death by a young sculptor who was dying of cancer. I had wanted to do a piece about death having watched my mother die over a long period of time, so I talked to a friend who was working in a hospice. I asked her if she thought anybody in the hospice would want to talk to me about their feelings, and she mentioned this young sculptor who was no longer able to work with his hands, but was interested in talking with another artist. He was a very beautiful person. We had a couple of conversations; he actually died just a few hours after our last talk. That piece incorporates his feelings about what he was experiencing and what he expected and his concept of death and his beliefs about it with environmental sounds: wind, some ocean sounds, and just ordinary human activity sounds: somebody jogging on a gravel road, somebody building out in the woods. And these wind sounds, which rise and fall throughout the piece, are interwoven with his voice.

It is a mixed media piece in that in addition to the playing of the tape, there is someone sitting and moving very, very, very slowly, almost imperceptibly slowly, which is sort of magnetizing when you watch it. At the same time the person is very slowly raising a couple of semicircles of a wooden hoop which has been split in half. These two semicircular parts of the hoop are finally joined together just after the taped voice finally finishes speaking, and then into the circle made by the hoop (which is about 4 feet in diameter) is projected a slide of very luminous blue that fills the hoop. And that is how the piece ends.

JR: So in each of the two compositions you have just discussed, there is a human—live—element.

AL: Yes. They're both performance pieces.

JR: Is this a consistent factor throughout your work?

AL: I haven't really done too many pieces which exist only in the form of tape without any live situation. I like live performance. I also do installations to run in galleries, different sorts of exhibition spaces. And those, of course, are walk-around experiences. You move through them.

JR: You have done a number of different installations in recent years and performance pieces, too.

AL: Yes, there is something traveling around Italy at the moment. There was a whole exhibition worked out in Italy, mostly of conceptual art relating to sound. The organizers wanted something from me, so I sent over the plans for one of my *Piano Transplants* from a whole series of them dating from the late sixties.

JR: What are those about?

AL: Transformed pianos. Pianos that are half-buried in gardens; there's a piano sitting in a lake in Texas—a little pond—that's drowning, called *Piano Drowning*. Then there's *Piano Burning* that I did and also permanently prepared pianos.

JR: The piece in Texas is there now?

AL: Sure. It's in Amarillo, Texas, and it's slowing sinking in a very shallow lake.

JR: What was the *Piano Transplant* that you sent to Italy?

AL: That's the most recent one, the one that I would most love to do, but have never been able to; to get hold of a grand piano and a sea anchor and anchor the piano in the tideland—one place that would be perfect is near Santa Cruz and the redwoods of the Henry Cowell Woods—and just have the tide wash it in and out for as long as it lasted, just anchored slightly off shore.

JR: Fascinating. Another example of one of your installations?

AL: I did something called *Conversations With The Ancestors* which is based on my tape recordings of two old women talking about their lives, one of whom had been a pioneer in medical social work in Boston, and one of whom had been a homemaker in the New York area. Each of them had a little sort of stage set—it was shown at the P.S. 1 Gallery space in New York—consisting of a mat and chair. In one case it was a rocking chair, and in the other case a sort of old-fashioned Victorian chair with little lace doilies on the back of the chairs, and a small ornamental table besides each chair with some object on it that each woman had possessed. In one case it was a little shell box that her father had bought her in Brittany, France, when she first went over as a child (age 12 for her first European tour). In the case of the other woman, it was an old baking tray for muffins, all blackened, and a very mysterious cup and saucer—the cup had a hole dead center in the bottom, no crack, no nothing, just a hole in the bottom of the cup. There was also a little album of photographs of them from when they were babies up through recent photographs that I had taken. It was quite elaborate; there was a big black and white blow-up of their faces behind a silk-screened quotation of one of the things they had said, and there was a color blow-up of their hands. You just slipped on a pair of headphones, and you could listen to either woman for as long as you'd like.

JR: How wonderfully intimate. Your most recent piece which you just premiered in England was . . .

AL: Oh, that's *The Sound Ball* which is a ball about 18 inches in diameter covered with open-celled foam, the sort of foam that microphone windshields are made of. Inside the ball are ten large speakers and an amplifier and a little Sony Walkman with a prerecorded tape. It is activated simply by a little on-off switch on the outside of the ball. The ball was designed by Bob Bielecki, a superb technician.

The piece was commissioned by two dancers in England, Miranda Tufnell and Dennis Greenwood; they just asked me for anything at all that I wanted to do. I had long wanted to put sound in a ball, and I thought it would be nice if the sound was something that dancers could move with in a physical object, instead of always coming to them from loud speakers with sound just drifting through the space, you know?

JR: And the kind of sounds that you put on that tape?

AL: Oh, natural sounds again; somewhat modified by speed changes, very simple modifications. It is three long phrases, essentially, of sound; and from one phrase to the next, one sound moves through into the next phrase, and the other sounds disappear. They had to be sounds that would sound good on small loud speakers: mid-range, mid-frequency, high frequency; there's very little low frequency in the sound, which was hard on me because I love low frequency sounds. But from speakers that small you can't have a good low range. So I just chose sounds which had a very strong presence coming through tiny speakers, such as crickets, very, very, very fast high staccatos.

JR: So you gave yourself a challenge in choosing the type of sound sources that would work.

AL: Yes, right. River water sounded wonderful on the speakers. It was amazingly distinct, clear, sharp, resonant—it's the Hudson because that's what I had been working on most recently. The river appears at the end of the piece. I decided I had really had enough of recording rivers, so the piece ends with the river going out and down my drain. (I have really resonant, noisy drains in this house.) I just recorded my drains and the river slowly and gently cross-fades with the drains and goes down the drain, which gave the dancers a very surprising ending. They didn't expect that at the end of the piece, and they had to deal with it in the choreography. It presented some funny problems.

JR: When you say you had had enough of recording rivers, I assume you're referring to your taping of a whole river anthology.

AL: The *River Archive,* yes. I think the Hudson River was probably the ultimate river project.

JR: How long did you spend taping the Hudson?

AL: I spent a year going up and down the river from its source to its estuary. I travelled all the way down the river just recording it at many, many spots and also recording the environment right at the river's side. The tape was used as one of several parts of an installation called *A Sound Map of the Hudson River* which was commissioned by the Hudson River Museum in Yonkers, New York.

JR: Had that been a long-planned project of yours—to tape one river all the way down its length?

AL: Yes, that was the logical extension of the *River Archive.*

JR: Where do you perceive yourself going from this point?

AL: I want to move away from environmental sounds, finally, I think. But I don't know; they are still very fascinating to me—very dynamic and complex. I am also becoming interested in using certain computer music programs, such as the CHANT program developed at IRCAM in Paris.

JR: Well, I look forward to hearing what comes out of your explorations. Thank you, Annea.

Judith Rosen: Ruth, as the moderator for the panel of composers of electronic and computer music, you weren't given an opportunity (or you didn't take the opportunity) to discuss your own music. I would like to remedy that now and ask you to say something about your own music.

Ruth Anderson: The members of the panel were chosen by Jeannie Pool, Annea Lockwood, and myself to represent the broadest spectrum of styles, concepts and ways of working with electronic music including both analog and digital studios as well as ad hoc installations.

My work has been involved with the use of electronic music as a source for creating meditation pieces which reduce stress. In this connection I found that sine tones [sounds containing only one frequency], which I used in a piece called *Points,* seemed to act as a kind of sonic acupressure. The persons who have listened to the piece have found after hearing it that they had an energy and a very alert state of mind. Some people have used it to get rid of migraine headaches or muscle spasm. But I'm not really interested in carrying this aspect of it further into what would really be therapy. I am simply interested in creating pieces which are meditations, which help a person to center herself or himself.

The piece which was done at the Congress involves biofeedback. I have four galvanic skin resistance sensors [GSRs] which are connected to four oscillators and essentially, the sensors detect the whole body state of the person wearing the sensor. If the person is very excited, then the pitch—which is controlled by the sensor—will go up, and if the person is very calm, the pitch will go down. The instructions for the dance, which I built around these GSRs and which is called *Centering,* are that the four persons wearing the GSRs focus their attention on the dancer and respond to his or her changes of energy level. The dancer is also then dancing to the music, so it makes a circle. The dancer is both dancing to the music and creating the music. I chose for a biofeedback sound, a sound which is close to sine tones. Generally, the biofeedback sound itself, from training devices to reduce stress through biofeedback, will be either a readout on a visual graph for which you have to keep your eyes open (which is stressful) or it will be a little repeating beep (which is a pain in the neck). So my idea was that the feedback signal, itself, should contribute to the well-being of the person.

JR: Was this piece *Centering* first performed at the Congress?

RA: No, the first performance was in Sweden at a "Festival of Arts and Consciousness" in 1979.

JR: Has it been performed elsewhere since the Congress?

RA: Yes, a number of times.

JR: And each time *Centering* is performed, do you as the composer get a very different sense at the outcome?

RA: No, I don't. [Chuckle] It invariably happens that a sense of unity is created among the five participants and a sense of unity is created with the audience and the participants in the piece. A meditative experience seems to occur from what one senses in the performance area and from what people say afterwards.

JR: So that what you have set out to accomplish within the terms that you have set up is achieved.

RA: Right.

JR: Do you have other pieces based on this concept of biofeedback? For instance, during your recent trip to Europe was a biofeedback piece performed?

RA: Well, it is not a piece in an audio sense. It's a clock, and the piece is an installation which is called *Time and Tempo*. It is just a Bulova schoolroom clock with a light and also GSRs which you attach to two fingers. It is designed so that when the clock light is off, the clock is running on normal time. As you turn an adjoining dial—in order to dial in your own particular range of sensitivity—the light goes on. At that point you're controlling the clock. If you are very excited, the clock hands race around, and if you are very calm, the clock hands slow and can even stop. So that there is a difference between clock time and your own tempo or the way you are able to use time.

JR: What were some of the responses from the participants?

RA: It was installed at a wonderful place called The Blackie in Liverpool. This is an art center which serves a working-class neighborhood. The people who came in—kind of tough little kids and some not so little—seemed to have no trouble with this clock at all. One little boy told me, "Oh, just a minute, I am going to stop the clock." And he turned his mind to a blank and stopped the clock. A little girl attached the two sensors to her *forehead* and said, "Oh, I am going to stop the clock. I am thinking of nothing." And she did just that. So, it was great fun.

JR: And gratifying too, I would think, to see the positive realization of your concept.

RA: Well, it is always gratifying if an electronic gadget works.

JR: In and of itself, right?

RA: Right. It's kind of interesting. There is one of the three major time museums in the world located in Liverpool, and a director who is seeking to expand the museum to include ways in which we relate to time, was very interested in having one of the clocks as part of their museum.

JR: How long have you been working with biofeedback as a source of compositional effort?

RA: Oh, a number of years. I had a wonderful technician in the studio [at Hunter College] named Jan Hall who was interested in these devices and made the first GSR for me. It has since been altered and changed and redesigned by Bob Bielecki, another wonderful technician. I couldn't possibly realize my designs without their intelligent know-how.

JR: Isn't that true with anyone who composes or creates any new idea. You need that technician. You need the machine shop, if it's a complex, mechanical invention.

RA: There are some composers who are able to do their own gadgetry—Liz Phillips is one.

JR: I think she's an exception. But to get back to your work. You say you are interested in meditative pieces. There was a time, however, when you didn't compose in this way. How did your work evolve into pieces that create meditative states?

RA: It evolved because it was something that I needed to do for myself.

JR: Do you feel that your work will continue in this direction or do you really have any idea as to where you will go from here?

RA: Well, I just did a little meditation called *Resolutions.*

JR: Which was?

RA: My first computer piece in which I took LaMonte Young's perfect fifth and resolved it from up in the sky to down in the basement. It goes over a period of about a half an hour, just falls down gradually. But, I am much more interested in the expanded horizons that computers can offer me, and I have a piece in mind with a number of applications for robots.

JR: Speaking of your work with computers, you had an amazing experience working with an individual and designing a computer to help him function. Would you talk a bit about that?

RA: I ran headlong into computers when I saw a friend who had become a quadraplegic. The essential person was still there; it was just that he couldn't move anything except his head. He had wonderful stories to tell—he could speak. I called all around the country and finally located a piece of equipment in Vancouver, another piece in Minneapolis, and another piece in Denton, Texas. Then finally I located a bioengineer—a half hour away from me after all of that—who was working on the same project at Burke Rehabilitation Institute [in White Plains, NY]. Next, a Swiss engineer, Christoph Meyer, worked with me. Finally after about six weeks of preliminary work, we set it all up and in two weeks more got all the equipment. So then the friend could use the telephone to call out and receive calls. He could turn on or off anything in his apartment, type out letters and keep files on anything he wanted to—such as recipes; he had been a great cook. He could get programs to learn something; he got a program to learn French. So that was my first encounter with computers personally, but I still didn't know how to use them. This past year I have been learning how to use an Apple II and now the Apple II will be connected both to an analog synthesizer, a Serge, and to a digital synthesizer, an AlphaSytauri.

JR: Does this mean you anticipate doing more work with computers?

RA: Right. Then I also have a GSR connection to this whole system; so I can use biofeedback again if I want to.

JR: How did you become interested In GSRs? How did they first come into your life?

RA: Through Jan Hall, the technician in the Hunter College studio.

JR: The electronic music studio you, yourself, founded?

RA: If you insist, yes.

JR: I insist.

RA: All right. That was the first operating studio in the City University [of New York] System set up in 1968. The only other studios in town, I think, were the Columbia-Princeton Studio and possibly Sarah Lawrence had a studio then, though I don't think so. I think that was later.

JR: What was some of the work to come out of that studio?

RA: I have been interested in installations and in games. In, I believe, 1975 I did an installation with Annea Lockwood which involved biofeedback and games. I had a game called *Tuneable Hopscotch* in which each of the numbers (on which you would jump playing hopscotch) was connected to a different oscillator. The pitch of the oscillators was controlled by a bank of dials on the wall, so that spectators could change the pitches. So you could make a fine piece by just playing the game of hopscotch. There were GSRs connected to audio signals and GSRs connected to light which was behind a mandala that a student had done—a very beautiful mandala [Indian design] on plexiglass. The idea was that if you relaxed enough and went into a meditative state, the light would go on behind the mandala, and you would be able to see it. Before that you were just looking at a black plexiglass.

JR: Your musical career has taken you in many directions and brought you in contact with many people. It was obvious to me when I saw you with Otto Luening on the Congress panel that your connection with him goes back a long way and that he appeared on the panel really because of your friendship with him. How long have you known Luening?

RA: I don't know how long—probably ever since I got to New York, 1951 or 1952.

JR: I need to interject something here. I have observed the response of audiences to your works; they *move* the people involved. That has to be a pretty great experience for you. I know if I were a composer, that is what I would like to know: that in one way or another I made some kind of impact on the audience. You do that well.

RA: Oh, thank you. You know this is about the fourth career I have had and so I, as a composer, am really quite young in comparison with all the other members of the panel. I have had a career as a flutist, as an orchestrator, as a professor, and it has only been recently that I have been able to concentrate more on composition.

JR: Which career do you . . .

RA: I love them all. I have loved everything.

JR: Do you sense that this career will be the one that will continue . . .

RA: Who knows? I enjoy everything.

JR: Particularly, what?

RA: Of course, composition—particularly music and people.

JR: That's a nice way of closing. Thank you, Ruth.

NOTE

1. For a discussion of Grigsby's own compositions, including her views on incorporating live performance with electronics, a description of her style, and a brief list of works to 1983, see "Women Composers of Electronic Music," *The Musical Woman: An International Perspective, 1983,* vol. 1 (Westport, Conn: Greenwood, 1984), pp. 177-79. In autumn 1984 Grigsby's opera, *The Mask of Eleanor* for soprano solo with the orchestral score realized on a Fairlight computer, was given at IRCAM in Paris; a subsequent performance in February 1985 was a highlight of the West Coast Women Conductor/Composer Symposium held at the University of Oregon in Eugene.

11

Mexico's Women Musicians

ESPERANZA PULIDO

To understand the very belated acceptance of Mexican women as composers and performers, as well as in other intellectual areas, one should be aware of at least two factors, both of which held a grip on women for centuries: *malinchismo* (a particular atavism) and *machismo* (an undesirable male trait).

Malinche was a young girl of coastal Mexico whom Hernán Cortés abducted and retained as interpreter (she had learned Spanish quickly). From 1519 on Malinche helped the conqueror a great deal in his first parliaments with the Aztecs; she also fell in love with him. She served Cortés well and proved to be a most intelligent assistant. Although Cortés had a son by Malinche, he committed a most ungrateful and discriminatory act in 1528 by yielding her to Alonso Hernández Portocarrero (another of the conquerors), whom she married.

Today *malinchismo* means an inferiority complex that manifests itself whenever a Mexican confronts a foreigner on important matters. It is especially obvious in the case of a young woman who consents to a foreign employer's sexual advances or his intellectual blandishments. *Machismo*—he-man-ship—refers to men's dictatorship in their home, as well as to their boasting about their power to attract women. Both traits are still rampant in certain Indian and mestizo social milieus but not so prevalent any longer among middle and upper-class Mexicans. In historical times and even in the recent past, both *machismo* and *malinchismo* loomed large as frustrating factors in the lives of those few women who dared to demand their freedom to acquire a wider range of musical knowledge, interfering with their ambitions both within their family circles and in their own thinking.

BRIEF HISTORY OF MEXICO

During the tenth century A.D. the Aztecs, otherwise known as Nahoas, inherited the great culture of the Toltecs. From the latter's deserted town of Teotihuacán (City of the Gods) the Aztecs proceeded on their pilgrimage through the Valley of Mexico—the "promised land"—where, according to an old saga, they were to settle down for good. Here they built the town of Tenochtitlan, which became in time the center of a great empire.

In 1520 Hernán Cortés (1485-1547) came to America as conqueror for the Spanish kingdom. One year later Tenochtitlan surrendered, and Cortés made Emperor Moctezuma prisoner by force of his firearms (unknown to the natives), plus the aid of another Indian race with whom he had formed an alliance after subduing them on his journey from Veracruz to Tenochtitlan. After the Aztecs were vanquished, Spain began sending large numbers of friars to Mexico for the express purpose of converting the natives to the Catholic faith. Among the first boatload of priests was one of Belgian ancestry, Fray Pedro de Gante, who became the principal Spanish teacher of Aztec Indians. As a musician, he soon discovered that his new pupils were quick in learning the new European sounds that were so strange to them, although they had never developed their own system for notating sounds. (Little is known of the Aztecs' own music. What we do know is that they had good music schools for both boys and girls, and that they were able builders of musical instruments as well as composers of artistic songs and ritual music of various kinds.)

New Spain (Mexico) remained a Spanish Viceroyalty until the beginning of the nineteenth century. In 1810 Don Miguel Hidalgo y Costillo (1753-1811) headed a conspiracy against the Viceroyalty; although Costillo and his collaborators were defeated and hanged, the insurgents persevered for ten years until 1821, when Augustín de Iturbide claimed victory. Over the next 40 years Mexico had two empires: Iturbide's (1821-1823) and that of the Emperor Maximilian of Hapsburg (1863-1867). During the second empire two political parties—liberals and conservatives—began squabbling over political power. The liberal Benito Juárez (1806-1872), who gave his country its *Laws of Reform*, won the elections.

In 1872 Porfirio Díaz (1830-1915) entered the Mexican scene and made a successful campaign for the presidency. For the following 35 years he remained Mexico's permanent president-dictator, until Mexico lost patience with him and Francisco I. Madero (1873-1914) raised an army of peasants and workers in 1910 and started the Mexican Revolution. After defeating Porfirio Díaz, Madero pacified the country, but a traitor murdered him in 1914. A few unsteady years followed, but in 1920 peace finally came to Mexico, along with cultural improvement. As secretary of public education, José Vasconcelos (1881-1959) began a series of cultural programs that brought the country to international notice, at least in the area of mural painting (through the works of Diego Rivera, José Clemente Orozco, and David Siqueiros). Vasconcelos campaigned for the presidency in 1929, but he was defeated due to some legally questionable maneuvers. Since that time several elections have been held, and Mexico, like most young countries, has managed to thrive amidst political ups and downs.

During the nineteenth century Mexico was dominated culturally, as well as politically, by other countries. In the middle of the century France and England invaded Mexico, but were chased out through the intervention of the United States. Mexico was obliged to yield a good part of its territory to its northern neighbor, but it did retain its independence. Not surprisingly, little of indigenous cultural importance occurred in Mexico during the nineteenth century and the first quarter of the twentieth. Since then, however, the country has produced some distinguished musicians, men such as Manuel M. Ponce (1882-1948), José Rolón (1883-1945), Carlos Chávez (1899-1972), Silvestre Revueltas (1899-1940), Julián Carrillo (1875-1965), Augusto Navaro (1893-1960), and the young musicians who sprang up after the Second World War: Jiménez Mabarak (b. 1916), Blas Galindo (b. 1910), José Pablo Moncayo (1912-1958), Eduardo Mata (b. 1942), Manuel Enríquez (b. 1926), Hector Quintanar (b. 1936), Mario Lavista (b. 1952), and others. Women's contributions—hampered by *machismo* as well as *malinchismo*—really come to the fore only in the most recent period.

MEXICAN COLONIAL MUSIC

During Mexico's four centuries of Spanish domination, Mexico's music had forcefully adapted itself to Spanish patterns. This most Catholic country in the world excelled in religious music. Cathedrals throughout Mexico had chapelmasters, choirs, and composers of masses, motets, villancicos, and the like; among the many notable composers and musicians of Colonial Mexico were Antonio de Salazar, Manuel Sumaya, Hernando Franco, and Juan Gutiérrez Padilla. Popular music also permeated many villages.

Up to the early twentieth century, Mexican history records only a solitary Mexican woman as a genuine artist and intellectual: Sor Juana Inés de la Cruz (1651-1695), a poet of great accomplishment and a woman of high learning, who could converse on equal terms with the wisest men of her time on philosophical and theological subjects.

She was born at the hacienda of San Miguel Nepantla. At age seven Juana asked to be sent to Mexico City's university, where she learned Latin and literary and religious subjects. In 1665, at the age of 14, she was asked to join the maids-in-waiting of the palace's first lady; from then on she made a very brilliant career as the greatest woman poet of the New World.

At the age of 18 she decided to enter the Convent of San Jerónimo, where she was allowed to live in a small apartment and be waited upon by a young maid. Intent on being useful to her convent mates, she taught herself music by means of theory books written by authors like the Neapolitan Pietro Cerone (1565-1625?), who had lived for a number of years in Spain. At the suggestion of the Viceroy's wife, Countess of Paredes (who was very fond of her), Juana started writing a music treatise that unfortunately appears not to have been preserved. But she wrote in one of her published poems the following verses:

I began writing a method
trying to condense in it
as many rules as prescribed.
Should memory fail me not,
I said there that harmony
is a spiral, not a circle,
and dared calling it a shell,
likewise revolving on itself.

The finest biography of Sor Juana Inés de la Cruz was published in 1983 by the distinguished Mexican poet Octavio Paz. This thoroughly researched work for the first time gives Sor Juana proper credit as one of Mexico's very best poets. In evaluating her musical gifts, Paz went as far as the lack of information and material would permit.

A "wonder woman" of Colonial times, Sor Juana is that rare exception—a figure who belongs in a class apart. Some of her principal works are: *Primero Sueño* (First I Dream); *El Divino Narciso* (The Divine Narcissus); *Carta Atenagórica* (Athenagorical Letter); and *Respuesta a Filotea de la Cruz* (Answer to Filotea de la Cruz—supposedly a pen-name for herself), which she sent to one of the wicked bishops who persecuted her during the last years of her short life. Several books of poems, villancicos, loas and other works also exist. (Some of her villancicos were written in the language of the Aztecs, Náhuatl; according to Robert Stevenson, the composer Antonio de Salazar set several of these to music.)

Only 28 years elapsed between Columbus's discovery of America (1492) and Mexico's conquest by Hernán Cortés (1521); while Columbus only got as far as Santo Domingo, on the Caribbean Sea, Cortés and his soldiers penetrated all the way to Tenochtitlan, proceeding on horseback and by foot after first landing at Veracruz. Everything was a novelty for the explorers: the sound of the Aztec drums—*huéhuetls* and *teponaztlis*—which seemed "infernal" to their ears, and later the beautiful dances which they saw and compared to "the best of Spain." The monk Bernardo Sahagún described the dances in detail and wrote *Psalmodia Christiana* (a copy of which exists in the Huntington Library in Los Angeles), which contains texts he adapted to Aztec music. Unfortunately, only the texts are notated, not the Aztec melodies.

Catholicism, the new religion, encouraged submission. Along with the loss of their freedom, women lost the right to appear in public songfests and dance performances.

One of the conquerors' (rather rare) virtues was intermarriage. There was, of course, a certain kind of Creole that would never mix with the aborigines, but many Spaniards did so, forming the basis of a new race. Women easily adapted themselves to their new duties as wives and mothers.

Convents enjoyed certain privileges. Chapelmasters were needed for religious services but men were not allowed in convents. Therefore it was necessary to open music schools for young women. Those who wanted to join a religious order but lacked the required dowry were taught enough music to be able to serve as chapelmasters if they showed musical talent. Names of some of these women appear in old archives.

What other music was available to the average colonial woman? Large towns like Mexico City, Guadalajara, Puebla, and Oaxaca had folkloric songs from Spain that the evergrowing population gradually assimilated and altered. But in faraway Indian towns and villages, old aboriginal tunes prevailed. A few of these have been handed down from generation to generation.

In large towns only privileged women could enjoy certain spectacles such as operas sent from Spain. In the late eighteenth century Cimarosa's *Il Fanatico Burlato* was heard in Mexico City, but people were more at home with *zarzuelas* and *tonadillas* performed by such popular female singers as Felipa Mercado (La Gata). Towns such as Morelia had music schools for girls; places at these schools, however, were reserved (with few exceptions) for the daughters of the wealthiest inhabitants.

MUSIC IN INDEPENDENT MEXICO

After independence, for some years music was at a standstill, but in 1827 the famous Spanish singer Manuel Garcia (1775-1832)—(father of Marie Malibran and Pauline Viardot-Garcia)—took his troupe to Mexico City for an opera season. That was the first of a very long succession of opera seasons presented by various opera companies, primarily Italian ones. During the nineteenth century Italian opera conquered almost the entire world, and Mexico was no exception; on the contrary, Mexico offered Italian opera a very rich soil.

During the four years of the Maximilian Empire (1863-67), private music schools were already teaching students to sing. At about that time Mexico had its first great international female singer, Angela Peralta (1845-83). Her father received a subsidy to take her to Italy, where she studied with the well-known vocal teacher Francesco Lamperti (1813-92); later she sang in various Italian, Spanish, and Russian opera houses. Back in Mexico she received a very enthusiastic welcome. During the short-lived French Empire, Maximilian granted La Peralta and her opera company funds to collaborate in the premiere of the opera *Ildegonda* by the Mexican composer Melesio Morales (1838-1908). She had already made several successful tours in Mexico with her own troupe; in 1883, in the course of one of these tours, she fell victim to a yellow fever epidemic in Mazatlán that killed her and other members of the company. Peralta had just turned 38.

Among her accomplishments were a number of compositions, including the *Album de Angela Peralta*, whose 20 pieces include waltzes, songs, mazurkas, dances, and fantasies for the piano, which were full of the runs and embellishments so dear to amateurs of those times.

The National Conservatory of Music was founded in 1866 in Mexico City by a group of enthusiastic musicians. One of its first graduates was Carlos J. Menéses (1865-1929), who became one of Mexico's best-known pianists, orchestra conductors, and teachers. He was to produce a host of women pianists and was partly responsible for Mexico's continuing piano cult.

MUSIC IN MODERN AND CONTEMPORARY TIMES

Menéses's prize pupil was Alba Herrera y Ogazón (1885-1931), considered a very brilliant pianist in her youth. It seems unjust that no Mexican dictionary or encyclopedia of music includes an entry on her. Together with Don Julian Carrillo (1875-1975), the celebrated Mexican microtonal composer, she gave the entire cycle of Beethoven's violin and piano sonatas, probably for the first time in Mexico, as well as some concerti with an orchestra conducted by Carrillo. But being very much attracted by musicology, she became Mexico's first female music critic and historian. Ogazón wrote several books: *El Arte Musical en México* (Musical Art in Mexico), *Puntos de Vista* (Viewpoints), *Historia de la Música* (History of Music), a translation of Josef Hofmann's *Piano Playing,* and others. At first her opinions concerning modern music were somewhat narrow-minded, but later she wrote more enlightened and

Figure 11.1 Choir of the University of Hermosillo, on the occasion of the première of Emiliana de Zubeldia's *Mass.* By permission of Emiliana de Zubeldia.

tolerant reviews of the music of Schoenberg, Prokofiev, and Ravel. Her judgments on Mexican musical matters of the time were accurate and to the point.

Many young women began voice training with the excellent vocal teachers to be found in Mexico in the latter part of the nineteenth century. Opera roles were opened to them, and international recognition soon followed. After Angela Peralta, Fanny Anitúa (1887-1967) was the next Mexican singer to be welcomed in Europe, as well as the first to sing in Milan's La Scala (in the role of Erda, in *Siegfried*). She was fond of less frequently performed operas, such as Gounod's *Sappho*, Gluck's *Orfeo*, and Saint-Saëns's *Samson et Dalila*. On the occasion of Rossini's centenary celebration in Pesaro, Italy, Anitúa was chosen as the best contralto in Italy.

After Fanny Anitúa, Mexico produced a succession of good opera singers who were capable of achieving international careers, such as María Luisa Escobar, María Romero (b. 1903), Mercedes Caraza (b. 1908), and Josefina Aguilar (1910?-1968). In the case of María Romero—a soprano of very beautiful voice and distinguished musicality—her family forbade the international career that could so easily have been hers.

In the field of lieder, María Bonilla (b. 1903) was unrivaled in Mexico. After receiving her conservatory degree, she moved to Germany with her parents. There, however, they prevented her from pursuing a Wagnerian career, so she returned to Mexico to teach at the conservatory and to give occasional recitals. Irma González and Julia Araya were her most brilliant pupils.

Currently there are a number of very able Mexican singers of the older generation still before the public on occasion, with Irma González (b. 1923) and Oralia Domínguez (b. 1924) at the head. Irma González is a fine example of excellent vocal training; she seems to sing better now than she did 30 years ago, singing opera, and excelling in cantatas and modern symphonic vocal parts. Oralia Domínguez spent many years in Europe as a much sought-after mezzo-soprano where her performances in Manuel de Falla's *El Amor Brujo* were famous.

María Luisa Rangel (b. 1924) has dedicated her career to Mexican vocal music, which she performs with proficiency. Mezzo-soprano Aurora Woodrow (b. 1920) has pursued a brilliant operatic career. María Luisa Salinas (b. 1925), a lyric soprano of graceful voice and impeccable musicianship, is currently much sought after for performances of symphonic vocal music. Rosa Rimoch (b. 1925) is another example of excellent vocal training; after a brilliant national and international career, she now specializes in lieder, Mexican as well as foreign. Margarita González (b. 1926) won a first prize in a Paris competition as the best foreign singer of French songs; with soprano Lupita Pérez Arias she now presents duet recitals. Belonging to the same generation are Maritza Alemán (b. 1925), a success in German opera for quite a number of years, and

Cristina Ortega (b. 1927), who, besides being an opera singer of considerable leggiero importance, sang Viennese operetta with great success. Martha Ornelas gave up a promising operatic career after marrying Plácido Domingo, but Hortensia Cervantes (b. 1940) elected not to give up hers, although she is the wife of a prominent Mexican baritone. Guillermina Higareda (b. 1942), one of Mexico's best sopranos, is also an accomplished pianist, which may account for her great musicality in both opera and art song. The same high degree of musicianship is observed in the performances of Rosario Andrade and Gilda Cruz-Romo—Mexican sopranos of well-deserved high international reputation.

Among the younger singers who have already had some success with their careers at Mexico's Opera Nacional are Estrella Ramírez, Margarita Pruneda, and Martha Félix.

OUTSTANDING WOMEN PIANISTS

In the early 1930s one of Mexico's best pianists of the century, Angélica Morales (b. 1913), was sent by the Mexican government to study in Germany in view of her accomplishments as a child prodigy. In Germany Morales studied at the Hochschüle für Musik with Egon Petri, with whom she worked closely in the development of her gifts. While still very young, she played, in four sessions, the entire 48 Preludes and Fugues of the *Well-Tempered Clavier* and appeared as a soloist with the Berlin and Dresden Philharmonic orchestras. Later she moved to Vienna to continue her studies with one of the last living pupils of Franz Liszt, Emil von Sauer (1862-1942), whom she later married. After Sauer's death she continued living and giving concerts in Europe until she was offered a position as teacher and concert pianist in residence at the University of Kansas. There she played a Liszt program on a piano that had actually belonged to the great Hungarian pianist-composer. From time to time she returns to Mexico to give recitals and play with Mexican orchestras. In the early 1980s she recorded a Liszt program in Mexico City, as well as the two volumes of Bach's *Well-Tempered Clavier*; all received excellent reviews in the North American press.

To Angélica Morales's generation belongs Esperanza Cruz (b. 1910). She was an exceptionally gifted pianist. In her youth the government of Veracruz sent her to Europe, where she studied initially with Isidor Philipp in Paris, later moving to Berlin to study with Petri and Felix Borowski (1872-1984). After quite a number of years, she married Mexico's famous philosopher and writer José Vasconcelos, who was considerably older than she; after his death she went to live in New York City. It may truthfully be said that her actual career did not fulfill its early promise.

But María Teresa Rodríguez (b. 1923) is a fine example of a great talent's promise truly fulfilled through assiduity of purpose, hard work, and élan.

Borowski, her last teacher, considered her a very special pupil, and Carlos Chávez cited her as his best interpreter at the piano. After Chávez's death she was given the task of recording the whole of his music for piano, which she is now ding in Mexico City under the auspices of the Secretaría de Educación Pública. Some years ago, when Olivier Messiaen's *Turangalîla* had its first Mexican performance, the French pianist who was to have played the very difficult piano part with the orchestra became ill. With only one day's notice María Teresa Rodríguez played the performance fluently as well as accurately. She is one of those rare persons who walk straight to their goal, without letting anybody or anything interfere.

Somewhat younger is Luz María Puente (b. 1925), another artist whose delicate touch and sound performances are a joy. She is the mother of Jorge Federico Osorio, one of Mexico's best young pianists.

María Elena Barrientos (b. 1940) now lives in Spain and enjoys there a well-earned reputation as an indispensable pianist of contemporary music. She holds an accompanist position at Madrid's School of High Vocal Training. (Mexico has probably lost her forever; quite a number of the country's best musicians still seem to think that it makes best sense to build their careers on foreign soil.)

Guadalupe Parrondo (b. 1945) was born in Peru of Mexican-Peruvian parents. She studied in Paris where she polished a very brilliant technique. Parrondo has lived in Mexico for a number of years, where she found favor with Señora Lopez Portillo, wife of Mexico's past president, who took Parrondo under her wing and gave her frequent engagements to play with the Orquesta Filarmónica de la Ciudad de México. In 1981 she was one of two soloists who went to Los Angeles and Washington on tour with the orchestra.

Other fine, contemporary women keyboard artists include Stella Contreras—one of Mexico's most brilliant and eclectic talents and a pianist and teacher of high standing who died in 1980 while still in her prime; and Carmen Betancourt (b. 1950), who, after being a competent concert pianist, is now making a name for herself as a new music specialist.

The intimate art of chamber music has attracted several outstanding Mexican women pianists. Carmela Castillo Betancourt (b. 1920) became a virtuosa after finishing her piano training in Mexico, but she changed focus after marrying the late distinguished violinist Higinio Ruvalcaba, whom she then regularly partnered. She still appears occasionally as a very able accompanist and chamber music player. María Teresa Castrillón has frequently appeared in duo with Georg Demus and has attained international recognition. She is also a concert pianist and music critic. Aurora Serratos (b. 1930), a well-regarded teacher at the Conservatory of Music, enjoys a solid reputation throughout Mexico and the southern United States, where she performs in duo with her husband, pianist Guillermo Salvador.

Education is an important part of musical life for several women keyboardists. Maria Teresa Naranjo, a concert pianist, is a professor at the Conservatory of Madrid. Holda Zepeda Alcangista was until recently director of musical programs of the Instituto Mexicano-Norteamericano de Relaciones Culturales and is also a fine concert pianist. Luisa Durón traded the piano for the harpsichord, studying that instrument in the Netherlands, then returning to Mexico, where she began to teach it at the Conservatory. She awakened an unusual enthusiasm in a large number of students and remains the indispensable keyboard player for important performances of Baroque music.

MODERN AND CONTEMPORARY WOMEN COMPOSERS

Mexicans should rightly consider the end of the Spanish Civil War and the end of World War II as the beginning of a new musical era for their country because then the country's doors and hearts were opened to a galaxy of many of the best Spanish composers, musicologists, and musicians. Among the women composers who then came to Mexico and did most of their important work there are Emiliana de Zubeldia, María Teresa Prieto, and Rosita Ascott (known as Rosa Bal y Gay).

Figure 11.2 Emiliana de Zubeldia. Photograph by E. Pulido.

EMILIANA DE ZUBELDIA (b. 1898) came to Mexico as a ready-made composer. During the period of the 1920s she had studied composition in Paris with Vincent d'Indy and Désiré Pacques and piano with Blanche Selva. Soon after arriving in Mexico she decided to continue her studies with Augusto Novaro, the prominent Mexican acoustician she had met in

New York City in 1933, the year in which he was travelling on a Guggenheim Fellowship.

Augusto Novaro (1893-1960), one of Mexico's greatest musical scientists, made important discoveries in the areas of acoustics, keyboard instrument tuning, and musical instrument building. His harmonic system was based on the natural overtone series interpreted in a new way. He devised his own scales and chords and also invented an acoustical device that fundamentally affected the tone-color of a keyboard instrument he himself designed and built called the *Novar.*

Emiliana de Zubeldia's enthusiasm for Novaro's harmonic theories induced her to change her musical language and to adopt his. Her earlier works included symphonies, piano music, songs, and other works written in tonal and polytonal styles. In 1931 she gave two recitals of her chamber music works in New York City with the collaboration (at a second piano) of Miirrha Alhambra. In the first of these concerts, given at Town Hall on February 12, they played a *Suite* in three movements, *Eight Basque Folk-Songs, Poem of My Mountains,* and nine *Folk Dances,* all in Zubeldia's own duo-piano arrangements made according to Novaro's theories. This concert was well received by the New York papers, garnering excellent reviews in the *New York Times, New York Sun,* and the *Evening Post.* The second recital took place on November 24 at the Roerich Museum; the program included the premiere performance of Zubeldia's own two-piano *Sonatine*; the composer also accompanied eleven of her songs and eight dances at the keyboard. The pianos for this concert were tuned according to Novaro's new system of tuning.

Typical of her style are the *Eleven Tientos.* During the Renaissance the term *tiento* (akin to the Italian *ricercare*) was applied to some sort of *preambule* used by the Spanish organ players. As Zubeldia was trying a new theory—Novaro's—she thought the word was most appropriate. Eleven of her *Tientos* were grouped together for publication, although she wrote many more. In the first *Tiento* the upper strand of the right-hand arpeggios seems akin to a scale in the Lydian mode, but the bass and the harmony show a succession of *natural chords with their *"reciprocals" and novel inversions (* indicates terms used in Novaro's harmonic theory). This *Tiento* is in ternary form: the outer sections use the texture already described. A kind of "broken" cadence introduces the middle section—a short Flamenco-like recitative that ends abruptly, going back to the first section. The piece moves through a fast progression of chords and inversions to finish on a A minor chord.

The composer herself analyzed a shorter *Tiento* with an introductory chart explaining her use of Novaro's harmonic theories.

In 1956 Emiliana de Zubeldia accepted a position at the University of Hermosillo (Sonora) to found a music school there. Here she has taught music to thousands of young people while bringing musical enlightenment to outsiders by means of broadcast lectures and music appreciation courses.

Figure 11.3 Excerpt from *Ier Tiento* by Emiliana de Zubeldia, mm. 17-22. Used by permission of the composer.

Figure 11.4 Excerpt from *Ier Tiento* by Emiliana de Zubeldia, m. 15. Used by permission of the composer.

Figure 11.5 Chart showing harmonic elements in Zubeldia's *Tiento*. Used by permission of the composer.

Figure 11.6 *Tiento* by Emiliana de Zubeldia. Used by permission of the composer.

MARIA TERESA PRIETO (1895-1982) was born in Toledo, Spain, where she began her musical education. In 1936 she came to Mexico as a refugee from the Spanish Civil War. Two years later she went to Manuel M. Ponce for lessons and then to Mills College in California to study with Darius Milhaud. Later, back in Mexico, she studied with Rodolfo Halffter and Carlos Chávez. Prieto loved the symphonic medium and had the pleasure of hearing some of her works conducted by Erick Kleiber, Herrera de la Fuente, and Chávez. Her whole output was written and premiered in Mexico. From 1942 to 1974 her principal works were *Impresión Sinfónica, Sinfonía Asturiana, Chichen Itzá, Sinfónia Breve, Variaciones y Fuga, Sinfónia Cantabile, Seis Canciones modales, Tema variado y Fuga,* and *Adagio y Fuga.* Prieto started out as a romantic nationalistic composer, but due to Halffter's influence, in her last years she wrote in the 12-tone idiom; yet the shadow of Bach was never far from her work.

GLORIA TAPIA (b. 1934) has been very active as a composer. In 1959 her *Quintet for Wind Instruments* won a prize from the Fine Arts Institute and the CENIDIM (Centro de Investigación, Difusión e Información Musical). Among her major works are a *Concerto for Clarinet and Chamber Orchestra,* a sonata for violin and piano, and *Allegro 72* for piano.

ROSA GURAIEB (b. 1931) received her musical education at Mexico City's conservatory. Her first composition teacher was José Pablo Moncayo; in 1970 she joined the Carlos Chávez Workshop and later studied with Mario Lavista and Daniel Catan. Previously she had studied at Yale University (1954) and in Bayreuth. Her principal works to date are two string quartets and a *Trio for Oboe, Bassoon and Piano.* She is now (1985) writing a *Concerto for Piano and Orchestra.*

For understandable reasons Mexican-born women only began studying composition a short time ago; the principal mitigating factor was a strongly-rooted *machismo.* Fortunately, since "women's liberation," Mexican women have learned to follow their own inclinations, and now they compose music as they wish and are admitted to men's circles; now they are even getting fellowships to study composition in foreign countries.

Among current women composers of fine art music, ALIDA VÁSQUEZ (b. 1942) is undoubtedly an example of how women can open up paths for themselves in foreign countries. Vásquez became a United States citizen but has never forgotten Mexico. With the aid of several grants and a prize from Pen Women of America, she earned a master's degree in composition at Columbia University, where she studied electronic music with Mario Davidovsky and Vladimir Ussachevsky. Some of her already-performed compositions are *Suite for the Piano, Electronic Moods and Piano Sounds, Acuarelas de Mexico* for voice and piano, and *Piece for Clarinet and Piano.*

Figure 11.7 Excerpt from *Piece for Clarinet and Piano* by Alida Vásquez (opening of movement I). Used by permission of the composer.

Piece for Clarinet and Piano, in two movements, begins with a rather long introduction played by the clarinet alone. In a very free style the clarinet goes through several contiguous 12-tone series.

After a long fermata on concert G-sharp, the piano enters with prestissimo impetus. Both instruments then continue together in a sensitive dialogue (with changes of meter in almost every measure) to the end. The second movement is a *giocoso energico* in 3/8 time that seems to hint at dance rhythms, always suggestively out of balance.

Lately, Vázquez has been equally interested in penetrating the secrets of the electronic music world and exploring new means of expression for acoustic instruments.

ALICIA URRETA (b. 1935) is a fine performer as well as composer. Having begun her career as a pianist, in 1957 she became the pianist for the Mexican Orquesta Sinfónica Nacional, a post she held for many years.

Figure 11.8 Alicia Urreta, composer.

Urreta entered the Conservatory in 1949 to study harmony with Rodolfo Halffter, chamber music with Sandor Roth, and other subjects. In 1964 she was soloist with the Harvard University Symphony Orchestra and gave recitals in the USSR and Czechoslovakia; in the same year she began composing incidental music for the theatre. From 1967 to 1968 she continued composition studies with Jean-Etienne Marie, and in 1973 she began organizing yearly festivals of Mexican-Spanish contemporary music in Mexico City and Madrid. In 1965 she was awarded a grant to study Spanish music with Alicia de Larrocha.

In 1972 Urreta's *De Natura Mortis*, or The True Story of Little Red Ridinghood, was premiered in Orléans, France. In 1983 the Orquesta Sinfónica Nacional premiered her *Concerto for Piano and Orchestra* with the composer as soloist. Other large-scale works are *Rallenti* for orchestra, the as-yet-unperformed opera *Romance de Doña Balada* and various works involving electronics.

For a long time Alicia Urreta has favored aleatoric music but, not wanting performers to have excessive freedom, she notates quite specific directions in her scores to firmly control the final performance. Specific markings indicate the exact durations in seconds of particular passages, precise dynamic contours, and so forth; pedalling being so important in a coloristic style, she never leaves it at random. These characteristics are clear in the following music examples from Urreta's *Salmodia*.

Among young Mexican women composers of art music are Marta García Renart (b. 1942), also an accomplished pianist and accompanist (she studied with Rudolf Serkin); Marcela Rodríguez (b. 1950); and Lilia Vázquez (b. 1955), a composition student at the CENIDIM who also plays the piano and

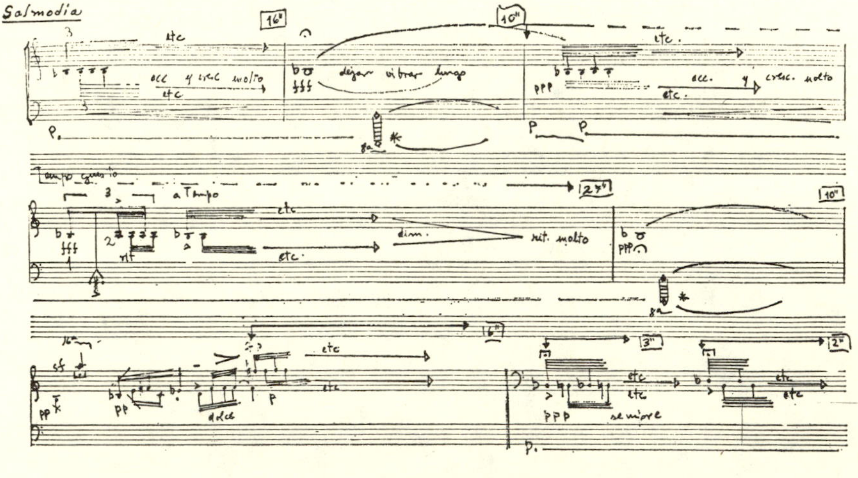

Figure 11.9 Opening of *Salmodia*, by Alicia Urreta. Used by permission of the composer.

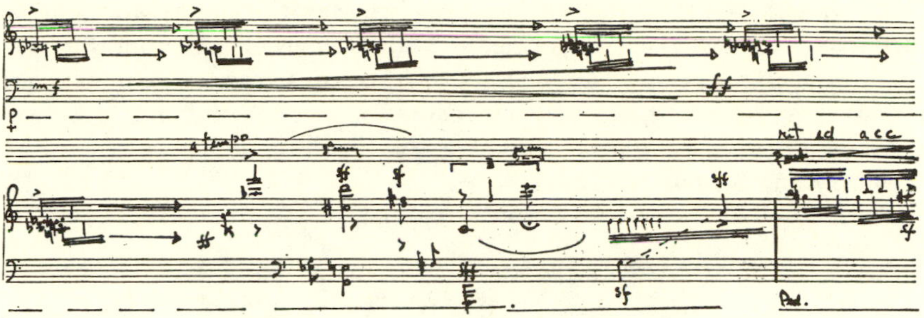

Figure 11.10 From *Salmodia*, by Alicia Urreta. Used by permission of the composer.

bassoon. Lilia Vázquez's symphonic work *Donde Habita el Olivado* (On the Site of Forgetfulness) was premiered in 1984 by the Orquesta Sinfónica de la Universidad with success.

Only in the field of popular music have works of Mexican women easily crossed the borders into other countries, especially the music of two composers: Maria Grever and Consuelo Velázquez.

MARIA GREVER (1884-1951) was a successful composer of romantic music. She was a self-taught composer who, in 1925, was asked by Paramount Pictures to write the music for various films on Latin-American subjects. Her first hit was the song *Júrame* (Swear to Me), followed by *Muñequita Linda* (Pretty Little Doll) and many more. Grever made the arrangements for the Broadway musical *Viva O'Brien* and conducted the orchestra for its run. Despite her recognition abroad, in her will she asked to be buried in Mexico.

CONSUELO VELAZQUEZ's (b. 1925) song *Bésame mucho* was a terrific hit among North American servicemen who fought in Asia and Europe during the Second World War. In 1962 the Beatles recorded the same song at Hamburg. Despite her love for classical and concert piano music, Velázquez's great successes pushed her to continue writing songs in the popular vein. In recent years she has presided over the important Sociedad de Autores y Compositores (Society of Authors and Composers) for two terms and has received many prizes and honors.

The royalties from her songs alone enable Consuelo Velázquez to enjoy a comfortable living. Even though in Mexico a composer's copyright does not last the entire lifetime of the creator, royalties from a single popular hit tune can amount to a considerable sum. Such composers rights were not enjoyed in Mexico until 1937. Before that time, composers like Manuel M. Ponce never got a penny in royalties from pieces such as his very popular *Estrellita* (Little Star), which was published and performed world wide.

Although Velázquez studied the piano with Ramón Serratos, she is a self-taught composer. The piano helps her to enrich the harmonies of her songs, even though she does not do her own orchestrations. She keeps up her keyboard technique, has performed the Saint-Saëns G minor and Ravel left hand concertos in public, and in late 1984 played, in concert, the piano part of a symphonic arrangement of three of her most famous songs—*Franqueza, Bésame mucho*, and *Que seas Feliz*—together with works by Debussy and Stravinsky.

Figure 11.11 Consuelo Velázquez, composer.

Another noted composer of popular songs is CARMEN MOLINA RIVERO (b. 1932), who specializes in children's songs, of which she has composed more than two hundred. Active for more than 25 years as a pianist, composer, and teacher, Rivero is beloved by children of all ages. Recently she was nominated to be the permanent conductor of a huge choir of 3,000 high school students, a chorus especially created to perform at official state functions.

MUSICOLOGISTS, CRITICS, AND SCHOLARS

Women in Mexico continue to show increased interest in music science, musicology, and criticism. In the early thirties, Manuel M. Ponce was the first Mexican musician to introduce an ethnomusicology class at the Conservatory. As a nationalistic composer, he induced young students to do field research in the area of Mexican folkloric musical materials. Some of his pupils devoted themselves fully to that task and wrote quite a number of books in the field. But at that time the Conservatory did not offer a musicology major in its curriculum.

The first Mexican woman to write a history of music, as well as other books on musical matters, was Alba Herrera y Ogazón (1885-1931), already mentioned as a pianist. After early piano studies with Carlos Meneses, Pedro Luis Ogazón, Alberto Villaseñor, and Ricardo Castro, in 1908 she was sent to New York City, where she learned the Virgil method of piano teaching—a system of teaching to produce perfect legato using silent keyboards with regulated touch, patented in the U.S. in 1892 by Almon K. Virgil—which she introduced to Mexico in 1910. But young students were, understandably, not very keen about having to practice on a mute piano, and so Ogazón returned to her first interest, musical research and criticism.

In 1917 she wrote her first book, *El arte musical en México* (Musical art in Mexico). It was published by the country's General Director of Fine Arts and was widely distributed in the schools. Beside the *History of Music,* she also published a collection of essays on musical criticism, *Puntos de Vista* (1921).

After Herrera y Ogazón's death, many years elapsed before Mexican women again showed interest in the scientific sides of music or the ways of exploring the art form in writing. After World War II women started trying their hand at in-depth concert reviews as well as criticism of concerts on a superficial basis.

In the 1970s women began to be interested in musicology. Emiliana de Zubeldia sent her talented pupil, Leticia Varela, to Berlin for a doctoral degree in musical science. Varela returned to Mexico in 1983 with honors, but she doesn't know what to do for a living with her diploma. Not until most of Mexico's universities establish musicology departments as part of their curricula will Mexican students get truly absorbed in scholarly or critical writing in large numbers. In the near past Mexico has had a good number of self-made scholars who could compete with university graduates, but that is not the ideal solution.

Carmen Sordo Sodi (b. 1934) is one of Mexico's most efficient and active ethnomusicologists. She earned a master's degree from the University of Southern California and another from Haifa's Hebrew University. For quite a number of years she was at the head of Mexico's Fine Arts Institute's Musical Research Department, where she convinced the institute to buy the important Sánchez-Garza collection of seventeenth- and eighteenth-century manuscripts of Mexican colonial music, as well as to ask Dr. Robert Stevenson from UCLA to transcribe most of that collection's villancicos [vocal works in madrigal style]. During her institute period, she exhibited a large collection of ancient and colonial instruments, gathered at her own initiative. In 1978, as part of Mexico's celebration of the centenary of Manuel M. Ponce's birth, she mounted a brilliant exhibition of the composer's music scores and personal memorabilia. The exhibition, open until March 1983, was enhanced by concerts of Ponce's music, lectures, and seminars.

During the last several years, Carmen Sordo Sodi has been busy with the Association of Mexican Women Musicians that she was instrumental in creating. She has also produced several series of concerts of colonial and folkloric music for students of university institutions; these performances are on a high artistic level and feature Sordo Sodi as one of the singers.

In 1980 a new Musicology Department was instituted at the Conservatory of Mexico under the supervision of three female and three male teachers. The women are Clara Meierovich, a young Uruguayan graduate of Montevideo's University; Angela Chapa, a young Mexican researcher; and myself. Meierovich is now conducting research on Carlos Chávez's more obscure material.

The Conservatory possesses large collections of old and uncatalogued papers that we intend to refurbish and research fully. We have already discovered a few very valuable documents. The three young men in the department—Juan José Escorza, Karl Bellinghausen, and José Antonio Robles Cahero—plan to write up their findings in several pamphlets with the intention of finally publishing a book.

Right now several women have centered their interest in music in the written word.

Elisa Osorio Bolio Saldívar (b. 1906), wife of the late music historian Gabriel Saldívar y Silva, is a pianist and musician in her own right. She was a tireless collaborator with her husband and a writer of books on kindergarten music (*Ritmos, Cantos y Juegos, Educadores del jardín de niños mexicano*). She is now preparing her husband's posthumous *Bibliografía de la Música Mexicana* (Bibliography of Mexican Music) for publication. Sẽnora Saldívar recently presented a concert of some of the colonial music contained in one of the original colonial codices owned by her late husband. Since his death, she has devoted herself to completing everything he left undone.

Music journalism—criticism and cultural reporting—has drawn several notable women into the profession. María Teresa Castrillón, a fine pianist—she earned a piano diploma from the Musical Academy of Vienna and has given recitals on two pianos with Georg Demus—is also an acute music critic for *El Heraldo de México*, one of the country's principal daily papers. Isabel Farfán Cano, a writer, poet, and amateur guitar player, has a fine instinct for sound musical judgment, as shown in her reviews for several papers, such as *Jueves de Excelsior*, *La República*, and *El Universal*. Other reviewers include Leonora Saavedra, Gloria Carmona, Angelina Camargo, and Magdalena Saldaña.

CONCLUSIONS

Right now the conservatory has some fine composer-teachers, for example, Mario Lavista and Daniel Catán, and the CENIDIM collaborates at times by arranging for good foreign teachers and conductors to come for longer or shorter periods to work with the students. The present generation of women composition students shows clearly the rewarding results of this nurturing. (Interestingly, they show *less* inclination toward nationalism in their work than most of their male peers.)

As we have seen, it almost seems to be "traditional" for Mexican performers to build their careers abroad; would it be easier for a Mexican woman to make a career in composition outside of Mexico? I would answer, Yes, of course—but provided that:

1. she has shown great specific talent for musical creation;
2. she has been sufficiently prepared in Mexico in harmony, counterpoint, analysis, and other theoretical basics;
3. she gets a grant for at least two or three years of study, or is supported independently;
4. she has chosen the right country and the right teacher or teachers;
5. she is willing and prepared to fight discrimination (should it be necessary);
6. she is like a fine filter that absorbs water and, after distilling the impurities from it, pours it back clear and brilliant, with magnificent results.

Up to now no Mexican woman composer of art music has won an international reputation for herself. But time has been short. I, for one, have faith in the future and know, almost for sure, that my country still holds many surprises in store.

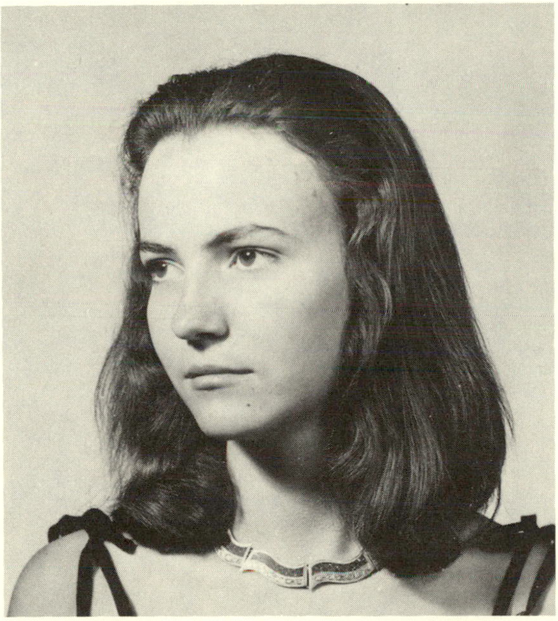

Figure 11.12 Marta García Renart, pianist and composer. Photograph by E. Pulido.

BIBLIOGRAPHY

Alvarez Coral, Juan. *Compositores Mexicanos.* México: Editores Asociados, 1971.

de la Barca, Marquesa de Calderón. *La Vida en México.* México: Editora Nacional, 1957.

de Saldívar, Elisa Osorio B. *In memoriam Dr. Gabriel Saldívar y Silva.* México, 1983.

Geijerstam, Claes. *Popular Music in Mexico.* Albuquerque: University of New Mexico Press, 1976.

Leiva, Raúl. *Introducción a Sor Juana.* México: Universidad Nacional Autónoma de México, 1975.

Mayer-Serra, Otto. *Música y Músicos de Latinoamérica.* New York: W. M. Jackson Inc., 1947.

Novaro, Augusto. *Sistema Natural de la Música.* México: Edición del Autor, 1951.

Olavarría Ferrari, Enrique. *Historia del Teatro en México.* Porrúa: 1967.

Paz, Octavio. *Sor Juana Inés de la Cruz, o Las Trampas de la Fe.* México: Fondo de Cultura Económica, 1983.

Pulido, Esperanza. *La Mujer Mexicana en la Música.* México: Ediciones de la Revista de Bellas Artes, 1958.

Stevenson, Robert. *Music in Mexico.* New York: Thomas Y. Crowell Co., 1952.

Vinton, John. *Dictionary of Contemporary Music.* New York: E. P. Dutton, 1971.

12

Spreading the Good News: Conferences on Women in Music

EDITH BORROFF

On 5-8 May 1983, Op. 2: Women in Music, the second such conference sponsored by the University of Michigan, was held at the University School of Music in Ann Arbor. The initial conference, held at the University on 12-14 March 1982, consisted of 30-odd sessions, starting with an anacrusis the evening of March 11—a recital of music by women working in the composition program of the university. It was an important anacrusis, for it emphasized the music itself, and in that sense it centered the university's series of conferences firmly in the area of living music.

About 175 conferees attended Op. 2, including several male attendees and male presenters. The conference participants included teachers, performers, musicologists, and a few persons representing less common pursuits (publishers, critics), plus one or two lay people. Most conferees attended most of the offerings. The participants were in general similar to those of the 1982 Conference, whose 200 or so participants—all but one of them women—were also largely music professionals or academics who came from 15 states and Canada, ranging from Maine to Saskatchewan and Texas to Virginia.

The 1983 conference again offered a rich panoply of recitals, concerts, lectures, panels, and other presentations (some difficult to classify, some clear hybrids, such as lecture/recitals). Running steadily from four o'clock Thursday afternoon until shortly after noon on Sunday, it was thickly and precisely scheduled, and, with the exception of Saturday evening's concert of organ works, heroically maintained. About 30 presentations, most of them dealing with more than one work, varied in length from ten to 40 minutes, with most at 20, 25, or 30 minutes.

The 1982 conference used the lovely half-circle theatre in the Rackham Graduate School; in 1983 all events but the banquet, the organ recital, and the carillon recital were held in one of the recital halls of the Moore Building at the School of Music, located at the more remote North Campus—a beautiful spot with excellent facilities but less convenient to local restaurants and other city attractions.

The Program Committee, chaired by Lynne Bartholomew, proved not only efficient but thoughtful. On Saturday, when the North Campus Commons was closed, box lunches were provided; and most presenters enjoyed local hospitality, an act of remarkable amenity and grace. Professor Marilyn Mason, the continuing mentor of the conference, is responsible for much of that grace.

Thus, although the Moore Building recital hall (attractive and efficient) could not compete with the sumptuous elegance of Rackham, the conference once more managed to provide a welcoming atmosphere and engendered a powerful esprit de corps unusual in professional meetings. The sense of kaleidoscopic input was turned into a strength in three ways: by adhering to the schedule (so that people could come and go with assurance), by having only one thing scheduled at a time, and by providing for all conferees a compendium of abstracts and programs—a thick booklet worth its weight in just about any metal you might mention—as a preview, an aid during the meetings, and especially in retrospect as a continuing reference. It is hoped that a published *Proceedings* will be made available for both conferences.

Standards were kept high, and it would be unfair to single out a few from the many stunning performances. As before, the focus of the conference was clearly on music and the performance of music. More than two-thirds of the presentations were recitals or lecture/recitals; interspersed were lectures on a variety of subjects, from biographical and analytical studies of particular persons and works to the music of Tunisian and Judeo-Spanish women. Three panel discussions bracketed the meetings: an opening panel (the only presentation on Thursday afternoon) dealt with "Women and Music in the College Curricula," and two closing panels (the only presentations on Sunday), "A Cross-Cultural Perspective on Women Musicians" and "Getting Women's Music Heard."

Thus, the heart of the conference, Thursday evening and all of Friday and Saturday, was a string of single, well-focused and well-prepared presentations that centered on the hearing of music. The complete agenda follows the body of this article.

Elizabeth Wood, a cosmopolitan mind and fine spokesman, gave the opening keynote address. She surveyed the changes in the acceptance of music by women and of college-level courses dealing with the music and with women in the profession. She made us all aware that forward steps are not necessarily permanent ("Survival is not inevitable"), she piqued our ambitions with reminders of how much remains to be done, and finally urged us to the open-minded acceptance of women in all phases of music. She particularly stressed the need to transcend both the "generation gap" and the "genre gap." Her presentation was a warm and wise invocation of thoughtfulness and generosity.

As banquet speaker, I tried to follow that wisdom with a metaphorical statement about the need to transcend those same gaps and particularly to tolerate—even welcome—the many approaches to the fight for women's music. I took my metaphor from the four humors, saying that we must incorporate all attitudes (citing happy, accepting, sad, and angry—the original sanguine, phlegmatic, melancholy, and choleric) and allow ourselves to help and be helped by all of them. Like Wood, I worked to foster the esprit de corps, and, since it was a postprandial offering, to buoy up the spirits of the men and women who were giving so much time to the meetings.

As a whole, I felt the conference to be a fine congeries of musical, anthropological, and sociological offerings, with a substantial preponderance of the fare solidly musical. Yet the musical offerings were not as well balanced as those of the first conference. And the luncheon discussion on Saturday, an open business meeting attended by a majority of the conferees, raised questions spawned by the conference itself, which give rise to questions about meetings on women's music in general.

Through the middle of 1983 two conferences sponsored by the University of Michigan have been held in Ann Arbor and two by the National Congress on Women in Music (now The International Congress on Women in Music), one each in New York and California. Patterns have been set by these two organizing bodies; patterns which are very different. The Congress is a broad-based organization with a National Advisory Committee of scholars, activists for women's rights, and representatives of publishers and national women's clubs (among others); I was one of the original committee members, and I spoke at the first (New York) Congress. Thus I am interested in both Congress and conference, and I feel strongly that we need both, with their differing approaches, differing strengths, differing ambiences.

THE CONSTITUENCY

Many issues in women's music confuse the concept of a national meeting. Clarification might well start with a determination of the nature of the persons to whom we wish to present programs and the nature of their needs. There are two main groups: those who come because of interest in women's studies and those who come because of interest in music. The pull toward sociological topics (particularly as panels) seems to represent the women's studies people; the pull toward recitals, concerts, and lecture/recitals seems to represent the musicians. It would be an oversimplification to characterize the Congress as more concerned with sociological aspects of these studies than the conference, but the programs of the four meetings can be used to support such a statement. A corporate performance or a recital with several performers, is a panel of sorts. Yet the panel discussion does, indeed, tend to educational, cultural, and business matters (as the titles of the three panels in Ann Arbor demonstrate). They are at their best stimulating, provoking, and useful; and at their worst they are nay-saying complaint sessions that may be therapeutic but are essentially boring when unfocused and nonconstructive. It may be that we need a National Gripe Session, a place to scream and be heard—I said something like that in my speech about the humors—but I am not sure where and when that should be. A session with a psychologist on how to handle rage might also be practical, but I am not sure where and when that should be either.

Academics comprise a healthy percentage of conferees; college and university faculty seemed to dominate the New York Congress, though that perception may have been skewed by the sample of the sessions that I attended and the one in which I participated. (Interestingly, I was invited as a *musicologist* by the Congress and as a *composer* by the conference.) The dilemma of the educator has often been reduced to a choice between method and content. My own belief is that our teachers (at all levels) need to expand content first and foremost and then launch a strong assault upon such musicological assumptions as have created the myth of "great music" that exists in the abstract (without performance!), which we are obliged not only to admire but to revere—music that has already been written and is therefore a completed corpus (pun intended), closed to American music, all ethnic music, however defined, and of course to music by women. Every marvelous work by a woman expands our sense of the human condition, but unless the structure of pretension is beaten down, such works cannot be acknowledged or incorporated into the canon of history—our works are still exceptions, oddities, parentheses. In women's studies, even more strongly than in traditional scholarship, the *implications* of new knowledge must be presented along with the knowledge itself, for the knowledge is the arrow and the comprehension of the *meaning* of the knowledge is the bow. An effort to add a few names and titles to the traditional lists of approved composers and works is essentially futile, an ounce of grapeshot against the parapets of prejudice.

The battle begins in history survey classes, and it may end there. After plowing through any of the general histories that inculcate the myth, a student is unable to assimilate exceptional materials. The same is true of Introduction to Music courses; every teacher who instills the traditional myth into her survey courses serves to perpetuate an audience of prejudging listeners. I no longer teach any course without including materials on women's music. Too many still do as I used to do: fight hard for women's music in special environments and then go back to the classroom and reinforce the myth. We must find the ways to supplant the myth, to work within a constructive matrix; we must evolve a new *basis operandi*. I have never heard a woman propose a retaliatory *basis operandi*, one that demands more for us than our due, and we certainly should not. But we *should* propose a *basis operandi* that will admit our existence and will welcome excellence wherever it be. Clearly, the academics have a job to do, a job of the most primary importance to the future of music in the United States. We cannot expect male academics, who have such a huge investment in the status quo, to man the battering rams; I suspect they will have to be womaned.

Performers are a vital component of the constituency. They serve us by bringing to life the music of women; they are served by each other and by the scholars who make fine music available to them. I have heard much excellent music at the conferences I've attended, *much* more than I conceived there would be, but have yet to hear these works with any frequency at general faculty recitals or on the programs of concert artists. If the musical arrows are to be shot, the scholar's bow is vital here. The music of women, in the cold cruel world of concerts, is too often rehearsed with insufficient time and perfunctory attention, performed poorly (often by a person or persons unwillingly assigned to the work), and dumped as the inevitable end of the self-fulfilling prophesy.*

Fewer concert groups program music by women than do university groups. Is it coincidental that the reluctant performers earn money directly from ticket sales for concerts and the willing ones give free concerts as part of their university duties? Would not the answers to such questions be vital in deciding the archer's target?

At the first conference in Ann Arbor, performers, private music teachers and college-level teachers made up the pith of the attendees; at the second, the focus was strongly upon composers. Eighteen of the 30-odd presentations were devoted to this vector, with overwhelming emphasis upon radical virtuoso works; the conferees were given much for their ears. Many of the difficult contemporary works were marvelously performed, and many were marvelously rich as music; also, it was interesting to have a majority of the composers present. But works of thorny musical and transcendent technical difficulty are not gifts to the teaching and performing repertoire; few of the works heard could readily be added to the repertoire for developing performers, and finding such music is a strong reason for attending these conferences on the part of teachers and performers. Three or four stunning performances of new music—something for the spirit as well as for the ear—would be effective and radiant gifts for those who come. But centering the conference in the promotion of new music is to turn the conference into another Composers Forum. Many societies already sponsor performances of new music, and, as close as this cause is to my heart, I cannot urge it upon the Congress and the conference.[1] Further, the new music component of such meetings (for I certainly do not suggest that that component be eliminated) should be balanced within the spectrum of conservative/radical styles, within the gamut of mediums (vocal and instrumental, solo and choral, solo

*As late as 1980, a work of mine was given a premiere "performance" by an all-male group, who actually had the bad taste to brag that they had not prepared it; there was no focus (because, not having looked at the score, they had no idea of the contrasting dynamic marks that indicated which instruments should predominate), the tempos were wacky (a movement designated at 80 quarters to the minute was played at 132), and they weren't together (one man ended four measures before the others). This was a nationally reputed chamber group, and I wish I could consider them aberrant. It is a good case in point, because in 1982 another group (also all-male) performed the work well, with fine reception, and have kept it in their repertoire.

chamber—a variety of combinations and sizes), within the gamut of difficulty (why not a recital by second- or third-year students? something comparable to—say—the Brahms *Intermezzi* rather than the *Paganini Variations*?). And the new music must not obscure the old: eighteen concerts of new music as against three of music from 1800-1970, two from 1600-1800, and two medieval concerts is not a balance.

FORMAT

Two chief styles of format have emerged in the meetings: the multiple-session format based upon the scholarly meeting, and the single-session format based upon the musical performance itself. Inevitably the two styles either reflect or engender the emphases with which they are associated. The first has been the preference of the Congress, the second of the conference. The association of panels as a vital force in the Congress programming and as ancillary or even peripheral in the conference further italicizes the basic difference. As against one panel in the first conference and three in the second, the second Congress had eighteen panels, ten in one day.

As with most of the differences between the conference and Congress, I feel that there is a place for both, but I have more difficulty with the multiple-session format than with any other facet of the meetings. I am not alone. The suggestion (at Op. 2's open business meeting) that the University of Michigan Conference switch to the multiple-session format was greeted with fervent negative response by the great majority of those attending. This may be attributed to the instinctive response to the congenial format by the performers, private teachers, and composers at the conference.

But the reason goes deeper than that; and in this case I feel that they were right. For one thing, esprit de corps, so salient a factor in the Michigan conferences, is based upon shared experience, not upon a choreography of confusion during which no two conferees will end up with the same schedule. But even more important, a gridlock of multiple sessions can be useful only to advanced scholars. At a national meeting of the American Musicological Society, for example, a Medieval specialist knows where to go—*if* one assumes that the business of a musicologist at a national meeting is to deepen the already narrow field. I reject that assumption for myself—I fear narrowness as much as I would a physical strait jacket—but I do not reject it for those who do not find it confining, and in any case I find a balance between breadth and depth constantly precarious. What I reject is the multiple format for a discipline as young as ours. *I do not know enough to know what I need to hear; I need to hear it all.*

The materials, obviously, are much more extensive, in amount as well as excellence, than anybody had envisaged. The preliminary report on the Women's Music Collection recently acquired by the University of Michigan and housed in the School of Music Library has revealed that it includes over 1,400 works of music by women published in Europe between 1780 and

1950—presumably with few or none by Americans (the collection has been catalogued for publication in the 1986-87 academic year)—and thus excludes the tremendous postwar spate. Yet it contains works by *over four hundred* composers. The vast bulk of this collection consists of unknown music; even the two or three boxes apiece devoted to the music of Dame Ethel Smyth, Cécile Chaminade, and Augusta Holmès are likely to contain some surprises. Is any one of us in the position to by-pass knowledge of this source in favor of something else going on at the same time?

The scheduling of as many as seven simultaneous sessions results in almost unbeatable odds in favor of chaos, makes it necessary to keep all sessions the same length, and forces the conferees to lose time triangulating among meeting rooms. And, of course, it inevitably means not being able to attend presentations upon which one has set one's heart. (In New York I couldn't go to the presentation I wanted most to hear because I was speaking at that time.) Are not three or four simultaneous offerings sufficient? The compensation is, of course, the great number of those who can be actively involved in a meeting; participation ensures brownie points for those in academe and, for many, carries with it expense funding as well. But this is, I think, offset by the price of talking only to ourselves. The private and high-school teachers who came to Ann Arbor had no backing nor did those performers not attached to universities; their contributions were substantial and their presence valued. The answer may lie in new financial setups; some universities make grants available to faculty members who propose to enhance course content and teaching effectiveness. Attending such meetings may well qualify.

If the simultaneous sessions can be an overkill, the single sessions can be too intense. Beginning at eight o'clock in the morning and going through to an evening concert is too heavy a day. The variable lengths, the interspersion of musical and verbal presentations, the coherence of the meetings, are relaxing, but 9:00-10:30, 10:45-12:15, 2:00-3:30, 3:45-5:15 (or any other deployment, regular or irregular, with five to six hours of solid fare), plus an evening that ends by 10:00, would seem a great plenty. Although in theory I know I can come and go quite freely, I always hate to miss the next presentation—and often the most exciting moments of a meeting lie in unexpected places.

GOALS

There are, in addition to national meetings, many forces at work for women's music. Many people in many places are laying the foundations for the future a stone at a time. Each of us probably knows one or two people who do excellent work. I know Marjory Irvin, Professor of Music (theory and piano) at Lawrence University in Appleton, Wisconsin, for example; she has performed (alone and with a singer) widely and lectured on music by women in general and on Augusta Holmès and Nadia Boulanger (both of whose songs she presented through Da Capo Press). And I have done my bits: chiefly two lectures (one historical and mild, one political and accusatory); my work on Elisabeth Jacquet de La Guerre (which stems from the 1950s and was not begun as an effort for women but simply as acknowledgment of that marvelous music); and a few articles. I regret that I am ignorant of so many of the others, but that is the way prejudice dissipates: by hundreds of small efforts made by hundreds of people unknown to each other.

Thus the national meetings should be seen as a more extensive and more broadly reaching representative of many small local presentations, all vital, all to be praised, all to be gratefully acknowledged.

The two directions represented by The International Congress on Women in Music and by the University of Michigan Conference on Women in Music are complementary; they should not merge, nor should either seek to emulate the other. The Congress, like most scholarly organizations, has no permanent home; the conference is based in a centrally located university which houses an important library resource that will surely grow.[2] Each style has something to offer, each has its own constituency. Neither should seek to absorb the other, for that would further one group at the expense of another. They are not rivals any more than my two hands are rivals. So young and so vital a discipline as women's music needs more than one hand, for it is known that we listen in vain for the sound of one hand clapping.

NOTES

1. The strong representation of new music clearly distinguishes the conference of 1983 from its predecessor. At the earlier conference contemporary music was treated like the rest, neither segregated (except in the opening concert of music by student composers) nor lionized *in ipso*. In such a context the not-quite-new can appear with honor, as can conservative composers in general.

2. Since this chapter was written, the International Congress on Women and Music has established a long-term connection with the Department of Music at California State University at Northridge from which base it issues a periodic newsletter and other publications; its incarnations as conference/festival continue, however, at other locations around the U.S. and abroad. By contrast, the Ann Arbor conference has now launched at least one subsequent edition in satellite form: "Op. 3: Women in Music Conference" took place at the University of Kansas at Lawrence, 28-31 March, 1985. (Editor's Note)

APPENDIX: AGENDA FOR WOMEN IN MUSIC, Op.2, THE UNIVERSITY OF MICHIGAN, MAY 5-8, 1983

Thursday, May 5

Panel Discussion: "Women & Music in the College Curriculum: Planning, Implementation, & Resources." Joan Swanekamp (Eastman School of Music),

Susan Borwich (Wake Forest University), Ellen Koskoff (Eastman School of Music), Susan Sandman (Wells College)

Opening Concert: Esquisses by Sharon Hershey (University of Michigan)

Emily Dickinson Songs by Gloria Coates, Kathryn LaBouff/soprano (Ithaca College), Susan Sobelevsky/piano (Ithaca College)

Five Love Songs by Thea Musgrave, Kathryn LaBouff/soprano, Pamela Kimmel/guitar (Roosevelt University)

Solitaire by Barbara Kolb, Naomi Oliphant/piano (Brock University)

Works of Elaine Lebenbom and Geraldine Schwartz, The Detroit Woodwind Quintet: Linda Dobbertin/flute, Sylvia Starkman/oboe, Lauran Mitchell/clarinet, Michael Wieland/bassoon, Ernestine Barnes/horn, Doris Euband/piano, with Joan Berndt/English horn

Friday, May 6

Keynote Address: "Opus 9: Notes on Survival." Elizabeth Wood (New York City)

Lecture-Recital: "Music from the University of California, Santa Barbara" (works of Emma Lou Diemer). Emma Lou Diemer/composer, Betty Oberacker/piano, Marjorie and Wendell Nelson/duo-pianists, Geoffrey Rutkowski/cello (University of California, Santa Barbara)

Lecture: "Problems of Women in American Music through the 1970's." Mary Brown Hinely (DeKalb Community College)

Lecture: "Sexism in Music Education: A Review of the Literature." Donna Pucciani (Rosary College)

Lecture: "How Women in Music Are Presented by Print Media." Laura Koplewitz (New York City)

Recital: "Music for Oboe & Harpsichord" (by Elisabeth-Claude Jacquet de La Guerre, Preethi de Silva, and Elizabeth Maconchy), Susan Hicks/oboe (University of Kansas), Susan Marchant/harpsichord (Pittsburgh State University, Kansas)

Recital: "Contemporary Harpsichord Works" (by Marga Richter, Barbara Pentland, Nancy Van de Vate, and Elizabeth Maconchy), Michelle Graveline/harpsichord (University of Michigan)

Lecture-Demonstration: "Women Composers of Piano Music in 19th-Century America." John Gillespie (University of California, Santa Barbara)

Lecture: "The Contribution of Women Pedagogues to the Piano Music of the 20th Century." Doris Allen (University of Oregon)

Lecture: "Dynamic Geometry—Hildegard von Bingen." Pozzi Escot (Wheaton College)

Lunch on Your Own (Student-Faculty Lounge or North Campus Commons suggested)

Lecture-Recital: "Song Cycle '*Twas My Own Glory* by Joyce Grill" (set to poems of Emily Dickinson). Wilma Scheffner/soprano (Winona State University), Joyce Grill/composer-piano (University of Wisconsin-LaCrosse)

Recital: "Songs by 20th-Century Composers" (Miriam Gideon, Rhian Samuel, Elizabeth Vercoe, Mary Howe), Sharon Mabry/mezzo-soprano (Austin Peay State University), Patsy Wade/piano (Nashville, Tennessee)

Lecture: "The Joyful Sound: Women in 19th-Century American Hymnody." Esther

Rothenbusch (University of Michigan), Mary Jane Montague/piano (University of Michigan)

Lecture: "The Making and Unmaking of a Composer: Ideals and Values in the Career of Mary Carr Moore, (1873-1957)." Catherine Parsons Smith (University of Nevada, Reno)

Lecture-Recital: "Compositional Techniques for Solo 'Cello." Gwyneth Walker/composer (Hartford Conservatory of Music), Mary Lou Rylands/'cello (University of Connecticut), Marsha Hogan/soprano (Trinity College)

Recital: "Piano Compositions of Ada Belle Marcus," Ada Belle Marcus/composer-piano (Des Plaines, Illinois)

Lecture: "Arthur P. Schmidt, Boston Publisher, and American Women Composers (*ca.* 1880-1945)." Adrienne Fried Block (Marymount Manhattan College)

Lecture: "American Women Orchestral Conductors: Factors Affecting Career Development." Kay D. Lawson (Michigan State University)

Recital: "Contemporary Music for Saxophone" (by Susan Hurley, Christina Kuzmych, and Lucie Robert), Jean Lansing/Saxophone (Wichita State University), Dorothy E. Crum/soprano (Wichita State University), Eleanor Kosek/violin (University of Michigan)

Recital: "Works by Germaine Tailleferre and Suzanne Demarquez for Violin and Piano," Norma Lewis Davidson/violin (Texas Woman's University), Joyce E. Strong/piano (Texas Woman's University)

Banquet Speech: "One or Two Words . . . " Edith Borroff, State University of New York, Binghamton

Entertainment: "Close Harmony Jazz Vocals—The Music of the Boswell Sisters, 1931-1933." Misbehavin' (Ann Arbor, Michigan): Susan Dawson, Jane Hassinger, Patricia Ward/vocals, Mark Tucker/arranger-piano, Peter Ferran/reeds, Paul Klinger/trumpet and bass saxophone, Ted Harley/bass, Bob Elliott/drums

Saturday, May 7

Lecture-Recital: "Judeo-Spanish Romances and Wedding Songs." Judith Cohen (Toronto, Canada)

Lecture-Demonstration: "Balkan Women as Preservers of Traditional Music and Culture." Patricia Shehan (Washington University)

Recital: "Black and White Women Composers of the 20th Century" (Margaret Brandman, Lili Boulanger, Philippa Schuyler, Undine Smith Moore, Elizabeth Szönyi, Vally Weigl, Dulci Holland), Selma Epstein/piano (Dickeyville, Maryland)

Lecture-Recital: "*Three Fantasy Pieces for Cello and Piano* by Shulamit Ran," Julie Bevan Zumsteg/cello (Brigham Young University), Sheila Philips Johns/piano (Washington, D.C.)

Lecture: "Musical Ensembles of Tunisian Women." JaFran Jones (Bowling Green State University)

Lecture: "Female *Tayu* in the Male-Dominated *Gidayu* Narrative Tradition of Japan." A. Kimi Coaldrake (University of Michigan)

Lecture-Recital: "The Harp: Henrietta Renie and Peggy Glanville-Hicks," Lucile H. Jennings/harp (Ohio University, Athens), Jill Bailiff-Reyes/harp (Eastern Michigan University)

Recital: "American Women's Harp Music—1975 to 1983" (works of Ruth Lomon, Amy Reich, and Elizabeth Vercoe), Susan Allen/harp (Newton, Massachusetts)

Lecture: "The Women's Music Collection of The University of Michigan." Peggy Daub (The University of Michigan)

Lecture: "Woman Sings Her Song: An Investigation into Woman-Identified Music." Karen E. Petersen (Northwestern University)

Recital: "A 21st-Century Woman," Suzanne Pierson/composer-soprano (Denver, Colorado)

Recital: "Contemporary American Women Composers" (Katherine David, Rebecca Clarke, Nancy Van de Vate, Mary Howe, Elizabeth Hayden Pizer, Karen Griebling), Marla Kensey/soprano (Olivet Nazarene College) Alice Edwards/piano (Olivet Nazarene College)

Lecture-Recital: "Two French Women Composers and Their Piano Compositions: Marguerite Canal and Suzanne Joly." Odette Goulon/piano (Paris, France)

Lecture-Recital: "Women and the Classic Guitar." Alice Artzt/guitar (New York City)

Recital: "Works of Black American Composers: Margaret Bonds and Jeraldine Herbison," Janis-Rozena Soprano (Old Dominion University), Alyce LeBlanc/piano (Norfolk, Virginia)

An Amy Beach Program

Lecture: "They Also Serve Who Only Succeed." Robert Plucker (Skagit Valley College)

Concert: The Music of Amy Beach. Works for Violin and Piano, Rose-Marie Johnson/violin (San Francisco)

Songs, Carolyn Heafner/soprano (New York City), Shirley Seguin/piano (New York City)

Quintet for Piano and Strings

Carillon Recital: Burton Tower (Main Campus) "Works of Margo Halsted, Emma Lou Diemer, Leslie Ellen Mahaffey, Mary Jeanne van Appledorn, Heleen van der Weel," Margo Halsted/carillonneur (University of California, Riverside)

Organ Program: Hill Auditorium (Main Campus)

Lecture-Recital "A Collaborative Creative Process for Organ," *Seven Portals of Vision,*" Ruth Lomon/composer (Cambridge, Massachusetts), Joanne M. Vollendorf/organ (University of Michigan)

Lecture-Recital: "Music by British and American Composers" (Ethel Smyth, Edith Borroff, Emma Lou Diemer), Jane Marcus/Smyth Scholar (University of Texas at Austin), Edith Borroff/composer (SUNY at Binghamton), Emma Lou Diemer/composer (University of California, Riverside), Marilyn Mason/organ (University of Michigan), Michele Johns/organ (University of Michigan)

Panel Discussion: "A Cross-Cultural Perspective on Women Musicians." Jane Bowers/moderator (University of Wisconsin-Milwaukee), Roxane Carlisle (Canadian International Development Agency), Ellen Koskoff (Eastman School of Music), Jennifer Quinn (Curator, Flanders Ballad Collection, Middlebury College), Judith Vander (ethnomusicologist)

Respite

Panel Discussion: "Getting Women's Music Heard." Judith Rosen/moderator (Encino, California), Jane Courtland Welton/recording executive (Los Angeles), Edwin London/composer-conductor (Cleveland State University; National Advisory Board, Meet the Composer), Nancy Shear/music consultant (Nancy Shear Music Services, NYC), Frances Steiner/conductor (Carson/Dominguez Hills Symphony: Baroque Consortium Chamber Orchestra; California State University, Dominguez Hills)

13

The Festivals of Women's Music, I–IV

KATHERINE HOOVER

In 1978 I began, under the sponsorship of the Women's Interart Center in New York, an unusual and ultimately rewarding project. We called it the "First Festival of Women's Music." At that time I stated the original aims.

> The First Festival of Women's Music was begun to fill a need, and to correct a misconception.
>
> It has been generally accepted by audiences, performers, and even composers, that women do not write music; or if they do, that it is a recent development or of limited nature. This is not the case. Women have written music for hundreds of years, from songs to complex orchestral works. Some women composers have been leading figures of their time (Elisabeth Jacquet de La Guerre, Isabella Leonarda, Amy Beach). There exists an immense body of works, a rich heritage which we have only begun to tap in this Festival.
>
> Furthermore, there are many excellent women composers active today, and though it is difficult for any contemporary composer to secure good performances, there is ample evidence to show that it has been more difficult for women.

As a composer myself, I had been aware of certain problems shared by all composers but felt more acutely by women. Most of those who have achieved some standing can get pieces performed, but to get them properly rehearsed and presented by a recognized group is a much more difficult matter. As a result, though all of us have tapes of our works, few of these are adequate for broadcast or submission to publishers or for competitions. The First Festival was designed primarily to meet these needs by stressing high-quality performances and tapes of professional caliber, as well as to bring to public awareness the large and excellent literature of women's compositions.

The success of the First Festival concerts and broadcasts led to three others, carrying through the spring of 1981. Each Festival consisted of four chamber music concerts, with two additional electronic music presentations included during the first year.

These Festivals were not the first of their kind; other concerts or groups of concerts of women's music had previously been held in New York and elsewhere. Furthermore, many have since developed, with wider publicity and expanded aims (papers, panels, and meetings added to a roster of concerts). Tremendous progress has been made in the last few years in the general knowledge and dissemination of women's music.

Festivals I through IV, however, maintain a unique place in this growth. They began early enough (1978) to be branded as radical by many who later accepted and respected their presence, and they constituted the first ongoing, yearly series. As the many letters from composers attest, the Festivals were rare in their commitment to high quality in performance and programming and in the variety of material presented. They also kept a steady focus on the importance of disseminating the performances through taping and broadcast.

This chapter will trace the history of this project, warts and all, from its inception to its untimely demise in 1981.

My own involvement with music began quite early with one-dollar piano lessons from a woman who lived around the corner; to her, the heights of music were reached by Mendelssohn's *Songs Without Words,* and it was all downhill after that. I knew no one who wrote music, nor was the subject ever discussed in my school system. From my reading and listening I rather presumed that no women had been composers. During my undergraduate years at the Eastman School of Music, I made some tentative efforts at composing and was ignored, and my attention was easily recentered on performing. I became a flutist and teacher of flute, ensemble, and theory. Still, composing continued to surface intermittently, until, finally, I made room for it and welcomed it into my life.

By 1977 I had been writing seriously for a few years with increasing success. That year a concert featuring some of my works was held at the Women's Interart Center in New York. Though it was underrehearsed, the players were excellent, and the enthusiastic response of the audience gave me great encouragement. I was grateful to the Center.

The Women's Interart Center (WIC) is an interesting place. It began in 1969 as shared space for women painters and sculptors and evolved into a production center with programs in drama, film, and music and a gallery and workshops. The women, both artists and administrators, represented a wide cross-section of style and age; the presentation of quality art was always its main concern. The Center has received numerous commendations and prizes for its productions of various kinds, particularly in drama and film.

The middle 1970s was a critical period for women composers. The League of Women Composers (later the International League-ILWC) and American Women Composers (AWC) were both founded during this period, and much of the scholarship that now constitutes primary source material on

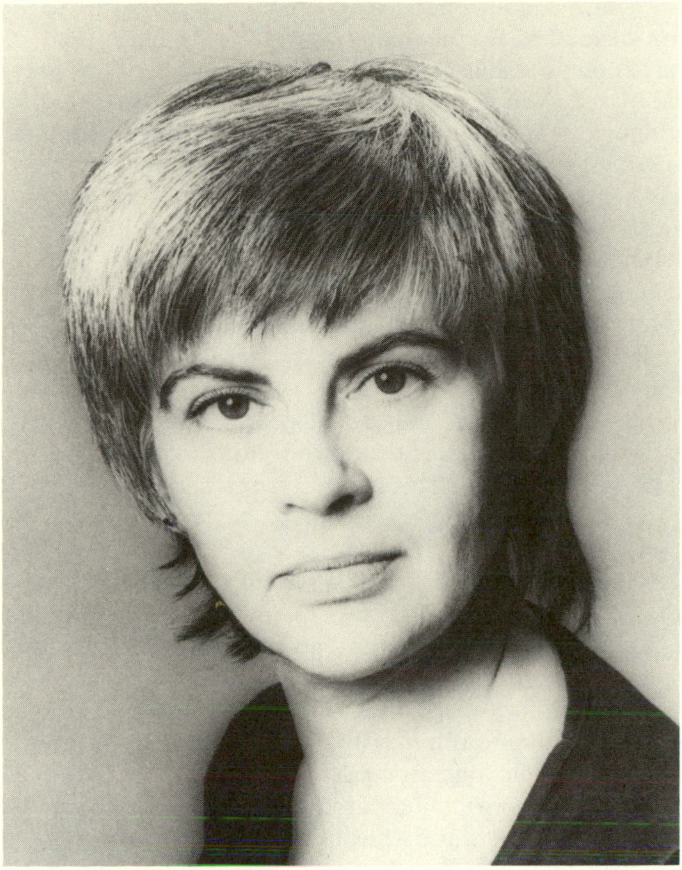

Figure 13.1 Katherine Hoover, composer, flutist, concert producer. Photograph by Frank Giraldi.

this subject was being written or printed at that time. Most women composers, however, were still working in isolation, without knowledge of their peers or their history, and with little or no access to such knowledge.

Shortly after the 1977 WIC concert of my works, Margot Lewiton, Director of the Center, spoke to me about possibly doing some sort of project to benefit women composers; that same year I attended some of the first meetings of the ILWC and AWC in New York and began to meet other composers and get an idea of common problems and needs. So, when the WIC project materialized, I already had a perspective and a set of goals from the composers' standpoint. Furthermore, after many years' experience as a freelance musician in New York, I knew many excellent players and had clear ideas of what performers need in order to present new or unknown material successfully.

Perhaps I should have been alert for administrative problems early on, for when I was asked definitely to begin there were only three weeks in which to organize a multiconcert series from scratch in order to meet grant application deadlines. Fortunately, my goals were fairly clear. Chamber music was the only feasible choice financially, and a series of four concerts was quickly fixed. Varied, interesting programs and quality performances were my highest priorities, along with documenting the performances via usable tapes and securing broadcasts of these tapes.

My first step, given the time crunch, was to secure the performers. Because an established group has a commitment to jointly understood musical standards and regularly scheduled rehearsals—both extremely important when dealing with busy players and unknown literature—I contacted the Dorian Wind Quintet and Rogeri Trio and took on recommendation of trusted colleagues the New York String Quartet and soprano Sheila Schonbrun. All but one were highly cooperative, in some instances (Sheila Schonbrun and Jane Taylor of the Dorian, particularly) adding to the programs fruits of their own research or aiding in the selection and preparation of material. This commitment was crucial in 1978 when the series was new and commonly viewed as an enterprise that was 90 percent political, and only 10 percent musical.

Later, after we were established as a serious musical endeavor (more on the order of 75 percent musical, 25 percent political) there was no difficulty in interesting performers, and most groups were delighted to help in selecting material by reading through works and also suggesting composers and pieces of which they knew. This enriched the series considerably. (We did have one last-minute disaster involving the choice of repertoire and deadlines in 1981, and one first-rate group was hurriedly replaced by another first-rate group willing to learn a substantive program. No lasting damage was done, but it was decidedly unpleasant for all concerned.)

My search for literature that first year was necessarily brief. I spoke to composers I had met at the ILWC and AWC meetings, did research at the American Music Center library, consulted with performers, and contacted people familiar with historical composers, particularly Marnie Hall (who had produced the recording "Women's Work" on the Gemini Hall label) and musicologist Judith Tick. In an amazingly short time the programs were in place. The music covered a span of nine centuries, from the Countess de Dia (1100s) to pieces written quite recently. This was the beginning of an education for yours truly, for it dawned on me that if four programs of good quality could be researched and collected in three weeks, what wealth must actually exist for those with time and resources to look for it? Later experience verified my suspicion. The Festivals could well have continued for many years, in terms of literature, tapping excellent unknown works and composers of both past and present.

The series attracted considerable interest. *New York* Magazine highlighted the first concert, and the *New York Times* gave it a serious and complimentary review. Byron Belt of *The Newhouse Newspaper Chain* mentioned the series in his weekly column several times, and there was a total of four interviews on WQXR and WNYC, New York classical music radio stations. The first concert was broadcast three times in March over the Voice of America, and WBAI (another New York station) presented electronic selections in July. The early and enthusiastic support of WNCN's music director David Dubal was extremely helpful in numerous ways: WNCN played the chamber concert tapes on prime time in September 1978 and highlighted them with a feature article that I wrote for their magazine, *Keynote*.[1] Since then there have been numerous other broadcasts throughout the country.

Figure 13.2 Excerpt from "Frühling," Op. 7, by Fanny Mendelssohn Hensel (c. 1840). Used by permission.

For the First Festival I collected complete translations and texts for the printed programs but I gave notes orally on performers and composers at some of the early concerts. Given the fact that many in the audience initially perceived the series as highly political, this was useful. It gave me a chance to set a tone appropriate for a substantial musical endeavor. Thereafter, all programs contained full notes as well as texts and translations.

Part of the offering in our first season was a noble experiment which, thanks to the efforts of Daria Semegen (head of the Electronic Music Studio at State University of New York—Stony Brook), came to some good. I had the idea of collecting pieces for electronic tape, making a "concert" program, and running it at intervals in the WIC Gallery for a couple of weeks at specified and advertised times, in conjunction with a current art show. I don't think this idea was ever seriously considered at WIC, and after several inquiries I was told it wasn't possible. We held, then, two Gallery concerts, where tapes were played that Daria had solicited and collected. Equipment was borrowed from a major electronic music center, and we had highly qualified personnel to run it, but it was old and rickety, and at one concert it broke down, forcing us to send the audience home and reschedule the performance! Full concerts of totally electronic works are a bit hard on a sedentary audience. Thereafter, electronics were incorporated into the regular chamber music concerts (and film one year as well), and equipment was obtained elsewhere. Daria arranged for several subsequent broadcasts of the electronic works, thus bringing some tangible benefit to the composers.

Since I determined from the first to concentrate money on performers and tapes, we didn't have much to spend on a hall. The first year taught me a gruesome lesson: Don't ever work in a large bureaucratic institution without having a key member of the institution, such as a department head, actively committed to the project in some way. The Graduate Center of the City University of New York had a new small hall and was openly looking for projects. However, within three weeks after we had reached an agreement to hold our series at their hall, financial cuts were imposed at the school and the concert manager who had made the agreement was fired and not replaced. Thereafter I dealt with eight separate offices and experienced contradictions, threats, incompetence, and political infighting of the most petty and frustrating kind.

As a result, we presented Festivals II through IV at another place, Christ and St. Stephen's, a small church four blocks from Lincoln Center. It is quite pleasant with nice acoustics; a touch noisy and uncomfortable in extreme heat or cold—but by far the best bet for the money. The staff are careful and cooperative about the use of their facilities, and it was a pleasure to work with them.

In scheduling, as well, the first year was a learning experience. Festival I spread its four concerts out over four months. This was too long. In the second year we tried four performances within two weeks. This was too short; we lost a lot of our repeat audience. Finally we settled on one concert a week for four weeks for the last two Festivals.

In 1979, Festival II of Women's Music presented compositions of 16 women not represented the previous year. (Two of the new pieces presented that year were among the ten semifinalists in the 1979 Kennedy-Friedheim Competition for new American music: works by Ruth Schonthal and Katherine Hoover.) The time span of the works presented was again nine centuries.

Media coverage was similar to the year before, with announcements on WNYC, WNCN, and an interview on Robert Sherman's *The Listening Room* on WQXR. Excellent reviews were published in the *New York Times* and by Byron Belt in the *Jersey Journal*. Tapes were made and deposited at the American Music Center; they were broadcast first on WNCN and subsequently on many stations throughout the country.

Figure 13.3 From the cantata *Jephté* by Elisabeth Jacquet de La Guerre; (c. 1700). Original notation.

Figure 13.4 From *Jephté*, by Elisabeth Jacquet de La Guerre. This transcription to modern notation, with fully realized figured bass by Katherine Hoover, was heard in performance during Festival III. Used by permission.

The third Festival was planned to consolidate and, if possible, extend the strengths of the preceding two. We continued to search out material by new composers, and by the end of Festival III we had included works by 55 women. One big step ahead that year was the request by National Public Radio to tape and broadcast our concerts live nationally. This they did. We also received backing from the National Endowment for the Arts as well as the New York State Council on the Arts, Meet the Composer, and the Mary Flagler Cary Charitable Trust.

Due to some unfortunate problems with a public relations firm, we had much less press coverage for Festival III (1980) and no major reviews. I did appear on Robert Sherman's *Listening Room* with some of the artists and composers (WQXR) and also secured an interview on WNCN.

National Public Radio had promised copies of its tapes numerous times, but they never arrived. As a result, neither the Women's Interart Center nor the American Music Center has its expected archival copies of the tapes from Festival III. NPR also asked all performers to sign releases to permit their performances to be broadcast; the release form specified an amount of about $20 to be paid each performer. These fees were never paid. Unhappily, there was worse to come.

Festival IV (1981), though continuing the successful format of four chamber music concerts at Christ and St. Stephen's, faced some unexpected difficulties. The year 1981 was one of increasing funding problems for many organizations. National Public Radio, after assuring us continually of their intent to broadcast Festival IV, pulled out the day before the first concert, leaving us with no broadcasts, tapes, nor any budget for their creation, and no time to tap other sources (which we could have done). Some last-minute taping was done, but so far, funds to construct the broadcast tapes and distribute them have not been found.

The concerts were, as usual, musically rewarding and underattended. There was very little publicity, despite the hiring of a better-known public relations firm. Again, I took artists and composers for an appearance on *The Listening Room* with Robert Sherman and gave a short interview on WNCN. There was a review in the *New York Times*, which was very helpful indeed to one composer but totally ignored the rest of the program. Thirteen new composers were represented.

Money was always a problem. The WIC had run programs before, and consequently we were able to begin with some funds from the New York State Council on the Arts. Various attempts over the years to find other sources were at times successful but generally haphazard due to confusion and changes at the Center as well as to limitations of foundations and the increasingly poor general economic situation.[2] We received one-time grants of varying sizes from the Beard's Fund, the Lucius and Eva Eastman Fund, and the Mary Flagler Cary Charitable Trust. The National Endowment for the Arts gave us backing the third season, which was cut severely in 1981 (like almost all such grants that unhappy year). Our continuing support and the backbone of our efforts came from the New York State Council on the Arts; Meet the Composer was also always helpful.

Program selection is an extremely touchy subject when one is dealing with contemporaries. What composer has adequate exposure these days? Certainly *none* of the talented women working! As a producer I was courted, flattered, dropped, and/or criticized by several on the basis of whether or not I was presenting a piece of theirs that year. I find this very sad and indicative of the pressing need for writers to learn how to organize performances or reach out to performers in other ways.

Our program selection was never formalized. I solicited lists of works from everyone I could, eventually accumulating over 60 lists. (*Contemporary Concert Music by Women* [the ILWC Directory] and the bibliographies by Adrienne Fried Block and Carol Neuls-Bates [*Women in American Music*] and Aaron Cohen [*International Encyclopedia of Women Composers*] have since made most of this work unnecessary. If only they had been available then!) Since the programs were generally historically balanced, I relied on the advice of a growing network of music historians. The format of the four concerts each year was decided by a brisk skimming of all my materials to determine where the most literature fell (string quartets, piano trios, etc.) Then I would make lists of possible pieces and solicit more in these categories. If time allowed I would use the ILWC newsletter, but that seldom worked out. I did do research at the American Music Center library and consulted all the active "networkers" among women composers that I knew as well as performers.[3]

Final selection was made by myself and the performing groups. The guiding criterion was, again, the creation of interesting programs of varied, strong music. Whenever possible I leaned toward a composer whose work had not been used before, and in our four seasons we used music by 69 women.

Our goal was to be representative rather than comprehensive. Many excellent composers were not heard (Talma, Diemer, Jolas, Kolb, for example) and some were heard more than twice, usually at the request of performers. (I limited my own compositions to one piece per year, with one short exception at the request of a performer.) Again, it was the total impact of each concert and each year's series on the listeners that concerned me. I wanted audiences to carry away an impression of strength, beauty, and professionalism; of art conceived and executed on a high level—and by and large they did.

Which brings me to reviews. We startled a lot of people, some of whom were more ready to listen than others. In general our reviews were quite good, though they ran the gamut from a rave to a strongly worded pan. The *New York Times* critics were usually reluctant to attend and were wooed personally by public relations people.[4] We were, after all, performing in halls not often covered by the *Times*; but that was not the basic objection. Though reviews were mostly favorable, some condescension lurks within them (with the exception of John Rockwell). I don't think we ever got past 60 percent artistic/40 percent political in critics minds, though getting that far was a considerable achievement. At least we were never put on the "Style" page!

Very little effort was made to reach the women's press; consequently, coverage here was sparse and sometimes ill-informed. Still, the single most comprehensive article to appear was a long, thoughtful treatment of the first three concerts of Festival II by Barbara Grant in *Women Artists News*, June 1979, titled "Art Music by Women: NYC Concert Series." It gives a very good sense of the series.

Here is an excerpt from our first review (Festival I, first concert) by John Rockwell in the *New York Times*, 1 March 1978.

> Monday's program consisted of a song recital by Sheila Schonbrun. . . . Ms. Schonbrun was at all times a sensitive and serious singer, with a fine musicality of phrasing and an idiomatic command of the seven or more languages she chose to sing. . . . The high point of the night came early, right after a pleasant opening Baroque cantata by Isabella Leonarda, in which the piano seemed rather too anachronistic. That highlight was a 12th-century Provençal troubador song by the Countess de Dia. . . . This single song and performance said more about Provençal culture than a whole evening devoted to the subject the night before.
>
> Thereafter a pretty lyrical song by Fanny Mendelssohn-Hensel, and three by Clara Schumann. . . . The first half closed with four very striking songs by Lili Boulanger, Nadia's sister.
>
> The music after intermission was likewise interesting, with one exception. . . . Otherwise there was an evocative four-song Hesse cycle by Ursula Mamlok, a very moving cycle to women poets by Judith Zaimont, and two fascinating Pablo Neruda settings by Vivan Fine. No sweeping generalizations about the place of women composers in history were possible on the basis of this music alone. But the music itself was often very fine.

That same year brought us our lowest blow. Despite the general reference at the beginning of the following review, this reviewer (Andrew Derhen) attended only one concert—our fourth one; and that after strong negative reaction to women's concerts had been openly expressed on the phone by *Musical America*'s editorial staff. This appeared in the June 1978 issue. It's hard to believe that it refers to the same series!

> The most exciting moments at the First Festival of Women's Music were provided by a whale. A recording of the plaintive moans and whines of the largest mammal were mixed with the live sounds of flute, cello and piano. . . . George Crumb and Alan Hovannes [*sic*] have also written music using taped whale cries, so [this] score with its grim chromaticism lacked even the virtue of novelty. Not that there was much to commend the other, cliquishly modern works heard. . . . The performances . . . sounded reasonably accurate. . . . Though it shows traces of the styles of husband Robert and the young Brahms, the two most influential men in her life, Mrs. Schumann's score [Trio] has its own Romantic individuality.

Note the "clever" use of male references (Crumb, Hovhannes, R. Schumann, Brahms) to put the women composers (Ulehla, Tower, Ivey, Cory, and *Mrs.* Schumann) in their place.

Fortunately, the second year brought us this, by Byron Belt in the *Jersey Journal,* 19 March 1979. The title was "Women's Music Program a Hit for Best Reasons."

> We attended the second program, which featured pianist-composers Ruth Schonthal, Doris Hays, Marga Richter, and Judith Lang Zaimont.
>
> It takes no reverse-chauvanism to state that the program was one of the most satisfying featuring contemporary music this critic has ever attended.
>
> One factor that made the program of major new works so pleasant was the fact that romantic works by such under-appreciated women composers as Louise Farrenc, Mary Bough Watson, and Cecile Chaminade were interlaced with the contemporary works. The other major factors were the superb pianism of the four composers, and a generally high level of quality in the recent works they presented.

Finally, here is a particularly revealing review in terms of attitude. Raymond Ericson of the *New York Times* covered the first concert of Festival II. The following, printed on 15 March 1979, constitutes the entire review, omitting only the listing of performers and composers at the beginning.

> There weren't any really dull moments in the program, and there was a goodly amount of stimulating material. What was interesting was the fact that the two most satisfying works—to this listener's ears, at least—were very much in strong traditions of the past. These were a set of eight German songs by [Josephine] Lang and "Einsame Nacht," a cycle based on poems of Hermann Hesse by Miss [Ellen Taaffe] Zwilich. If the Lang works sounded like a great many other 19th-century lieder, they nevertheless were thoroughly enjoyable. The rippling piano accompaniment had undeniable charm, and there were surprising twists in the treatment of the texts.
>
> Miss Zwilich's cycle of six songs looks back to the 20th century Viennese school of Berg, Schoenberg and Webern, suitable, certainly, to the Hesse texts. The composer works very smoothly within the style, and it would have been hard to fault the placement of a note in such concentrated music. The cycle was written in 1971, and whether the composer is developing a more individual style remains to be seen. But here her craftsmanship and expressive powers are first-rate.
>
> Miss [Gloria] Swisher's "Sisters" had the benefit of three fine poems, by Alice Dunbar Nelson, Angelina Weld Grimke and Aphra Behn, and the musical settings in a fairly conservative style, did justice to them. Miss [Victoria] Bond, too, had chosen a brilliant text for her work, namely Wallace Steven's "Peter Quince at the Clavier." She turned it into an ambitious and quite diverting monodrama for soprano and piano, with the singer using a number of percussion instruments.
>
> A duet from Miss [Peggy] Glanville-Hicks's opera "Nausicaa" was in that composer's deceptively simplistic style, with a basis in early Greek music. All the performances were competent and often more than that. They deserved praise for the whole-hearted devotion they represented.

Figure 13.5 Excerpt from *Trio* (1921) by Rebecca Clarke, programmed during Festival II.

Some people found this review excellent; others were angered by its tone. It prompted me to pen the following reply-in-kind (purely for my own perspective; in this business one cannot afford to send such a note).

Dear Sir:

Thank you for your not unkind review. Though it read like many others it was, nevertheless, rather enjoyable. It didn't contain any really dull sentiments, and it would be hard to fault the placement of commas, paragraphs, etc. It deserves praise.

Obviously critics vary widely in their outlooks and perceptions. Some are open to and anxious for interesting musical experiences no matter where they might appear. Others have various prejudices. Most of these (though clearly not all) are, I think, the result of a conviction that if any of this material were worthy, they, as experts, would know of it after so many

Figure 13.6 Excerpt from *Nocturne* (1979) by Judith Lang Zaimont, performed by the composer during Festival II. Used by permission of the composer.

years in the field. Indeed, it is a mark of the sad, twisted history of women's compositions that so many scholars and critics don't know of them.

In terms of planning and direction, the Festivals were largely a one-person effort. The Women's Interart Center was indispensable in many respects, and when the administrator who worked with me was an experienced, settled one (which was the case for a while) the operation ran fairly smoothly. The WIC has a reputation for impressive artistic success and an equal reputation for administrative problems. In my experience both are deserved. WIC provided the opportunity for the Festivals and gave me a free hand and much encouragement. It also undermined them by disorganizing my plans because of serious confusions, lack of deadlines, frequent changes of personnel, and fiscal mismanagement. (As of June 1986 I am still owed a rather large sum, and no date of payment has been set.) It should come as no surprise to learn that when I decided to leave, I could find no able administrator to continue the Festivals under such conditions.

WIC took my plans and information and wrote grant applications, designed and mailed the handsome brochures, and printed programs; in our third year they also took over relations with the church. Their handling of money was a continuing problem, and I was obliged to spend a great deal of effort in soothing people and securing late payments. They hired public relations firms, who, with one partial exception, were useless, consuming lots of my time, effort, and material and generating nothing—partly, but only partly, because the WIC owed them money. I was left with considerable doubts about "PR" as a field.

Still, despite the awkward operating conditions, there is room for pride for all concerned; the Women's Interart Center, myself, and Jill Pollack, who assisted in the last Festival.

Figure 13.7 Excerpt from Katherine Hoover's *Trio* (1978) for violin, 'cello and piano. The work was performed during Festival II and subsequently recorded on disc on the Leonarda label (LPI 103). Used by permission of the composer.

By 1981 our accomplishments were:

- Performances of works by 69 women and broadcasts to literally millions of listeners nationally and abroad.
- Participation in four recordings (music by Farrenc, Boulanger, Clarke, Hoover, Tailleferre, Ulehla, Beach, Schonthal, Mamlok, Aderholt, Vellère) as well as indirect influence on other recordings, including work by Lang, Mendelssohn-Hensel, Zwilich, Van Appledorn, and Clara Schumann.
- Repertoire learned for these concerts has been performed on other programs by the Rogeri Trio, the Da Capo Chamber Players, Western Wind, The Dorian Quintet, The Crescent Quartet, Virginia Eskin, and several other individual performers, both here and abroad.

- The group Ariel, under a separate grant, has performed several concerts away from New York involving women's music, partially sponsored by the Women's Interart Center. This is a direct offshoot of their appearance in Festival III.
- Tapes made under the auspices of these Festivals have been widely used by composers for further submissions for grants, contests, and broadcasts.

I have been asked why I began the Festivals in the first place. For one thing the opportunity arose when a personal loss had left a gaping hole in my life, and I welcomed a project that would collect my energies and focus them in a worthy area. As mentioned, the ILWC and AWC gatherings had alerted me to the cruel isolation of women composers and their common problems. Here, suddenly, was a way to begin to attack those problems. It seemed that I was the right person at the right time, being connected to both the composers' and performers' worlds and having had experience at concert organization.

I spent a tremendous amount of time and energy on the Festivals, with some very great rewards. They connected me with my own history and my colleagues, many of whom have become valuable friends. Certainly the success of the concerts brought me credibility and exposure. Furthermore, they gave considerable encouragement, not to mention performances, broadcasts, and tapes, to many women who needed and deserved them, and clearly they helped to make a wide public more aware of the strength and variety of women's compositions. All these things brought me a very personal joy.

Sadly, with the passage of time, the rewards began to dwindle as financial problems became exacerbated and plans for sharing the administration and beginning new facets, such as commissions, were undercut by difficulties at WIC and tight money everywhere. The last-minute pullout by NPR in 1981 was a telling blow, coupled with the refusal of a group to find time to learn a short work written for the series (though they said it was the best piece ever composed for them!). These events, coupled with the growing debt to me and at least three others connected with the project, prompted my resignation in June 1981.

I hope I haven't smoothed over too many glitches. Because I was overburdened, I wasn't always able to carry through as I would have wished; and there was at least one glaring mismatch of performer and piece and a few questionable choices of literature—though surprisingly few. Our average was high, as attested by the repeated use of materials by performers in other situations and our success in broadcasts.

I've saved the best for last. My personal contacts at New York's classical music stations turned into pure gold, for since they knew me, they were willing to listen and then air lots of material from the Festivals. The tapings also led to success in another area. Marnie Hall was beginning Leonarda Productions, Inc., which has since become well-known nationally for its recordings of historical women's and contemporary men's and women's compositions. Some of our early efforts were combined to the advantage of all and led to recordings that continue to be heard. Other broadcasts and recordings grew from the Festivals, resulting in repeated quality performances and considerable exposure for many deserving composers. We have reached, literally, millions. This, I believe, was our greatest contribution. Despite the bitterness of debt, it is an experience I shall always remember with gratefulness, fatigue, and pride in all concerned—composers, performers, supporters, friends, and the many people at WIC who truly worked and cared.

Figure 13.8 Excerpt from *Seven Dramatic Episodes* (1976) by Ann Callaway (opening of the third movement), a work programmed in Festival IV. Used by permission of the composer.

NOTES

1. K. Hoover, "Fanny and Lili Who?" *Keynote* (September 1978), p. 15.

2. One of the latest fashions in grant-giving is the one-year, nonrenewable grant.

3. Historical women composers wrote overwhelmingly for voice and keyboard, the media to which they were generally restricted as performers. Consequently every Festival had one vocal program, and after the first year virtually all our chamber groups included keyboard.

4. The *Times* reviewed only three of the eighteen concerts given, though invited to all of them.

APPENDIX I: NOTES FOR CONCERT PRODUCERS

Anyone wishing to put on concerts has to deal with performers. Having been on all sides of this situation—organizer, composer, performer, I'd like to note a few guidelines, for over the years I've seen a lot of unnecessary tension caused by carelessness or ignorance in the following areas.

- Use performers whose work is known to be of high standard and, whenever possible, people who work together regularly.
- Consult the players early about literature, and give them some choice whenever possible. Consult them about performance needs (hall rehearsal, *readable* scores and parts, heat, lighting, stands, piano tuning, etc.) Keep in mind that you all have a common goal—a first-rate performance. Do insist on a good, balanced program.
- If possible, use players who are aware of and interested in women composers. There are many, both men and women. If they are unaware but curious, give them goodies to listen to.
- Set and *keep* deadlines for program decisions, delivery of scores and parts, publicity activities, and financial commitments. (My aforementioned 1981 debacle could and *should* have been avoided this way.)
- Arrange for broadcast if you possibly can; make sure your performers *know* about any broadcasting plans at the time you hire them, and obtain the necessary written clearances well ahead of time.

Your attention to the performers' needs will almost always be rewarded by better performances, not to mention more pleasant relations and the creation of a good basis for future endeavors.

APPENDIX II: PROGRAMS

First Festival of Women's Music, February 27, 1978, 8 P.M.

Sheila Schonbrun, soprano; Morey Ritt, pianist

O Flammae	Isabella Leonarda (1620-1700)
A chantar m'er de so qu'ieu non volria	Countess de Dia (c. 1140-?)
Die Mainacht	Fanny Mendelssohn-Hensel (1805-1847)
Liebst du um Schönheit Ich stand in dunklen Träumen Er ist Gekommen in Sturm und Regen	Clara Schumann (1819-1896)
Deux ancolies Vous m'avez regardé avec toute votre âme Si tout ceci n'est qu'un pauvre rêve Les lilas qui avaient fleuri	Lili Boulanger (1893-1919)

Four German Songs (1958)	Ursula Mamlok
Ueber die Felder	
September	
Schmetterling	
Nachtgefuehl	
Greyed Sonnets (1975)	Judith Lang Zaimont
Soliloquy	
Let It Be Forgotten	
A Season's Song	
Love's Autumn	
Entreaty	
American Indian Song Suite (1976)	Jeanne Singer
Pawnee	
Maliseet	Composer at the Piano
Kiowa	
Laguna	
Two Poems of Pablo Neruda (1971)	Vivian Fine
La Tortuga	
Oda al Piano	

Figure 13.9 Soprano Sheila Schonbrun.

Figure 13.10 The Dorian Wind Quintet: Karl Kraber, flute, Gerald Reuter, oboe, Jerry Kirkbride, clarinet, David Jolley, horn, Jane Taylor, bassoon.

Monday, March 13, 1978, 8:00 P.M.

The Dorian Quintet: Karl Kraber, flute; Charles Kuskin, oboe; Jerry Kirkbridge, clarinet; Robin Graham, horn; Jane Taylor, bassoon

Pastorale	Amy Marcy Beach (1867-1944)
Divertimento for Woodwind Quintet (1948) Andantino Allegretto	Miriam Gideon
Quintet for Wind Instruments (1956) Molto vivo Andante tranquillo Allegro molto	Ursula Mamlok

Suite for Wind Quintet (1952) Allegretto Lento rubato Allegro possible	Ruth Crawford Seeger (1901-1953)
Homage to Bartok (1975) Allegro agitato Arioso Vivace	Katherine Hoover

Tuesday, March 28, 1978, 8 P.M.
Electronic Music Concert

Lagoon (1975)	Wendy Chambers
Targets (1972-73)	Margo Greene
Quadratura Circuli (1977-78) (premiere)	Anne LeBaron
ARC: Music For Dancers (1977)	Daria Semegen
Invisible Chariots (1975-77) Movements 1 and 2 (premiere)	Priscilla McLean
Clockworks (1975)	Laurie Spiegel
Farewell To A Hill (1975)	Alice Shields

Monday, April 24, 1978, 8 P.M.
The New York String Quartet: William Fitzpatrick, violin; Brian Dembow, violin; Robert Becker, viola; Steven Erdody, cello

Quartet IV Cantabile Minuet	Maddalena Lombardini Sirmen (1735-?)
String Quartet No. 2 (1958) Largo Andante sostenuto-allegro-largando-allegro	Marga Richter
String Quartet (1931) Rubato assai-Leggiero-Andante Allegro possible	Ruth Crawford Seeger (1901-1953)
Modes for String Quartet (1968) Moderato Adagio Allegro	Dorothy Rudd Moore
String Quartet (1974) Maestoso Allegro moderato et vigoroso Lento et tranquillo Rhapsodico	Ellen Taaffe Zwilich

Monday, May 8, 1978, 8:00 P.M.
The Rogeri Trio: Karen Clarke, violin; Carter Brey, cello; Barbara Weintraub, piano; Assisted by Katherine Hoover, flute

Elegy for a Whale (1975) Flute, Cello, Piano, Tape	Ludmilla Ulehla
Platinum Spirals (1976) Violin	Joan Tower
Epithalamium (1973) Flute	Eleanor Cory
Tonada (1966) Violin, Cello	Jean Eichelberger Ivey
Ode (1965) Violin, Piano	Jean Eichelberger Ivey
Trio Violin, Cello, Piano	Clara Schumann (1819-1896)

June 24, 1978, 3 P.M.
Electronic Music Concert

Electronic Composition No. 1 (1971-72)	Daria Semegen
Episode (1976)	Ann McMillan
Invisible Chariots (1975-77) 3rd Movement (premiere)	Priscilla McLean
Quadratura Circuli (1978)	Anne LeBaron
Voyage in C (1976)	Lois Wilcken
Sitar (1978) Scene from the opera "Shaman" (premiere)	Alice Shields
Patchwork (1976)	Laurie Spiegel
Targets (1972-73)	Margo Greene
Cortege—For Charles Kent (1969)	Jean Eichelberger Ivey

Second Festival of Women's Music, Tuesday, March 13, 1979, 8 P.M.
Janet Steele, soprano; Patrick Mason, baritone; Michael Fardink, pianist

Sequence "O virgo ac diadema"	Hildegarde von Bingen (1098-1197)
Two Arias Non volete ch'io mi dolga (Opus 7) Bel desio che mi tormenti (Opus 6)	Barbara Strozzi (1619-after 1664)
Lieder Am Flusse Sehnsucht Mignon's Klage Gluckliche Fahrt	Josephine Lang (1815-1880)

An den See
Sie Liebt Mich
An Einer Quelle
Scheideblick

Two Duets from *Le Déluge* Aux Mortels Gage de Paix	Elisabeth Jacquet de La Guerre (1664-1729)
Sisters (1976) I Sit and Sew Tenebris The Cabal at Nickel Nackeys	Gloria Wilson Swisher
Einsame Nacht (1971) Uber die Felder Wie sind die Tage schwer Schicksal Elisabeth Wohl Lieb ich die finstre Nacht Mückenschwarm	Ellen Taaffe Zwilich
Peter Quince at the Clavier (1977)	Victoria Bond
Duo, from *Nausicaa* Act II, Scene 5	Peggy Glanville-Hicks

March 15, 1979, 8 P.M.

Pianist-Composers: Ruth Schonthal, Doris Hays, Marga Richter, Judith Lang Zaimont

Etude no. 10, Opus 26	Louise Farrenc (1804-1875)
In Homage of . . . (24 Preludes) 1978	Ruth Schonthal

1. Andante molto
2. Un poco molto
3. Allegro ben marcato
4. Very flowing and with great tenderness
5. Tranquillo, semplice
6. Fast and wild
7. Very slow and majestic
8. Fast and delicately
9. With a slightly melancholy air
10. Agitato
11. Delicatissimo
12. Quasi Recitativo
13. Agitato
14. Waltz Tempo
15. Risoluto e pesante
16. Tempo rubato (sempre dolce)
17. Poco agitato
18. Tranquillo
19. Agitato
20. Tranquil, but not too slow

21. Serioso
22. Slow and majestic
23. Fast, as delicately as possible
24. Allegro molto agitato

Ruth Schonthal, pianist

Momenti 4 (1978)	Vivan Fine
Sunday Nights (1976)	Doris Hays
Dishrag (c. 1905)	Mary Baugh Watson
Wildflowers (1978) Pipsissewa Passion Flower Pink Turtlehead Trailing Arbutus	Doris Hays

Doris Hays, pianist

Requiem (1978)	Marga Richter

Marga Richter, pianist

Selections from *A Calendar Set* (1974-78) January: "Whose morning drumbeat, following the sun, circles the Earth." —Daniel Webster February: Palace of Ice May: "As full of spirit as the month of May, and gorgeous."—Shakespeare June: "Then, if ever, come perfect days." —James Russell Lowell July: THE GLORIOUS FOURTH! August: "Dry August and warm . . ." —Thomas Tusser September: "Where blue is darkened on blueness, Down the way Persephone goes, just now, In first-frosted September." —D. H. Lawrence	Judith Lang Zaimont
Appassionato: Etude de Concert no. 4, Opus 35	Cécile Chaminade (1867-1944)
Nocturne: La Fin de Siècle (1978)	Judith Lang Zaimont

Judith Lang Zaimont, pianist

Tuesday, March 20, 1979, 8 P.M.

Da Capo Chamber Players: Patricia Spencer, flute; Laura Flax, clarinet; Joel Lester, violin; Andre Emelianoff, cello; Joan Tower, piano

Sonata for Flute Adagio Allegretto Allegro ma non troppo	Anna Amalia, Princess of Prussia (1723-87)

For an Actor— Monologue for Clarinet (1978)	Shulamit Ran
Anais (1977)	Diane Thome
Nocturne D'un Matin de Printemps	Lili Boulanger (1893-1918)
Responsive Resonance with Feathers (1979) (premiere)	Joan La Barbara
Amazon (1977)	Joan Tower

Thursday, March 22, 1979, 8 P.M.

The Rogeri Trio: Karen Clarke, violin; Carter Brey, cello; Barbara Weintraub, piano; Assisted by Katherine Hoover, flute

Trio in E Minor, Opus 45 (c. 1850) Allegro deciso Andante Scherzo; vivace Finale; presto	Louise Farrenc
Trio (1921) Moderato ma appassionato Andante molto semplice Allegro vigoroso	Rebecca Clarke (1886-1979)
Three Biblical Masks (1960) Haman Esther Mordecai	Miriam Gideon
Trio (1978) (premiere) Moderato—Allegro con fuoco Cantabile Allegro con brio	Katherine Hoover

Third Festival of Women's Music, March 6, 1980, 8 P.M.

The Ariel Ensemble: Julia Lovett, soprano; Jerome Bunke, clarinet; Michael Fardink, piano; with guest artist Linda Eckard, mezzo-soprano

"Jephthé Revient," from *Jephthe*	Elisabeth Jacquet de La Guerre (1664-1729)

Ms. Lovett, Ms. Eckard, Mr. Fardink

From *Juhan Liiv'i* (1974) Helin Üks suu Sa tulid paikene	Helen Duesberg

Ms. Lovett, Mr. Fardink

Three Pieces (1968) Tranquillo	Daria Semegen

Figure 13.11 Mezzo-soprano Linda Eckard.

Scherzando
Quasi Rubato

Mr. Bunke, Mr. Fardink

Lieder — Fanny Mendelssohn-Hensel (1805-1847)

Schwanenlied (Op. 1)
Mayenlied (Op. 1)
Gondelied (Op. 1.)
Frühling (Op. 7)
Im Herbste (Op. 10)
Verlust (Op. 9)
Vorwurf (Op. 10)
Nach Suden (Op. 10)

Ms. Lovett, Ms. Eckard, Mr. Fardink

"A Naughty Boy" (1979) (John Keats) — Loretta Jankowski

Ms. Lovett, Mr. Bunke, Mr. Fardink

In meines Vaters Garten (Hartleben) — Alma Mahler (1879-1964)

Ms. Eckard, Mr. Fardink

From "Six Moods" (1953) (Mark van Doren) — Judith Dvorkin
Old Ben Golliday
Down Dip the Branches
He Cut One finger
Ms. Eckard, Mr. Fardink

Selima, or, Ode on the Death of a Favourite Cat, Drowned in a Tub of Goldfishes (Thomas Grey) (1979) — Katherine Hoover
Ms. Lovett, Mr. Bunke, Mr. Fardink

Figure 13.12 The Ariel Ensemble (left to right): Jerome Bunke, clarinet, Julia Lovett, soprano, Michael Fardink, piano.

March 13, 1980, 8 P.M.

Performers: Virginia Brewer, oboe; Mary Ann Brown, piano; Katherine Hoover, flute; Carey Lovelace, reader; James Preiss, percussion; Louise Schulman, viola; Glen Velez, percussion

Daysongs (1974) — Nancy Chance
Sun Greeting
Noonjoy
Moonsoft
Ms. Hoover, Mr. Velez, Mr. Preiss

Trio (1960) — Thea Musgrave
Ms. Hoover, Ms. Brewer, Ms. Brown

The Insistent Murmur of Resemblance (1979) film by Roberta Friedman text by Carey Lovelace, in collaboration with Grahame Weinbren and Roberta Friedman	Carey Lovelace
Ms. Lovelace, Mr. Velez, Mr. Preiss	
Five Capriccios for Oboe and Piano (1968)	Ursula Mamlok
Ms. Brewer, Ms. Brown	
Variations for Solo Flute (1961)	Ursula Mamlok
Ms. Hoover	
Music for Viola, Percussion, and Piano (1976) I II III	Nancy Van de Vate
Ms. Schulman, Ms. Brown, Mr. Velez	

March 20, 1980, 8 P.M.

Virginia Eskin, pianist; assisted by Ann Silsbee, pianist and composer

Sonata No. 3 Allegro Andante Allegro	Maria Anna Martinez (1754-1812)
Etudes F Major E Major	Maria Szymanowska (1789-1831)
No. 2 No. 8	Grażyna Bacewicz (1913-1969)
Four Piano Pieces Syncope Toccata Chromaticon Ostinato	Marion Bauer (1896-1955)
Lament (1977)	Katherine Hoover
From "Snazzy Sonata" (1972) Lazy Beguine Be-Bop Scherzo	Judith Lang Zaimont
with Ann Silsbee	
Variations on a Balkan Theme, Opus 60	Amy Cheney Beach (1867-1944)
Soundings (1975)	Ruth Lomon
with Ann Silsbee	
Doors (1976)	Ann Silsbee
Ms. Silsbee	

Set of Five (1978) — Mary Jeanne van Appledorn
- Ostinato
- Blues
- Improvisation
- Elegy
- Toccata

Figure 13.13 Pianist Virginia Eskin.

March 27, 1980, 8 P.M.

Mitchell Stern, violin; Toby Appel, viola; Diane Walsh, piano

Danceries (1953) — Jacqueline Fontyn
- Pavane et Gaillarde
- Allemande
- Branle de Poictou

Mr. Stern, Ms. Walsh

Sonata Pastorale (1956) — Lillian Fuchs
Fantasia
Pastorale

Mr. Appel

Sonata in Three Movements (1973-74) — Ellen Taaffe Zwilich
Liberamente; Tempo giusto
Lento e molto espressivo
Allegro vivo e con brio

Mr. Stern, Ms. Walsh

Sicilienne — Maria-Theresia von Paradis (1759-1824)

Mr. Appel, Ms. Walsh

Four Caprices — Grażyna Bacewicz (1913-1969)

Mr. Stern

Sonata for Viola and Piano — Rebecca Clarke (1886-1979)
Impetuoso
Vivace
Adagio-Allegro

Mr. Appel, Ms. Walsh

Fourth Festival of Women's Music, May 19, 1981, 8 P.M.
The Arden Trio: Suzanne Ornstein, violin; Clay Ruede, cello; Thomas Schmidt, piano; with Keith Underwood, flute; and Charles Pistone, speaker

Bulgarian Trio (1972) — Esta Blood
Allegro Vivo
Deliberatamente; Moderato
Freely; Andantino; Freely
Allegro Deciso

Mr. Underwood, Ms. Ornstein, Mr. Schmidt

Duos III (1980) — Nancy Chance

Ms. Ornstein, Mr. Ruede

Seven Dramatic Episodes (1976) — Ann Callaway

Mr. Underwood, Mr. Ruede, Mr. Schmidt, Charles Pistone

Plein Chant (1977) — Elaine Barkin

Mr. Underwood

Trio (Opus 11) — Fanny Mendelssohn-Hensel (1805-1847)
Allegro Molto Vivace
Andante Expressivo
Lied, Allegretto
Allegro Moderato

Ms. Ornstein, Mr. Ruede, Mr. Schmidt

May 26, 1981, 8 P.M.

Composers and Friends: Tania J. Leon, Frank Dodge, Julie Kabat, Katherine Hoover, Mary Ann Brown, Wendy Chambers, Hal Freedman, Boris Policeband, Pam Sklar, Glenn Velez

Scherzo in C minor — Clara Schumann (1819-1896)

Ms. Leon

Sonata for Cello (1981) (premiere) — Tania J. Leon
- Allegro
- Lento, doloroso
- Montuno
- Vivace

Mr. Dodge, Ms. Leon

The Idea of Order in Key West (1977) — Julie Kabat
(poem by Wallace Stevens)

Ms. Kabat

Tapestry (1976) — Julie Kabat

Ms. Kabat

Pastorale (1942) — Germaine Tailleferre

Ms. Hoover, Ms. Brown

The Medieval Suite (1981) (premiere) — Katherine Hoover
- Virelai
- The Black Knight
- The Drunken Friar
- Demon's Dance

Ms. Hoover, Ms. Brown

Busy Box Quartet (1980) — Wendy Chambers

Mr. Freedman, Mr. Policeband
Ms. Sklar, Mr. Velez
Ms. Chambers, Conductor

June 2, 1981, 8 P.M.

Crescent Quartet: Nancy McAlhany Diggs, violin; Alicia Edelberg, violin; Jill Jaffe, viola; Maxine Neuman, cello

String Quartet (1978) — Sarah W. Aderholdt
- Moderato-Più Mosso-Moderato

String Quartet (1962) — Ruth Schonthal
- Very slow and expressive
- Moderato
- Tempo di recitativo
- Allegro molto, un poco scherzando
- Moderato
- Slow Valse
- Allegro molto agitato
- Lento

Allegro con spirito	
Lento	
Moderato (dance like)	
String Quartet (1956)	Tui St. George Tucker
Allegro	
String Quartet No. 3 (1951)	Lucie Vellère
Allegro	(1896-1966)
Presto	
Andante	
Vivo Spiccato	
String Quartet No. 3 (1975)	Gloria Coates
Marcato	
Spiegel Kanon	
Agitato	

June 9, 1981, 8 P.M.

The Western Wind Vocal Ensemble: Ma Prem Alimo, soprano; Janet Sullivan, soprano; William Zukof, countertenor; Lawrence Bennett, tenor; William Lyon Lee, tenor; Elliot Levin, baritone; with Dixie Ross Neill, piano; Maxine Neuman, cello

Crossworlds (1978)	C. Jane Wilkinson*
Auf dem See in tausend Sterne (C. Reinhold)	Josephine Lang
Wie glanzt so hell dein Auge (A. von Calatin)	(1815-1880)
Sie liebt mich (Goethe)	
Four Hebrew Madrigals (1973) (Rahel)	Tzipora H. Jochsberger*
Aviv (Spring)	
Velu (If only)	
Matai (My dead)	
El Heharim (To the mountains)	
Do Not Press My Hand (Gabriela Mistral) (1981)	Marga Richter*
O Mistress Mine (Shakespeare) (1969)	Judith Lang Zaimont
Away Delight (Ben Jonson)	Rebecca Clarke (1886-1979)
Weep you no more sad fountains (Dowland)	
Sleep (Fletcher)	
I got me flowers (George Herbert)	Alice Parker
My spirit like a charmed bark doth float	Rebecca Clarke
Dolcissimi Respiri	Barbara Strozzi
L'Usignolo	(1619-after 1664)
Pietossisimo Amore	

*Written for the Western Wind Vocal Ensemble.

14

String Quartets by Women: Report on Two Conferences

JUDITH LANG ZAIMONT

In the minds of many, writing a string quartet most surely takes the measure of a composer's gift. Here the composer has no recourse to the variety and richness of orchestral textures and tone colors. Indeed, she or he is required to be inventive and infinitely resourceful with a mere four instruments of similar timbre and to be disciplined enough to express original thought completely in a medium pared down to essentials.

The challenge of the medium has continued to draw composers to it for more than two centuries, with the result that the repertoire for string quartet is a rich, varied, and sustained record of the progress of musical thought. Whether a composer's string quartet music is central to his oeuvre—as in the case of Ludwig van Beethoven or Elizabeth Maconchy—or, seemingly, a diversion from his principal area of interest—as with Giuseppi Verdi or Kurt Weill—these compositions often comprise the individual creator's most telling statements, displaying the quintessence of his or her art.

It should be surprising to no one that women composers have devoted a proportional share of their creative energies to writing string quartets. Yet, *this* repertoire is all but unknown. Even scholars and performers already alerted to the contributions of women composers throughout history might be hard put to name more than one or two women composers of string quartets.

The first steps in shedding light on this music were taken in 1980 and 1981 on the East and West Coasts of the United States, respectively, with two conferences devoted to string quartets written by twentieth century women composers.[1]

On 8 March, 1980, an all-day Conference/Workshop on Twentieth Century String Quartets by Women Composers was held at the Trinity School in New York. The program, jointly directed by Jeannie G. Pool and Doris Hays, was sponsored by the International League of Women Composers and the First National Congress on Women in Music. Funding was provided by grants from Meet the Composer; the Alice M. Ditson Fund of Columbia University; Broadcast Music, Inc.; American Society of Composers, Authors and Publishers; the New York Council for the Humanities; and individual contributors.

The aim of the Conference/Workshop was "to bring Twentieth Century string quartets by women composers into the performance mainstream by presentation of an all-day program and evening concert for string players, teachers, composers, musicologists, music critics, and the general public". The event included:

- thorough examination through performance, analysis, scholarly presentations, and discussions of a wide selection of string quartets;
- survey of the repertoire through open rehearsals and coached sight-reading sessions;
- day-long score library/listening lab for perusal by musicians, musicologists, and composers;
- panel discussion of musicologists and composers to discuss the repertoire in detail.

Planning sessions for the Conference/Workshop began in July 1979 (committee members were Jeannie Pool, Doris Hays, Nancy Corporan, Jill Jaffe [violist with the Crescent Quartet], and Jane Pipik), and a benefit concert to raise money for the event was given by Virginia Eskin, Lucille Field Goodman, Suzanne Ornstein, and Adrienne Fried Block on 24 February, 1980 at Barnard College.

The event proved to be exciting and intellectually stimulating, even if it did not draw the general audience the sponsors had hoped to attract. Perhaps its most significant components were the two concerts, during which eight quartets were performed, and the impressive score library/listening lab that resulted from string quartet submissions from women composers around the globe.

The schedule of events included two formal concerts, lecture discussions on specific pieces to be performed, unprepared sight-reading sessions, and two panel discussions. Eight works were given polished performances in the formal concerts, and another eleven were read at sight.

Schedule of Events, 1980 Conference/Workshop on Twentieth Century String Quartets by Women Composers

Dedicated to the memory of Ruth Crawford Seeger

Registration

Lecture/Demonstration: Manhattan String Quartet with composers Zwilich, Hays, and Ulehla

Panel Discussion: "Meet the Composer." Moderator: James G. Roy, BMI; Composers: Sarah W. Aderholdt (North Carolina), Gloria Coates (Munich, Germany), Doris Hays (New York City), Ruth Schonthal (New York City), Ludmila Ulehla (New York City), Nancy Van de Vate (Honolulu), Ellen Taaffe Zwilich (New York City)

Recital: The Crescent Quartet: *Quartet in D* (1968) by Alice Parker, *String Quartet* (1962) by Ruth Schonthal, *String Quartet* (1978) by Sarah W. Aderholdt (awarded first prize in the 1979 Search for New Music Competition sponsored by the International League of Women Composers), *String Quartet No. 3* (1974-75) by Gloria Coates

Panel Discussion: "Survey of 20th Century String Quartets by Women Composers." Moderator: Martin Bookspan, ASCAP; Panelists: Dr. Ruth Anderson (Hunter College, City University of New York), Ruth Julius (Graduate Center, CUNY), Dr. Otto Luening (Professor Emeritus, Columbia University), Jeannie G. Pool, (National Coordinator, First National Congress on Women in Music), Eric Salzman (Composer and Writer, New York City), Dr. John Reeves White (Graduate Center, CUNY).

Sight-Reading Sessions: Crescent Quartet: quartets by Tui St. George Tucker and Joelle Wallach

String Players from the audience: quartets by the Baroque composer Maddelena Lombardini Sirmen.

Quartets by Blythe Owen, Margo Greene, Paula Kimper, Zenobia Powell Perry, Julia Smith

Quartets by Norma Wendelburg, Judith Lang Zaimont, Ruth Anderson, Nancy Van de Vate

Evening Concert: Manhattan String Quartet: *String Quartet* (1931) by Ruth Crawford Seeger, *Tunings for String Quartet* (1979) by Doris Hays, *String Quartet* (1974) by Ellen Taaffe Zwilich, *Contrasts and Interludes for String Quartet* (1979) by Ludmila Ulehla.

Both of the Conference/Workshop's concerts were taped by National Public Radio and, along with interviews of the composers represented, were broadcast nationally later in 1980 as part of a special six-part series entitled "Woman's Work is . . . Music." Additionally, the Crescent Quartet—an all-woman ensemble that made its debut appearance at the conference—later recorded an album of string quartets by women on the Leonarda label that included two of the works they had programmed at the conference (quartets by Ruth Schonthal and Sarah Aderholdt).

The planning committee for the 1980 conference had hoped to present similar conferences on the same subject in other parts of the country. For financial and logistical reasons these plans had to be suspended. Instead, a totally separate enterprise was begun in California, resulting in a Conference on Contemporary String Quartets by Women Composers given on 7 and 8 August, 1981 at the San Francisco Conservatory of Music.

The San Francisco conference was conceived by composer Deena Grossman after she heard a report on the 1980 New York String Quartet Conference given by Jeannie Pool at a mini-conference on women in music held at the San Francisco Community Music Center in March 1980. Pool had hoped that the New York Conference would generate enough interest in exploring women's contributions to the genre that additional regional conferences throughout the United States on the same subject would be undertaken independently as self-contained events featuring music by

Figure 14.1 The Crescent Quartet (left to right): Jill Jaffe, viola, Alicia Edelberg, violin, Maxine Neuman, 'cello, Nancy McAlhany, violin. Photograph by Lisa Kohler.

women of individual regions. The San Francisco conference was posited on that basis; only later in the planning stages did it take on a broader scope.

Grossman organized a planning committee that met through the summer and fall of 1980 to discuss the scope and format, funding, and scheduling of the conference. Original planning committee members were writer and agent Anne Worthington Prescott; Susan Endrizzi, pianist and head of California Artists Management; composer Leslie Richards; composer/cellist/improvisor Gwendolyn Watson; and conductor and pianist Joan Gallegos. When, after the initial planning meetings, the press of other commitments severely limited participation by Richards, Watson, and Gallegos, four more composers joined the committee—Jeffrey Davis, Sandra Cotton, Marjorie Rusche, and David Holloway—along with Elizabeth Pizer and Lucretia Wolfe, librarian of the San Francisco Conservatory of Music.

During the second phase of meetings, the San Francisco conference began to diverge from the regional-conference model. Both because national funding and coordination did not materialize and because inquiries and expressions of interest began to come in from Europe, Canada, Australia, and Japan as well as the United States, it was decided not to treat this conference as one with a limited focus—national/regional—but to try to represent women composers around the globe. So, too, a decision was made to program quartets by living composers exclusively.

The planning committee also outlined additional guidelines for the conference:

- Works for string quartet would be solicited widely. Selection of pieces to be performed would be made by an independent jury.
- The event would last one full day, with an opening concert and registration on the preceding evening. This format permitted the scheduling of *two* evening concerts, plus a midday prepared sight-reading session, without the need for concurrent presentations. Both formal concerts and the prepared reading session would be given by paid professional ensembles.
- An exhibit of scores and a listening lab would be open for inspection/use throughout the conference.
- In order to attract an audience of both music professionals and general public (men and women), panel discussions would be held on three topics targeted separately to the educator, composer, and listener/music presenter.
- In addition to the regular artists' fees paid to the three participating string quartets who would perform at the conference, jurors, panelists, and committee members would receive honorariums.

In order to solicit scores and raise funds in an orderly way, these activities began in the fall of 1980; sufficient funds were received or pledged by an intermediate "go or no-go" deadline of 30 January 1981 to enable the conference to proceed as scheduled. The deadline for score submissions was 20 February 1981. Thirty-two works were submitted, of which fourteen were finally presented in the two concerts and prepared sight-reading session. The panel of judges consisted of Elinor Armer, composer and faculty member at the San Francisco Conservatory of Music; Bonne Hampton, cellist and faculty member of Stanford University; Lou Harrison, composer and faculty member of Mills College; Paul Hersh, pianist, violist, and member of the faculty at San Francisco Conservatory of Music; and Daniel Kobialka, violinist, composer, and faculty member of San Francisco State University.

Local Bay Area quartets were engaged to perform. Friday night's concert featured the Aurora String Quartet playing *Piece for String Quartet in Two Sections* (1980) by Deborah Van Ohlen (Connecticut); *Estampie* (1976) by Darleen Cowles (Chicago, Illinois); *String Quartet III* (1975) by Junko Mori (Japan); and *String Quartet* (1962) by Ursula Mamlok (New York).

The Saturday afternoon prepared readings were performed by the San Francisco String Quartet. The pieces heard were *Musical Portrait of Thomas Jefferson for String Quartet* by Radie Britain (Hollywood, California); *String Quartet No. I in 5/4* (1979) by Renee Leach (Novator, California); *String Quartet* (1980) by Lori Dobbins (Valencia, California); *Quartet for Strings* (1981) by Marjorie M. Rusche (Berkeley, California);

and *Glass Walls for String Quartet and Tape* by Wendy Reid (Oakland, California).

The Ridge String Quartet played Saturday night's concert of five works: *String Quartet* (1967) by Janice Giteck (Seattle, Washington); *Terra in F* (1981) by Patricia McKann-Mancini (Oakland, California); *String Quartet* (1969) by Teresa Procaccini (Rome, Italy); *Clay* (1979) by Linda Smith (Canada); and *String Quartet* (1969) by Nancy Van de Vate (by that time resident in Washington, D.C.).

While the principal focus of the conference was undoubtedly the performances, the three shrewdly-targeted panel discussions had much to do with drawing the large and varied audience that attended. The first panel, "Contemporary Music Education," dealt with the problems of teaching contemporary (string) literature and techniques to elementary, high school, and college students. Composers, private teachers, and school educators were presented with new approaches to aural training as well as a discussion of current trends in the repertoire. Carolyn Lindeman, a specialist in middle-school education and member of the faculty at San Francisco State University, was the moderator; the other panelists were Marilyn Blanc, cellist and teacher; Daniel Kobialka; Hermann LeRoux, pianist, singer, and member of the faculty of the San Francisco Conservatory of Music; Gwendolyn Watson; and composer Ursula Mamlok.

The second panel, "How to Publish, Record and Protect Yourself," focussed on the problems the composer faces in getting contemporary music into the marketplace. Participants were James Roy, moderator (BMI); Judith Cody (Kikimora Press); April McMahon (KPFA-FM radio); Roger Reynolds, composer (representing Meet the Composer); Carolyn Sachs (CRI, C.F. Peters); and composer Nancy Van de Vate.

The third panel, addressing the complex challenges involved in attracting and building an audience for contemporary music, took place under the direction of moderator Vicky Holt, Director of The Lively Arts at Stanford. Panel participants were George Heussenstamm, Director of The Coleman Chamber Music Association of Pasadena; Victor Ledin, programming director of KQED-FM radio; Kent Nagano, conductor of the Berkeley Symphony; Richard Pontzious, music critic for the San Francisco *Examiner*; and Eva Soltes, formerly the concert director for the Arch Street Concerts and now an independent producer.

In many respects this conference was successful. Certainly it drew an appreciative, involved audience. According to the planning committee's final report, "the audience for both the concerts and the panel discussions was well-mixed and all were equally free in their participation in the question and answer periods. The panels were a definite contribution to the depth of the entire event and allowed for a greater [audience] involvement than the concerts [alone] could provide." From the financial standpoint, too, the conference was successful. Contributions from regional and local foundations and corporations, ASCAP and BMI, plus in-kind contributions totalled $14,765. Total expenses for the one-and-a-half day conference were $13,750, leaving a surplus of more than $1,000, which the planning committee decided to put toward some similar project to be undertaken in the future.

Most important, the conference was successful as a musical undertaking. "After some initial balking by local critics at the idea of the conference, critical response to the events was generally favorable" (committee member's report):

> Unlike most conference or festival programs of modern music, these were beautifully organized. The brevity of the music—pieces ranged between six minutes' duration to about fifteen—made for compact experiences that tired neither the ear nor one's patience.—Heuwell Tircuit, San Francisco *Chronicle,* 10 August 1981

> In the words of Eva Soltes, independent producer, "Presenting contemporary music in a professional way is very important!" This, in addition to the generally excellent music that was played, was an undeniable conference achievement.—Richard Pontzious, San Francisco *Sunday Examiner & Chronicle*, 16 August 1981.

> If these concerts proved anything, it was that women composers write about the same music, and experience the same technical and aesthetic problems of influence, as their male colleagues.—Heuwell Tircuit, San Francisco *Chronicle*, 10 August 1981.

As a final parallel to the New York conference, a commercial recording also resulted from the San Francisco conference. Nancy Van de Vate extended her stay in California to supervise a special taping of her quartet by the Ridge Quartet (who had performed it at the Saturday night concert), which was subsequently released on disc on the Orion label.

Select investigations into women's contributions to the genre have occasionally taken place since the East and West Coast conferences, usually as part of some larger conference or festival, for example, the 27 March 1982 concert of nine quartets by women composers of Europe and America which was part of the Third Edition of Rome's *Donne in Musica* annual festival. In the future, one would hope to see Jeannie Pool's original idea of a round-robin of regional—or global—string quartet conferences put into practice. To illustrate the wealth of literature that awaits exploration, we provide the following list of 129 string quartets by twentieth century women composers of varied nationalities (although primarily American) as a starting point.

List of Works

The following selective list of string quartets by women was created by cross-referencing titles from a half-dozen sources, notably Aaron Cohen's *International Discography of Women Composers* (pub. 1984) and the International League of

Women Composers' directory, *Contemporary Concert Music by Women* (pub. 1981) (both Greenwood Press publications), along with the 51 works presently on deposit at the American Music Center. Due to the nature of the sources, works by American composers predominate. An asterisk (*) denotes quartets on deposit at the American Music Center, 250 West 54th Street, Room 300, New York, NY 10019; where such works also have a publisher of record noted, please consult the individual publisher first before requesting a perusal copy of the work from AMC.

Aderholdt, Sarah W. *String Quartet*. 1978
Allen, Judith Shatin. *Constellations*. 1979. American Composers Alliance.
Anderson, Beth. *Music for Charlemagne Palestine*. 1973
Anderson, Ruth. *Two Movements for String Quartet*.
Armer, Elinor. **String Quartet*. 1983.
Bacewicz, Grazyna. *String Quartet No. 1*. 1938.
String Quartet No. 2. 1942.
Quartet No. 3 for Strings. 1947.
String Quartet No. 4.
String Quartet No. 5. 1956.
String Quartet No. 6. 1960.
Quartet for Strings No. 7. 1965.
Barberis, Mansi. *Cvartettino Pentru Coarde in Stil Neo-Classic*.
Barkin, Elaine. **String Quartet*. 1969.
Beach, Amy. *Quartet for Strings*. 1929.
Beglarian, Eve. **Quartett-Satz*. c. 1981.
Britain, Radie. *Epic Poem—Musical Portrait of Thomas Jefferson*. 1927. Music Library University of California, Los Angeles.
Prison (Lament). 1935. UCLA.
String Quartet. 1934. UCLA.
Brogue, Roslyn. **Quartet for Strings*. 1951.
Cecconi-Bates, Augusta. *Quartet Brevis*. 1976.
Coates, Gloria. **String Quartet No. 3*. 1975.
Coulombe Saint-Marcoux, Micheline. *Quatuor* à Cordes.
Coulthard, Jean. *String Quartet No. 2 (Threnody)*.
Cowles, Darleen. **Estampie*. 1975.
Crawford Seeger, Ruth. *String Quartet*. 1931.
Danforth, Frances. *String Quartet*. 1967.
Dobbins, Lori. **String Quartet*. 1980.
Drake, Elizabeth Bell. **First String Quartet*. 1958.
Fontana, A. *Quartetto No. 1*. 1982.
Gentile, A. *Diaresis*. 1981.
Gideon, Miriam. **Lyric Piece*. 1955. American Composers Alliance.
**Quartet for Strings*. c. 1946. American Composers Alliance.
Giteck, Janice. **String Quartet*. 1967.
Gould, Elizabeth. **String Quartet No. 2*. c. 1977.
Greene, Margo. *String Quartet*. 1968-69.
Greif, Marjorie. **Composition for String Quartet*.
Gyring, Elizabeth. **String Quartet No. 4*.
**String Quartet No. 5*. 1953. American Composers Alliance.
Hays, Doris. **Tunings*. 1979. Quinska-Hays Music.

Hier, Ethel Glenn. **Carolina Christmas.* c. 1952. American Composers Alliance.
Hsu, Wen-Ying. *String Quartet No. 1.* Wen-Ying Studio.
String Quartet No. 2. 1968. Wen-Ying Studio.
Ivey, Jean Eichelberger. **String Quartet.* 1960.
Johnson, Elizabeth. *String Quartet.* 1938.
Jolas, Betsy. *Quatuor III (Nine Etudes) for String Quartet.* 1973.
Kimper, Paula M. *Underground Dream Suite.* (1979-80.)
Lackman, Susan Cohn. *String Quartet No. 1.* 1976.
String Quartet No. 2. 1977.
Loudova, Ivana. *String Quartet No. 2. (Dem Andenken an Smetana).* 1976.
Lutyens, Elisabeth. *String Quartet Op. 25,* No. 6 1952.
Maconchy, Elizabeth. Twelve *String Quartets.* Between 1933 and 1979. Of these the following are recorded:
String Quartet No. 5. 1948.
String Quartet No. 9.
String Quartet No. 10. 1972.
Mamlok, Ursula. *String Quartet.* c. 1962.
Marcus, Adabelle Gross. *String Quartet No. 1.*
**String Quartet No. 2.*
McKann-Mancini, Patricia. *Terra in F.* 1981.
Mell, Gertrud Maria. *String Quartet No. 1.*
Mori, Junko. *String Quartet 3.* 1975.
Musgrave, Thea. *String Quartet.* 1958. J. & W. Chester.
Obrovska, Jana. *String Quartet.*
Owen, Blythe. *Quartet for Strings No. 2.* 1951.
Parker, Alice. *Quartet in D.* 1968.
Pentland, Barbara. *String Quartet No. 1.*
String Quartet No. 3.
String Quartet No. 4.
Perry, Zenobia Powell. *Three Designs for Four Strings.* 1964.
Pistono D'Angelo. *Quartetto No. 1.* 1982.
Pizer, Elizabeth Hayden. **Interfuguelude, Op. 43.* 1977.
Preobrajenska, Vera N. **Classical Menuetto.* 1947.
**Hebraic Suite.* 1968.
**Le Petit Sonatine.* 1962.
Preludium.
Procaccini, Teresa. *Quartetto, Op. 42.* 1962.
Rainier, Priaulx. *String Quartet.* 1939.
Rapoport, Eda. **Quartet in G, Op. 16.* c. 1939. M. Weaner.
**String Quartet on Hebrew Themes.* c. 1944. Transcontinental Music Corp.
Richter, Marga. *Ricercare.* 1958. Carl Fischer.
**String Quartet No. 2.* 1959. Carl Fischer.
Rusche, Marjorie M. **Quartet for Strings.* c. 1981.
Schonthal, Ruth. **String Quartet.* 1962.
Semegen, Daria. *Composition for String Quartet.* 1965. American Composers Alliance.
String Quartet No. 1. 1963.
String Quartet No. 2. 1964.

Silsbee, Ann. *Quest*. 1977. American Composers Alliance.
Silverman, Faye-Ellen. **String Quartet*. c. 1976. Seesaw Music Corporation.
Simons, Netty. **Facets 4*. c. 1964. American Composers Alliance.
 **String Quartet*. 1950. American Composers Alliance.
Smith, Julia. **Quartet for Strings*. 1964. Mowbray Music Publishers.
Smith, Linda Catlin. *Clay*. 1979.
Spencer, Williametta. **String Quartet No. 1*.
St. John, Kathleen. **Quartet of a Prophecy*. 1980.
 **A String Quartet to a Swan*. 1967.
Stanley, Helen. **String Quartet*. 1951.
Stilman, Julia. **Etudes for String Quartet*. American Composers Alliance.
Tailleferre, Germaine. *Quartet for Strings*. 1918.
Terzian, Alicia. *Three Pieces on Armenian Folk Material for String Quartet, Op. 5*.
Tucker, Tui St. George. *String Quartet*. 1956-57.
Ulehla, Ludmila. *Contrasts and Interludes for String Quartet*. 1979.
Van de Vate, Nancy. **Music for Student String Quartet*. 1977.
 **String Quartet No. 1*. 1969.
Van Ohlen, Deborah. *Piece for String Quartet in Two Sections*. 1980.
Vallère, Lucie. *Troisième Quatuor*. 1051.
 Quatrième Quatuor. 1962.
Vito-Delvaux, Berthe di. *Suite for String Quartet*.
Wallach, Joelle. **Movement*. 1968. American Composers Alliance.
Weigl, Vally. **Adagio for Strings*. American Composers Alliance.
 **Andante for String Quartet*. American Composers Alliance.
 **To Emily*.
Wendelburg, Norma. *String Quartet No. 2*. 1956.
Witbeck, Ariel Lea. **Motet for String Quartet*.
Witni, Monica. **String Quartet in E Minor*. 1969.
Wylie, Ruth Shaw. *String Quartet No. 1, Op. 1*. 1942.
 String Quartet No. 2, Op. 8. 1944.
 **String Quartet No. 3, Op. 17*. 1962. Cor Publishing Company.
Zaimont, Judith Lang. **De Infinitate Caeleste (Of the Celestial Infinite)*. 1979.
Zechlin, Ruth. *Four String Quartets*.
Ziffrin, Marilyn J. **String Quartet*. 1970.
Zimmermann, M. **Quartetto No. 1, Op. 7*. 1979.
Zwilich, Ellen Taaffe. **String Quartet*. 1974. Margun Music, Inc.

An additional source for repertoire is the "Listing of String Quartets by Women Composers" compiled by Jeannie G. Pool, issued in conjunction with her report on the 1980 New York Conference on String Quartets by Women (*Working Papers on Women in Music* No. 1, International Institute for the Study of Women in Music, California State University-Northridge, June 1985).

Note

1. This chapter is based on personal observation of the New York conference, original research, and materials distributed by the planning committees of both conferences.

15

Women Band Directors in American Higher Education

CAROL ANN FEATHER

Every year several thousand music education majors graduate from American colleges and universities; large numbers of these are women whose applied major was instrumental music. A significant number of these women later earn graduate degrees in music education, applied music, or education. Yet, comparatively few of them become band directors at the postsecondary school level. Those few who have obtained such positions seldom are recognized nationally, nor do they otherwise gain appreciable visibility and thus do not serve as role models for young women who might aspire to careers as college band directors.

Female musicians are only just now starting to receive acclaim in the areas of composing for band and performing on traditionally *male* band instruments, such as the trumpet and tuba. "Bands, especially marching bands, seem to be the last frontier for women in music. There are fewer women composers, conductors, and teachers for bands than in any other part of music education."[1] And the very title *band director* evokes the image of the traditional male director standing on his podium, dressed in his uniform trousers, jacket, and hat with baton in hand. Names such as John Philip Sousa (1854-1932), Patrick S. Gilmore (1829-1892), Edwin Franko Goldman (1878-1956), Paul V. Yoder (b. 1908), and William D. Revelli (b. 1902) come to mind. Seldom, if ever, can one recall the name of a woman director.

Is band directing still a male citadel, or are women successfully beginning to make their place within the conducting profession? Has the ground been properly broken for women to become *directors* of bands and wind ensembles, by virtue of their plentiful presence as *performers* within these groups?

Historically, it was the forming of women's orchestras, beginning around 1870, which first provided openings for women as performers and, more significantly, as conductors. These orchestras were generally founded by women instrumentalists or conductors in order to provide performance opportunities for themselves and other women.[2] Although the main thrust of the women's orchestra movement had subsided by the end of World War II, these orchestras demonstrated clearly that women instrumentalists were able to perform standard symphonic repertory and that women were fully capable of conducting that repertory.[3]

With the burgeoning women's movement of recent years there has been a refocusing of attention on women conductors.[4] Along with this attention has come an acknowledged list of hurdles which must be successfully negotiated by the present-day woman conductor, particularly if she aspires to conduct a mixed ensemble which includes both male and female players.

A main cause of women's lack of success as orchestral conductors, according to Robert Jones (former critic for *Time* Magazine and *Cue*), is the sum of their physical attributes.[5] Women's slighter stature and personal attractiveness can tell against them when they attempt to establish themselves in positions of command and authority, Jones noted in 1976. He reported one musician in Sarah Caldwell's orchestra as saying, "If she'd been a babe, we'd have walked right over her," speculating "One also wonders whether musicians in her orchestra would have treated her like Caldwell if she happened to look like [Marilyn] Monroe. Probably not."[6]

Regardless of the reason given, women have found it difficult to build successful conducting careers. Women have seldom been hired for conducting positions which hold prestige and which have provided great visibility. Few, during their school years, have been encouraged to compete as serious conductors. When Margaret Hillis, conductor of the Chicago Symphony Chorus, graduated from Indiana University in 1947, she was told that a woman could not succeed as a symphonic conductor.[7] Twenty years later, Victoria Bond was told much the same thing.[8] Even the most successful women conductors have felt discriminated against at one time or another. As Antonia Brico remarked in a 1975 interview, "I think it's perfectly tragic that when I want to conduct, when I'm capable of it, when I've had the training, that people should look twice because I'm a woman."[9] Joyce Johnson, conductor of the Oakland Symphony Orchestra, found that, "Men always have an edge. It is as if men are judged competent until they prove themselves incompetent, and women are judged incompetent until they prove themselves competent."[10] Voicing similar concerns, one of the leading women choral conductors, Elaine Brown of Temple University, said that in order to be judged as equal to her male colleagues, she has had to be more qualified than they were, and has had to do a better job than they.[11] Margaret Hillis was a little more optimistic when she commented, "Some people are amazed that the orchestra sounds well when I conduct it. Life isn't fair, and this is one of the unfair things, but it's changing."[12]

Clout is needed if women are to succeed in influencing the use of more women in all aspects of music. "Since women are rarely in a position to bestow professional favors, they rarely receive them,"[13] thus setting up a vicious cycle: The lack of successful female role models in conducting and other segments of the music profession inhibits other women from entering the field and perhaps changing the nature of the situation overall. (David Truman underscores the importance of visible role models in noting the almost perfect correlation which exists between women achievers and the number of women on the faculty of the college these achievers attended.[14])

Yet, within the last one-and-a-half decades, the picture has slowly changed. A few nationally-noted women conductors have become role models for younger women just entering the field. The influence of one of these, Sarah Caldwell, was recognized when she was named by *Harper's Bazaar* (1977) as one of the ten most powerful women in the United States.[15]

Discriminatory practices against women have been especially blatant in bands, where admission as instrumentalists was late in coming. College officials responsible for admitting students to membership in marching bands were guilty of sexual discrimination, and marching bands were the last type of musical ensemble in which membership as instrumentalists was granted to women. And only after many years of experience as instrumen-

Figure 15.1 Kathryn B. Scott, Director of Bands at the University of Alabama. By permission of University of Alabama.

Figure 15.2 Kathryn B. Scott conducting the University of Alabama's "Million Dollar" Band in formation at a football game. By permission of University of Alabama.

talists in the marching bands did women begin to express the desire to direct marching ensembles. Even through recent years, it has been difficult to find successful women directors of marching bands. Part of this problem was related to the history and tradition of the marching band, which evolved from the military, in which there were no women.[16] With the outbreak of World War II, "Many formerly all-male college bands accepted women members. . . . When the war ended, the bands became all-male again."[17]

In 1954, the director of the University of Minnesota marching band presented his solution to the problem of women who desired to be a part of the band. Although he gave no reason for his opinion, he wrote, "Our experiences have shown us that it is generally ill-advised for men and women to march together in one large unit."[18] He went on to describe his deployment of a separate woman's unit. Much of the time the women presented separate short shows or played only in the stands. The women's unit occasionally appeared in block formation along with the men, to form a letter in a word-spelling formation or to provide a fuller woodwind sound.* He guarded the femininity of the women by having their uniforms designed in a feminine style but still similar to those of the men. Even certain music and perfor-

*Women were frequently channeled toward playing the "feminine" small woodwind instruments while men were encouraged to play the "masculine" brass winds and percussion instruments. This practice has now begun to change, and increasing numbers of women have begun studying the formerly taboo instruments.

mance styles were considered either feminine or masculine. "Shows and music will be especially written for the women's band with particular care given to the dignity of performance which should be characteristic—'ladylike'."[19] The director claimed that such "careful" preparation allowed women to participate in the marching band on an equal basis with men. The fact that each girl had to purchase her own uniform, while the men had their uniforms provided by the university, did not seem of any consequence to the director.[20] Therefore, it was little wonder he did not see some of his other policies as being discriminatory. His summary statement presented a not uncommon philosophy that served to propagate the idea of the masculine marching band. "Men have enthusiasm and drive; let's not forget it. However," he continued, "let's not forget the great importance of the women in our band."[21] The inferences from that statement are characteristic of sexual discrimination.

Over the last 30 years women have made tremendous progress in their struggle to become equal participants with men in both concert and marching bands.[22] The director of the 1954 University of Minnesota marching band would have been shocked to read that, by 1975, women were not only marching in most college and high school bands along with the men, but that 5 percent of the combined college and high school band directors were women.[23] In that year, however, a published study disclosed that the majority of women band directors did not hold the more prestigious positions, as, "sixty-five percent of women instrumental teachers teach in elementary or junior high school; thirty-three percent in high school; and only two percent in colleges and universities."[24] The 1975 study also reported that women were not granted equal recognition within the profession. "The select American School Band Directors Association has 18 women out of a membership of 960. The most prestigious organization, the American Bandmasters Association, of 275 members has none; while Phi Beta Mu, the bandmasters honorary fraternity, in the past few years has had one honorary and several state chapter women members."[25] This situation has moderated somewhat since 1975. As of July 1984, the membership of the American School Band Directors Association (ASBDA) included 71 women.[26] The American Bandmasters Association (ABA) as of June 1984 had approximately 275 active members, including the first and only woman member. This woman, a high school band director, was accepted into membership in March 1984.[27] Phi Beta Mu had approximately 80 women, including two state chairpersons out of a total membership of over 1,400, as of June 1984.[28]

While a career in the field of band music in higher education is more accessible to women today, few women plan for or aspire to the profession. Little is known about the women who do successfully direct bands in junior or community colleges, four-year colleges, and universities, and the women directors themselves frequently are not aware of other women who function in similar positions.

I am a former band director on the four-year college level. Following my graduation from Morehead State University in Kentucky, where I majored in instrumental music and theory, and a one-year position as a choral director in the Elko County Schools in Elko, Nevada, I was employed as the band director at Pikeville College in Pikeville, Kentucky. I held that position from 1965 to 1969. In September 1969, I moved to Dyersburg, Tennessee, to build a music program in a new community college. I am currently an associate professor of music at Dyersburg State Community College and conductor of the Dyersburg Community Orchestra.

Figure 15.3 Carol Ann Feather. Photograph by Angie Galloway.

While completing my doctoral studies at the University of Mississippi, I was encouraged to conduct research in some area of women's studies. Reflection upon my past experiences as a woman band director led me directly into a study of the status and number of women employed in such positions. My feelings of isolation while I was so employed gave me a sense of urgency in trying to locate and encourage women who were caught in the same isolation. How well I recalled attending professional meetings of band directors where I was the only female in attendance! During my entire four-year tenure as a college band director, I never met another woman in a similar position. It was only in the public school systems that I had met any women band directors. In undertaking this study I finally had the opportunity to determine if other women were facing situations I had encountered ten years earlier. A key reason for initiating it was to gather data that could be used to generate greater visibility for the women who have succeeded as band directors, and by spotlighting successful professionals, to provide the potential for encouraging newcomers to enter the field.

The study was formally designed and carried out during the academic year 1979-80. Data was gathered on American women band directors in place in higher education at that time, and a comparison of their circumstances with those of their male colleagues was carried out. In order to accomplish this, several key questions or sets of questions were posed to all survey participants, male and female, via a sequence of formal questionnaires (followed up as necessary by individual telephone interviews). Although the actual questionnaires were multi-page documents, the basic questions guiding their organization were the following:

- What is the educational preparation and professional experience of the women?
- Job circumstances—In what kinds of institutions are they employed? What are their primary job responsibilities? What financial compensation do they receive?
- What are some of the personal characteristics of these women? Do they face unique problems in their professional lives due to being female? How do they feel these problems can best be faced or solved?

Locating the women to participate in the study was not a simple task. By systematically tracking down all female members (or those with possible female first names) on the 1979-80 membership lists of the Women Band Directors National Association, the College Band Directors National Association, and the list of college band directors distributed by the College Music Society, I was able to come up with a basic population of 43. Subsequent referrals from male respondents to the survey added another 10 names to the original list of women, thus identifying a total population of 53 American female potential respondents. Because this number was so small, the entire 53 were queried, disclosing that only 21 were in fact college band directors during the 1979-80 academic year. The bulk of the useful data, then, was generated from the responses of these 21 active women band directors.

(Of the remaining 32 women who were not then active as band directors at the college level, 11 reported they had never been band directors at any level of education; six were high school band directors, including four who had taught college band in the past; five were no longer teaching, including one who had retired and one who had opened a music store; three had been college band directors in the past, but had moved into other positions at their colleges; one had become a department chairperson; one voluntarily moved into classroom teaching; and one was moved into classroom teaching involuntarily during the 1979-80 academic year when she was replaced by a male band director. The seven remaining included two women who had been college band directors but who had left college work to become band directors in elementary schools; two who worked only with college flag corps, majorettes, and rifle teams; and one college band director who was on a leave of absence for the 1979-80 academic year. The final two gave no specific data.)

The male population for comparison was easily located. A random sample of 10 percent (181) of the total 1979-80 male membership of the College Band Directors National Association and the list of college band directors distributed by the College Music Society was prepared. Eventually, 154 of the 181 total sample participated in the survey, 141 of whom qualified as band directors in higher education, a response rate considered adequate enough for the purpose.

After the questionnaires were completed and returned, the data was analyzed and certain conclusions were reached.[29]

Statistical evidence presented in the study indicated that women held 1.25 percent of the jobs as band directors in American colleges and universities, accounting for 21 of the 1,679 qualifying professionals as of June 1980. Thus, it is evident that the career field of band directing in higher education continues to be dominated by males.

The 21 women who were identified as college band directors were not employed in the larger or more prestigious institutions, as was evidenced by the 53.38 percent (11 women) who were employed at four-year, private institutions with enrollments of less than 3,000. Of the ten women who were employed in public institutions, five did not hold positions of high status. Two of these five were part-time faculty, while the other three were assistant band directors who worked under the supervision of male head directors.[30] In comparison, men directors were more often employed in public institutions or in the larger, more prestigious private institutions. (see Table 15.1).

Doctorates were held by 42.86 percent of the women (9 women) compared to 26.28 percent of the men, but only 52.38 percent of the women directors were in professorial ranks, compared to 73.38 percent of the men. A larger percentage of women than men held the rank of full professor; however, proportionally fewer women than men held ranks of associate or

Table 15.1
Number and Percent of Female and Male Band Directors in Higher Education by Type of College Where Employed

	Responses			
	Female[a]		*Male*[b]	
College type	Number	Percent	Number	Percent
I. Level of training				
A. Four-year college	18	85.71	104	73.76
B. Two-year college	3	14.29	37	26.24
II. Type of governance				
A. Private college	11	52.38	51	36.17
B. Public college	10	47.62	90	63.83
III. Sex of students				
A. Coeducational	19	90.48	141	100.00
B. Women's (private college)	2	9.52	0	0.00

[a]Based on twenty-one responses.
[b]Based on 141 responses.

assistant professor. At least a portion of this difference in ranks is attributable to two factors: (1) the men directors averaged five years more teaching experience than the women; and (2) the men had a mean tenure in their present position of 8.79 years compared to 4.81 years for the women. The effects of these two factors should have been offset somewhat, however, by the greater proportion of doctorates held by women directors (see Table 15.2).

Although 10 of the women (almost 48 percent) and a comparable 57 of the men (about 41 percent) went directly into college band directing, with no previous experience at precollege schools, the majority of each group of respondents had had such experience. Three of the women had had prior experience as elementary school band directors, two had been junior high school band directors, and nine had had experience as senior high school band directors. Eleven of the male respondents had taught band on the elementary school level, 20 had been junior high school band directors, and 76 had been band directors in senior high schools (see Table 15.3).

Bands directed by women were of smaller size than those directed by men, with mean enrollments of 65 and 88 players, respectively. The primary reason for this difference in size was related to the smaller enrollments in the institutions in which the women were employed; this was particularly evident in the private institutions.

Women and men band directors in higher education were most commonly found as directors of concert bands, symphonic bands, or wind ensembles. Relatively few women directors (19 percent, as compared to 39 percent of the men) directed marching bands. (These findings bore out similar findings from a 1977 study which reported that it was rare to find successful women directors of marching bands even though women were meeting with success as conductors of concert bands.[31] Similarly, only 19 percent of the women directed jazz or stage bands, compared to almost 40 percent of the men (see Table 15.4). Such differences may be attributed to one or more of

Table 15.2
Comparison of Level of Professional Training to Academic Rank of Female and Male College Band Directors

Academic rank and level of professional training	Females		Males	
	Number[a]	*Percent*	*Number*[b]	*Percent*
I. Instructors				
Bachelor's Degree	2	33.33	1	3.33
Master's degree	2	33.33	14	46.67
Master's degree plus one year	1	16.67	8	26.67
All but dissertation	1	16.67	5	16.66
Doctoral degree	0	0.00	2	6.67
Total	6	100.00	30	100.00
II. Assistant Professors				
Bachelor's degree	0	0.00	1	2.70
Master's degree	1	20.00	11	29.73
Master's plus one year	1	20.00	9	24.33
Educational Specialist	0	0.00	1	2.70
All but dissertation	0	0.00	6	16.22
Doctoral degree	3	60.00	9	24.32
Total	5	100.00	37	100.00
III. Associate Professors				
Master's degree	0	0.00	9	21.95
Master's plus one year	0	0.00	12	29.27
All but dissertation	0	0.00	5	12.20
Doctoral degree	1	100.00	15	36.58
Total	1	100.00	41	100.00
IV. Professors				
Master's degree	0	0.00	4	18.18
Master's plus one year	1	20.00	7	31.82
All but dissertation	0	0.00	2	9.09
Doctoral degree	4	80.00	9	40.91
Total	5	100.00	22	100.00

[a]Based on a total of seventeen women in traditional academic ranks who reported both rank and professional training.

[b]Based on a total of 130 men in traditional academic ranks who reported both rank and professional training.

Table 15.3
Teaching Experience by Level as Reported According to Sex of Band Director in Higher Education

	Females		Males	
Teaching Level	*Number*[a]	*Percent*	*Number*[b]	*Percent*
No previous experience	6	28.57	28	19.86
Elementary school	3	14.29	11	7.80
Junior high school	2	9.52	20	14.18
Senior high school	9	42.86	76	53.90
Other college	6	28.57	51	36.17

[a]Several of the twenty-one female directors indicated experience on more than one teaching level.

[b]Several of the 141 male directors indicated experience on more than one teaching level.

Figure 15.4 Dorothy Cacchio, Band Director of Caldwell College, New Jersey.

the following three factors: (1) many small private colleges do not have the enrollments to support marching and jazz or stage bands in addition to some type of concert band—these are the very colleges that employ over half of the women band directors, (2) administrators who hire band directors are more resistant to hiring women directors for certain kinds of bands, and (3) women directors do not always have prior experience with these types of bands and therefore do not feel adequately prepared to direct them.

The most serious discrepancy between the women and men band directors in higher education was in the area of financial compensation. In both the private and public institutions, women directors were paid less than men when compared on a rank-to-rank basis (see Table 15.5). The mean salary

Table 15.4
Types of Bands Directed by Women and Men Band Directors in Higher Education by Sex of Director

	Females		Males	
Type of Band	*Number*	*Percent*[a]	*Number*	*Percent*[b]
Marching	4	19.05	55	39.01
Concert, symphonic, or wind ensemble	17	80.95	126	89.36
Jazz or stage	4	19.05	56	39.72
Pep	3	14.29	4	2.84

[a]Based on twenty-one responses.
[b]Based on 141 responses.

Table 15.5
Mean Salary, Salary Differential, and Percent of Terminal Degrees According to Traditional Rank Held by Women and Men Band Directors in Higher Education Employed on a Full-Time Basis[a]

	Number Reporting		Mean Salary		Salary	Percent with Terminal Degree	
Traditional rank	*Females*	*Males*	*Females*	*Males*	*differential*	*Females*	*Males*
Instructor	5	25	$12,840	$15,226	$2,386	0.00	6.67
Assistant professor	5	34	12,941	15,720	2,779	60.00	24.32
Associate professor	1	36	16,920	18,444	1,524	100.00	36.59
Professor	5	22	20,356	23,919	3,563	80.00	40.91

[a]All salaries converted to a nine-month basis.

for full-time women band directors was $14,840 compared to $18,126 for full-time men. Surprisingly, the greatest inequity was in the full professor rank, where the mean salary of women directors was $3,563 less than that of the men, even though 80 percent of the women who were full professors held doctorates compared to 41 percent of the men. Thus, regardless of educational preparation, women band directors in higher education were paid less than men, even when the women and men held positions of equal rank and responsibility.

Further evidence of the salary discrepancy was provided by data that showed women band directors taught a heavier weekly contact hour load than did their male colleagues. The mean number of contact hours for women was 20.53 compared to 18.79 hours for the men. In essence, the women band directors worked longer hours than did the men and earned less money. Even though male directors averaged five more years of teaching experience than did the women, the greater percentage of doctoral degrees held by women directors along with a heavier work load should have resulted in equalization of salaries.

The data also revealed that the mean age of the women was 35.76 years, compared to 41.44 for the men. Perhaps related to the age factor were the revealing figures showing that two-thirds of the women band directors were single compared with only 15 percent of the men. Implications regarding these data are varied, and no firm conclusions can be reached based only on the evidence in this study. It may be hypothesized, however, that many women band directors leave the profession upon being married due to increased family responsibilities and restraints on the time available to concentrate on professional growth in a demanding profession.

Thus, in virtually all respects, the women band directors share in the same difficulties with regard to finding and sustaining their place within the profession as do the more well-known women orchestra and opera conductors. These include: lack of role models; active discouragement by mentors or advisors*; seldom finding employment in the more prestigious institutions (here, colleges and universities); inequities in salary levels and in number of hours of assigned work load, when contrasted with their male colleagues; and negotiating the ever-present conflicts that arise from balancing the requirements of a career against those of marriage and a full home life.

The women in this study seemed to suffer particularly from the effects of perceived isolation as women band directors*, and from attitudes of distrust or skepticism on the part of the men with whom they would work. The three most frequently reported problems were (1) attitudes of skepticism from others concerning the ability of women to handle the position of

*Two of the women in the study stated that they were openly discouraged from entering the band field by their college advisors. These advisors indicated that women could not function successfully as band directors and that they would encounter numerous problems due to their sex.

*None of the women band directors was able to name another woman holding a position as a college band director, while twenty-one male directors in the study named one woman, and one man named two women, whom they believed to be band directors in higher education.

Figure 15.5 Paula Holcomb, Band Director at Central College, Pella, Iowa. By permission of Central College.

band director (31 percent); (2) their belief that men directors considered them a threat to their power or position (31 percent); and (3) reluctance on the part of administrators to hire women band directors (23 percent).

In addition to these general plaints, the women also noted problems in dealing with sexual advances from male colleagues, negative attitudes from conservative towns, problems in coping with colleagues' jealous wives, the struggle to gain the students' acceptance as the person who would be conducting the band, and perhaps a certain added difficulty in obtaining assistance from a biased administration. These, as well as other professional problems—coping with discipline problems, lack of experience with marching bands, and so forth—were written about with remarkable candor by the women in the study. The full text of their responses to the open-

Figure 15.6 Rebekah C. Covell, Band Director at the Crane School of Music in New York, conducting the ceremonial band for the awards ceremony at the 1980 Winter Olympics in Lake Placid. On the podium with Dr. Covell is Jim Craig, goalie for the U.S. Hockey Team, ''assisting'' with Sousa's *Stars and Stripes*. Note the Gold Medal around his neck.

ended section on ''unique problems'' will be found as an appendix to this chapter.

The women themselves made several recommendations on a personal level that may well be effective for others who are thinking of entering the profession: Prove yourself—first and foremost, and, to the greatest extent individually possible, be strong. Also important is to work within the system and function effectively by being firm with discipline, asserting your program needs, and being supportive of other band directors.

To these personal recommendations for courage and persistence on the job may be joined more general suggestions for the field as a whole:

- College advisors should present the career option of ''band director'' to women students who major in instrumental music.
- College administrators should be encouraged to give equal consideration to women applicants for positions as band directors in higher education.
- Qualified women should be encouraged to apply for positions as band directors in higher education in general and especially for positions in public colleges and universities and in large, prestigious private colleges and universities.

- College administrators should take precautions to give equal consideration to women band directors in the areas of promotions, financial compensation, and work load.
- Women who major in instrumental music education should be encouraged to gain equal experience with men in marching bands and stage or jazz bands.
- In order to eliminate the isolation experienced by these women professionals, a communications network should be established through the Women Band Directors National Association (Barbara Lovett, President, WBDNA, 3703 26th Street, Lubbock, Texas 79410), the College Band Directors National Association, or independently, to provide a means of discussing common interests, experiences, and problems.

Additionally, for the purpose of further study, it is recommended that:

1. This study be replicated periodically in order to measure any change in data concerning women band directors in higher education.
2. A study be conducted to determine why two-thirds of the women band directors in higher education were single, compared to only 15 percent of the male directors.
3. A comparative study of career aspirations of women and men students who major in instrumental music education be conducted. Such a study would be of added value if the aspirations of the women and men were compared both upon entering college and upon graduation, in order to measure any significant change in aspirations by sex during the period of college training.

Figure 15.7 Professor Paula Holcomb conducting a stage band at Central College.

The problems encountered by the women band directors reflect general attitudes faced by any minority group when it tries to gain acceptance in situations or career areas previously closed to it. As more capable women gain employment as college band directors, precedents will be set that will eliminate much of the skepticism about women's abilities as band directors, as well as eliminating the reluctance by administrators to hire women for such positions. When the number of women in the field increases, men will become accustomed to working with women band directors as peers, just as they are now adapting to working with women in other fields which were, at one time, dominated by males.

COMPLETE RESPONSES OF WOMEN BAND DIRECTORS IN HIGHER EDUCATION REGARDING UNIQUE PROBLEMS FACED DUE TO WORKING IN A PREDOMINANTLY MALE CAREER FIELD AND THEIR RECOMMENDED SOLUTIONS TO THESE PROBLEMS

Response No. 1

I experienced no difficulties in public schools; however, there have been difficulties in my college job. Band directors more than others seem to display the 'little god' syndrome. I'm a threat to their power.

1. Resentment by high school directors of my job. First time I have ever been accused of sexual advances. (not true)
2. I have had what may be described as major difficulties in the attitudes of very conservative, Southern, 'churchly town.'

Response No. 2

No particular problem now—twenty years ago, maybe. I'm a strong individual. I know what has to be done and I do it.

Response No. 3

The first problem was at the graduate level where I sensed a definite attempt on the part of my major professor to steer me away from the instrumental area into elementary general music.

A second time—in my first college job, I experienced successful attempts at excluding me from the band conducting area. This occurred with a change of administration during which time I was taken away from the band job in order that the new chairman might bring in his own *man*.

At this present job, I have felt no prejudice and sense a great deal of respect for my position and my capabilities and the quality of my work.

Response No. 4

I met with problems several years ago when applying for high school jobs. They were reluctant to hire females. They were afraid that a woman couldn't handle the job and would have discipline problems.

Response No. 5

After proving myself as a woman conductor, the jealousy problems I had were corrected in my first year.

Response No. 6

Only that students coming directly from high school groups with male directors—[*sic*] they feel they must 'get used to' a female, but they do adjust very quickly and even seem to be proud of having a female (i.e., it's something different!).

Response No. 7

Yes! I've always been told that I would encounter problems if I went into band directing, and I was ready to face them. What I wasn't prepared to face was the fact that most of the problems come from other women. I have not had even one mishap because of men. In addition to band directing I play ____* and do free-lance work in ____*. There are several booking agents who hire me. They are the most courteous people I have ever dealt with. They ask what part I wish to play and who else I would prefer to fill out the rest of the section! The other brass players have been men and they too are wonderful. Guys who have been in the field 30 years help me feel comfortable (I'm 26) and are always helpful and encouraging. However, there are about three or four women brass players in this area who have been auditioning judges. I find it interesting that in one year of over 20 auditions, I have won every one (14 by count) except the ones where those women preside. Further, their attitudes could give most men lessons in how to be unfair, cruel, and unprofessional. How to handle it—I work very hard at being very good. I do not attend to other women who spend precious time looking for 'soap' boxes and opportunities to throw their weight around. Choose any great women—Ruth Slenczynska, Marilyn Horne, Marie Curie, Janet Baker, Margaret Hillis, etc. If you look into their daily schedules, most of them work hard most of the time to be great in their field. (As do all the great people in their field.) I study and practice very hard, and if I continue and become really good at what I do, and if other people do not get so sick and tired of incompetent women with big mouths, and unnecessarily put me into that category—maybe I will continue to get good jobs.

Response No. 8

At contests in previous positions (high schools) I was treated coldly. In my present position I feel I'm a threat to the large band and orchestra director personnel. They are slow to fraternize.

Response No. 9

When I graduated from college I was unable to find a high school band position. All positions available required four years of university marching band experience. At that time no females were allowed in the band, thus, I became a junior high band director. My junior high band was performing at a level that was superior in almost every way to the bands at the four high schools that my students transferred to. I

*Information deleted to protect confidentiality.

gradually moved into a supervisory capacity, with several male band directors to work with. The stories of my efforts, finally positively rewarded, to enlist their cooperation and reduce their animosity are lengthy. I now am primarily involved in behavioral band research and ____* performance. I am very well known among ____* and have a number of high ranking professional responsibilities. Yet I still face repeatedly the following situations.

1. Unless I am personally known, I am not chosen by my credentials and tapes for a job. It seems that committees have a hard time imagining a 39-year-old ____* conductor relating to their 19 year olds (usually male) ____*. Thus, everything that has happened in my career seems to have come about as a result of personal contact.
2. The people (usually male) with whom I have closely worked have, after we had worked together for some time, told me that the initial adjustment to working with me was difficult for them. The problem stems from my 'dual image.' I am an attractive, fun-loving blond. And I do have a good time in life. On the other hand, when it is time for business I prefer logical thinking and don't care to tolerate sloppy planning and lack of thoughtful consideration of students and beautiful music. My mind works rapidly; I am well-read and well-thought in arenas other than music. Thus I am threatening to many males until they realize that I know how to cooperate, *be supportive*, and work within the system. Yes, I go out of my way to be positively supporting where possible, and caring of colleagues. This so helps them with their fears.
3. Wives of colleagues can be an even worse problem. I also am a pianist who specializes in ____* accompanying. Thus, between____* gigs and piano accompanying, I am in demand for all sorts of activities out of the classroom. Of course wives are suspicious and resentful of the off hours, extra rehearsals, etc. I go to extra efforts to include wives; if they are interested I keep them up-to-date on the activities and decisions—their husbands forget to tell them; I choose to remember countless birthdays, graduations, etc., of children. This all seems to help.
4. I deal with all sexual advances as gently and thoughtfully as possible. I *never* let a male colleague think he is sexually uninteresting to me. But I make sure they are aware that I value them and their friendship far too much to chance letting sexual activities foul up our good relationship.
5. I am quite certain that my family status (husband and four children) counts against me as I seek promotion.

Response No. 10

Generally I find attitudes favorable. The only problems I have encountered were my senior male students last year. They tended to try to relate to me as a peer. I occasionally feel that being an 'authority figure' is important to the current generation of students, and it's not my way. I feel that I am more noticed, given more praise and more negative criticism by students and colleagues because I'm female. It's inevitable with any visible minority.

---

*Information deleted to protect confidentiality.

Response No. 11

My feelings are that administrations don't want to take you as seriously as you would like, due to the fact that you are a woman. To meet this problem I believe that you have to be fairly aggressive and make yourself known and heard. You have to have the background that they will respect.

I believe it is harder to discipline your groups as a woman, especially an instrumental group which has traditionally had male leadership. I think many times that students try to take advantage of your more understanding nature and give you a hassle when they may not have given a man the same hassle. The only way to meet this is to handle your problems in a firm but fair way and stick to your guns.

I feel that it is harder to get money out of administrations as a woman. A man's word as to what he needs for his work is more seriously taken into consideration from the approach that he tends to get [*sic*] treated more as a colleague, etc. Again, you have to keep asserting your needs and this may also require careful documentation to prove your needs.

Response No. 12

Just skepticism—not after I proved myself. 'They hired a what?' was a remark from an area band director.

Response No. 13

Some administrative problems—run-arounds that former band directors didn't have. Just stick in there.

NOTES

1. Suzanne Shields, "Women Musicians—In Step with the Times," *The School Musician, Director and Teacher* 49 (November 1977), p. 66.

2. Christine Ammer, *Unsung: A History of Women in American Music* (Westport, Conn.: Greenwood Press, 1980), p. 108.

3. Carol Neuls-Bates, "Sources and Resources for Women's Studies in American Music: A Report," *Notes* XXXV (December 1978), p. 277. For detailed information on the geographical distribution of these ensembles and individual histories of particular all-women's orchestras see Carol Neuls-Bates, "Women's Orchestras in the United States, 1925-45," in *Women Making Music: The Western Art Tradition, 1150-1950*, edited by Jane Bowers and Judith Tick (Urbana and Chicago: University of Illinois Press, 1986), pp. 349-369.

4. Ibid., p. 280.

5. Robert Jones, "Walking into the Fire," *Opera News*, XL (February 14, 1976.)

6. Ibid., pp. 11-12.

7. Barbara Jepson, "American Women in Conducting." *Music Club Magazine*, LVI (Autumn 1976), p. 15.

8. Victoria Bond, statement made in interview, cited in "Career Alternatives in Music," *The Instrumentalist*, XXXI (December 1976), p. 34.

9. Antonia Brico, statement made in interview, New York City, 1974, cited by

Judith Trojan, "Portrait of Antonia," *Film Library Quarterly*, VIII (January 1975), pp. 28-29.

10. Joyce Johnson, statement made in interview, cited by Jepson, op. cit., p. 13.

11. Elaine Brown, statement made in interview, cited by Carole Glenn, "In Quest of Answers," *The Choral Journal*, XVI (December 1975), p. 24.

12. Margaret Hillis, statement made in interview, cited by Glenn, p. 24.

13. Nancy Van de Vate, "Notes from a Bearded Lady: The American Woman Composer," *International Musician*, LXXIV (July 1975), p. 9.

14. David Truman, "Recycling Women's Opinions: Awards as Incentives, and Vice Versa," *Women in Fellowship and Training Programs* (Washington, D.C.: American Association of Colleges, 1972), p. 13.

15. "America's 10 Most Powerful Women," *Harper's Bazaar*, CXI (November 1977), p. 151.

16. Shields, "Women Musicians," p. 65.

17. Ibid.

18. Gale L. Sperry, "Women Are Here to Stay," *The Instrumentalist*, VIII (March 1954), pp. 30-31.

19. Ibid., p. 31.

20. Ibid.

21. Ibid.

22. Shields, "Women Musicians," p. 66.

23. Gladys Wright, "Career Opportunities for the Young Woman Graduate," *The School Musician, Director and Teacher* XLI (June-July 1975), p. 41.

24. Ibid.

25. Ibid.

26. Information provided by Gladys S. Wright, a member of ASBDA, in a telephone interview, West Lafayette, Indiana, 5 July 1984.

27. Information provided by Jack H. Mahan, secretary of the ABA, in a telephone interview, Arlington, Texas, 18 June 1984.

28. Information provided by Richard Crain, executive secretary of Phi Beta Mu, in a telephone interview, Houston, Texas, 19 June 1984.

29. Carol Ann Feather, "Women Band Directors in Higher Education," (Ph.D. diss., University of Mississippi, 1980.)

30. None of these women worked on a band staff that included another woman, and none of the men who responded worked on a band staff that included a woman director. But three women were head band directors on band staffs that included one or more male directors.

31. Shields, "Women Musicians," p. 66.

BIBLIOGRAPHY

Books

Ammer, Christine. *Unsung: A History of Women in American Music*. Westport, Conn.: Greenwood Press, 1980.

Friedan, Betty. *The Feminine Mystique*. New York: W. W. Norton, 1963.

Kerlinger, Fred N. *Foundations of Behavioral Research*. 2d ed. New York: Holt, Rinehart and Winston, 1973.

Periodicals

Alexander, Lucille Dillinger. "A Double Career—Band Directing and Marriage: Is It Possible?—Is it Advisable?" *The School Musician, Director and Teacher* 48 (April 1972), pp. 58-59.

"America's 10 Most Powerful Women." *Harper's Bazaar* 111 (November 1977), pp. 150-51.

Apone, Carl. "Victoria Bond: Composer, Conductor." *High Fidelity/Musical America*, 29 (April 1979), pp. 28-29, 35.

Barnes, Nancy, and Carol Neuls-Bates. "Women in Music: A Preliminary Report." *College Music Symposium* 14 (Fall 1974), pp. 67-70.

Block, Adrienne Fried. "The Woman Musician on Campus: Hiring and Promotion Patterns." *High Fidelity/Musical America* 25 (June 1975), pp. 22-23.

______. "Women in the Profession in Higher Education." *College Music Symposium* 14 (Fall 1974), pp. 60-66.

Burns, Don. "The Distaffed Composers." *Music Journal* 32 (March 1974), pp. 16-17, 32-37.

"Career Alternatives in Music." *The Instrumentalist* 21 (December 1976), pp. 34-39.

Elrod, Elizabeth L. "Women in Music: Results of the CMS Questionnaire." *College Music Symposium* 16 (Spring 1976), pp. 1-3.

Glenn, Carole. "In Quest of Answers." *The Choral Journal* 16 (December 1975), pp. 24-25.

Jepson, Barbara. "American Women in Conducting." *Music Club Magazine* 56 (Autumn 1976), pp. 12-16.

Jones, Robert. "Walking into the Fire." *Opera News* 40 (14 February 1976), pp. 11-21.

Lee, Marcella. "I Wonder Where the Women Went." *The Choral Journal* 18 (December 1977), pp. 35-37.

Neuls-Bates, Carol. "Sources and Resources for Women's Studies in American Music: A Report." *Notes* 35 (December 1978), pp. 269-83.

Shields, Suzanne. "Women Musicians—In Step with the Times." *The School Musician, Director and Teacher* 49 (November 1977), pp. 64-66.

Sperry, Gale L. "Women are Here to Stay." *The Instrumentalist* 8 (March 1954), pp. 30-31.

Taylor, Nora E. "Raisin's Conductor Began at Age 3." *The Christian Science Monitor* 68 (7 January 1976), p. 12.

Trojan, Judith. "Portrait of Antonia." *Film Library Quarterly* 8 (January 1975), pp. 24-28, 30.

Van de Vate, Nancy. "Notes from a Bearded Lady: The American Woman Composer." *International Musician* 74 (July 1975), pp. 9, 22.

Wright, Gladys. "Career Opportunities for the Young Woman Graduate." *The School Musician, Director and Teacher* 41 (June-July 1975), pp. 41, 49.

Interviews

American Bandmasters Association. Telephone interview between Jack H. Mahan, secretary, and the writer. Arlington, Texas, 18 June 1984.

American School Band Directors Association. Telephone interview between Gladys S. Wright, member, and the writer. West Lafayette, Indiana, 5 July 1984.

Exxon/Arts Endowment Conducting Program. Telephone interview between Kate Akos, Manager of Special Programs with Affiliate Artists, and the writer. New York, New York, 2 July 1984.

Phi Beta Mu. Telephone interview between Richard Crain, executive secretary, and the writer. Houston, Texas, 19 June 1984.

Other Sources

Collins, Judy, and Jill Godmilow, dirs. *Antonia: Portrait of the Woman*. With Antonia Brico, Judy Collins, et al. New York: Phoenix Films, 1974.

Feather, Carol Ann, "Women Band Directors in Higher Education," Ph.D. dissertation, University of Mississippi, 1980.

Good, Carter V., ed. *Dictionary of Education*. 3d ed. New York: McGraw-Hill, 1973.

Lovejoy, Clarence E. *Lovejoy's College Guide*. New York: Simon and Schuster, 1976.

Podolsky, Arthur, and Carolyn R. Smith, eds. *Education Directory, Colleges & Universities 1978-79*. Washington, D.C.: U.S. Government Printing Office, 1979.

Short, Craig R., comp. and ed. *Directory of Music Faculties in Colleges and Universities, U.S. and Canada 1976-78*. Binghamton, N.Y.: College Music Society, 1976.

Truman, David. "Recycling Women's Opinions: Awards as Incentives, and Vice Versa." *Women in Fellowship and Training Programs*. Washington, D.C.: American Association of Colleges, 1972.

16

Women's Contributions to Modern Piano Pedagogy

DORIS ALLEN

Pedagogy—especially in reference to piano study—is a term frequently used in music and academic circles, yet the word itself seems to elude clear definition. Does it mean simply "teaching"? Does it refer primarily to the study of methods and materials? Is it the examination of certain teaching systems and techniques? Can it be interpreted in the more rigid sense of "teacher training"? Or does the word mean something far more inclusive, also encompassing a general sense of communication and human relationships? In a technical sense, "pedagogy" may be defined as "the art, science, or profession of teaching; the study of language which includes principles and methods of formal education." But the word becomes much more formidable when we take into account the fact that pedagogy has as its subject the *person*. Pedagogy is a centering process to which the teacher, or pedagogue, and the learner are mutually committed. It is also a discipline that helps to bring to maturity the talents and sensitivities of a person and aims to develop the full range of a student's capacities.

The word "pedagogy" itself comes from two Greek words that mean "child" and "to lead." When translated directly from the original source, a pedagogue is "one who leads a child" and pedagogy is his craft, as teacher.[1] Throughout history women have most often been responsible for "leading the children" and for playing major roles in teaching music, poetry, writing, crafts, and other forms of artistic expression to children.

This survey of women musicians of the twentieth century points out the prejudices they have faced and the problems encountered as they have worked to become recognized as educators and composers—as pedagogues who are as talented and as capable as are their male counterparts in demonstrating a high degree of skill and imparting that knowledge to others.

History has recorded for us the contributions of many gifted women musicians who have broken through traditional biases and barriers to become recognized as leaders in a profession dominated by men. The list of women who have had a significant impact on the growth and development of piano study, performance, literature, and education is lengthy and impressive. In selecting a few teachers, performers, and composers to represent the contributions of women to the piano pedagogy of the twentieth century, an effort has been made to focus especially on those who have made unique and innovative contributions to the profession.

"It is as teachers that women musicians have been most visible. Women began to teach music in America in the eighteenth century or perhaps even earlier. Though the masters of singing schools were invariably men, private music teachers frequently were women."[2] However, even before 1900 many women were teaching in music schools of various kinds. Judith Tick estimated that by 1870, 60 percent of all music teachers were women.[3] The August 1908 edition of *Etude Magazine* cited a figure of 75 to 80 percent women teachers. Daniel Batchelor said,

> When we come to the regular music lessons of the children, we see that this is nearly all done by women, and rightly so, because this is women's sphere. Probably if parents were asked why they had engaged a lady teacher in preference to a man, the general answer would be that it was cheaper. Unfortunately, that is true, but it is not just. Work of equal merit should receive equal compensation, regardless of sex. But, in truth, pay is not the determining factor in this case. Women teach children because they are better fitted for the work than men. They are in closer touch with children and can therefore work along the line of the child's sympathies. . . . Of course, some of our women teachers will work with more advanced students, but that is a work which men can do equally well—in some cases, perhaps, better. What I would emphasize is that woman's greatest work is in developing the musical faculty in the children. Others will reap where she has sown, but her glory will be equal.[4]

Attitudes similar to Mr. Barchelor's were common and often shared by women themselves. "If music teaching is genteel enough for women, the man who teaches is showing that he lacks something."[5]

By the close of the nineteenth century, America was beginning to assume a more significant role in the areas of piano study and performance. The first music schools and conservatories in this country were being established: Peabody in 1857; Oberlin in 1865; New England Conservatory, Cincinnati Conservatory, and Chicago Musical College in 1867; and the Philadelphia Conservatory in 1877.[6]

Companies such as Steinway, Mason and Hamlin, Knabe, and Chickering began to manufacture pianos in America, and by the end of the century thousands of families had pianos in their parlors. The new interest in music-making was so strong that "by the beginning of the twentieth century there were more pianos and harmoniums in the United States than bathtubs."[7]

Although figures and statistics may vary, we do know that many children received their weekly lessons in the living rooms of their own homes. It was common for the piano teacher to travel about the community rather than asking the students to come to her. However, it was not deemed proper for men to enter the homes of their students to teach, so they usually had studios where the older and more advanced students came to study. Thus, the teaching of the young was primarily the responsibility of the women.

This turn-of-the-century interest in music in America provided more than commercial opportunities for piano manufacturers. It also created a need for more and better qualified teachers. Class piano teachers and private teachers of younger students—usually women—were generally trained at "normal" schools, whereas performing artists and studio teachers—usually men—were studying at conservatories in America or abroad. These two groups, along with the educational psychologists (followers of Jung, Piaget, and others), were apparently unaware of one another's endeavors and did not recognize how the knowledge and experiences of one could benefit the others. In the course of the twentieth century, the processes, ideas, and techniques of these three groups have coalesced and have greatly influenced contemporary pedagogy.[8]

Unfortunately, at the beginning of this century, as today, there were no clearly defined standards for piano teachers and no systems of control to separate the unqualified or indifferent teacher from the trained and experienced. Consequently, the profession had a low status, and women teachers often failed to regard their work seriously. Many students and parents regarded piano lessons as a social grace rather than as a serious educational pursuit, so teachers were not necessarily expected to work for the development of high musical standards.

Many women pedagogues of the early 1900s were not satisfied with their secondary role and did a great deal to elevate the status of the profession. While women musicians and teachers may not have seemed a very formidable force, the profession was ranked fifth in the vocations most frequently pursued by women at the beginning of the twentieth century. Music followed elementary school teaching, medicine, social and religious work, and law.[9]

In 1909, Harriette Brower, a teacher and frequent contributor to music journals, was asked about the preparation, ability, and opportunities for women in music as compared to men. She responded: "If the estimate comes near the truth, namely, that women do about 80% of all the music teaching which is done in this country, this answers the question of preparation and ability." She believed that while a woman "may not have the business ability to push and advertise herself as the man has, she has the conscience to do solid, patient, competent work." Brower was also a strong proponent of teaching piano in groups as well as including piano study in the public school curriculum. She spoke out against the prejudice that allowed men, but not women, to become professors and thus to achieve higher status in the profession. "It is sex, name and price that count, and so the Professor secures the coveted prize." She anticipated the time when there would be equality between men and women teachers and asserted that the American woman teacher was equal to the task.[10]

Amy Fay, born in Bayou Goula, Mississippi, in 1841, became a successful teacher and pianist of international acclaim and was also an early champion of women's rights. In 1869, after study at the New England Conservatory, she joined the then-popular migration to Europe, where she studied with Carl Tausig, Theodore Kullak, Ludwig Kieppe, and Franz Liszt. Letters describing her life and studies there were collected and published by her sister, Melusina Fay Pierce, under the title, *Music Study in Germany*. The book, which had a great impact on women musicians and teachers, had 21 printings in the United States alone by 1900. Through these writings, Fay was said to have influenced thousands of Americans to study abroad. She returned to America in 1875 and enjoyed a successful career as a performer and teacher in New York and Chicago. Her experiences as a professional woman are chronicled in an article, "The Woman Teacher in a Large City," in *Etude* in January 1902. She found that while lesson fees were high ($5.00 on the average), the teaching year was shortened because people left the city for the summer months in the country: "The music teacher is left, high and dry, alone in her glory." She discovered that "a woman is at a disadvantage on account of her sex, and the reason is that, as a rule, boys and men do not study music and young girls find it more interesting to take of a man teacher. . . . Fix it as you will, the woman teacher usually comes out at the small end of the horn."[11]

In an earlier article, "Women and Music," written for *Music* in October 1900, Fay expressed more of her feelings about the woman's role as teacher.

> Women have been too much taken up with helping and encouraging men to place a proper value on their own talent, which they are too prone to underestimate and to think not worth making the most of. Their whole training from time immemorial, has tended to make them take an intense interest in the work of men and to stimulate them to their best efforts. . . . But now, all this is changed. Women are beginning to realize that they, too, have brains, and even musical ones. They are, at last, studying composition seriously, and will, ere long, feel out a path for themselves, instead of being mere imitators of men. . . . If it has required 50,000 years to produce a male Beethoven, surely one little century ought to be vouchsafed to create a female one.[12]

In the post-Civil War period, as the great rush to study in Europe was reversing itself and Europe's trained musicians were coming to America to teach, women were at work founding and directing many of this country's schools of music. Many of these colleges and universities, first established in the late 1800s, have continued to operate over the years and have grown to become top-ranked conservatories of the twentieth century.

Clara and Bertha Baur had founded the Cincinnati Conservatory of Music in 1867 using some of the great conservatories of Europe as models. After coming to this country to visit her brother, Clara stayed on to teach piano and later decided to establish her own school of music. Because she was eager to see a conservatory in this country such as she had known as a child in Stuttgart, Germany, she returned to Europe to study teaching methods and administration of schools. Her school in Cincinnati had its beginnings in a few rented rooms, where students were trained to be performers and teachers by a faculty of both European and American professors. Three years after its founding the school expanded to include piano study for children, establishing what was probably the first "preparatory division" in this country. Clara's school could boast other firsts, for it was innovative in providing a residence for women, was among the first schools to include summer study programs for students, and pioneered in offering a placement service to assist graduates in finding jobs. Clara's niece, Bertha, gave up her own interest in studying medicine to become her aunt's assistant in 1897 and later assumed the directorship of the school. By the time of Bertha's retirement in 1930, when the school was bequeathed to the city of Cincinnati, the Conservatory had expanded to include an opera department and a large instrumental program, staffed by members of the Cincinnati Symphony Orchestra.[13] Today the nearly 1,000 full-time students enrolled at Cincinnati may participate in any of a wide offering of performance ensembles: choruses, chamber vocal groups, marching or concert bands, opera workshop, symphony orchestra, or jazz ensembles.[14]

Janet Daniels Schenck (1883-1976), a graduate of the New York School of Social Work and of the American Institute of Applied Music, founded the Neighborhood Music School in New York's Upper East Side. When she organized the school in 1917, Schenck persuaded her former teacher pianist Harold Bauer and the cellist Pablo Casals to serve on the Artist Auxiliary Board. In 1938 the name of the school was changed to the Manhattan School of Music. The *American Musician's Handbook* in 1980 listed a student body of 800, with 17 full-time and 162 part-time faculty members. With a library of over 92,000 volumes, 4,000 music scores and 26,000 recordings, the Manhattan School of Music has become recognized as one of the country's outstanding degree-granting music conservatories.

If a woman who had intended to become a doctor and another who had trained as a social worker were to become the founders of music schools, it would seem reasonable that a music critic might also undertake such an endeavor.

Like Clara Baur, May Garrettson Evans (1866-1947) was interested in providing excellent musical training for children. As a child, she had studied piano with her mother and later earned a certificate in music from the Peabody Conservatory of Music in Baltimore, where she also played violin in the Peabody Symphony Orchestra. During her college years Evans had assisted her brother with his newspaper work on the *Baltimore Sun*. From this experience her interests in teaching and performing music expanded to include writing about music. Although it must have taken some courage to venture into the field of reporting at a time when women were seldom seen in public without an escort and few actively pursued professional careers, May Evans applied for a job with the *Baltimore Sun* and became the music critic for this prestigious newspaper.[15] After six successful years in this position, she pursued a second career. In 1894 she and her sister, Marion

Dorsey Evans, established a school of music specifically for children in Baltimore. The new enterprise was an immediate success, and a year later Evans left her job as music critic to devote full time to the school, which was to merge with the Peabody Conservatory in 1898, becoming its Preparatory Division. By 1930, when she retired from the directorship, enrollment in the division had grown to over 3,200 students. The Peabody Preparatory Division continues today as one of the largest and most comprehensive such programs in America.

While some of the schools that were begun by women in the nineteenth century have grown to become fully accredited, degree-granting institutions, others have continued to offer music instruction at the precollege level. Many new community piano programs and college-related preparatory divisions have been established by women in the twentieth century.

Angela Diller (1877-1968) studied piano with Edward MacDowell and Percy Goetschius at Columbia University in New York and later headed the theory department of the Music School Settlement in New York. Diller met Elizabeth Quaille (1874-1951) while both were on the faculty of the Mannes College of Music, and together they wrote a highly innovative piano-teaching series, the Diller-Quaille piano books.[16] They also founded their own school, the Diller-Quaille School of Music in New York, which continues today, offering music instruction to children from very young ages to precollege levels.

The Crane School of Music at Potsdam, New York, had its beginnings in 1831, when the first music teacher was hired to provide music instruction to students enrolled in the Sarah Lawrence Academy. Julia Etta Crane (1855-1923) was appointed to the faculty in 1884 and initiated a two-year curriculum for the preparation of public school music teachers, which was offered through the New York State Normal and Training School at Potsdam. In 1926 the Crane School of Music was incorporated into Potsdam College, which in turn became the State University of Arts and Science at Potsdam. Founder Julia Crane was succeeded by Marie Anna Schuette (serving as director 1923-1930) and in 1930, by Helen M. Hosmer (b. 1899). Hosmer, now Dean Emeritus of Crane School, had spent most of her life in Potsdam and completed courses at Crane. Following study at Potsdam, she went on to Cornell University and later to the American Conservatory at Fontainebleau, France. Here she studied with and became a close friend of Nadia Boulanger. When she was appointed to the directorship of Crane in 1930, Hosmer initiated many changes. More instrumentalists and more male students were recruited and a credit/no credit marking system, where students worked individually with faculty and on their own, was initiated.[17] The increased male enrollment enabled her to establish the Crane Chorus, conducted by Nadia Boulanger at a Carnegie Hall concert in 1941, and, on other occasions, by Robert Shaw. When she retired in 1966, Helen Hosmer was honored by having the school's concert hall named for her; it is the only building in the State University of New York system to be named for a living person. Much of the credit for the success of this school, with its present enrollment of over 450 students and a full-time faculty of 50 artist-teachers, must go to this innovative woman.

The Community Arts Music School at Radford University, Virginia, was begun in 1976 and is directed by its founder, Kathryn Obenshain (b. 1931). It is a part of the larger Community Arts School, which encompasses the four disciplines of art, dance, music, and theatre. This broad scope provides comprehensive training in the arts for young people and also serves to create a community awareness of the arts. After graduating from Mary Washington College in Fredericksburg, Va., Ms. Obenshain followed the same route as many women who have earned music degrees: a few private piano students; church organist; director of a children's choir. In 1966 she enrolled in the newly established Master's Degree in Music Program at Radcliffe College, "to get out of my teacher-housewife rut," but with her degree came an offer to join the faculty of the University as an instructor of music. She went on to earn a doctorate in education, but Obenshain says that her pedagogical training was gained "from practical experience, much reading and research, workshops and master classes." With this background, she began a class piano program at the university in 1974, instituted the addition of a piano lab two years later, and proposed a piano pedagogy course, which has since become a part of the university's regular curriculum offerings. In addition to her work as director of the Community Arts School Music Program and a heavy teaching schedule, Kathryn Obenshain has also founded and is currently directing a summer piano camp for precollege students and a related annual Music Teacher's Workshop.

Another institution that has responded to this new interest in community music programs is Baldwin-Wallace College in Berea, Ohio. The Preparatory Department, which began in the fall of 1975 by offering individual lessons for voice and most instruments to members of the community, has grown to include private study in 22 different areas, 5 ensemble groups which range from beginning strings to a senior youth orchestra, Dalcroze eurhythmics classes, and a new program for children and adults with special needs. Mary Lou Hunger (b. 1936) has served as director of the program since its beginning nine years ago. After receiving her bachelor of music degree in piano from Baldwin-Wallace, Ms. Hunger began her college teaching career as an instructor in a music class for elementary education majors. Following her appointment as instructor of theory for the Baldwin-Wallace Conservatory of Music, she became involved in the Dalcroze eurhythmics program as a teacher and administrator and earned her Dalcroze Eurhythmics Certificate from Carnegie Mellon University. The rapid growth and acceptance by the community of the wide variety of programs offered in Berea is representative of the need and the interest in Community and Preparatory Programs today throughout this country.

Frances Clark (b. 1906) is well known for her untiring work as a lecturer, clinician, author, and teacher of master classes and as the author of the

Frances Clark Library for Piano Students, but her contributions to piano pedagogy go far beyond her reputation as a writer and music educator. She has exerted considerable influence on the relatively new movement in higher education to offer more extensive pedagogy courses, as well as undergraduate and graduate pedagogy degrees. She is also a strong proponent of pedagogical training for the hundreds of pianists who graduate each year from major colleges, universities, and conservatories with performance degrees.

Perhaps Dr. Clark's most significant contribution to pedagogy is the founding of the New School for Music Study in Princeton, New Jersey. Established in 1960 by Louise Goss and Frances Clark, the school has become a professional training center for piano teachers and a laboratory for continuing research in the nature of music and the nature of learning. In its 25 years of existence, the New School has grown in size and in stature and now offers a masters degree in Piano Pedagogy in conjunction with Westminster Choir College.

As an undergraduate student at Kalamazoo College, Michigan, Ms. Clark first became interested in the teaching-learning process while doing practice-teaching in English literature.

> My supervisory teacher in that situation, Miss Bender, was a model of excellent teaching and as a mentor and as a critic was one of the most formative influences in my life. It was here that I learned that to teach meant knowing the subject and, in addition, knowing how to teach. I wondered why the piano teachers I had had (and there had been two "big name" teachers) did not use such basic and sensible principles in their teaching, and I determined that my own teaching would be based on the theoretical and practical insights gained in my experience with Miss Bender. That big event occurred 50 years ago, and has been my field of exploration ever since.[18]

Frances Clark continued her education, working with Guy Maier in Ann Arbor, Ernest Hutcheson at Juilliard, and Isidor Phillippe and Marcel Herrenschmidt in France. In 1945 she returned to her alma mater, Kalamazoo College, to develop the first four-year credit program in piano pedagogy in an American college and probably in the world. This degree program, set in a small, liberal arts college, became a model for many later programs in a variety of academic settings. Among them, Westminster Choir College (1955-60), under Dr. Clark's direction; University of Tulsa, Oklahoma (Richard Chronister); Southern Methodist University (Louise Bianchi); Goshen College, Indiana, and Columbus College, Georgia (John O'Brien); and more recently, the University of Oregon (Doris Allen). The basic format of lectures, demonstration teaching with discussion, practicum teaching with observation and critiquing, as developed at the New School in Princeton, has been followed in varying degrees in these and many other college and university programs. The materials that she developed during these years were first published in 1953 when the Summy-Birchard Publishing Co. commissioned what is now a 50-volume series, the *Frances Clark Library for Piano Students*.

Figure 16.1 Frances Clark, teacher, innovator and author of the multi-volume *Frances Clark Library for Piano Students.* By permission of New School for Music Study.

Dr. Clark's earlier work became the model for the program established at the New School for Music Study in Princeton, New Jersey, in 1960. Here over 100 full-time graduate students earned certification in the program between 1960 and 1982, when a new master's degree, offered jointly with Westminster Choir College, was introduced. Many of these students have gone on to positions of leadership in the field of piano pedagogy, some of them heading programs that, in turn, offer pedagogy degrees. Dr. Clark says of her work:

> From the start to finish, it has been based on what I learned with Miss Bender. First, that the soundest educational principles can apply with equal power and effectiveness to any area of learning, and second, that high teaching standards cannot be taught by lecturing or even by demonstrating, but only by providing the beginning teacher with extensive opportunities to teach under observation, each observation followed by a one-to-one critique.[19]

She believes a successful pedagogy program requires the depth and breadth of the student teacher's opportunities for hands-on experiences, with various types and levels of students, working in both private and group teaching modes. Frances Clark was awarded an honorary doctorate degree by Kalamazoo College in 1953, citing her for her outstanding achievements in the field of music.

Women are assuming roles of leadership throughout the country as the field of piano pedagogy matures. The 1982-84 *College Music Society Directory of Music Faculties in Colleges and Universities, U.S. and Canada*, lists 20 schools that offer advanced degrees in piano pedagogy, 12 of which have women as directors of the programs. Many more offer courses in pedagogy and have preparatory divisions and community piano programs that are directed by women.

Although women may have been forced to compete for their status as teachers, performers, and composers of music in the late nineteenth century, they had one powerful force under their own control, the club movement. Women often gained access to careers in music through closed systems such as clubs, all-women orchestras, and private music teaching, all of which were available to them regardless of racial, regional, or socioeconomic backgrounds.

The phenomenal growth of the club movement in the early years of the twentieth century afforded middle- and upper-class women new opportunities for self-development and social outreach. Because men in America had traditionally demonstrated little interest in culture and the arts, women became the promoters and consumers of music, art, drama, and literature. In 1876 Fanny Raymond Ritter, in an address to the Association for the Advancement of Women, challenged women to join together to become participants in and patrons of the arts in their individual communities.[20]

Fourteen years later Fanny Morris Smith addressed this same issue in an article in *Etude*. "It is a longing for more life, fuller life, that brings women together in club work. . . . Spend a day at the music club and enter into feelings of the working girls assembled there. Lend a hand in starting the young artist. . . . Share her hopes and fears."[21] In addition to her active involvement in the club movement, Fanny Smith edited a full-page column in the *Etude* for several years, "Women's Work in Music."

While women comprised most of the membership of the Music Teachers National Association (MTNA), the fourth annual meeting of the MTNA in 1880 did not include a single woman's name in either its program or in its list of officers. Women held office at the local levels, but national programs only occasionally included a female performer or two, such as pianist Fannie Bloomfield-Zeisler, who was invited to perform at several national conventions in the late 1800s.

Pianist and composer Florence Sutro (1865-1906) wrote and published a controversial and prophetic book on women's roles in the professions, *Women in Music and Law*. She was most active in opening new opportunities for women in the MTNA and through her efforts a "Women's Department" was begun in 1895. After setting up a program of papers and compositions by music club women at the New York Convention in 1897, Mrs. Sutro was elected president of an initially temporary organization whose purpose it was to bring together the various music societies. She later assumed the leadership of the new, now permanent, National Federation of Music Clubs.

The National Federation, always a strong supporter of women musicians, was organized early in the twentieth century. Fanny Morris Smith wrote about the Federation in her July 1901 column in *Etude*. The organization had established a bureau of reciprocity, through which members could learn of others who were willing to present recitals and lectures for low fees, and also served as a source of information on constitutions, by-laws, and other organizational data. In 1907 there were an estimated 600,000 members in 4,500 local clubs.[22] The Federation continues to offer support and encouragement to women performers, teachers, and composers through its various contests and competitions, most recently by dedicating the years 1975-1985 a "Decade of Women," which helped American women musicians to be heard.

The same social, professional, and personal needs that provided the impetus for the women's club movement at the turn of the century were probably responsible for the formation of the all-women's orchestras. Women—other than harpists, and even they were seldom hired on a regular basis until the 1930s—were not welcomed into major orchestras. Out of necessity, they banded together to form their own music ensembles.

Professional music fraternities were another outgrowth of this need for group support in the women's music movement. Mu Phi Epsilon was founded on 13 November 1903 at the Metropolitan College of Music, Cincinnati, Ohio, by Dr. Winthrop Sterling and faculty member Elizabeth Mathias. Membership in the organization is limited to music majors and minors, faculty members, and graduate students enrolled in schools where chapters exist. Today the 135 collegiate chapters and 85 alumni chapters are still working toward the advancement of music in America and throughout the world.[23]

Public attitudes and those of the larger music establishment toward women's roles in music have been slow to change, but various women's clubs and organizations have fostered and strengthened individual member's careers in music through festivals and competitions. They have done a great deal to improve the quality of education for young people and have set high standards for both teachers and students. The advancement of women from traditional patterns of supportive, secondary roles to primary roles as educators, performers, composers, and conductors may be attributed in many ways to the club movement of the early 1900s.

During the first half of this century, women pianists, as artist-performers, were not a rarity—either in Europe or America. In the twentieth century piano study and performance, displacing the role it had played in the eighteenth and nineteenth centuries as a simple social grace, became a more serious endeavor for many women. However, while women pianists outnumbered men as teachers in music schools and conservatories early in the century, comparatively few were able to become recognized performers or master teachers; it was primarily the male pianists who achieved fame during this era. Nevertheless, several women have had successful careers both on the performing stage and as teachers of advanced students. Included among those women are Teresa Carreño, Julie Rivé-King, Fannie Bloomfield-Zeisler, Amy Fay, Olga Samaroff, Guiomar Novaes, Myra Hess, Lili Kraus, Alicia de Larrocha, and Rosalyn Tureck. Of this list of women pianists, most have been known as teachers and lecturers as well as artist-performers.

In the early 1800s the only women who dared to perform in public were child prodigies. Sophie Hewitt, born in New York in 1800, began her public career at age seven with a debut recital at City Hotel. Her next recorded public performance was in Boston in 1814.[24] A few years later, she returned to New York, where she began her teaching career at Mrs. Brenton's Boarding School. In 1820, an advertisement carried in Boston's leading music periodical of the time, the *Euterpiad*, read, "Miss Hewitt begs to inform her friends that she teaches the Pianoforte, Harp and Singing. Her terms may be known by applying at Mrs. Rowson's, Hollis Street, or at the Franklin Music Warehouse, No. 6 Milk Street."[25] Adequate records remain to verify her success as a performer, accompanist and teacher in Boston, New York, and Portland, Maine.

Teresa Carreño, born in Venezuela in 1854, and the composer of that country's national anthem, was eight years old when she made her debut in New York. The following year she was invited to the White House, where she entertained President Lincoln by improvising on his favorite song, "Listen to the Mocking Bird." She was to return to Washington 55 years later to perform again for a president, Woodrow Wilson. Teresa celebrated her tenth birthday by performing two of her own compositions in a concert in Boston. After a short-lived marriage and the birth of a daughter, Emilita, Carreño retired briefly from public performance. She returned to the concert stage in 1875 and pursued again an active and busy concert career.

A brilliant pianist, she attracted large, enthusiastic audiences, which thrilled to her fiery interpretations of romantic music. One reviewer referred to her as the "Goddess of the pianoforte." In addition to her active concert career, Carreño put a great deal of time and energy into teaching and writing, with articles on teaching piano appearing in many music journals. By the early 1900s she had toured throughout the world and had gained an international following. In the spring of 1917 Madame Carreño became ill while on concert tour and died shortly thereafter.

Lucy Marie Olga Agnes Hickenlooper was born in 1882 in San Antonio, Texas, and became the first American woman to win a scholarship for piano study at the Paris Conservatory. When Lucy Marie married a Russian, Boris Loutzky, she retired from performing. Three years later, after an annulment, she returned from Europe, intending to make her debut as a concert pianist. Finding that she could do so only with a great deal of money or with European notices to her credit, she took a gamble, hired Carnegie Hall, and changed her name from Lucy Hickenlooper to Olga Samaroff. The gamble paid off. Subsequently she received many concert engagements for which she earned fees higher than any woman pianist before her, though still considerably less than those received by men. After her marriage to Leopold Stokowski in 1911, she gave up performing once again and turned her energies to writing about music in journals and books, thus proving herself to be a serious scholar. When she and Stokowski divorced in 1923, Samaroff returned to the recital circuit. Two years later, when she injured her arm in a fall and was no longer able to perform, she accepted a teaching position at the newly formed Juilliard Graduate School. Here she worked with her former teacher, Ernest Hutcheson, with Rosina and Josef Lhevinne, and other masters. At the same time she accepted a position as music critic for the *New York Evening Post*. This was a short-lived venture, and she soon turned her full attention again to teaching at Juilliard, where her students included Willy Kappell and Rosalyn Tureck. Her major work, *The Listener's Music Book*, was published in 1947. Shortly before her death in 1948, Olga Samaroff received the honorary degree of doctor of music from the University of Pennsylvania.

Other women pianists of the early twentieth century discovered that one way to overcome the problems of prejudice against women performers was to specialize. A contemporary of Samaroff's, Polish pianist Wanda Landowska (1879-1959), battled the odds by concentrating her exceptional talent on an instrument from the Baroque period, the harpsichord, and the literature of that era. In spite of strong objections of friends and colleagues, she pursued her ambition to produce an instrument designed as closely as possible after the instruments used in the mid-1700s. She studied harpsichords in museums intensively and finally convinced the master craftsman, Pleyel, to build an instrument based on her specifications. Manual de Falla and Francis Poulenc were among the composers who wrote the first modern works for harpsichord, especially for Madame Landowska. In 1925 she founded her own school, the École de Musique Ancienne near Paris. It was intended especially for the experienced musician who was ready to work seriously to improve performance skills and who wanted to study the instruments of the seventeenth and eighteenth centuries. The school was abandoned in the forties, when the Nazis were approaching Paris, resulting in the tragic loss of her library of over 10,000 volumes and a collection of rare instruments. In addition to her success as a performer, teacher, and specialist on the music of Bach, Landowska is to be remembered as a lecturer, critic, author of several books, and composer. With her deep compassion for people and her phenomenal ability to communicate through her music, Madame Landowska was fully responsible for the revival of the harpsichord and for the rediscovery of literature that had been written a century or more before.[26]

Another concert artist who was to contribute many firsts to music, and who also chose to limit her career to one area of performance was Rosalyn Tureck. Born in Chicago in 1914 to a family of Russian and Turkish descent, she won a scholarship at the age of 16 to study with Olga Samaroff at Juilliard. An exceptionally talented student and brilliant woman, she became proficient on the harpsichord, piano, organ, and clavichord. Although her teachers advised against a career specializing in the music of a single composer, Tureck became the twentieth century's outstanding authority on the keyboard music of Bach. In regard to her work, she said, "I had to form new ways of thinking about music, new keyboard techniques of phrasing, dynamics, touch and endless means of performance. I had to create a totally new tonal and physical piano technique to match this deeper perception of what Bach's music and structure really is."[27] At age 19 Tureck made the finals of the prestigious Naumberg competition, for which she presented an all-Bach program. She lost the Naumberg, but the following year won the Schubert Memorial Award. At age 22, Tureck received the first Town Hall endowment award for "most distinguished performance of the New York season." Ironically, the award, which was presented to her by Walter Naumberg, was given for the six-week series of concerts, where she had performed exclusively the music of Bach. These performances had included all 48 of the Bach Preludes and Fugues. In 1966 she founded the International Bach Society. Tureck has been the recipient of four honorary doctorate degrees: from Colby College (1964), Roosevelt University (1968), Wilson College (1968), and Oxford University (1977).

Her vast and distinguished career as a Bach authority, performer, scholar, conductor, lecturer, and teacher continues with her soon-to-be-published editions of the music of Bach. She has become a living legend, as a musician, scholar, and leader of women in music.

Still another pedagogue of the twentieth century who chose to specialize was Abby Whiteside (1881-1956). She became known for her study of piano technique rather than as a performer. Whiteside studied intensively the movements of dancers, athletes, jazz pianists, jugglers, and instrumentalists. She observed the ways in which each class of artists used the body to achieve desired effects in their individual pursuits. She also studied the processes by which the pianist transfers the lifeless visual images of music notation into sensitive and meaningful musical sounds. Whiteside came to realize that by utilizing the full power and control of the body—the torso plus the upper arm as the center of energy, with the forearm, wrist, and fingers serving as the peripheral levers—the pianist could achieve maximum power and maintain efficient control. These ingenious theories on the utilization of the body's basic natural rhythm are detailed in her book, *Indispensables of Piano Playing*.[28]

Russian-born Rosina Lhevinne (1880-1976), a woman who ranks as one of the great piano teachers of all time, must be credited with contributing as much as any other single individual to the standards of teaching in this century. A child prodigy, she studied at the Moscow Imperial Conservatory. Following her debut with the Moscow Symphony Orchestra in 1895, Lhevinne toured widely in Europe and the United States. Returning to Moscow to complete her studies, Madame Lhevinne received a gold medal upon graduation in 1898. The same year she married Josef Lhevinne and thereafter limited her public appearances to two-piano performances with her husband. When they came to America after World War I, both were appointed to the faculty of the Institute of Musical Art in New York (later the Juilliard School). Even so, Rosina considered Josef to be the great musician, and herself the great teacher. Her greatness is evidenced by the list of successful pianists whom she taught: Van Cliburn, John Browning, Daniel Pollack, Mischa Dichter, David Bar-Illan, and Garrick Ohlsson. Her depth of understanding is revealed in this quotation:

> In my long career at Juilliard I have had a great number of talented students, but talent alone is not enough to become a great success. Personality is the determining factor in the make-up of a great teacher. To develop and grow musically as an individual one must be constantly reading—not just on music, but one must develop an acquaintance with the other arts, go to museums, lectures, one must travel—all these are a great help to continue the growth and development of the personality. . . . The teacher must really be interested in teaching, and want to help his students.[29]

Adele Marcus, master teacher at Juilliard, believes, as did Rosina Lhevinne, that every artist must discover and develop her own technique. She feels that a student of any age must be spiritually and physically excited by the music and that it is upon this individual motivation that a teacher can build. She has earned herself a reputation as a dynamic but often controversial teacher who cares deeply about each student's personal growth, seeing talent as a creative process that involves the total personality. Marcus's students number such successful pianists as Augustin Anievas, Thomas Schumacher, Horacio Gutierrez, and Byron Janis. She has served on international juries, on the faculties of the Aspen Summer Festival in Colorado, and the Temple University Festival at Ambler, Pennsylvania, and is much in demand for her master classes and demonstration lectures.

Adele Marcus advises teachers to reach out for the understanding of all the new trends in music, even if it is music that does not particularly appeal to them, like avant-garde music, electronic music, and so forth. "We must all be conversant with what is going on in the world around us, and we all need to broaden our horizons. . . . I think the personal contact with workshops, with master classes, and with participation in local, state and national organizations has a very broadening effect."[30] She urges teachers to get back to the piano and to practice at least a little each day. Adele Marcus is one of the outstanding pedagogues of the twentieth century and lives by the conviction that "we are women first, and musicians, afterward."[31]

While women had been recognized as teachers—especially of early stringed instruments, keyboard instruments, and voice—throughout the history of music, they had not been generally accepted as serious composers before the twentieth century. Women have traditionally been successful as composers of so-called "educational music" and their accomplishments in this field have been well received, but prior to 1900 few women who wrote concert music could hope to have their works performed. In 1895 Florence Sutro related her difficulties in finding any books about women composers. A book salesman explained that because there were no women composers, no books had been written about them. Such was certainly not the case, for women had been composing since the earliest recorded history of music, although often forced to publish under their brother's or husband's names or to use male pseudonyms. It took some perseverance for Mrs. Sutro to find any information about women who were writing music in the 1890s. Ninety years later one must still persevere to find adequate information about women composers—not because they have not existed, but because history too often has failed to include them.

At the beginning of the century there were reasons to be optimistic about the future of the woman as composer. Otto Ebel's list of over 800 names in his 1913 book about women composers included Fannie Crosby, Cécile Chaminade, Harriette Brower, Amy Marcy Cheny (Mrs. H.H.A. Beach), Lili Boulanger, Carrie Louise Dunning, and Germaine Tailleferre.[32] Fanny Morris Smith comments optimistically on the status of the woman composer: "She has come to stay. Will she write the great opera of the 20th century?" Yet she also had an understanding of women as an economically powerless social class. In too many instances, women simply could not afford the education necessary to become great composers.[33] Several women did find the means to study composition and became a part of the pre-World War I generation that awakened a new musical consciousness.

Nadia Boulanger, born into a musical family in Paris in 1887, seemed destined from the beginning to have a profound and far-reaching influence on the music of the twentieth century as well as on the changing attitudes toward the role of women in music.

As a young child Nadia wanted to be a doctor, but in the 1890s such a profession was not acceptable for a woman. Music was a more accessible career, especially when one's father was a professor at the Conservatoire and one's mother was a singer. In addition to possessing a lovely singing voice, Russian-born Madame Boulanger was a strict disciplinarian who expected perfection from her children. The demands placed upon Nadia as a child, combined with her own inquisitive spirit, were to shape the course of her life. By the age of five she was applying herself to the rigors of the French musicianship courses, and she began to study organ with Louis Vierne when she was eight. The following year Nadia was admitted to the Conservatoire National du Musique in Paris to learn solfège. In 1898 the 11-year-old student captured first place in the school's solfège competition, although she was the youngest entrant.[34] Six years later she accepted her first piano students, some of whom were her own age.

As a young woman, Nadia continued to adhere to the strict disciplines and self-imposed goals that had been a part of her childhood. Her students loved her, respected her, and responded without question to the demands of their taskmaster. For whatever reasons, it was also Nadia's nature to rebel against convention. As a small child she had dressed in the black velvet suits usually worn by boys, and throughout her life, Boulanger wore only black, mannish clothes. She went about by day or night unchaperoned—quite unheard of for the aristocratic life of Paris in the early 1900s. Throughout her life Nadia lent her name to radical causes and was always eager to pursue new ventures or to explore innovative ideas. This same self-determination was evident when she entered the prestigious Prix de Rome competition in 1907. Although she did not win upon her first entry, she tried again the following year and won second place. It was a victory against enormous odds. The feminist press was ecstatic and Nadia Boulanger became a celebrity.[35]

In 1910 she was granted a professorship in elementary piano and piano accompaniment at the Conservatoire National and shortly thereafter began to teach at the American Conservatory at Fontainebleau. Here some of her early students included Aaron Copland, Marion Bauer, Melville Smith, and Douglas Moore. By 1922 the works of Nadia Boulanger and of her students were being heard throughout America.[36]

Up until 1920 Boulanger had focused most of her energy on her performance career, but the demands of teaching, practicing, performing, and composing began to take their toll, and she suffered regularly from severe migraine headaches. Nadia, a strict Catholic, retreated to a convent for periods of rest and began to concentrate her energies on her work as composer and teacher. By 1923 her health had improved and she was teaching in Paris during the academic year and at Fontainebleau in the summers. Along with the heavy demands that Boulanger placed on her students were the rewards of close companionship; it was an honor to be invited to her regular Wednesday afternoon teas and a very special privilege to attend one of her dinner parties. Students were as welcome in Boulanger's home as they were in her studio. By 1923 she had taught over 100 American students. It was her aim to mold them into well-schooled, intelligent musicians who understood the art and craft of composition.

As she came to better understand the dynamics of the teacher-student relationship, Nadia began to regret the estrangement that had occurred 16 years previously with her own teacher, Gabriel Fauré. At her initiation, this friendship was renewed and continued throughout their lives. Another composer who was an influential figure in Nadia Boulanger's life was Igor Stravinsky. When his *Firebird* had its sensational premiere at the Paris Opéra in 1910, Boulanger was among those who applauded this controversial work. Her faith in his composition was reaffirmed 13 years later when she heard his *Octet for Winds* performed for the first time in the same opera house. Their friendship and mutual respect for one another's work continued over the years, with Stravinsky sharing manuscripts of new music with her before they were premiered and in 1935 collaborating with her in teaching composition classes at the Ecole Normale.[37]

As more and more American students sought her out, Boulanger set a new goal for herself: a concert tour to America. In 1925 she was finally able to make her mark in America as a lecturer and recitalist—not as a virtuoso performer, but as a master teacher. Her popularity with American students continued, with most of them remaining in Europe to study with her for at least three years. She continued to extend herself far beyond the usual role of teacher, helping students to find inexpensive lodging and entertaining them regularly at her Wednesday afternoon teas.

Following the American tour several women who were later to become prominent composers travelled to Europe to study with Boulanger. Helen Hosmer was an especially dedicated student whose friendship with her mentor was to last for more than 40 years. Boulanger journeyed to Hosmer's school in Potsdam, New York, to lecture and conduct, and Hosmer in turn led study groups to Europe to attend Boulanger's classes.

Pianist Louise Talma began her study with Boulanger in 1928 after discovering that they shared an enthusiasm for twentieth century music. It was at Nadia's urging that Louise began to work seriously as a composer. Talma later became a professor at Hunter College in New York and arranged Boulanger's second American tour in 1937.[38]

Hosmer, Talma, and Boulanger shared more than their love of twentieth century music and interest in composition. Each of these women also devoted several years of her life to the care of an invalid mother, while at the same time pursuing her own busy career. Each one also made the conscious choice at some point in her development to concentrate most of her time and energy on teaching rather than on performance.

After her mother's death in 1935, Nadia found more time to travel and made her first trip to England. On her second tour to America she presented lecture-recitals at Radcliffe, Wellesley, and Hunter colleges, gave several radio broadcasts, and became the first woman to conduct the Boston Symphony. She scored a triumph when she conducted the New York Philharmonic in a Carnegie Hall concert.

She continued to attract new talent after her return to Europe. Harold Schonberg paid her this tribute in 1950: "If there is one person who shaped the course of music from 1920 to 1940, that person has been Nadia Boulanger." She continued to teach and to meet with her devoted students until her death on 22 October 1979.[39]

Boulanger's pedagogy and subject matter were impervious to the changes that were going on in the musical world by this time, for she continued to want a quality of restraint and a complete mastery of technique in the work of her students. She expected them to acquire a broad knowledge of music in general and an ability to project their own enthusiasm for each detail as well as for the overall form in every composition that they produced. Boulanger always wanted her students to present an image to the world that was as well crafted as were their harmony and counterpoint exercises. Her own electric personality brought distinction to everything that she did and influenced the great numbers of her students who have become, in turn, prominent teachers and composers of the twentieth century.

Whatever educational and economic limitations may have been imposed upon women as they struggled to become recognized as composers of concert music, they have been acknowledged as authors of educational music and materials for nearly a century. Mrs. John Spencer Curwen, a piano teacher from Dublin, Ireland, brought the art of teaching piano into the world of twentieth-century pedagogy with the publication in 1886 of her book, *The Child Pianist*, and its accompanying manual, *The Pianoforte Method*.[40] Marienne Uszler, writing on early teaching methods, says of her ideas,

> Curwen's "method" demonstrates repeatedly that the educational psychology underlying most of its premises and suggested techniques is solid, informed and extensive. Many teachers today might still regard some recommendations as innovative or, at least, controversial. Most impressive is the care taken to explain the teaching of rhythm (functional counting: 1 for each quarter-note, 1-2 for each half, regardless of meter or metric placement); reading by interval; [and] the introduction of key signature only after the idea of key has been experienced by the child.[41]

Other teaching methods written in the early 1900s were often designed for use with specific teaching environments, such as class piano, private study, public schools, and so on. Children were learning the early rudiments of music from Mrs. Crosby Adams's *Very First Lessons at the Piano* (1902); *The Virgil Method*, written in the same year by Antha Minerva Virgil; *Piano Technique for Children*, Julia Lois Caruthers (1903); or Florence Goodrich's *Synthetic Series of Piano Pieces* (1907).[42]

These early twentieth century educators led the way and influenced future pedagogues and composers of music for children, many of whom were to use folk music as resource material for their work. Ella Mason Ahearn, Louise Robyn, Angela Diller, Elizabeth Quaille, Gail Martin Haake, and Ruth Crawford-Seeger all made use of the rhythm and repetition as well as the humor and tone play of folk songs to varying extents in their educational materials.

Ruth Crawford-Seeger (1901-1953), who had proven her ability as a musician at an early age, earned her tuition for study at the American Conservatory in Chicago by teaching piano and theory. She studied piano there with Diane Lavoie-Herz, through whom she became acquainted with many influential musicians, but it was through her work and close association with Louise Robyn that Crawford developed her interest in music for children. Before she had completed her master's degree, four of her *Nine Piano Preludes* were published in the *New Music Quarterly*, followed in 1929 by publication of *Piano Study in Mixed Accents*. Her compositional style at this time included such advanced techniques as tone clusters and heterophony. In 1930 Crawford became the first American woman to win a Guggenheim fellowship for study in Europe. When she returned to America and married her former composition teacher, Charles Seeger, they decided together to put aside their interest in what seemed like elite concert music to concentrate their energies on the serious study of folk music. While mothering a family of six children, Crawford-Seeger transcribed over 1,000 folk recordings from the archives of American Folk Songs in the Library of Congress and taught music at three different nursery schools. She wrote the piano accompaniments for a large collection of folk songs for children and collaborated with ethnomusicologists John and Alan Lomax on the publication of "Our Singing Country."[43] Throughout these years Crawford-Seeger remained active as a teacher; she returned to composing concert music in 1950, completing a "Suite for Wind Quintet" shortly before her sudden death at age 52. During her lifetime, Crawford-Seeger taught music to thousands of children. Her three books of folk music, *Animal Folk Songs for Children*, *American Folk Songs for Children*, and *American Folk Songs for Christmas* have been used widely in schools and music studios.[44] Mary Mathilde Gaume said of her, "Ruth Crawford must be counted among those who have contributed appreciably to the 20th century musical scene in the United States. She represents the best in American pioneer spirit and tradition. She has contributed a solid core of durable musical ideas which have helped to enrich America's cultural legacy in the 20th century. She possessed and developed a very great talent, perhaps genius."[45]

Among those women who have authored or coauthored more recently published teaching materials for young children are Frances Aronoff and Donna Wood. Frances Weber Aronoff, Professor of Music and Music Education at New York University, is recognized as an artist-musician who has developed many contemporary approaches to music in education. Included in her graduate and undergraduate courses at NYU are Dalcroze eurhythmics and a course that Aronoff likes to call "Anti-Methods." Her work and her writings involve the principles of eurhythmics as developed by Emile Jacques-Dalcroze (1865-1950), based on the time-space-energy relationship of body movement. The rationale for this approach may be explored in her *Music and Young Children*, a work that has been translated into Spanish, Portuguese, and Russian.[46] In 1982 she published a companion "workbook for adults—parents and teachers with little or no musical training," *Songs and Activities for Young Children*.[47] Both books include many folk songs and related keyboard explorations. Frances Aronoff is an untiring, innovative teacher who teaches as she believes, that music for young children should combine intellectual and emotional growth and that the music and body movement are inseparable in the child's learning environment.

Canadian-born Donna Wood is on the faculty of the Royal Conservatory of Music, where she has developed preparatory music classes for children from three to five years of age. As a leader in the field of music in early childhood, she frequently conducts workshops and seminars for teachers and parents. Her book, *Move, Sing, Listen, Play*, is a guide to the ages and stages of childhood development and offers guidelines for the musician who wishes to enter the world of early childhood education.[48] Mrs. Wood believes in the fun of creative musical learning through play, game, and song.

Although we are very near to the end of this century, with only a decade and a half remaining before the year 2000, many composers of early-level

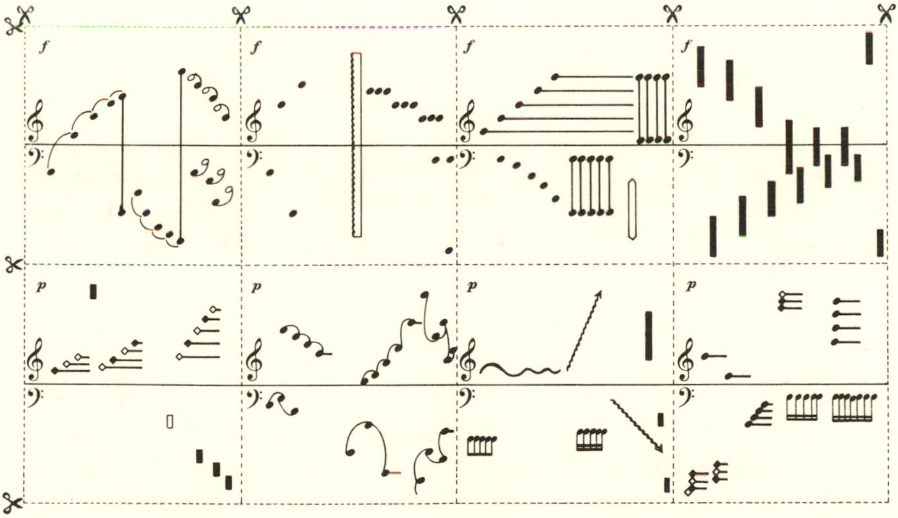

Figure 16.2 "Kartenspiel" for piano solo by Gertrud Firnkees. The player decides how to interpret the graphic notation, which sections will be played and in what order. Used by permission of the composer.

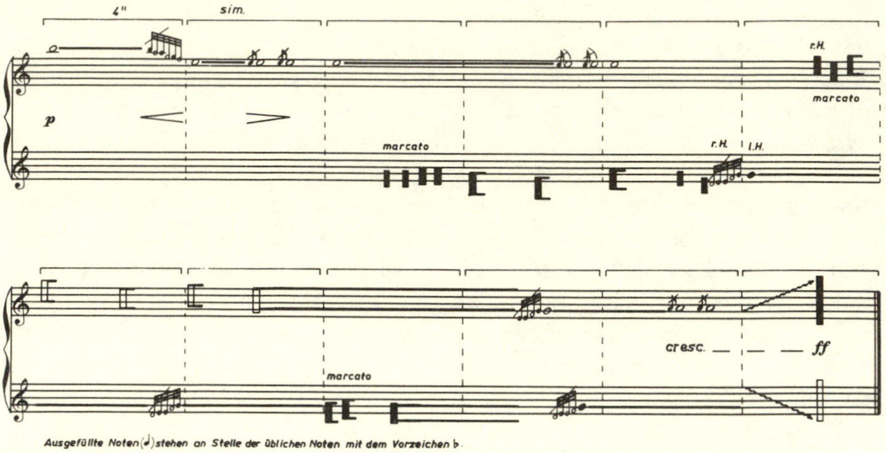

Figure 16.3 "Collage" by Gertrud Firnkees. Used by permission of the composer.

piano study materials have yet to pay heed to the techniques of twentieth century music. Most of the methods and materials written for and used in the teaching of children and older beginners continue to focus on out-dated methods and concepts—such as the "middle C approach" and inflexible common meters—while avoiding any hint of dissonant tonalitites and freeform or flexible rhythm patterns. Few pedagogues or method books encourage creativity or the exploration of new sounds, but rather limit the student to the methodical reading of traditional notation. Perhaps Frances Aronoff's "anti-method" course should be packaged and sent about to the thousands of piano teachers who have yet to venture beyond these traditional texts and materials for the beginning student. Because many of the piano study methods available today have been and are being written and edited by women, they must assume responsibility for the musical education of the upcoming generation of children. Several of these writers are exploring the new sounds and free rhythms of contemporary music and are making available to teachers and to students music that is representative of this generation.

Gertrude Firnkees experienced the same frustration as many teachers when she began to teach at the artist gymnasium near her home in Munich, Germany. She could not find materials that she liked and which she would wish to have played in concert, so she began to write her own "piano tutor" in the style of Bartok's *Mikrokosmos*. Beginning with five-finger patterns, she developed technique exercises that included opportunities for improvisation as they moved on to extensions and contractions, changing fingers, full chords, and playing two voices in one hand. Firnkees, who was born in Heidelberg in 1925, studied at the Mozarteum in Salzburg, where she earned her masters degree in piano performance and pedagogy. Her *Miniaturen*,

Figure 16.4 No. 5 from *Time Twisters,* by Joan Last. Reprinted by permission of Oxford University Press.

published by Bote and Bock in Berlin in 1976, consists of 13 experimental pieces that include tone rows, clusters, chromatic scales, graphic notation, and the interplay of black against white keys. She teaches music in Wolfenbüttel, West Germany, and as she says, "It's improv all the way!"

Betty Beath, born in the Queensland, Australia, town of Bundaberg, concentrates her pedagogical interests on transcultural composition, drawing from the music of eastern Asia. Her works for children fall primarily into the category of music drama. The results of research carried out in

Indonesia, Bali, and Java include "Spice and Magic," "Reflections from Bali," and musical settings for the poetry of Indonesian writer Goenawan Mohamad. Betty and her husband, David Cox, are presently working on "Poems from the Chinese," settings of Kenneth Rexroth's translations of classical Chinese poetry. Beath's work is used in schools throughout Australia and has been recorded by the Australian Broadcasting Commission. She is a music specialist at St. Margaret's Girls School in Albion and is accompanist with the Queensland Conservatory of Music.

The melody flows from one hand to the other in a free rhythm; the player should feel the stretch of interval as the line lifts and falls in smooth waves. A contour drawing might aid in hearing it, such as the opening phrase:

Figure 16.5 "Floating" by Barbara Pentland, from *Music of Now.* © by Waterloo Music Company Limited, Waterloo, Ontario, Canada. All Rights Reserved. Used by permission.

Like many of her colleagues, Joan Last had early ambitions to become a concert pianist. She was born in Littlehampton, Sussex, England, in 1908 and received her early musical training at the Godalhin School, Salisbury. Her more advanced piano study was done with Mathilde Verne, who had been a pupil of Clara Schumann. A severe accident to her hand limited Last's piano study and she began to concentrate on teaching and writing. "I soon found that I had ideas of my own so I became independent of any kind of guidance. . . . My newer ideas of freedom for beginning pieces (instead of on five notes) were the forerunner of much that has followed in educational writing." After earning her Teacher's and Performer's Diplomas, Last was invited in 1959 to join the faculty of London's Royal Academy of Music, where she taught until 1981. In 1975 she was awarded the Honorary R.A.M., the highest honor given to a musician of international standing who was not a student at the Academy. The listing of Joan Last's published works is lengthy: over 100 albums of teaching pieces that are imaginative and varied in style, ranging through many levels of advancement. Joan Last says, "My aims in both my music and my teaching are freedom of movement in the earliest stages and beauty and balance of tone and touch."[49] Her success in reaching these goals is evident in the outstanding records of her students over the years as well as in the charm and challenge of her compositions. While Ms. Last claims that "my style is not very modern today even though I add many chromatic harmonies," the compositions themselves prove quite the contrary.[50] Pieces of only 12 to 20 measures may flow through several changes of meter or use chromatic harmonies to complement a tightly woven melodic line. She utilizes the full range of the piano with even early-level pieces cavorting about over a range of three or four octaves. Her work is evidence that Joan Last is indeed, as she says, "Going strong at age 76."

Although her parents regarded the idea as eccentric, Barbara Pentland began to compose at the age of nine. She persisted, and after her piano debut in 1936, the Canadian-born (1912-1978) pianist received a fellowship to study composition at Juilliard. While studying with Aaron Copland she wrote "Sonata Fantasy," which was reviewed as "radical" when it premiered in Toronto in 1948. Pentland was unique among mid-twentieth century composers of pedagogical material, for her works encompass many contemporary techniques. For example, Book two of her teaching series, *Music of Now*, introduces tone-clusters, mixed meter, retrograde and inversive canon, and free nonmetered rhythms.[51] She set a positive example for both teachers and composers of educational materials in encouraging improvisation with each new idea and musical pattern as a means of fully exploring each particular tonal area before moving on to another.

Composers who work in twentieth-century idioms are usually faced with more than the usual difficulties when they try to publish. An enterprising woman in Boulder, Colorado, circumvented this problem by forming her own business, Myklas Press. Mary Elizabeth Clark has not only written a

The double-notes in the L. H. are held without sounding, so that they vibrate when the melodic phrases are played in the R. H. Listen to the "echoes". The melody should be vigorous and non legato.
Moderato
non legato f
(Hold down L.H. notes without sounding)
non legato f
(Hold down L. H. notes without sounding)
(Listen)
(Listen)

Figure 16.6 "Vibrations" for piano duet by Barbara Pentland (from *Music of Now.*) © 1970 by Waterloo Music Company Limited, Waterloo, Ontario, Canada. All Rights Reserved. Used by permission.

great deal of music using contemporary techniques herself, but has also encouraged and supported the work of many other composers. Her teaching series, *Piano Tomorrow,* was published in 1981. Composers from all over the country work for Myklas Press on a freelance basis, just as Ms. Clark herself continues to freelance for other publishers. She has had music published in Japanese, French, German, and Swedish and has worked under the pen names of Meredith Barrett and Lawrence Grant.

Contempo II (1974) is representative of Myklas Press publications. It contains 17 early-level pieces written by four male and five female composers and employs a wide range of compositional techniques, such as quartal harmonies, a six-tone row, the Japanese scale, various modes, and one work with tape. Myklas Press fulfills a great pedagogical need in making the music of many twentieth-century composers readily available to students and teachers. In addition to her work as a composer and lecturer,

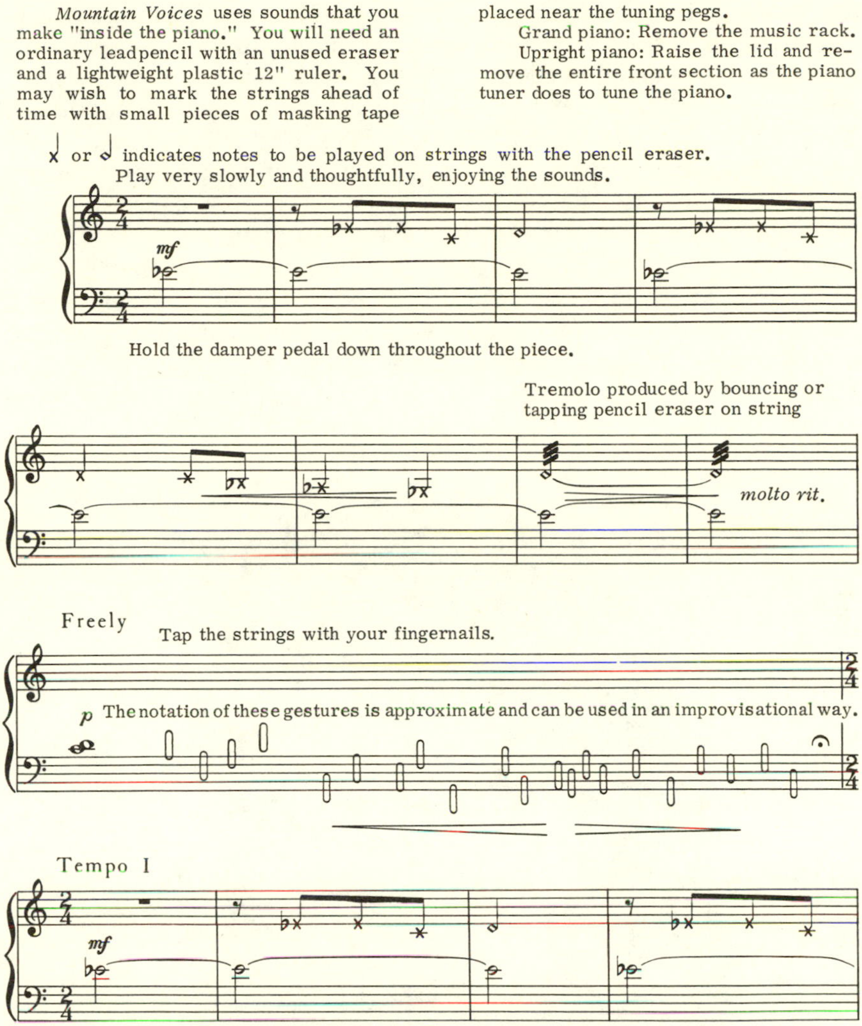
Mountain Voices uses sounds that you make "inside the piano." You will need an ordinary leadpencil with an unused eraser and a lightweight plastic 12" ruler. You may wish to mark the strings ahead of time with small pieces of masking tape placed near the tuning pegs.
Grand piano: Remove the music rack.
Upright piano: Raise the lid and remove the entire front section as the piano tuner does to tune the piano.
or indicates notes to be played on strings with the pencil eraser.
Play very slowly and thoughtfully, enjoying the sounds.
mf
Hold the damper pedal down throughout the piece.
Tremolo produced by bouncing or tapping pencil eraser on string
molto rit.
Freely
Tap the strings with your fingernails.
p
The notation of these gestures is approximate and can be used in an improvisational way.
Tempo I
mf

Figure 16.7 "Mountain Voices" by Eloise Ristad, from *Contempo II*, a publication of Myklas Music Press. © Copyright 1974 by Myklas Press, Box 929, Boulder, Colorado 80302. All rights reserved. Used by permission.

Ms. Clark continues to manage the business with the help of one musical assistant and a support staff, yet finds time to travel, to be active in the community, to climb mountains, and to enjoy her home and family.

Composer, concert pianist, and teacher, Ruth Schonthal, born in Hamburg, Germany, of Viennese parents, is on the faculties of New York University and of the College Division of the Westchester Conservatory. Her talent was recognized early when, at the age of 5, she entered the Stern

Conservatory in Berlin. Eight years later she was again the youngest student accepted in the history of a school when she enrolled in the Royal Academy of Music in Stockholm, Sweden. In 1946 she received a scholarship to study composition at Yale University with Paul Hindemith. Her compositions, which are published by Oxford University Press, Carl Fischer, Inc., Galaxy Music Corp. and Shawnee Press, range from works for the elementary piano student to vocal and instrumental chamber music, a ballet suite, and two piano concerti. She has been the recipient of many awards and prizes and has had her works performed in major concert halls and festivals throughout the world. In spite of a demanding teaching schedule and a steady output of new compositions, Mrs. Schonthal finds time to present lectures and workshops. Her educational writings include *Miniatures* (Galaxy), *Minuscules*, *Near and Far*, and *Potpourri* (all C. Fischer). This

Figure 16.8 Composer Ruth Schonthal.

latter volume, a collection of ten piano pieces, is representative of the charm and imagination of this talented composer. The ostinati fourths in "Festive Sounds," the $\frac{3}{4} + \frac{2}{4} + \frac{2}{4}$ meter of "Dance," and the gently moving broken chords of "Gathering Sea Shells" give each piece the imaginative character implied by the title. Of her pedagogical writing, Ruth Schonthal says, "My philosophy in writing educational music is to write *real* music, that is designed with specific musical and technical problems in mind—and always then to make the most with the least."[52]

Judith Lang Zaimont has had an active and varied career. While she is perhaps best known as a composer and has been the recipient of many commissions and grants, including a Guggenheim Fellowship for 1983-84, Zaimont has toured extensively throughout the United States as a member of a duo-piano team. She is on the theory faculty of the Peabody Institute/Conservatory of Music in Baltimore, Maryland, and has also written and edited articles and books on music, including "Twentieth Century Compositional Techniques" and "A Selective List of 20th Century Repertoire for Piano" in *Teaching Piano*.[53] Zaimont's description of herself as a "highly dramatic composer with non-traditional but tonal underpinnings to her work" is evident in her *Calendar Collection*, a set of 12

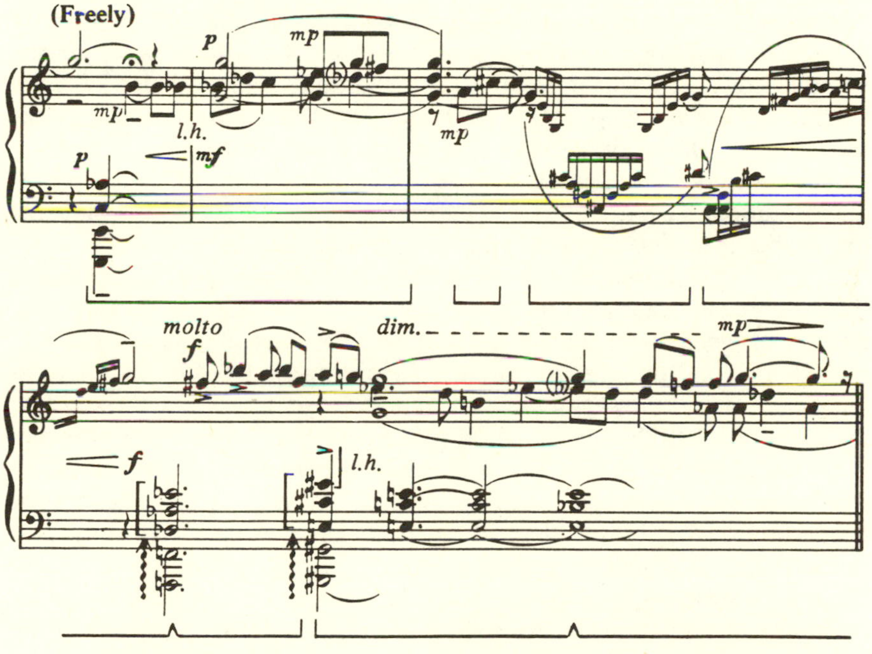

Figure 16.9 Excerpt from "April: Recitative" by Judith Lang Zaimont, one of 12 preludes for the developing pianist in the *Calendar Collection*. © Copyright MCMLXXIX by Alfred Publishing Co., Inc. Used by permission.

descriptive preludes, published by Alfred in 1979. For example, "April"'s slow, rubato arpeggios and broken chords encompass over five octaves of the piano keyboard, while the "secret thunder" of "November" is concentrated primarily in the lower range of the keyboard, utilizing the dramatic effects of extended trills and sudden dynamic changes. She says of her work, "My style is essentially chromatic, and non-contrapuntal."[54] Her work as a composer has earned her many awards and she lectures frequently before university audiences and for music teachers' groups.

Many of the texts used in college pedagogy courses and teacher-training programs have been written by women. Yvonne Enoch coauthored *Creative Piano Teaching* with James Lyke.[55] Isabelle Byman wrote *The Piano Teachers Art* in 1978.[56] Alice Kern was the author of *Guidebook to Piano Literature.*[57] A significant pedagogy text that deals exclusively with twentieth century piano literature is *Teaching and Understanding Contemporary Piano Music*, written by Ellen Thompson.[58] Mildred Portnoy Chase wrote *Just Being at the Piano* in 1981.[59] *The Young Pianist, a New Approach for Teachers and Students*, written by the British pedagogue, Joan Last, has become an essential part of every teacher's library since its publication in 1954.[60]

Adjunct to these pedagogy texts are several books recently published on the general subject of women and their contributions to music: *Unsung, a History of Women in American Music*, by Christine Ammer; *Women in Music*, an anthology of source readings from the Middle Ages to the present, edited by Carol Neuls-Bates; and the three volumes of Jane LePage's *Women Composers, Conductors and Musicians of the 20th Century* (Vol. 1, 1981; Vol. 2, 1983; Vol. 3, projected for 1988.)

At the schools where many of these master teachers are affiliated—leading institutions such as Juilliard, Peabody, Curtis, NYU—women students outnumber men, but the faculty remains predominantly male.

In a 1975 article written for *High Fidelity/Musical America*, Adrienne Fried Block cited statistics that pointed out the vast disparity between the number of women trained and the number of women employed in music-related positions in higher education.[61] Figures taken from a U.S. Government publication, the *Digest of Educational Statistics*, 1968-71, showed that in the period 1970-71 women had earned 55 percent of all bachelor's degrees in music, almost 50 percent of the master's degrees and over 16 percent of the doctorates. But figures issued by the National Association of Schools of Music in 1973-74 showed that during this period women held only 21.4 percent of music faculty appointments. Of these, 49.2 percent of all piano faculties were women. Women held 12 percent of the full professor positions, 37 percent of the associate professor positions, 50 percent of the assistant professor jobs, and 50 percent of the instructor assignments. They held 71 percent of the part-time piano faculty jobs.

Anne Mayer of Carleton College compiled a statistical study from the College Music Society (CMS) Directory of 1972-74. Her research indicated that 31.3 percent of the applied music teachers were women and that in the areas of voice and piano the highest concentration of women was at the rank of instructor. In violin and flute the highest number of women were employed as part-time instructors. Women exceeded men in the teaching of class piano (60 percent) and equalled them in individual piano and accompanying. In the more specific area of applied music, out of 123 who held the rank of professor, only 7.5 percent were women. 14.2 percent were associate professors (out of 233 total); 21.5 percent were assistant professors (out of 333), 25.2 percent ranked as instructors (out of the total 414), and 22.4 percent were assistant instructors (out of 368).

In this CMS report, Judith Tick of Brooklyn College of the City of New York showed a total of 2,520 faculty members teaching music history and musicology. Of these, 608, or 24 percent, were women.

Anne Mayer concludes, "The sad fact remains that the majority of women in applied music teaching are concentrated at the lowest ranks, and as part-time instructors they have little chance of advancement or salary commensurate with their ability or years of service." Unfortunately, the situation has not changed significantly during the past ten years.[62]

Adrienne Block sums up these statistics,

> What seems apparent from this sample is that there is a pattern of employment for women that depends not on the number of women in a music department available and qualified in a field. Can there be an unwritten, perhaps unconscious, limit on the number of women in a music department, and on the number promoted to the upper, often highly visible positions? And what has happened to the women who do not teach on college faculties—the other 30% who were trained?[63]

One must hope that through the research being done by Bloch and others a new awareness will emerge, and through such an awareness more opportunities will open for those who are best qualified—be they men or women—to teach and to contribute their talents to all areas of the profession.

A pedogogue, in whatever particular area of specialization—performance, composition, conducting—is a teacher. We teach all the time by what we are and by what we do. In a like manner, we learn all the time, by what we see and feel and think and do. A good teacher, then, learns from her students as she teaches them. It takes a sensitivity to others as well as a very good ear to hear and to see that which is present in a student, be that a child or an adult.

To be deeply understood, pedagogy needs to be seen not as an activity nor as a means to earning a livelihood, but rather as a process in which both teacher and learner are mutually committed and involved. While the outdated image of the long-skirted, compliant piano teacher may accurately symbolize the role that women have played for too long, "leading the children," present-day women pedagogues are being more widely recognized for their skill as musicians as they continue to move from the parlor into the concert halls, from teachers' desks in kindergarten and grade-school classrooms into college and university offices and lecture halls. It is a slow and often difficult process, but it is clear that we are in the midst of a climate of change, thanks to the perseverance of thousands of dedicated women musicians who have insisted on being heard and fully respected within the profession. Women are responding to the pedagogical challenges of these final years of the twentieth century.

NOTES

1. Mary Caroline Richards, *Centering in Pottery, Poetry and the Person* (Middletown, Ohio: Wesleyan University Press, 1962), pp. 96-129.

2. Christine Ammer, *Unsung* (Westport, Conn.: Greenwood Press, 1980), p. 225.

3. Judith Tick, "Women as Professional Musicians in the United States, 1890-1900," *Yearbook for the Inter-American Research in Music* 9 (1973), pp. 95-133.

4. *Etude Music Magazine* (September 1901), p. 319.

5. *Etude Music Magazine* (May 1907), p. 291.

6. Ammer, *Unsung*, p. 225.

7. Gerald Carson, "The Piano in the Parlor," *American Heritage* 17, no. 1, (December 1965), p. 58.

8. Marienne Uszler, "The American Piano Method: View and Viewpoint—Part 2: Roots and Branches," *The Piano Quarterly* (Winter 1982-83).

9. Rudolph C. Blitz, "Women in the Professions, 1870-1970," *Monthly Labor Review* (May 1974), p. 56.

10. "Women's Opportunity in Music," *Etude Music Magazine* (August 1909).

11. Carol Neuls-Bates, *Women in Music* (New York: Harper & Row, 1982), p. 187.

12. Ibid., pp. 217-18.

13. Ammer, *Unsung*, pp. 227-28.

14. *The American Music Handbook*. (N.Y.: Macmillan, 1974), p. 524.

15. Barbara Jepson, "Women Music Critics in the United States," in *The Musical Woman*, ed. Judith Lang Zaimont (Westport, Conn.: Greenwood Press, 1983), pp. 245-46.

16. Ammer, *Unsung*, p. 228.

17. Karen Deans, "The Affirmative Approach," *Music Educators Journal* (March 1984), pp. 23-86.

20. As cited in Neuls-Bates, *Women in Music*, p. 188.

21. As cited in Neuls-Bates, *Women in Music*, pp. 190-91.

22. Ammer, *Unsung*, p. 230.

23. Mu Phi Epsilon Information Bulletin, 833 Laurel Ave., Highland Park, Illinois.

24. As cited in *Unsung*, pp. 9-10. Harold Earle Johnson, *Musical Interludes in Boston, 1795-1830* (New York: Columbia University Press, 1943), pp. 84, 99.

25. Boston, *The Euterpiad*, 8 April 1820.

26. Jane LePage, *Women Composers, Conductors and Musicians of the 20th Century*, Vol. I. (Metuchen, N.J.: The Scarecrow Press, 1980), pp. 133-44.

27. Ibid., p. 243.

28. Abby Whiteside, *Indispensables of Piano Playing*. (New York: Scribner's, 1961).
29. James Bastien, *How to Teach Piano Successfully* (Park Ridge and La Jolla: General Words and Music Co., Neil A. Kjos, Jr., 1973), pp. 397-400.
30. Ibid., p. 414.
31. Ylda Novik, "On Being a Woman Musician," *Clavier* (February 1976), pp. 10-12.
32. Otto Ebel, *Women Composers* 3rd ed. (Brooklyn, N.Y.: F. H. Chandler, 1913).
33. Fanny Morris Smith, *Etude Music Magazine* (September 1901), p. 317.
34. Leonie Rosenstiel, *Nadia Boulanger* (New York: W. W. Norton, 1982), p. 38.
35. Ibid., p. 68.
36. Ibid., p. 173.
37. Ibid., pp. 167-70.
38. Ibid., pp. 222-23, 270-71.
39. Ibid., p. 353.
40. Uszler, "American Piano Method: Part 2: 1850-1940, Crisscrossing Threads," *The Piano Quarterly* 121 (Spring 1983), p. 16.
41. Ibid., p. 18.
42. Ibid.
43. Ruth Crawford-Seeger, *Our Singing Country*, ed. John and Alan Lomax (N.Y.: MacMillan, 1941).
44. Ruth Crawford-Seeger, *Animal Folk Songs for Children* (Garden City, N.Y.: Doubleday and Co., 1948); *American Folk Songs for Children* (New York: Doubleday, 1948); *American Folk Songs for Christmas* (Garden City, N.Y.: Doubleday, 1953).
45. Mary Mathilde Gaume, "Ruth Crawford-Seeger: Her Life and Works" (Ph.D. diss., Indiana University, 1973).
46. Frances Aronoff, *Music and Young Children*. (New York: Turning Wheel Press, 1979).
47. Frances Aronoff, *Songs and Activities for Young Children* (New York: Turning Wheel Press, 1982).
48. Donna Wood, *Move, Sing, Listen, Play* (Toronto, Canada: Gordon V. Thompson, Ltd., 1982).
49. Letter to the author, dated 15 February 1984.
50. Ibid.
51. Barbara Pentland, "Music of Now," Book 2 (Waterlook, Ontario, Canada: Waterloo Music Co., Ltd., 1970.
52. Letter to the author, dated 3 March 1984.
53. Denes Agay, *Teaching Piano* (New York: Yorktown Music Press, Inc., 1981), pp. 489-548.
54. Letter to the author, dated 20 February 1984.
55. Yvonne Enoch and James Lyke, *Creative Piano Teaching* (Champaign, Illinois: Stipes Publishing Co., 1977).
56. Isabelle Byman, *The Piano Teacher's Art* (New York: G. Schirmer, 1978).
57. Alice Kern and Helen M. Titus, *The Teacher's Guidebook to Piano Literature*. (Ann Arbor, Mich.: Edwards Bros., Inc., 1969).
58. Ellen Thompson, *Teaching and Understanding Contemporary Piano Music*. (San Diego, Calif.: Kjos West, 1976).

59. Mildred Portnoy Chase, *Just Being at the Piano* (Culver City, Calif.: Peace Press, Inc., 1981).

60. Joan Last, *The Young Pianist, a New Approach for Teachers and Students* (London: Oxford University Press, 1960).

61. Adrienne Fried Block. "The Woman Musician on Campus, Hiring and Firing Patterns," *High-Fidelity/Musical America* (June 1975), *Musical America,* pp. 22-23.

62. Barbara Hampton Renton, "Status of Women in College Music, 1976-77," College Music Society.

63. Block, "The Woman Musician," p. 23.

BIBLIOGRAPHY

Ammer, Christine. *Unsung: A History of Women in American Music.* Westport, Conn.: Greenwood Press, 1980.

Barnes, Edwin C. *American Women in Creative Music.* Washington, D.C.: Music Educator's Publications, 1936.

Bauer, Marion. *Twentieth Century Music.* New York: G. Putnam & Sons, 1933.

Drinker, Sophie. *Music and Women—The Story of Women in their Relationship to Music.* New York: Coward, McCann, 1948.

Elson, Arthur. *Women's Work in Music.* Boston: L. C. Page, 1913.

Hixon, Donald. *Women in Music.* Metuchen, N.J.: Scarecrow Press, 1975.

Kendall, Alan. *The Tender Tyrant: Nadia Boulanger.* Wilton, Conn.: Lyceum, 1976.

LePage, Jane. *Women Composers, Conductors and Musicians of the 20th Century.* Vol. I, Vol. II. Metuchen, N.J.: Scarecrow Press, 1983.

Loesser, Arthur. *Men, Women and Pianos.* New York: Simon & Schuster, 1954.

Mach, Elyse. *Great Pianists Speak for Themselves.* New York: Dodd, Mead, 1980.

Neuls-Bates, Carol. *Women in Music: An Anthology of Source Readings.* New York: Harper & Row, 1982.

Richards, Mary Caroline. *Centering in Pottery, Poetry and the Person.* Middletown, Ohio: Wesleyan University Press, 1962.

Rosenstiel, Leonie. *Nadia Boulanger: A Life in Music.* New York: W. W. Norton, 1982.

Samaroff, Olga. *An American Musician's Story.* New York: W. W. Norton, 1939.

Stern, Susan. *Women Composers: A Handbook.* Metuchen, N.J.: Scarecrow Press, 1978.

Whiteside, Abby. *Indispensables of Piano Playing.* New York: Scribners, 1961.

Schonberg, Harold. *The Great Pianists.* New York: Simon & Schuster, 1963.

17

A Survey of College Music Textbooks: Benign Neglect of Women Composers?

DIANE JEZIC and DANIEL BINDER

At a time when the scholarship on women in music continues to proliferate, when the mainstreaming of women's studies continues to challenge tradition, and when publishers of elementary and middle-school textbooks continue to reevaluate and overhaul their wares, just how often are women composers being mentioned and discussions of their works being integrated into current college-level music history and music-appreciation textbooks? As teachers in two undergraduate universities, we decided to scrutinize these texts and find out.

The undertaking of this project occurred to us independently, though almost simultaneously. Why? First of all, we were tired of waiting for the ideal text to appear, one that could conscientiously be adopted for our classes. Secondly, since we both work in universities that have strong commitments to women's studies, we had become sensitized to that discipline's order of the decade: to mainstream, or integrate directly into the text and curriculum, the latest scholarship on women. Thirdly, we felt a real concern for our female students who, according to the latest statistics, now comprise more than one-half of the entire student population and in our experience, clearly outnumber men in undergraduate music courses.[1]

We wanted to believe that the college texts are/were making a good faith effort to mainstream women composers, but we needed evidence. If we could show exactly how many and which women composers the recent texts include, contrasted with texts of previous decades, we would have legitimate data for our friends, colleagues, and publishers, who might believe, as we did prior to this study, that "things really are better now in the '80s; consciences have been raised concerning women, blacks, and minorities." Easy to believe, but, we discovered, impossible to substantiate. In spite of the last decade's considerable activity in terms of books and articles written, musical scores located and made available, recordings released, conferences and congresses held, proliferating performances and recitals of women's music, and separate courses instituted on Women in Music, little, if any, of this vast amount of material has trickled down to the basic introductory and music history textbooks.

What follows is the result of our two separate surveys. During the spring semester of 1985, Dr. Jezic surveyed 14 of the most frequently used Introduction to Music (Music Appreciation) texts published between 1976 and 1985. Dr. Binder's survey, undertaken earlier in the academic year of 1984-85, includes 47 music history texts, both specialized and general, dating from 1940 through 1985.

The central concern of both surveys was simply to document the evidence, presented in table form and interpreted in the following pages. Although we surveyed two different types of publications—those directed toward either the huge music appreciation market of the general college and/or high school student, or the smaller market of music majors, undergraduate and graduate—similar sketchy representation of women composers and their music appears to be common to both categories of text. Once this became apparent, some discussion of *how* and *why* this situation arose was mandatory. Our results confirm that the reconstruction of textbooks is long overdue. Women's creative contributions to music should be embedded in the fabric of music history, recorded not just as a twentieth-century phenomenon, but mentioned, as appropriate, throughout. Authors, editors, and textbook publishers must be held accountable for this integration effort; they owe it not only to today's heavily enrolled female student population, but to all music students and teachers of future generations.

This chapter, then, is divided into three parts: (1) Dr. Jezic's annotated discussion of Music Appreciation courses and the survey of 14 texts; (2) Dr. Binder's discussion of the nature of musicology in relation to the study of music history, and a summary of his textbook survey findings; and (3) a joint conclusion with suggestions as to what can be done beyond the classroom to correct the current imbalance of representation of women composers in these key source materials.

Tables 1-4 embody the results of the separate investigations. As expected, texts that mention women composers and their music most frequently are those music history texts specializing in either twentieth-century music or American music. Unexpectedly, particularly in the music appreciation category (see tables 1 and 4), the most recent texts often do not contain as many references to women composers as do those of an earlier date!

What these tables do *not* show is how many *men* composers were mentioned in comparison to the number of women composers. Thus, a text containing references to five hundred men and two women would be a considerably worse representation than a text that mentioned one hundred men and two women composers.[2]

MUSIC APPRECIATION TEXTS SURVEY

The music course that most frequently fulfills the Fine Arts/Humanities core curriculum requirement is one with a title similar to "Music Appreciation." Here the student is introduced to an established canon of Western art music, which includes the works of historical and modern masters, and certain genres of composition, such as Medieval chant, Renaissance masses, Baroque oratorio, and Romantic opera. American jazz, after gaining sufficient respectability, has finally been admitted to the course; gradually, other elements of American classical and popular music have also been added. One of the most recent additions has been in the area of world music, in growing recognition of the fact that, while important, the Western tradition in music is but one of many musics, and students should become acquainted with at least some of the music of the world's other cultures.

All of these additions and changes—non-Western music, music of American popular culture, American art music, as well as evidence of the recent avant-garde—have altered and reshaped the music appreciation courses to reflect the results of recent specialized musical study mainstreamed into the introductory level course. But music written by women has been virtually left out.

A cursory look at table 17.1 will reveal that very few texts discuss women composers and their music, except under the heading of "Contemporary Music." Furthermore, only four record anthologies that accompany these texts include any example of women's music, again usually a contemporary piece (see table 17.2). Thus, our students study and hear a world of music that is comprised almost exclusively of music by male composers.

Yet the fact remains that "Introduction to Music," Music 101, is the bread-and-butter course of music departments. Whether part of a core requirements or a general elective, Music 101 keeps music departments in business. Sooner or later, most undergraduate music professors will have taught this course, and sooner or later, a large percentage of the undergraduate population will have passed through its doors.

Students of 101 are a wonderfully diverse group: the biology major who played in the high school band, the business major who "likes music" but never participated in making music, the returning older student who may have discovered the classical music station or may have accompanied a friend to the symphony, and the new breed of music minor, who was happily engaged in music-making before college but whose practical goals now focus perhaps on a career in computer science.

Our responsibility as educators is probably greatest right here in Music 101. In this course we are educating not only future audiences and consumers, but also future symphony board members or corporate sponsors of the fine arts.

Unfortunately, the current group of texts for this course, as seen in table 1,

Table 17.1
Music Appreciation Textbooks Ranked in Order of Number of Women Composers Mentioned

Author, Book Title, Publisher, Date	Number of Pages	Total Number of Women Composers Mentioned	Number of Music Examples Composed by Women	Number of Complete Paragraphs Discussing a Particular Woman Composer	Names of Composers
Levy, Kenneth, *Music: A Listener's Guide*, Harper & Row, 1983	491	13	0	3	Casia Hildegard of Bingen Clara Schumann Francesca Caccini Barbara Strozzi Elisabeth Jacquet de La Guerre Maria Teresia von Paradis Cécile Chaminade Ethel Smyth Amy Beach Barbara Kolb Thea Musgrave Pauline Oliveros
Kerman, Joseph and Vivian, *Listen*, Worth, 1980	545	7	0	5	Clara Schumann Fanny Mendelssohn Hensel Barbara Strozzi Beatriz de Dia Gormunda of Montpellier Joni Mitchell Carole King

Politoske, Daniel, *Music*, (3rd ed.), Prentice Hall, 1984	450	5	0	0	Esther Williamson Ballou Pozzi Escot Thea Musgrave Clara Schumann Toshiko Akiyoshi
Borroff, Edith, and Marjory Ivin, *Music in Perspective*, Harcourt Brace Jovanovich, 1976	303	4	0	2	Marie de Bourgogne Joan Baez Carole King Germaine Tailleferre
Wingell, Robert, *Experiencing Music*, Alfred, 1981	453	4*	0	0	Joan Baez Joni Mitchell Judy Collins Janis Joplin
Machlis, Joseph, *The Enjoyment of Music*, (5th ed.), Norton, 1984	608	3	1	9	Julia Perry Ruth Crawford Thea Musgrave
Manoff, Tom, *Music: A Living Language*, Norton, 1982	468	2	0	26	Joni Mitchell Karla Bonoff
Hoffer, Charles, *The Understanding of Music*, Wadsworth, 1981	512	2	0	0	Amy Beach Pauline Oliveros
Kamien, Roger, *Music: An Appreciation*, McGraw-Hill, 1984	589	1	0	5	Miriam Gideon
Bamberger, Jeanne, and Howard Brofsky, *Developing Musical Perception*, Harper & Row, 1979	369	1	0	0	Miriam Gideon

Table 17.1 *continued*

Author, Book Title, Publisher, Date	Number of Pages	Total Number of Women Composers Mentioned	Number of Music Examples Composed by Women	Number of Complete Paragraphs Discussing a Particular Woman Composer	Names of Composers
Komar, Arthur, *Music and Human Experience,* Schirmer 1980.	468	0	0	0	
Byrnside, Robert, *Music, Sound and Sense*, William C. Brown, 1985	383	0	0	0	
Reimer, Bennett, *Developing the Experience of Music*, (2nd ed.), Prentice-Hall, 1985	264	0	0	0	
Ferris, Jean, *Music—The Art of Listening*,. William C. Brown, 1985	359	0	0	0	

*All composers of popular music.

Table 17.2
Recorded Examples of Music by Women Composers Included in Albums Accompanying the Music Appreciation Textbooks

Author	Book Title	Composer	Recorded Example
Borroff, Edith, & Irvin, Marjory	*Music in Perspective*	Marie de Bourgogne (fl. ca. 1450)	Basse Danse (instrumental ensemble)
Levy, Kennth	*Music: A Listener's Guide*	Pauline Oliveros	"Sound Patterns" (for chamber choir)
Kamien, Roger	*Music: A Appreciation*	Miriam Gideon	"Questions on Nature" (chamber vocal)
Machlis, Joseph	*The Enjoyment of Music*	Ruth Crawford (Seeger)	String Quartet, 1931

is unresponsive overall in depicting women's historical and continuing creative contributions to music.

The statistics cannot be ignored: 28 percent of the books published since 1979 mention no women composers. More than 50 percent of the 14 texts published since 1979 mention one or none. If one discounts the Wingell book's mention of four popular singer-composers, there are only five books out of 14 that mention three or more women composers—roughly one-third. Likewise, only four of the 14 (28 percent) include recorded examples, and all but one of those come from the twentieth century. When one considers the large number of women composers who might have been mentioned, these are hardly impressive numbers.

In looking more closely at the individual texts, the *context* in which women are presented seems as important as the actual number of times they are mentioned.

The book that appears most sensitive to women composers and which mentions 13 of them, is Kenneth Levy's *Music: A Listener's Guide* (Harper and Row, 1983). The book starts out rather convincingly, when, in the chapter on the Middle Ages we read:

> In an era when musical composition was largely an anonymous all-male affair, there were two women who won renown in sacred monophonic styles like those of Notker and Adam. One was Hildegard of Bingen, the saintly twelfth-century abbess of Rupertsberg on the Rhine, who wrote spiritual songs that earned her the nickname of

"The Sibyl of the Rhine." The other was the Byzantine nun Casia (b. ca. 820) who produced orthodox Church hymns that are still sung in the liturgy today. Casia was one of the outspoken feminists of the Middle Ages. (p. 31)

Women composers are next cited in the chapter on electronic music—a leap of seven centuries—when the music of Pauline Oliveros is discussed along with that of Mario Davidovsky.

Further along in Levy's discussion of twentieth-century music, Barbara Kolb's *Solitaire, for Piano and Vibes* (1971) is mentioned in the same paragraph with George Rochberg and Luciano Berio, and Thea Musgrave and her *Night Music* receive an entire paragraph, interpolated between discussions of Charles Ives and George Crumb. So far, this appears to be a reasonably mainstreamed text, even if seven centuries of women composers were omitted. However, the following "catch-all" paragraph is relegated to a section entitled "The Women's Movement." Here we read:

No survey of the contemporary scene would be complete without noting two social issues that profoundly influence the course of music. One is the effect of the women's movement. The other is the economic plight of today's serious composers. The women's movement launched in the 1960's enhanced the awareness of women's gifts as composers. For a long time, women enjoyed high status as musical performers, but only grudging acknowledgment as creators. The obstacles to professionalism of any sort meant that gifted women in past centuries rarely attempted music composition. There were exceptions. Francesca Caccini (1587-1640) produced ballets and lyric works for the Medici in early seventeenth century Florence. (p. 399)

Levy then lists the names, dates, and major genres of the other women composers noted on the table: Barbara Strozzi, Elisabeth Jacquet de La Guerre, Maria Theresia von Paradis, Clara Wieck Schumann, "who composed chamber music in a style closer to her husband's" (p. 400), Cécile Chaminade, Ethel Smyth, and Amy Beach. Laudable mentions all, but in the wrong place.

The book's concluding paragraph, while not completely true, reflects an all-too-common assumption:

The early twentieth century saw an increase in the number of notable women composers, particularly in France and the United States. But it was only with the breakthroughs of the 1960's—the generation of Oliveros, Musgrave, and Kolb, among others, that substantial numbers of first-rank women composers began to find congenial environments for creation and to assert themselves as equals to their male contemporaries. Women's compositions are at last being savored as art works in themselves rather than as art works by women. (p. 400)

Regardless of the inconsistency of Levy's book in integrating only five out of 13 women composers into the chapters where they logically belong, this volume clearly represents the best attempt, so far, at getting women composers into the text. Additional noteworthy features of this textbook are the inclusion of Pauline Oliveros's "Sound Patterns" on the record album accompanying the book, and the large number of illustrations (photographs or drawings) of women instrumentalists. In the chapter on the Renaissance, women are shown in six out of eight pictures. They are shown playing the lute, organ, bass recorder, tenor viol, a virginal, and singing a four-part madrigal.[3]

Considering music appreciation's commitment to today's diverse student population, it is hardly surprising that Joni Mitchell ties for first place with Clara Schumann and Thea Musgrave, and that Carole King and Joan Baez share second place with Miriam Gideon, Pauline Oliveros, and Amy Beach in the number of references to women composers in all 14 texts (see table 17.3).

Table 17.3
Total Mentions of Women Composers in All Fourteen Music Appreciation Texts Surveyed

One Mention	Two Mentions	Three Mentions
Hildegard of Bingen	Joan Baez	Joni Mitchell
Karla Bonoff	Amy Beach	Thea Musgrave
Marie de Bourgogne	Miriam Gideon	Clara Schumann
Francesca Caccini	Carole King	
Casia	Pauline Oliveros	
Cécile Chaminade		
Judy Collins		
Ruth Crawford		
Beatriz de Dia		
Pozzi Escot		
Fanny Hensel		
Elisabeth Claude Jacquet de La Guerre		
Janis Joplin		
Barbara Kolb		
Gormonda of Montpellier		
Maria Theresia von Paradis		
Julia Perry		
Ethel Smyth		
Barbara Strozzi		
Germaine Tailleferre		
Esther Williamson Ballou		

Vivian and Joseph Kerman's book *Listen* (1980) devotes two pages, complete with photographs, to "Carole and Joni" in their final chapter, "Popular Music in an Electronic Age." However, like several of the other textbooks, *Listen* lumps women composers together at the very end of the book, almost as an afterthought. (Or was it too costly for the publishers to do otherwise?) Here, under the heading "Carole and Joni," we read:

> Women composers have come late to popular music, but they have not been exactly thick on the ground in classical music either. Obviously this is not a matter of artistic talent . . . but a matter of social convention. While a number of names can be brought forward from the twentieth century, few can be found in earlier times. Clara Schumann, wife of the composer Robert Schumann, and Fanny Mendelssohn, sister of Felix, were both promising composers whose menfolk made it clear that their place was to be home—not music-makers. At the time of Monteverdi, there was a very good composer-singer named Barbara Strozzi; a well-placed courtesan, she was therefore free from the restraints that kept respectable married women in more traditional feminine pursuits. Oddly, it is back in the age of chivalry that we hear of some woman troubadours and trouveres who may have written the music as well as the words to their songs, as King and Mitchell have today. (pp. 526, 527)

While the Kermans do not tell us what Clara Schumann, Fanny Mendelssohn Hensel, or Barbara Strozzi composed, at least this book implies that talent knows no gender. But their attempts at integrating women into the text are inconsistent. Just like the Levy text, in the chapter on The Middle Ages II, one happily discovers this: "There were also highly regarded women poets, such as the troubadour Countess Beatrix of Bie [*sic*] and the trouvere Gormonda of Montpellier" (p. 93). Even though Countess Beatriz's place of origin is incorrect, and even though, historically, a woman troubadour was referred to as a "trobairitz," the errors can be excused in the light of the authors' integrating these two trobairitze into the text where they belong.[4]

The third edition of Daniel Politoske's *Music* has added one woman composer to its 450 pages in the five years since the publication of its second edition (1979): Toshiko Akiyoshi, mentioned in passing in the chapter on jazz. The new edition also adds the names of Joan Baez and Janis Joplin, referring to each, respectively, as a folk and a rock singer. It is puzzling, however, that in the index under "musical examples," a song by Baez is listed for page 471. No such example appears in the text, and there is no indication that it is included on the record album.

In both the second and third edition of Politoske's book, Clara Schumann is mentioned several times in the text in relation to her husband and to Brahms; the one tribute to Clara Schumann as a composer is found in small print under her picture.

Once again, the disturbing trend of lumping the other women composers together at the end of the book recurs. Even after five years, the third edition of the Politoske book does exactly what the second did, which is to conclude the entire book with a single paragraph:

> Another important aspect of modern music is the increasing participation and acceptance of women, not only as performers, but also as conductors and composers. While women have been active in the writing and performing of music for centuries, their role has grown enormously in the twentieth century. Women singers have enjoyed great prominence and prestige ever since the seventeenth century, but women composers and conductors have rarely enjoyed the success and

popularity of their male counterparts, most often due to social restrictions. In recent decades Margaret Hillis (b. 1921), conductor of the Chicago Symphony Chorus, and Sarah Caldwell (b. 1928), conductor of the Opera Company of Boston, have been acclaimed for their particular genius. Composers Thea Musgrave (b. 1928), Esther Williamson Ballou (1915-1973), and Pozzi Escot (b. 1933) have all gained international repute. Hopefully the barriers to recognition of female composers and conductors will all soon fade.

If the author, editors, or publishers really do hope that "the barriers will soon fade," why are these women so trivialized by segregating them—regardless of their particular styles or genres, let alone titles of their work—into the last paragraph in the book, "Increasing Roles for Women"?

A book clearly sensitive to women, one which is coauthored by two women, Edith Borroff and Marjory Irvin, is *Music in Perspective* (Harcourt, Brace, Jovanovich, 1976). Since Dr. Borroff is herself a composer, this text raises interesting questions regarding which women composers are/are not included, and why only four women composers do appear.

A unique feature of this book is its inclusion of a "Basse Danse" by the composer Marie de Bourgogne (fl. ca. 1450) in the accompanying record album. This is the only recorded example of early music by a woman in all the albums.

However, the only other women composers mentioned in the text are Joan Baez (specifically as a composer rather than singer), Carole King, and Germaine Tailleferre. It seems distinctly odd that the Baroque composer Elisabeth-Claude Jacquet de La Guerre does not appear in this book, especially since Dr. Borroff is the author of a book on de La Guerre.[5] It is hard to believe that Borroff "neglected" to include de La Guerre in her own music appreciation textbook! Again, who is responsible?[6]

As does the Levy, this book includes many pictures of women as performers and lists many women jazz pianists and singers—Ma Rainey, Marion McPartland, and Marian Anderson, to name a few. A number of women in other creative arts also receive attention: Isadora Duncan, Edna St. Vincent Millay, Edith Sitwell, and the poet Marie Borroff (sister of Edith Borroff). In the section on medieval jongleurs, such phrases as "these men and women" show that the authors, editors, and publishers are really aware that women did compose during the Middle Ages.

Another textbook that also includes four women is Robert Komar's *Music as Human Experience*. However, all four of the women mentioned are contemporary popular singer-composers: Joni Mitchell, Joan Baez, Judy Collins, and Janis Joplin. In a text whose title makes a commitment to "human experience," one could expect a greater variety of women composers.

In Tom Manoff's *Music—A Living Language* (Norton, 1982), the woman who gets all the attention (except for one mention of popular singer-composer Karla Bonoff) is Joni Mitchell. A full nine pages are devoted to discussing her style, her place in popular music, and four of her songs, taken from several of her albums, from 1967 through the song cycle "Hejira" (1976), described by the author as "a modern masterpiece." This text, then, holds the distinction of having devoted more pages to a single woman composer than any of the other texts. It may well be that the author has anticipated what his young audience's main interests are, and so he re-echoes their current belief; that is, in these modern times, women in popular music really have made it. The general tone of his text—"Good music simply means that which moves the listener" (p. 457)—would seem to make it ideally hospitable to women composers. But, alas, not even in the chapter on "Song—The Universal Impulse" is one woman composer mentioned!

The only concession to historic women composers in the Manoff book occurs in a paragraph about the Mozart family. In reference to Wolfgang's sister, Nannerl, we find: "but like so many gifted women of the past, her career was submerged by the traditional social restrictions of the eighteenth century." (p. 214) (Is one to assume, then, that the careers of the two Anna Amalias, Maria Theresia von Paradis, Corona Schroeter, Maddalena Lombardini-Sirmen, Maria Teresa d'Agnesi-Pignotti, and Julie Candeille were also submerged? Hardly. But who's to know?)

Manoff uses one listening example which *could* have been attributed to an historic woman composer. When he describes, twice in the text, the anonymous "Bressay Lullabye," could he not have *suggested* that its "anonymous" composer might have been a woman? Are we to believe that all lullabies, throughout history, have been composed by men?

One of the best-selling Music Appreciation textbooks is *The Enjoyment of Music* by Joseph Machlis, now in its fifth edition (1984). It has been 30 years since its initial publication (1955). The most recent book's 608 pages now include three women, all from the twentieth century: Thea Musgrave, Ruth Crawford, and Julia Perry. Amy Beach, mentioned in the revised (second) edition, has been dropped. In 1984 Clara Schumann is still referred to as a gifted pianist, wife of Robert Schumann, and an inspiration for Brahms; Alma Mahler remains Gustav's wife and the patron who backed the production of Alban Berg's *Wozzek*; Pauline Viardot-Garcia is mentioned only as a singer, and the only Boulanger mentioned is Nadia. However, there is an attempt to include women composers in the chronological charts in the Appendix of the book. Here we find the names and dates of Amy Beach, Ruth Crawford, Julia Perry, Thea Musgrave, Ellen Zwilich, and Laurie Anderson.

The most notable inclusion is the musical analysis of Ruth Crawford's *String Quartet* from 1931. There is a brief biographical sketch and a picture of Crawford, although one sentence gives only a half-truth assessment of why Crawford essentially stopped composing after 1932: "There was, however, no audience in America for what she had to say. Like Ives and Ruggles, she gave up composing when she should have been at the height of her creativity." (p. 553)

It would have been more correct to include the fact that Crawford's husband, Charles Seeger, persuaded his new wife, and step-mother of his five children, to give up her original composition to concentrate, as he did, on re-presenting American folk songs. (Charles Seeger felt that this activity was more consonant with the social climate and political concerns of the Depression years.)

Regardless of those details, one applauds the inclusion of musical analysis, the presence of five short music examples (all by Crawford), and, above all, the recorded string quartet in its entirety. The Machlis text is, at least, an excellent beginning in getting women composers' *music*, not just names, into the texts.

While *The Enjoyment of Music* is careful not to group all the women together at the end of the book, it certainly could have included more American women in the 33 pages devoted to American music. The only one mentioned is Julia Perry, one name among five in a sentence listing black composers of the modern American school.

In books like the Machlis, which list other more specialized texts in their "Suggested Reading" columns, one looks long and hard to find titles of books whose subject is women in music, or, more specifically, women composers. Only one such reference was found in all the texts surveyed: *Unsung*, Christine Ammer's history of women in American music (Greenwood Press), is included on the "Suggested Reading" list in Roger Kamien's *Music: An Appreciation* (1984).

The most praiseworthy aspect of Kamien's volume is that it includes on the record album and in the text an entire composition by a woman composer, Miriam Gideon's vocal chamber work "Questions on Nature" (1964). The discussion of the piece is correlated in the text with a discussion of George Crumb's *The Ancient Voices of Children* (1970).

Even though Gideon is the only woman composer mentioned, as such (Clara Schumann remains pianist and wife; Alma Mahler remains wife and patron), one has the feeling that Kamien is sensitive to at least naming and providing photographs of other musical women: Lil Hardin, Elizabeth Sprague Coolidge, Marie de Medici, Nadia Boulanger, and several black singers—Ella Fitzgerald, Aretha Franklin, Billie Holiday, Bessie Smith, and Diana Ross. In Appendix I—Chronology, several women writers are named: George Sand, Emily Dickinson, Gertrude Stein, Virginia Woolf. However, the only women composers included on that chronological chart are Ruth Crawford and Miriam Gideon.[7]

Another popular Music Appreciation textbook, in its fourth printing as of 1979, is *The Art of Listening—Developing Musical Perception*, by Jeanne Shapiro Bamberger and Howard Brofsky.

This text differs from the others in that it emphasizes the development of listening skills over historical and stylistic knowledge. Thus, music history, as such, is not introduced until Part Four of the book, "Historical Context," where the great masters and their masterpieces are assigned less than seventy pages. This approach, relying on short listening examples for three-fourths of the book, could make an ideal framework in which to include women composers. However, in spite of the fact that one of the authors is a woman, this text makes almost no effort to mention women, much less women composers.

There is only a fleeting hint of sensitivity to women composers, and that involves occasional instances of the use of "his/her" pronouns. Actually, the only "her" mentioned in this book is Miriam Gideon, who appears on a composite list of names under "Suggested Listening." And again, following the usual pattern of "Suggested Reading" assignments, no mention is made of books about women composers, even though several books and articles were already in print by 1979.

Of the four Music Appreciation texts that mention no women composers, three are the most recent publications: Ronald Byrnside's *Music, Sound and Sense* (William C. Brown, 1985); Bennett Reimer's *Developing the Experience of Music*, 2d ed. (Prentice Hall, 1985); and Jean Ferris's *Music: The Art of Listening* (William C. Brown, 1985). The latter, written by a woman, mentions only three women: folksingers Joan Baez and Judy Collins, and Nadia Boulanger, a famous teacher of famous men. One is tempted to blurt out, "We've come a long way! (in 1985)—right back where we started from!"

It ought to be very simple to create the woman-integrated Music Appreciation textbook. Since the aim of this course is not the educating of future musicologists, there really is ample opportunity to mainstream women, blacks, and other minorities. For instance, the 101 student usually gets several introductory chapters on the musical elements—rhythm, melody, harmony, form, and tone color—before approaching the canon of masterpieces. What more logical place than here to mainstream women composers? A Fanny Hensel song can teach the concept of melody, Ethel Smyth's *Trio* can introduce $\frac{5}{4}$ meter and syncopation, de La Guerre's keyboard sonatas can teach the tone color of the harpsichord, Louise Farrenc's *Piano Trio* or *Nonet* can teach the concept of sonata form, and the list goes on.

Actually, our sister discipline of music theory appears to be ahead of us in its inclusion of printed music examples by women in its texts. Recently the 1980 theory sequence *Practical Beginning Theory*, 4th ed., by Bruce Benward and Barbara Garvey Jackson (the Florence Price scholar and author of many articles about women in music) has come to my attention.[8] Musical examples by Cécile Chaminade, Elisabeth-Claude Jacquet de La Guerre, Fanny Hensel, Anne Miller, Lady John Scott, and Clara Schumann are included for the student to analyze. Also an entire historical anthology of music by women is currently in development, scheduled for publication in 1987. Edited by Dr. James Briscoe of Butler University, the volume reprints the music itself—complete movements or short works—with critical introductions by scholars who specialize in researching particular composers.

How many times have we all heard the concern voiced by teachers of the one-semester music appreciation course, "But there's so little time to include all those 'extras:' " (meaning world music, popular music, jazz, American music, women, blacks, and other minorities). Our response? These are not "extras." Expanding the repertoire of the course will not cause the great monuments to fall into silence, but *not* to mention women composers just might cause *their* music to sink deeper into the silence that already pervades our radio stations and concert halls.

MUSIC HISTORY TEXTS SURVEY

A review of many music history textbooks reveals that music is here treated as object: intensive analyses of discrete pieces form the bulk of these books, a methodology peculiar to historical musicology.[9] This approach only further reinforces the relativist point of view. Thus emerges a "canon" of monuments created by great geniuses that, unfortunately, is not placed in any sort of social or cultural context. This "great man/great works" view continues to influence the shaping of music history as it is both written and taught. Many texts and courses move from one "great man" to the next as though they represent the normal levels of human endeavor in a given age.

There are at least three problems with this approach: (1) the students will receive the mistaken impression that the past consisted only of a succession of geniuses who, by the way, were all male; (2) they will perceive as typical for an age what was often atypical; and (3) the silence surrounding women's music communicates the strong message that musical composition is not an activity to be engaged in by women.

A review of 47 music history texts of either the one-volume comprehensive history or the one-volume period study indicates that twelve fail altogether to mention women composers, while 17 books mention only one or two. Most often, when women composers are mentioned, it is not as composers but as performers, teachers, or in relation to a husband, father, or brother. For example, the most commonly used music history textbook (Grout) mentions two different women composers four times, but never in the context of being composers. Only 12 books actually include one or more paragraphs on a woman composer, and they are books on either American or twentieth-century music. Not surprisingly, only one text includes any musical examples by women. Again, not surprisingly, Nadia Boulanger's name is the one most frequently mentioned, but always in relation to someone else; her intrinsic importance as a composer is never discussed. Clara Schumann is talked about in relation to Robert, but rarely as a composer. Germaine Tailleferre is frequently mentioned, but always as being one of the unimportant members of Les Six.

There are, however, *some* interesting tidbits to be found if one looks long enough or hard enough. For example, in the third edition of Donald

Ferguson's *A History of Musical Thought* is found, in a footnote, a statement that Francesca Caccini was perhaps a greater talent than her father.[10] Another example is found in Paul Henry Lang's monumental volume *Music in Western Civilization.* He briefly discusses women's role in music in ancient Rome and later briefly presents an interesting account of Renaissance women in the roles of patron and musician.[11] One final example is found in Henry Raynor's *A Social History of Music*, when he mentions Maria Antonia Walpurgis, the Princess of Bavaria, as a composer of some accomplishment. He then qualifies this statement by saying that she was also a person of unlimited ambition who published her works under a pen name.[12] There is no attempt to explain why it may have been necessary for her to publish her works under another name, or to observe that if she wasn't ambitious about her music, who, in that period, would have been?

Table 17.4 reflects the situation as it is. We applaud Leonie Rosenstiel's *The Schirmer History of Music* (Schirmer Books, 1982), but wonder why this woman author of the *Life and Works of Lili Boulanger* (Madison, N.J.: Fairleigh Dickinson University Press, 1976) managed to include only six women composers in the 900-page book of which she was editor.

What conclusions can be drawn, then, about the recent music history texts' sporadic sensitivity to women composers? A glance at Table 4, listing those music history texts in order, from the most responsive down to the least responsive, shows that several recent publications bear little or no improvement over the earlier ones. For example, the best selling music history text, Donald Grout's *A History of Western Music* (Norton, 1980), mentions two women composers in 752 pages, while Paul Henry Lang's classic of 40 years earlier, *Music in Western Civilization* (Norton, 1941), also mentions two women composers. Another recent music history text, Milo Wold's *An Outline History of Music* (W. C. Brown, 1985), mentions three women composers, but the David Poultney text, *Studying Music History* (Prentice Hall, 1983), mentions no women composers. Compare this to Homer Ulrich's *A History of Music and Musical Style* (Harcourt, Brace, Jovanovich, 1963), written 20 years earlier, where six women composers are mentioned.

We applaud the fact that Joseph Machlis, in 1979, lists 21 women composers in his *Introduction to Contemporary Music*, 2d ed. (Norton)! This is an excellent beginning. However, we wonder why the Machlis, which is a general survey of twentieth-century music, had little or no impact upon the more specialized Cope book published two years later, *New Directions in Music* (W. C. Brown, 1981), which contains only six women composers. William Austin's classic *Music in the Twentieth Century*, published 18 years earlier, mentioned six women composers. That the Peter Yates book on twentieth-century music (Minerva Press, 1967) could not manage to mention one single twentieth-century woman composer in 342 pages is most regrettable.

As regards American music texts, Gilbert Chase did as well in 1966 with his *America's Music* (McGraw-Hill) as Charles Hamm did 17 years later in his

Table 17.4
Music History Textbooks Ranked in Order of Number of Women Composers Mentioned

Author, Book Title, Publisher, Date	Number of Pages	Number of Women Composers Mentioned	Number of Music Examples Composed by Women	Complete Paragraphs Discussing a Particular Woman Composer	Total Number of Women Musicians Mentioned
Machlis, Joseph, *Introduction to Contemporary Music*, Norton, 1979	600	21	0	25	40
Hitchcock, H. Wiley, *Music in the United States: A Historical Introduction*, Prentice-Hall, 1974	237	7	0	0	16
Cope, David, *New Directions in Music*, Wm. C. Brown, 1981	319	6	0	1	29
Austin, William, *Music in the Twentieth Century*, Norton, 1966	537	6	0	1	14
Rosenstiel, Leonie, ed., *Schirmer History of Music*, Schirmer, 1982	944	6	0	2	9
Ulrich, Homer, and Paul A. Pisk, *A History of Music and Musical Style*, Harcourt Brace Jovanovich, 1963	663	6	0	0	11
Borroff, Edith, *Music in Europe and the United States: A History*, Prentice-Hall, 1971	715	5	2	1	11
Martin, William R., and Julius Drossin, *Music of the Twentieth Century*, Prentice-Hall, 1980	373	5	0	1	14
Abraham, Gerald, *The Concise Oxford History of Music*, Oxford University Press, 1979	863	5	0	0	9

Table 17.4 *continued*

Author, Book Title, Publisher, Date	**Number of Pages**	**Number of Women Composers Mentioned**	**Number of Music Examples Composed by Women**	**Complete Paragraphs Discussing a Particular Woman Composer**	**Total Number of Women Musicians Mentioned**
Chase, Gilbert, *America's Music*, (2nd ed.), McGraw-Hill, 1966	692	4	0	6	24
Ferguson, Donald N., *A History of Musical Thought*, Appleton, Century, Crofts, 1959	638	4	0	0	9
Hamm, Charles, *Music in the New World*, Norton, 1983	657	4	0	3	9
Einstein, Alfred, *Music in the Romantic Era*, Norton, 1947	362	4	0	0	4
Salzman, Eric, *Twentieth Century Music*, Prentice-Hall, 1974	201	4	0	0	5
Kingman, Daniel, *American Music, A Panorama*, Schirmer, 1979	563	4	0	0	1
Southern, Eileen, *The Music of Black Americans*, Norton, 1983	554	3	0	5	7
Headington, Christopher, *History of Western Music*, Schirmer, 1974	305	3	0	0	5
Wold, Milo, and Edmund Cykler, *An Outline History of Music*, Wm. C. Brown, 1985	340	3	0	0	0
Plantigua, Leon, *Romantic Music*, Norton, 1985	461	2	0	0	11
Hanson, Peter, *An Introduction to Twentieth Century Music*, Allyn & Bacon, 1978	415	2	0	1	7
Klaus, Kenneth, *The Romantic Period in Music*, Allyn & Bacon, 1970	545	2	0	0	7

White, John, *Music in Western Culture, A Short History*, Wm. C. Brown, 1972	361	2	0	0	4
Bukofzer, Manfred F., *Music in the Baroque Era*, Norton, 1947	411	2	0	0	4
Grout, Donald Jay, *A History of Western Music*, (3rd ed.), Norton, 1980	752	2	0	0	4
Reese, Gustave, *Music in the Middle Ages*, Norton, 1940	424	2	0	0	2
Lang, Paul Henry, *Music in Western Civilization*, Norton, 1941	1,030	2	0	3	2
Boroff, Edith, *The Music of the Baroque*, Wm. C. Brown, 1970	135	1	0	0	4
Mellers, W. *Music in a New Found Land*, Hillstone, 1964	439	1	0	0	4
Longyear, Rey Morgan, *Nineteenth Century Romanticism*, Prentice-Hall, 1973	279	1	0	0	3
Canon, Beekman C., Alvin H. Johnson, and William G. Waite, *The Art of Music*, T. Crowell, 1960	465	1	0	0	2
Thomson, James C., *Music Through the Renaissance*, Wm. C. Brown, 1984	250	1	0	0	2
Sachs, Curt, *Our Musical Heritage*, Prentice-Hall, 1955	333	1	0	0	1
Hughes, D., *A History of European Music*, McGraw-Hill, 1974	496	1	0	0	1
Raynor, Henry, *A Social History of Music*, Schocken, 1972	555	1	0	0	1
Robertson, *The Pelican History of Music*, 1963	915	1	0	0	0
Abraham, Gerald, *A Hundred Years of Music*, Aldine Publishing Co., 1964	298	0	0	0	0

Table 17.4 *continued*

Author, Book Title, Publisher, Date	Number of Pages	Number of Women Composers Mentioned	Number of Music Examples Composed by Women	Complete Paragraphs Discussing a Particular Woman Composer	Total Number of Women Musicians Mentioned
Brown, Howard Mayer, *Music in the Renaissance*, Prentice-Hall, 19--	373	0	0	0	0
Crocker, Richard, *A History of Musical Style*, McGraw-Hill, 1966	526	0	0	0	0
Einstein, Alfred, *A Short History of Music*, Vintage, 1954	205	0	0	0	0
Hoppin, Richard, *Medieval Music*, Norton, 1978	524	0	0	0	0
Palisca, Claude, *Baroque Music*, (2nd ed.), Prentice-Hall, 1981	282	0	0	0	0
Pauly, Reinhard G., *Music in the Classic Period*, Prentice-Hall, 1973	199	0	0	0	0
Poultney, David, *Studying Music History*, Prentice-Hall, 1983	228	0	0	0	0
Reese, Gustave, *Music in the Renaissance*, Norton, 1959	883	0	0	0	0
Wiora, Walter, *The Four Ages of Music*, Norton, 1965	197	0	0	0	0
Yates, Peter, *Twentieth Century Music*, Minerva Press, 1967	342	0	0	0	0
Harmon, Alec, Anthony Milner, and Wilfrid Mellers, *Man and His Music*, Oxford University Press, 1962	1,068	0	0	0	0

Music in the Western World (Norton, 1983). And Gustav Reese, writing in 1940, found two women to mention in his *Music in the Middle Ages* (Norton, 1940); and Manfred Bukofzer, in his *Music of the Baroque Era* (Norton, 1947), also found two women composers to mention. The fact that both Bukofzer and Reese, writing specialized period books in the 1940s, managed to mention more women composers than 20 of the 47 books included in this study, leads one to believe that the authors/publishers of 40 years ago were fairly sensitized to including women composers in their books.

It is possible that the books published in the 1940s were somewhat more responsive to women as musical creators since American women composers in the first half of this century were hardly invisible. Amy Beach, Marion Bauer, Mabel Daniels, Mary Howe, Ethel Leginska, and Florence Price all achieved recognition either through performances of their works or through attention in newspapers and periodicals to their careers as composers. Books on women composers had been written long before the 1940s: Arthur Elson's *Woman's Work in Music* (Boston: L. C. Page, 1904), Louis Elson's *Woman in Music* (New York: The University Society, Inc., 1918), and Otto Ebel's *Women Composers: A Biographical Handbook of Woman's Work in Music*, 3d ed. (Brooklyn: Chandler-Ebel Music Co., 1913), to name a few. Furthermore, a quick glance through Oscar Thompson's *International Cyclopedia of Music and Musicians* (Dodd Mead Publishers, 1939), which is a reference work, not a text, reveals an astonishing number of historic and contemporary women composers. Titles, genres, performances, publications, and dates of their works are consistently included. Is it any accident that the composer-author Marion Bauer and the American Music historian Gilbert Chase (whose book *America's Music* lists four women composers in 1966) were members of the Board of Associates of that 1939 *International Cyclopedia*?

As for hard statistics, twelve out of the 47 music history texts surveyed here mention no women composers—roughly 25 percent. Twenty-one out of the 47 mention only one, or none at all—45 percent. Twenty-nine mention two, one, or none—61 percent. Of the twentieth-century books where one could expect to find the most women composers, out of the five texts, only one (Machlis) lists a representative number. Of the American music texts, two books mention six, two mention four, and one mentions none! As for musical examples by women in the history books, there are two—both appearing in the same text (Borroff, *Music in Europe and the United States*). The two examples in that single text, out of all the music examples in the 47 texts, afford a grand total of .02 percent of musical examples composed by women.

JOINT CONCLUSIONS

The central questions remain. Just who *is* responsible for the unbalanced representation of women composers and their music in our music textbooks? Is it the authors? editors? publishers?

Why is the representation of women composers in some of the most recent texts no better and sometimes worse than those published earlier?

We would like to address certain suppositions, based on our first-hand acquaintance with the academic environment in which these books are framed and issued.

The old adage that "we parent as we were parented" has often been rephrased, "we teach as we were taught." This truism applies by and large to our colleagues, the professor-authors of these texts.

If no one at their university ever taught "Women in Music," or if the person in charge of ordering books, records, and scores has heard only of Ellen Zwilich (whose 1983 Pulitzer Prize at least made the newspapers), how could these authors have become sensitized to the quantity and quality of materials out there (including the scores and many recordings) about women composers? If these professor-authors attended any of the national professional meetings and conferences in the late seventies, they may have stumbled into panel discussions of women composers (though, unfortunately, not at American Musicological Society's national meetings in the 1980s!). The only professional forum for addressing the entire subject in any conscientious detail still remains the all-women music conference, and we have yet to see these authors at those meetings.

One very real problem with the professor-authors is their perception of how impossible it is to keep up with their own specialties, let alone learn about others. We certainly sympathize with this. Yet being pressed for time is no excuse for being fundamentally uninformed at a time when so many doctoral dissertations are being written on women composers. How can one reconcile women's diminished presence in current textbooks with the scholar's presumed commitment to broad expert knowledge of the field?

One possible reason for the inclusion of women composers in the textbooks of the 1940s might have to do with the history of musicology in America, a discipline that was in its infancy in the 1930s. Once the first generation of American musicologists (including those naturalized Americans who were born and educated in Europe) had written their books and taught their students about the canon of Western musical monuments, women composers were somehow eclipsed. An easy way out for a present-day musicologist-author is to make the false claim (but do they know it is false?) that it is "the women's movement" or the "progressive sixties and seventies" that discovered and permitted the activity of composition by women (therefore relegating them to the back of the book).[13]

Now, what about the publishers and editors? We would like to suggest that it is the editors and publishers who have "tacked on" the women composers at the end of the books. Maybe they sincerely believe in the legitimacy of sequestering/bunching the references in this fashion; or perhaps it is just too costly to integrate women composers directly into the text, especially for later editions of an already-existing book. Our key question here is: If the publishers of *public school* music texts can be held accountable for their representation or misrepresentation of women, blacks, and minorities, why are the publishers of *college* texts seemingly exempt?

A professional colleague, under contract in 1985 with a major publisher of public school music books, has been assigned the task of rewriting the current middle-school (grades 5-8) texts in that particular series. The publisher has already supplied him with a list of women, black, and other minority music makers. He has permitted the following quotation to be used here:

> No one can hope to publish any [grade- or high-] school text now (1985) without due representation and sensitivity to the way minorities are portrayed. I am not required to be an expert on the new scholarship in these fields, but the editors and publishers commission those who *are* knowledgable. My job is unacceptable until I have communicated with those experts, have looked at their materials, and have included representative samples. Did you know that some states have refused to adopt certain texts which have not corrected their stereotypes? As you are finding out, the publishing of *college* music texts is something else entirely. Recently I received a college Music Appreciation manuscript to review from a well-known publisher. I am so accustomed to looking out for the rehashings of stereotypes and the status quo, that I sent the manuscript back to the publisher, commenting, "Unacceptable as is—No mention of women composers."[4]

Who sensitized our colleague to that kind of automatic response? The publishers! No inclusion of minorities means no sales to certain states. This may not be the kind of pressure we in higher education would espouse, but the implication is clear: College music-book publishers are not at this time vulnerable to the "community sensitivity = economic gain" mandate. A pity.

If certain states can pressure publishers, who, in turn, can pressure their editors and authors, then *we* must begin to pressure the publishers ourselves for new texts that fully integrate women's music into the narrative. After all, publishers won't change until they see that a mere rehashing of old material, with a token smattering of the new (resulting in misrepresentation), is no longer financially viable for them. We must begin preparing and submitting manuscripts, lists, and bibliographies to the publishers. We must also write angry letters and send them articles such as this one, which include the hard statistics. We must insist on representation of publishers, authors, and women composer scholars at national meetings. If our author colleagues, publishers, or editors should admit that they don't know enough about women composers, we should supply them with the names of scholars who do. And if our author friends were to suggest, as we suppose they might, that their inclusion of women composers got relegated by the editors and publishers to the end of the text, against the author's better judgment, we must alert the publishers to the enormous disservice they are rendering students and colleagues.

If it is true that every generation must write its own history, then the task of this generation is to write a history in which women composers and their music are no longer ignored, or worse, trivialized. Women and their music must come up from the footnotes and be fully integrated into the study of music history. After all, if we are at all interested in offering our students a historically accurate account of Western (and world) music, we must include the accomplishments of women, not because they are women, nor because they are women of accomplishment, but rather because these are accomplishments of a culture inconceivable without accomplished persons, both men and women. We must remember that whatever else the arts may be, they are also a record of people's creative responses to life in their time.

Music has traditionally lagged behind the other arts and intellectual disciplines in effecting change of any sort. As the musicologist Joseph Kerman, in his new book *Contemplating Music: Challenges to Musicology*, has observed: "Musical thought travels behind the latest chariots of intellectual life in general. . . . Post-structuralism, deconstruction, and serious feminism have yet to make their debuts in musicology."[15] Kerman is right in his assessment of the snail's pace of musical thought—but is it too much to ask that publishers, editors, and authors try to hasten the process?[16]

NOTES

1. "More Women than Men Now Attending College," *Chicago Sun Times*, 18 October 1984, p. 58.

2. A factor possibly accounting for a greater number of references in the Music History tables may reflect a difference in the way the separate statistics were compiled. The Music Appreciation charts do not credit any mention of a woman composer that neglects to cite her as a *composer* (e.g., the frequent tendency to name Clara Schumann simply as a pianist, or "wife of"). The Music History statistics are considerably more charitable; here, credit was given for *any* inclusion of the name, even if the woman is not mentioned specifically as a composer.

3. Such sensitivity to women as composers, and pictured as performers, might possibly be accredited to the publishers, Harper and Row. Did the editors there become sensitized to Women in Music through their publication of Carol Neuls-Bates's book of that title (Harper and Row, 1982)? It may well be only a matter of time before this sensitized publisher will come out with a completely integrated text, placing the historic women composers in the chapters where they belong, and including women composers throughout history on chronological time lines and charts.

4. Ian Parker, "Beatriz de Dia," *The New Grove Dictionary of Music and Musicians* (New York: Macmillan, 1980); Edith Borroff, "Women Composers: Reminiscence and History," *Symposium, the Journal of the College Music Society*, Vol. 15 (Boulder, Colorado, Spring 1975), p. 28.

5. Edith Borroff, *An Introduction to Elisabeth-Claude Jacquet de La Guerre*, (Brooklyn, N.Y.: Institute of Medieval Music, 1966).

6. According to co-author Marjory Irvin, the *authors* insisted on including a recorded example by a woman composer, resulting in de Bourgogne's 59-second example. However, Dr. Irvin recalls that *her* knowledge of women composers, in 1974, when the book was written, was practically nil. She has permitted the following quotation for this chapter:

I only became involved in learning about women composers *after* writing the book. At my university, the Women's Studies people were actively rediscovering women in their own disciplines, and so it occurred to me that I should be doing research on and performing the compositions by women composers. I don't recall any specific battles with the publishers in 1974-75, because I was not sensitized at that time to women composers. But *now* I consistently program women on recitals; I worked with Da Capo Press, and wrote the Foreword for their volume on Augusta Holmès, and *now* I can't do enough for the cause of women composers. It's too bad the book preceded my raised conscience.

Marjory Irvin, Interview with Diane Jezic, 7 July 1985.

7. Since the author's mother, Anna Kamien, is a composer, one might suppose that Roger Kamien would have been in favor of including more women composers. Who, then—editor or publisher—is responsible for including in the text proper of this otherwise woman-sensitive book only one woman composer?

8. Bruce Benward and Barbara Garvey Jackson, *Practical Beginning Theory*, 4th ed. (Dubuque, Iowa: W. C. Brown, 1980). According to an unpublished article by Adel Heinrich (organist and theory professor at Colby College, Maine), the Benward-Jackson text is particularly sensitive to women composers.

9. Robert Copland, "Music Historiography in the Classroom," *Symposium, the Journal of the College Music Society*, Vol. 19, no. 1 (Spring 1979), p. 147.

10. Donald Ferguson. *A History of Musical Thought*, 3d ed. (New York: Appleton, Century, Crofts, 1959), p. 256.

11. Paul Henry Lang. *Music in Western Civilization* (New York: Norton, 1940), pp. 35, 301.

12. Henry Raynor. *A Social History of Music* (New York: Schocken Books, 1972), p. 295.

13. An illustration of how musicologists/professors often tend to believe that women composers are a product of the twentieth century comes from a young woman on an East Coast campus. Unfortunately the incident that she reported to us is not an isolated one. She had already taken a "Women in Music" course when she enrolled in an upper-level Music History course. Inquiring of the professor as to just why there were no women composers in music history before the twentieth century (of course, *she* knew otherwise), she reports his answer—"because of the old social constraints, women were never encouraged to compose until recently, so, of course, there were no women composers of note until the twentieth century." Did that professor know what he didn't know? How many professors are fortunate enough to have a student in undergraduate music history who can provide the class and the professor with names, evidence, bibliographies, and discographies to disprove the texts' and professors' misinformation?

14. Dr. Vincent P. Lawrence, interview with Diane Jezic, July 1985.

15. Joseph Kerman. *Contemplating Music: Challenges to Musicology* (Cambridge, Mass.: Harvard University Press, 1985), p. 17.

16. Some of these basic changes appear to be happening. According to Karen Speerstra, acquisitions editor for William C. Brown publishing company, a new music history text is currently in development that will integrate fully into discussions of individual historical periods approximately 50 women musicians, at least 30 of whom are or were noted primarily as composers. The textbook, entitled "The Development of Western Music: A History," is due to appear in 1988. (Editor's Note)

18

*Tarquinia Molza (1542–1617): A Case Study of Women, Music, and Society in the Renaissance**

JOANNE RILEY

> Why is it that the pages of all history glow with the names of illustrious men, while only here and there a lone woman appears who, like the eccentric comet, marks the centuries?
>
> Susan B. Anthony[1]

The life and career of Tarquinia Molza (1542-1617), an Italian musician of the late Renaissance, provide an illuminating response to Susan B. Anthony's question. Molza worked at the Este court of Ferrara in the 1580s with several other women collectively referred to at the time as the *concerto delle donne*. The vocal virtuosity of this group of women supposedly inspired famous male composers to write madrigals featuring ornamented soprano parts that undermined the "equal-voiced" madrigal ideal and paved the way for the "concertante" principle of the Baroque.[2] However, contradictions and questions still surround the historical contribution of the "singing Ladies of Ferrara"—questions that can be satisfyingly answered only after examining the roles of *both women and men* in the musical life of sixteenth-century Italy. As historian Gerda Lerner insists, "Gender must be included as an analytical category to history. When gender is considered with race, class, ethnicity and religious affiliation in analyzing any given period or event, an entirely new dimension is added to social history."[3]

This chapter will examine Tarquinia Molza's life and career in light of Lerner's exhortation. It will offer, in a substantial revision of the traditional view of secular song in sixteenth-century Italy, some striking conclusions: that women and men had distinctly separate musical styles in the first half of the century and that Tarquinia Molza, who was trained in both styles, was largely instrumental in their eventual combination in the luxuriant madrigal, an important musical development of the late Renaissance. The accuracy of these conclusions was confirmed late in the research process by the delightfully unexpected rediscovery of a document written in 1577 by

*This article was awarded Third Prize in the first Pauline Alderman Prize competition for new scholarship on women in music (1986). Research for the article was made possible by a generous grant from the S and H Foundation's Beinecke Memorial Fund.

Figure 18.1 Tarquinia Molza. Used by permission of Giovanna Molza de Gazzolo.

Molza's friend Francesco Patrizi, which gives priceless details of her life and musical practice. Information from that manuscript will be presented toward the end of this chapter as corroborative evidence.

MOLZA'S LIFE AND CAREER: THE TRADITIONAL VIEW

Tarquinia Molza is mentioned in most of the standard sources dealing with music in the Renaissance. A composite overview of her life—unchallenged until recently—as compiled from the works of such researchers as Vandelli, Solerti, Einstein, and Reese would look like this:

Tarquinia Molza was born in 1542, the oldest of nine children born to a noble family in the city of Modena. Her father allowed her to study along with her brothers, Ludovico and Niccolo, with the best masters he could find. Tarquinia proved herself to be something of a prodigy, learning Greek, Latin, Hebrew, astronomy, and philosophy at a very early age, writing commendable poetry, and teaching herself music from books. All of these endeavors were highly praised by the most learned scholars and musicians of her time.

In 1582, after her husband died, Signora Tarquinia was recruited by Duke Alfonso II d'Este of Ferrara as a lady-in-waiting to his bride, Margherita Gonzaga. In that capacity Tarquinia won great fame as a virtuoso singer, along with two other ladies who sang with her at court functions. These "Three Ladies of Ferrara" as they were called, had such beautiful voices that they inspired gifted composers such as Giaches Wert, Luca Marenzio, Giulio Caccini, and many others to compose madrigals that featured three prominent soprano parts against the two lower parts, an exciting new style.

Tarquinia was banished from court in 1589 because of a love affair with Giaches de Wert, a low-born musician considered unfit company for a woman of her noble rank.[4] So she retired to her hometown, where she was surrounded by literati and musicians who delighted in her knowledge and ready wit. In 1601, Tarquinia Molza was made an honorary citizen of Rome, the only time that privilege was ever accorded a woman. She died in 1617 at the age of 75, leaving behind a will made out in Latin, Greek, and Italian.

This, Tarquinia Molza's "official" biography, offers us a familiar picture of an educated, talented Renaissance woman inspiring men of genius. But does this portrayal explain Molza's inclusion in Western music history? The female "muses" of countless male composers are never given historical recognition—why is she? Furthermore, why is she consistently singled out for special mention over the other Ladies of Ferrara, if their function was supposedly the same? Why were her composer/admirers so numerous (Wert, Caccini, Striggio, Virchi, Luzzaschi, and more) when the inspiring muse of most male artists was an exclusively personal romantic figure? Could it be that *active creative influence*—and not merely admiration for voice, face, and body—obliged historians to include Molza in their accounts, albeit recast as a passive, minor figure? With these questions in mind, let us briefly review the social and musical history of women and men in sixteenth-century Italy in the generation preceding Molza's birth.

SOCIAL AND MUSICAL LIFE IN SIXTEENTH-CENTURY ITALY

Sixteenth-century life was separated into two well-defined spheres—public and private. Among the aristocracy, the inner court circle constituted the private sphere, presided over by women responsible for maintaining standards of cultural sensibility. The inner court circle was the birthplace of

Figure 18.2 The opening measures of Giaches Wert's madrigal for five voices, "Tu canti e cant'anch'io." In this example of proto-concertanta style, Wert highlights the ornamented trio of women's voices for three measures before bringing in the paired tenor and bass. © Copyright 1970 by Armen Carapetyan/Hänssler-Verlag, 7303 Neuhausen-Stuttgart. Used by permission.

the *frottola* and related secular song forms generally performed as solos to lute or keyboard accompaniment by *women*. Improvisation was a defining element of these early secular song forms, both in the extemporaneous creation of verses and melodies and in the often intricate embellishment and ornamentation of the melodies. The verses for these songs were usually unsentimental, "cheerful, sensuous, ironic, with a tendency to parody even in expressions of pain," and the music was homophonic, with the accompaniment supplied by the singer.[5]

Women's role as principal performers of this style is rarely acknowledged by historians. But it is abundantly clear from sixteenth-century sources that proficiency in secular song performance was a required part of the noble female role, as indicated by the following sampling:

Annibal Guasco to his daughter Lavinia re the proper manners of a court lady: "Her eyes should be held on linen and needle, on clavichord or songbook, or whatever she is occupied with, not darting them here and there."[6]

"As to what Signora Irene [Spilimbergo] learned in playing, and in singing to the lute, the harpsichord, and the viol, and how on each of these instruments, far beyond the usual custom and intellect of women, she approximated the very best in these arts, I say nothing, for it would take too long."[7] (my translation).

Not only would I have [the ideal court lady] engage in robust and manly exercises, but even in those that are becoming to a woman I would have her practice in a measured way . . . And so, when she dances, I should not wish to see her make movements that are too energetic or violent; nor when she sings or plays, uses those loud and oft-repeated diminutions that show more art than sweetness, likewise the musical instruments that she plays ought to be appropriate to this intent.[8]

No mention is made here of *whether* a woman should perform or not, but only that *when* she play or sing she do it with discretion, in which case it is altogether "becoming to a woman," "well-suited to a woman,"—an integral part of her role.[9] This kind of language presses for the inference of an extended tradition of female performance in the private court sphere. Many, many women sang and played; some were spectacular, like Irene Spilimbergo, some were terrible, and the majority were most likely mediocre, but all were necessary to give substance to the musical style.

The public sphere of life in the sixteenth century consisted of the church, the battlefield, and the political arena, then as now dominated by men. At the dawning of the century, the attention of noble males was occupied with matters of church and state, and secular music-making was rigorously discouraged for its supposedly deleterious effects on men's commitment to the public realm. As Castiglione had one of his characters state in his widely popular handbook on court etiquette: "I think that music, along with many other vanities, is indeed well-suited to women, and perhaps also to others who have the appearance of men, but not to real men; for the latter ought not to render their minds effeminate and afraid of death."[10]

Noble men were educated in the science of acoustics and the theory of counterpoint, but their experience by no means extended to the performance of secular songs about love, which was deemed a frivolous waste of time.[11]

Over the course of the sixteenth century, the public sphere became a realm of tension and defeat for the Italian aristocracy, as an increasingly dismal set of circumstances spelled out their diminishing power. Giuliano Procacci details this process in his *History of the Italian People*; a synopsis of part of his argument follows.

Beginning with Charles VIII's invasion of Italy in 1494, France and Spain fought out their battles for control of Western Europe on Italian soil, with the Italian city states as pawns in the game. On another front, the Roman Catholic church, long aligned with the Italian aristocracy, was undergoing the profound upheaval of the Protestant Reformation and the Counter-

Reformation. Yet one more threat to the stability of the aristocracy was the so-called price revolution of the latter 1500s, when vast amounts of silver imported from the Americas "acted as a solvent of existing social relations, and, gradually, as the midwife of new social groups and classes."[12]

This complicated knot of social problems, plus the simple fact that after the 1529 Treaty of Cambrai, noble men were in residence at the court instead of on the battlefield, caused noble men to withdraw into the inner court circle to explore the diversions offered there. For unlike the then tumultuous, unstable public sphere, the inner court was a controllable arena where a magnificent world of pomp and refinement providing diversion, security, and image reinforcement for the beleaguered aristocracy could be constructed.[13]

Thus, during the early 1500s, noble males gradually began to take a more active interest in the secular song style. Such a step was not easy for noblemen, due to the social stigma hitherto attached to secular song performance on their part, so a gradual process of acclimatization was necessary.[14] In part, noble men were drawn into the performing circle in the early 1500s by the far-reaching efforts of a noble woman, the prodigious Isabella d'Este (1474-1533). Isabella routinely solicited poetic offerings from noble male friends, which she then set to music and performed or else had one of her court musicians set to music.[15] Consider the following excerpts from her correspondence:

1504—Isabella d'Este to Niccolo da Correggio: "Since I want to have a canzone of Petrarch set to music, I beg of Your Excellency to select one that pleases you, and to send me the initium, along with one or two of your own verses."[16]

1505—Pietro Bembo to Isabella d'Este, including 12 of his own poems begging Isabella to perform them: "I would really like to have my verses sung by your Highness, remembering as I do the sweetness and elegance with which you sang the others on that happy evening."[17]

1494—Antonio Tebaldeo to Isabella d'Este: "I have seen the *strambotto* composed by Your Ladyship on the plants stripped of their foliage, and I like it very much."[18] This poem appears in Petrucci's *Book II*, but is listed as anonymously composed.

Isabella's artistic activities place her squarely in the midst of the humanist campaign to upgrade Italian poetic sensibility, based on the Petrarchan revival led by the Pietro Bembo. Creating verses subject to critical appraisal by their noble peers provided a desirable combination of national pride, diversion, and image-reinforcement for the nobility. Especially important for noble men was the supposed literary refinement and exclusiveness newly associated with the writing of verses.

There is no evidence to indicate that noble men musically *performed* the sentimental verses they so copiously poured out at this early stage—that had to wait until the "frivolous" music of the *frottola* took an analogous step up in "refinement." They did not have to wait long, for "the musicians of the early 16th century, at first Netherlands composers working in Italy

Figure 18.3 An excerpt from an early frottola (a) plain form, ca. 1460-1470) and (b) embellished form, ca. 1505. Quoted from Ernst Ferand's "Improvisation in Nine Centuries of Western Music" in *Anthology of Music* Volume 12. Used by permission of the publisher, MCA Music.

(Verdelot, Willaert, Arcadelt), cooperated with the poets in order to achieve a new style of artistic refinement and expression."[19]

It is extremely significant that the earliest composers of this new courtly style were Netherlanders, for it suggests a predisposition to "refine" the *frottola* by applying the ideal of a polyphonic texture. The Netherlands style was characterized by a level of contrapuntal complexity unknown to the homophonic *frottola*. The infiltration of the *frottola* by the "learned" contrapuntal techniques of the Netherlanders can be traced in Petrucci's publications, the result being the famed Italian madrigal, usually considered the century's sublime form of musical expression. The madrigal can be defined as a nonimprovised polyphonic piece based on the motet principle of equal, independent voice lines, through-composed, and often performed a cappella.

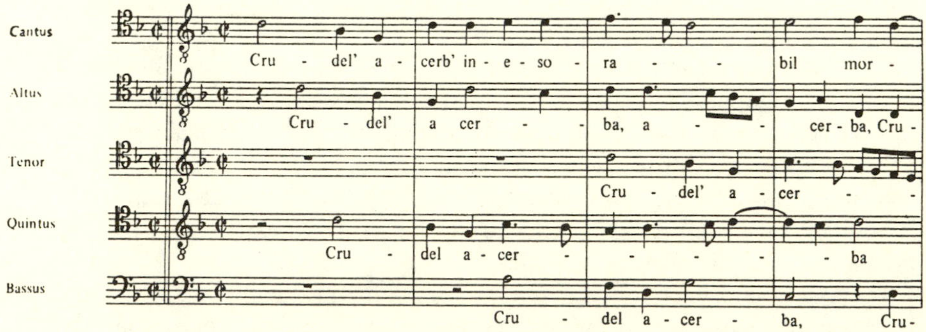

Figure 18.4 The opening of Arcadelt's madrigal of 1540, "Crudel'acerb'inesorabil morte." © Copyright 1969 by Armen Carapetyan/Hänssler-Verlag, 7303 Neuhousen-Stuttgart, Used by permission.

The displacement of the homophonic solo song style by the madrigal is described as a smooth, organic musical development by most musicologists. But Alfred Einstein uses the following vehement language: "The transition from song form to motet form about 1520 had been one of the greatest revolutions in music history. The secular counterpart of the motet, the madrigal, had as it were degraded the song forms proper, one after the other, to a less aristocratic level, the level of second-rate music."[20] To his credit, Einstein alone recognized that the transition was anything but a natural development. A revolution had, indeed, taken place, with sociocultural as well as musical implications. The social role and personnel involved in aristocratic secular music had been transformed based on the needs and aims of noble men.

The performance of the classic madrigal was decidedly reserved for men, as evidenced by the fact that "early madrigals were scored for . . . men's voices—bass, two tenors and falsetto." "The woman," Einstein observed, "is the object of all these serenades and mattinate. She takes part in them only as a listener."[21] Noblemen at last felt comfortable performing a style of music all their own, a style projected as elite, fashionable, and intricate. *"It was considered elegant to follow one's part in a complex ensemble, more elegant, certainly, than to appear as a singer to lute accompaniment."*[22] (emphasis mine). Moreover, secular music-making suddenly became, with the madrigal, a style aimed at the delectation of the *performer*, instead of the audience. Noble males saw themselves as subjects in the artistic process, not as entertaining objects to be observed and admired, which is how they perceived women musicians. And so, the role of the audience was altogether dispensed with, as men entertained themselves and each other in the activity of performing. (A new cultural institution in Italy, the musical academy, was developed during this time. The music academies brought together noble males and professional male musicians for musical discussions and performances—women were not allowed, except in rare, token instances. I consider the musical academy to have been a setting contrived by aristocratic men who wished to enjoy some of the diversions and atmosphere of the inner court circle without the presence of women.)

Skill at sight-reading and part-singing was assumed in madrigal performance, as well as vertical improvisation (not to be confused with the linear improvisation of embellishments and diminutions found in the solo song style). Vertical improvisation involved adding yet another voice to a contrapuntal texture or using one voice of a madrigal as a *cantus firmus* and adding other voices to it.[23]

While men were cultivating the classic madrigal, what were women doing, musically speaking? They continued to develop the solo song forms, just as they had before the motet principle and noble men invaded secular song, bringing the spotlight of history along with them. In the 1520s and 1530s, women added to their repertoires reductions of contrapuntal madrigals, arranged for solo voice and lute accompaniment. Unfortunately, we have no clear record of innovations made by women musicians during these

Figure 18.5 "A mente counterpoint" by Gioseffo Zarlino. A canon at the unison on a plainsong melody. The procedure is the same as the 16th-century technique of adding improvised lines to one of the voices of a madrigal. Quoted from Ernst Ferand's "Improvisation in Nine Centuries of Western Music" in *Anthology of Music* Volume 12. Used by permission of the publisher, MCA Music.

years, since their improvised performances were seldom, if ever, notated.

We do know that in the evolution of musical style, homophonic textures were the wave of the future, to be the dominant texture in Western secular music from 1600 to the present. The classic madrigal, in Einstein's judgment an "aberration, a deviation from the natural course of development initiated by the frottola," was destined to give way sooner or later to the reassertion of the homophonic principle.[24] The first signs of a reversal in the polyphonic trend crop up in midcentury, when a few male composers (e.g., Willaert) experimented with writing more "tuneful" madrigals (*madrigali ariosi*), in which "musical interest was not centered on the interplay of equal voices but rather in the progress of a melodic upper voice placed against a harmonic background.[25] In effect these composers were applying the ideal of the homophonic song forms to the polyphonic texture of the madrigal. Other significant features of the women's solo style were soon incorporated into the written madrigal—virtuoso vocal display and intricate melodic embellishment, both of which automatically undermine the equal-voice ideal of the madrigal.[26] In view of women's traditional expertise in the solo song style, it is not surprising that they entered the madrigal scene as performers at precisely the same time that the key elements of their song style were creeping into the written madrigal. Women's crossover into the polyphonic style is evident in rising vocal registers and new scorings for mixed voices in manuscripts from the 1550s onward. At this crossroads, Tarquinia Molza enters the picture.

TARQUINIA MOLZA'S MUSICAL CAREER

Tarquinia Molza was, predictably, proficient at playing the viola da mano, clavier, and lute and improvising verses to her own accompaniment as part of her socialization into the noble female role. However, there is evidence to suggest that unlike most women of her time, Molza also studied contrapuntal theory. One of her earliest biographers, Domenico Vandelli, wrote in 1750:

As a child, Tarquinia began to learn music for enjoyment, and as a diversion from her more serious studies, such that in the briefest time, she surpassed by far all of the women who had sung to great acclaim. . . .

She acquired control of her voice according to the true rules from books, not by memorizing the words of masters in the art, some of whom had the laudable desire to be able to show her something unusual in this profession. These were, among others, Giaches Wert, Luzzascho Luzzaschi and Orazio [della Viola[27]] on which instrument [*viola bastarda*[28]] she used to musically play one part, uniting to it another part with her voice. She did this with such skill and knowledge that one could not hope for better.[29]

For Vandelli to specify Molza's ability to skillfully "play one part, uniting it to another part with her voice" is to refer to the *polyphonic style*. For the art of providing accompaniment for solo songs was referred to in sixteenth-century documents as *cantando al liuto* ("singing to the lute") or *accompanandosi* ("accompanying oneself"). Moreover, the musicians he lists were all associated with the polyphonic style—Wert and Luzzaschi as madrigalists and della Viola as a virtuoso on the *viola bastarda* and famous for his madrigal transcriptions and contrapuntal improvisations.[30]

If Molza was in fact an expert in the techniques of both the solo song style (learned as part of her enculturation into the noble female role) and the contrapuntal style (learned from books and from interactions with established male musicians), then her contribution to the music of the late Renaissance becomes clear. She actively aided in synthesizing two distinct

Figure 18.6 (a) four measures of Cipriano de Rore's widely popular madrigal "Anchor che co'l partire," with two ornamented lines by dalla Casa (b and c). The last was intended for performance on the *viola bastarda*. From *Embellishing Sixteenth Century Music* by Howard Mayer Brown (1976). By permission of Oxford University Press.

musical traditions, solo and contrapuntal. The result of this synthesis was the so-called luxuriant madrigal, understood to be "the most significant [development] in the history of the style of the madrigal during the 1580s."[31] The luxuriant style represented the final stage in the breakdown of the equal-voice madrigal, for it involved simultaneous diminution of the rhythmic values of several voices, those diminutions eventually being employed in a thematic way.[32]

Musicians involved in developing this new style would necessarily have to be well-schooled in the solo song style practices (i.e., linear improvisation), and the polyphonic style (note-reading, rules of harmony, vertical improvisation). As we have seen, Molza appears to have provided herself with precisely this training.

One puzzling feature of historial accounts of the *concerto delle donne* is

Figure 18.7 An excerpt from a madrigal in the luxuriant style, "O dolcezze amarissime d'amore," by Luzzasco Luzzaschi, court organist at Ferrara. From Luzzaschi's "Madrigali per cantare e sonare. . . ." Used by permission of Bärenreiter-Verlag.

that, after her arrival at court in 1583, Molza is never explicitly mentioned as a *performer* with that ensemble but as a respected singer and instrumentalist known to have played some significant role in the group. Her absence from the roster of singing ladies can now be reasonably explained by assuming that she organized and taught the trio of women musicians who caused such a stir, passing on to them a unique approach to the stylistic problems related to simultaneous improvisation. We know these women rehearsed from two to six hours daily and that they succeeded in deeply impressing musically astute listeners as is reflected in the following excerpt from a letter written by composer Alessandro Striggio to his patron in 1584:

This *concerto delle donne* is truly exceptional. [a] *These ladies sing excellently both with instruments and from partbooks, and they are sure in improvisation.* [b] *The Duke showed me in writing all the works which they improvise upon, with all the runs and passages that they do.* (Emphasis mine; see discussion below) I hope that your excellency will soon permit me to return to Mantova . . . and there I will be able to compose more easily some pieces for Your Highness' ensemble, in imitation of these songs of Ferrara.[33]

This is but one example of the many encomia directed to the women by professional musicians, several of whom profess a desire to imitate the ladies' style, while others attest to the wondrous changes wrought in their own madrigals by the women's innovative improvisations. But every musicologist commenting on this phenomenon insists that the women's influence was limited to their virtuosic ability in singing runs and embellishments at sight, thus inspiring composers to supply them with repertoire. To support this theory, otherwise astute scholars pass on astonishing examples of faulty translation and misinterpretation. Consider, for instance, two lines from Striggio's letter in the original Italian:

[a] Quelle Signore cantano eccellentement et nel loro conserto [*sic*] e a libro, e alimproviso son sicure.

[b] Il Sig. Duca mi favorisse di continuo di mostrarme in scritto tutte le oppere che cantano a la mente, con tutte le tirate e passaggi che vi fanno.

The operative words here are *alimproviso* and *a la mente*, which in *modern* Italian usage mean "impromptu" and "by memory," respectively. But in sixteenth-century Italian, as used by Striggio, both words were meant to describe the women's proficiency at *contrapuntal improvisation*. Definitive proof is supplied by Ernest Ferand, on the basis of his exhaustive study of sixteenth-century musical treatises:

The most widely accepted term by which the entire practice of improvised counterpoint became known, especially in Italy, was *contrappunto a mente*, or *alla mente* . . . , literally "mental counterpoint". . . . In Italian treatises, the singing of counterpoint was referred to as *contrapuntizzare*, and it could be performed *alla sprorovveduta, all'improviso, al'improvista, de improviso,* . . .[34]

"Alimproviso" and "ala mente," therefore, were both terms for contrapuntal improvisation.

That musicologists over the centuries have assumed that the Ladies of Ferrara were imitative rather than creative musicians becomes painfully clear from translations of the above passages by two of the most meticulous scholars in the field. Anthony Newcombe mistakenly translates "alimproviso" as "without rehearsal," then adds a semicolon and passes over a comma in the original, so that his translation reads:

[a] Those ladies sing excellently; both when singing in their *concerto* (from memory) and when singing at sight from part books they are secure.

[b] The Duke favored me continually by showing me written out all the pieces that they sing by memory, with all the diminutions [*tirate e passaggi*] that they do.[35]

Alfred Einstein properly translates "alimproviso son sicure" as "they are sure-footed in improvisation," but he reveals his bias in the next line of the letter, when he takes "a la mente" to mean rote memory:

[b] The Duke . . . show(ed) me in manuscript everything that they sing by heart.[36]

Perhaps Einstein was misled by the information that Duke Alfonso presented his visitor with a book containing the women's repertoire—surely an impossibility if the music were improvised. But no, the existence of such a book does not undermine the fundamentally improvisatory nature of the women's work. As the theorist Vincentino advised in 1555 in his paradoxically entitled chapter "Modo di comporre alla mente sopra i canti fermi" (How to compose extemporaneously upon a cantus firmus"):

[Even in a well-prepared group] the true counterpoint—or rather the true composition—will be one in which all the voices that are sung *alla mente* are written down.[37]

Apparently it was a highly regarded practice during this period to write down previously improvised parts, in order to study them or to work out problems—problems of simultaneous diminution in the case of the women of Ferrara.[38]

The Ladies of Ferrara were also famous for their renditions of currently popular madrigals, but again, scholars claim their reputation was won by vocal quality and sight-singing ability, whereas eyewitnesses credit their creative use of improvisatory techniques. Paolo Virchi, court organist, in the dedication of his *First Book of Madrigals a 5* to Duke Alfonso II, in 1584, wrote

I do not attribute [the success of my madrigals] so much to my own artifice as to the sweetness of the voices of the Illustrious Ladies who sing them, who, with a marvelous new approach (*dispositione*) and in a new way—not fully understood—of diminutions and ornamentation, easily increase the pleasure of my music, so that I am not equal to their reputation for such excellence.[39]

In this gracious and matter-of-fact way, Virchi confirms our premise that the women of Ferrara were independently creative musicians with a genuinely avant-garde aura. By extension, he also gives weight to Ernest Ferand's rarely honored exhortation:

> In the vocal and instrumental music of [the Renaissance and early Baroque] we have . . . a practice in which . . . the performer's contribution often exceeded that of the composer. It should never be forgotten that the compositions of that time that have come down to us in manuscript or print often present only a pale outline of how they actually sounded, and that the composers themselves often considered it to be their task merely to sketch their work on paper, to present a skeleton and to leave the details of clothing it to the performing singers or players.[40]

Thus, the *concerto di donne* of Ferrara, with Tarquinia Molza as its mentor, contributed much more to sixteenth-century music than lovely stage presence and coloratura voices. They actively effected a synthesis between two distinct musical styles.

To recapitulate, the use of untapped historical documents and the reinterpretation of familiar material have led to these conclusions:

- Tarquinia Molza was instructed in the art of solo singing, including linear improvisation (diminution and embellishment) as part of her training into the noble female role.
- In addition, Molza learned contrapuntal theory and vertical improvisation, considered the preserve of males.
- At the court of Ferrara, Molza was involved in developing a style of music that employed simultaneous improvised diminution in a contrapuntal setting—a synthesis of contrapuntal and solo song styles known as the "luxuriant madrigal."
- Tarquinia Molza taught and guided the Ladies of Ferrara, whose public improvisations in this new style excited well-known male composers to imitate them in written compositions.

CORROBORATIVE EVIDENCE: PATRIZI'S MANUSCRIPT

Having reached this point in my research in 1979, I was to some extent confronting an impasse. On the one hand, the process had yielded sensible solutions to recurring contradictions in the scholarship on this period. On the other hand, the amount of supporting documentation was minimal, given the dearth of published information about women and the prohibitive distance of Italian archives and libraries. Especially lacking was further corroboration of Tarquinia Molza's involvement in the contrapuntal style, a critical link in the chain. Imagine, then, the excitement I felt when I stumbled upon the priceless document *L'Amorosa filosofia*, written by Molza's good friend Francesco Patrizi when she was 35 years old and still residing in Modena.

Patrizi had known Molza since she was a child, and in 1577 he set down a detailed, though unfinished, account of her personality, appearance, philosophical theories, and musical practice. Since Patrizi's manuscript was neither revised nor published in his lifetime, it is remarkably free from the conventional flattery that distorts much biographical writing of the Renaissance. The original manuscript gathered dust in the library of Parma until 1963, when it was edited and published in the original Italian by John Charles Nelson, a scholar interested only in those parts of the text dealing with philosophy. Nelson's interest was in Patrizi himself and in Platonic philosophy; he was unbelievably supercilious regarding Molza's philosophical views as aired in the manuscript and passed over the detailed references to her musicality with the words, "her musical ability cannot be easily documented." And so this document escaped the notice of musicologists for 15 years, while it circulated lamely among philosophers and academics. Finally, in 1978, two self-described "musical dilettanti," Anna Martellotti and Elio Durante, brought Patrizi's work to the attention of musicologists. In their brilliantly insightful book, *Cronistoria del Concerto*, they used Patrizi's account to accurately assess Tarquinia Molza's guiding role in the work of the *concerto delle donne*, although they did not recognize the significance of her knowledge of counterpoint. The following are excerpts from Patrizi's manuscript—his first-hand observations of Tarquinia Molza's education and musical practice.

Education

Cavalier Camillo [Tarquinia's father] kept a certain Don Politiani at the house, a man of rare goodness, and learned in Latin, Greek, and Hebrew, and entrusted to him the care of his sons [*figli maschi*]. Tarquinia, along with her sisters, was set to the feminine pursuit of needlework by their mother, an exercise she used to flee from whenever she could. Tarquinia so longed to hold a book in her hand—even before she knew her alphabet—to look at when her mother wasn't present, that she smuggled one to hide under her mantle—a little girl who didn't yet know her ABC's! She was caught many times in this noble thievery, both by her mother (who disapproved of it), and by her father (who took infinite delight in it). And Tarquinia so pleaded with her father to let Don Giovanni teach her along with her brothers that he just had to give in to her charms. . . . Thus, while still a young girl, she showed such a lively intellect that she effortlessly learned all of the reading and grammar taught her by her instructor, and surpassed, not only her brothers, but all the others who also came there to learn.

Tarquinia's father and teacher died within a short time of each other, and Tarquinia, again under the authority of her mother, gave up the studies and books to which she was so strongly drawn, and attended to those activities of home and self that young ladies engage in. She occupied herself in this fashion for five years, until she was married.[41]

What a difference there is between this compelling eyewitness report and the romantic claims of historians that women and men had equal access to education in the Renaissance![42] The two brothers with whom Molza begged to study were both *younger* than she—their education was considered a birthright, hers a fond concession to a charmingly persistent child. The formal education Molza fought so hard for was brought to an end upon the death of her father when she was only 13 years old. Patrizi goes on to inform us that she picked up her studies again of her own accord ("with her husband's permission") five years after her marriage, and at that time secured teachers for herself.[43]

Patrizi's observations delineate two spheres of activity within one household: a literary sphere occupying the male children, presided over by the father; and a female domestic sphere presided over by the mother. Tarquinia Molza's refusal to be relegated to the domestic sphere as a young child was but the first of the crossovers she was to make into the public sphere—an act she invariably accomplished with the persistence and brilliance that marked her early, hard-won education.

Musical Training

It happened one day that Cesarino came upon Tarquinia sitting by the fire, singing some poem or other by Petrarch as a song, which she knew how to do. Upon hearing the sweetness of her voice, the placement, the grace of her control, he was astounded, and wanted her to learn to sing in all ways.

And so, unknown to her husband, he began to teach her. And not a month had passed before she was singing securely everything he had shown her. Then she was found out by her husband, but when he saw the effect, he was happy to have her continue. She succeeded so incredibly that within three months she was accomplished enough to sing by note, effortlessly and gracefully, any music whatsoever that they place in front of her, no matter how difficult and embellished it might be.[44]

What could be more clear? At a point when she was already proficient at singing improvised verses, probably to her own accompaniment, Molza's ability so impressed a male musician that he insisted on teaching her another style of music—an undertaking so unconventional that she had to hide her efforts from her husband! But Patrizi wants there to be no mistaking the fact that this extraordinary woman was indeed engaged in two different styles of music. So he deluges us with endless fascinating details, the following of which is only a sampling:

No woman has a voice so sweet and round in singing, nor such pleasing of every manner of trills, runs, and diminutions. Neither is any woman so secure in any difficult composition, nor able to sing so angelically to the lute, to play the bass on the viola and sing the soprano at the same time, nor to so understand counterpoint and the art in its entirety.[45]

And she does many things excellently—not through mere practice, nor because they were shown her by her teachers, as is the case with women who sing nowadays . . . ,

> but rather due to her marvelous and unusual ear, which detects both errors and excellence, however minute, and due to her accomplished knowledge of counterpoint. In evidence of this last is the counterpoint I saw which she superimposed on Cipriano's famous madrigal "Anchorche col partire."[46]

> One day Pietro Vinci arrived while she was singing some of his madrigals, and stationing himself rather far away where he could listen with careful attention, onlookers saw him raise his hands to heaven . . . , weeping from the sweetness of it. And when she finished singing, he rushed to embrace her, saying, "Oh, my child, I thank God and you for giving me the consolation of hearing my works sung as I never would have thought I should, or could, hear them." And he spoke many words in this fashion, thus testifying to the elements of her singing style.[47]

Patrizi's manuscript breaks off after 94 pages, the last dated 27 August 1577—six years before Molza's arrival at the court of Ferrara. But although we are sadly deprived of his observations of her career at court, Patrizi does describe Molza's introductory performance for Alfonso II d'Este, her eventual patron, in 1568. Note well the references made to two entirely different areas of expertise: singing a contrapuntal madrigal, and solo performance to her own accompaniment of a poem by Petrarch.

> On that occasion, His Highness wanted to hear her perform some difficult madrigals of Vincio in the company of the top musicians of his *cappella*. In that test, everyone else missed certain passages, while she held firm and sustained (her note) so as to give the others a chance to recover. And so the Duke, after reproving his musicians, praised her, saying that he had never heard anywhere a more secure part than hers.[48]

> But there is nothing to be heard in the whole world that is more sweet, wonderful and divine, than her singing to lute accompaniment. This singing amazed Duke Alfonso and Duchess Barbara. . . . Signora Tarquinia sang various things for them, but the Duke's very favorite was Petrarch's sonnet "Hor ch'il ciel," which—because of the wonder he found in it—he had her repeat four to six more times.[49]

Before this episode occurred, Alfonso II had taken no particular interest in music, his activities being generally of a more "manly" sort: horsemanship, arms, ball-playing, alchemy. He did maintain the usual *cappella di musica*, which supplied music for court functions, but the soprano parts in all cases were taken by males, whether young boys, falsettists, or castrati.[50] No wonder, then, that Alfonso was intrigued by the novelty of Molza's range, expertise, and innovations. Durante and Martellotti suggest that it was precisely the experience of hearing Molza that sparked Alfonso's interest in female singing practice of a particular, highly innovative kind. In the succeeding two decades, Alfonso energetically promoted women singers, to the point where his involvement was deemed almost obsessive by his noble peers. The "Ladies of Ferrara" became renowned throughout Italy and beyond, at first due to their performances within the female accompanied song style, and then, after Tarquinia Molza's arrival in 1583, as innovators of the "luxuriant madrigal" style, which combined solo and contrapuntal techniques.

IMPLICATIONS FOR MUSIC HISTORY

This brief analysis of the secular music scene in sixteenth-century Italy is neither polished nor fully documented. We still know too little about the standards for the solo song style and how they were determined, details of the linear improvisation practice, the identities of the women who were masters of that style, the reactions of female musicians to the "madrigal revolution" of the 1520s, and much more.

It is possible that after further investigation we will conclude that Western music history between the mid-fifteenth and the seventeenth centuries formed a continuum held together by women, based on the development of the homophonic ideal of a single expressive line supported by functional harmonies—a continuum broken for a few years by the interloping madrigal. "The madrigal is artificial," wrote Einstein, "in every sense of the term: in its origins, its practice, and as a work of art."[51] But because Einstein did not apply gender as an analytical category, he was at a loss to explain the phenomenon he so rightly observed regarding the madrigal, simply marvelling "strange are the ways of history!"[52] Strange, indeed, are the ways of a historical process that ignores the contributions of half the population, then wonders why the results seem patchy! How, then, shall we answer Susan B. Anthony's haunting question? Why *do* history's pages glow with the names of illustrious men while a woman appears only here and there? Here is Gerda Lerner's reply: "Women have been left out of history not because of the evil conspiracies of men in general or male historians in particular, but because we have considered history only in male-centered terms. We have missed women and their activities, because we have asked questions of history that are inappropriate to women."[53]

Tarquinia Molza's life and career amply fortify Lerner's words. Reams of untapped resources, like Patrizi's manuscript, are waiting in libraries and archives all over the world, ready to give up their secrets in response to the appropriate questions. We have finally achieved the ability to conceptualize a history of women and men; there remains now only our happy responsibility to give it substance. *Avanti*!

NOTES

1. Susan B. Anthony, speech entitled "The True Woman," delivered in 1857, autograph housed at the Schlesinger Library, Radcliffe College, Cambridge, Massachusetts.

2. "*Concertante*: music that is in some sense soloistic, with a contrasting element, or "concerto-like." In the Baroque period it was sometimes used, more or less interchangeably with *concertato*, to describe a group of mixed musical forces, generally vocal and instrumental or comprising a larger ensemble and a smaller one." *The New Grove Dictionary of Music and Musicians*, ed. Stanley Sadie, vol. 4 (London: Macmillan, 1980), p. 625.

3. Gerda Lerner, *The Majority Finds Its Past: Placing Women in History* (New

York: Oxford University Press, 1979), p. 172.

4. Tarquinia Molza was indeed dismissed from court due to her relationship with the brilliant and cultured musician Giaches de Wert. However, Tarquinia insisted that their relationship was warm friendship ("I confided in him," she is quoted as saying), and that rumors of a supposed love affair were mere gossip circulated by a certain "Vittorio" out of professional jealousy. (See A. Ramazzini, "I musici fiamminghi alla corte di Ferrara, Giaches Wert e Tarquinia Molza," in *Archivio Storico Lombardo*, 6, 1879). Tarquinia's defense is supported by a brief note recently unearthed from the archives by Durante and Martellotti. The note was written by a courtier named Alfonso Fontanelli to a friend on 11 November 1589: "Signora Tarquinia is leaving court, dismissed by His Highness, and Vittorio remains here in that same lord's service—so that, on all accounts, the Signora's case grieves me." (E. Durante and A. Martellotti, *Cronistoria del Concerto delle Donne Principalissime di Margherita Gonzaga d'Este* [Florence: Studio per edizione scelte, 1979], p. 185.)

5. Alfred Einstein, *The Italian Madrigal*, vol. 1 (Princeton, N.J.: Princeton University Press, 1949), p. 110.

6. Ruth Kelso, *Doctrine for the Lady of the Renaissance* (Urbana: University of Illinois Press, 1956), p. 223.

7. Einstein, *The Italian Madrigal*, p. 50.

8. Baldassare Castiglione, *The Book of the Courtier*, trans. Charles S. Singleton (Garden City: Doubleday, 1959), p. 210.

9. It must be noted that comments of this sort reveal more about the perceptions and determinations of the male author than they do about the talent and aspirations of the female artist. Further illustrating this point is a letter written by Abraham Mendelssohn to his daughter Fanny in 1820, when she was 15 years old: "Music will perhaps become [your brother Felix's] profession, while for *you* it can and must be only an ornament, never the root of your being and doing. . . . [It] does you credit that you have always shown yourself good and sensible in these matters. . . . Remain true to these sentiments and to this line of conduct; they are feminine, and only what is truly feminine is an ornament to your sex." Despite this energetic discouragement of her talent, Fanny continued to compose, and three published pieces in Felix's Opus 8 and three in his Opus 9 were actually written by Fanny. See *Women in Music: An Anthology of Source Readings from the Middle Ages to the Present*, ed. Carol Neuls-Bates (New York: Harper and Row, 1982), p. 143.

10. Castiglione, *The Book of the Courtier*, p. 75.

11. See George Conklin, *Aspects of Renaissance Culture* (Middletown, Conn.: Wesleyan University Press, 1953), p. 155.

12. Giuliano Procacci, *History of the Italian People*, trans. Anthony Paul (London: Weidenfeld and Nicolson, 1970), pp. 105, 117.

13. For further development of these points, including a description of a remarkably similar phenomenon in sixteenth-century Java, see Joanne Riley, "The Influence of Women on Secular Vocal Music in Sixteenth Century Italy: the Life and Career of Tarquinia Molza" (Masters thesis, Wesleyan University, 1980) pp. 35-41, 101.

14. A pathetic example of one courtier's difficulties in adjusting to the new role can be found in the case of Signor Giulio Cesare Brancaccio, an ex-military man with a superb bass voice who was called into the service of Duke Alfonso of Ferrara. From the archives:

[Letter of February 1581] The Duke accepted Signor Brancaccio into his service principally to enjoy his singing ability. Before [Brancaccio] arrived here, the Duke made a pact with him not to talk about things of war, but I don't believe he was informed that he would serve as a musician—and perhaps he doesn't, since he only performs in private in the company of ladies.

[June 1581] Signor Brancaccio always takes part in these entertainments, and is generally good enough about it. However, I know that at certain times it profoundly bothers him—especially that time when Cardinal Farnese was here, since not only the Cardinal but also his entire court attended the performance. Brancaccio tried to take comfort in the fact that on such occasions the Duke introduces him with the words, "and would Signor Giulio Cesare also care to do us the honor—??" and allows him to remain seated when he sings.

[August 1583] The arrival here of the Duke of Joyeuse has caused the departure of Signor Brancaccio. Duke Alfonso had already lost patience with him and his ways, because Brancaccio always wanted to discuss war topics, to the Duke's annoyance. . . . Now, during the visit of the Duke of Joyeuse, the Duke wanted Brancaccio to sing in the company of the ladies as usual (that being the reason he took him into his service). But Brancaccio resolutely refused to do it, and so, after Monsignor de Joyeuse had left, he was fired. (Archival excerpts in the original Italian in Durante and Martellotti, pp. 140, 161f.)

15. Certain professional male musicians, such as Marco Cara, Bartolommeo Tromboncino, Giovanni Testagrossa and others, were involved and influential in the solo singing style. Their numbers were few compared to the numbers of women involved in the style, but they received virtually all of the public recognition because they had been designated "professional" musicians.

16. Walter Rubsamen, *Literary Sources of Secular Vocal Music in Italy ca. 1500* (New York: Da Capo Press, 1943), p. 24.

17. Einstein, p. 552.

18. Ibid., p. 44.

19. Willi Apel, *The Harvard Dictionary of Music* (Cambridge: Harvard University Press, 1972), p. 497.

20. Einstein, *The Italian Madrigal*, p. 552.

21. Ibid., p. 182.

22. Ibid., p. 153.

23. Ernest Ferand, "Improvised Vocal Counterpoint in the Late Renaissance and Early Baroque" in *Annales Musicologiques*, vol. 4, 1956, p. 132.

24. Einstein, *The Italian Mdrigal*, p. 153.

25. Anthony Newcombe, *The Madrigal at Ferrara 1579-1597*, vol. 1 (Princeton, N.J.: Princeton University Press, 1980), p. 18.

26. Ibid., pp. 48, 49.

27. Orazio della Viccola is one of the appellations of Orazio Bassano, also known as Orazio della Viola, ?1540-?1609. See Newcombe, *The Madrigal*, p. 194.

28. "*Viola bastarda*: an Italian 16th and early 17th century term for a small bass viol especially suitable for improvising rapid passage-work. Since its compass was so large, it was not limited to carrying a single line, but could skip from voice to voice of a polyphonic composition." *The New Grove Dictionary*, vol. 19, p. 814.

29. Domenico Vandelli, "Vita di Tarquinia Molza detta L'Unica" in P. Serassi *Delle poesie volgari e latine di Francesco Maria Molza*, vol. 2 (Bergamo: Lancellotti, 1750), p. 7.

30. *The New Grove Dictionary*, vol. 2, p. 253.

31. Newcombe, *The Madrigal*, p. 49.

32. Ibid., p. 78.

33. Durante and Martellotti, *Cronistoria del Concerto*, pp. 164-5.

34. Ferand, "Improvised Vocal Counterpoint in the Late Renaissance and Early Baroque," p. 141.

35. Newcombe, *The Madrigal*, p. 55.

36. Einstein, *The Italian Madrigal*, p. 846.

37. Ferand, "Improvised Vocal Counterpoint in the Late Renaissance and Early Baroque," p. 148.

38. Adriano Cavicchi, ed., *Li Madrigali per Cantare e Sonare a Uno, Due e Tre Soprani* (1601), by Luzzasco Luzzaschi (Brescia-Kassel: Barenreiter-Verlag, 1965), Preface by the editor, p. 17.

39. Durante and Martellotti, *Cronistoria del Concerto*, p. 166.

40. Ernest Ferand, "Improvisation in Nine Centuries of Western Music," in *Anthology of Music*, vol. 12, ed. K. G. Fellerer (Cologne: Arno Volk Verlag Koln, 1961), p. 13.

41. Francesco Patrizi, *L'amorosa filosofia*, ed. John Charles Nelson (Florence: Felice Le Monnier, 1963), pp. 18-19, 60.

42. Historian Jacob Burckhardt sets forth the standard misperception of a supposedly utopian equality between men and women in this period, in his classic *The Civilization of the Renaissance in Italy* (New York: Random House, 1954), p. 294. He writes: "There was no question of 'women's rights' or 'emancipation' simply because the thing itself was a matter of course. The educated woman of that time strove, exactly like the man, after a characteristic and complete individuality. The same intellectual and emotional development that perfected the man was demanded for the woman."

43. Patrizi, *L'amorosa filosofia*, p. 60.

44. Ibid., p. 38.

45. Ibid., p. 40.

46. Ibid., p. 41.

47. Ibid., p. 38.

48. Ibid., p. 38.

49. Ibid., p. 42.

50. Durante and Martellotti, *Cronistoria del Concerto*, p. 52.

51. Einstein, *The Italian Madrigal*, p. 153.

52. Ibid.

53. Lerner, *The Majority Finds Its Past*, p. 178.

BIBLIOGRAPHY

Apel, Willi. *Harvard Dictionary of Music*. Cambridge: Harvard University Press, 1972.

Brown, Howard. *Music in the Renaissance*. Prentice-Hall, 1976.

Burckhardt, Jacob. *The Civilization of the Renaissance in Italy*. New York: Random House, 1954.

Castiglione, Baldassare. *The Book of the Courtier*. Translated by Charles S. Singleton. Garden City: Doubleday, 1959.

Cavicchi, Adriano, ed. Luzzasco Luzzaschi, *Li Madrigali per Cantare e Sonare a Uno, Due e Tre Soprani* (1601). Preface by the editor, pp. 7-23. Brescia-Kassel: Bärenreiter-Verlag, 1965.

Conklin, George N. *Aspects of Renaissance Culture.* Middletown, Conn.: Wesleyan University Press, 1953.

Durante, Elio and Anna Martellotti. *Cronistoria del Concerto delle Donne Principalissime di Margherita Gonzaga d'Este.* Florence: Studio per edizioni scelte, 1979.

Einstein, Alfred. *The Italian Madrigal.* Princeton, N.J.: Princeton University Press, 1949.

Ferand, Ernest. "Improvised Vocal Counterpoint in the Late Renaissance and Early Baroque," in *Annales Musicologiques,* vol. 4, 1956.

______. "Improvisation in Nine Centuries of Western Music," in *Anthology of Music,* vol. 12. ed. K. G. Fellerer. Cologne: Arno Volk Verlag Koln, 1961.

Kelso, Ruth. *Doctrine for the Lady of the Renaissance.* Urbana: University of Illinois Press, 1956.

Lerner, Gerda. *The Majority Finds Its Past: Placing Women in History.* New York: Oxford University Press, 1979.

Luzzaschi, Luzzasco. *Li Madrigali per Cantare e Sonare a Uno, Due e Tre Soprani* (1601). Edited by Adriano Cavicchi. Brescia-Kassel: Bärenreiter-Verlag, 1965.

MacClintock, Carol. *Giaches Wert (1535-1596): Life and Works.* American Institute of Musicology, Neuhausen-Stuttgart: Hanssler-Verlag, 1966.

Molza, Giovanna Jana. *Alfonso II d'Este e Torquato Tasso nella vita di Tarquinia Molza.* Modena: S.T.E.M.-Mucchi, 1971.

Neuls-Bates, Carol, ed. *Women in Music: An Anthology of Source Readings from the Middle Ages to the Present.* New York: Harper and Row, 1982.

Newcombe, Anthony. *The Madrigal at Ferrara 1579-1597,* vol. 1. Princeton, N.J.: Princeton University Press, 1980.

Patrizi, Francesco. *L'amorosa filosofia.* Edited by John Charles Nelson. Florence: Felice Le Monnier, 1963.

Procacci, Giuliano. *History of the Italian People.* Translated by Anthony Paul. London: Weidenfeld and Nicolson, 1970.

Rammazzini, A. "I musici fiamminghi alla corte di Ferrara, Giaches Wert e Tarquinia Molza." In *Archivio Storico Lombardo VI,* 1879.

Reese, Gustav. *Music in the Renaissance.* London: W. W. Norton, 1954.

Rubsamen, Walter. *Literary Sources of Secular Vocal Music in Italy ca. 1500.* New York: Da Capo Press, 1943.

Solerti, Angelo. "Ferrara e la corte Estense nella seconda meta del secolo decimosesto." In *I Discorsi di Annibale Romei Gentiluomo Ferrarese,* Citta di Castello, 1900.

Vandelli, Domenico. "Vita di Tarquinia Molza detta l'Unica." In P. Serassi, *Delle poesie volgari e latine di Francesco Maria Molza* vol. 2. Bergamo: Lancellotti, 1750.

Wert, Giaches. *Collected Works.* Edited by Carol MacClintock. American Institute of Musicology, Neuhausen-Stuttgart: Hanssler-Verlag, 1968.

DISCOGRAPHY

The following discography, by no means exhaustive, represents a variety of stylistic approaches to the music of Tarquinia Molza's era.

Anthologie Sonore Vol. 2, Record 3 "The Italian Madrigal at the End of the Renaissance." Luca Marenzio Ensemble. Reissue Everest 3179.

The Art of Ornamentation in the Renaissance and Baroque. Bach Guild HM-47-8.

Bartolommeo Tromboncino: Frottole. The Consort of Musicke. Decca DSLO 593.

Claudio Monteverdi: Madrigals. Raymond Leppard, con. Philips 670305, 679906, 6747416.

Claudio Monteverdi: Selected Works. Nadia Boulanger, cond. Angel COLH 20.

Court Music of the 16th Century. Nonesuch 71012.

Ecco la Primavera. Early Music Consort of London. London ST S-15583.

A Florentine Festival: Music for Ferdinand de Medici. Musica Reservata, Argo ZRG 602.

Giaches Wert: Music from the Court of Mantua. Denis Stevens, dir. Vanguard VCS 10083.

Historical Anthology of Music. Bach Guild 1972-.

History of Music: Middle Ages to Baroque. 3-Lyr 7278.

History of Music in Sound; Archiv Production. RCA-DGG.

Instruments of the Middle Ages and the Renaissance. 2-Ang SZ 3810.

Italia Mia: Songs and Dances of the Italian Renaissance. Waverly Consort. CBS 7464-36664-1.

Italian Airs and Dances (1500-1540). Argo ZRG 923.

Italian Madrigals. Abbey Singers. Decca DL 10103.

Italian Music in the Age of Exploration. Fleetwood Singers. LLST 775.

Italian Recorder Music. Tel 642335.

Italian Songs, Sixteenth and Seventeenth Centuries. Reissue Westminster 9611.

Italienische Frottolen der Renaissance. Monterosso, cond. Candide-Vox CEC 1017.

La Mantovana: Italian Airs and Dances of the Early Baroque. London Early Music Group. Nonesuch 71392.

L'Amfiparnasso. Deller Consort, Collegium Aureum. Harmonia Mundi 1CO-65-99816.

The Late Sixteenth Century: Parts 1 and 2. Pleides 255, 256.

Madrigals of Luzzasco Luzzaschi. Five Centuries Ensemble. Italia ITL 70050.

Monteverdi's Contemporaries. Early Music Consort of London. Ang-S-37524.

Music at the Courts. 3-Nonesuch 73014.

Music from the Time of Boccaccio's Decameron. Musica Reservata. Philips 802904.

Music from the Time of Christopher Columbus. Musica Reservata. Philips 839714.

A Musical Banquet at the Court of the Estense. Nuova Capella Musicali. Bongiovanni GB 5001.

Orlando Lassus: Chansons. Alfred Deller. Bach SRV 298 SD.

Orlando Lassus: Madrigals. Noah Greenberg, dir. MCA 2513.

Petrucci: First Printer of Music. New York Pro Musica. Decca DL 79435.

Pleasures of the Royal Courts. Early Music Consort of London. Nonesuch 71326.

Renaissance Lutes. C. and R. Strizich. Titanic 15.

Secular Vocal Music of the Renaissance from Spain, Italy and France. Denis Stevens, dir. Dover 5262.

Seraphim Guide to Renaissance Music. 3-Seraphim S6052.

Teresa Berganza: Venetian Music for Voice and Instruments, (16th and 17th Centuries). Claves D-8206.

Virtuose Verzierungs Kunst um 1600. Schola Cantorum Basiliensis. Harmonia Mundi IC 165-99 895/96.

Vocal Music of Claudio Monteverdi. New York Pro Musica. Columbia ML5149.

19

Gender and Genre in Ethel Smyth's Operas

ELIZABETH WOOD

It is difficult to separate the creator from her compositions in the case of Dame Ethel Mary Smyth (1858-1944).[1] This is not because her operas may be less colorful, less vital, less passionate than she, but because her music—"these coherent chords, harmonies, melodies (she has spun) from her center"—is but one expression of her work.[2] Their themes and concerns echo personal and political views expressed more directly in her writings and memoirs; and she, heroic protagonist in the romantic drama of her own life, is more fascinating than are her fictional characters.

Much has been written of her, not always fondly, not always accurately.[3] She frightened and confused many critics, most of them men; the force of her affections and her rage apparently distracted them from a truthful account of her work.[4] It is also probable that her music has not received serious scholarly attention because she was a woman artist working against the enormous odds of time, place, profession, genre, and gender. She suspected her work would not have its due from the "Male Machine," arbiter of musical taste and values, until "naught remains of me but sexless dots and lines on ruled paper."[5]

English-born, she (like America's Amy Cheney Beach) has now been dead for 40 years, and many of the conditions under which women make music have changed as Smyth insisted they must and had labored and fought to ensure. Yet her own music is not heard. Her manuscripts are in the British Museum; much of her music was published although only her *Mass in D* has been reprinted; and other than some performances recorded for the British Broadcasting Company (BBC), there has been only one commercial recording, no longer current, of Sir Thomas Beecham's performance of the Overture to *The Wreckers*, one of the few operas to have been revived in recent years. Smyth's speeches, radio lectures, diaries, and many letters have yet to be published, and her nine published books are hard to find.[6]

Yet she is one of our most outstanding women composers. Her music is fresh, lively, well-made. It compares favorably with that of better-known composers of the period. While her output is quantitatively less than Edward Elgar's, she has more flair and originality than most of her British contemporaries such as Hubert Parry, Charles Stanford, Rutland Boughton, Arthur Sullivan (in his serious vein) or later composers like Arthur Bliss, Arnold Bax, Edward German or Arthur Benjamin.

She is distinctive for writing large, varied, and ambitious forms (six operas, a choral symphony, Mass, and concerto) and for attempting a range of subjects in them. *The Boatswain's Mate* and *Fête Galante* were novel operas for their time, and *The Wreckers*, if not novel in a post-Wagnerian sense, is possibly the most distinguished English opera of the twentieth century before Benjamin Britten. Smyth's other music, especially her string quartet and many lovely songs, is unjustly neglected. She set parts of several of her operas as separate choruses and orchestral pieces (not merely from overtures but sets of dances too), and her chorus, *Hey Nonny No*, to a sixteenth-century Christchurch manuscript is probably the finest, most spirited mixed chorus by any British composer. While her dramatic and theatrical gifts show best through opera, her abstract works are equally well-wrought in counterpoint that is Brahmsian in cast but with a particular rhythmic vitality and an originality of unexpected, almost daring harmonic ideas that stamp the music as her own.

Then, she is more than a gifted composer: a conductor, pianist, polemicist, brilliant writer and witty raconteur, superb friend, suffragist, feminist; an "army orphan" yet social snob whose regal or rich sponsors were chiefly women; candid lesbian when homosexuals were censored or encoded; a woman jailed and knighted; avid golfer—keening in old age for the hunt, tennis, cricket, the sports and adventures of her ardent youth. Throughout her life she shouted for recognition, hungered for her audience, and worked daily on her orchestrations in a quiet rose-filled cottage in the Surrey countryside with her sheep dogs, her solitude; deaf, lame, dressed in dull grey tweeds, "mannish" collar and tie with matching porkpie hat, thick stockings, heavy shoes like the turn-of-century mountaineer and pioneer bicyclist that she was. She weathered an extraordinary life of 86 years, navigating the shoals and scaling the peaks in a manner as romantic, as heroic, as chromatic as the very settings, plots, and counterpoint of her operas.[7]

Given both her personality and her early musical training in Leipzig from 1877, it is not surprising she was drawn to dramatic composition. Like so many of her contemporaries who studied in Germany at that time, she acquired technique from her teachers and tradition from the musical environment.[8] The genres she worked in are steeped in the conventions of German romantic drama, fantasy, and comedy. Although on her return to England early in the twentieth century she rediscovered English themes and idioms, her operas remain in that romantic tradition, and she was among the first in Britain to revive a romantic national opera through the post-

Wagnerian Celtic poetic drama movement and in vernacular chamber operetta.

She lost interest in her first opera, *Fantasio* (composed 1894-98), and made a bonfire of all the published scores she could retrieve. It had a complicated libretto adapted by her philosopher friend Henry Brewster from Alfred de Musset's story, with a through-composed setting, despite Brewster's recommendation for a number opera with spoken dialogue. Smyth's orchestration, largely self-taught, was praised then, as it often has been since.[9]

Der Wald (1901) is a romantic-magic work that belongs to the timeless spirit and folk world of Weber's *Silvana* (1812) or E.T.A. Hoffmann's *Undine* (1815), where the rites and spirits of the natural world dominate a simpler human one; in which the forest itself is the "mother" (depicted as shelter, roof, childhood playmate, mighty heart, eternal love) that nurtures, protects, and regenerates yet which has spawned evil from nature's womb. Iolanthe, Lady of the Forest, embodies both worlds: witch and whore, possessing demoniac and supernatural powers and the bold, seductive, carnal adventurousness of the woman—once betrayed—who must destroy. She, like the setting, is both terrible and beautiful; her musical motif is a troubling yet arousing hunting horn call.

The opera was a popular if not a critical success, with performances in Berlin, Covent Garden, and the New York Metropolitan Opera House.[10] The Wagnerian theme of salvation through death, of the choice of a "love that is deathless and mighty" over "life which is weak and brief," is pronounced and framed within Prologue and Epilogue choral numbers with contrapuntal chorales. Nine scenes intervene, linked by orchestral passages that reiterate melodic or rhythmic motifs from surrounding vocal numbers. Smyth contrasts dramatically her pairs of lovers (aristocratic/peasant; evil/good) through musical means: folklike simplicity in peasant chorus and dance, the poor pedlar's patter song, or pious Röschen's "Sancta Maria" as she awaits her doomed marriage to the woodsman Heinrich, contrast with florid, lyrical duets, accompanied recitative, and strophic arias for the chief characters Iolanthe and Rudolph, always unified by on- and offstage hunting motifs.

Her third opera, *The Wreckers* (1906), is her major work.[11] Henry Brewster's libretto was based on a symbolic Cornish story Smyth first heard in the Scilly Isles in 1886 and described as: "Two lovers who, by kindling secret beacons, endeavoured to counteract the savage policy of the community (that wrecks ships through the use of false lights)—how they were caught in the act by the Wreckers' Committee, a sort of secret court which was the sole authority they recognized—and condemned to die in one of those sea-invaded caves"—such as the Piper's Hole, a cave she explored on the "desperate, rugged Cornish coast where caves run out under the sea—you hear the waves over your head—the soft thunder of rocks pushed by the tide."[12]

It is a vision of the underworld. The cave engulfed by water is also a female symbol of the womb as sanctuary and as a seal of sexuality. The opera links beacons and cave, light and darkness, to religious superstition, oppression, crime, and punishment. The cave is also prison and grave. The secret, deceptive beacons that the wreckers light to lure ships on the rocks for plunder become symbols for forbidden love between Thirza, the heroine, and her lover Mark, who light safe beacons to warn approaching ships of the treacherous coast and are themselves illuminated by the dawning light of love and self-knowledge. The poetic symbolism reverses, ironically, Plato's simile of the cave for the realm of reality, by its progress from shadowy and shackled illusion to the dazzling source of enlightenment within the tomb-cave itself.[13] The symbolism is clearly Wagnerian, with its theme of self-sacrifice and redemption through an illuminating suffering. The music is often reminiscent of *Der Fliegende Holländer* (1841), with its use of leit-motif, dense contrapuntal writing, ballad arias, and large colorful orchestral forces.

There is also much in common between *The Wreckers* and *Peter Grimes* (1945).[14] Britten portrays an ambivalent outsider who becomes an outcast punished by an intolerant, hypocritical community. He puts to sea to die, for the sea is the main protagonist; it gives the opera its dramatic intensity and its musical structure. Both operas have a historical Cornish coastal setting, orchestral sea interludes, and an offstage chorus against onstage soloists. In each, the poetic drama is both desperate and dreamlike. The sea, bringer of booty, taker of life, and the reiteration of waves, dominates both scores.

Smyth's later orchestral song cycle, *Three Moods of the Sea* (1913), with its stormy or tranquil arpeggiated rhythmic patterns, belongs to the idiom of Edward Elgar's *Sea Pictures* (composed 1897-99, published 1900).[15] It was as natural for British islanders to write sea pastorals and dramatize sea imagery as it was for composers of romantic operas to depict storms, voyages, and wrecks, inspired by the nineteenth-century Gothic imagination of disaster and its preoccupation with a "bildungsroman" journey of life that pitted faith and survival against the forces of nature.

The Wreckers reveals Smyth's mature techniques. Themes announced in the Overture, including the wreckers' horn signals of warning and of hope and their quasi-liturgical pietist chorale, recur throughout in multiple melodic variations and are transformed at major dramatic moments and recapitulations. The work is dramatically sustained and impressively coherent. Orchestral passages are bridges, intermezzi, and theatrical effects that correspond to entrances, exits, and lighting or scenic changes. The chorus is an active participant in the drama. When dawn and the incoming tide begin to engulf the final cavernous scene and the superstitious community starts to falter without strong leadership, the choral lines break and cross. Orchestrally accompanied recitative and the longer lyrical solos and duets are based on speech patterns that seem to fall more naturally in German than in English. The solo voice, especially the female, meets formidable demands, tricky key and tempo changes, and thorny chromaticism, which all require considerable agility and range. Smyth insisted on the subservience of vocal considerations to dramatic necessities and terrorized her singers to keep up the lyrical flow, especially when she herself conducted.[16] This sense of driving intensity is conveyed through an ever-shifting density of texture and colorful orchestral timbres.

Her next opera, *The Boatswain's Mate* (1916), was written after Smyth's two-year stint in active suffrage service (1911-13) and is the most frequently performed of her operas, suited as it is to intimate, small-scale and even amateur production.[17] She described it as a "conversatzione" piece, but critics have been chary of the manner in which a traditional first-act ballad opera with spoken dialogue and set numbers becomes through-composed in the second act. This seems quite musically and dramatically appropriate and effective, for the second act, a parody of *opera seria*, contains the action, while the first merely introduces players, setting, and plot. There are five soloists, one of whom, the servant girl, is a speaking part, and a chorus. In comparison with all Smyth's previous operas, it is a thoroughly English chamber opera, set entirely in the interior of the Beehive Inn, presided over by a strong-willed, independent landlady, the "queen-bee" Mrs. Waters.

Like other late-nineteenth-century British domestic comedies, the cast (a former sailor, Harry Benn; former soldier, Ned Travers; and a policeman) is contrasted emphatically and humorously through literary as well as musical language.[18] The amorous plot is treated ironically and underlined by hilarious musical pastiche: folksongs, adaptations of English nursery songs ("Ding, dong, dell; pussy's in the well"), a march-spoof on the "Marche Militaire," and parody of "The Bells of Big Ben" to accompany Benn's drinking song and to introduce a tipsy chorus, which enters to a staggered canonic refrain.

There is also the time-honored burlesque tradition of introducing Smyth's own earlier music: both "The March of the Women" (1913) and her suffrage march "1910" appear in the Overture not merely to salute her most popular music but to hint at contemporary politics and feminism. For Mrs. Waters is modelled on Emmeline Pankhurst, Smyth's friend and mentor during their suffrage struggles and imprisonment.[19] Mrs. Waters "needs no man's protection" and in fact has turned man's world upside-down and is "on top" as boss of a typically working-class male domain, the English pub.[20] She outwits her suitors, who come by stealth to frighten her into submission, for, of course, they insist she needs their protection. She makes them appear ridiculous. Is it, however, merely an operatic convention that finds her in the ending coyly, coolly contemplating marriage with Travers while her maid silently smirks in approval? Or is this a mean form of revenge on an aloof, formidable Mrs. Pankhurst whose relationship with Smyth ended in argument and distrust?[21]

The chief success of this work is in the deft coordination of a contemporary "verismo" story with recognizable characters and easily identifiable music. A highlight is Travers's boastful song in strophic ballad form, where the voice repeats a passacaglia theme while the orchestra accompanies in a set of ironic, irregular rhythmic variations. Dramatic movement is maintained through reiterated fragments of themes heard first in the Overture and in subsequent vocal passages and orchestral transitions.

Her other short comedy, *Entente Cordiale* (1925), a wartime farce, was her last work for the theatre.[22] It also resembles a ballad opera in its free adaptation of traditional French folk materials and Smyth's insertion of seven bright, brittle bugle calls, which here recall her affection for her military childhood. (In contrast, the bugle call "The Last Post," cited in *The Prison* (1930), serves a more sombre, symbolic purpose).[23] This opera is also scored for a chamber ensemble with six soloists, four speaking parts, and a small soldiers' chorus. Such economy of means suited amateur or touring companies, who faced limited resources, especially in the period between the wars. Twelve musical numbers include an orchestral Overture, intermezzo, and finale, a solo song for each player, a trio, quartet, lovers' reconciliation duet, and some jaunty choral refrains. The most delightful number is Bill's patter-song portrait of an English eccentric, presumably modelled on General Smyth himself, which begins: "My father said a thing one day, that ought to be stuck in a hymn and sung, 'Unless you've something pleasant to say,' said he to the children, 'Hold your tongue' " and ends: "And if you harbour a foolish desire to be loved (falsetto voice)—*don't* be a character" (normal voice).[24]

The really disappointing aspect of this work is its total failure to realize Smyth's own call for a "new departure in British comic opera" (in her "Iron Thesis on Opera").[25] She hoped for a contemporary, realistic British opera that might renew the popularity of Savoy operetta traditions and gain a huge music-hall following. Like its Broadway contemporaries, *Entente Cordiale* too often nears banality.[26] Its topical clichés (such as a pack of oafish British "tommies" ogling a married French soubrette), its Eliza Doolittle-style cockney coarseness, and its patriotic farce routines lure the piece into the shallow backwaters of opera obsolescence. It misses simultaneously the timeless comic conventions of Gilbertian satire and the equally effective, if equally superficial, romanticism of other early-twentieth-century chamber operas of the "verismo" school of Puccini, Giordano, or Charpentier.[27]

Fête Galante (1922) is another matter.[28] It almost achieves Smyth's "new departure," as it was completed three years after Stravinsky's first neo-classical ballet, *Pulcinella* (1920) and shortly before the young William Walton's modernist satire of neo-classicism and pastiche in his setting of Edith Sitwell's poems in *Facade* (1922). Smyth embarked on a work that is genuinely neo-classical in story, scene, and form, but which retains a rich romantic style. Described as a "dance-dream," it is a one-act fantasy on "fickleness, betrayal, and love-strife" with a classical setting of a Watteau garden complete with temple (or is it Folly?), tidy hedges, marble seats, and promenades. This spacious outdoor formality reflects both the internal classical forms—dance movements such as the Sarabande, musette, and waltz, played by on- and offstage musicians and choruses—and the sense of physical distance and movement Smyth creates through acoustic effects, echoes, and spatial groupings. The rhythmic, diatonic dances accompany masquerade while cloaked puppets mime to the play-within-a-play "commedia dell-arte" characters of Pierrot, Harlequin, Colombine, and Pantaloon, watched by the "real" players, the King, Queen, and Lover with retinues and guests, all heavily disguised in cloaks and masks.[29]

Such conventions belong to the English burlesque tradition which sets transformation scenes amid ironic and amorous metamorphoses in a mimed end-harlequinade. Here, Maurice Baring's story is bitter-sweet; courtly love is mocked by Pierrot's "real" death, for only Pierrot "keeps love hidden in his heart"; but players, puppets, and audience no longer know who is player, which is play, which is "life." Dramatic ambiguity is aided by a score that includes an *a capella* setting of a madrigal by John Donne and dance music arranged from Smyth's previously published chorus, "Hey Nonny No." Much of the music sounds reminiscent of Engelbert Humperdinck's *Hansel and Gretel* (1893), with similar simple, rather sentimental, folklike melodies and orchestral whimsy.[30] However, its themes of deception and disguise, traditionally the "feminine" in art, and the contradictions between what you play and what you are, are common to most of Smyth's operas.

Just as the masks and codes of this opera are indicative of sex and gender ambiguities, the accompanying music exposes the innuendos of dissonance between theatrical fiction and reality. Until the Queen's last words to the Lover ("Think you disguise will save you? The park is full of eyes and tongues"), intermittent moonlight chases and clouds the inner subtleties and treacheries of the text, while the play-within-a-play-within-a-play simultaneously distances—through parody and deception—even as it invites gasps of recognition from among both the onstage players and their audience, who is "in the know." This form of theatrical legitimacy, of legitimizing the coding of costumed roles, and the mimetic as well as symbolic overtones in the action, has interesting similarities with Virginia Woolf's last novel, *Between The Acts* (1941), which also places its pageant players in a formal garden and which depicts as both leader and outcast the character of Miss La Trobe, modelled on Ethel Smyth herself. Literary critic Sandra Gilbert has suggested that Miss La Trobe is "an ironic version of the lost Shakespearean sister Woolf imagined in *A Room of One's Own*, who holds many mirrors up to the nature of Western culture in order to show that all our roles, even those which appear most fated [*sic*], are merely costumes."[31] Both Woolf in her novel and Smyth in *Fête Galante* find costume inseparable from identity and declare that "we are what we wear."

The contradiction between appearance and identity, between artistic vision and actuality, is thrilling and maddening to both Ethel Smyth and Miss La Trobe, who, as lesbian and as artist, has the power and the desire to "stir in her listeners and players their unacted part" (*Between The Acts*, page 107). She paces the stage, rallies her players, and frets behind the hedge in gnawing frustration: "Hadn't she, for twenty-five minutes, made them see? A vision imparted was relief from agony . . . for one moment . . . one moment. Then the music petered out on the last word WE. . . . She hadn't made them see. It was a failure! As usual. Her vision escaped her." (page 72)

The gardens of Pointz Hall in *Between The Acts* and of *Fête Galante* both resemble the moral as well as symbolic English garden maze of Michael Tippett's *The Knot Garden*, an opera written in 1970.

It would appear that opera was Smyth's chosen means—and perhaps the mask—through which she contrived to reveal and reshape her lifelong struggle with what she called the "eternal sex problem between men and women."[32] While Mrs. Waters is her authentically "new" opera heroine, all Smyth's leading women are warm-toned, strong mezzo-sopranos rather than dramatic high sopranos; they partner high tenors, not the more compatible baritone; and they struggle to define a gender-free reality beneath and behind myth and history and operatic stereotype. So doing, they are perceived more as evil and destructive than heroic. Her heroines, like Smyth herself, personify and dramatize sexual ambiguity and the double image of women drawn close into a natural world powerful and protective in its maternal myths and female symbolism. Thirza, whose character is related to George Gissing's novel of that name, is scorned but feared by the wreckers' community, at first because she has sexual power over their leader, an old man; second, because she "seduces" a younger outsider; and third because, in her goodness, she wrecks their livelihood and thus their community, and thus their faith.[33] She must, then, be a witch who must be tried, found guilty, and destroyed by drowning. At her moment of self-knowledge and fulfillment, she becomes their victim.

Ethel Smyth consistently refused to be a victim herself. As Virginia Woolf depicts her, she too is a wrecker: "She drew the enemies' fire and left behind her a pathway. . . . She smashed, and broke, and toiled, and drew upon herself hostility and ridicule in order that it might not be wicked . . . or disgraceful for women now . . . who come after her."[34] What confounds and confronts both Miss La Trobe the artist and Ethel Smyth the composer is Woolf's metaphorical sense of time. For the fictional artist: "Time was passing. How long would time hold them together? It was a gamble, a risk . . . and she laid about her energetically." (*Between The Acts*, page 106)

For Smyth, especially in the "shabby, sordid" octogenarian years, time was also against her. She wrote to Woolf in 1930: "I am in love with death—with turning away—[with] disengaging the eternal from the temporal, the personal from the impersonal in my own heart and imagination."[35] The prism of time encapsulates the recurring theme of the prisoner in much of her work. There is no lasting escape, no sure rescue. Three operas end in death, one in capitulation. Smyth's "prisons" are natural as well as psychological states that demand deception, renunciation, even death, to enable the protagonist to "pass," to belong.[36] The liberation of self-awareness or reconciliation is rewarded by further sacrifice. The theme of punishment and redemption through suffering is a Christian one; Smyth's theme of the captive, the oppressed, is sexual. To be freed from her own betrayals, Iolanthe destroys Heinrich and her own sexual impulses and causes an innocent Röschen to fall lifeless on her lover's body. Their first kisses release sexuality for both Thirza and Mark at the moment they are engulfed by time and tide. When the disguised Queen wearily abandons her King, Lover, and Jester and hides in the hedgerows of the *Fête*, Pierrot, "keeper" of her love, silently dies.

In Beethoven's *Fidelio*, Smyth's favorite opera, it was a woman, disguised as a man, who rescued the prisoner and whose courage brought the anguish of joy after the release of strain and suffering. In her last work, the choral and symphonic setting of Henry Brewster's philosophical dialogue, *The Prison* (1930), Smyth was drawn to the depiction of captivity, dread, the pallor of prisoners, the agony of not being able to communicate with one's lover, and of hope deferred.[37] Deaf, bedridden, alone, Smyth called her last nurse-companion her "warder," yet remembered happiness in the sanctuary of an old friend's tower at Windsor Castle, Lady Ponsonby's "The Prisons." When Nelly Benson, a younger friend, had suddenly died, her mother, wife of the Anglican Archbishop, had read with Smyth for solace a copy of Brewster's *The Prison*. On Smyth's own death, her soldier-brother scattered her ashes on the golf course opposite her Woking cottage to her music from *The Prison*. Yet, fettered by time, she had wanted most to die as had Elizabeth I and Elizabeth Cady Stanton, "standing up," a fighter to the last post.[38] The composer who conducted imprisoned suffragists in singing her "March" to freedom for women, beating time with her toothbrush through her cell bars in Holloway Prison, insisted she must never be silenced nor her music barred.[39]

NOTES

1. Earlier versions of this essay include "Dame Ethel Smyth: Radicalism and Respectability," read at the First National Congress on Women in Music, New York University, March 1981; "Behind Bars: Dame Ethel Smyth (1858-1944)," read at the Festival of Women in the Arts, Princeton University, April 1981; and "Gender and Genre in Ethel Smyth's Operas" read at the first Conference on Women in Music, University of Michigan, Ann Arbor, March 1982. I wish to thank Jane Bernstein, Jane Marcus, and members of the Columbia University Seminar on Women in Society for their support and stimulating criticism in the development of this essay.

2. Virginia Woolf, *A Writer's Diary* (London: Hogarth Press, 1954), entry dated 4 February 1931, p. 168.

3. A short bibliography is appended to this essay.

4. Samples include "an eccentric" (Edward Sackville-West) "harasser" (Jerrold

Moore) "unnatural" (Joseph Joachim), "obsessive" (Nigel Nicolson), and "mediocre" (critic W. J. Turner); see bibliography at end of essay.

5. Ethel M. Smyth, *A Final Burning of Boats* (London: Longmans, Green and Co., 1928), p. 54. An example of sexist criticism is in the entry on Smyth in *The Grove Dictionary of Music and Musicians*, 5th ed., ed. Eric Blom, vol. 7 (London: The Macmillan Co., 1954). "The most striking thing about [her *Mass*] was the entire absence of the qualities that are usually associated with feminine productions; throughout it was virile." (p. 860) Smyth's comments on the "Machine," which she also calls "The Gang" who blocked the "gangway" to women in music, recur in her writings; see *As Time Went On* (London: Longmans, Green and Co., 1936), p. 292, 294-95.

6. The *Mass in D* is reprinted by Da Capo Press, New York, 1981, with foreword by Jane Bernstein. Jane Marcus is preparing the correspondence between Smyth and Virginia Woolf for publication with The Women's Press, London, under the title, "One's Own Trumpet; Dame Ethel Smyth and Virginia Woolf—A Portrait in Letters." Books published by Smyth are: *Impressions that Remained*, 2 vols. (London: Longmans, Green and Co., 1918; reprinted, New York: Da Capo Press, 1981); *Streaks of Life* (London: Longmans, Green and Co., 1921); *A Three-Legged Tour in Greece* (London: Wm. Heinemann, 1927); *A Final Burning of Boats* (London: Longmans, Green and Co., 1928); *Female Pipings in Eden* (London: Peter Davies, 1933); *Beecham and Pharoah* (London: Chapman and Hall, 1935); *As Time Went On* (London: Longmans, Green and Co., 1936); *Inordinate (?) Affection* (London: Cresset, 1936); *Maurice Baring* (London: Wm. Heinemann, 1938); and *What Happened Next* (London: Longmans, Green and Co., 1940).

7. Woolf has described Smyth in memorable ways. See her review of Smyth's *Streaks of Life* in *The New Statesman*, 23 April 1921, and in many of her letters to Smyth following the first printed in *The Letters of Virginia Woolf*, ed. Nigel Nicolson and Joanne Trautman, vol. 4 (1929-31) (New York: Harcourt Brace Jovanovich, 1979), and subsequent volumes. Further portraits are in the biography by Christopher St. John, *Ethel Smyth: A Biography* (London: Longmans, Green and Co., 1959); Margaret Cole, *Women of Today* (London: T. Nelson & Son Ltd., 1938), ch. 1 on "Ethel Smyth," pp. 3-29. I am grateful to Mr. Chalkley, Keeper of the Mayford and Woking Historical Society, Surrey, for excerpts from their materials. Smyth's *Impressions That Remained*, 2 vols. (London: Longmans, Green and Co., 1918), is still the best autobiographical source.

8. Her main but short-term composition teacher in Leipzig was Carl Heinrich Reinecke (1824-1910), composer of six operas, two of which are one-act "Märchenoper" or romantic fantasies with "singspiel" and hybrid forms. St. John considers that Smyth learnt more from the Leipzig musical environment than from formal studies and was particularly influenced by *The Magic Flute* and *Fidelio*, which she saw produced there. (An Australian writer-composer wrote an excellent musical novel based on her own musical training and experience as a contemporary of Smyth and similarly a musical expatriate student in Leipzig; see Henry Handel Richardson (Ethel Richardson), *Maurice Guest* (London: 1908, reprinted Melbourne: Sun Books, 1965). What *is* surprising is that Smyth wrote six operas, a genre few women had then attempted and where fewer still achieved performances and revivals as Smyth did.

9. *Fantasio*, written in 1894, premiered 20 May 1898 at Weimar, was revived at Karlsruhe in 1901. Smyth's attempts to have performances at Munich (through

Levi), Karlsruhe (under Mottl), Dresden, Leipzig, Cologne, Hamburg, and Wiesbaden had been previously unsuccessful before Weimar; St. John, *Ethel Smyth*, pp. 89-94.

10. *Der Wald* (The Forest), music drama with Prologue and Epilogue in one act (Mainz: Schott, 1902). Vocal score with preface and argument by Henry Brewster, 115p. First performed Berlin, 22 April 1902; Covent Garden, 18 July 1902; New York, 11 March 1903. See Smyth's chapter, "A Winter of Storm" in *Streaks of Life*, pp. 139-64, describing Dresden's rejection of the score just after she had completed the orchestration in July 1901. On the London production, see St. John, *Ethel Smyth*, pp. 96-98. Smyth had begun the work in 1895.

11. *The Wreckers* (*Strandrecht*) a lyrical drama in three acts adapted from the Cornish drama, "Les Naufrageurs" by Henry Brewster (London: Universal Edition, 1916). Vocal score, 285pp. First performed Leipzig, 1906; His Majesty's Theatre, London, 22 June 1909; Covent Garden, 1910. The score was finished in September 1904, and Smyth began the tedious process of "hawking" it to opera directors, including those of the Brussels Théâtre de la Monnaie, Leipzig (Nikisch), Prague (Neumann), Leipzig (Hagel), and Vienna (Mahler and Bruno Walter); see St. John, *Ethel Smyth*, pp. 105, 108-9; and Smyth, *What Happened Next* (London: Longmans, Green and Co., 1940), pp. 269-77. Brewster died shortly after the first (concert) performance in London, when Arthur Nikisch gave the first two acts in Queens Hall, 28 May 1908, with the London Symphony Orchestra (L.S.O.) and Blanche Marchesi as Thirza with her singing pupils in the chorus. Nikisch gave the Prelude to Act II in an L.S.O. concert that same month. Beecham conducted the 1909 stage production in his first season of British opera, having met Smyth through harpsichordist Violet Gordon-Woodhouse; see Osbert Sitwell, "Noble Essences," in *Left Hand, Right Hand*, vol. 1 (London: Macmillan 1945). John Coates sang Mark. Walter prepared *The Wreckers* for the 1914-15 season at Munich; St. John, *Ethel Smyth*, p. 169. During the 1920s, London concerts of Smyth's music became more plentiful. Her diary records a 19 April 1921 performance of the love scene from Act II, and on 21 June of the Overture; see St. John, *Ethel Smyth*, p. 175. The full opera was revived at Sadler's Wells in 1939; Eric Walter White, *The Rise of English Opera* (London: John Lehmann, 1951), p. 263.

12. Smyth, *What Happened Next*, p. 234, and "Iron Thesis on Opera," in *A Final Burning of Boats* (London: Longmans, Green and Co.), p. 186.

13. Desmond Lee, ed., *Plato's Republic*, 2d rev. ed. (London: Penguin Books, 1981), Book 7, pp. 316-25. Jane Marcus informs me that a London bar frequented by lesbians in the 1920s was called the "Cave of Harmony," where writer Vera Brittain, a friend of Smyth's, then covering the obscenity trials of Radcliffe Hall's novel *The Well of Loneliness* (1928), met both Hall and Katherine Mansfield. Another contemporary writer who links symbolism of the cave, death, and women is E. M. Forster in *A Passage to India*, and Woolf uses sea imagery in many novels, especially *The Waves*, *To The Lighthouse*, and *The Voyage Out*. After Brewster died, Ethel Smyth "felt like a rudderless ship, aimlessly drifting hither and thither," (St. John, *Ethel Smyth*, p. 131), but it was Woolf who more fittingly described Smyth as a wrecker herself; see n. 34 below.

14. I am grateful to Jane Bernstein for her original remarks on *Der Fliegende Holländer*. She informs me that Peter Pears told her Britten did not know of *The Wreckers* and that the copy of its score in the Britten Library arrived after his death. Britten's ignorance seems unlikely. Jane Bernstein, "Shout, Shout, Up With Your

Song!: Dame Ethel Smyth and the Changing Role of the British Composer," chapter in *Women Making Music*, eds. Judith Tick and Jane Bowers (Urbana and Chicago: University of Illinois Press, 1986). Even distant Australian composers knew Smyth's work; see my unpublished dissertation, "Australian Opera (1842-1970), A History of Australian Opera with Descriptive Catalogues" vol. 1, p. 118, n. 170 which discusses the efforts of Anglo-Australian composer G. W. L. Marshall-Hall to emulate Smyth in having his operas translated into German to attract both German and British productions.

15. Smyth's songs set poems by Arthur Symons, translated into German by R. St. Hoffman, including "Requies," "Before the Squall," and "After Sunset," for mezzo-soprano with orchestra (Leipzig: Universal Edition, 1913). The cycle of Smyth's settings of poems by Henri de Regnier that Debussy apparently admired includes "The Dance," "Chrysilla," and "Odelette," published with her setting of Leconte de Lisle's "Anacreontic Ode," all for mezzo-soprano with chamber orchestra or ensemble of violin, viola, cello, flute, harp, and percussion (London: Novello, 1909); St. John, *Ethel Smyth*, p. 112.

16. Smyth practiced her conducting techniques by tying herself to a tree and looking in a mirror to control any excessive bodily movement. She conducted a concert of her works to raise funds for the Women's Social and Political Union (WSPU) on 8 April 1911 at Queens Hall and was praised by Bernard Shore, leader of the viola section in the BBC Symphony Orchestra in his study of conductors, *The Orchestra Speaks*, quoted by St. John, *Ethel Smyth*, pp. 159-61. When Edith Craig, daughter of Ellen Terry, produced *The Boatswain's Mate* at the Leeds Art Theatre but told Smyth the singers were "having trouble," the composer insisted she would brook no changes; St. John, *Ethel Smyth*, pp. 150, 162-66.

17. *The Boatswain's Mate*, comedy in one act and two parts after W. W. Jacob's story of that name, dramatized for music and composed by Ethel Smyth (London: Forsyth, 1915), vocal score 156pp. First performed 1916, Shaftesbury Theatre, London, and 1921 at the Old Vic. The opera was also translated into German and accepted by the Intendant of Frankfurt Opera; St. John, *Ethel Smyth*, p. 170. Smyth was too deaf to hear the orchestration at the London premiere. Beecham produced it at Drury Lane with his British National Opera Company in 1919; the Old Vic production opened 1 April 1921, produced by Lilian Baylis; and on 17 July 1923 both this opera and *Féte Galante* ran for two weeks at the Birmingham Repertory. *Boatswain's Mate* was revived at Covent Garden also in 1923 by Eugene Goossens with Rosina Buckman as Mrs. Waters; St. John, *Ethel Smyth*, pp. 177-85.

18. Alfred Cellier's highly popular *Doris* (1889) and *Dorothy* (1888) and Cecil Sharp's *Dimple's Lovers* (1890) are precursors. The genre was repugnant to George Bernard Shaw, *London Music in 1888-1889* (London: Constable & Company, 1937), pp. 107, 213-16, 217, 255, 262, 368.

19. In Smyth, *Female Pipings in Eden* (London: Peter Davies, 1933), pp. 185-290, Smyth drew her portrait of Mrs. Pankhurst (1858-1928), "a theme the gravity and importance of which had alternatively attracted and terrified [her] for years," observed Vera Brittain in her review of the book titled "A Musician's Challenge," typescript, not dated but probably 1933, in *Vera Brittain Archive*, Mills Memorial Library, McMaster University, Ontario. Their 11-year comradeship had ended in bitter, chilly silence. Smyth's "1910" for mixed chorus with or without band, and "March of the Women," were printed together in 1911 with "Laggard Dawn" for unaccompanied women's chorus; Kathleen Dale, "Ethel Smyth's Music: A Critical Study," in St. John, *Ethel Smyth*, p. 301. The similarity between an Abruzzi folk

tune and "March of the Women" is discussed by St. John, *Ethel Smyth*, p. 151.

20. For a brilliant study of role inversion to imagine worlds in which women exercise power over men, using the stage as context and the parody-play as genre, see Froma I. Zeitlin, "Travesties of Gender and Genre in Aristophanes's *Thesmophoriazousae*," *Critical Inquiry* 8, no. 2 (Winter 1981), pp. 301-27.

21. A revenge akin to that practiced on Smyth by E. C. Benson, son of Smyth's dear friend Mrs. Benson, wife of the Anglican Archbishop, in his novel *Dodo* (London: Century Company, 1893), in which the character of Edith Staines is a caricature of Ethel Smyth.

22. *Entente Cordiale*, a postwar comedy in one act (founded on fact), written and composed by Ethel Smyth, ("Bengal Military Orphan") (London: J. Curwen, 1925), vocal score 106pp. First performed 1925, Royal College of Music; 1926, Theatre Royal, Bristol.

23. Smyth inscribed the first five bars of that bugle call in a copy of *The Prison* by Brewster signed by Smyth on 24 February 1931 with an inscription to Virginia Woolf; Jane Marcus, *One's Own Trumpet*, typescript, in preparation for The Women's Press (London), p. 65 and n. 37 below. Smyth began work on *Entente Cordiale* in February 1923 and completed the score on 21 November 1924. Its premiere at the Royal College of Music was on a double-bill with *Fête Galante*, 25 July 1925. Both Baring and Gordon-Woodhouse found it "intoxicatingly gay," St. John, *Ethel Smyth*, pp. 188, 190.

24. Vocal score, no. 2, pp. 8-16; the verses make ironic reference to the suffragists and other contemporary social and political events.

25. Discussed in "Iron Thesis on Opera," pp. 180-99, and in "A New Departure in Comic Opera," both printed in Smyth, *A Final Burning of Boats*, pp. 180-99, 200. Smyth seeks "the human side, pathetic and funny, in ordinary workaday clothes, in romance and comedy from contemporary life, rather than the burlesque." The libretti for both *The Boatswain's Mate* and *Entente Cordiale* are reprinted in Smyth, *A Final Burning*, pp. 203-34, 234-63.

26. Irving Berlin's *Yip, Yip, Yaphank* (1918) or *The Belle of Cairo* by Australian Arthur Brewster-Jones (1921) are among many ephemeral wartime operettas; Gilbert Chase, *America's Music* (New York: McGraw-Hill Book Co., 1955), p. 625.

27. Unlike, for example, operas by Arthur Benjamin, *The Devil Take Her* (1931) or *Prima Donna* (1933) and other then-contemporary English light opera; E. Walter White, *The Rise of English Opera*, pp. 271-73.

28. *Fête Galante*, a dance-drama in one act after Maurice Baring's story of that name, dramatized and composed by Ethel Smyth, poetic version by Edward Shanks, vocal score (Vienna: Universal Edition, 1923), 72pp. First performed 17 July 1923, Birmingham Repertory (with *Boatswain's Mate*). Smyth had long wanted to write the opera but did not begin work until 15 December 1921, afterwards receiving her knighthood as Dame Commander of the Order of the British Empire, January 1922; St. John, *Ethel Smyth*, p. 177. Both *Fête* and *Entente* were revived together on 25 July 1925, Royal College of Music; St. John, *Ethel Smyth*, p. 188.

29. Contemporary operas also adopting neo-classical "commedia dell'arte" and puppet traditions include Busoni's *Arlecchino* (Zurich, 1917), and Manuel De Falla's *El Retablo de Maese Pedro* (Paris, 1923), the latter also employing the play-within-a-play device.

30. Humperdinck (1854-1921) was a student at Munich when Smyth studied in Leipzig; *Hansel und Gretel* was produced in London in 1894 and described as a "dream-pantomime"; *Die Königskinde*, another of his post-Wagnerian

"Märchenoper," was first performed in 1910. Smyth's chorus "Hey Nonny No" was written prior to her suffrage service and was greatly admired by Gustav Holst and Percy Grainger; their letters are quoted in St. John, *Ethel Smyth*, pp. 152-53.

31. Sandra Gilbert, "Costumes of the Mind: Transvestism as Metaphor in Modern Literature," *Critical Inquiry* 7, no. 2 (Winter 1980), pp. 391-417. The edition of *Between The Acts* used here is London: Penguin, 1953; see also a recent discussion of Miss La Trobe in Nora Eisenberg, "Virginia Woolf's Last Words on Words: *Between The Acts* and 'Anon'," in *New Feminist Essays on Virginia Woolf*, ed. Jane Marcus (Lincoln: University of Nebraska Press, 1981), pp. 253-66.

32. Her comments on "sex-antagonism" recur in her writings but especially in *As Time Went On*, pp. 294-95, and *Final Burning*, pp. 47, 54.

33. I am grateful to Dorothy Litt for this information and to Jane Marcus for further notes. Gissing's novel was published in London in 1887, in which Thyrza (*sic*) is a rustic but powerful heroine. Gissing (1857-1903) wrote at least 27 books; see Bernard Bergonzi's introduction and biography in the Penguin reprint of Gissing's *New Grub Street* (London: Smith, Elder, & Co., originally published in 1891, reprinted 1978), pp. 9-27.

34. Virginia Woolf, "Speech before the London/National Society for Women's Service, January 21, 1931," text transcribed from an untitled typescript with manuscript corrections, of 25 pages in the Berg Collection, New York Public Library, reprinted in *The Pargiters; The Novel-Essay Portion of 'The Years'*, ed. Mitchell A. Leaska (New York: Harcourt Brace Jovanovich, 1978), pp. xxvi-xliv. A much-reduced version of this speech, almost completely omitting references to Smyth, was published by Leonard Woolf as "Professions for Women," in *The Death of the Moth and Other Essays* (London: Hogarth Press, 1942), pp. 149-54.

35. Ethel Smyth, letter to Virginia Woolf, 11 August 1931, quoted by Marcus, *One's Own Trumpet*, typescript, pp. 85-90.

36. For a discussion of "silence" and forms of homosexual coding as "passports into the territory of the dominant world," see Catharine R. Stimpson, "Zero Degree Deviancy: The Lesbian Novel in English," *Critical Inquiry* 8, no. 2 (Winter 1981), pp. 363-79.

37. Henry Brewster (1850-1908), *The Prison: A Dialogue* (London: 1891), reprinted by William Heinemann, 1931); reprinted with a memoir by Ethel Smyth in 1930. Smyth's setting for soprano (the Soul), bass-baritone (the Prisoner), chorus and orchestra was first performed by the Bach Choir under Sir Adrian Boult at Queens Hall in 1931. Smyth's words on *Fidelio* and her fascination with the theme of prisoner are found in *Final Burning*, pp. 148-49, 150.

38. Ellen Carol DuBois, ed., *Elizabeth Cady Stanton, Susan B. Anthony*; *Correspondence, Writings, Speeches* (New York: Schocken Books 1981), p. 265.

39. A performance touchingly described by eye-witness Beecham in his *A Mingled Chime*; *An Autobiography* (New York: Putnam's Sons, 1943), p. 158ff.

SELECTED BIBLIOGRAPHY

Bayliss, Stanley. "The Operas of Dame Ethel Smyth." *Musical Opinion* (September 1939), pp. 1045-46.

Beecham, Thomas. *A Mingled Chime: An Autobiography*. New York: Putnam's Sons, 1943.

Bernstein, Jane, " 'Shout, Shout, Up with your Song!'; Dame Ethel Smyth and the Changing Role of the British Woman Composer." In *Women Making Music*, eds. Judith Tick and Jane Bowers. Urbana and Chicago: University of Illinois Press, 1986.

______, ed. *Mass in D Major by Ethel Smyth*. New York: Da Capo Press, 1981.

Boult, Adrian. *Music and Friends: Seven Decades of Letters to Adrian Boult*. Annotated by Jerrold N. Moore. London: Hamish Hamilton 1979. Pp. 60-64, 81-82.

______. *My Own Trumpet*. London: Hamish Hamilton 1973.

______. *Thoughts on Conducting*. London: Hamish Hamilton 1963.

Canarina, John. "The Legendary Dame Ethel Smyth." *Helicon Nine; A Journal of Women's Arts and Letters* (Spring 1981), pp. 7-13.

Cole, Margaret. "Ethel Smyth." In *Women of Today*. London: T. Nelson & Son Ltd., 1938. Pp. 3-29.

Dale, Kathleen. "Ethel Smyth's Music: A Critical Study." In Christopher St. John, *Ethel Smyth: A Biography*. London: Longmans, Green and Co., 1959. P. 301 with Appendix, pp. 305-8.

______. "Ethel Smyth's Prentice Work." *Music and Letters* 30, no. 4 (October 1949), pp. 329-36.

______. "Dame Ethel Smyth." *Music and Letters* 25, no. 1 (1944), p. 191.

Lambert, Constant. *Music Ho!* London: Faber, 1934.

Marcus, Jane. *One's Own Trumpet*; *Dame Ethel Smyth and Virginia Woolf—A Portrait in Letters*, London: The Women's Press (in preparation 1986).

______. "Thinking Back Through Our Mothers." In *New Feminist Essays on Virginia Woolf*, ed. Jane Marcus. Lincoln: Nebraska University Press, 1982. Pp. 1-30.

Nicolson, Nigel, ed. *The Question of Things Happening: The Letters of Virginia Woolf*. Vol. 2, 1912-1922, London: The Hogarth Press, 1976.

Nicolson, Nigel, and Joanne Trautman, eds. *A Reflection of The Other Person: The Letters of Virginia Woolf*. Vol. 4, 1929-1931. London: Hogarth Press, 1959. (See also vols. 5 and 6 published in New York by Harcourt Brace Jovanovich.)

St. John, Christopher. *Ethel Smyth: A Biography*. London: Longmans, Green and Co., 1959.

Tovey, Donald. *Essays in Musical Analysis*. Vol. 5, London: Oxford University Press, 1937. Pp. 136-37.

White, Eric Walter. *The Rise of English Opera*. London: John Lehmann, 1951.

Wood, Elizabeth. "Women, Music, and Ethel Smyth: A Pathway in the Politics of Music." *Woman: The Arts 1*. Special issue of *The Massachusetts Review* 24, no. 1 (Spring 1983), pp. 125-39.

20

Gallery: Another View of Five Composers

A good gauge of a topic's timeliness may be to keep track of how many different ways the topic surfaces, in print or visual treatments, as the featured element or even a secondary theme. With this in mind, the editors of *The Musical Woman* are happy to be able to share with our readers the following excerpts from a recent, very different publication also devoted to musical women, the *Woman Composers* coloring book.

Coloring books function, like all books, as a stimulus for the mind, in addition to being a time-honored recreation for children of all ages. *Woman Composers*, published by Bellerophon Books in 1984, presents 26 composers through lively biographies and line drawings to color in a chronological sequence from Sappho to Cathy Berberian. Five of these 26 are composers discussed in depth in the present volume of TMW: Molza, Beach, Smyth, Tailleferre, and Akiyoshi; their entries from the coloring book are reproduced on the following pages.

Woman Composers, by Carol Plantamura, includes drawings from various sources by Nancy Conkle and the staff of Bellerophon Books. The excerpts are reprinted by kind permission of the publisher. The book is copyright © 1984 by Bellerophon Books, 36 Anacapa Street, Santa Barbara, California 93101.

Tarquinia Molza

born in Modena, Italy in 1542 - died in Rome in 1617

Tarquinia Molza was born, raised and married in the Northern Italian town of Modena. She was the daughter of a prominent merchant and, like every well-bred young lady of her time, she learned to sing and to play the lute and the viola da gamba. But Tarquinia's musical ability was exceptional, and when she was widowed at the age of twenty-seven, her life took a new turn.

By the time of her husband's death she was widely known for her beautiful voice and her keen intellect. News of her talents had reached the court of Alfonso d'Este, the Duke of Ferrara.

The duke had just married and wished to present his new wife, who loved music and dancing, with three splendid musicians as ladies-in-waiting. The duke's ambassadors sought out Tarquinia and proposed that the court would "buy" her and provide for her needs for the rest of her life. It was unusual for anyone not of noble birth to be accepted at court, but the beauty of Tarquinia's voice gave her the key to a new and promising life.

The court of Ferrara was the cultural center of Northern Italy at that time. Among its residents were the famed poets Torquato Tasso and Giovanni Battista Guarini and the musicians Giaches de Wert, Luca Marenzio, and Luzzasco Luzzaschi. The ladies-in-waiting were expected to produce frequent well-polished musical performances. The work was demanding. But Tarquinia thrived on it. Her music improved and she found time to perfect her art as a composer. She became so highly regarded that the poet Tasso wrote several poems in her praise, and the duke fought a joust in her honor.

Tarquinia, however, was also endowed with a lively and willful spirit which was to get her into trouble. She did as she pleased and, finally, after a love affair with the composer Giaches de Wert was revealed, she was exiled from the court.

After her banishment, Giaches de Wert languished and died, but Tarquinia continued to apply herself to life. She returned to Modena where she gathered together a sophisticated group dedicated to music, poetry, art and humanism. In 1610, because of the talent and energy she had devoted to the arts, she was made an honorary citizen of Rome, a distinction usually reserved for men.

Tarquinia wrote in the new monodic style of the late 1600's. In her life she composed more than 40 monodies, melodies written for a single voice. Until her death in 1617 she continued to be an active musician and a leader of others.

TARQUINIA MOLSA UNICA
PUDICITIÆ EXEMPLAR, MUSAR, OCELLUS,
ET SCIENTIARUM DELICIÆ.

Dame Ethel Smyth

born in London in 1858 - died in Surrey in 1944

Young Ethel Smyth was definitely not a prim and proper Victorian lady. She insisted on travelling to Leipzig to study composition when she was only nineteen. There she composed music which was performed in Germany and England (often with herself conducting) and attracted the attention of such giants as Brahms, Dvorak, Clara Schumann, Grieg and Tchaikovsky. But her success as a composer did nothing to soften her image as a non-conformist.

Besides music, she wrote ten books in which she discussed everything that interested her, from feminism and the state of the British Empire to Old English Sheepdogs, which she raised throughout her life. She was a militant feminist and was at one time locked up in Holloway Prison for her suffragette activities. Undaunted, she wrote a piece entitled "The March of the Women," which she conducted from her prison cell with a toothbrush. In spite of her maverick reputation, she was made a Dame of the British Empire in 1922.

She wrote six operas, the most famous of which is *The Wreckers.* Another, *The Boatswain's Mate,* in which she voiced her political inclinations, became part of the standard repertory of the Old Vic. Scholarly publications speak of the "sincerity and seriousness" of Dame Ethel's works, but in her own opinion she never became "even a tiny wheel in the English musical machine." She admitted to having the helpful attributes of "an iron constitution, a fair share of fighting spirit, and, most important of all, a small but independent income" without which she was sure that loneliness and discouragement would have vanquished her.

Compared with the conventional music of the late nineteenth century, Dame Ethel's music contains some unusual harmonic experiments. In *The Wreckers,* for instance, there is an odd blend of the styles of Richard Wagner and Sir Arthur Sullivan. Her deafness, which began in the 1920s, may have had something to do with this. Hers is never "comfortable" music. It is as curious and intriguing as the woman herself.

ETHEL SMYTH after John Singer Sargent, National Portrait Gallery, London

Amy Beach

born in New Hampshire in 1867 - died in New York City in 1944

By the age of fifteen, Amy Beach had already made a place for herself in music history. In this year, 1882, the New York Philharmonic Society performed the work of an American woman composer for the first time — a concert aria which Amy wrote when she was thirteen. Around the same time, the Handel and Haydn Society performed her Mass in E. Again, this was the first time they had performed music written by an American woman. And in this same year Amy produced the first full-fledged symphony ever written by an American woman, the *Gaelic* Symphony.

Amy's contributions didn't stop here. Just after her marriage, at the age of eighteen, she made her professional debut as a pianist with the Boston Symphony. Unlike many other woman composers, Amy didn't allow marriage to hamper her career. She continued composing music throughout the next twenty-five years.

Following the death of her husband, in 1910, Amy began to perform more actively in concert. From 1911-1914 she toured Europe playing from the standard Romantic piano repertory — Beethoven, Lizst, Schumann, Chopin, and Brahms — as well as her own work. When her First Symphony, the *Gaelic*, was performed in Berlin and Leipzig, Europeans gained respect for the musical ability of the Americans, whom they had previously scorned as cowboys.

At the beginning of the first World War, Amy settled in New York and spent the next 30 years composing and making concert tours. During this time she wrote her only opera, *Cabildo.*

In her life she wrote over 150 pieces including songs, piano music, chamber music, symphonies, large works for chorus and orchestra, and the one opera. Her creativity was helped by her ability to freely make use of European musical tradition and avoid a restricted "American style." She felt that music is and should be universal.

Germaine Tailleferre

born near Paris, 1892 - 1983

"Tailleferre" means "iron-cutter." The people who once had this job had to be very strong, and Germaine was like them. She took piano lessons like all well-educated girls of her time, but she was better and more serious than her parents had expected. They considered music an improper career and she had to fight hard to enter the Paris Conservatory when she was twelve. While she was there, she won prizes in almost every field. Most important, she studied composition with Maurice Ravel, a leader in the new style of French music which had been developing for the last twenty years. The music was light and elegant, avoiding the heavy harmonies and repetitive forms of the German music which had dominated the nineteenth century.

A newer, more radical French composer was Erik Satie. While at the Conservatory, Germaine became friends with composers Georges Auric, Darius Milhaud and Arthur Honegger, all followers of Satie. They were later joined by Louis Durey and Francis Poulenc in forming a group of composers calling themselves "the New Youth." After their artist-writer friend Jean Cocteau drew a group-portrait of them, they became known as "*Les Six*" ("the six"). They founded a cabaret in the colorful Montmarte district of Paris, where they could perform their music and friends like Cocteau their plays. They let an ox graze on the roof of the cabaret to attract attention.

"*Les Six*" were full of fun and energy and active in art, poetry and drama as well as music. They kept a loose association throughout the 20s, then went more their own ways. They were never formal or academic; many outsiders considered them frivolous; but their work was always new and always important. Germaine herself was constantly experimenting with new techniques — she even wrote pieces in Arnold Schoenberg's extremely rigid twelve-tone serialism — but the style was always her own, fresh and spontaneous. She wrote stage works (one with Cocteau), chamber music, vocal music and music for film, radio and television.

Germaine Tailleferre outlived the others in "*Les Six*" and died recently.

Toshiko Akiyoshi

born in Manchuria, 1929

Hampton Hawes was beginning to make it as a be-bop pianist when he was drafted and sent to Japan. One night in 1952, a friend took him to the "Harlem Club" in Yokohama. "I sat in the back," he later wrote, ". . . and . . . this little chick in a kimono sat down at the piano and started to rip off things I didn't believe, swinging like she'd grown up in Kansas City."

Though only 23, Toshiko Akiyoshi was already a star in the fanatical Japanese jazz world. Like her new friend Hawes, she emulated the master bop pianist, Bud Powell, and she came to the U.S. in 1956 to study and play. In the next decade she developed a name here and in Europe as well as in Japan, working mostly in small combos with her husband Charles Mariano, with Charles Mingus, J.J. Johnson and others.

By the mid-1960s, Toshiko's piano style had become more studied, her creative horizon far wider. As much a composer and arranger as a pianist now, she turned more and more frequently to the larger and subtler format of the big band. In 1972, she settled in Los Angeles with her second husband, Lew Tabackin, and started the 16-piece Toshiko Akiyoshi-Lew Tabackin Big Band. Today, polls of jazz fans and critics usually place the band at the top of the big band category and Toshiko first among composers and arrangers.

Although the Akiyoshi-Tabackin Band has been a leader in the revival of big bands, it hardly resembles the swing bands that flourished from the 30s to the 50s. Toshiko's music is extremely complex and difficult, requiring unusual concentration and long rehearsal; in concert the band has the intensity of a small symphony orchestra. The band has the traditional core of brass and woodwinds, but can include singers, speakers and even Japanese instrumentalists.

Toshiko's music understandably contains Japanese forms as well, and some unstated Japanese influences, especially in her rhythms. Many people would call her a "fusion" composer, but she insists on her commitment to jazz. "Jazz is a certain rhythm," she says. "It's how you play, not what you play. It's a street music, with a certain earthiness . . . I'm trying to draw from my heritage and enrich the jazz tradition without changing it. I'm putting into jazz, not just taking out."

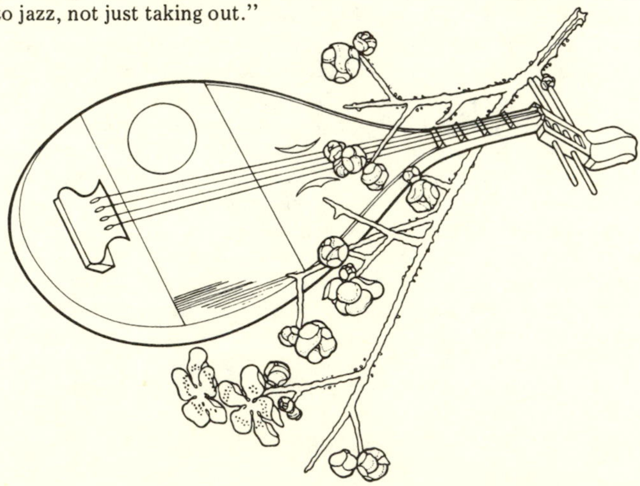

TOSHIKO AKIYOSHI, above

Index

Numbers in italics denote illustrations.

Index prepared by Catherine Overhauser

About the Editors and Contributors

JANE GOTTLIEB is presently head librarian at The Juilliard School. Her previous affiliations include 2½ years as head librarian at Mannes College of Music, 2 years as reference librarian at the New York Public Library at Lincoln Center, and 5 years at the American Music Center. She holds a Bachelor of Arts in Music degree from the State University of New York at Binghamton, and a Master of Science in Library Service from Columbia University.

CATHERINE OVERHAUSER is music director and founder of the Hopkins Symphony Orchestra, a community orchestra based at the Johns Hopkins University in Baltimore, Maryland. She is also assistant conductor of the Prince George's Philharmonic and music director of the York Youth Symphony, and has served as assistant conductor to the Aspen Music Festival. As guest conductor with Res Musica Baltimore she has conducted world premiere performances of many works by distinguished American composers.

JUDITH LANG ZAIMONT is a prize-winning composer. Among her awards are a Guggenheim Fellowship in music composition, grants from the Presser Foundation and the National Endowment for the Arts, and composition fellowships from the Maryland State Council on the Arts, the Woodrow Wilson Foundation, and Alliance Française. Many of her works are recorded and published and have been performed in Europe, Canada and Australia as well as in the United States. She is the coeditor of *Contemporary Concert Music by Women* (Greenwood Press, 1981).

* * *

DANIEL A. BINDER is a professor of music at Lewis University in suburban Chicago where he teaches music history. Dr. Binder founded the music department at Lewis and was its chairman for 14 years. He holds a doctorate in historical musicology from Ball State University and bachelor and master degrees from the University of Denver. He has written extensively on women's music, American music and the introductory music course and has presented papers to such organizations as the College Music Society, Sonneck Society, and conferences on women and women in music.

ADRIENNE FRIED BLOCK has a doctorate in Musicology from the City University of New York, where she has taught. She has also taught at Pace University. She now is at Marymount Manhattan College and the Dalcroze School of Music, both in New York. A specialist in both French sixteenth-century music and music by American women composers, Dr. Block was coeditor and compiler of *Women in American Music: A Bibliography of Music and Literature* (Westport, Conn.: Greenwood Press, 1979). More recently her two-volume study, *The Early French Parody Noël*, was issued by UMI Research Press of Ann Arbor, and "Timbre, texte, et air" appeared in a recent issue of *Revue de Musicologie*. She is currently at work on a biography of Amy Beach, under a fellowship from the National Endowment for the Humanities.

EDITH BORROFF was born in New York City and had her early training in music there; she appeared as a pianist from the age of four and was composing soon thereafter. After receiving a B. Mus. and M. Mus. in composition, working with Irwin Fischer at the American Conservatory in Chicago, Borroff went on to earn a Ph.D. in History of Music at the University of Michigan. She has taught at several universities, including the University of Wisconsin—Milwaukee; Eastern Michigan University; and, since 1973, the State University of New York at Binghamton. Among her books are a study of Elisabeth Jacquet de La Guerre (1966), *Music in Europe and the United States: A History* (Prentice-Hall, 1974), and *Music in Perspective* (Harcourt Brace Jovanovich, 1976).

JOAN BRICCETTI joined the Saint Louis Symphony Orchestra in 1980 to oversee the orchestra's artistic and production operations. A native of Somers, New York, and a 1970 graduate of Bryn Mawr College, Briccetti began her career in Indianapolis, Indiana, as administrative assistant to her brother, conductor Thomas Briccetti, and program editor of the Fine Arts Society of Indianapolis, a nonprofit, classical music radio service. In 1972 she was appointed director of public relations of the Richmond (Va.) Symphony, and in 1973 she became general manager, a position she held until her appointment in St. Louis. She has served as chairman of the Orchestra and Recording panels of the National Endowment for the Arts; on advisory panels for the Virginia, Tennessee, and Kentucky Arts Commissions; and as vice president of the Regional Orchestra Manager's Association. Briccetti is a member of the Standing Committee on Artistic Affairs for the American Symphony Orchestra League and an advisor for its national Orchestra Management Fellowship Program. At home she is a director of the St. Louis Forum, an organization of executive and professional women.

CAROL ANN FEATHER, an experienced conductor and educator, holds undergraduate and graduate degrees in music and education, including a Ph.D. in Higher Education with a concentration in music from the University of Mississippi. She is presently associate professor of Music at Dyersburg State Community College in Tennessee, where in 1969 she set up the school's curriculum for music and organized its music department. In 1965 Feather organized both concert and marching bands at Pikeville College in Kentucky; she conducted these bands as well as countywide band festivals and clinics over the next four years. She has held broad and continuing assignments conducting bands, orchestras, choruses, and local productions of Broadway musicals over the last 20 years.

KATHERINE HOOVER, composer and flutist, is a National Endowment Composer's Grant recipient, with music published by Theodore Presser and Carl Fischer, among others. Her works have been performed worldwide, and her recordings on the Leonarda label have been well received. She appears often as a recitalist and has recorded solo and chamber repertoire for various labels. A graduate of Eastman, Hoover taught at the Manhattan School of Music for several years and currently works with graduate students at Teacher's College, Columbia University.

DIANE JEZIC, currently on the music faculty of Towson State University in Baltimore, received her Doctor of Musical Arts degree from the Peabody Conservatory of Johns Hopkins University. As a pianist, she has performed widely in the Baltimore-Washington area and has issued three piano solo recordings on the Educo label. She is the author of a book on emigré composers in the U.S., *The Musical Migration, 1933-41* (1987), and articles and reviews in *Signs—The Journal of Women in Culture and Society*, the *Music Educators' Journal*, *The American Music Teacher*, the Canadian *Music Journal*, and the *Journal of the International Congress on Women in Music*. She has presented papers on women in music at several national meetings, and presently is at work on a book inspired by the pianist, composer, program director and entrepreneur: her mother, entitled *Women Performers in the Golden Age of Radio*.

LAURA KOPLEWITZ is a music journalist, press consultant, and student of music composition. Raised in Vermont and currently living in New York City, she received her Bachelor of Arts degree in feminist literary criticism and music from Hampshire College (1979), Amherst, Massachusetts. She has recently completed requirements for a Masters degree in interdisciplinary arts from the Gallatin Program at New York University, where she concentrated on studies of twentieth-century women in music as well as original composition.

Koplewitz is the music editor for a new women's magazine based in Washington, D.C., *Quarante*; she has contributed to *The New Grove Dictionary of Music in the United States*, *Ms. Magazine*, *High Fidelity/Musical America*, *Connecticut Magazine*, *Medical World News*, *East-West Journal*, and *Symphony Magazine*, among others. Her current projects include research about music and memory, medical issues in the performing arts, and the lives and works of contemporary women in music.

LAURA MITGANG graduated from Oberlin College magna cum laude in 1982; her study of Germaine Tailleferre began there as an honors thesis. Recently she has been working in music management and booking at Columbia Artists Management, Inc. and has continued extensive research here and abroad toward a full-length biography of the composer.

KAREN MONSON is the author of *Alban Berg* (Houghton Mifflin, 1979) and *Alma Mahler, Muse to Genius* (Houghton Mifflin, 1983; Collins, 1984). The former head of the Music Critics Association's Education Committee, she has contributed to a wide variety of newspapers and magazines, most recently (1984-86) as music critic for the *Baltimore Sun*.

CAROL NEULS-BATES, a musicologist, holds a Ph.D. from Yale University and has taught on the faculties of the University of Connecticut, Yale University, and

Hunter and Brooklyn Colleges of the City University of New York. She is the author of numerous articles and books, including, with Adrienne Fried Block, *Women in American Music: A Bibliography of Music and Literature* (Westport, Conn.: Greenwood Press, 1979), which was funded by the National Endowment for the Humanities and the Ford Foundation. She has also edited *Women in Music: An Anthology of Source Readings from the Middle Ages to the Present* (New York: Harper and Row, 1982), and she has contributed articles to the forthcoming *New Grove Dictionary of Music in the United States* about women musicians and other related topics. Currently she is an Account Supervisor with the John O'Donnell Company, a management consultant firm in New York City.

BARBARA A. PETERSEN, who earned her Ph.D. in musicology at New York University, is manager of concert research at Broadcast Music, Inc. Author of *"Ton und Wort": The Lieder of Richard Strauss* (Ann Arbor: UMI Research Press, 1980), she gives lecture-recitals on Strauss and Wagner with her husband, baritone Roger Roloff, and also writes on contemporary music.

ESPERANZA PULIDO, a native of Mexico, studied at the National Conservatory of Music in Mexico City and the Manhattan School of Music in New York. Her graduate work in musicology was with André Schaeffner and Lazar-Lévy in Paris on a fellowship from the French government. Pulido is the editor-in-chief of *Heterofonia*, a scholarly musical periodical published by Mexico's National Conservatory of Music, and the author of many articles on musicological subjects including one on Mexican musicians for the *Dictionary of Contemporary Music* (John Vinton, ed. New York: Dutton, 1974).

JOANNE RILEY holds a bachelor's degree from Wellesley (1977) and a Master of Arts in Ethnomusicology from Wesleyan University (1980). She pursued her research on Tarquinia Molza in Bologna, Italy, as the recipient of a Beinecke grant from the S and H Foundation's Beinecke Memorial Fund. Riley taught music at the Park School in Baltimore for several years.

From 1979 through 1985 JESSE ROSEN was responsible for the design and implementation of new programs for Affiliate Artists Inc., overseeing the administration of Affiliate Artists Residencies, the Exxon/Arts Endowment Conductors Program, the Seaver Conducting Award (a major awards program for career development begun in 1985), and the Xerox Pianists Program. Born in New York City in 1952, Mr. Rosen received a Bachelor of Music from the Manhattan School of Music and did graduate work at the Juilliard School. After working as a freelance trombonist, he became an intern in the Music Program of the National Endowment for the Arts. Mr. Rosen joined the staff of Affiliate Artists Inc. in 1977, leaving in 1985 to become the Orchestra Manager of the New York Philharmonic.

JUDITH ROSEN is a researcher and lecturer on the subject of women composers. She has participated in numerous radio broadcasts and coordinated music festivals featuring women's works. Her articles have appeared in a number of publications including *High Fidelity* and *The Musical Woman* (Volume 1). She is a contributor to *The New Grove Dictionary of Music in the United States.*

SUSAN WADSWORTH was born in New York City. Her major piano studies were with Mieczyslaw Munz, and she also studied the violin. She continued her musical studies at Vassar College, at the Fountainebleau Conservatory in France, and at the Mannes College of Music in New York. In 1961, Susan Wadsworth founded Young Concert Artists, Inc., a nonprofit organization dedicated to discovering and developing the careers of gifted young musicians. Mrs. Wadsworth has served on numerous music competition juries and as a consultant to the New York State Council on the Arts and the National Endowment for the Arts. She is a member of the National Advisory Committees of the Avery Fisher Prize Program, the Van Cliburn Competition, and Young Audiences, Inc. Mrs. Wadsworth and her husband Charles Wadsworth live in New York City with their daughter, Rebecca.

ELIZABETH WOOD is a musicologist and freelance writer who lives in New York City. An Australian by birth and education, she has taught music history courses at Queens and Hunter colleges, has presented scholarly papers on women composers at several American colleges and conferences, and is a regular contributor on women in music to *Ms. Magazine.* Recent publications include an article on the music of Grażyna Bacewicz (*The Musical Woman*, Volume 1); an autobiographical essay, "Music Into Words," in *Between Women* (Beacon Press, 1984); a study of American women in the contemporary musical avant-garde (June 1983); and a study of music historiography and feminist biography for the sixth Berkshire Conference of Women Historians (June 1984). She is a member of the New York University Institute for the Humanities Biography Seminar and is preparing materials for her new biography of the life and music of Dame Ethel Smyth.